The
Nourishment For Life Cookbook

Lisa & Neil:
Best of
health

Rachel
& Don

RACHEL ALBERT-MATESZ & DON MATESZ

Nourishment For Life Press

The Nourishment For Life Cookbook

Disclaimer: This publication is designed as an educational tool. Any and all recommendations contained within are based upon the study and personal and professional experience of the authors. Because any material can be misused, the authors and publisher are not responsible for any adverse consequences resulting from the application or misapplication of any of the recommendations given herein. However, the authors and publisher believe that this information should be available to the public.

Publishers Cataloging in Publication

Albert-Matesz, Rachel, 1965—

Matesz, Donald, 1961—

The Nourishment For Life Cookbook/Rachel Albert-Matesz & Don Matesz.

Includes index.

SUMMARY: A collection of recipes and tools for instructing individuals in the art of ecological, macrobiotic, vegetarian, whole foods cooking.

Pre-assigned LCCN 94-66937

ISBN 0-9641267-0-2

Printed in the United States of America

Cover design by Barb Rowan

Back cover photo by Patricia Poggi

Illustrations by Susan Moore

Design & layout by Robin Sharpe

Edited by Danielle Williams & Rachel & Don

For additional copies, use the order form at the back of this book or write to:

Nourishment for Life, customer inquiries,

2210 N. 42nd, Suite #A, Seattle, WA 98103, Tel. # (206) 545-4325

Dedication

To our fragile planet, Gaia; to present Earth-Savers; and to future generations

Why We Created This Book

In our every deliberation, we must consider the impact of our decisions on the next seven generations.

—The Great Law of the Six Nations Iroquois Confederacy

How are we to eat? That is a question each of us has to deal with every day. And its answer affects both personal and planetary health. In the spirit of The Great Law of the Six Nations of the Iroguois people we have worked to produce a book which offers guidance to those who love this planet. We have endeavored to provide a means of cooking and eating that will benefit not only ourselves but the next seven generations, on this fragile planet. In the pages that follow, we offer guidance for people interested in developing a dietary pattern that is sustainable in all senses of the word. This is really a handbook for learning and practicing a practical, economical, healthful, and environmentally sustainable way of eating.

Although the science and practice of ecology is relatively new to the West, it has had a long and illustrious history in many traditional cultures around the world, particularly in traditional Chinese culture. In fact, one of the pillars of Chinese culture, Taoism, can be considered a natural, ecological science par excellence. Taoist teachings form the foundation of Chinese science and medicine, and the essence of these teachings is expressed in a fundamental maxim of Chinese science, "Humanity and Earth are not two." For over 5000 years, the mind of the Chinese scientist has been directed toward realizing harmony with Nature in order to magnify human health and potential. Traditional Chinese Medicine developed from this approach to the world, and it continues to teach that the Way to well-being is through harmony with Natural Order. It is a beautiful, holistic science and we have chosen to draw on it in developing an ecological way of eating. Consequently, this cookbook is spiced with references to traditional Chinese medicine. The capitalization of certain words in this book such as Damp, Cold, and the names of some organs such as Spleen and Kidney follow the conventions of Oriental medicine. In Oriental Medicine, when these terms are capitalized, they refer to specifically defined conditions and/or the sphere of energy associated with the organ, not just the physical organ itself as is referred to in Western medicine.

Unlike most other cookbooks, *The Nourishment For Life Cookbook* provides information, tools, and techniques to not only enable you to eat an ecological, sustainable diet, but also to liberate you from dependence upon this or any other cookbook. As stated elsewhere in this book, we believe that truly excellent cooks are made, not born; they are made through the practice and mastery of basic techniques. In the culinary arts, as in every skilled activity, daily practice of basic techniques and procedures enables the artist to endlessly develop his or her skill.

Although a cliche, practice does make perfect. May your practice bring pleasure to many palates as well as to our planet and the generations to come.

Acknowledgements

Although I had been teaching and studying natural foods and macrobiotics for many years, and had written two vegan/macrobiotic cookbooks (and published one of them already), I was not healthy when I first met my husband in the Spring of 1988. At that time, I was suffering from candidiasis, food allergies, digestive problems, chronic fatigue, manic depression, and overweight. Don and I became best friends shortly after meeting, and it was he who literally nursed me back to health and renewed my faith in the power of macrobiotics. With his support I was able to study and honestly practice this healing way.

In the fall of 1990 we moved in together. In the summer of 1991 we were officially married. Through our union came, among other things, the marriage of our cooking styles and the conception of this book, our literary baby. During the following three and a-half years of pregnancy and labor our book changed shape and form many times. I wanted to capture the essence of our daily cooking, weekly cooking classes, and Friday night dinners. It was not an easy task. I have never worked so hard and so long to bring something to completion. An often overwhelming experience, the creation of this book became my major preoccupation and a source of great frustration and excitement.

I am eternally grateful to Don for supporting this creation. From the day I moved in with him, he helped with daily meal planning, cooking, and weekly shopping and housecleaning. Although I spent most of my time at the computer, when I wasn't teaching, cooking, walking, eating, writing magazine articles, or helping with the housecleaning, it is Don who fathered this book. He came up with more than half of the recipes, wrote his share of the text and taught me about basic procedures, measuring, meal planning, and cooking with purpose. With his support and guidance I have become a much healthier, happier, and more centered person, a more confidant cook, an organized teacher and writer, and a walking recipe rolodex.

Throughout the process of birthing this book Don helped me to avoid burn out by encouraging me to take regular breaks, inviting me to join him on long daily walks, sharing leisurely meals with me each day, and reminding me to take one full day off each week. He helped me to better nourish myself and our "baby." I am forever grateful to him for being my best friend, confidant, constant companion, husband, cooking buddy, co-creator, editor, and source of inspiration and love. Without him I would not be who I am today and we would not have this wonderful book to share with you.

We owe our thanks to the editors of *Veggie Life, Vegetarian Times, Vegetarian Gourmet, Vegetarian Journal, Let's Live, New Body, Qi magazine, The Sound Consumer, Central Co-op News* and *Natural Health* for buying so many articles over the past few years. We owe further thanks to all of our dedicated students in Ann Arbor, Michigan and Seattle, Washington for their confidence, encouragement and practice of our methods and recipes as we shaped and reshaped the manuscript. A special thanks to our Friday night dinner guests for taste testing so many of our old favorites and new concoctions. These organizations and individuals were, and still are, our bread and *sesame* butter.

We owe gratitude to our past, present and future teachers. We are especially grateful to our macrobiotic teachers, to the late Weston Price, D.D. S., Ronald Schmid, Udo Erasmus, and others who have influenced our work. We also thank Julia Ferré for her wonderful book, *Basic Macrobiotic Cooking,* which exposed first Don, then I and my students, to the idea of basic procedures. We also thank Danielle Williams, Healther Crimson, and Mary Goodell for the many hours she spent testing our methods and editing and Robin Sharpe, who organized the design of the book, and the layout crew (Julie Panusis, Vic Turner, and Janine Chevalier).

Finally, a heartfelt thanks to my father, Joe, and his wife Marcia for first exposing me to the delicious joys of macrobiotic food during the Christmas vacation I spent with them in 1980 when I was a sophomore in high school, and later during the Christmas vacation I spent with them in 1983, when I was in college. Little did they know the path that would lead me down this road. I also owe my thanks to my mother, the late Martha Albert, for instilling in me the confidence to do anything that I set my mind and heart on. I am sure she would have enjoyed this book.

Rachel Albert-Matesz, July 1994

Table of Contents

Index
Due to financial and time constraints an index is not provided in this issue. We apologize for any inconvenience this may cause. We hope that the table of contents and chapter organization will adequately guide you through this book. We will have an index supplement available after February of 1995. Write to use after this date to receive your free copy. We apologize for any inconvenience.

> **Note:** *The sea salt called for in our recipes is a special unrefined, sun dried sea salt. It is particularly rich in trace minerals (83 different trace minerals) and contains less than half of the sodium found in commercial table salt or even so called "sea salts" found in most health stores. Thus, it is important to seek out a reliable source of true sea salt. (See Resources.) If refined salt/sea salt is used, halve the amount called for in recipes.*

Foreword

Two years ago we started publishing the Matesz' words of wisdom and recipes in the pages of *Veggie Life,* a new magazine for vegetarians and those interested in going meatless. Issue after issue we accepted their articles; I tested their recipes for bagels, amasake, soups, porridge, tempeh, sea vegetables...Issue after issue, I ate well. Fairly new to macrobiotics, I drew on the knowledge that accompanied their recipes. They taught me how to plan meals and reminded me to prepare ahead. From their words, I learned to eat seasonally, locally and healthfully without sacrificing taste. I began to understand my food choices and to listen to my body's needs.

Don't consider this just another cookbook; it isn't. Rather, it is a macrobiotic primer, a vegetarian encyclopedia. There's a lot of information to digest here. I don't suggest you read it all in one day. Why not follow Rachel and Don's approach to life as you progress through the book? Learn a little each day. Start with their approach to stocking your kitchen. Try a new chopping technique on another day, and put it to use in an unusual soup. For those of you cook book junkies out there, you'll find the explanations as fascinating as the recipes. As you incorporate their suggestions into your diet, you'll feel your body respond—with gratitude. Keep reading. Take everything in. Be open to all their information; although you may not be familiar with all the foods they use, try them without discrimination. They're not hard to find, and they may be just what your body needs.

Some of the information in this book has already appeared in national magazines; maybe you've clipped some of the recipes for your files already. While the rest may be new to you, rest assured that it is not new to Rachel and Don. They work hard, these two—with the prime motivation of teaching what they have learned from years of study and experimentation both in the classroom and at home.

As Rachel puts it, it's been a long labor to get this book finished. Put it to good use—wisely and often. You now have all the information you need to get your kitchen in order and your body in tune. And join me in thanking this wonderfully down-to-earth couple for being willing to make the effort to teach us what we all need to know.

Lauren Mukamal
Former Food and Nutrition Editor
Veggie Life

Our Purpose

Traditional Oriental Medicine is the oldest, most complete, effective, and theoretically sound system of naturopathic and energetic medicine in use today. It is also the system most rapidly finding acceptance among American patients and practitioners. Due to the simplicity, common sense, and truth of its theoretic foundations, it has the potential to explain and incorporate all other forms of medicine. Thus, we think it is the medicine of the future.

Most practitioners and patients of Oriental medicine are familiar only with massage, herbs, and acupuncture. Most practitioners and patients of Western medicine are familiar only with drugs, surgery and other invasive treatments. However, these techniques only address the symptoms of disease; they do not move the causes. It is an axiom of Oriental medicine that disease is a manifestation of a lifestyle that opposes the Way of Nature. It is through our dietary choices that we most intimately contact Nature. Therefore, incorrect diet is the fundamental cause of most diseases. Consequently, traditional Oriental medicine has its roots in a dietetic approach to wellness. In fact, as Bob Flaws, O.M.D., points out "diet is such an important part of our daily life and existence that unless one's diet is well adjusted and appropriately regulated, no amount of herbs, acupuncture, or other medicines can achieve a complete and lasting cure." Therefore, is is imperative that patients and practitioners of medicine to know how to eat well.

There are two aspects of knowing how to eat well. The first is theoretical knowledge, knowing what to eat and drink and in what proportions, and what to avoid. The second is practical knowledge, knowing how to choose and prepare health-promoting foods, how to translate abstract proportions into actual servings, and how to integrate new ways of food preparation into an ongoing life. In this book we have endeavored to supply both aspects of "how to" knowledge with respect to providing nourishment for life according to the principles of traditional Oriental medicine. Our purpose is to help the reader understand what to eat, why to eat it, and how to prepare it so that is is as delicious as it is nutritious.

How To Use This Book

To get maximum benefit from this book, we suggest reading through the first three chapters carefully a couple of times in oder to assimilate their contents fully. There you will find an explanation of the basic philosophy and practices which underlay the oriental way of cooking and eating. Since mastery of basic cooking techniques is key to creating a health sustaining way of cooking, and for proper technique one needs to have certain pieces of equipment, we recommend outfitting your kitchen with some of the basic tools and supplies (such as a vegetable knife, pressure cooker, etc.) described in chapters one and two. Next, read through the chapters which deal with the basic foods. One can then begin to practice the basic techniques, using seasonally and bioregionally appropriate foods.

The meal and menu planning section of this book, chapter 3, will show you how to compose meals using basic cooking techniques. The appendix offers additional menus and several months of meals, all planned out. The book as a whole will help orient you to the philosophy of seasonal eating. We encourage you to go beyond our seasonal adaptations and to adapt your own dishes to the foods in your own region that are locally and seasonally available and most appropriate for you.

It is our desire that this book enable you to maintain your health and inspire your native creative ability in the kitchen. Daily practice of these techniques will lead to mastery of them. We believe that truly excellent cooks are made, not born. As the saying goes, "practice makes perfect." Toward that end, we offer *The Nourishment For Life Cookbook*.

The Myth of the Gift
What it takes to be a good cook

"The heart of the martial arts is in understanding techniques"

Bruce Lee, The Tao of Jeet Kune Do

Good cooking, like the mastery of martial arts, depends upon knowledge and practice of basic skills. Like anything else worthwhile, it takes practice. It is a learned art. Even those who seem to effortlessly produce consistently fabulous meals have worked to get to this point. Indeed, good "freeform cooks" are made, not born. To get to the freeform stage, to transform care-less cooking into care-ful cooking, one must have a long period of discipline. Certain steps are essential to the discipline. This is not to say that learning to be a good cook is an arduous task. Quite the contrary. Cooking can be joyful, meditative, creative, and rewarding. But it is still a learned skill. Like any other skill—driving a car, playing the piano, building a house, or practicing a martial art—good cooking takes practice and is learned through a step by step process.

The process of learning to cook

Though you might not consciously experience all of the steps, the learning process usually goes as follows:

1. You become aware of something you want to do (be a good cook, turn out tasty food, etc.)

2. You realize that certain skills and needed to accomplish this.

3. You have some perception of what learning the skills entails.

4. You have a desire to learn and master these skills. (This is crucial. It will drive you to read, study, practice, and keep going even when things seem awkward or difficult.)

5. You come to understand at least some of the reasons behind the instructions you are given.

6. You experience the process. (You have the actual experience of following the basic steps and procedures, stringing them together, and getting good results or learning from mistakes.)

7. You come to master the basics skills. (This happens when you consistently practice the skills and can predictably produce good results in the kitchen. You are not done or *there* but you have shown some mastery, tasted some success, and are *beginning* to really cook.)

8. You forget the skills. (Actually you forget that there are steps because now there is a flow. The skills have become a part of you—you've internalized them and can now call on them at will. The basic recipes no longer seem like formulas. Now you can string them together to create your own form that fits the given day, season, ingredients, or moment. This is free-form cooking.

Where To Start

Try starting at the beginning.

The Beginner Stage

To be a good cook you must first learn the basics by studying from a book at home, by taking classes, by learning from a friend, or by combining several of these modalities. You start by building knowledge of basic procedures and proportions and of what is needed to produce the proper quantities and qualities of food. With this knowledge, you become confident that your food will be a success ahead of time. This is confidence born of planning, using the proper tools, and measuring.

Using The Tools of The Trade

Good cooks, like good carpenters or draftsmen, use the tools of the trade. Measuring cups, spoons, and appropriate knives, pots. and pans are just some of the tools for producing delicious food. A skilled carpenter has a plan, measures, uses a knowledge of basic proportions, and works methodically doing each task in the proper order. You cannot expect to build a strong, solid or attractive house without first having an idea of what you wish to create. Once you have a plan, you must methodically measure and follow basic step-by-step procedures that will bring your idea into reality. The same goes for cooking. If you don't have a plan, don't use the tools of the trade, and don't use basic proportions to guide you in the assembly and preparation of foods, chances are good that your results will be erratic; sometimes your food will be rather good; other times it may only be fair; at worst it may be totally unpalatable.

The difference between a good cook and a cook who often produces disappointing results is one of accuracy and practice. Good cooks use the available tools to their best advantage. They use their sense of taste, smell, touch, and sight. They memorize basic proportions so that they know how much of what to add and when. Though you may not see them following recipes, they are usually following a formula in their heads, where they have stored the basic recipes that they use the most. It only *looks* like they are winging it.

Cracking the Myth of the Gift

Many people have the impression that good cooks never measure and that they have a "gift" which allows them to throw things together that magically turn out. Some refer to this as the gift of intuition. We do not believe in this sort of "intuition" or inborn talent. We believe that being a good cook requires practice and mastery of basic kitchen tools and skills. We are not born with mastery, rather it comes through practice and attention. Every good cook became good through practice and anyone can become a good cook.

A good cook knows how much dry grain, vegetables, beans, salt, water, oil, and seasoning to use in a particular dish for a particular number of people. Measuring is an essential first step in becoming a good cook which helps you produce consistent and pleasing results. Your food will be enjoyable and your family and guests satisfied if you measure, and measure carefully and consistently.

Practice Makes Perfect

Becoming a good cook (or carpenter, musician, or martial artist) takes time. You have to put more time in at the beginning, until you learn the ropes or basics, then you can gradually be more efficient. If you follow any procedure enough times, paying attention to the basic ingredients and proportions, the recipe will become etched in your brain and you will gradually create a repertoire of recipes—like a mental recipe card file—that you can access at any time. Gradually you will no longer need to look at a printed page to know how to make your favorite dishes. You may vary the ingredients according to what you have on hand, but the organizing principles—the procedures and basic proportions—will be in your head to guide you. You can then be confident (even before you step into the kitchen) that you will produce fabulous food. In a short time your skill level will build as you add to your repertoire of basic recipes (or basic procedures as we call them). Your confidence will build through both your successes and your failures. Most failures arise from not planning, measuring, or following procedures (basically being care-less or inattentive). Learning from those failures strengthens your foundation.

Paring Away the Inessentials

To be a good cook you must get rid of "bad" habits and pare away the inessentials. As you study and practice successful and healthful cooking techniques, you will discover your own "bad" habits. Once you know what these are, you can let them go.

Laying the Groundwork for Success

At first it may feel awkward to measure and precisely follow directions but such steps are essential to learning anything new, whether it is driving a car, building a house, or learning a martial art. Practicing these steps builds knowledge, confidence and skill level. Without measuring, how will you know what worked or didn't? How can you replicate the same results next time, if the results were good, or improve upon what you did, if the results were not satisfying? How will you know how much grain, beans, or vegetables to make? How much water or stock to cook your rice, cereal, pasta, beans, soup or vegetables in? How will you know how much water or yeast to add to the flour to make bread How much sea salt, miso, tamari, or herbs to use to season a soup or stew? How will you decide how much food to make for a particular number of people or meals and how long to cook each dish? In short,.how can you be confident that your food will turn out if you don't measure, follow a recipe, or use basic proportions and time-tested procedures? If you do not have a plan or do not follow specific steps to carry it out, your cooking and meals will be left to chance, and chances are that it won't work. It certainly won't get good meals on the table on a day-in, day-out basis.

Measure—Why Bother?

If you don't measure, you may find, as many of our students have, that sometimes your food is too watery while at other times it is too dry. Sometimes it is too salty while at other times it is bland and unappealing. Sometimes you will burn your rice while at other times it may be under-done. Other problems may also arise from lack of measuring or failure to use basic procedures and proportions.

Attention to Details

Good cooking requires careful attention to details such as allowing your bread to rise fully before baking or soaking your beans prior to cooking. Proper equipment is another important detail that is too often overlooked. Many problems can arise from using the wrong equipment (such as trying to bake a pie in a casserole dish and ending up with a soggy crust or no crust at all). Temperature is another key element. Not using the correct temperature may result in a wilted and grey stir fry, bread which is hard on the outside but raw on the inside, or seeds which are charred and bitter.

Following Along

Not following the instructions completely, failing to measure, using the wrong equipment, using the wrong temperature, or cooking a dish either too long or not long enough, can produce disappointing results, The point to remember is that learning to do anything will requires practice, *and* it is usually easier to learn from the successes and failures of others who have come before you. There's no need to reinvent the wheel. If you study with good teachers who pass on their wisdom and experience, your chances of success are greater than if you fumble around with no clear direction.

We are not beginners, yet we plan, measure, and follow recipes. We keep a Beginner's Mind and this is what keeps us on our toes and allows us to produce predictably good food. We also have a solid foundation from which to experiment and create with success. This foundation is the result of years of practice and study. In this book we offer what we have learned so that you may have good food and good health. We give you the necessary information so that you can have fun and play with intention.

To learn to do anything will requires following instructions. This is not to say that you won't make mistakes. You will. This is part of the learning process. However, planning ahead, measuring and following instructions will prevent many, if not most, mistakes. That is the way to learn. It can save weeks, months, or even years of frustration and fumbling in the kitchen. It can keep you from burning pots, pans, the food, or yourself, and from making yourself or your guests sick.

You do not get to be good at driving a car by throwing yourself onto a busy freeway the first time out. First you must start with the basic maneuvers—standing still, then driving in parking lots, on quiet streets, and eventually on well-traveled roads. You do not build a solid, comfortable house by haphazardly hammering nails into pieces of wood, And before entering martial arts competition, you must first learn basic stances, blocks, kicks, and punches. It is the same with cooking.

Getting Where You Want To Go

If you master a handful of basic techniques, adding a few here and there, you will soon have a head full of recipes that you can call on at will. As you build on your knowledge, cooking becomes more fun because you can experiment with confidence. You will be able to cook with whatever is on hand and be assured of producing good results. You will then be able to make substitutions, vary recipes, and even create new dishes with success. Even if you've never before been a *good* cook, if you practice the basic procedures outlined in this book, success—and rave reviews—will be yours!

Remember, you will make mistakes. (Even we make them now and again!) That's part of the learning process. You will have some disappointments. You will burn some things, over or under cook others and probably lose your cool now and again. But such disappointments can be greatly minimized by referring back to our basic procedures. Look for what you may have done wrong, see if you can fix the mistake, and see what you can do to improve your results next time Eventually your cooking will no longer be left to chance.

TROUBLE SHOOTING COMMON PROBLEMS

We have had many students who have said, "I made your_____ but it was too salty, too bland, too soggy, or just didn't turn out like yours." After further questioning, we often discover that they made one or several critical mistakes.

They usually consist of:
(a) not having a plan before entering the kitchen
(b) not measuring or not measuring accurately
(c) not reading the recipe before staring
(d) not following the basic steps or proportions in the recipe or following only partially
(e) leaving out crucial ingredients
(f) leaving out crucial steps or adding different steps that changed the results
(g) not using the right equipment
(h) not using the correct temperature
(i) not cooking for the proper time, leading to over or undercooked food
(j) getting distracted and losing your place in the process, or losing track of time

Measure For Measure

Besides measuring with a cup and spoon, many cooks have learned to measure with the pots and bowls they use most often. They know just how much to fill a certain saucepan to make a certain number of servings of hot cereal, and how many serving bowls full of cut vegetables will make a given amount of stir fried vegetables. They know that a two-finger pinch of sea salt or herbs is equal to an eighth of a teaspoon while a three-finger pinch is equal to a quarter teaspoon and they learn how many of their ladles it takes to make a cup of soup. They improvise, but they do so with knowledge. Though they may not incorporate standard measuring tools, the measuring techniques that they do use are still tools, and what they do still constitutes measuring.

How We Measure

We know roughly how much dry rice, rolled oats, or flour to figure per person and per meal that we are cooking for. We know how much dry beans, herbs, tofu, tempeh, and vegetables we need per person and per meal for soups and stews. We also have a general idea of the quantity of raw vegetables needed to make a given amount of stir fried, pressed, boiled, or steamed vegetables. We know how much salt to put into the grain pot or bread bowl, how much soy sauce or sea salt to add to vegetable dish, etc. The same goes for other foods and dishes that we make. This comes from having "rules of thumb" for everything and from the study and practice of basic formulas and procedures.

We use both methods: the measuring cup and spoon method, and the eye-ball, hand, and common pot-bow-or spoon method. In most cases, however, we use measuring cups and measuring spoons so that we will make just the right amount of food to last for the right number of meals. This saves time and energy, eliminates food waste, and assures us that we will make enough food without making too much. Indeed, we find that using measuring cups and spoons is necessary, if not crucial, for repeated success in the kitchen—and not just for the novice cook! At first, using such tools may seem constraining, particularly if you are used to just guessing and throwing things together. Aside from measuring and paying attention in the kitchen we cannot think of a better way to produce consistently good food. The more you measure the more it will become habit. Your cooking will be better for it too.

Intermediate Stage

Cooking is about proportion and timing. You can continually try new recipes and procedures which will help you to accumulate more knowledge. At the intermediate stage, when you have built your knowledge of basic procedures, proportions and quantities, "intuition" comes into play. You have built confidence through success and learned from your failures. You have gotten rid of careless "bad habits," memorized basic formulas, and now improvise with ingredients and techniques.

We Never Really Create Anything New

Freeform cooking is about using your senses and knowledge to make the most of what you have. There are only so many ways to cut, toss, mix, and cook foods. Most cooks don't re-invent the wheel; they merely rearrange the parts to make them seem new and different. This intuition" is often just a matter of using time-tested methods to put together new and interesting combinations of ingredients— be they they different beans, grains, vegetables, herbs, spices, or other seasonings. There's really nothing mysterious about it. It is not an inborn talent, rather it comes from practice. It is the same thing that skilled martial artists, musicians, painters and carpenters do. They take different techniques and elements and string them together in different ways, emphasizing some, de-emphasizing others, throwing out some, and modifying others. Thus, what creative cooks and other artists do is nothing really new but simply variations on old themes.

Advanced cookery

A cook's knowledge is vast. After many years of study and practice, measuring becomes second nature. Anything can be eyeballed and wonderful food can be consistently created without effort or struggle. The food is cooked "just right," the quantity is "just right, " and the taste is "just right." At this stage, you can "freeform" cook. That is, you can draw on your experience and knowledge to create tasty food with flair. Your "new" dishes are really just creative use of basic procedures, with the special spark of your personality. However, even at this stage success requires a Beginner's Mind. The best cooks are very humble, and part of being humble is knowing that you do not know all there is to know. This humility assures that you continue to improve upon what you do, learning from your mistakes and progressing forward. Through discipline comes true "freedom."

Modifying Old Recipes & Creating New Ones

When we create new recipes we rarely if ever test or taste them before serving them to guests. We rarely have to make a dish repeatedly to "get it right." Some people wonder how we do this. How do we keep coming up with new recipes that taste so good? How do we do it without having first tested and modified the recipes? Why do we have so few failures in the kitchen? The answer is: we follow certain predictable steps or basic procedures which we have either created or adapted from what others have done. We start with a plan; we measure whenever we cook; and we practice. All of these acts allow us to produce predictably nutritious and delicious food.

In many cases we rely on our basic everyday recipes (referred to in this book as *Basic Procedures)* to create new recipes. The Basic Procedure recipes followed by three stars (***) are the recipes that we and our students use most often and have memorized. For variety we just change the ingredients a bit, substituting different beans, grains, vegetables, or seasonings. Through this may seem undisciplined, it is simply improvisation of basic ingredients, techniques, and procedures. And believe it or not, we never tire of these basic recipes.

We also create seemingly new recipes by looking at other cookbooks and magazines (many of which are not-vegan or vegetarian) or by remembering a dish we've eaten at a restaurant, potluck, or friend's house. Any of these can serve as inspiration or guidance for the creation of new recipes and procedures. In fact, when looking at someone else's recipe we search for the basic procedure. We ask ourselves: What steps are called for and why? What ingredients are called for? Which elements do we want to save? This recipe is then used as a map, formula, or stepping stone for creating new dishes. Though we may change the ingredients or modify the proportions—slightly, or more drastically—we try to keep the essence or flavor of the original recipe.

When adapting recipes to make them our own, we greatly reduce the amount of oil, butter, nuts, or seeds called for. In some cases we eliminate the oil altogether. We also omit the meat, fish, poultry, dairy products, and eggs, replacing them with smaller portions of lower fat and/or higher quality vegetarian ingredients such as tofu, tempeh, wheat meat and/or miso. And we always omit margarine, shortening, sugar, MSG canned food, artificially preserved food, frozen vegetables, enriched white flour, chocolate, and out of season produce. When making substitutions, some products can be substituted one for one; however, you cannot do this with everything. For example, you cannot replace three pounds of meat with three pounds of wheat meat. You have to know how much to use per person and how to flavor it. Daunting as this may seem, once you have learned the basics you will have a better idea of how much of what to chop, when to add it, how long to cook it, and how to season it.

When we do use dairy products—milk, yogurt, cheese, etc.—we don't bake or cook them into dishes; rather, we serve them in small portions as condiments in a meal. For instance, we may use yogurt as a topping for hot cereal, as the soak liquid for vegetable muesli, in a dressing, or as a side dish. If we use cheese, we grate it and serve at the table, sprinkled over warm rice, bread, millet, pasta, or vegetables. If we make drip cheese from homemade yogurt, we may use the whey when puréeing warm "cream of vegetable" soup or to thin hot cereal that is too thick. When we use eggs, we use them very sparingly, figuring just one per person. We poach the eggs, steam them in oiled custard cups, or scramble or stir fry them with tofu, tempeh, or vegetables then serve them over hot cereal, bread, rice, or millet. We don't use them to bind casseroles or in our desserts though. If we use butter or ghee, we may use them in sautéing vegetables or as a table condiment for hot cereal, whole grain, pasta, bread, or vegetables. Or, we may use butter or ghee in baking. Ghee (clarified butter) is far more heat stable and more suited for use in cooking than is unclarified butter (which burns easily) or vegetable oil.

Milk, yogurt, and cheese are best served in an uncooked form. Cooking, particularly at a high heat, destroys heat labile nutrients and denatures their proteins, rendering them less nutritious and a nemesis to our digestive and circulatory systems. Although one may use eggs and/or dairy products daily, it is unnecessary and inadvisable to throw them into every dish in a meal. Such practices waste these precious foods and can lead to diseases of excess. When used, these precious foods should always be used consciously, sparingly and with reverence. A little bit can be made to go a long way. (Don't waste a thing. The solids left from making ghee can be used as a table condiment and the egg shells can be used to make a bone-building soup stock.)

If you choose to use fish, it can be added to a soup, stew or stir fry or steamed or poached for use as a side dish or topping for grains or vegetables. For example, you might substitute red or white meat fish for wheat meat in our Seitan Stroganoff, Hungarian Goulash, Tuscan Tempeh Casserole, or Tempeh & Vegetable Stew. Or, fish bones may be cooked all day or overnight (with a teaball full of dried hawthorn berries) until they are soft enough to mash. At this point the bones and the broth can be used in their entirety, as a bone-building base or stock for a bean or vegetable soup or stew, as is common in many traditional cultures. (Of course you needn't eat fish or fish bone stock to build healthy bones. Raw goat milk or yogurt, egg shell stock, greens, tofu, and sea vegetables cooked with high quality, unrefined, cold pressed seed or nut oils or ghee will also help to build strong teeth and bones.)

The recipes in this book will give you new ingredients, ideas and substitution tips that you can play with and use to adapt other people's recipes. It is not difficult to upgrade other people's recipes once you get the hang of it. Understanding and mastering the basic cooking tools, procedures, and proportions used in this book will allow you to successfully create and adapt recipes that come out tasty the first time, and every time. Whether you choose to follow a vegetarian, vegan, macrobiotic, or mixed diet, we hope that this book will bring joy to you and to all who eat your food.

Where To Go From Here

Start reading and get cooking! And remember, there is no substitute for practice.

Nourishment For Life:
Eating the Orient-al Medicine Way

The people do not understand how to apply the five methods in order to get well from their diseases. The first method cures the spirit; the second gives knowledge of how to nourish the body; the third gives knowledge of the true effects of poisons and medicines; the fourth explains acupuncture; the fifth tells how to treat the viscera. These five methods are drawn up together so that each has one that precedes it.

Yellow Emperor's Classic of Internal Medicine

Originating perhaps three thousand years ago, the *Nei Ching Huang Ti Su Wen,* or *Yellow Emperor's Classic of Simple Questions on Internal Medicine* (hereafter referred to simply as the Classic or Simple Questions), is a dialogue between Ch'i Po and the Yellow Emperor concerning the fundamentals of medicine and the Way of Nourishing Life to prevent and heal disease. It is one of the texts forming the theoretical foundations of Oriental medicine.

As we see above, according to Ch'i Po, education is the essence and first method of both the preventive and remedial applications of traditional Oriental medicine. The *Oriental* physician's first task is to "cure the spirit" of ignorance and re-orient the patient to a life in harmony with nature's way, the Tao. Ch'i Po, the Yellow Emperor's chief physician, advised "those who rebel against the basic rules of the universe sever their own roots and ruin their true selves," while "those who follow the laws of the universe remain free from dangerous illness." Hence, before all else, the Yellow Emperor's Classic advises that disease should be prevented and treated by correction of faults and disorder in the patient's way of life, providing guidance in the Way of Nourishing Life.

Attention to proper diet is a fundamental concern of the traditional Oriental Way of Nourishing Life. After education, it is the primary preventive and remedial technique. As the Classic states, "If people pay attention to the five flavors and blend them well, their bones will remain straight, their muscles will remain tender and young, breath and blood will circulate freely, the pores will be fine in texture, and consequently breath and bones will be filled with the essence of life." Since all of our bodily organs and their functions are formed and nourished by the food we take everyday, any dietary deficiency or excess will result in malformation and/or malfunction of those organs. Hence, proper diet — a way of eating in accord with the fundamental order of the universe — is the foundation for health and necessary for complete treatment of disease. And, conversely, improper, disorderly diet, is one root of dangerous illness.

Understanding Foods: Full and Empty

In traditional Oriental medicine, there are Eight Principles used for differentiating between phenomena. Of those eight, the most important to us here are Yin and Yang and Full and Empty. Using these four principles, we can understand the various foods available to us as manifesting a continuum of nourishment. This in turn can enable us to understand the effects of foods on our health, and to choose those foods which enable us to avoid dis-ease.

The principle of Yin-Yang is fundamental to Oriental medicine. Roughly speaking, Yin refers to the dense material aspect of phenomena, while Yang refers to the subtle energetic aspect or potential of phenomena.

In Oriental medicine, if something is replete with both matter and energy, this is called a Full condition—Full of both yang and yin, or, in the case of foods and people, both Qi (vital energy) and Blood.For example, an overweight and very warm person is very Full. On the other hand, if something is relatively lacking in both yang-energy and yin-matter, or both Qi and Blood, then it is said to be Empty. For example, an underweight and cold person is very Empty.

Among foods, raw salad vegetables, fruits, and sugar are all relatively Empty. That is, they have very little substance, and very little energy, to offer to us. We commonly refer to them as "light" foods. On the other hand red meats, eggs, and dairy foods are all extremely Full; they are very rich in very dense, energy-rich fat, and protein and other materials that build the body substance and weight. We commonly refer to them as "substantial" or "rich" foods.

Cooked green leafy, root, and round vegetables, and cooked fruits are on the Empty side of things, but not as Empty as those cited above. On the other hand, eggs are not as Full as fish, poultry, meat and so on. Whole grains strike a balance between Filling and Emptying—the endosperm is Filling, the bran is Emptying.

This leads us to a systematic and very sensible way of understanding foods. When people eat Full foods to excess, they become Full. Diets that include copious amounts of meats, eggs, and dairy foods tend to create overweight, overheated, uncomfortable people with Hot diseases. When people eat Empty foods to excess, they become Empty. Diets rich in raw vegetables and fruits, and sugar, create people who are underweight (very light is yang) but also cold (yin). Thus they suffer from cold disorders.

The so-called Standard American Diet is composed primarily of these two extreme groups of foods. People in Western countries eat meals composed largely of Full meats, eggs, or dairy foods, with Empty side dishes of white bread, white rice, potatoes, fruit and salad, followed by or washed down with Empty coffee, sweet desserts, fruit juices, or soft drinks. In this way, the average American seeks a sort of "balance" between Filling and Emptying.

From the traditional Oriental perspective, this way of eating causes immense stress to the internal Organs. The Full foods are too Full—too dense and hard to digest. On the other hand, the Empty foods are too Empty—that is, practically devoid of any redeeming nutritional value. The result is a diet that creates degenerative dis-eases, complex conditions that combine both accumulated extreme Excess—stress, obesity, high cholesterol, tumors, and so on—and severe Deficiency—nutritional deficiencies, fatigue, poor circulation, depression, and so on.

Traditional Oriental medicine recommends that, rather than build our diets around such extreme foods, we choose foods that are more neutral or balanced in and of themselves. Those are whole grains and legumes. Cooked and raw land and sea vegetables, and some of the highest quality animal foods complement one another and supplement this core. Everything else is an option rather than a necessity. You may choose to Nourish your Life with a purely vegetarian diet supplemented with some eggs or raw dairy foods. Others may choose to eat a purely vegetarian diet supplemented with fish. Still others may opt for a mixed diet. The option is yours.

Nourishment For Life
Spectrum of Foods

More Yang Foods

These foods have denser protein thicker fat, and/or excess minerals.

More Yang Foods

Over consumption causes heaviness, dullness, density, heat, irritability, and stagnation.

Refined Salt

Meat

Poultry

Hard cheese

Whole Undried Salt

Shellfish

Fish

Miso/Tamari

Eggs

Soft cheese

Yogurt

Seeds & Nuts

Natural Whole Foods

these foods have a balance of nutrients, liquid, and fiber.

Beans & Peas

Whole Grains

Root Vegetables

Ground Vegetables

Natural Whole Foods

Regular consumption creates a healthy condition.

Leafy Vegetables

Sea Vegetables

Vegetable Oils

Local Fruits

Refined Grains

More Yin Foods

These foods and drugs have more fiber water, sugar and/or relatively few nutrients.

Tropical Fruits

Refined Sugars

Coffee, Alcohol

Drugs

More Yin Foods

Over consumption creates cold-weak-wet-soft deficiency conditions

Nourishment For Life Food Guide Pyramid

The Food Groups of traditional Oriental medicine can be graphically displayed as a pyramid with successive stories made of receding discs, the grain level twice as large as the vegetable level, the vegetable level twice as large as the supplementary foods level, and the supplementary foods level twice as large as the seasonings and condiments level.

5%
salt/oils
nuts, herbs, fruits

supplementary foods
animal foods— ~10%

tertiary vegetable foods
beans and sea weeds—10-15% of daily meals

secondary vegetable foods
green leafy and deep orange and sea vegetables—
25-30% of daily meals

whole grains—principal food
40-50% of daily meals—cereals, pasta, bread, rice

We can also view the food groups as pieces of a pie or dinner plate.

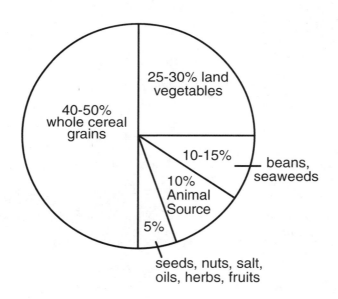

Note: Percentages in this chart refer to volume, not weight or calories.

This vision of what constitutes nourishment for life is in complete harmony with the dietary guidelines recently published by leading experts in western governments. Most of us grew up with the Four Food Groups of the U.S.D.A.– the Meat and Meat Alternatives Group, the Bread and Cereals Group, the Fruits and Vegetables Group, and the Dairy Products Group. Recently the U.S.D.A. reorganized the Four Food Groups into a Food Guide Pyramid, which appears to urge Americans to use grain products as the base of their diet, which fruits and vegetables as foods of secondary importance, and meat, meat alternatives, and dairy products as foods of tertiary importance. This most recent dietary guide comes remarkably close to the 3000 year old guidelines of traditional Oriental medicine. Ancient Oriental truth is slowly becoming known to modern western medicine.

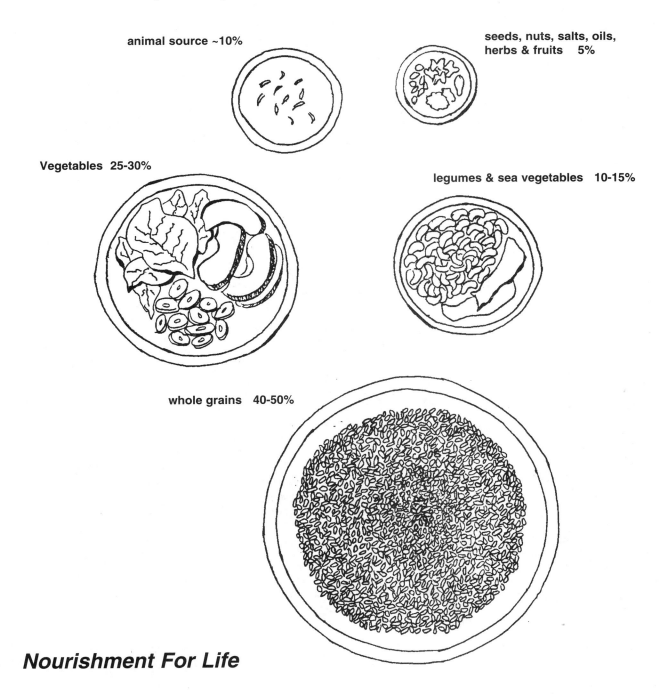

animal source ~10%

seeds, nuts, salts, oils, herbs & fruits   5%

Vegetables 25-30%

legumes & sea vegetables   10-15%

whole grains   40-50%

Nourishment For Life

Comparing The Popular Diets

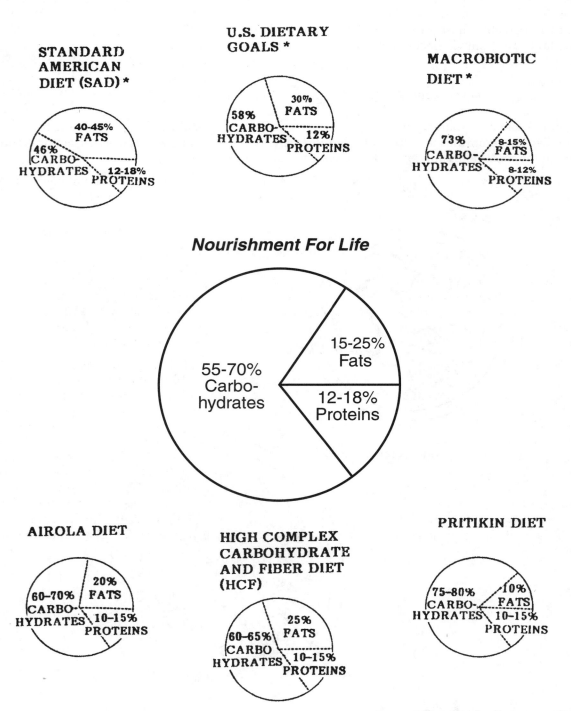

STANDARD AMERICAN DIET (SAD) *

40-45% FATS
46% CARBO-HYDRATES
12-18% PROTEINS

U.S. DIETARY GOALS *

30% FATS
58% CARBO-HYDRATES
12% PROTEINS

MACROBIOTIC DIET *

73% CARBO-HYDRATES
8-15% FATS
8-12% PROTEINS

Nourishment For Life

55-70% Carbo-hydrates
15-25% Fats
12-18% Proteins

AIROLA DIET

20% FATS
60-70% CARBO-HYDRATES
10-15% PROTEINS

HIGH COMPLEX CARBOHYDRATE AND FIBER DIET (HCF)

25% FATS
60-65% CARBO-HYDRATES
10-15% PROTEINS

PRITIKIN DIET

10% FATS
75-80% CARBO-HYDRATES
10-15% PROTEINS

Note: The percentages above refer to the percentage of calories that typically comprise each diet.

Nourishing The Earth: The Ecological Side of Diet

Probably the founders of traditional Oriental medicine were the very first ecologist. The Classic emphasizes that human nature is inseparable from the Heavens and the Earth, and that nourishment for life is to be found in harmonizing with natural cycles. Thus the goal of Oriental science is to make human lifestyles ecological. This is reflected in the guidelines of traditional oriental dietetics. In fact, Oriental dietary guidelines are but reflections of the inherent order of living nature.

Since the foundation of life on Earth is the vegetation, ecological nourishment is primarily vegetarian. Since grasses are the most abundant forms of plant life, grains—the progeny of grasses—are naturally the most abundant of agricultural crops. Mother Earth naturally gives birth to more grasses than succulents, and more succulent vegetation than fruits or fish. The most natural way of farming flows with, rather than against, the river of life, and will produce more grains than vegetables, and more vegetables than animals or fruits. Such ecological agriculture, harmonizing with the Tao of life on Earth, exemplifies the Oriental scientific principle of wu wei—non-egocentric action—and will produce the most nourishment, with the least human toil and trouble.

Of course, an ecological diet will also reflect this order. The dietary advice of Oriental medicine urges us to re-orient our meals to reflect the Tao, by eating more grains than vegetables, and more vegetables than animal foods or fruits.

How Much Does It Cost?

Many popular dietary plans sound simple on paper, but in practice they often cost an arm and a leg. This is especially true of those plans that are built around imported Japanese foods, fruits, juices, animal foods or expensive nutritional supplements. Economic stress, over-work, and "drudging for dollars" at Spirit-breaking jobs are major causes of modern illnesses, and any dietary plan that increases financial burdens cannot be considered to be true Nourishment for Life.

Since the dietary way of Oriental medicine is based upon the most abundant and least expensive foods available — whole grains — and uses little of the less abundant and most expensive foods — animal products, fruits, nuts, and imported delicacies — it is, without effort, a very economical way to eat. The economic cost of a food reflects its ecological position in relationship to the consumer. That is, those foods that are close at hand and easily produced are inexpensive, and those foods which come from far away and are difficult to produce are more expensive. For example, since it takes 16 pounds of grain food to produce one pound of beef, one pound of beef steak costs (at least!) sixteen times what one pays for a pound of grain. Similarly, when one considers the nutrient value of vegetables in comparison to fruits, fruits are very uneconomical foods. In China, where fruit cultivation is not artificially supported by intensive irrigation systems, fruits are very expensive, reflecting their relatively insignificant position in more natural ecosystems and agricultural production. Finally, imported, out of season foods and delicacies are far more expensive than locally produced, in-season, more "coarse" foods.

In Keeping with the Seasons

Produce is the primary part of our diet that needs to change with the seasons, although even here the change may be minimal, depending upon where you live. Many of the staple vegetables that we use can be grown and harvested and/or stored throughout most of the year. Examples include cabbages, collards, kale, mustard greens, carrots, winter squash, burdock root and onions. Throughout the year you can follow the same basic meal plans based on whole grains. You can use the same grains, beans and legumes. Whatever the season, it is important to eat grains and vegetables at every meal and to rely mostly on whole grains, supplemented by some breads and noodles. Basically, you can use the same cooking techniques and recipes, with only slight variations, throughout the year. By varying ingredients in subtle ways, according to the season and what you have on hand, you can keep your meals interesting.

There is no need to make radical changes in either cooking techniques or diet as the weather changes. You don't have to switch from short grain to long grain brown rice. You can still pressure cook your rice. You do not have to reduce the amount of salt you use in cooking or the amount of grain you eat. It is also advisable to have a cup of miso seasoned vegetable soup and/or stews every day, regardless of the weather. As for breakfast, even in warm weather it is best to continue to break your overnight fast with soft, warm or hot cereal, millet, rice, or noodles, with cooked greens or pressed salad, seed condiments; sea vegetables and soup, stew or a yellow/orange vegetable side dish. These foods are as appropriate as breakfast side dishes in warm months as they are in cold months.

The Middle Way

A healthy diet is a "centered" grain-based diet. This means using foods and preparation techniques that are neither too heating nor too cooling. For centuries, this ancient, timeless knowledge originating in the Orient has successfully helped people to maintain optimal health. At the core of this knowledge is the idea that the human body is a warm organism generating its own heat through metabolic processes. To function optimally, it needs to stay warm internally. This inner warmth or inner fire of life is sparked and maintained by consuming foods that are primarily warm in nature.

According to the Oriental system of medicine, foods and cooking techniques can be classified on a continuum ranging from cold to hot. Grains fall in the middle of this continuum and are considered neutral to cooling. For this reason, they should be the primary foods in all seasons. A grain-centered diet helps the body's maintain an even, relatively warm temperature. They will cause us to neither over-heat nor cool us off too much. Most seeds, nuts, and beans fall just outside of grains—with beans being a bit more cooling than grains, and seeds and nuts being a bit more warming. However, these foods are still very neutral when compared to vegetables, fruits, or animal products. Most vegetables and fruits fall on the cooling to cold end of the spectrum with fruits and tropical origin vegetables being more cold than temperate climate produce. On the other end of the spectrum, most animal products are warming to hot. Flesh foods, particularly warm-blooded animals, are the most warming while dairy foods and eggs are less warming.

Of preparation techniques, raw preparations are more cooling, while cooked preparations are more warming. Baking and deep frying are more heating while stir frying, sautéing and soup making are more neutral. Steaming and simmering are more cooling than either of the latter methods. It should be noted that these methods are relative, that is, they are more warming or cooling "relative" to each other. Deep fried vegetables are more warming than stir fried, steamed, or simmered vegetables, but none of the vegetables are as hot or yang as meat or poultry. Likewise, steamed vegetables are more light and cooling than stir fried vegetables, but they are certainly *not* as cooling as raw salads or fruits. Similarly, cooked fruit is less cooling than raw fruit, but it is still very cooling relative to vegetables, and it is even more cooling relative to grains or meat.

From the Oriental medicine perspective, it is important to eat warm foods (cooked or at least room temperature) most of the time, even during warm weather. Summer is the time to store warm energy for the coming fall and winter. Cold and raw foods disperse and expel body heat; thus, eating too many of cool and/or raw foods in any season can deplete the body's vital energy stores and injure the Spleen and Stomach (the digestive fire) and the Kidney fire (the fire of life). If you eat too many cold and/or raw foods in the summer, you will likely create health problems that will not show up until fall or winter, when you will tend to become very cold and find it difficult to adapt to winter weather. To maintain health, store up cooling energy for the spring and summer in the fall and winter by eating seasonal vegetables and cooked meals, with small to moderate amounts of raw foods. By eating mainly cooked foods and avoiding an excess of cold temperature, cold energy, or raw food in the spring and summer, we can store up the warmth of summer and conserve some of our internal heat so that we will have it in the coming fall and winter.

Just as too much cold and raw foods in the summer makes us ill adapted to fall and winter weather, a lack of lightly cooked leafy green vegetable dishes in winter can lead to imbalances and an inability to adjust to the coming summer. The best way, as always, is the middle way. This means basing your diet on whole cereal grains with cooked vegetable and bean side dishes throughout the year. Just as a diet which contains excessive amounts of vegetables, fruits, or raw foods can create a Cold and deficient condition (by emptying one out), too many animal foods, whether flesh or dairy, can plug us up creating problems of excess and pathological Heat. According to the principles of Oriental medicine, it is particularly important to focus the diet on middle-range foods—avoiding overly heating or overly cooling foods and eating enough warming, well-cooked foods.

The teachings of Oriental medicine recommend that we harmonize with the weather or a body temperature consistent with the outdoors. Trying to be too warm in the winter or too cool in the summer is, in effect, going against nature (or against the grain). By minimizing the difference between our body and the external environment, we come into balance and naturally feel more comfortable whatever the weather. By eating a centered diet, you will more easily adapt to both hot and cold weather. Eating a diet of extremes (both extreme Cold and extreme Hot foods), you will likely have a harder time adjusting to the changes in your environment and may become more dependent on artificial temperature regulators such as air conditioning and over-heating.

Since nature provides the necessary balancing qualities in the foods of each season, eating with nature will naturally bring us into balance. A centered diet provides a balance of foods in each season—some of it warming, some of it cooling, and with most of it neutral. A centered diet balances the right amount of grains with appropriate volumes of vegetables, beans, seeds, nuts, fruits and animal foods.

So what aspects of your eating do you need to change with the seasons? The types of vegetables you choose, and to some extent the cooking times, cutting techniques, and serving temperature may shift according to the season. In reality, some of these elements will change only slightly, others may vary more, depending upon our condition and the severity of the climactic change. In general, warmer weather dictates using slightly shorter cooking times for some foods. Cutting vegetables into smaller pieces to facilitate shorter cooking times is also helpful. Eating slightly more pressed and raw salads and leafy greens than root and round vegetables can also be helpful. You may also enjoy serving more of your food at room temperature during warmer months. In contrast, colder weather usually requires some longer cooking times, and thus, cutting some vegetable foods into larger pieces for hearty stews or baked casseroles. Colder weather also dictates eating all or most foods hot from the oven or stove top. In cooler weather, your should endeavor to eat slightly more root, round, and ground vegetables and slightly less leafy vegetables. However, these are not absolutes. Some individuals, due to their state of health or dis-ease, would be well advised to eat more roots, rounds, and ground vegetables than leafy greens regardless of the season or weather. In actuality, the most striking change with each season will be varying the selection of vegetables from your local environment, though even some of these are locally available and/or storable and thus suitable for use throughout most of the year.

Seasonal Vegetables

Choosing Seasonal Produce

Depending upon where you live, there are many vegetables that can be grown year round, with or without the use of cold-frames or other protective devices. However, there are others that are strictly seasonal (or regional). To eat with the seasons, you must first familiarize yourself with the season's offerings. Start a year-round garden or shop either at your local farmers market or a store that supports local growers. (Farmers' markets are making a comeback.) One of the best things you can do for yourself would be to rip out your lawn, if you have one, and plant a garden. This will provide fresh, seasonal produce for you and yours. Eating locally and regionally produced foods puts you in sync with your environment. Eating foods from other climates acclimates you to those other climates but does nothing to help you adapt to the climate in which you live. Thus, consuming out of season foods on a regular basis inevitably weakens the body by making us ill-adapted to the immediate environment and sets the stage for dis-ease.

Warm Weather

Many of late spring and summer's vegetables are watery, tender and juicy —examples include lettuce, wild salad greens, cucumbers, bell peppers, zucchini, summer squash, spinach, mustard greens, sweet corn, chives, arugula, endive, escarole, parsley, dill, mustard and turnip greens, various leafy Chinese vegetables, and tomatoes. Most of these vegetables ripen quickly and spoil rapidly, though some are fairly hardy. Those familiar with summer gardening know that in extremely hot weather, these tender leafy vegetables will often burn out. In contrast, their hardier counterparts are able to withstand extremes in temperature and weather. You can still find some hardy root and round vegetables (carrots, beets, baby turnips, icicle radishes, leeks, scallions, and onions) in the summer, even though the delicate vegetables are the most popular and are typically grown in greater abundance. Hardy greens—such as collards, mustard greens, and kale—are well-adapted and resistant to warm weather as well as cool seasons and grow well in all climates. Thus, these greens, in combination with root and round vegetables, should still form the bulk of our vegetables. By eating mainly vegetables that can withstand both warm weather and cold weather, and those from our region or bio-region, we become well-adapted to seasonal changes. (Winter squash is often ready to harvest as early as late July or early August.)

Cool Weather

Hard, dense, hearty material vegetables are prevalent in the fall and winter. These include winter squashes, rutabaga, turnips, carrot, parsnips, cabbages, brussels sprouts, kale and collard greens, etc. (those that have stored the heat of summer yet that keep far longer than summer's juicy produce). Root, round, and ground vegetables, including hard cabbages, keep for months at a time while kale, collards, and brussels sprouts are hardy enough to withstand freezing temperatures. Some vegetables, such as parsnips, carrots, and Jerusalem artichokes, can be left in the ground over the winter and picked in spring. In the fall you may also be able to enjoy the remnants of summer's produce, including various tender greens and lettuce, parsley, chives, zucchini, bell peppers, and tomatoes.

Seasonal Fruits

Warm weather

Just as with summer vegetables, summer fruits tend to be juicy, tender, and prone to rapid decay. Melons, berries, peaches, apricots, nectarines, plums, and may other fruits are bountiful in warm seasons and climates.

Cool weather

Like Fall and cold weather vegetables, apples, pears and other fall fruits are hearty, dense, and keep for long periods of time, much longer—even at room temperature—than the tender fruits of summer.

Cutting & Cooking For The Seasons

Vegetables

Most vegetables have a cooling energy, though the degree to which they are cooling varies with the vegetable and the method of preparation. To create harmony with our external environment, through-out the year we use leafy green vegetables as well as root, round, and ground vegetables. We also prepare vegetables in soups, boiled salads, pressed salads and sautées and stir fries, pickling, steaming and quick-boiling in every season.

Warm Weather

Cut vegetables into smaller pieces to facilitate quicker cooking. Emphasize lighter cooking techniques such as boiling, quick-boiling, steaming, stir frying, pressing, marinating, and pickling. You can steam hearty vegetables such as winter squash, parsnips, yams or sweet potatoes (cut into 1 to 2-inch cubes) in the the spring and early summer and continue to use them in soups. Even in warm weather soups should be eaten once or twice a day—just make them a bit thinner use local produce. In hot weather, we make marinated and quickly pressed salads. On the hottest days you may wish to eat some cooked, cooled soups or an occasional uncooked vegetable soup. You might as enjoy very small daily servings of raw vegetables prepared as salads or relishes, if your digestion is strong.

Emphasize an equal or slightly greater volume of leafy green vegetables over root and round vegetables in the spring and summer, unless you have a cold or weak condition. In this case, you would want to use about slightly more of the root and round vegetables than leafy vegetables. Bok choy, nappa cabbage, tender spring greens and wild salad greens are good choices. Upward growing leeks or scallions can replace onions more often, and pickles can be made from radishes, cucumbers, sweet and spring onions, zucchini, and other summery vegetables. On the whole, you will harmonize with your environment by simply making your regular soups, stews, stir frys and other recipes using spring and summer produce. You might cut the vegetables smaller so that they cook more quickly, make more steamed and stove-top dishes, and avoid overly heating cooking techniques such as baking. (See the vegetable chapter for more on seasonal vegetables selection and cooking technique.)

Cold Weather

In cooler or cold weather cut some of your vegetables into larger pieces or leave them whole. It is also appropriate to cook some of your vegetables for longer periods of time. Yet, even in cold weather it is not a good idea to cook everything for a long time, nor to cook everything in the oven. Make baked vegetables often, but also try nishime and kinpira style vegetables daily or at least several times per week. Emphasize more quick-boiled and sautéed vegetables and boiled salads rather than raw or pressed salads. Though you can still prepare cabbage, kale, or collard-green based salads throughout the fall and winter months by using pressing, marinating, quick-boiling, or parboiling techniques, avoid or minimize tossed salads. Also be careful not to eat too large a volume of pressed salad (a small portion several times per week or once per day is plenty). You may wish to briefly steam your pressed or marinated salads before serving to take the chill off. Also, pressed cabbage-type salads should be pressed for a longer time (8-24 hours) as you move into late fall and winter. Aside from pressed or marinated salads, hardy cabbage-family vegetables can be cooked into soups, stews, sautées, and stir fries.

Gravies, sauces, and hearty root vegetable soups and stews are appropriate fare in cold weather. Although you will want to use a slightly greater proportion of root, round and ground vegetables than greens in the fall, winter, and early spring, don't neglect leafy greens altogether. It is still essential to have the upward energy and fresh, dark, green, leafy vegetables or cabbages at every meal (or at least twice per day) throughout the year. It is best to minimize or skip the tossed lettuce salads as you move into late fall and avoid them altogether in the winter. Fall and winter are good times to emphasize cabbage and root vegetable pickles.

Seasonal Grain Preparations

Most grains can be used freely in any season. In fact, seasonal shifts require only slight variations in the selection and preparation of these central and neutral foods. For example, pressure cooking is appropriate throughout the year, though boiling can be used more in warm weather or for morning porridge in any season.

When cooking vegetables and grains together, use the vegetables of the season (turnips or sweet winter squash in fall, winter, and early spring; cauliflower or sweet corn in summer and fall, etc.) Rolled oats and other rolled grains which cook up quickly can be used any time of year. Hot or warm grain porridge is perfectly appropriate in any season. Grain porridge generally has a harmonizing effect, cooling us when we are hot, warming us when we are cold.

Warm Weather

As the weather warms in the spring, you might continue to use brown rice and millet as primary grains, just toss some barley in with your rice or morning millet once in a while or make barley-rice porridge on a weekly basis. Sprouting grains such as wheat, rye, spelt or kamut berries and cooking them in with rice is also nice now and then and it is an ideal way to add a spring-like sprouting energy to your meals. Use sweet rice less often as you move into warmer weather. In warmer weather, you may wish to use polenta or cornmeal more often, either alone or combined with rice, millet, or rolled oats. Corn tonifies the Heart. Since polenta is made from corn, and summer is the time when the Heart is most active, it is an especially good time to use this food. Masa harina—a specially prepared instant corn dough used for tamales, dumplings, and tortillas—is particularly nice during summer though it can be eaten in any weather. Steamed tamales, corn dumplings, and corn tortillas made from masa are particularly good in these seasons. Buckwheat is also a good cooling grain for the warmer seasons, either used alone or combined with rolled oats, teff, sweet corn, or mixed with precooked brown rice for dinner grain or breakfast porridge.

As the weather warms up, you might use noodles more often and use more millet or polenta slices to replace baked corn and loaf breads. You can also make more rice balls, nori-maki sushi rolls, and occasional whole grain or noodle salads as the weather warms up. Use mochi and sweet rice much less often. Emphasize breads that are steamed or cooked on a griddle rather than baked. When you do bake breads, emphasize focaccia, bagels, chapatis, pita and other quick-baked varieties over dinner rolls, loaf breads, and other long baked, heat-holding, energy intensive breads. Minimize or save pizza for late summer and early fall. To lighten and freshen leftover breads, steam heat them instead of toasting. When using rolled oats, combine them with vegetables or a second grain such as rolled barley, spelt flakes, millet, cornmeal, leftover noodles, leftover cooked rice, or kasha (roasted buckwheat).

Warm porridge or dinner grain is still your best bet for breakfast, even in warm weather. You can let your hot cereal cool off a little before you eat it. You can also serve warm porridge or rice with room temperature, cooked vegetables or leftover pressed, marinated, wilted, boiled, or tossed salad. Skip the whole oat groats and overnight stove-top cooked cereals in hot weather, however. Steamed or nishime cooked winter-type squash is a good side dish with breakfast in the spring and summer (sweet corn is good in late summer and fall). During the hottest days of the year try Cold-Cooked, Counter Top Oats or Vegetable Muesli. Or, add sweet corn or fresh peas to morning cereal or dinner grain during the peak of the season. If you get really fresh, really tender corn, you can occasionally eat it in a raw, uncooked form in the heat of summer--off the cob, in a salad, or in a gazpacho-type soup.

Cool Weather/ Cold weather

As the weather cools, use sweet rice, mochi, and steel cut or whole oat groats more often, all have a heavy and sticky quality more suited to winter weather. We like sweet rice combined with millet often with the addition of beans or sweet root or round vegetables. You can also cook winter squash or dried chestnuts in with your grain. (If you live in a two-season climate or a geographical area which gets very little warm or dry weather, you may use these grains throughout the year, even in the alleged "spring" and "summer.") Occasionally, add some nuts or seeds to the grain pot before cooking dinner grain or breakfast cereal for added warmth, energy, and a change of texture.

In the fall and winter, you can make many of the same breads and whole grain dishes as in the spring and summer, but now you can add in more loaf breads, rolls, and baked grain casseroles. Though pasta and noodles can be eaten in these seasons, you will want to serve them warm and with a sauce or various toppings or condiments. Definitely avoid making chilled noodle or rice salads in the winter. Also avoid Counter Top Oats and Vegetable Muesli during the late fall and throughout the cold season. Instead, make overnight cooked cereals more frequently during the colder months or make simmered or pressure cooked breakfast cereals.

Beans

Beans, legumes, tofu, tempeh, and wheat meat are good to use in all seasons. We also cook beans and legumes in with our rice or millet, and we make bean, tofu, tempeh, and wheat meat burgers now and then in every season. We use these products in soups, stews, sauces, and stir fries through out the year. What changes from season to season is the vegetables we add to them, though it need not change much. The cooking techniques and cooking times for these foods change little, if at all. The serving temperature for these foods may change slightly, with some bean products served at room temperature, though most are served warm throughout the year.

Warm Weather

You may wish to make bean, tofu, and tempeh dips, spreads, and salads more frequently as the weather warms up. Refried beans and tofu sour cream are particularly tasty in the warmer months and soups are always a hit. Emphasize tofu slightly more than wheat meat, perhaps using tofu several times per week, if your condition permits. (If you are cold a lot or have digestive weakness, it is usually best to minimize the use of tofu in any season). Avoid long baked bean dishes. Better yet, opt for stove top bean, tempeh, tofu, and wheat meat side dishes and casseroles. Also, prepare more fermented bean dishes in these seasons—such as natto made from chickpeas or other beans; miso or umeboshi pickled tofu; tempeh, etc.

Cool & Cold Weather

During the colder months, use beans, tofu, tempeh, and wheat meat in baked casseroles, thick stews, and hearty sauces and gravies. You can also cook beans or legumes into the rice or millet pot. In colder seasons, make your bean soups and stews a bit thicker and pair them up with the season's hardy roots and round vegetables. Try sweet rice and millet combined with beans, or chestnuts with azuki beans and sweet winter vegetables. Hungarian Goulash, Stroganoff, and wheat meat loaves are also wonderful in the colder seasons. The occasional pan fried tempeh, tofu, or wheat meat can also add extra warmth in the dead of winter.

Sea Vegetables

There are no major seasonal changes in our use of these foods except that we may occasionally use them in baked casseroles in colder weather and in raw, tossed, marinated, or dressed salads in warmer weather. When preparing sea vegetables with land vegetables we simply pair them up with the produce of the season. Occasionally we combine them with dried vegetables as well. (See the sea vegetable chapter for more specifics.)

Desserts

Though most of our desserts are suitable for any season, some have definite seasons. In general, amasake puddings, chestnut desserts, and fruit compotes and sauces are good any time of year. When using fruits, however, use what is in season in your local area and use those moderately, even in the heat of summer. (**Note:** Just because it's at the market doesn't mean it is in season in your area) Search for foods grown in our area, or as close to home as possible. There are, however, some changes that should be made in our selection and preparation of desserts. Cakes, bars, brownies, and most baked cookies should be saved for infrequent use. When you do have them, it is best to have them in the fall and winter since they are baked and heavy and hold a lot of heat. Save the baked apples and most pies for the colder months as well. As the weather warms up, lighter desserts such as fruit gels and aspics are more appropriate. Raw fruits may also be used occasionally. Baked fruit crisps, steamed or no-bake cookies, and similar desserts are also suitable for occasional use in warmer weather.

Seasonal Serving Tips

In warm weather it is helpful to plan to do the bulk of your cooking in the early morning, before the temperature gets too hot. If you set aside a good hour in the morning, you can cook food for the day, with some leftovers for the next day—then leftovers can be reheated for lunch or supper as needed. Fill in dishes, such as stir fries, sautés, steamed vegetables, or pressed and marinated salads can be made any time as these take little time and won't overheat the house. And don't forget the Thermal Cooker (a special thermos-like cooking unit). If you have one, you can cook soup for just ten minutes on top of the stove, slip it into the insulated jacket, then let it cook for one, two, or up to eight hours off the stove. This can help you cook, without overheating, in even the hottest weather. Other foods can also be made in this ingenious, ecological, cooker.

In warmer weather, you may want to serve some of your food at room temperature, while in the winter it is best to serve most foods fresh from the oven, stock pot, skillet, or steamer tray. Leftovers are more often heated in cold weather and more often unheated in warm weather, though you can still eat both room temperature and warmed foods throughout the year. For example, leftover steamed, stir-fried, or sautéed greens or mixed vegetables should be served at room temperature throughout the year because reheating them weakens and over-cooks them. With millet, rice, or bread, regardless of season, grains are most digestible and flavorful when steam heated before serving. When eating away from home, they can be eaten at room temperature, although they are more enjoyable when served with a thermos cup of warm soup. Microwave ovens should be avoided at all times.

When its super hot outside, serve more cool or room temperature foods if your digestion is good. (If it is poor, it is prudent to serve most foods warm so as to avoid putting out an already weak digestive fire). You may wish to serve one or more dishes in a meal at room temperature. Don't serve foods ice cold from the refrigerator, however. Ice-cold foods paralyze the stomach and weaken the digestive fire. Leftover or prepared soups, stews, bean dishes, noodles, rice, millet slices, steamed or stir fried veggies, potatoes, steamed winter squash, corn on the cob, tofu or beans dishes, and many other foods are delicious and satisfying when served cool, at room temperature. In many cases (particularly in warm weather), they needn't be reheated before serving: simply take them out of the refrigerator 30-90 minutes before serving and serve them cool, perhaps with one warm or freshly made dish.

Sample Week of Summer Meals

	Breakfast	**Lunch**	**Dinner**
Wed.	Buckwheat & Teff Cereal	Daikon-Onion Alaria Soup	Cream of Summer Squash Soup
	Seed Condiment or seed oil	Brown Rice	Leftover rice
	Leftover sautéed greens	Leftover pressed salad + oil	+/- Panfried Tempeh Cutlets
	Roasted nori or kelp	Seed condiment	Leftover seed condiment
	Chive or parsley garnish	Sprout or parsley garnish	Leftover pressed salad +/- flax oil
Thurs.	Millet-Polenta Porridge	Leftover daikon-alaria soup	leftover summer squash soup
	Cooled, Boiled Greens	Leftover rice	Polenta-Rice, topped with
	with 1-2-3 Dressing	Seed condiment and/or oil	+/- Leftover tempeh cutlets
	Roasted dulse or nori	Marinated salad or greens	Seed Condiment
	Seed condiment or egg	Parsley or scallion garnish	Leftover greens with dressing
	Fresh dill garnish	Corn on the cob	Red radish, onion, or daikon pickle
Fri.	Millet & Oatmeal	Buckwheat or Spelt Buns	Cream of Carrot Soup
	Roasted dulse or nori	Tofu Spread or Quark	Leftover polenta-rice topped with
	Steamed winter squash	Dulse Flakes	Seed condiment or seed oil
	Sunflower seed condiment	Boiled Salad	Sea Vegetable Flakes (to top grain)
	Leftover marinated salad	Pickles	Leftover boiled salad + oil
	Fresh parsley garnish	Fruit Gel or Amasake	Onion, radish, or daikon pickles
Sat.	Cold-Cooked Oats	Leftover cream of carrot soup	Plain noodles topped with
	Grated carrot +/- apple	Leftover Buns	Diluted Miso-Tahini or seed condiment
	Shredded salad greens	Leftover tofu spread or quark	Sea Vegetable Condiment or Sea Flakes
	Minced celery & dill	Sautéed Greens	Leftover sautéed greens or pressed salad
	Soy or goat yogurt or milk	Onion or radish pickles	Beet Root Relish
Sun.	Noodle & Oat Porridge	Cream of Zucchini Soup	Chili-Bean Stew with seitan or tempeh
	Pumpkin Seed Condiment	Rice with sweet corn	Leftover buns or tortillas
	Stir Fried Vegetables	Seed condiment	Millet Butter or other spread
	Roasted dulse or kelp	Leftover sea vegetable	Boiled Salad + sesame-soy dressing
	Parsley or dill garnish	Leftover stir fry	Chive, parsley, or scallion garnish
	Steamed or Nishime Squash	Leftover beet root relish	Sauerkraut or other pickles
Mon.	Rolled Barley & Oatmeal	Leftover chili-bean stew	Leftover zucchini soup
	+/- ume or apriboshi paste	Leftover buns or tortillas	leftover rice with sweet corn
	Roasted dulse or kelp	or rice with sweet corn	Pumpkin or sunflower seed condiment
	Seed condiment or seed oil	Pressed salad + seed oil	Sea vegetable flakes or condiment
	leftover boiled salad	Pickle +/- spread or seeds	Glazed Greens or Mixed Vegetables
	Chives, scallions or parsley	Chives or scallions	Chives or parsley
Tues.	Corn-rice porridge (leftovers)	Yogurt or Milk w/ginger	Quick Miso Soup
	Roasted dulse or nori	Tortillas or chapatis	Brown Rice
	Seed condiment or seed oil	Cooked, Mashed Squash	Stir Fried Mixed Vegetables
	Leftover glazed vegetables	Miso-Nut Butter Spread	Corn on the cob with umeboshi
	Chives, scallions, or dill	Leftover pressed salad	Chives, scallions, or dill
	Onion pickles or beet relish	Parsley or scallions	No-Bake Cookies or Fruit Gel or Aspic
Wed.	Vegetable-Muesli, soaked in	Corn Soup (from leftovers)	Leftover squash, cooled and mashed
	plain soy/goat milk/yogurt	Leftover rice	rolled in tortillas, chapatis, or other bread
	Lettuce, carrot, corn	Seed Condiment	Walnut or Peanut Butter-Miso Spread
	Roasted or raw nuts or seeds	Leftover stir-fried veggies	Quick-Boiled Greens or Pressed Salad
	Roasted dulse	+/- Tempeh Cutlets	Onion pickles, and chives or scallions
	Scallions or chives	+/- Leftover dessert	Plain soy/goat milk/yogurt

Chapter 1
What's in the Kitchen

Basic Staples for a Nourishing Diet

Your initial start up costs may at first seem high; however, once you have stocked up on the basics, it won't cost much to buy fill in ingredients. Most people find that they can eat amazingly well on about $100-$120 per person per month. The foods we use most are the least expensive. These will balance out the cost of some of the more expensive or gourmet type items.

If you can find or start a bulk buying club in your area it will allow you to buy natural foods in bulk, at wholesale, and can cut your food bill by about 40%. See our mail order resource list if you cannot find all of the foods you need at your local co-op or health food store.

A general shopping guide is provided to help you stock your pantry and freezer. You may already have some of these items on hand. It may look like a lot of food, but you will soon discover that it is far easier to plan and prepare daily meals if you have a ready supply of basic dry goods, enough to last for several weeks or a month at a time. You will then be able to plug these staples into a wide array of recipes and meals and you won't have to rush off to the store for last minute ingredients. Of course, you may need to adjust the amount of dry and fresh goods you buy, to meet your budget, family size, and needs. But the more dry goods you have on hand the easier it will be to start cooking and to keep the ball rolling.

It is best to buy fresh produce as needed, once or twice a week. On the weekend you may want to make a rough meal plan for the week, then make a list of any special ingredients that you need to purchase but don't have on hand. Slowly you may add to or replenish your supply of dry beans, various whole grains, flour, pasta, sea vegetables, spices, herbs, seasonings, etc. as you run out or decide to venture into new territory.

Eventually you will want to stock up on the foods you use most. For example, buy the grains you use most in 25-50 pound bags. You will go through them remarkably quickly eating a grain-based diet. You may also wish to buy some pastas in bulk (say in ten pound boxes). Flour, however, is best freshly ground. If purchased, it should be used up within a couple of weeks. Beans, which are used in smaller amounts, are best purchased in one to five pound quantities. You can purchase several varieties of sea vegetables (each in a one or two pound bags) directly from the harvesters. You may wish to purchase several types of miso, each in three, five, nine, or ten pound tubs. Tamari, shoyu, umeboshi and many other products can be purchased by the case or the gallon at a discount. Good quality sea salt can be purchased in one to five pound bags to last for months or for a year or more at a time.

Dried herbs and spices, seeds, nuts, nut butters, yeast, oil, and other highly perishable items are best purchased in smaller amounts that can be reasonably used up within several months. (You can extend the shelf life of nuts and seeds by storing them in the freezer or refrigerator.) These items do not retain their vitality or flavor for nearly as long as whole grains, beans, or sea vegetables. Breads, tempeh, tofu, wheat meat, and other items can be purchased fresh from a local source if you do not make your own, or you may wish to keep some in the freezer for emergency use.

WHOLE CEREAL GRAINS AND GRAIN PRODUCTS

WHOLE CEREAL GRAINS (& WHOLE GRAIN FLOUR)

Primary Grains	Secondary Grains	More Occasional Use
Millet	Sweet brown rice	Mochi
Medium grain brown rice	Chestnuts	Brown rice cakes
Short grain brown rice	Amaranth	Long grain brown rice
Barley	Quinoa	Brown basmati rice
Buckwheat	Teff, ivory or brown	Popcorn
Whole dry corn	Rolled barley	Flour made from any of these
Whole oats	Rolled oats	
Wheat berries	Rolled rye	
Rye berries	Rolled wheat	
Spelt berries	Rolled kamut	
Kamut berries	Rolled spelt	
Pearl or pot barley	Wild or wehani rice	
Flour made from any of these	Flour made from any of these	

WHOLE GRAIN PRODUCTS

Regular Use	Occasional Use
Masa harina	Essene sprouted grain bread
Bulgur wheat	
Cracked wheat	
Steel cut oats	
Corn grits	
Whole wheat couscous	
Other cracked grains	

WHOLE GRAIN FLOUR PRODUCTS

Regular/Daily Use	Seasonal or Occasional Use
Whole wheat noodles	Baked whole grain loaf breads*
Whole spelt noodles	Other baked whole grain breads
Other whole grain noodles	Whole grain crackers*
Dumplings	
Steamed whole grain bread*	
Chapatis or flat breads*	
Tortillas and arepas	
Pita & other quick	
Baked breads **	

* Choose whole grain flour products without sweeteners, with no oil (or very little oil), and without baking powder, baking soda or other artificial leavening. You may choose naturally leavened (sourdough or desem) bread if you prefer it to yeasted products, though yeasted products which meet the above standards are perfectly acceptable for frequent or daily use.

**Quick baked breads baked less than 20 or 30 minutes are preferable to long baked loaf breads. These take less energy, hold less heat, and tend to be more light, moist and easy to digest. See bread chapter for recipes. Loaf breads are more ecological only if made in large batches.

VEGETABLES

Primary use, in season	Secondary use, in season	Infrequent use, in season
(Most nutritious)	(Moderately nutritious)	(Fair source of nutrients)

Leafy greens & cruciferious vegetables	*Other:*	*Other:*
Arugula	Endive	Artichoke
Bok choy	Escarole	Bamboo shoots
Broccoli	Curly dock	Eggplant
Brussel sprouts	Celery	Fennel
Cabbage	Chives	Ferns
Carrot tops	Corn on the cob	New Zealand spinach
Cauliflower	Cucumber	Plantain
Chinese broccoli	Green beans	Potato
Chinese cabbage	Green peas	Spinach
Collard greens	Green and red bell peppers	Salsify
Daikon greens	Kohlrabi	Swiss chard
Romaine lettuce	Mushrooms	Sprouts
Dandelion leaves	Mushrooms, shiitake	Sorrel
Kale	Patty pan squash	Tomato
Mustardcress	Purslane	Other
Mustard greens	Shepherd's purse	
Parsley	Snap beans	
Red cabbage	Snap pea	
Turnip greens	Summer squash	
Watercress	Jinenjo mountain yam	
Other seasonal greens	Wax beans	
Other edible flowers	Zucchini	
Other hard greens		

Root, Round & Ground vegetables

Acorn and danish squash
Beets
Burdock
Butternut squash
Carrots
Daikon radish
Dandelion roots
Delicatta and sweet dumpling squash
Hubbard squash
Jerusalem artichoke
Kabocha, sweet mama, and honey delight squash
Leeks
Lotus root
Onion
Parsnip
Pumpkin
Radish
Rutabaga
Scallions
Sweet potato/"Yams"
Turnip

BEANS

Aduki beans***
Anasazi beans
Black-eyed peas soy beans
Black turtle beans***
Calypso beans
Chickpeas (garbanzo beans)***
Great Northern beans
Kidney beans***
Lentils (green or brown)***
Lentils (red)
Lima beans
Mung beans
Navy beans
Peas (whole dried), green***
Peas, split (yellow, green, or other)
Pinto beans
Small red beans
Soybeans
Other beans

OPTIONAL, FISH & SHELLFISH

White meat fish
Shellfish
Deep sea fatty fish

BEAN PRODUCTS

Bean curd, dried
Natto (fermented beans)
Tempeh
Tempeh Burgers and/or gluten sausage*
Tofu, fresh or dried
Vegetarian Burgers or sausages*
Wheat gluten (seitan; wheat meat) or spelt gluten
Soy yogurt (unsweetened, non-fortified)
Soy milk (unsweetened, non-fortified)

OPTIONAL, EGGS
Free range /fertile eggs from naturally raised, animals

(Use the whole egg—not just the whites)
Chicken eggs
Duck eggs
Quail eggs
Other birds' eggs

OPTIONAL, CERTIFIED RAW AND/OR ORGANIC DAIRY PRODUCTS
From free-range, naturally raised, grass fed animals; unpasteurized; hormone- free

Cultured butter
Ghee/Clarified butter
Organic raw butter
Raw milk yogurt
Kefir or quark
Raw goat milk

---

* Vegetarian burgers— should be free of preservatives, additives, artificial flavorings or colorings, MSG, fruit juice, or sugar. Homemade burgers are ideal. Low-fat varieties are best, preferably made in your city, state, region, or bio-region. Avoid vegetarian luncheon meats; these are highly processed. Avoid most vegetarian hot dogs or limit their use to special occasions. (They are also highly processed food.)

**It is best to avoid the so-called "dairy-free" cheeses. These are highly refined and processed and typically contain casein (milk protein) albeit in an imbalanced form. Like cheese they tend to be high in fat, hard to digest (often more difficult than cheese) and mucous producing. Many have the same or worse effect on digestion and health as cheese: you would do better to have a small serving of raw milk cheese less often; or to use tofu, soy milk, white miso, grated mochi, arrowroot, rolled oats, and/or nutritional yeast to produce creamy, cheesy, or dairy-like tastes and textures.

***These are the beans we use most and find to be the most balanced. Your personal preferences may of course vary.

******About using Fish & Shellfish:** Select fish or shell fish over poultry or meat. Fish heads or bones, sardines, or small dried fish or shellfish would be most ecological. Fish bones could be used to make soup stock.

*******About Using Dairy Products:** If you use dairy products, ghee could be used to replace vegetable oil in cooking or ghee or raw or cultured butter may be used to replace seed or nut condiments as a table condiment for grains or vegetables. (Replace 1 tsp. oil with 1 tsp. ghee or butter; replace 1-2 Tbsp. seed or nut condiment with 1-2 tsp. ghee or butter.) Milk, cheese, or yogurt should be used raw, uncooked, and at the table as a condiments or side dish.

SEA VEGETABLES

Use on a daily basis. We recommend the following sea vegetables harvested off the shores of the American continent (if you live in the United States) or your own continent (if you live elsewhere) rather than those imported from other continents. If you choose to use sea vegetables imported from other continents, we suggest using them infrequently

Alaria
Digitata kelp
Dulse
Fucus (bladderack)
Kelp or kombu
Nori, wild (or laver)
Ocean Ribbons
Sea palm
Silky sea palm
Pacific coast wakame
Sea cress
Other sea vegetables native to your region or continent

CONDIMENTS, GRAIN TOPPINGS, VEGETABLE SEASONINGS

Use appropriate salty condiments to season foods to taste at the table. Do not add salt, tamari, shoyu, ume vinegar, or soy sauce directly to foods at the table; instead, use seed condiments, roasted, crumbled sea vegetables, sea vegetable flakes, sea vegetable condiments, miso-vegetable condiments, or light dressings, sauces or gravies. (See also seasonings below.)

Daily Table Condiments (For daily use as desired)	Other Daily Condiments (For daily in small amounts)	Land and/or Sea Vegetable Condiments
Fresh dill*	Flax oil or seed condiment	Alaria condiment
Fresh or dried chives*	Sunflower seed condiment	Apriboshi vinegar**
Fresh arugula	Pumpkin seed condiment	Brown rice vinegar
Fresh parsley	Sesame seed condiment	Dulse or other sea vegetable flakes
Fresh scallions	Other seed condiments	Kelp or nori condiment, etc.
Other green garnishes	Seasoned nut condiments	Miso-vegetable condiment
Sea vegetable flakes	American umeboshi	Umeboshi vinegar**
	American apriboshi	Tekka

**Ume and apriboshi vinegar, tamari or shoyu soy sauce (which are very salty) are best used by the cook—to season pressed, marinated or parboiled salads, to toss over steamed vegetables, or in making quick pickles, dressings, spreads or sauces—rather than at the table. A very small amount of ume or apriboshi paste, however, may be stirred into or spread over the top of breakfast cereal now and then. Be sure to get a brand that is free of sugar, MSG, artificial colorings or flavorings. Look in a health food store, co-op, or see our Mail Order Resources.

SEASONINGS

For cooking or seasoning foods at the table

Daily or regular use
(Daily if in small amounts)

Optional use
(Use in small volumes, if at all)

Prefered oils:
Light or toasted sesame oil
Flax oil (use raw; do not cook with this)

Raw butter, cultured or uncultured
Ghee, clarified butter

Other cold pressed or unrefined oils:
Olive oil
Sunflower oil
Pumpkin seed oil
Corn oil
Hazelnut, walnut, or other oil
Seasoned or spiced oils
Low-fat/low oil salad dressings

Other seasonings

These should be free of preservatives or additives, sugar and artificial ingredients, and preferably of local origin (from your state, region, bio-region, or continent).

Daily use	Occasional/weekly use	Less Frequent Use
Miso	Brown rice vinegar	Mirin cooking wine
Barley miso		Sake
Brown rice miso		Other cooking wines or sherry
Buckwheat miso		Honey or rice malt
Chickpea miso		Szechuan sauce**
Millet miso		Teriyaki sauce**
Other types of miso		Sweet & Sour Sauce**
Natural organic shoyu		
Natural organic tamari		
Sun dried sea minerals		
Sun dried sea salt		
Umeboshi vinegar or paste		
Apriboshi vinegar or paste		

Note: Umeboshi and apriboshi vinegars are not true vinegars; rather, they are the juice drained from ume-apricots or ume-plums after drying and pickling with sun dried sea salt and shiso leaves. They are both sour and salty; thus, they may replace all or part of the tamari, shoyu, or miso in many recipes. If used to replace true vinegar, reduce or eliminate the salt or salty seasonings in a recipe.

**These are best used very infrequently, if at all. Select those made without sugar, MSG, preservatives, or artificial ingredients. Check health foods store for more natural versions of conventional sauces. Many can also be made at home without sweeteners or with rice malt or barley malt. (Refer to an Asian natural foods cookbook for ideas and/or recipes.)

Garnishes

(Use freely to top or soups, stews, grains, or beans. Use fresh, when in season or use dried varieties anytime. May be grown indoors in pots, for year round use)

Arugula and arugula flowers
Beet, grated
Basil, minced
Carrot, grated
Celery tops, minced
Cilantro, minced
Chives, minced (fresh or dried)

Dill weed, minced
Edible flowers
Parsley, chopped
Scallions, minced
Sprouts, especially sunflower
Other fresh, pungent greens

Spices & Seasonings for use in Cooking

European or American herbs, fresh or dried

Daily or frequent use
Anise seed
Bay leaf
Black pepper
Basil
Caraway seeds
Chili pepper powder
Anaheim, Ancho or chipotle)
Cilantro
Cumin, seed or powder
Dill, weed or seed
Fennel, seeds
Garlic, fresh or dried
Ginger root, fresh, grated
Ginger, dried
Horseradish, grated
Marjoram
Mustard, seeds (brown or yellow)
Mustard, yellow or brown powder
Mustard, prepared stone ground*
Oregano
Paprika
Poppy seeds
Rosemary
Sage
Savory
Tarragon
Thyme

Occasional use
Asefotida
Cayenne
Cardamon
Chili powder
Cinnamon
Coriander
Curry
Garam masala
Mace
Nutmeg
Pumpkin pie spice
Other

* Prepared mustard should be a natural, preservative and sugar-free, such as is found in health food stores and co-ops, or homemade.

** Use a light hand with spices, particularly hot spices and those derived from leaves. ❏

PICKLES

A small volume of pickle may be eaten daily—as a condiment for various grains, or added to salads, soups, stews, casseroles, or other dishes. Pickles are to be made only with sea salt or sea minerals, tamari, shoyu, miso, umeboshi vinegar, apriboshi vinegar, brown rice vinegar, and/or natural quality apple cider vinegar. One's selection need not be limited to dill pickles and sauerkraut. Almost any vegetable can be pickled: onions, leeks, red and green cabbages, cucumbers, daikon (white radish), small red radishes, garlic, ginger, carrots, celery, baby turnips, etc. Briefly marinated sprouts or grated vegetable relishes may also stand in for regular pickles now and then.

Natural sauerkraut or natural, vinegar-free true cucumber pickles can be found in natural foods stores. It is best to avoid the pickles sold in most Oriental markets as these typically contain sugar, MSG, dyes and other unnatural ingredients. The pickles sold in most grocery stores contain poor quality salt, preservatives, additives, and low-quality, artificially produced vinegar.

(See above for examples of vegetable options)

Rice bran pickles

Brine pickles (made with salt, tamari, shoyu, ume, or apriboshi)

Miso pickles

Pressed pickles

Sauerkraut

Tamari or shoyu pickles

Umeboshi or apriboshi pickles

Quick pickles

FRUIT

Cooked, dried, or fresh, in seasonal, northern climate fruit (i.e., from your region or bio-region). Serve in small volume, generally less, usually not more than once or twice per week. Any cooked fruit or prepared fruit sauce should be free of sugar or other sweeteners. Try a pinch of sea salt, raisins or other dried fruit, apple juice and/or chestnuts. Amasake can also be used in fruit desserts. Use of syrups and concentrates should be kept to very infrequent use; these are largely unnecessary if fresh fruits are used with any of the above items. Of syrups, rice syrup and barley malt are preferred sweeteners.

Apples

Apricots

Blueberries

Blackberries

Cantaloupe

Cherries

Crenshaw or other

Honeydew or other

Lingonberries

Marionberries

Nectarines

Peaches

Pears

Plums/prunes

Raisins

Raspberries

Strawberries

Watermelon

SEEDS

These are best raw or very lightly dry roasted (without oil or butter) then seasoned with tamari, shoyu, or salty brine, or ground with sea salt or sea minerals, and used as a table condiment in place of the salt shaker or soy sauce bottle. Seed condiments may also be used to replace butter or oil on whole grains, breakfast porridge, or vegetables.

Regular or daily use

Flax seeds
Pumpkin seeds*
Sunflower seeds
Sesame seeds (black or brown), unhulled
Other seed from your locale
Seed butters
    Sesame butter, raw or roasted
    Sesame tahini, raw or roasted
    Sunflower butter
    Other seed butters

* The pumpkin seeds referred to here are not the same as those you scoop out of pumpkins and squashes. These are green and raised specifically for eating—their outer hull is thinner and they are easier to dry roast and grind, and are much tastier.

**Seed butters should be natural and minimally processed--free of sugar or other sweeteners preservatives, additives, hydrogenated oils, etc. Sea salt may be added by the manufacturer. This poses no problem and actually adds flavor, benefits digestion, and prolongs shelf life. Buy salted or unsalted varieties. Nut and seed butters are very concentrated and best used infrequently or in very small amounts.

Note: We generally mix nut or seed butters with an equal volume of water then add a small amount of miso, tamari, shoyu, or umeboshi then use them as a spread or in sauces, dressing or gravies Or, we use them as an ingredient in some other dish.

NUTS

Raw or very lightly dry roasted, locally grown-nuts may be used in very small volumes as condiments in a meal, or occasionally cooked into or used to garnish desserts or breads, or bean, whole grain, pasta, bread, or vegetable dishes several times week or month. They may be used slightly more often, if used in small amounts, for growing children, pregnant or lactating moms, or those who are active. They should be limited for strict low-fat healing diets, weight loss, or for those or are relatively inactive.

Almonds
Hazelnuts
Peanuts
Pignolias (pine nuts)
Walnuts
Other nuts from your locale
Nut butters*
    Peanut butter
    Almond butter
    Hazelnut butter

* Nut butters should be natural and minimally processed—free of sugar or other sweeteners, preservatives, additives, hydrogenated oils, etc.. Buy salted or unsalted. Added sea salt is not a problems with these products and makes them more flavorful.

Note: Nut butters may be mixed with tamari, shoyu, miso, or umeboshi and water, to dilute them and to aid in digestion.

SWEETS

Sweets for daily use

The sweet taste can be had at any meal by incorporating the following sweet vegetables:

Cabbage
Carrots
Corn, fresh sweet

Daikon radish
Onions, red and white
Kale or collard greens
Parsnips
Rutabaga
Sweet potatoes (or red garnet or jewel "yams")

Squash, winter varieties
Buttercup
Corn, whole dried (posole)
Delicatta
Hokaido pumpkin
Honey delight
Kabocha
Sweet dumpling
Sweet mama
Other

Sweets for weekly use
(Instead of fruit or combined
with fruit or other ingredients)

Amasake, pudding or nectar
Amasake with fruit
Barley malt
Brown rice syrup
Chestnuts, dried or fresh
Chestnut flour in baking/steaming
Raisin purée in dessert making
Apple juice in desserts
Fruit aspics
Fruit puddings or gels
Grain puddings

Celebration use
sweeteners—-
(Not for daily
or frequent use)

Honey*
Maple syrup

Infrequent use desserts
(Not recommended for
frequent use. Once or twice per
month is plenty.)

Cookies (steamed, baked, or other)*
Cakes, steamed or baked*
Biscuits
Pies
Sweet buns, steamed*
Sweet breads, baked or steamed*
Sweet pastries, steamed or baked*

* As much as possible, occasional and infrequent use desserts should be made from whole grains or whole grain flour and should contain very little or no added fat. High quality, minimally processed ingredients should be used—cold pressed vegetable oils, etc. with little or no eggs, milk, butter, ghee, or other dairy products. (Avoid using margarine, vegetable shortening, or other hydrogenated oils. Butter and ghee are far more digestible and healthful than margarine or other hydrogenated fats.) Refer to the dessert chapter or index for further information on sweets and sweeteners.

BEVERAGES

Daily use	Occasional use	Infrequent use (for holidays and celebrations)
Grain coffee, brewed	Corn silk +/- corn cob tea	Northern climate fruit juices
Instant grain coffee	Mu tea	Northern climate vegetable juices**
Barley, roasted	Apriboshi tea	Naturally brewed beer
Chicory root, roasted	Umeboshi tea	Naturally brewed sake
Corn tea, roasted	Other herb or spice teas*	Spiced or mulled cider**
Dandelion root, roasted	Sweet vegetable broth*	Non-alcoholic beer
Licorice tea	Peppermint or camomile tea	
Purified spring or well water	Rosehip or red clover tea	
Other roots and stems	Other herb teas (without fruit)	
used in tea	Soy milk, plain, unfortified	
Kukicha (twig tea)	Northern climate vegetable juices**	
Umeboshi Kuzu Drink		

* Spiced and many herb teas are best used under the counsel of an herbalist or acupuncturist. They have a very strong effect (e.g., hot teas such as cinnamon or cardamom are appropriate for someone with a Cold condition but contraindicated for Hot conditions; conversely, peppermint or camomile tea would be appropriate for one with a Hot condition but not for a Cold person or Cold condition. Sweet vegetables—onions, carrots, winter squash, parsnip, corn, etc. may be brewed singly or in combination then strained to make a sweet tea.

**Juices and cider can be diluted half and half with water or herb tea to lessen their strong dehydrating and thirst-producing effect and to dilute their sugars. Use them very infrequently. Juices are too concentrated in sugars for use on a regular or frequent basis. They are also very expensive and unecological. It is better to eat whole-foods with the fiber and substance intact. (See dessert chapter for more about juices.) If you do choose juice as an occasional beverage, snack, ar dessert, beverage juces (such as carrot) are a better choice than fruit juice and are more nutritious.

OTHER PANTRY STAPLES FOR COOKING & BAKING

For general cooking/baking:
Cal (lime powder for softening whole dried corn/posole)
Koji (culture for amasake making)
Natto spores (for making homemade fermented natto beans; not essential)
Rapid-Rise Yeast *or* Active-Dry Yeast
Wood ash or Tequesquite (a Mexican leavening agent) for corn breads or softening posole
Arrowroot powder/arrowroot starch
Kudzu or kuzu root starch

For cleaning and deodorizing:
Baking soda (for cleaning burned pots and stove top!)
Cheap vinegar (for cleaning burned pots and stove top!)

For dessert making, baking or cooking:
Agar agar flakes or other vegetarian gelatin (for jello making; not essential)
Amasake beverage (comes in several flavors, plain, original, almond, etc.)
Apple syrup (made from cooked down apple cider; not essential)
Unsweetened fruit juice (for baking, dessert making) NOT FOR USE AS A BEVERAGE
Unsweetened apple sauce (this can also be used in baking, to replace oil, butter, or margarine)
Soy milk, unsweetened, plain, fresh, locally made, non fortified—NOT FOR USE IN DESSERTS

START UP STAPLES
BASICS TO HAVE ON HAND

GRAINS & GRAIN PRODUCTS

Brown rice, short grain	10-25 lbs.
Millet	5-25 lbs.
Wild Rice, Amaranth, or Quinoa	1 lbs. of one or each
Rolled oats	3-5 lbs.
Kasha, roasted buckwheat	1 lb.
Corn meal or polenta	1-3 lbs. lbs.
Flour, whole wheat bread flour	
and/or hard white wheat or spelt	5-10 lbs. of one or several
Barley flour	1-5 lbs.
Noodles, domestic udon or soba, or wheat,	
spelt, kamut or other variety	1-4 lbs.
Brown rice cakes, thick, dense variety	1-2 pkgs.
Whole wheat pita or chapatis	2 pkgs.
Loaf bread, wheat, rye, or spelt;	1-2 loaves
(sweetener & oil free, yeasted or sourdough)	

BEANS & BEAN PRODUCTS

Azuki, kidney, or small red beans, dried	1/2-1 lb. of one or each
Chickpea (garbanzo beans), dried	1/2-1 lb. of one or each
Lentils or black turtle beans, dried	1/2-1 lbs. of one or each
Green peas, whole dried or split	1/2-1 lb.
+/- Tempeh, fresh or frozen	1 or 2, 8 oz. blocks
Wheat meat	1-2 frozen pkgs.
+/-Tofu, fresh, firm or silken	1 lb.
+/- Vegetarian burgers (low-fat variety)	

SEASONINGS & OILS

Toasted sesame oil	12-16 oz. bottle
Flax oil, light sesame and/or olive oil	12-16 oz. bottle
Miso:	
Light, sweet, yellow, or mellow miso	1 lb. tub
3-year, dark barley or soy bean miso	1 lb. tub
Tamari	16-32 oz. bottle
Brown rice vinegar	12-16 oz. bottle
Umeboshi plums or apriboshi	1/2-1 lb.
Umeboshi or apriboshi vinegar	12-16 oz. bottle

Sun dried, mineral rich sea salt (macrobiotic quality)	1 lb.
Sesame tahini or sesame butter	1/2-1 lb. tub or jar
Sunflower or peanut butter	1/2-1 lb. tub or jar
Raw, whole flax or sesame seeds	1/2 lb.
Raw, whole, shelled pumpkin seeds	
2nd/or sunflower seeds	1/2-1 lb.
+/- Walnuts or almonds	1/2-1 lb.

SEA VEGETABLES

(Preferably from this continent):

Kelp or kombu, dulse, alaria	1 small pkg. of each or 1 lb.
+/-Sea palm, ocean ribbons, or other	1 small pkg. or 1 lb.
Sea vegetable flakes (dulse or other)	1 small pkg.or 1 lb.
Optional, sushi nori	1 50 sheet package

BEVERAGES

Instant grain coffee (Inka, Pero, Kaffree Roma, etc.)	1 bottle or canister
Brewable grain coffee:	
Roasted barley (mugi cha) or Barley Brew	1 pkg.
Roasted chicory and/or dandelion root	1/2 lb. of one or each
Camomile, peppermint, rosehip or other herb tea	1 pkg. of one or each

DRIED VEGETABLES, HERBS & SPICES

Bay leaves	1/3 cupful
Sage, rosemary, thyme, marjoram, basil, oregano, ground cumin, dill, paprika, cinnamon, ginger, etc.	1/4 cupful of some or all
Mild red pepper powder-ancho, Anaheim, or chipotle	1/4 cupful
Dried onion flakes	1 cup
Garlic granules	1/3 cupful
Dried chives	1 cup
Prepared, natural preservative-free mustard (yellow, stone ground or dijon)	1 small jar

OTHER:

Rapid-Rise Yeast and/or Active-Dry Yeast	3 pkgs. or 1 jar
Arrowroot powder (for thickening)	1/2-1 lb.
Agar agar flakes or vegetarian gelatin	1 pkg.
Amasake, plain or flavored, aseptic or fresh	1-4 pkg. or bottles (8, 16, or 32 oz.)
Popcorn	1 lb.
Rice syrup and/or barley malt	16-oz bottle of one or both
Liquid smoke/Hickory smoke	1 bottle
Raw dairy products, eggs or fish	

FRESH VEGETABLES

(Amount needed will vary with family size; kind will vary with the season).

Onions, white or yellow	3-5 lbs.
Scallions	1-2 bunches
Garlic, fresh	1-2 heads
Ginger root	1-2 pieces
Carrots	3-5 lbs.
Winter squash (*kabocha, buttercup, butternut, sweet dumpling, delicatta, hokaido pumpkin etc.*)	1-3 of one or several varieties
Kale, collards, or Chinese greens	1-2 bunches total
Cabbage, green or Chinese variety	1-2 heads
Broccoli or cauliflower	1 bunch or head
Mushrooms, button, crimini or shiitake	1/4 lb.
Daikon or red radish	1 bunch or 1-2 large pieces
Parsley or chives	1 bunch
Sweet potatoes (red garnet, jewel or white)	2-4
Other seasonal vegetables (*celery, rutabaga, beets, Jerusalem artichoke, turnip, sweet corn, etc.*)	as desired

FRUIT

(Buy organic, local fruit if possible . Fruits are usually heavily sprayed.)

Apples pears, peaches, or nectarines	2-6 pieces
Other fresh, in-season, local fruit	1-2 pints or several pieces
Raisins (for dessert making)	12-16 oz. bag

Kitchen Prep, Washing, Chopping & Storage

Before you dive into the recipe section, there are a few key points that we think are vital to your success. We have listed these below.

1. **Washing Produce:** It is assumed in all recipes that you will wash fresh vegetables and fruits before cutting them and/or using them in a recipe. It is best, however, to only wash the amount of fruit or vegetables that you expect to use within a meal or a day or two. Vegetables contain a natural coating which helps to preserve their freshness; therefore, we do not wash an entire bunch of greens at once, unless we plan to use the whole bunch at once.

To wash leafy vegetables, run them under cold or lukewarm water. If they are particularly sandy (parsley, kale, mustard greens, lettuce, watercress, etc.) dunk them in a bowl or basin of water, swish them around, then remove them from the water. Root, round, or tuberous vegetables should be run under water and scrubbed with a natural bristle brush to remove dirt. (Burdock root, Jerusalem artichoke, and leeks need a bit more attention in washing as they tend to be very sandy, however, they do not need to be peeled—just scrubbed extra well. Leeks should be cut in half down the center then run under water. You will want to run your fingers and the water between each layer of the leek to remove all of the sand.) Most fruits need a gentle rinsing in a strainer; apples, pears, nectarines, and peaches, however, can use a light scrub with a natural bristle brush.

Do not wash or rinse *dried* land vegetables or sea vegetables. Washing removes a good deal of the flavor and minerals found in these foods. These may be used straight away or soaked, chopped, then added to a particular dish or cut with kitchen shears while still dry.

2. **Peeling Produce:** Vegetables do not need to be peeled. Ninety-nine percent of the time we refrain from peeling our vegetables and fruits regardless of whether they are organically grown or not. Peeling is an unnecessary step.

The outer skins of fruits and vegetables are quite nutritious and delicious, even the skins of winter squash are highly edible and tasty. In a few recipes, for appearance sake or texture, you may wish to remove the skins from winter squash, yam, sweet potatoes, or white potatoes before puréeing (say for pie, pudding, sauce, or a mashed potato-type dish). In most mashed dishes, we leave the skins on squashes and parsnips, though. We often peel beets before cooking (when adding them to a soup, stew, or puréed sauce) or after cooking (when they will be cooked whole then sliced and marinated or pickled). We do this to remove the bitter flavor found in the beet's skin. These are the exceptions to the rule. We never peel our apples; we leave the skins on, even when making apple sauces, puddings, compotes, apple pies, crisps, and cobblers.

3. **Waste Nothing:** Use as much of a food as possible. When cutting vegetables—onions, carrots, parsnips, brussel sprouts, squashes, kale, broccoli, scallions, etc.—remove as little of the ends as possible. You will get more flavor, value, and nutrition for your money if you use as much of a food as possible. We always use both the white and the green part of leeks and scallions (green onions). We remove only the roughest looking parts, tossing them into the soup stock bowl. When cutting broccoli—after removing the florets—we peel the stems, then use them. The same goes for cauliflower cores. When cutting kale or collards, we cook and eat the stems as well. (They are very tasty when cooked until tender.) Any vegetable cores and stems can be peeled, sliced, diced, grated or minced then added to soups, stews, stir fries, sautes, pressed salads, steamed dishes. Cores and stems can also be left whole and added to the soup stock pot with other miscellaneous vegetable bits. The tops from carrots can be used to make a tasty condiment when properly cooked and seasoned. Broccoli leaves and brussel sprout, daikon, and turnip greens are all edible. Practice will acquaint you with the best techniques for preparing the parts of a vegetable that are most commonly discarded.

If you cut and use only a portion of a root or round vegetable, simply toss it into the crisper bin (you don't need to put it in a bag, plastic wrap, or a plastic container) or toss it into an uncovered bowl in the refrigerator. Any leafy vegetables that are not used right away are best stored in a cotton or linen storage bag, also in the refrigerator. Half-pieces, quarter pieces, quarter-cupfuls, or tablespoons of cut vegetables can be added to almost any dish, so you needn't waste a thing.

Most cut vegetables should be used within about a week. (Keep ginger root out of the refrigerator, though; it does best in an uncovered bowl on the counter. Kept in a bag, under plastic wrap, in a closed container, or in the refrigerator, fresh ginger collects moisture and molds.)

4. **Use an appropriate knife:** A Mac or Caddie knife is of the utmost importance when working the vegetables. This particular type of knife is designed for vegetables. It has a square blade (6-inches long by 1 1/2-1 1/3/4-inches wide) and a sturdy handle. It will give you crisp, clean cuts and maximum control. A serrated edged knife is designed for sawing back and forth and cutting flesh—and you don't want to cut your own (flesh)! A narrow or pointed blade is completely unnecessary when cutting vegetables and fruits; in fact, such a blade is downright dangerous. A vegetable knife is not meant to be used like a saw; rather, it should be used with a different motion altogether. The motion is more straight up and down or circular and the food is generally cut with the center part of the blade rather than with the tip. In essence, the knife should be viewed as an extension of your arm and should be wielded with your entire body, not just your hand or wrist.

5. **Look after your knife:** Wash your knife and dry it immediately after use. Store it on a magnetic rack, in a wooden rack with slits designed to protect the knife, or keep it in an egg carton so that the blade will not be exposed when you open the drawer. Also, avoid putting a sharp knife in the dish drain as this can lead to a loss of fingers! It is better to wash a sharp knife right away, then put it in its proper place. Better safe than sorry.

Keep your knife sharp. You are more likely to cut yourself with a dull knife than a sharp knife. With a dull knife you will likely end up exerting more force than is necessary and may even saw back and forth, or even slip. A good vegetable knife will need to be sharpened every month or every few months (though some people sharpen weekly), either with a wet stone, sharpening rod, or by a skilled friend or machinist!

To prevent dulling of the blade, avoid scraping your knife across the cutting board, instead use the back of the knife to move cut foods out of the way. Also, use kitchen shears (not your good knife) to open plastic or other packages of food. If you are right handed it is best to sharpen only the right side, if left handed sharpen the left side. Sharpening only one side of the knife adds more control.

6. **Use appropriate cutting techniques:** There is no getting around it, cutting is part of cooking. However, it needn't take up an excessive amount of time if you prepare vegetables in the proper proportions. Since they are not the main dish on a Nourishment for Life Diet, you shouldn't have to spend hours chopping.

We recommend against buying pre-cut vegetable; they are less fresh than those you would wash and cut yourself. We also recommend against using a food processor for cutting vegetables. A processor limits the range of cutting shapes available. It is far better to put as much of your energy into the food as possible, under the premise that you get out what you put in. A food processor cannot turn out match stick slices, irregular wedges or chunks, squares, or other such shapes. Many vegetables turn watery when put through a food processor. (A blender may be used for puréeing soups, sauces, puddings, and the like; but even here a Foley food mill or suribachi will often do the trick. We do not banish all electrical appliances; rather, we use them only when necessary or most effective for the task at hand.)

The way you cut vegetables matters. So how much does it matter? A lot. Small pieces cook more quickly than large pieces; thin slivers cook more quickly than fat chunks. The way you cut a vegetable affects its cooking time, taste, texture, and appearance. Since we eat with all of our senses, you will want your food to be visually pleasing; mastery of a variety of cutting techniques is, therefore, of paramount importance. For a stir fry to turn out right, the vegetables must be cut in thin slices to expose maximum surface area in a minimum of time. If the vegetables are not cut finely enough, they will not be done in the allotted time. For a hearty stew to turn out right, the vegetables must be in larger chunks or wedges so that they maintain their shape during longer cooking. If they are minced or diced, they will dissolve into nothing at the end of the prescribed period of cooking. To be a good cook, you must pay careful attention to what you are doing. Mastery of basic cutting techniques will go a long way to making your food pleasing on all levels. Read on for a rundown of basic cutting techniques.

7. **Keep your work area clean:** A cluttered work area is a safety hazard. If your knife is near the edge of the counter, or pointing toward the edge of the counter, it can easy be knocked off and may cause irreparable damage. Clear sufficient space to comfortably work. If you feel crowded when cutting vegetables, you are more likely to cut yourself than if you have ample room to work and move freely. If you can get in the habit of cleaning up as you go you will have less of a mess to attend to once your meal is ready.

When preparing vegetables, we always keep a number of small to medium sized bowls on the counter. After cutting each vegetables, we arrange them by kind in separate bowls or in a large measuring cup if the vegetables will all be added to a dish at once. We measure out other ingredients and often arrange them in appropriate sized dishes too. This keeps the counter clean and makes it easy to add the ingredients in the order they are called for in a recipe.

8. **Organize your kitchen for maximum efficiency:** Keep the tools you use most within reach. We keep several crocks or ceramic vessels on the counter, filled with the ladles, spatulas, rice paddles, wooden spoons, serving spoons, whisks, blanching spoons, and other tools we use regularly. We keep two sets of measuring spoons on hooks near the sink and stove. Pot holders, cloth trivets, and

heat deflectors or flame tamers are hung near the stove. Measuring cups and a blender sit in the corner on the counter. The water purifier sits next to the sink. The wok and bamboo steamers nest under the cutting block. Pot lids sit in a metal rack atop the refrigerator, next to a jar of sea salt, and a bowl of fresh garlic and ginger root. Tamari, shoyu, umeboshi and other common seasonings are tucked into a nearby cabinet as are the herbs, spices, and the like. The pots, pans, and bowls we use most often are within easy reach as well. Your kitchen may vary from ours, but the point is that the things that you use most often should be kept in a handy place within easy reach.

9. **Organize your pantry & refrigerator for maximum efficiency:** We organize both the pantry and the refrigerator so that we know what we have and are sure to use up old containers of food before buying or opening new ones. The organization is purely practical.

In the pantry, we keep the grains next to the grains; pasta with pasta; beans next to other beans; seasonings next to other seasonings; sea vegetables with all other sea vegetables; dried fruits next to other dried fruits; boxed foods next to other boxed foods (by kind); sweeteners with other sweeteners, etc. Onions are kept in hanging sacks or baskets (in the pantry or kitchen). Apples, winter squashes, and sweet potatoes are kept in a cold box (a cabinet with shelves and a vent to the out doors) until they are cut or cooked, after which they go into the refrigerator. We also keep winter squashes on the mantle piece or on shelves, with space in between each one to avoid spoilage or growth of mold. By storing like foods with like foods, it is easy to find what you are looking for.

In the refrigerator, we keep all the pickle jars next to each other. We also keep all of the miso containers next to each other. Ditto for nut and seed butters, etc. We keep all of the greens near other greens (in dampened cloth or canvas storage bags). We keep the roots with other roots (in the crisper bin or in cloth bags on the shelves above).

FOOD STORAGE

Note: The following storage tips refer to uncooked foods unless otherwise noted.

Grains: Keep whole grains, rolled and cracked grains, and flour products in airtight containers. Whole, cracked, and rolled grains may be stored in large plastic bins with snap on lids, stored in a cool dry place (pantry, closet, etc.). Flour products should be kept in jars in the refrigerator or in bags in the freezer. If you have a cold box or a cool basement, room, or pantry then you may store your flour there, in sealed bins. (Tape a bay leaf to the inside portion of the lid to discourage pests. It is also helpful to hang a special non-toxic bug trap in your pantry or dry goods closet.)

Whole grains will keep for at least a year or up to several years. Rolled and cracked grains should be used within about six months to one year though they will keep longer if refrigerated or frozen. Flour should be used within several weeks; frozen or refrigerated flour may be kept longer. Fresh is always best, though. For truly fresh flour, you must grind it yourself.

Dried chestnuts & chestnut flour: Store peeled, dried chestnuts in sealed bags or jars in the refrigerator, in freezer containers, or in sealed bins or jars in a very cool, very dry place. Refrigerate or freeze chestnut flour.

If chestnuts are inadvertently exposed to dampness and become soft or watery, or if they become buggy, dry roast in the oven at 200-225° F for several hours then return to airtight containers. Fresh, unpeeled chestnuts may be stored at room temperature in a sealed bag, jar, or canister. Use fresh chestnuts within one year, and dried chestnuts within three years. Use chestnut flour within six months.

Noodles/pasta: Store dry pasta/noodles in airtight jars, bags, or bins, in a cool dry place. Dry pasta will keep for years. Fresh pasta should be refrigerated and used within one week. Frozen pasta should be used within one year of purchase and several days of thawing.

Bread: Store in cellophane or paper bags at room temperature for one week, in a cold box for one to several weeks, or the refrigerator for up to a six weeks. Unsweetened, oil-free breads, par-

ticularly desem, natural leaven or sourdough bread, will often keep for up to six weeks (without being frozen) and without molding.

Note: Moist breads such as tortillas, chapatis, and pancakes do not keep as long as most other breads. Refrigerate if they will not be used within 24 hours, or freeze if they will not be used within one or two weeks. Corn bread, batter breads, and muffins may be kept at room temperature but should be used within about one week. When freezing bread, put it in an airtight cellophane or plastic bag. Do not discard bread which has become hard or dry; steam moisten it instead. See the bread chapter for more about bread storage, reheating and remoistening.

Mochi: Store in the freezer for up to several years. Once thawed, or if fresh, use within about ten days of purchase or thawing. Scrape off green mold if it develops and use the unspoiled portion. Aseptically packaged mochi is much more expensive but may be kept at room temperature for years; it can be handy when camping or traveling.

Dry beans: Store in jars or sealed bins or jars, in a cool dry place. Use within several years.

Tofu & tempeh: Keep refrigerated and use within one week of purchase or freeze for longer storage. (See Bean Chapter for specifics). Use frozen tempeh or tofu within one year.

Seeds & nuts: Store shelled seeds and nuts in the refrigerator or freezer to prevent rancidity Store nut or seed butters in the refrigerator after opening. (Gomashio or other salted, roasted seed condiments may be kept at room temperature, though they should be used within two weeks.) Unsalted, roasted nuts or seeds should be refrigerated and used within about one to two months. Store unshelled nuts as per shelled nuts above. Use nuts, seeds, or opened jars of nut or seed butter within one year. (Frozen nuts or seeds may be kept longer.)

Oils: Store in the refrigerator or a cold box. (Olive or toasted sesame oil may be kept at room temperature, in a cool, dry place, away from direct sunlight or in the refrigerator.) Use oils within several months of opening. Oils go rancid quickly. (**Note:** Cloudiness or thickening, as with toasted sesame oil or olive oil, is temporary and not harmful. Oils return to liquid state at room temperature or when held under warm water for one minute.)

Sea vegetables: Store in airtight bags, jars, or bins, in a cool, dry place. These will keep for years and never spoil. If they are inadvertently exposed to dampness and become soft or watery, dry in the oven then return to airtight containers. (Dry roasted sea vegetables are best stored in a sealed glass jar or in an open skillet in a gas oven.)

Dried land vegetables: Store in sealed jars, in a cool dry place such as a cabinet, away from direct sunlight. These will keep for years.

Herbs & spices: Store in small spice jars or bottles; dark glass is preferable as it slows down oxidation and flavor loss. For optimal flavor and longevity, buy spices whole if possible (whole cumin, caraway, fennel, mustard seeds, etc.) and grind them yourself, using an electric coffee-spice mill or suribachi. Store away from moisture or the heat of the stove. A cool closet or cupboard is best. Use dried herbs and spices within one year, if possible. Discard if flavor or aroma become weak.

Dried fruit: Store in sealed jars or inside plastic bags inside jars, in a cool dry place, away from heat or direct sunlight. Or refrigerate. Use within several years.

Tamari & shoyu: These need no refrigeration as the salt preserves them naturally. Store at room temperature, in glass bottles, in a cupboard, cold box, or on the countertop. These last indefinitely and, like wine, improve with age.

Umeboshi/apriboshi vinegar, umeboshi/apriboshi paste, pickled shiso leaf: These need no refrigeration; the salt acts as a natural preservative. Store at room temperature, in glass bottles or jars or in a cupboard, cold box, or on top of the counter. These keep indefinitely.

Miso: Store in wide-mouth glass jars or ceramic crocks with lids, in the refrigerator or a very cool dry place or cold box. Light miso is more perishable than dark miso and should be refrigerated. Because it is fermented, miso keeps indefinitely and, like wine, improves with age. It will keep for years with no loss of potency or flavor. Longer aged miso will have a stronger flavor and unrefrigerated miso may take on a more wine-like aroma.

If a white mold like coating appears on the surface, do not throw the miso away. Simply stir the white stuff back into the miso. This white "mold" is the koji (the fermentation agent or starter) rising to the surface. (Tekka miso—a special condiment made from long sautéed burdock root, carrot, lotus root, ginger, and miso, until it is dry and crumbly—needs no refrigeration; it will keep for at least six months out of the refrigerator if homemade. Store bought tekka is dryer than homemade tekka and should be used within 1 year after opening the package.)

Fresh vegetables: Avoid storing vegetables in plastic bags; this invites mold and suffocates the vegetables. They will keep longer in dioxin-free, natural fiber bags and will be better for it.

Leafy greens, scallions, leeks, chives, and celery: Store in cotton/flannel bags in the refrigerator and use within several days to one week. If possible use bags with a double thickness which may be wet and wrung out to retain moisture.

Hard cabbages: Store in a cold box, cold porch, or directly on shelves in the refrigerator. Use within several weeks or several months. Store brussel sprouts in cloth bags in the refrigerator or if attached to the "tree" they grew on, store on a cold porch, or in the crisper bin of the refrigerator. Use within several weeks.

Tender, watery cabbages, bok choy, Chinese cabbage, etc.: Store in the refrigerator shelves or in cloth/muslin bags. Use within one to two weeks, depending on kind and freshness.

Hardy roots: Store carrots, beets, turnips, rutagaga, parsnips, daikon radish, jerusalem artichoke and burdock root directly in the crisper bin of the refrigerator, no plastic bags are needed. Cellophane bags may be used if desired though we prefer to put them in cotton/flannel or muslin bags on the shelves above the crisper. These vegetables will keep for months in the refrigerator or they may be stored in bins on a cold porch, in a root cellar.

Onions: Round onions with a dry covering keep for months in bins on a cold porch, in a cold box, or in wire baskets away from direct sunlight, moisture or heat, or in a root cellar. Fresh onions which have not been dried on the outside and are sold with their green tops on, (called spring onions) should be refrigerated.

Cut away any moldy spots. Refrigerate portions of cut onions in an uncovered bowl. Store leeks and scallions in the refrigerator in cloth bags.

Winter squashes: Hardy varieties such as kabocha, buttercup, and sweet mama may keep for six to eight months out of the refrigerator if kept dry and in a cool place. Do not allow the squashes to touch each other or moisture will collect and cause molding. We keep them on a shelf above the fireplace (if we are not using it) or in a crate or box with newspaper or cellulose peanuts underneath and between each squash. More delicate squashes such as butternut, delicatta, sweet dumpling, or honey delight may be stored in the same manner but not kept as long. Refrigerate if soft spots develop and cut away soft, moldy spots. Refrigerate a squash after cutting.

Note: If you do not use an entire squash at once, cut out wedges that you need or cut in half and leave the seeds in the unused portion to keep it from drying out. We put the unused portion in the refrigerator, on a shelf, without any plastic wrap or wrap of any kind. The edges will dry out a bit but there will be no flavor loss. Use a cut squash within a week to ten days. If you have a cold box, cut squash may be kept there for several days.

Sweet potatoes & yams: Store red garnet, jewel or white sweet potatoes (popularly called yams but not true yams) in a cool dry place such as a hanging basket or the shelves of a cold box, on a cold porch, or refrigerate if they develop soft spots. Use within several weeks to one or two months . Refrigerate cut portions directly on a shelf in the refrigerator.

Other vegetables: Most other vegetables should be refrigerated after purchase, directly on refrigerator shelves, in natural cloth bags on shelves, or in the crisper section. Put tomatoes in a bowl; keep sweet corn in the husk; and keep bell peppers in cloth or paper bags.

Ginger root: Fresh ginger root should not be refrigerated (this invites mold and spoilage) nor should it be stored in plastic bags. Store in an uncovered bowl on top of the refrigerator, on the counter away from direct sunlight, or in a cold box. It will not dry out or lose flavor kept this way. It should last for several months.

Fresh garlic: Store as per fresh ginger or keep in hanging baskets in the kitchen, away from the steam of the stove. Or, store in a ceramic crock. Use within several months to one year, depending on type and freshness.

Fresh fruit: Store apples in a cool-dry place, in baskets or bowls on the counter, on thop of the refrigerator, or on shelves or stacking wire baskets in a cold room or old-fashioned cold box. Fresh apples—hearty varieties—will keep for at least a month at room temperature or longer in a cold room or cold porch. Refrigerate apples if they become soft or are not used within a month or two (unless you have an alternate cold storage place). Store unripe fruits in a bowl and/or paper bag on the counter. Refrigerate once they become ripe. Store berries and other juicy fruits in bowls covered with a plate, in cellophane bags, or in other sealed containers in the refrigerator.

Pickles: When purchasing ready made pickles in jars, refrigerate after opening and use within about six months to one year. Pickles purchased in sealed plastic bags should be transferred to jars after opening and refrigerated. Use these within about one year or so. Store homemade pickles in the refrigerator after pickling for the recommended time period. Use within several weeks to several months, or keep for a longer time if pickled with more salt. ❏

Chapter 2
Tools, Tips & Techniques

Tips for a Non-Toxic & Natural Kitchen

1) Save glass jars: Glass jars of any size— cup, pint, quart, or half gallon. They are particularly handy for storing bits of this and that— from small amounts of leftover pressed salad, roasted seeds and sea vegetables, or sauce, to pints, quarts, or gallons of dried beans or rice.

2) Use non-toxic storage containers: Plastic storage containers cannot be used to reheat foods the way that glass and steel containers can. It is best to store cooked foods in glass, pyrex, and stainless steel. (See advantages of glass, ceramic, and stainless steel for storing, heating, and serving, below.) Also buy cotton storage bags for produce.

3) Store, reheat and serve in the same containers whenever possible: Glass, stainless steel, and ceramic bowls can be used to store and reheat leftovers. These types of containers are durable, work well, and do not add to our pollution and waste problems. They also cut down on the number of dishes you have to wash since you can store, heat, and serve from the same containers! (This can also simplify meal planning and prep too!)

4) Avoid plastic serving bowls, spatulas and mixing spoons: Plastic utensils and bowls don't hold up to heat well. They emit noxious fumes and toxic gasses such as formaldehyde. They also impart a less than enjoyable taste. We urge you to choose non-toxic and natural materials.

5) Avoid using teflon pans: Teflon is unnatural, and its safety has not been proven. It is a product of the petrochemical industry and is an incredible waste of money and precious resources. Teflon pans do not conduct heat as well as cast iron, glass, or heavy duty stainless steel materials, nor are teflon pans as durable. Teflon and other artificial coatings peel and chip easily. (People have gotten by without teflon for ages and we can too! You will be amazed at how little oil is needed, even for pancakes, if you use our tips. In many cases, you can cook without oil, even without using a non-stick pan.)

6) Avoid aluminum cookware: Aluminum can leach into food and its safety is questionable at best. Better results may be achieved using more traditional cooking methods and by mastering basic cooking techniques! You may pay a bit more for stainless steel and glassware but it's worth it! Heavy-duty stainless steel pots and baking pans as well as glass and enamel-lined cast iron all conduct heat well and are just as long-lasting, or moreso, than high-tech artificial cookware. They are safer too!

7) Avoid plastic wrap: Plastic wrap contains toxic byproducts which have been shown to be carcinogenic. Plastic is also a non-biodegradable material and only adds to our overflowing landfills. Far better and safer alternatives exist for storing and heating foods. We use ceramic or glass plates to cover bowls of food instead of plastic wrap. You can also invest in several sets of stainless steel lunch boxes (usually comprised of stacking round, flat-bottomed bowls which are placed on top of each other for easy storage and transport, all held together with a metal bracket.)

8) Buy cellulose, wax paper, or brown paper bags: These are non-toxic, bio-degradable, and handy for bread, sandwiches, and other baked goods. We use both large and small brown paper sacks for storing breads, arepas, biscuits, buns, etc. We roll or fold them over to close. They work incredibly well and don't invite mold as plastic wrap does! We use the same bags again and again.

9) Avoid aluminum foil as much as possible: Aluminum foil is not biodegradable. It is best used only infrequently, if at all (for example , if you need but do not have a lid for a particular baking pan). Foods can be easily stored in jars or ceramic, glass, stainless steel or pyrex bowls covered with saucers or plates.

10) Buy canvas or mesh shopping bags and storage bags: Invest in several of these and be sure to take them on all shopping adventures (with a supply of old paper and plastic bags). This will minimize the use of non-renewable resources this way and lessen the load on the landfills! Small mesh or tightly woven, double-layered cotton, linen, or canvas bags are also sold for storing produce—they are very handy. It is nice to have six to ten of these. Wet thick ones before putting leafy greens, leeks, or scallions inside to keep them fresh.

Save and reuse plastic bread and produce bags. Wash them; turn them inside out; put them over a bottle or wooden pegs—to air dry—then tuck them away in a drawer for later use. Old plastic bags can also be used for storing bread or leftovers. Keep some on hand for shopping trips.

11) Avoid buying and using plastic silverware: Save the earth and money too—pack a spoon, fork or chopsticks, and a butter knife, in your purse, back pack or briefcase for meals away from home. Avoid picking up disposable utensils in restaurants or tea shops.

12) Avoid paper plates and paper bowls: Ask your friends to bring their own dishes for picnics, potlucks, and parties. If you use your own dishes for big parties, enlist the aid of your guests or friends in washing the dishes.

13) Avoid paper napkins and paper towels: Buy cloth napkins and dish towels. They can be washed and used millions of times. When they're too worn or stained, use them as cleaning rags. Or, cut old towels or table cloths and sew the edges to make napkins.

14) Avoid cans and most boxes: Buy bulk foods whenever possible. Also buy fresh, local, regional, whole-foods which are minimally processed and minimally packaged. Avoid or severely limit the purchase of expensive and environmentally polluting canned and frozen foods. Instead, make your own convenience foods by planning and cooking ahead. Buy dry goods and wet goods from bulk bins when possible, using your own containers. Stock up on the items you use most. The average person throws out their weight in packaging every month! Such waste is totally unnecessary and won't change if you don't!

Use large metal cans or heavy duty thick plastic tubs for storing large bags of dry whole grains, flour, and beans. If you do buy some products, such as miso or nut butter, in small plastic tubs,then reuse the tubs so that they do not immediately go into our landfills!

15) Buy non-toxic, non-biotoxic cleaning products: Clean your entire house the natural way. The best cleaning products are baking soda and vinegar. or natural, cruelty-free products derived from plant extracts and free of preservatives, parabens, petroleum derivitives, M.E.A, Butyl, and other harmful substances. Most commercial household cleaning products contain toxic ingredients which pollute our homes, plants, animals, soil, water, and air. (The average home contains 10-40 times the pollution found in outside air! It makes sense to reduce unnecessary indoor air pollution as much as possible.) Look for natural and non-toxic products in your local health food or specialty store, or mail order catalogs. There are many options. It helps to have at least one plant in every room. Plants filter out toxins in the air; while at the same time enriching and adding oxygen to your home environment. Some plants are better than others for cleaning the air, check with your local garden or plant shop.

Important Kitchen Tools

We strongly urge to get these items, now or later, so that your work in the kitchen goes smoothly, safely, and efficiently. These are what we consider the essentials. While it may seem unnecessary to have a particular kind of pot, pan, or other utensil, it can make a world of difference in the preparation and the results you produce. In some cases, the right tools can make or break the success of a recipe. We urge you to slowly fill your "tool box" so that you will be equipped for any task you undertake.

Every cook has different needs and your essentials will depend on the cooking techniques you use most; however, a wide variety of tools will give you a wider variety of possibilities. You needn't get everything at once, in fact it is best to do it in stages so that you can develop familiarity with each tool as you add it to your kitchen.

We suggest buying used pots, pans, bowls, plates, and utensils whenever possible. You'll save both money and resources. You needn't pay an arm and a leg to equip your kitchen.

Many of the tools we use in the kitchen can be found for a bargain at thrift stores, garage sales, and discount merchandise outlets. We have found incredible pots, pans and dishes for a fraction of the cost of new ones and many of these had never actually been used. For new items look in department stores, chain drugstores, upscale grocery stores, kitchen shops, and ethnic and Asian markets.

For all of the cookery pots and pans listed in this section, we recommend glass, stainless steel, or enamel-lined cast iron rather than aluminum or teflon coated pots and pans. Low-fat, tasty, and oil-free cookery can be done in stainless steel, carbon steel, or cast iron pots with the techniques outlined in this book.

Apple corer: It may not sound essential, but for making baked stuffed apples or other apple desserts, the corer can save time and keep you from cutting yourself. Skip the plastic and ferret out an apple corer with a wooden handle. It's a tool worth having on hand.

Assorted glass jars: Save glass jars from prepared foods or mason jars with lids. These can be used to store gravies, soups, stocks, sauces, pressed salads, desserts, pickles, and condiments. They may also be used to make pickles, to grow sprouts, and to store uncooked grains, beans, dried land and sea vegetables, and herbs and spices. Jars are also handy for making and storing yoghurt. Ask friends to save jars, rescue them from the recycling bins in your neighborhood, or look for them at garage sales, grocery stores, and kitchen shops.

Baking pans and pots: We suggest having two stainless steel cookie sheets and one or two 9-inch stainless steel cake pans, two standard loaf pans, and one or two 9-inch glass pie plates. An oblong 14 x 9 x 2-inch pan for making millet squares or baking squash, sweet potatoes, or fruits (whose syrupy juices would otherwise drip onto the bottom of the oven). Cookie sheets can be used to bake flat or loaf breads, rolls, pizza, turnovers, and other items.

Glass loaf pans with lids are helpful for small casseroles, baked fruit, or sweet vegetable dishes. A dutch oven pot with a lid, or a Creuset pot (a heavy enamel-lined cast iron pot with a lid), is especially handy for baking vegetables, bean stews, apple crisps, casseroles, cakes, brownies, batter breads, even loaf breads and dinner rolls. Baking breads and other items in a heavy, covered pot seals in moisture and allows you to bake with little or no added oil, producing moist and flavorful products. Corn bread can also be baked in a cast iron skillet.

Bamboo rice paddles: Thick bamboo rice paddles are perfect for mixing and serving porridge, rice or millet or for dry roasting grains, seeds, and other foods. These are durable and much better than plastic spoons which melt when exposed to heat. (To prevent steam burns, we recommend two short rice paddles and two long, thick-handled paddles to prevent steam burns when stirring pots of grains, beans, hot cereal, etc.)

Bamboo sushi mats: Purchase three to five of these, even if you never plan to make nori-maki sushi rolls. Bamboo mats are useful for covering cooked foods on the table or counter (retaining warmth while allowing air to circulate around the food.) Tightly covered pots of food will continue to cook long after the heat's been turned off; this results in sticky, mushy rice or water-logged and grey vegetables. It is best to remove grains and vegetables from pots immediately after cooking and transfer them to serving bowls covered loosely with a bamboo mat.

Bowls, serving and storage: Wood, glass, or pottery bowls are attractive and durable. Get several different sizes: 1, 2, 3, and 4-quart bowls. Also get a few assorted sized, decorative pottery or wood bowls for displaying, serving, and storing fresh and leftover foods. Warm foods are best transferred to a bowl and covered with a bamboo sushi mat to keep in heat, while allowing air to circulate. (Leftover rice or millet may be kept on the counter for up to two days, in this manner, covered with a bamboo mat. Other leftovers may be stored in glass or stainless steel bowls then covered with dinner plates or small saucers, in the refrigerator.)

Blender: A blender will be your best ally in creating creamy soups without cream as well as smooth sauces, salad dressings, puddings and custards. It can also be used to grind seeds, nuts, and some whole grains if you purchase a small attachable mini-blend (osterizer) containers. Skip the fancy blenders with 22 speeds, they're usually the same as the 6-8-speed versions, they just have a higher price tag and fancier names for their functions.

Bowls (porridge/cereal): Eating a nourishing breakfast requires a glass or wood breakfast bowl that holds a substantial amount of porridge. Standard 8-ounce bowls just won't accommodate a meal-size serving of hot cereal, much less the condiments and vegetables served on top. Find pottery, glass, wood, or ceramic bowls that will hold 2 1/2-3-cups worth of food. These are also handy for noodle based meals. (You can even resteam leftovers on a steamer tray with such bowls!)

Bowls (stainless steel, mixing): Pick up a variety of stainless steel mixing bowls. Small sized bowls are invaluable for heating and resteaming leftovers to prevent burning and retain flavors. They are also useful for steaming stove-top casseroles; pressure cooking one or two different types of grains or beans at the same time; resteaming (uncovered) leftover rice, millet or hot cereal; heating leftover soup, stew or sauce (in a covered bowl-within-a-pot); or cooking foods in small batches inside the pressure cooker. Stainless steel bowls are also invaluable for storing leftovers in the refrigerator, covered with a plate or saucer, ready to heat at the next meal. We suggest getting three or four 16 to 24-ounce stainless steel bowls for this. Extra-large stainless bowls (12- to 16-cup size) are helpful for mixing enough pressed salad for the week or kneading bread dough!

Bowls, (serving) plates and platters: Choose glass, stainless steel, wood or ceramic bowls and platters to display prepared foods and to store leftovers in the refrigerator. Plates and saucers can be used to cover bowls in the refrigerator. Leftovers can be reheated in a stainless steel bowl (See index for Bowl-Within-A-Pot Method.) Ceramic, pyrex or glass bowls can be used for warming up leftovers, provided they are placed on top of a bamboo steam tray, a metal steamer basket, or on top of a meat rack or trivet. (See Reheating Tips & Techniques.)

Colander: Usually larger than a mesh strainer, a colander can be used for draining pasta, rinsing vegetables or straining vegetable stock scraps. Be sure to purchase a stainless steel colander rather than plastic or aluminum.

Cooking thermometer: This is essential for heating water to the precise temperature for making yeast-risen breads, natto, amasake, yogurt, and other fermented products. A small slender metal stem candy thermometer (5 1/2-inches long) works best and is fairly inexpensive.

Cooling Racks: Invest in at least one sturdy square or oblong stainless steel cooling rack for just-baked breads, cookies, biscuits, rolls, steamed buns, and the like.

Cotton or linen kitchen towels: These towels should be white. (Colored towels can bleed ink on foods during steaming) They may be wrapped around tortillas, biscuits, bagels, rolls or other breads to keep them warm. They can also be wrapped around meal size servings of stale, dry, or leftover breads or other baked goods you wish to steam heat and freshen. The towel will keep the steamer clean and keep the bread from getting soggy. We suggest getting at least three of these towels for steaming bread products. **Caution:** do not use cotton terry; it will leave fuzzies all over your bread!

Custard cups and ramekin dishes: These are handy, not only for individual sized custards, but also for steaming up individual portions of savory dishes such as fruit desserts, eggs, custards, tofu omelets, or for storing and/or reheating leftovers. You can portion out several meals worth of pressed salads or cooked vegetables in the 6-ounce cups, then stack and store them in the refrigerator for ease of use. The 10-12 ounce sizes are perfect for individual pot pies too! The larger ones are good for storing stews and other items. Your best buy is a set consisting of eight 6-ounce, four 12-ounce, and one 32-ounce bowls which come with plastic lids (for storing, not cooking). All should be made of heat-proof, pyrex, CorningWare, or similar material.

Note: When cooking or heating foods in heat proof glass, do not put the dish directly on the bottom of a pot. Instead, place the dish on a wire, stainless steel or bamboo steamer tray or basket to avoid breakage or put a meat rack or trivet in the bottom of the pot, with the fragile bowl(s) on top. Don't use the plastic lids in cooking! Use them for storing foods only.

Cutting boards: Select a thick square or oblong, wooden cutting board. Plastic and other synthetic boards can dull your knife. Keep your board clean using a damp sponge. Rub it down periodically with vinegar or vinegar and baking soda. Oil it occasionally with block oil to keep it from cracking. The cutting board can also be cleaned with a non-toxic, non-biotoxic cleaner which contains live natural cultures. (These are available in most health food stores and co-ops or through the mail.) The live bacteria in the cleaner will digest any food left on the cutting board that might otherwise be problematic.

Flame Tamers, heat deflectors, heat diffusers: This is a light metal pad or plate that has tiny holes in it, available in most hardware or kitchen supply stores. It distributes the heat evenly and can prevent foods like rice, hot cereal, thick bean dishes or stews from burning on the bottom. The heat diffuser, flame tamer, or deflector is placed between the pot and the burner once the contents have come to a full boil or up to pressure. Flame tamers are helpful for cooking on both gas and electric stove tops. You will need 2-3 of these inexpensive tools for proper cookery and convenience.

Fine wire mesh strainers: Two strainers with different sized holes are handy. Be sure to get one fine enough to wash tiny sesame or sunflower seeds or grains such as quinoa or millet. Strainers with slightly larger holes can be used to rinse uncooked beans or rice or for draining small portions of cooked pasta. Plastic is best avoided. Plastic off-gasses formaldehyde and other toxic chemicals and is not durable. Use stainless steel or a fine mesh screen strainer.

Fry pans and skillets, stainless steel: These aren't essential if you have a good cast iron skillet or two. Stainless steel fry pans are handy, though they don't work as well as a wok or cast iron skillet for dry roasting grains, nuts, seeds, or flour. Stainless steel fry pans are useful for sautéing, sauce making, or small steaming jobs.

Fry pans and skillets, cast iron: A cast iron skillet adds a wonderful flavor to sautéed vegetables and other stove top dishes. In addition, very little oil is needed if salt is used to draw out moisture from vegetables. Cast iron skillets add extra iron to the diet and are the best choice for dry roasting seeds or nuts for condiments, flour, whole grains, and whole spices. They also work marvelously for oven roasting sea vegetables; baking skillet breads (such as corn bread); cooking or heating tortillas; making pancakes; light ly sautéed sea vegetables; and scrambling tofu or pan frying tempeh or wheat meat cutlets.

Clean your cast iron skillet with a damp sponge. If food sticks, just put some water in the pan and let it sit until the food loosens, then scrub with a natural bristle brush then rinse. Avoid lengthy soaking. To prevent rusting, dry your cast iron pan immediately after each use (on the stove top over a moderate flame to keep moisture from collecting in the pores). Oil the skillet lightly after washing or periodically after use to build up a coating. (Refer to the seasoning instructions that come with your skillet.)

Note: Cast iron skillets should always be rinsed then dried on top of the stove with the heat turned on before being put away; however, enamel lined cast iron pots, should never be dried on top of the stove—they will chip and wear out if they are heated when empty!

Graters: Porcelain or stainless steel graters with tiny teeth work best for grating ginger so that you can extract the juice. Larger "cheese"-style graters are good for grating hard cheeses. (If you eat cheese, grating it and using it as a garnish at the table will allow you to make a little bit go a long way, We mostly use our grater for carrots, daikon, onions, rutabaga, beets. or ginger It is useful for making instant soups, relishes, or for grating mochi for use as a cheese-like casserole topping or sauce thickener. A special wooden box with an angled blade for grating cabbage and other vegetables can be a real timesaver. This is especially handy for making coleslaw, pressed salad, or sauerkraut.

Knives: Stainless steel or carbon steel vegetable knives with squared-off ends are the most efficient and effective for vegetable cutting. Pointed edged knives or those with serrated edges are mainly for cutting flesh foods or for tearing foods. Squared off knives (also called Mac or Caddie knives) rely on a gentle back and forth, almost circular motion. They offer more control and accuracy and are better suited to cutting vegetables. Get one with a 6-inch long by 1 1/2-inch wide blade. (Most cost just $15-20 through mail order catalogues or in Asian or macrobiotic specialty stores.) Get two if you can afford it and have two cooks in the house.

A small paring knife is useful for cutting apples or slicing small food items. Butter knives or a few wide frosting spreaders are good for slicing buns or rolls at the table or spreading nut, seed, or vegetable butters, bean dips or patés, on bread, or smoothing the tops of desserts.

Ladles: Buy one or two large stainless steel ladles, 4-8 ouncers, for scooping out breakfast cereal, soups and stews. Stainless steel or wood is preferable to plastic because these won't melt under heat. Wood is also preferable to metal because it won't scrape the finish off of clay pots or enamel lined cast iron pots. A few small 2 or 4-ounce ladles or gravy spoons are helpful for serving up gravies, sauces, stir fried or steamed vegetables, marinated salads, and other items.

Lunch boxes, non-toxic: Small stainless steel lunch box containers may be purchased in many Korean, Chinese or Indian grocery stores for transporting pack lunches and travel food. Food sits directly in these vessels, unlike the more common lunch boxes which hold a thermos and plastic containers. Some are round and are comprised of 2 to 4 stacking trays (each holding 1-2 cups worth of food). These come with a lid, and a bracket and handle for carrying. Other stainless steel boxes are square or oblong with clamp-on lids to keep foods air tight. These containers are ideal for stacking and storing leftovers in the refrigerator and can go directly to the table, to the top of a bamboo steamer tray, or to the bottom of a pot-- for easy reheating! Get several of these if you can; they will last for years on end.

To keep food cool when traveling long distances or taking day trips, pack a freezer gel bag or dry ice pack (wrapped in a sealed plastic bag) next to or under, your stainless steel lunch box or other container to keep sandwiches, grain and vegetable salads, or eggs or dairy foods cool. A canvas sachel or tiny hand-held cooler may also be helpful for transporting pack lunches or travel meals. (Most foods can be eaten room temperature and don't need to be chilled or cooled with a cold-pak. This includes breads, buns, leftover rice, millet slices, noodles or salad. A thermos of hot soup or stew to accompany your room temperature leftovers will make your meal warming enough.)

Measuring cups and spoons: Sound too obvious? Many students have come to us claiming not to own or use measuring spoons or cups. Needless to say their cooking is generally inconsistent, yet they wonder how we consistently come up with delicious recipes. Our secret? We always measure! Invest in a set of sturdy stainless steel measuring cups for dry food, and a couple of pyrex measuring cups (both 2 and 4-cup size). Metal measuring spoons are also a must in every kitchen.

Pickle press/salad press: We often use a plastic pickle press to simplify making pickles and pressed salads. These plastic vessels have a screw on lid which allows varying degrees of pressure to compress and submerge vegetables in a marinade. A 3 1/2-4-quart size is ideal, though you may also want a small one for making pickles. (Large pickle presses are particularly handy for making pressed salads when camping in KOA's, motels, or the boonies.)

If finances are tight, you can improvise with a glass or stainless steel bowl or a ceramic crock plus a small saucer which can double as a cover and press, and a rock, dumbbell, or a jug full of water used as a weight on top. We used the bowl method for several years before investing in a pickle press.

Potato masher: This is invaluable for mashing squash, parsnips, sweet potatoes, refried beans, lumpy breakfast cereal, cooked millet for loaves or squares, and other such things. Get a good stainless steel potato masher with a firm handle.

Pots (soup & stew) & sauce pans: Stainless steel, enamel or glass pots work best for stews, boiling pasta, parboiling vegetables, or for steaming left-over or fresh foods. Bamboo steamer trays may also be placed atop a wide rimmed pot of boiling water for easy steaming of one or several different dishes--for example, steam cooking buns or cooking vegetables while at the same time reheating leftover rice, polenta or bread.

You'll need a few different sized pots for convenience. Two small sauce pans (1-or 2-quart size) will do for heating sauces or making small quantities of soup or stew. Two 3-to 4-quart pots are handy for heating up leftovers or cooking stove top casseroles and whole grains. When cooking for large families or gatherings, or making boiled salads, cooking pasta, steamed buns, or for reheating leftovers on stacking bamboo trays, a 4-to 8-quart pot is ideal . Be sure pots have tight fitting lids to prevent heat, taste and water loss.

A 4-quart, heavy duty, enamel-lined cast iron pot (such as a Le Creuset brand) is helpful— both for stove-top simmering of breakfast cereals, dinner grains, stews, bean dishes, and hearty vegetable dishes. In overnight cooking, nishime cooking, stewing, and steam-baking, such a pot helps to retain moisture and flavors. Be sure to use a wooden ladle and wooden spoons with these pots so as not to scrape and ruin their delicate finishes. (If you are making breakfast cereal for just two people, you don't need a 4-quart pot; a 2-quart pot will do)

Pot holders & oven mitts: No house should be without three or four pot holders and at least one set of oven mitts. You'll prevent nasty steam burns and blisters if you hang these from hooks right next to the stove. In a pinch they can double as trivets for hot pots. If you have two sets, one will be clean even if the other is in the washing machine.

Pressure cooker: Purchase one or two 4 quart stainless steel pressure cookers or a 4- quart and a 6-quart model (avoid aluminum ones!). Even if you are cooking for one, a 4-quart cooker is most versatile; you can set a small stainless steel bowl inside the pot to cook smaller quantities of rice, beans, or dessert if needed. A good pressure cooker will last indefinitely if you take good care of it.

Pressure cookers are invaluable for cooking rice, millet, and many other whole grains and for beans. Pressure cooking produces more tender and digestible grains and beans than does boiling. Beans often take hours to soften if boiled but become tender in 15-30 minutes under pressure. Many other foods like starchy vegetables, sea vegetable dishes and fruit desserts can be pressure cooked in a fraction of the time required with conventional methods, and without added fat.

Presto pressure cookers are some of the most reasonably priced and most easily located. Other good brands include Innova, Aeternum, Cuisinart, and T-fal. The brand you get should be one which you can easily get replacement parts for. It pays to shop around. Be sure the one you buy is stainless steel. Some are enamel lined; these are also good but are more pricey but very durable if used and cleaned properly.

Note: Be sure to keep your pressure cooker clean, especially around the top, sides and pressure release valves. Use a pipe cleaner, tooth brush or vegetable scrub brush to keep these openings clean and to prevent blockage. Replace the gaskets and rubber fittings every year, or as needed. When your cooker stops keeping a tight seal and fails to come up to pressure properly, it probably needs a new gasket. These cost several dollars and must be replaced periodically (usually once a year).

Saucers and plates (heat-proof), extras: Buy a half a dozen or so of small to medium-sized heat-proof saucers. They are invaluable for cooking and as covers for bowls of leftovers. Use these to top small stainless steel bowls for pressure cooking, pressure steaming, or steam-poaching in a large pot or pressure cooker (with the covered-bowl-within-a-pot method.) They will eliminate the need for plastic wrap or foil in food storage as well. Be sure to have several larger plates (8-9-inch) for use atop a bamboo steamer tray for steam cooking buns, rolls, cut squash, or reheating leftover millet loaf, polenta, or other such items. They're really handy!

Slotted spoon or basket, large: These are essential for making blanched and parboiled vegetable salads. One with a 6 to 8-inch wide basket is optimal for quickly removing vegetables from their cooking water. Smaller slotted spoons don't work: vegetables will become soggy by the time you fish them out of the water! Get a large one with a long handle and a sturdy basket or a curved bowl-like center with small holes. Often these are sold as skimmers or deep fry baskets. Use smaller slotted spoons for serving foods at the table.

Spatulas: Spatulas are great for cleaning out pots, pans, or dishes, scraping out the blender, or mixing. Get two rubber tipped spatulas with wood handles for mixing and scraping. Get one metal pancake turner with a sturdy wooden or metal handle; you'll need it to flip tortillas, pita, arepas, and pancakes or crêpes as they cook. They're also handy for flipping and turning cutlets and grain, wheat meat, or bean patties as they pan fry and for removing biscuits and other goods from baking trays.

Spoons, mixing: Wooden spoons are best for mixing batters, stirring soups, sautéing or stir frying vegetables, and roasting grains, flour, and seeds. Wooden utensils won't scratch the surface of pots or melt under high heat, nor will they impart a metallic or plastic taste to your food. For mixing bread dough, however, you will want a long handled, sturdy stainless steel spoon that won't break under pressure.

Steamer trays and baskets: Get one and preferably two large and sturdy sets of stacking bamboo steamer trays. Look for a 10 1/2 inches diameter (9 3/4-inches from inside edge to inside), with a thick and tight weave and very little space between the thick slats. Even larger ones are available but you must make sure that you have a large 4-5 quart pot with a matching diameter upon which to place your steamer trays for steaming, or a wok.

A wok is not as efficient and won't work for using the bowl-within-a-pot method *and* the bamboo steamer trays at the same time. A large steamer and pot will provide maximum kitchen efficiency, thereby allowing you to cook several different items at a time, using the same pot, the same burner, and the same steam!

If you get two sets of bamboo steamers you will save a great deal of energy and time. Many items you'd normally bake can be steamed, and in a fraction of the time—breads, rolls, greens, or the occasional tofu & egg omelet, even cookies! Leftovers—breads, pasta, rice, casseroles, burritos, pot pies, polenta, and many other foods—can also be reheated by steam at the same time new foods are cooked, and without flavor mixing! We use our steamer trays more than any other device in the kitchen. In fact, we sometimes use them at every meal!

Also available are stainless steel steamer baskets which fit inside a saucepan or pot. (We use ours often.) These work wonderfully for steaming single dishes of food or cooking up vegetables, though they are not nearly as versatile as the bamboo stacking trays which allow you to cook or heat many different items at once. If you get just one of these, you can use it in a pinch when the bamboo trays are full. The metal steamer can even be placed in the bottom of the pot, underneath your bamboo steamer trays. Using both steamers at the same time will allow you to cook or heat even more dishes at once.

Suribachi with a wooden pestle: This ceramic Japanese-style mortar has ridges on the inside that spiral out from the center. It comes with a wooden pestle called a suricogi. This tool set is invaluable for grinding seeds; mashing vegetables or beans into dips, spreads, or sauces. It can also be used to make dressings, to dissolve miso into soup, or to mash apriboshi or umeboshi plums into a paste. Buy a medium sized (9-10-inch) suribachi; small ones are less practical and usually result in mess on the counter, the floor, or both! An extra large (12-inch) suribachi is handy for making pressed or marinated salads or quick pickles as it makes the crushing of the vegetables go more quickly.

Tea strainer: Get a small metal or bamboo strainer. Use it for straining roasted corn or barley tea, dandelion, chicory, or grain "coffee" beverages, or raw herb teas. A tea ball can also be handy for making grain coffee or herb tea. Be sure to get stainless steel rather than aluminum.

Tea pot: Teas can be simply brewed and simmered in a sauce pan, then ladled into cups through a small tea strainer. A stainless steel stove-top percolator is especially handy for making delicious grain "coffee" on top of the stove and can be left on top of the stove for several days, with the liquid heated up just before serving and extra water or tea added to the basket as the tea runs out or gets weak. The same results can be achieved with the sauce pan, though, so don't worry if you are not able to locate such a tea pot. Other glass or ceramic tea pots may also be used.

Note: A glass or ceramic tea pot is essential for making Chinese medicinal teas. Metal pots are unacceptable for this purpose, since they may react with the contents of various medicinal herbs. Such pots can, however, be used for general use teas as well.

Thermos: Hunt around in hardware stores for a Nissan Thermos Brand, or Stanley-Alladin stainless steel thermos with a wide-mouth opening. These are perfect for thick soups and stews or for packing a big bowl of breakfast cereal if you must take breakfast away from home. They come in several sizes (some are perfect for casseroles, warm beans, etc.) and are well worth the investment.

If you can't locate a good stainless steel thermos, look for one with a glass rather than plastic liner (thrift stores are best for this). A narrow thermos is more suitable for tea or grain "coffee." If you can only find or afford a plastic lined thermos, so be it. Since soups and stews are really important for meals, it is essential to have a good thermos for every member of your family.

Trivets: Any well equipped kitchen will boast 3 to-5 counter-top trivets which provide a safe resting place for hot pots and pans. Trivets may be made of wood, thick cork, quilted fabric, ceramic or tile. Keep them handy to avoid burning table and counter tops.

Another type of trivet, consisting of a small, round, metal disk, fits inside a pot and is used to lift pyrex bowls and ramekin dishes off the bottom of a cooking pot. These trivets are made to get wet and often come with pressure cookers. They allow you to use the bowl-within-a-pot method to steam-cook foods or to reheat leftovers in CorningWare, Vision-Ware, or pyrex-type bowls which would ordinarily break if set on the bottom of a pot. Some meat-racks may also be used as trivets for small bowls of food you wish to steam or steam-simmer in a pot. (Roasting pans come with a metal rack which can also be used for steaming plates or dishes of food.)

Vegetable scrub brush: A small, round scrub brush made from natural bristles is perfect for scrubbing root and round vegetables. Also get an extra brush for cleaning your cast iron pots. (It is not a good idea to use the same brush for both.)

Wok: A wok is not just for stir-frying! These traditional rounded Chinese pans can be used for steaming, water- or light- sauteing or even dry roasting. You can even cook hot air pop corn in a wok with a lid. Heavy carbon steel woks are most durable and hold heat best, though many varieties abound. Get one with a flat bottom which doesn't require a ring or stand between it and the burner. Also buy a cover so that you can steam or simmer in your wok. Use cooking chop sticks or a wooden spoon to stir in the wok so as to avoid scraping the finish. As with a cast iron pot, do not soak the wok, simply wash it with a damp sponge, or a natural bristle brush and always dry it on the stove top with heat underneath to prevent moisture from collecting in the pores. Periodically rub it lightly with sesame oil to prevent rusting.

Other helpful kitchen tools:

While not essential, many of these items are worth collecting. Some will save you time or energy in preparation or cooking; some will assure you fresher foods or better nutrition; others will allow you to create more interesting, exotic or appetizing dishes. Get what you can when you can and remember to check out the garage sales, estate sales, thrift shops, bulletin boards and the like. Used products are a real bargain and often quite abundant.

Cooking & eating chop sticks: Extra long cooking chop sticks are good for sauteing, pan frying, cooking noodles, or tossing salads. They stir food without breaking them apart and will not add a metallic taste. Cooking chopsticks consist of two long sticks held together loosely at the end with a string. These are user friendly even for those normally awkward with chopsticks.

Shorter chopsticks make good eating utensils and will not burn your tongue nor do they impart a metallic taste as a hot or metal fork will. Eating chop sticks come with tapered, pointed tips (these are the Japanese kind) or squared off/blunt ends (these are the Chinese variety). The squared-off and thicker sticks are much easier to use and more practical than the pointy, often shiny, thin sticks. With practice anyone can become skilled in their use. We find them handy with rice, millet, polenta, and even for eating noodles, salads, and even some dessert! (We find chop sticks most enjoyable for eating almost everything.) Chopsticks can even be used to cut cooked foods at the table, making extra utensils unnecessary. They can also help to slow you down if you typically eat too fast.

Crocks: Ceramic crocks are helpful for making pressed salads or pickles in large quantities. It is often helpful to have an assortment of sizes so that you don't use up all of your bowls. Crocks can be found in most kitchen shops and Oriental markets and do not need lids, only saucers which fit inside the rim of the crock and securely cover the contents.

Crock pot: This isn't essential, though it can be helpful for busy folks or those who are at first overwhelmed by the idea of cooking. (Crock pots are quick and easy to use; however, food cooked in a crock pot never tastes as good as food cooked on a gas stove. Regardless, the tradeoff may be worth it in some cases. What has a front has a back.) You can cook soups and stews overnight or while you're out for the day. You can also cook whole or rolled grain breakfast cereals, or bake winter squash, yams, or sweet potatoes, while you sleep or are away. A crock pot can also be used to cook apple sauce, essene sprouted grain bread, Boston Brown Bread (in cans), rice, pudding, casseroles, beans, and many other foods. Also called slow cookers, these pots are energy efficient, safe, and convenient, allowing you to cook things without having to be near the kitchen or in the house. If you travel, and stay in motels, you can cook some amazing things in a crock pot. (We have!)

Get a crock pot with a glass rather than plastic lid. And get a big one to cook for more than one person. Get two pots if you have a hard time putting meals together--you can cook two soups, stews, or side dishes simultaneously during the day or night. Smaller, one-person crock pots are handy for traveling. With these, you can even cook hot cereal for breakfast (for one person), overnight, in a hotel or motel room. (See index for Overnight Cereal.) Most crock pots come with instructions booklets which will help you to adapt your favorite recipes to crock pot time.

Drop lids: These can be useful for pickle crocks or in cooking. They are sold in most Oriental grocery stores or through macrobiotic mail order catalogs. Typically made of wood, they are meant to fit inside a pot, directly on top of foods as they cook, to prevent moisture loss. (They may also be used to cover crocks full of miso that have first been covered with cheese cloth.)

Foley Food Mill: This can stand in for a blender or food grinder. These stainless steel hand food mills can be found easily and very affordably (they usually cost about $6-$7). You simply place this lightweight utensil on top of a bowl, pour food into the top, then crank the handle around to press the food through screen-like holes in the bottom. Any pulp can be scraped into the purée with a spatula if you like. We use ours often for making creamy puréed soups, bean and vegetable sauces or spreads, puréed amasake, chestnut or fruit puddings, tofu dips, etc. Though a blender can be handy, this utensil uses no electricity and takes only a minimum of hand power.

Food Dehydrator: Read on for more on this.

Ice cream scoop: We don't use this for ice cream; we use it to scoop out perfect portions of rice, millet, Millet "Mashed Potatoes," or bread pudding. Many other grain, bean, and starchy vegetable dishes look attractive when served by the scoopful. A 6-ounce scooper is good for dinner grains and desserts. For condiment sized portions of Tofu Sour cream, Millet Butter and the like, a smaller melon ball sized scoop is best.

Garlic press: This is not essential but may be handy. We prefer to mince our garlic, to cook or roast it whole, or to mash it in a suribachi. Use whatever works best for you.

Grain mill: This is essential if you are going to make bread on a regular basis. Fresh flour is of the utmost importance. If you do not have a local mill to get flour from, it would be a good idea to invest in a flour mill as soon as you are able. After 48-hours, flour starts to oxidize (break down and lose nutrients and flavor). The taste of fresh flour is incomparable.

A flour mill is an investment in your health and your future! (Grain is the staff of life. If you wish to use flour, only freshly ground grain will truly nourish.) If you can't get a flour mill, try to buy flour from a store with a rapid turnover of product, preferably from a local flour mill, then store it in a cool, dry place or the freezer or refrigerator, and use it up within 1-4 months.

New flour mills often cost between $200 and $300 though used ones are much less expensive. Look around and compare prices. Get a home flour mill that uses a low rather than high temperature; high temperature grinding "cooks" the flour and can destroy many of its nutrients.

Pasta maker: By no means is this essential, though you will save a small fortune if you like to eat pasta but hate to pay outrageous prices for good, fresh, egg-less, whole grain pasta. Pasta machines come in many varieties so you'll have to shop around and compare (or get one used). Some are priced at $70. Pasta making isn't difficult; in fact, you can use our simple spanokopita pie crust recipes or our won ton dough for making pasta. You can use all sorts of different flour combinations, too. You may want to get a sturdy rack for drying your pasta if you plan to make it in big batches once or twice a month.

Rolling pin: If you don't have a tortilla press, chances are you'll need a rolling pin if you plan to make pizza, tortillas, won tons, ravioli, pita, or other flat breads. A large wooden one works best. If you're tight on funds, a glass jar or a suricogi (wooden pestle) with smooth sides will work if you flour it. (See tortilla presses; they can be used for many of the same tasks.)

Shears, kitchen: Special kitchen scissors are invaluable for cutting open plastic or paper packages, snipping fresh herbs, dried sea vegetables, dried tomatoes, or dried fruits, etc. Kitchen scissors are essential. (You will dull your vegetable knife if you use it to open plastic packages. A regular knife is ill-equipped to deal with food and moisture.)

Small electric coffee-spice mill: Not essential—but very helpful for grinding spices or turning amaranth, millet or other soft shelled grains into flour or "meal," these tiny mills usually cost $15-20 at most department or drugstores. With it you can also grind flax seeds (for an egg replacer in baking). Most blenders can be equipped with Osterizer mini-blend containers (a plastic mini-blender container which screws onto the blender blade). This makes it possible to whip or blend small volumes of liquid or semi-solid food which would otherwise be difficult in a large blender. It can be used to mix salad dressings or small amounts of sauce, to purée fresh tomatoes, or to grind amaranth, quinoa, millet, or seeds to a flour or meal.

Thermal Cooker: This is like a crock pot but without the cord. It's a real lifesaver and energy saver. It allows you to cook foods using only five to ten minutes of electric or gas fuel. You cook the dish on top of the stove for five to ten minutes in a special stainless steel pot, then transfer the pot to the insulated container and allow it to sit for as long as your recipe needs to cook or several hours or all day. No overcooking, no-fuss, no mess, no-kidding! Nissan Thermos Co. was the first to come out with this ecological cooking unit.

Toaster oven: We rarely if ever toast bread; we prefer to steam heat it instead, for better taste, nutrition, and added moisture). We don't even own a toaster; however, a small toaster oven can be of benefit for those who live alone. Baking in a small toaster oven saves energy. It doesn't make sense to heat up a big household oven for just one or two burritos, a small pot pie, or a hot sandwich. With your toaster oven you can bake two sweet potatoes, whole onions, stuffed peppers or small squash halves, or a small casserole, or meal sized portions of oven "fried" tempeh or wheat meat. This is far more efficient and ecological than using a conventional oven! Look for a toaster oven that will hold a small casserole or mini-broiler pan if you want to get the most from your unit.

Tortilla press: A real must! Instead of rolling out dough with a rolling pin, we use a tortilla press. These are often made of cast aluminum (this is okay; you won't be cooking in it so it poses no health risk) We use this for flattening dough for pita, souvlaki pita, calzones, individual pizzas, flat breads, pot pies, won tons, ravioli, and the like. They are not expensive and are a real time-saver. The are a lot less messy to use than a rolling pin and floured cutting board. All you have to do is dip your ball of dough in flour then press it between the two round metal disks that comprise the press. Or, place the ball of dough between two pieces of wax paper or parchment paper, between the press.

Special Tools:

Cooking without Cooking: Using an Insulated Thermal Cooker

Do you dream of being able to:

(a) cook while you work, sleep, play, or workout?

(b) cook with no chance of burning or over cooking?

(c) transport a hot dish to a potluck, party, or picnic without spilling?

(d) leave food cooking unattended without worrying about safety?

(e) prepare foods hours ahead of time and know that they will be cooked to perfection when meal time rolls around?

(f) or start a dish cooking then go on to other things ?

Well, now you can. The Nissan Thermal Cooker (a.k.a. The Thermal Chef) gives you the benefits of a stove, a crock pot, and an oven —anywhere. You can take it camping (as long as you have a camp stove to bring the food up to a boil). You can also use it at home when you need an extra burner on the stove but don't have it.

To use the Thermal Cooker you simply put the recipe ingredients into the "cooking pot," bring it to a boil, cook it over a moderate heat for five or six minutes, then remove it from the heat and slip it into the "thermal pot." Cover it then let it stand for the recipe cooking time, or longer. Your food will stay hot for up to 8 hours without overcooking. It can reduce your electric or gas bill significantly since a dish that would ordinarily take 30, 60, 90, or 120 minutes will only need 5-10 minutes of stove top heat if you use the Thermal Cooker to do the rest.

It really works. You can make fabulous soups, stews, chilis, gravies, sauces, stuffed cabbage leaves or bell peppers, steamed vegetables, rice, millet, sweet potatoes, fruit compotes and much much more. You can start your dish cooking first thing in the morning, then come home to a piping hot lunch or supper. You can start foods cooking in it before bed, then wake up to hot cereal, baked squash, or what have you. You can use it in the heat of summer to avoid overheating the house, or any time of year.

Since we have an apartment-size gas stove but entertain eight to twelve guests every Friday night, the cooker has been just the thing to simplify preparations and save energy. With it we've made wonderful borscht, Southern-style gravy, creamy split pea soup, cream of celery soup, and many other tasty concoctions. It's the most fail-safe, convenient, economical, and ecological cooking unit since the crock pot. In fact, once you try one you might want two!

Well known chef Graham Kerr is coming out with a thermal cooker cookbook. When it comes out you can adapt his recipes. Until then, experiment with your favorite recipes.

These cookers retail for $92.00 and can be found in many chain department stores and kitchen stores. If you can't find them in your area, call The Thermos Company, (815) 232-2111. Or, write them at 1555 Illinois, Route 75, East, P.O. Box 600, Freeport, Illinois 61032-0600.

Why Dry?

Drying foods is good for you and mama earth too!

A dehydrator is the perfect gift to give to lovers of low-fat, all-natural, dried treats and crafts. A dehydrator makes delicious, nutritious, economical and ecological snacks or foods to add to your favorite cooked dishes.

Drying has several advantages over freezing or canning. Drying saves space. Most foods dry to 1/3-1/16 their original size. Comparing fresh foods to dried foods, you'll find that you can store 25 pounds of onions in a one gallon jar as onion rings, flakes, or powder. Comparing dried foods to canned foods is impressive. Dried foods weigh 85% less than canned goods and take up 1/3-1/2 the space. For example, 76 tomatoes, once dried, will fit in a one quart jar! If these same tomatoes were canned they'd fill up 16 quart jars and 16 times as much space. You can store 38 sliced or 76 powdered apples in a one quart jar. A one pound block of tofu can be stored in an 8-12 ounce jar sliced, diced, or minced, and dried. Countless other foods can be dehydrated including easoned wheat meat.

Drying saves energy. It takes far less energy to dry foods—one or two pennies per hour—than to store them in the refrigerator or freezer. The drying process is complete after 4-12 hours, but most people store fruits, vegetables, and prepared foods in cold storage for far longer than this. Needless to say, enormous amounts of energy are wasted in food storage that could be saved or put to better use. With a dehydrator you'll reduce your impact on the environment.

Drying helps reduce your reliance on packaged, processed, and so-called "convenience" foods. This translates into fewer cans, boxes and bags in your home and our landfills. By some estimates, the average American throws out his or her weight in packaging every month. Do you? Even health conscious, health-food store shoppers often buy heavily packaged foods. Why not make your own instant foods? With dried fruits and vegetables you can make spice blends; instant soups; dip sauces and stuffing mixes; soup "helpers" and extenders; desserts; powdered dessert sweeteners; fruit and vegetable leathers; tofu or veggie-jerky; and much more.

Drying saves money. You can save money on nutritious dried foods by drying them yourself. Sun dried tomatoes often cost upwards of $12 a pound; dried chives often cost $28 a pound; and shiitake mushrooms can cost $20 to $40 per pound depending on the grade. Dried apples cost upwards of $10 per pound; dried apricots and peaches often cost $15 per pound; and most other dried spices and seasonings are equally expensive. In most cases, you can save up to 90% by drying foods at home. (Efficient dehydrators dry foods in hours, not days. They expand to hold many trays and most cost just a few pennies per hour to operate.)

Drying is convenient. Dehydrators don't require any attention except for occasional checking to see if the foods are as dry as you like. You don't need any special storage containers either. Dried foods can be stored in old peanut butter, mustard, jam, or spice jars or in zip-lock bags that you've been saving and reusing. Empty (plastic) miso tubs can be used for short term storage of dried food destined for the refrigerator (for storage of several weeks to a month). Further, your favorite foods can be dried during the day, while you're at home or away, or at night while you sleep! What could be easier ?

Drying is less work than canning or freezing. There's no pot watching, stirring, or fussing. You can collect fresh apples, peaches, pears, blueberries or cherries when they're perfectly ripe, then dry them for use throughout the year. Vegetables and herbs can also be dehydrated for adding to soups, stews, stuffings, casseroles, and even desserts. Make the most of the summer's sweet corn, tomatoes, bell peppers, chili peppers, peas, parsley, chives, leeks, edible flowers, scallions and other fragile fare. You can stock up on fall and winter weather squashes and sweet potatoes, Jerusalem artichokes, onions, parsnips, carrots and other finery too. Burdock root, wild and cultivated mushrooms, okra, and other exotica can also be dried. With such a marvelous invention you'll be able to use produce from the garden from the farmers' market, or from good deals on seasonal produce at the grocery store.

Drying is the healthy way to go. Drying fruits, vegetables, soy products, and other items at home, ensures that your meals and desserts are free from preservatives, refined sugar, and other additives. This is a big plus in a day and age where so many healthy foods have been adulterated to the extent that they no longer nourish us and actually cause health problems. Overall, you'll be benefitting your own health and the health of our fragile planet by drying.

Here are just some of the foods you can dry:

Fresh fruits
Fresh vegetables
Fresh fruit and vegetable purées
Fresh herbs and spices
Seasoned tofu, tempeh, and other bean products
"Meaty" vegetarian loaves, burgers, and croquettes
Soups and stews
Dips
Sauces, purées, and puddings

Here are some of the things you can make with dehydrated foods:

Soups and soup "helpers"
Stews and chilis
Sauces for pasta, pizza, or rice
Stuffings
Salsa
Seasoning mixes
Stir fry additions
Pilafs
Pot pie fillings
Casseroles
Loaves and burgers
Chutneys & relishes
Dips & dressings
Garnishes for soups, stews, beans & casseroles
Fat-free or low-fat vegetable chips
Cereal sprinkles
Puddings and purées
Fillings for pies, turnovers, and pastries
Glazes & toppings for desserts
Stewed fruit sauces and compotes
Dessert "helpers"
Granulated fruit sweeteners
Granulated grain-malt sweeteners (from amasake)
Fruit or vegetable leathers
Granola bars

Cooking Tips, Special Tools & Techniques

Variety

For the most part, variety comes in using the vegetables of the season (from your region or bio-region). Following the seasons one will naturally eat a varied diet. Variety in cooking technique is also important. You may vary the following aspects of your cooking within each day, week, month, and season:

1. The selection of foods within the following categories—whole grains; cracked grains and flour products; soups and stews; vegetables; beans and bean products; wheat meat, sea vegetables; condiments and seasonings; culinary herbs; pickles; and beverages.

2. The methods of cooking—boiling, steaming, sautéing, simmering, pressure cooking, etc.

3. The ways of cutting vegetables—both in the size and shape of pieces.

4. The amount of water or type of liquid used—pure water, pasta water, or vegetable stock.

5. The amount and kind of seasoning and condiments used—sun dried sea salt or sea minerals, type of miso, tamari or shoyu soy sauce, umeboshi or apriboshi, pickle juice, etc.

6. The length of cooking time—longer cooking dishes in cold weather, shorter cooking times in warmer weather, a combination of both of these within each meal, day, and season.

7. The combination of foods and dishes.

8. The seasonal cooking adjustment—little or no baking in warm weather, some baking in cold weather; more steaming and light cooking in hot weather, etc.

Preparation

A traditional and sustainable way of cooking employs simple ingredients. Cooking is the key to producing meals which are nutritious, tasty, and attractive. The cook has the ability to change the quality of the food. More cooking, the use of pressure, marinating, salt, heat, and time, makes the energy of food more concentrated. Quick cooking, the use of herbs and spices, and little salt preserves a lighter energy. A good cook improves the health of those for whom he or she cooks by varying the cooking styles and the ingredients to make harmony with the season and one's needs. Strengthening cooking is essential ingredient for good health.

METHODS OF COOKING AND FOOD PREPARATION

Regular use
Pressure cooking
Soup/stew
Waterless/nishime
Boiling
Quick-Boiling
Steaming
Stir frying
Sautéing and water sautéing
Pressing & marinating
Dry roasting
Pickling
Raw

Seasonal use
Broiling
Long Simmering
Baking
Barbequing & Grilling

Electric and Microwave Cooking: A Holistic Perspective

A wholistic way of understanding electric and microwave cooking is multi-dimensional. We do not recommend cooking with either electric or microwave stoves or ovens for the following reasons:

1. Sensory appeal:

Both electric and microwave cooking utensils limit the sensory appeal of our cooking by imposing limitations on the creativity of the cook and negatively affecting the taste and textures of foods prepared on or in them.

Electric and microwave ovens and stoves do not have the infinite adjustability of stoves with gas flames, so the cook can only use the heat settings that are allowed by the stove itself. In addition, in microwave cooking, the cook is not able to perform such basic cooking techniques as stir frying, sauteing, pan frying, browning, or other operations which require contact with the food while it is over a heat source. This limits the variety of effects that can be obtained in cooking and thus limits the sensory appeal and variety of one's overall diet. Lack of variety in cooking also limits our capacity to change cooking style in response to daily and seasonal variations in available produce and climate. This limits our adaptability to our environment.

Anyone can verify that the taste and appearance of food cooked on electricity or in microwave ovens is considerably different and less satisfying than food cooked on a gas or wood stove. The popularity of the American cook-out lies in large part in the sensory appeal that food has when cooked over a natural wood flame. A potato baked in a gas stove or over a wood fire has considerably more flavor and a more appealing texture than a microwaved potato. Broccoli steamed on a gas stove is much fresher in taste and appearance than that prepared over an electric coil or in a microwave oven.

From a wholistic perspective, sensory satisfaction is an important part of nutrition, and cooking techniques and tools should allow us maximum variety and vitality of taste and textures. Since electric and microwave cooking limit variety and noticeably affect vitality of produce, they are not recommended for daily or even frequent use.

2. Scientific objections.

To this point in time, no studies have been performed which demonstrate the nutritional safety of cooking with either electric or microwave utensils. However, there are a number of reasons to believe that these tools have detrimental effects on the nutritional quality of our food as well as the general safety of our home environments.

Both electric and microwave stoves produce heat in food by alternating currents. On an electric stove, the heating element itself is a contained alternating current of electrons which is producing thermal energy, which is in turn is transferred to the cooking pot and then to the food in the pot. In a microwave oven, microwaves penetrate the foodstuffs and heat by alternating the polarity of the molecules of which they are composed. In both cases, the natural electromagnetic field of the foodstuff is probably altered by the cooking utensil.

The electromagnetic field of any substance is the force maintaining the integrity of the molecular structures in that substance. If the field is in any way damaged or altered, the substance may lose its integrity and degenerate. In fact, epidemiological and other studies show that biological organisms do undergo structural degeneration in the presence of electromagnetic fields. For example, a study of children in Denver who died of cancer between 1950 and 1973 "found that children who lived near electrical distribution lines were twice as likely to develop cancer as those who did not." Exposure to microwave radiation has been linked in numerous studies to a long list of health problems including cataracts, testicular degeneration, tinnitus, cancer, and genetic defects.

Fresh vegetable food is living tissue. It is not unreasonable to expect that electromagnetic fields and nonionizing radiation from electric stoves and microwave ovens can damage the structure and nutritional value of the foods cooked on or in them. In the case of an electric stove, the heating coil produces an electromagnetic field that may alter the electromagnetic field of the food cooked on it , in the same way that the fields surrounding power lines may alter the shape and function of human cells toward cancer. Microwave ovens directly alter the polarity of the molecules of the food that is cooked in them. It certainly should not be surprising if any study would find that food cooked in a microwave is less nourishing — or even toxic — due to subtle alterations in the molecular structure cased by the radiation.

In fact, one study reported in Lancet (Dec. 9, 1989) showed that microwave heated milk develops D-amino acids and cis-amino acids, both of which are known to have neuro- and hepato-toxic effects. Another study reported in the Journal of American Dietetic Association (May 1989) concluded that microwave heating of human milk destroys vital immunoglobin A and is inappropriate for that reason. Yet another study suggests that fats are denatured by microwave radiation (Lipids, 1988; 23:367-69), which is not surprising, since it is well known that fats are easily changed to free radicals—highly reactive and carcinogenic substances—by excessive exposure to heat or light. And John Ott reports experiments that he has conducted (in his book *Light, Radiation & You*) that suggest that consumption of microwave treated foods can immediately reduce normal muscle strength. This field must be investigated more thoroughly before anyone can legitimately claim that microwave heating of food is safe and sane.

In the absence of any evidence that these tools are indeed unquestionably safe, we consider use of them to be nothing other than an act of blind faith in the benevolence of modern technology and the electronics industry. Given its track record, we have no reason to believe that modern technology is intrinsically benevolent and harmless. In fact, rather the opposite would seem to be a more reasonable assumption, given the undeniable fact of the degeneration of our environment and human health since the advent of industrial technology. The burden of proof on this matter lies with the manufacturers and purveyors of these appliances. Our view is that it is better to be prudent and avoid their use, than to accept them as unavoidable or convenient, only to end up sorry when the evidence comes in.

3. Social objections:

a) Ethics.

Since neither electric nor microwave cooking appliances have been tested for long term safety, those of us who are using them are unwillingly taking part in a nutritional experiment that may, and probably will, fail to prove beneficial to our personal health, and certainly fails to support planetary healing. This is a breach of personal freedom.

b) Economics.

Using an electric stove or a microwave to heat food is analogous to using a chain saw to cut butter. Natural wood, coal or gas flame heats food directly and therefore economically. There is no need for high technology hardware or power plants for this simple household task. Both electric and microwave appliances are economically costly because of the high energy and materials input required to build them and maintain their power sources.

c) Environment.

Electric and microwave appliances are ecologically undesirable because they cannot be built or operated without expenditure of nonrenewable resources and consequent material, thermal, and radiation pollution of our environment. They also increase demand for and reliance upon nuclear power plants.

d) Political.

Electric and microwave appliances are part of a social structure which concentrates socioeconomic and political power in the hands of scientists and business people who have intellectual or economic investments in high technology and centralized energy transformers (such as electric or nuclear power plants). These appliances therefore represent decline in political and socioeconomic freedom, and concentration of power—literally—in the hands of the few "experts." They limit our personal freedom in energy resource management.

e) Cultural.

Electric and microwave appliances are not part of traditional cooking styles, and cannot duplicate many traditional dishes coming from traditional cultures. They therefore reinforce the modern tendency toward cultural homogeneity and loss of traditions and cultural diversity. Since cultural diversity developed out of local adaptations to bioregional environmental conditions, it represents a stock of simple cooking and other technologies which have enabled human beings to adapt to variations in climactic and other environmental conditions. Reduction and loss of cultural cooking diversity thus produces a less interesting world and a less adaptable human population.

f) Cross-cultural adaptability.

It is simply impossible, due to limitation of resources, for everyone in the world to own and operate electric and/or microwave appliances. The energy, material, and ecological costs of these appliances are too great to make their universal application possible. Therefore, we cannot recommend their use. We recommend use of cooking tools and techniques which can be employed now (and in the sustainable future) by all human beings without exception.

4. Philosophical objections.

Electric and microwave appliances do not promote the spiritual growth of humanity. They encourage the continuation of abuse of our planet and the separation of humanity from the earth, due to their heavy resource cost, which can only be met by continued abuse of the planet's nonrenewable resources. They also encourage antagonism between people, because there must be competition for non-renewable resources in order to continue to build and expand their use. Since they tend to create these antagonisms, which are against the spirit of brotherhood that underlies true spiritual development, these appliances are not recommended.

Further, these appliances are a reflection of, and perpetuate, an impatient, immature, convenience-oriented mentality. This is harmful to our biological and spiritual development as individuals and a species. Difficulties strengthen us spiritually and biologically, developing our flexibility and adaptability. "Convenience" makes us soft and weak. Just as automobile use results in atrophy in leg muscles and dependence on machines for transportation, use of electric stoves and microwave ovens especially results in a spirit of childish dependence and demanding impatience, contrary to the highest qualities of the human spirit—freedom, stamina, endurance, self-reliance and maturity. Therefore we cannot recommend their regular use.

Everything at its extreme turns into its opposite. The convenience of the automobile turns into the inconvenience of the clogged freeway. Likewise, the convenience of the microwave will be proven to turn into the inconvenience of human physiological degeneration. The bigger the front, the bigger the back. Microwave and electric appliances look very promising — that is exactly why we should be wary of them. Their drawbacks must be as big as their promises. We must consider these things very carefully if we are to maintain our health and happiness into a sustainable future.

A Matter of Life & Death

Microwaves rob foods of their vital life force energy. But steam cooking adds energy to foods. Microwaves works by friction, agitating or rearranging the molecules in foods until heat is created. In contrast steaming adds heat (yang) and moisture (yin) to foods. The result of steaming, an energetically balanced cooking technique, is moist and flavorful food. The result of microwaving is neither pleasant nor nutritious. When bread is heated in a microwave oven, it is warmed initially but then turns rubbery and hard as a rock. A microwave literally zaps the energy (yang), moisture (yin), flavor, aroma, and nutrients right out of food.

Researchers have discovered that the the flavors produced by microwaving are chemically different from those produced by conventional cooking. In "Microwaving Means Microflavors," in the Sept./Oct. 1992 issue of Natural Health, Joanne Crerand reports that "Conventional cooking gives flavor to food through a series of chemical reactions between the sugar molecules and the amino acids." These reactions, known as the *Maillard effect,* create volatile compounds that account for the browning of food and for flavor development. In particular, the rich, meaty, buttery, nutty and caramel-like flavors are absent from microwaved foods. Yet the deleterious effects of microwaving foods go far beyond flavor.

Microwaving alters the molecular structure of foods. In particular, it has been found to destroy non-nutritive but beneficial substances in foods, leaving them devitalized. For example, the immunoglobin A in human mother's milk is destroyed when the milk is heated in a microwave oven. Immunoglobin A is a protein necessary for a baby's proper physical development; and for building natural immunity. Since immunity is the cornerstone of life and health, microwave ovens can be viewed as Qi (life energy) destroying, anti-life machines. If they destroy the essential building blocks in mothers milk, they will most certainly destroy other proteins and highly beneficial substances in other foods. It should be avoided by any who wish to have lasting health and vitality.

Steam Cuisine

Bamboo steamers

Bamboo steamers, an ancient Chinese cooking tool, have many more uses than you might imagine. They can simplify your job as a cook, allowing you to turn out varied meals with a minimum of time, energy, and effort. Steaming is also a very nutritious way to cook. When steamed, most foods can be cooked without added fats or oils. Not only that but they become far more tender, moist and digestible than when baked, broiled, or deep fried.

If you get two large sets of bamboo steamer trays, you will have the tools to save precious time and energy. Bamboo steamers allow you to cook one dish or several dishes at the same time, using the same pot. When using bamboo steamers, you can cook several dishes without having to tend too many pots or wash a sink full of pots, pans, or bowls. Because using a bamboo steamer allows you to cook several dishes with one pot on one burner, it is perhaps one of the most ecological and economical cooking tools, after the wok and pressure cooker. Cooking with this tool uses a fraction of the fuel that conventional ovens use and steamed foods often cook in less time than those cooked using other techniques.

Steaming isn't just for vegetables. Many items you would normally bake, broil, saute or fry can be steamed in a fraction of the time otherwise required. Breads; rolls; meat-less meat balls; root, round, ground and green leafy vegetables; fish; even cookies and pastries are fabulous when steamed. (Eggs and omelets can also be steamed, in oiled custard cups, if you choose to include eggs in your diet.) Leftover pasta, rice, casseroles, burritos, pot pies, polenta, dried out bread, and many other foods can also be reheated by steam.

Unlike the western metal steamer basket, Chinese-style steamers are comprised of several bamboo trays which neatly stack atop one another. These bamboo trays can be placed in a wok or for greater efficiency the trays can be placed on top of a large stainless steel or enamel pot. Either way, you can stack one, two, three, four, or even six bamboo trays on top of one another In China, in shops where Chinese steamed buns and pastries are made, many more trays than this are stacked on top of one another. However, in the home kitchen two to six trays would be a more reasonable height. More than this and you may have difficulty tending the trays or reaching them safely.

Metal vegetable steamers

Metal vegetable steamers are most common in America, though they are a relatively new invention when compared to the thousands of years-old Chinese steamers. The stainless steel steamer basket adjusts to fit neatly inside a saucepan or pot. (The center pin in the metal basket can be unscrewed and removed to allow a bowl or plate to sit directly on the basket.) These steamers work well for steaming single dishes of food or cooking a small amount of vegetables but are not nearly as versatile as the bamboo stacking trays which allow you to cook and/or heat many different items at once.

If you don't have access to a bamboo steamer set, you can get by using two metal steamer baskets and several stainless steel bowls. However, when using a metal steamer basket you will need to have a separate pot and burner for each bowl of food you wish to reheat for a given meal.

A metal steamer basket (about $5-$6) can be use it in a pinch when all of your bamboo trays are full, or for small jobs. This basket can even be placed in the bottom of a pot underneath one or more bamboo steamer trays, giving you the ability to cook or heat even more dishes at once.

Another option is a special metal steamer insert that comes with its own pot. This steamer basket fits the contours of the pot and has handles which extend out from the pot. These sets usually usually consist of one pot and one or two baskets of varying sizes. Sometimes these are used to cook pasta so that the pasta—immersed in the water—may be removed easily. These particular steamers do not work for making steamed buns because the metal sides of the container collect water and will turn your dough to mush. They will work for steaming vegetables or reheating bowls of food though.)

Steaming bowls

Many foods can be steamed in stainless steel bowls. You will want to collect several of these bowls in various sizes from 16-ounce to 64-ounce. If possible, get bowls with flat rather than rounded bottoms. You will also need several small heat-proof saucer which fit snugly atop the bowls (look in thrift stores and at garage sales) so that you can steam heat foods with a cover when needed. We use the uncovered bowl-within-a-pot method and the covered-bowl-within-a-pot method daily, for heating leftovers and cooking fresh foods. These techniques will be discussed in detail later in this chapter and will be referred to throughout this book.

Starting to Steam

Below are some of the most commonly asked questions about steam cooking. You will also find some simple diagrams designed to take you through the various steaming techniques that we use. Beware, once you start you may be hooked. Steaming opens up a whole new world of culinary possibilities. Once you discover these, your cooking will never be the same!

Common Questions

What kind of bamboo steamer should I use?

Bamboo steamers come in many different sizes of varying quality. We suggest purchasing bamboo steamer trays which measure 9 3/4 inches from inside edge to inside edge and 10 1/2-inches from outside edge to outside edge. These are usually sold as 10-inch steamers. This size followed by the next larger size (12-inch) seems to be the most versatile. (With smaller sizes, you cannot efficiently cook steamed buns or other items in a reasonable quantity.) The trays should be of sturdy bamboo or wood construction with a tight fitting weave and very little space between the slats. For maximum efficiency, purchase at least one set (two trays plus a lid), and preferably two sets.

What kind of pot should I use with bamboo steamer trays?

You will need a pot whose diameter matches that of the bamboo steamer trays or a wok that you can place the steamers in. For the best and most efficient steaming the pot should be 3-4-inches deep and 10-inches across for a 10-inch steamer. (Bamboo steamer trays work best with 2- or 3-inches of space between the bottom of the tray and the boiling water so that steam is allowed to rise.) For 10 inch trays (outside edge to outside edge) we use a 4 or 5 quart pot which is 10-inches across. For a set of 12-inch steamers, you will need a wider pot. A stainless steel pot works well. If you can't find a large pot of this description, an enamel stock pot which is slightly deeper yet has the appropriate diameter will also do. Another option is to rest the steamers inside a flat bottom wok on top of the stove. (If using a wok, the water may cover the bottom 1/2-1 inch of the bamboo tray but should not come in contact with the food or plates of food.)

If all else fails, you may use a large, round electric skillet whose diameter matches that of the bamboo trays (these are deeper than conventional stove top skillets so they will allow the steam to rise properly). We prefer using a pot and keeping it on or near the stove at all times to steam up leftovers before meals and/or to cook new foods with ease. We also use the wok for steaming, from time to time.

Matching your pot and steamer trays

As mentioned above, the sides of your bamboo steamer trays should nearly match or be slightly smaller than the width of the pot you place them on. If the bamboo steamer trays are larger in diameter than the pot, heating will not be efficient and water and cooking juices will leak onto the stove top and make a terrible mess. If the bamboo trays are smaller in diameter than the pot, the pot will sit in the water and your food will become soggy because steam is not allowed to rise through or around it. Try to make the diameters match, or use a wok.

How much water should I put in the pot?

When using a metal steamer basket, the water in your pot should not touch the bottom of the basket. In most cases you will need about one or two inches of water. When using bamboo trays, you only need 1-2-inches of water in the pot and this water should not touch the bottom of the tray unless a wok is used. When using the bowl-within-a-pot method to steam cook or reheat foods, you will need to add enough water to the pot so that the water level comes up to one-third to one-half the height of the bowl.

Does the foods location affect cooking time?

The distance between the food and the steaming hot water will affect the cooking time. Ideally, the steamer trays should be several inches above the water level (or immersed in about 1/2-inch of water if a wok is used). Foods closest to the heat source will cook or heat faster than those farther away.

Cooking time will vary slightly depending upon whether you are using bamboo steam trays or metal steamer baskets. It is important to layer the food in your steamer according to required cooking times and to be conscious of the distance between the food and the water.

When bread is steam heated (to remoisten and freshen), it should be placed on the top tray of a series of one or several stacked steamer trays, placed on top of a 4-inch deep pot filled with two inches of water. In this way, the bread can be left to steam for 20-25 minutes while a soup or stew heats in a covered bowl on the bottom of the pot and/or other foods cook in another tray. The bread will not get soggy this way.

To steam heat bread more quickly you may use a metal steamer tray; however, the bread must be removed within 5-10 minutes or it will become soggy. For either method, the bread should be wrapped in a white, cotton/linen towel before being put on the steamer tray to avoid soiling the tray or making soggy bread.)

Can I put foods directly on the bamboo trays?

To prolong the life of your bamboo steamers and for ease of serving and clean-up, foods with a soft, watery, sticky, or oily texture or consistency or small size should be place in shallow dishes or on heat-proof plates. At the very least, put them on a layer of unbleached baking paper or whole cabbage or collard leaves, not directly on the floor of the bamboo or metal steamer basket or tray. (For example, steamed bun dough, won tons, dumplings, or gyoza should always be placed on oiled heat-proof plates before being placed on the steamer trays. Similarly, tamales should be wrapped in corn husks, tamale wrapping paper, a cotton-linen towel, or parchment paper before being placed on the bamboo slats.)

Winter squash, or sweet potatoes may be placed directly on bamboo or metal trays, but you will have to scrub the bamboo trays afterwards. To avoid soiling the bamboo trays, put cut winter squash on a plate then put the plate on the tray, or put the squash on a metal steamer basket (which is easier to clean). If beets are steamed on bamboo trays they should be in bowls or on plates to prevent staining the bamboo. Green vegetables may be placed, whole or cut, directly on the tray or basket. Other vegetables, cut in thin slices or small pieces—mushrooms, peas, green beans, onions, leeks, carrots, radishes, rutabaga, corn, bean sprouts, and the like—may also be placed directly on the trays or basket.

What's the best pot to use with a metal steamer basket?

When using a metal steamer basket, any saucepan will do. The basket will open out to occupy more space in a wide pot or fold in to fit inside a small pot. We often use this type of steamer in conjunction with bamboo steamer trays stacked above the pot or we use it in combination with the bowl-in-a-pot method (using two pots). When using a metal steamer basket on its own, we typically use a 1 1/2-2-quart saucepan with a tight fitting lid.

What temperature should I use for steaming?

When warming or cooking foods by steam, it is not necessary to use a high flame for the entire time. Start the pot on a medium or medium-high heat. Once the water comes to a full boil, reduce the heat to medium but be sure to maintain a rolling and vigorous boil with rising steam throughout the process. If the steam stops rising, you turned the heat too low and will need to bring the water back to a boil. However, if you leave the pot on high for the entire cooking time you will waste energy and may may steam up all of the windows in the kitchen, the living room, etc. Of course, some window steaming is inevitable. If pictures start falling off of the wall and the wall paper starts peeling, you *may* need to lower the heat under your pot.

How often should I check the water?

When cooking items over steam with a relatively high heat or items that will take *more than* 30 minutes, check the water level periodically and/or be sure to add enough at the beginning to keep the pot from boiling dry. In order to maintain steam, and cooking, use *boiling* water to replenish the water below your bamboo steamer trays. Sufficient water is necessary to create and maintain steam, yet adding too much may flood a bowl-within-a-pot or a bowl-on-a-rack/basket.

When do I start timing a steamed dish?

Start timing once the pot comes to boil and steam rises out the top. For example, if a dish must steam for 15 minutes, start counting the time *after* the pot has come to a full boil.

When should food be removed from steamer trays or baskets?

Generally speaking, once an item is through cooking, remove it (or the tray that is holding it) from the pot. When cooking fresh vegetables, the dishes should be removed from the heat source immediately or they will over cook. Vegetables left to sit in a warm pot in a tray, above steam, or with a lid on, will turn to mush and lose their color, flavor and appeal in no time. Steamed eggs (in oiled custard cups) will continue to cook for a several minutes even after removal from the heat, so they should be taken out *before* they and their yolks have become totally hard, otherwise you will have a hard-cooked rather than soft-boiled or poached egg.

While vegetables must be removed immediately from the steam, there are some foods which benefit from remaining above the steam after cooking time has elapsed. Steamed buns must sit above the steam, covered, for 10-15 minutes *after* the cooking time has elapsed, to allow the cooking process to come to completion. Don't leave the buns over the steam too much longer or the plates may collect too much water. When being reheated, leftover whole grain or bread may sit above the steam even after the heat has been turned off; this will only add moisture and usually won't harm them. Watch out for leftover noodles, burritos, or thin breads like tortillas, or chapatis, though. These will get soggy if over-steamed or left to sit over the heat. (As a rule, the latter items need only brief steam heating and should not be left unattended.)

The easiest way to serve from steamer trays

When cooking items in small dishes such custard cups, ramekin or souffle dishes, stainless steel bowls, or other heat-proof bowls or dishes, it is easiest to remove the dish with a pot holder and transfer it directly to the counter or dining table. Most foods can be cooked, served, and even stored in the same dish. This is very convenient if you don't like to wash many dishes.

Handling steaming hot bowls of food:

Use oven mits, to take warm bowls of food directly from the steamer tray. Place them on trivets or placemats or inside an attractive larger serving bowl such as a pottery dish. This will keep you from leaving ugly burn marks on your table-top. Warm bowls of grain can be placed inside a bigger bowl and covered with the bamboo steamer lid to keep them warm, or they may be covered with a bamboo sushi mat.

Serving freshly steamed or warmed bread or whole grain: Loaf bread, buns, tamales, or dumplings can easily served from the steamer trays at the table. Place the steamer tray (or stack of trays) on a larger platter; on top of a medium-sized glass or wooden mixing bowl; or inside a larger glass, pottery, or wooden bowl. Bread that has been wrapped in a cotton-linen towel and steam heated can be placed, still wrapped in the towel, in a large bowl and covered with the bamboo steamer lid to keep it warm. (Placing food items in trays or on a bowl will keep the hot steam from dripping water and dampening or soiling your table top or table cloth.)

Using one pot to cook or heat several foods

You can cook or heat a whole meal at the same time using only one pot. Depending on the size of your steamer trays and dishes, you can place one or more dishes on each tray. To make most efficient use of a single burner, you can also place a single bowl of food (covered or uncovered, depending upon the dish) directly in the bottom of the pot. This can be filled with leftover soup stew, rice, a casserole, etc. Or you can place a metal steamer basket in the bottom of the pot then put a bowl of leftover rice or millet on a tray above. Stacking bamboo trays filled with uncooked vegetables, towel wrapped bread, or shallow dishes of tofu-based custards or plate-fuls of tamales or dumplings can also be placed on top of a pot and... voila! You will have a full hot meal ecologically and economically heated on one burner.

Do I need to change the position of the bamboo trays during cooking?

Several bamboo trays may be stacked on top of each other for efficient cooking. With some foods you may find it necessary to change the position of the tiers partway through cooking since the foods closest to the steam will cook more quickly, yet this is unnecessary in many cases. (You can leave the tiers in place while cooking steamed buns. However, when rising buns over steam you may wish to change the position of the tiers once during the rising period.) In most cases though, this step is unnecessary if you put thicker, slower cooking foods on the bottom layer and lighter foods on top.

When stacking trays, how do I decide which level to put the different foods on?

When cooking several items at once you will need to decide the most efficient method of cookery. You must first decide how to place the foods inside the trays. Some items are best heated using the-bowl-with-a-pot method page; for others, it is best to use the bowl-on-a-rack method; and still other foods can be efficiently heated or cooked using either method. If foods will be cooked and/or heated on different tiers, it is helpful to put the items which require the highest heat or longest cooking on the bottom tier(s). These can steam by themselves for as long as is necessary. Add trays with items that take less time to cook later so that all of the dishes will be done at the same time. Or put quick cooking dishes on at the start and *remove* them as soon as they are done. If several different types of vegetables are cooked together on one tray (such as carrots, onions, and cabbage), cut the toughest and hardest vegetables move finely to that they will be done at the same time. Arrange vegetables in small piles or sections directly on the steamer tray(s) alongside each other. You can also layer several different vegetables on top of one another, placing the quickest cooking and most tender vegetables on top.

You may also opt to reheat two different dishes in separate bowls within separate pots or on separate metal steamer racks. For example, rice may be heated in an uncovered bowl-within-a-pot in one saucepan, soup may be heated in a covered-bowl-within-a-pot in a second pot while a root vegetable side dish may be reheated in a bowl on a rack, or pudding may be cooked in a covered bowl in a third pot.

Can I cook buns, tamales, ravioli, and dumplings with a steamer?

Yes. To make steamed buns or dumplings, divide the dough (see index for recipes) into small pieces. Shape them appropriately then put them on oiled plates. Put the plates on bamboo steamer trays, leaving a little bit of room (about 1-inch) between the balls of dough to allow for expansion (less for doughs which will not rise). Also allow 1/4-1/2-inch of space between the sides of the plate(s) and the sides of steamer trays to allow steam to rise up and around the dough. Instead of placing them on plates, dumplings or tamales can be wrapped in parchment paper or corn husks and placed directly on the steamer tray for cooking.

What containers work best for reheating leftover rice, millet, or polenta?

To retain or add moisture and flavor, and for efficient warming and serving, leftover rice, noodles or other grains should be placed in uncovered bowls rather than directly on the bottom of steamer trays or baskets. These bowls of grain may be placed on a steamer tray or rack. Stainless steel bowls can be placed directly in the bottom of a pot and surrounded with a small amount of water to steam. Polenta, millet slices or mounds, or millet a or polenta loaf can be warmed on heat-proof plates placed on top of a bamboo tray or metal steamer basket. Leftover cooked noodles can also be heated in a bowl on a rack or within a pot, though they take less time than rice.

Reheating and remoistening leftover breads or baked goods

To reheat breads, rolls, bagels, biscuits, buns, muffins, and even cookies, wrap them in a white cotton-linen towel—one with no fuzzies and wash the towel with a non-toxic and natural detergent—and place on the bamboo tray. Pancakes, sticky danishes, or tortillas are best placed on a heat-proof plate, wrapped in a cotton-linen kitchen towel before being put on your steamer tray to keep them from getting soggy. Cake, if warmed by steam, should be placed on a plate and steam heated for only a few minutes.

How long does it take to steam heat leftover whole grain, pasta, or breads?

Reheating time will vary with the dryness, type, and amount of whole grain or bread you are heating, and the size and depth of the pot. How far the food is from the boiling water also makes a difference. Old, dry or thick breads or deep bowls of rice take longer to heat than moister breads or smaller bowls of grain. Practice will acquaint you with the proper time needed to reheat leftover foods.

In general, we heat leftover rice or millet for 20-25 minutes and bread for 10-20 minutes. (We usually heat leftover soup, stew, gravy, or sauce at the same time below the trays in a covered-bowl-within-a-pot or we heat these liquids in a covered bowl within a separate pot for 10-15 minutes.) Leftover noodles are usually warm enough after 10 minutes, depending on the type, volume, and how close the bowl or tray is to the boiling water.

Leftover green or tender vegetables should not be reheated, but taken out of the refrigerator—30-60 minutes before a meal—and served at room temperature. Hearty root and round vegetable dishes, however, can be either served at room temperature or reheated in a covered bowl for 15 minutes or an uncovered bowl for 5-10 minutes. Soups and stews; casseroles; gravies; or tempeh, wheat meat, or tofu dishes can be heated using the covered-bowl-within-a-pot method. This covered steaming method prevents over cooking and keeps excess moisture from pooling in the bottom of the bowl. (Whereas leftover rice or millet should be heated in an uncovered bowl—because they have a tendency to dry out and need to be remoistened—you don't want a leftover soup, stew, or casserole to collect more water and become soggy and diluted; thus, we cover very wet foods when re heating with steam.)

Cooking desserts with steam

Fruit and whole grain or bread-based puddings may be cooked or reheated in a covered bowl-within-a-pot. Arrowroot or flour thickened puddings cook well with steam in a covered bowl-within-a-pot; this eliminates the need to stir such puddings as they cook. Whole or halved fruits can also be cooked in uncovered shallow custard cups or bowls on top of a metal or bamboo steamer tray. Stiff cookie dough (the consistency of refrigerator cookies, or bread, won ton, tamale, or pasta dough) can also be placed on oiled heat-proof plates on top of steam trays for efficient steam cooking and this produces moist, and delectable cookies.

Care and cleaning of bamboo steamers

Bamboo will have a strong smell when you first use it. Some sources recommend thoroughly wetting a new set, soaking for an hour or two, then steaming, then air drying to cure the bamboo. The bamboo will naturally darken with age. Periodically wash it in cool water with little or no soap. (We use a natural bristle brush to remove any food residue.) You won't have to wash the trays very frequently if you place most foods on plates or bowls rather than directly on the bamboo slats. Thoroughly air dry your trays on a rack or a sunny porch after use. We keep our bamboo steamers stacked on a shelf underneath our butcher block for easy access. Occasionally, you may wish to rub the bamboo trays with vegetable oil to prolong their life.

Special techniques for heating leftovers or cooking new dishes:

The great benefit of the following cooking and reheating methods is that they are simple. They require little attention: no stirring, pot watching or stress. You needn't worry about burning your food as a result of distractions such as telephone calls, visitors, or work. However, it is a good idea to set a timer to prevent over cooking and boiling a pot dry.

Covered bowl-within-a-pot method

Tools:

1 1/2-5 quart pot with lid
Small or medium sized stainless steel bowl
Heat proof saucer

1. Place food in a stainless steel bowl (small to medium size, depending upon volume of food).

2. Add enough water to the pot to surround the bowl by 14-1/3 of its height.

3. Cover the bowl with a heat proof saucer.

4. Put a lid on the pot. Or, if you wish to cook other dishes above, put one or more stacking bamboo trays on top of the pot.

5. Bring the pot to boil and steam until food is cooked or heated through.

Use this method to:

• Reheat soups, stews, sauces, or gravies

• Reheat leftover casseroles

• Cook new soups or stews while other dishes cook or heat above on stacking bamboo trays

• Cook fruit sauces or grain puddings on top of the stove so without stirring or burning.

• Cook grain pilafs, stove-top casseroles, fish, or meat-less loaves efficiently

Note: The covered-bowl-within-a-pot method works with stainless steel bowls only. For breakable bowls use the covered bowl on a trivet method.

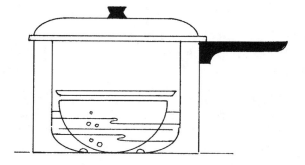

Covered-bowl-on-a-trivet method

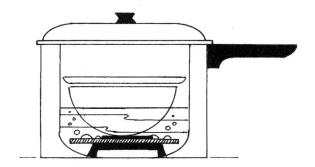

Tools:

Small to large (1 1/2-5 quart) pot with lid
Trivet or meat rack
Heat-proof saucer

1. Place food in a Pyrex, Corningware, or other heat-proof bowl.

2. Place a small trivet or metal disk in the bottom of the pot. Put the bowl of food on top of this trivet or rack.

3. Cover bowl with a heat proof saucer.

4. Surround about one-third to one-half of the bowl's height with water; cover the pot; and cook or heat as for covered-bowl-within-a-pot method.

• See uses for covered-bowl-within-a-pot method

Covered-bowl-on a rack, steamer basket or tray method

Tools:

Medium to large pot or roasting pan with lid
Shallow heat-proof stainless steel bowl
Heat proof saucer

1. Place food in a shallow heat-proof bowl.

2. Put the bowl directly on a metal steamer basket, bamboo steamer tray, or elevated meat rack in a large pot or roasting pan.

3. Cover bowl with a heat-proof saucer.

4. Add water to the pot, to reach just below the level of the metal steamed basket or meat rack. To use bamboo steamers, fill a pot with l-2 inches of water and place the bamboo trays on top of the pot.

5. Cover the pot or bamboo trays with a lid and bring pot to a full boil. Reduce heat and steam until food is cooked or heated through.

Use this method to:

• Steam-souffles, delicate puddings, custards, fish or seafood, or stove top casseroles.

• Reheat grain, bean, wheat meat, or vegetable casseroles.

Uncovered bowl-on-a-rack, steamer basket, or tray method

Tools:

Medium to large (11/2-5-quart) pot with lid
Heat-proof bowl to fit inside of pot
Steamer basket, steamer tray, or meat rack

1. Put about 1-inch of water in a large pot and put a meat rack or metal steamer basket inside the pot or bamboo trays on top.

2. Place food in a heat-proof glass, pyrex, ceramic, or wood bowl.

3. Leave the bowl uncovered and place it on top of a metal steamer basket, bamboo steamer tray, or elevated meat rack inside or on the pot.

4. Cover pot or bamboo tray with a lid; bring water in pot to a boil; and steam food until cooked or heated through.

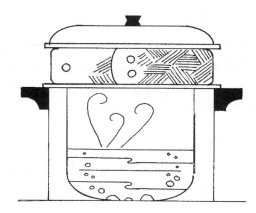

Use this method to:

• Reheat and freshen leftover rice, millet, hot cereals, or plain noodles

• Steam eggs, custards, omelets, or pressed salad (in custard cups or shallow dishes)

• Steam wheat "meat" balls

• Steam cook chunks of root vegetables

• Steam whole or halved pieces of fruit

Uncovered-bowl-within-a-pot method

Tools:

1 1/2-5 quart stainless steel pot with lid
Stainless steel bowl to fit inside Inside pot

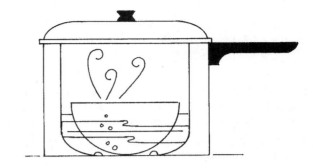

1. Place food in a small stainless steel bowl to fit inside the larger pot; use a large bowl for larger volumes of food.

2. Add water to the pot to surround the bowl by 1/4-1/3 of its height.

3. Leave the bowl uncovered but put a lid on the pot. If you wish to cook other dishes above, put stacking bamboo trays on top of the pot instead.

4. Bring the water to boil and steam until food is cooked or heated through.

Use this method to:

- Reheat and freshen leftover rice, millet, hot cereals, tamales, or plain noodles

- Steam wheat "meat" balls

- Steam whole or halved pieces of fruit

Steaming on-a-steamer-basket (or bamboo tray) method

Tools:

Large pot with a lid
Steamer basket or bamboo steamer tray

1. Place metal steamer basket in a pot.

2. If using a metal steamer basket, add water until it reaches just below the level of the basket. if using bamboo steamer trays fill a pot with 1 to 2-inches of water and put one or more stacking bamboo trays on top of the pot. (Diameter of bamboo trays must match diameter of the pot for proper heating.)

3. **To cook vegetables:** Put vegetables directly on the metal rack or bamboo trays. When using several varieties, cut the longest cooking vegetables in small or thinner pieces; arrange in layers with longest cooking vegetables the bottom.

Notes: Whole, uncut small to medium-sized potatoes, sweet potatoes or yams may be cooked directly on the metal steamer basket or bamboo tray if desired.

Heating leftover bread: Wrap buns or other pieces of bread in a white cotton-linen dish towel and put on basket.

Cooking tamales, masa balls, or dumplings: Wrap in a white cotton-linen towel, parchment paper or corn husks.

4. Bring water to a boil and steam food until cooked or heated through.

Use this method to:

- Cook whole or cut green leafy vegetables or cabbage leaves

- Cook mixed, cut vegetables and salads

- Steam cook chunks of winter squash, sweet potatoes, yam, or small whole potatoes

- Cook tamales, masa balls, or dumplings

- Reheat dry or old loaf bread, rolls, biscuits, bagels, muffins, buns, cake, bread sticks, or other breads

Steaming on-a-plate method

Tools:

Medium to large pot with lid
Metal steamer basket or bamboo trays
Heat-proof plate to fit inside bamboo steamer tray or on top of metal basket

1a.Using a metal steamer basket: Unscrew and remove the center pin from basket. Put basket in a pot and add water to the pot to reach just below the level of the basket.

1b.Using stacking bamboo steamer trays: Fill a pot with 2-inches of water then place stacking bamboo trays on top of pot. (Sides of pot must match the diameter of the steamer trays for proper heating.)

2a.Using a metal steamer basket: Put a heat proof dinner plate On top of basket.

2b.Using stacking bamboo trays: Put each plate on a stacking bamboo tray (leaving at least 1/4-inch of space between the sides of the plate and the sides of the steamer tray.

Notes: if reheating millet or polenta slices: Put a whole loaf of sliced grain on one or more heat-proof plates. Alternatively, layer slices of top of the heat-proof plate or plates.

If cooking tamales, dumplings, masa balls, won tons, gyoza, ravioli, cookies, filled pastries, or steamed buns (bread dough formed into small buns): Place grain product on oiled heat proof plates.

3. Cover the pot or bamboo trays with lid. Bring water in pot to a boil; reduce heat to medium and steam food until cooked (recommended time) or reheated through.

Note: Steamed buns or yeasted pastries must rise on the plates before being steamed. See index and specific recipes for further details.

Use this method to:

- Cook filled or unfilled steamed buns (raw dough) after rising
- Cook tamales, dumplings or masa balls
- Cook won tons, gyoza, or ravioli
- Reheat polenta or millet loaves or slices
- Cook chunks of squash or sweet potato
- Steam cookies (this only works for cookie dough with a very stiff and dry consistency like that of refrigerator cookies, rolled cookies, or sugar cookie dough)
- Reheat leftover cakes, bars, or muffins (heat for only 3-5 minutes or they will turn soggy)

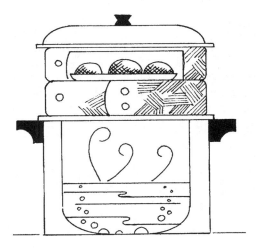

30 Minutes until dinner: How to orchestrate a meal in a jiffy

By incorporating leftovers and using only 1-3 pots, you can cook a whole meal in 30 minutes. If you need a new soup, stew, or whole grain from scratch allow 45-60 minutes until dinner.

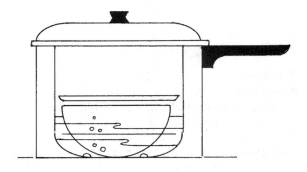

1. **Soup:** Heat leftover soup or stew in a covered-stainless steel bowl-within-a-pot. Or, cook a soup from scratch in a separate saucepan.

2. **Grain:** Heat leftover rice, millet, or noodles using the uncovered-bowl-within-a-pot method or bowl-on-a-rack method. Or, heat leftover bread, arepas, tamales, or dumplings in a cotton kitchen towel on a metal steamer basket or on a bamboo tray stacked above the covered bowl of soup or stew. Or, cook a fresh pot of pasta, rice, millet, or polenta in a separate pot. Start cooking the grain before beginning other dishes. Brown rice takes one hour to cook after reaching a boil or pressure. Millet takes 30-35 minutes. Noodles take 10-12 minutes. A First batch of mochi waffles will be ready within 10 minutes; remaining batches can be cooked at the table while you eat the first one, then the second, then the third, etc.

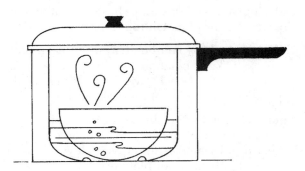

3. **Vegetable side dish:** Steam cook greens or mixed vegetables on another stacking tray unless you have leftover pressed, marinated, boiled or raw salad, or cooked vegetables on hand. Or, stir fry, sauté, quick-boil, or parboil vegetables, or make a quick marinated or pressed salad while other foods cook or heat.

Note: When stacking several steamer trays, put hard or hardy vegetables and/or whole grains on lower trays; put the most tender greens or mixed vegetables, or bread on the top tray(s).

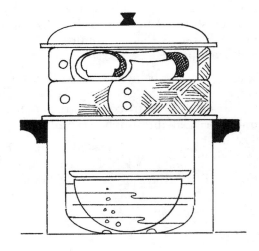

Pressure-steaming-on-a-rack method

Tools:

Pressure Cooker
Trivet or stainless steel vegetable steamer
or meat rack, or stainless steel rack

1. Place trivet, metal steamer basket, or rack in bottom of pressure cooker.

2. Add water to the pressure cooker to reach just below the bottom of the metal steamer basket, meat rack, or trivet.

3. **To cook whole vegetables:** Place vegetables directly on a metal steamer basket or stainless steel meat rack.

   To cook pudding: Put the pudding ingredients in a heat-proof stainless steel or pyrex bowl or a pudding mold designed for steaming. Cover bowl with a heat-proof saucer. If the bowl is fragile, put it on top of a trivet, steamer basket, or meat rack. A stainless steel bowl may be put directly in the bottom of a pot then surrounded with water to rise up to one-third of the bowl's height.

4. Seal the pressure cooker; bring to full pressure over medium-high heat; reduce heat to medium-low and cook for the recommended time.

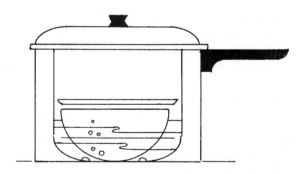

Use this method to:

• Cook whole potatoes, sweet potatoes, or beets quickly and efficiently

• Cook steamed pudding (actually a cake cooked in an attractive mold). See also Covered-bowl-with-in-a-pot method for cooking steamed puddings

• Cook vegetarian "sausage" or raw gluten loaves, burgers, etc.

Reheating Leftover Grains ***

Leftover dinner grain can be easily reheated and remoistened with the methods below. These methods revive the grain *and* enhance its flavor, but also require no attendance, leaving you free to do other things while your grain reheats.

Note: To serve 1-2 people, use a 2-quart saucepan and a small to medium-sized stainless steel bowl which holds 1-3 cups rice (for 1 person) or 3-5 cups of cooked grain (for 2 grain eaters). Or, use a 4-6 quart pot to reheat a bowl of grain while simultaneously cooking or heating other foods in stacking trays above. Use a large pot to reheat larger volumes of grain. Use the-bowl-within-a-pot method to reheat whole grain or casseroles on the bottom of a pot while at the same time steaming vegetables or other foods on stacking trays above. Or, steam grain in a bowl or on a plate atop a bamboo tray when heating leftover soup, stew, or sauce in a covered bowl-within-a-pot below.

Bowl-within-a-pot method:

1. With a rice paddle, spoon desired amount of cooked grain into a small stainless steel bowl.

2. Put the bowl on the bottom of a saucepan. Add water to the pot to surround it by about 1-2 inches (or 1/3 the height of the bowl). (Don't add too much water or the water will take too long to boil or boil into the rice or onto the stove. Too little water and the pot will boil dry or not generate sufficient steam.)

3. Leave bowl uncovered. Cover the pot with a lid, or stack one or several bamboo trays over the pot. Cover the pot with a lid. (The sides of the steam trays should match the pot's width).

4. Bring the pot of water to boil over medium-high heat. Reduce heat to medium making sure enough steam continues to rise. Steam 15-30 minutes, as needed.

5. Transfer bowl of rice to the table and cover with a bamboo mat.

Tips:

- **Reheating casseroles made from noodles, rice, or beans:** Cover the bowl with a small heat proof saucer before steam heating. This will keep excess moisture from pooling in the bowl and making everything soggy.

Bowl-on-a rack method:

1. Put leftover cooked grain in a wood, ceramic, pyrex or heat-proof bowl. (See notes below for heating leftover polenta, grain loaf, or bread.)

2. Place the bowl on a metal steamer basket, bamboo steamer tray, or on top of a metal disk (meat rack or trivet) placed in the bottom of a saucepan to protect the bowl from breakage.

3. Add 1 to 2-inches of water to the pot. (Water should not touch the metal basket or tray.) If a trivet is used, add water to the pot to surround the bowl by 1/3-1/2 of its height. Put a cover on the pot, but leave the bowl uncovered.

4. Bring pot to boil; reduce heat to medium, and steam for 10-20 minutes until grain is warmed through. Exact time will vary with the amount and type of grain you are reheating.

Tips for Reheating:

- **Millet or polenta slices:** Place the loaf or slices on a heat proof plate, put the plate on a metal or bamboo steamer tray. Heat as above.

- **Leftover pasta:** Place it in a bowl, as above, but reheat for just 5-15 minutes, until warm.

- **Leftover bread, pancakes, biscuits, or cookies:** Wrap in a white linen or cotton kitchen towel. Place on a bamboo steamer rack, high above the water. Put lid on steamer. Steam for 10-30 minutes (time will depend on the dryness and thickness of the food). If heating on a metal steamer tray which is closer to the water, heat just 3-8 minutes to prevent bread from turning soggy.

Reheating Leftover Soups, Stews, Sauces & Gravies

We store leftover soups, stews, sauces, and gravies in ready-to-heat small stainless steel bowls covered with heat-proof saucers. These can be stored in meal-sized portions then reheated using the covered-bowl within a pot method. (You can often find small stainless steel bowls and heat proof saucers and plates at garage sales, thrift stores, and second hand shops. Stock up on these for handy food storage and heating).

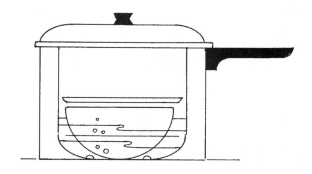

1. Approximately half an hour before you plan to eat, take out your stainless steel bowl full of soup, stew, sauce or gravy, and place it in the bottom of a saucepan.

2. Add water to the saucepan, to surround and reach one-third the bowl's height.

3. Cover the bowl with a heat-proof saucer then put a lid on the pot or cover with a bamboo tray holding other food to be reheated.

4. Bring the pot to boil then reduce the heat to medium-high, enough to keep the steam rising. Either let contents steam for 20-30 minutes while you set the table or cook or assemble some last minute vegetable side dishes, condiments, sauces, or garnishes. Alternately, let the contents steam for 10 minutes then turn off the heat but allow the bowl to sit in the warm pot for another 15-20 minutes before serving. Time will depend upon the dish being heated. (Use the shorter time for soups, stew, or gravies which have already been seasoned with miso.)

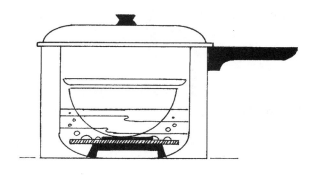

5. Season your soup, then ladle into serving bowls and garnish. Transfer all dishes to the table, and serve.

Note: Soups may be heated directly in a saucepan; however, this requires continuous stirring to avoid burning. Special care is needed when reheating soups, stews, or sauces which have been seasoned with miso. Such dishes should not be allowed to boil during warming or the live cultures in the miso will be destroyed. Use a low simmer, directly in a pot or the covered-bowl-within-a-pot method.

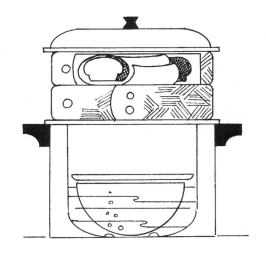

Cutting Techniques

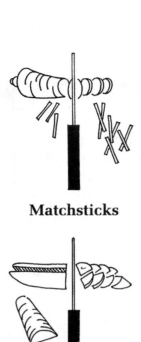

Matchsticks

Cubes

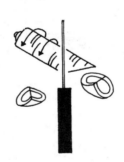

Half & Quarter Moons

Mincing

Rolling Cut

Squares

Cresents

Cutting Squash

Chapter 3
Meal & Menu Planning

Making It Happen

No Dish Stands Alone

In Western styles of cooking, dishes are often prepared as self-sufficient units or "courses" in a meal, each to be consumed by themselves. For example, the soup is usually served as a starter instead of or followed by a dressed salad. Buttered bread is also supposed to stand on its own. Then comes the entrée. Even the side dishes accompanying the main course are often as substantial as the main course, with exciting and rich flavors and textures. Oftentimes each dish is sauced or dressed to the hilt. This reflects a view that the dishes are independent of one another.

In contrast, dishes of traditional Oriental cuisines are viewed as dependent upon one another—like pieces of a puzzle. Thus, while incomplete on their own, they fit together to form a beautiful picture. For example, it is rare for Americans to eat plain cooked rice as part of a meal. Instead, if rice is served, it usually fried or dressed with butter or oil, spices, nuts, and other rich additions so that it can stand on. In contrast, in Oriental cuisine the rice is served plain, as a main dish, with soup and various side dishes served *along side* to complement and enhance it. In such a cuisines, no dish stands alone. The rice needs the side dishes—by virtue of its relative blandness—while the side dishes are small, well seasoned, richly flavored, and not substantial enough to serve as a meal on their own. Thus, the side dishes require the rice to balance and fill them out. While this practice may seem odd to most Americans, it is common in many traditional cultures around the world. In the cuisines of Ethiopia, India, Mexico and Greece, various breads are often used to scoop up vegetables, beans, and other side dishes. In these cuisines breads are often served as the main dish, in the same way that rice or millet are served as main dishes in China, Africa, or Japan. Oftentimes these cultures feature not one but *two* grain dishes in a meal. Cracked wheat, cornmeal, buckwheat, or various flour products may be served along with rice, bread or noodles. For example, pasta or polenta with bread; rice with won tons or gyoza; lasagna with bread; tabouli with pita bread; or rice with tortillas.

This *orient*-al way (or re-*orientation*) is the way of eating we offer as Nourishment for Life. In meals based upon whole grains, all other dishes are served along side and in relatively small quantities. Consequently, you may find that our recommended portion sizes for side dishes (beans, vegetables, etc.) are considerably smaller than what you are used to while those for grains may be larger than you are used to. However, on a low-fat vegetarian diet it is necessary to eat a large volume of grain in order to maintain energy and strength. Vegetables, being far less calorie dense and often harder to digest, should be eaten in smaller amounts. Also, beans (or condiments such as nuts or seeds) tend to be very rich and also relatively difficult to digest. Thus, they too should be eaten in small amounts. When eaten in large quantities beans, seeds, and nuts can lead to digestive disorders and other health problems. When you stop seeing meals as being composed of independent "courses," and instead view them as a composition of inter-dependent dishes—with grain as the center—you will begin to make the transition to a healthier life and more planet-supporting diet. This is the way to Nourish Life.

Suggestions for serving and partaking of a grain-based meal

The Elements of a Grain-Based Diet

At first it might seem strange to have some fairly bland or unseasoned dishes in a meal. It might also seem odd to serve the entire meal at once rather than in course, but we think that once you start eating in this way, you will like it and even find that your old way of serving foods seems "strange."

Serving it all at once

On a grain-based diet, the soup or stew, and vegetable side dishes are served with the grain—brown rice, millet, noodles, bread, etc.— rather than in courses. This benefits digestion. Serving a soup or stew with the meal eliminates the need for beverages which can disturb digestion when taken with your meal. It also reduces the need for oily and rich spreads you use, without sacrificing taste or enjoyment. Soups or stews can even be used as bread spreads or to stand in for sauces on pasta or polenta. Likewise a gravy or sauce can stand in for soup or stew in a meal. Bread or millet "slices" can also be dunked in the soup, stew, or gravy or used to scoop up tender morsels of food. If rice is served along side a soup or stew, it can be eaten with or followed by spoonfuls of soup. Seasoned roasted seed or nut condiments can be used in any meal to "dress up" rice or other grains. Cooked root vegetables; sea vegetables; boiled, pressed or marinated salads; seasoned beans, tofu, tempeh or wheat meat; and pickles may serve as additional condiments and toppings for whole grain, pasta, or bread.

Order of eating

Although everything is served at once, eating is a progressive activity. That is we eat from yang to yin, eating the most dense, warm, cooked foods first—mostly grain, along with the soup, stew, or hearty root vegetables—progressing to more cooling foods such as cooked greens or salads. This protects and kindles the Spleen (digestive fire). This is best done by alternating a bite or two of grain with a bite of soup or stew.

(The grain needn't be eaten "plain;" it may be topped with seed or nut condiments, sea vegetables, or other savory toppings and condiments.) Once the soup or stew is gone, alternate a bite of grain with a bite of side dish, eating beans or roots before cooked greens or salad and saving pickles for the end of the meal. By alternating mouthfuls of grain with bites of side dishes about 50% of the volume in each meal will be grain. Eating this way—eating warm, cooked foods first—also helps prepare your Stomach for the rest of the meal, thereby facilitating good digestion and assimilation. Cold foods literally paralyze the Stomach. Thus, eating the salad, cooked greens or root vegetables, or pickles at the start of the meal—before sufficient warm foods have been eaten—can put a real "damper" on digestion. When eaten too soon in meal, or in too great a quantity, these foods can extinguish the digestive fire and impair its functioning. This is because such foods are Damp and Cold by nature and the Spleen (the digestive fire in Oriental terms) is, by nature, warm and must stay that way to burn up the food we eat.

Don't put out the fire

From the Oriental medicine perspective, raw vegetables are Cold and Damp. Even cooked vegetables have a Cooling, Damp energy. Therefore, it is inadvisable to start a meal with a salad or steamed vegetables or to eat meals consisting entirely or primarily of vegetables or fruits. Warm (or at least room temperature) soups and grain are the best "starters" for meals. Though soups are often served as an appetizer in restaurants and in many homes, they are best and more appropriately served and eaten with grain throughout the first half of a meal. This enhances both digestion and the flavor of a grain-based meal. Even after the soup is gone, when eating the recommended amount of grain, there will be ample grain leftover to be eaten with the vegetables toward the second half of the meal.

If dairy products—such as goat milk or yogurt—are served in a meal, they should always be served at room temperature, or slightly warmed, rather than ice cold from the refrigerator because cold foods can put out the digestive fire.

The Middle Burner Space (The Fires)

In Oriental medicine, the human body is divided into three "burning spaces," the Upper, Middle, and Lower Burners. Life is conceived basically as a flame that must be properly nurtured for the maintenance of health. The Middle Burner Space is the site of the Spleen and Stomach (which are the primary organs of digestion and assimilation). Digestive problems are generally a result of dysfunction of the Spleen —due to unbalanced dietary and lifestyle habits. In fact, many other problems are also rooted in dysfunction of the Middle Burner. In Oriental medicine it is said that "if the Stomach Qi is weak, the body will be weak." These Organs are responsible for the transformation of food and fluids. Without proper transformation (digestion and assimilation) of food and fluids—the *zhen Qi,* or true basic vitality, cannot be maintained and disease results.

The image of a Middle Burner is to be taken quite seriously. Oriental medicine identifies the Spleen as a "digestive fire," and the Stomach as the container for the fuel that feeds that fire. The digestive fires work by the same principles as a bonfire or fireplace. To burn cleanly the fuel must be appropriate, both in quantity and quality. Also, if a fire—in this case, the fire of life— is to be sustained, it must be fed regularly. If too much wood (or food in this case) is put on the fire, it will be smothered and put out. On the other hand, if too little fuel is put on the fire, it will not be able to sustain itself and will also go out. If one throws greasy or oily substances on the fire, it will smoke and smolder (often producing gaseous fumes!). Douse a fire with something cold or damp (whether food or beverages) and it will be rapidly extinguished and not easily lit again. Try to build a fire in a damaged container and it will not heat or burn efficiently.

Don't add fruit to your meals

Raisins and other dried fruits, fresh fruits, and other sweets should be left out of the dishes for a meal. When eaten, they should be reserved for after or between meals, as dessert or a light snack. Sugars are digested at a different rate than complex carbohydrates, fats, and protein.

Eating sweets in a meal can inhibit proper digestion and lead to fermentation and flatulence. Fruit and grain combinations are best reserved for infrequent desserts after a meal or as a light snack.

Sit down

Eat only when sitting down—saliva produced when standing lacks digestive enzymes.

Just eat

Too many people in our culture have become habituated to eating meals on the run—in a hurry, standing, walking, working, driving, watching television—or in between other hurried activities. This does nothing for our digestion, much less our overall health and enjoyment. Practices such as eating with the radio pumping out fast tunes that our jaws try to harmonize with, balancing our checkbooks while unbalancing our meals, and working over meals are so common than few even question such practices. Now it is time to start questioning. .

Chew well

Cooking is the first step in the digestive process. Chewing is the second step. The goal of chewing is to break food down into small particles, mixing it with saliva—which contains digestive enzymes if you are relaxed and sitting down— then sending it on to the stomach as a "soup." Proper chewing during the meal produces sufficient saliva (and stimulates production of digestive enzymes) to moisten food. If food is not chewed thoroughly, incomplete digestion often results. At the very least, insufficient chewing often leads to a feeling of heaviness and bloating after meals, often accompanied by strong thirst.

Thorough chewing means chewing your food until it is liquified, like soup. This usually means chewing each mouthful 50 times. You can chew fast yet thoroughly and still eat your meal slowly. While this may sound strange, or even impossible, it can be done. It just takes attention and practice. (Just keep pushing the food forward in your mouth with our tongue, so it doesn't go down your throat prematurely.) You will have to count your chews at first, until you get a feel for it Then it will feel natural to turn your food into soup or "milk" before swallowing. Proper mastication also takes time. Thus, you will need to set aside plenty of time for meals, usually 45-60 minutes for each meal.

Don't drink and eat

Drinking beverages with meals leads to only partially chewed food being washed down. Instead of drinking liquids with meals, take a cup of warm soup or stew at once or twice a day (or you might replace your soup or stew with a small cup of raw milk or yogurt now and then if you use such products.). Eat and sip the soup, stew, or gravy with your food. Tea, grain coffee or water should be served after or between rather than during meals to avoid diluting the digestive juices or overloading the Spleen and Stomach with too much fluid at once. (If you can wait at least 30-60 minutes after eating before drinking a beverage, all the better.) Cooked grains and vegetables contain plenty of water already. Proper chewing will produce additional fluid in the form of saliva. There is no physiological need to drink fluids with meals. It is just a habit. And habits can be changed.

Be an early bird

If possible, allow one hour between the time you get out of bed and when you eat breakfast. (Your digestive system needs time to wake up too!) And whatever you do,. don't skip breakfast. If you skip any meal or eat lightly—make it the evening meal. You don't need to fuel up before bed and you will sleep better if you go to sleep on an empty stomach.

Don't be a midnight muncher

Avoid eating after 7 p.m. The digestive organs slow down and come to a screeching halt as the day wears on and night falls. Food taken after this time is poorly digested and leads to food stagnation and excess accumulations. If you can be done with your last meal earlier, all the better.

Eat whole meals

It is best to eat three balanced meals each day and avoid snacking. Or, eat two large meals early in the day (breakfast plus a late lunch) then take a light snack in the late afternoon or early evening. Digestion is work, and the Spleen (analogous to the stomach and intestines in the West) needs to rest between meals. Snacking over stimulates and exhausts the digestive organs making them work overtime. To avoid having to eat between meals you will want to eat enough at meals (plenty of grain) to allow 4-5 hours before you are hungry again. If you are hungry after cutting out snacks, then it means that you simply need to eat more at meal-time. It's that simple. By the same token, don't wait until you are hungry to start cooking, and don't wait until you are ravenous to eat. Plan ahead and you will avoid problems here.

Meal spacing

If possible, eat at fairly regular times each day. The body likes and performs best with rhythms. It is also important to take in the bulk of your food in the early part of the day, when your body needs the fuel and is most able to utilize it. Therefore, breakfast and lunch should be the largest and most leisurely meals of the day. This is the way people have eaten in traditional cultures. Dinner—or supper, which comes from the same word as soup—should be light and taken early to avoid overloading the digestive system.

While it is best to allow 4-5 hours between meals for thorough digestion to take place, if you are eating just two meals per day (a large breakfast and a large mid-day or early afternoon meal), you may allow 10-18 hours of fasting between your lunch and breakfast the next day. This stimulates metabolism and immune function. If you are used to eating at night, when you begin skipping the evening meal you may experience great hunger at first, but if you persevere and resist the urge to eat at night, you will have a wonderfully strong morning appetite in no time (and improved digestion too!). You will then be able to eat a much larger breakfast and lunch. This will re-set your body clock and metabolism to work more efficiently then it will feel normal to eat in such a fashion. After several months of eating two meals a day you may want or need to add a light snack in the early evening, depending upon your needs and activity level.

Meal times

If you take just two larger meals a day, you might want to try spacing them as follows:

> **Breakfast** at 6:30 or 7 a.m.
> **Lunch** at 1, 1:30, or 2 p.m
> **Optional, light snack or mini-meal** at 5:30 or 6 p.m.

If eating three meals per day, you might try:

> **Breakfast** at 6:00, 6:30, or 7 a.m
> **Lunch** at 11:30 and 12:30 p.m
> **Dinner** at 4:30, 5, 5:30, or 6 p.m.

For those with increased nutritional needs (children, athletes, heavy laborers, or pregnant or lactating women), it is usually necessary to take three meals per day; however, the bulk of your daily food (at least two thirds of your daily calories and food volume) should still be consumed over breakfast and lunch combined.

It's not really that difficult

At first all of this order and way of eating might seem overly complicated and troublesome but hang in there! When people try this way of eating, they usually find that it is really quite simple and that it makes a world of difference in the enjoyment of and digestibility of meals. The more you practice this, the sooner it will become habit. Once it has become habit, you will experience freedom (the kind that comes from discipline). When you eat a predictable volume of food, at regular times, and in an orderly way, the time between meals will then be more pleasant and productive; you will enjoy your food more; and you will be free from the distracting thoughts about food that arise when meals are skipped, eaten at irregular times, or taken in a disorderly way.

A Guide To Daily Food Choices

FOOD GROUP

GRAINS...
Bread, Cereal, Rice, Barley
Millet , Oats, Pasta, etc.

VEGETABLES ....
Dark Green Leafy, Orange,
Yellow, White & Red Vegetables

SEA VEGETABLES...
Dulse, Sea Palm, Nori, Kelp,
Ocean Ribbons, Sea Cress,
Alaria, Fucus, Agar Agar, etc.

BEANS, BEAN PRODUCTS
& MEAT ALTERNATIVES ....
Tofu & Tempeh; Dried Beans
& Peas; Wheat Meat /Seitan

FREE FATS ....
Cold Pressed/Unrefined Vegetable Oils &
Ghee (Clarified Butter) or Raw Butter

NUT & SEEDS ....
Seeds, Nuts, Seed & Nut Butters

BEVERAGES ....
Pure, Filtered or Spring
Water, Instant or Brewed Grain
"Coffee," Herb Tea

FRUITS & DESSERTS ....

SUPPLEMENTAL, ANIMAL FOODS ....
(Unfortified, unpasteurized raw dairy foods:
hormone/antibiotic-free, from local, naturally
raised, free-ranging animals)
Yogurt, Kefir, Quark, Yogurt Cheese,
Buttermilk, Cheese, Milk;
Whole, Fertile, Free-Range eggs;
or Fish or Fish Head or Bones

Suggested Number of Daily Servings

8-12 servings from entire group daily. 12-18 servings for athletes, very active adults and teens, growing kids, or pregnant or breast feeding women.

4-10 servings daily: 2-4 leafy greens, 1-2 orange or yellow vegetables. Also and 2-3 small servings of raw green garnishes. Use round, ground, vine vegetables often. Include pressed, marinated, or raw salads daily.

1-3 servings daily; 2-3 if pregnant or nursing. (Servings needn't be large; sea vegetables are very concentrated.)

1-2 servings from entire group per day.

1-3 measured tablespoons oil (or part oil, part ghee) per day. For essential fatty acids, most or or all of the oil should be raw, uncooked. (Do not cook with flax oil.)

2-4 Tbsp. nuts or seeds or 1-3 Tbsp. nut or seed butter per day; slightly more for teens, active adults, growing children or pregnant or lactating women.

Use sparingly, according to thirst. Avoid ice cold or chilled beverages of all kinds. Avoid soda; coffee; and beverages with artificial flavorings, colorings, sweeteners, preservatives, chemicals, or other additives. Use vegetable or fruit juice infrequently (in warm weather), if at all.. Avoid alcohol or limit naturally fermented beer, wine, or sake to special occasions.

Limit to 2-4 servings *per week*. Amasake drink; amasake pudding; chestnuts; sweet starchy vegetables; whole grains and flours; grain sweeteners; cooked seasonal, fresh and/or dried, local fruit or juice; occasional raw fruit; +/- trace amounts of oil, nuts, or seeds.

1-2 servings from entire group daily. Emphasize at least one calcium rich dairy food or mineral rich bone broth/soup daily. When using eggs, use the whole egg—not just the whites. Goat milk products are preferable to cow's milk. Avoid pasteurized and homogenized dairy foods. If only pasteurized milk is available, bring it to a full boil before drinking or making yogurt or cheese. If using flesh food, use cold water or deep ocean fish or seafood, or fish heads, bones or scraps. If poultry is used, use infrequently and use the bones.

WHAT COUNTS AS A SERVING?

1 slice of bread; 1 flour or 2 corn tortillas
1/2 bagel, bun, english muffin, or pita bread
1/2 large or 1 small roll, biscuit, or muffin
1/2 cup cooked cereal, brown rice, millet,
polenta, buckwheat, barley, or oats
1/2 cup spaghetti, noodles, or other pasta
1 oz. dry breakfast cereal or whole grain crackers
4 cups dry popped corn or 1-1 1/2 rice cakes
1 1/2 oz. mochi (uncooked)

1/2 cup raw or cooked vegetables
1/2 cup pressed, marinated, or wilted salad
1/2-1 cup soup or stew made with vegetables
1 cup veggie soup with tempeh, beans or seitan
1 cup raw leafy greens (lettuce, endive or Mesclun)

1/8-1/2 cup loosely packed, roasted
2-4 tsp. sea vegetable flakes or powder
3-5" strip in a pot of soup, stew, or grain
1-3 Tbsp. cooked sea vegetable condiment
2 sheets of sushi nori or other;
1/4-1/2 cup sea & land vegetable dish

1/4-1/2 cup cooked beans or legumes
1/4-2/3 cup bean dip, sauce, gravy, or spread
2-3 oz. /1/3-2/3 cup tempeh, tofu, wheat meat/seitan
1 cup bean or vegetable-bean soup or stew
1/2-1 cup unfortified soy milk or soy yogurt

1 tsp. unrefined flax, sesame, sunflower or olive oil
1 tsp. ghee or organic raw or cultured butter

1 Tbsp. seeds or nuts (or seed or nut condiment)
1 1/2 tsp. nut or seed butter

1/2-1 cup spring, well, or purified water
1/2-1 cup herb tea
1/2-1 cup grain coffee/roasted grain beverage
1/2-1 cup vegetable broth
1/2-1 cup vegetable juice (infrequently)*

2/3-1 cup amasake pudding or beverage
2/3-1 cup grain pudding or chestnut dessert
2/3-3/4 cup cooked fruit, sauce, or compote
1 whole fruit— apple, pear, peach, or other
1-2 whole grain cookies or biscuits
1 slice fruit or vegetable pie, pastry, or cake
1/2-1 cup fruit or vegetable juice (infrequent)

1 whole medium to large egg or 2 small eggs
1-1 1/2 oz. raw or cultured milk cheese
4-6 Tbsp. grated raw or cultured milk cheese
1/4-1/2 cup raw milk cottage cheese or ricotta
6-8 oz. raw or cultured milk, yogurt, or kefir
1 cup of soup made from fish bones or scraps
2-3 oz. fresh fish or 1/4-1/2 oz. dried fish
2-4 oz. fish or fowl scraps for bone-building-stock

SUGGESTIONS & USAGE

Use whole or minimally refined grains, prepared simply. Use some whole, uncracked and unground grains daily. Cook grains alone or with beans, sea or land vegetables; seeds or nuts; beans, etc. Use in porridge; stuffings; fillings for vegetables; soups, sauces, gravies; or as wrappers for tamales, tacos, burritos, tortillas, calzones; in breads, crusts.

Prepare alone or with root, round, ground, or vine vegetables or with beans or sea vegetables. Use in soups, stews, sauces, spreads, stir fries, sautés, casseroles, or boiled, pressed, or marinated salads or as fillings for calzones, burritos, etc.

Cook into soups, stews, whole grain or breakfast cereal; cook with root, round, or leafy green vegetables; add to grain, bean, or vegetable salads; use as a garnish; use in making condiments, or in stuffings, fillings, spreads, sauces, etc.

Use in soup, stews, spreads, and sauces; dressings and dips; burgers, loaves, and casseroles; fillings, stuffings, and sandwiches; grain or vegetable salads and stir fries; add to a pot of rice or millet; or combine with eggs, yogurt, or fish.

Use in dressings, spreads, sauces; stir fries and sautés or spooned over cooked grains, vegetables, or salad at the table.

Make raw or roasted, ground or whole, salted or unsalted condiments for grain or topping dessert or vegetables; use in puddings, casseroles, doughs, or a pot of rice or hot cereal.

Drink water, grain coffee or tea after or between meals according to thirst. Use soup or stew as liquid at meals. Use dairy or grain, soy, or seed/nut milk or yogurt at the end of a meal or as a snack. Serve warm or room temperature.

Prepare simple fruit-, chestnut-, or grain-puddings, custards, compotes, sauces, gels, or aspics. Use only small amounts of nuts, seeds, or oil, in cookies, cakes, crisps, or bars.

Use to top plain whole grain, pasta, hot cereal, bread, or beans. Avoid cooking dairy products into dishes; instead, use sparingly and consciously at the table. (Grate cheese to sprinkle over cooked grains, vegetables, or beans. Poach, scramble, or steam eggs to spoon over whole grain, cereal, bread, or vegetables. Use yogurt as a beverage or topping for cereal or vegetables. Use ghee to sautée or as a table condiment. Cook fish or fish scraps and bones to make a stock, or steam or stir fry fish to use as a topping for grain or veggies.

Using the Guidelines & Basic Meal Formats

The recommendations to follow are rough guidelines to help you put together a diet that supplies a sufficient quantity of food to meet your basic nutritional needs. Serving sizes are outlined in the chart on the previous pages. In most cases, if you eat a larger portion count it as more than one serving. For example: 1/2 cup of rice counts as one serving; two cups counts as four servings, etc. One slice of bread is one serving; three slices equals three servings; and so on. If you eat a smaller portion than the serving suggested, count it as part of a serving. When combining foods from different food groups into one dish, simply estimate how many servings from each group are included in the dish. A dish of stir fried tofu with broccoli counts in the bean group and the vegetable group; a bean burrito counts in the grain group (tortilla and/or rice) and the bean group; and so on. These measurements are provided only as a general guide.

At first it might be helpful to measure your food into individual serving dishes so that you know how much your soup cups and cereal bowls hold. In this way you can get an idea of how much you typically eat. This can also help you eat food in the proper proportion. However, it is unnecessary to measure all of your food. Being obsessed with how much you eat is not the way toward a balanced diet or life. The point to remember is that the bulk of your diet (40-60% by volume) should consist of grain. If you eat regular meals at regular times every day you will find that you eat a fairly consistent amount from meal to meal and day to day. Knowing what this amount is will help you plan meals, it will help you figure out how much food to prepare for a given meal or a given two day period and it will prevent waste because you will not put food on your plate that you cannot finish.

About Under eating:

Under eating *causes* uncontrollable hunger and overeating. Thus it is senseless to try to restrict your food volume excessively. Your appetite is not the enemy; it is there for a reason (you need food, energy, and nutrients). Feed it well and it will be your best ally.

A Pattern For Nourishment

The basic Nourishment For Life meal pattern lends itself endless variety. It is also sustainable, meaning that you can put together healthy and tasty meals without making it an all day affair and without going to great expense. Of course, you may need to spend more time in the beginning until you get your system down. And you may initially spend more money to stock your pantry with new staples. However, in the long run, the methods outlined in this book make meal planning and prep a snap. In fact, if you regularly practice our methods, your meals will almost make themselves. (Really!)

No-fuss cookery: Simplicity is the key. Unlike most cookbooks, this one does not recommend complicated steps nor do the recipes have long lists of ingredients. Most of the work is done not by elaborate mixing, constant stirring, or standing over a hot pot, but by simply combining healthy ingredients then leaving them to cook. With this no-fuss approach, many foods can be cooked while you are doing other things such as showering, dressing, exercising, washing dishes or laundry, or eating a meal.

Procedure oriented cookery: Our emphasis is on procedure oriented cookery for daily practice. Most of our recipes can be used on a daily, weekly, and year round basis yet they need never become boring. You can vary the ingredients or combination of ingredients in each recipe by using different grains, beans, land vegetables, sea vegetables, herbs or spices. You can also mix and match different dishes to create new meals.

Variety: Variety comes from making little changes here and there. For example, you can cook brown rice several times a week or even daily make it a bit different every time. Combine it (before cooking) with a second grain such as millet, barley, sweet rice, polenta, amaranth or rye berries. Another time you might cook nuts, seeds, chestnuts, or dried beans into your rice, or perhaps some seasonal vegetable like sweet corn, cubed winter squash, or green peas. You can do similar things with millet.

With our simple bread making methods you'll be afforded incredible variety with a single dough recipe. This recipe can be infinitely varied by using different flour combinations or by forming it into different shapes prior to cooking. In fact, this same flexible approach applies to the dishes in every chapter, whether they be grain, bean, vegetable, or fruit. The ingredients are interchangeable, while the basic recipe or procedure acts as a guide.

(**Simple =Sustainable!**): We keep everyday meals simple, consisting of just three or four dishes rounded out with basic condiments that we make to last for several days or a week at a time. The dishes needn't be complex. We like to have at least one dish in a meal that contains just one or perhaps two main ingredients. We also like to have one bland or lightly seasoned dish in a meal (this is usually the grain). This balances more complex dishes which contain several major ingredients. Alternately, we may choose to have several simple dishes in a meal, sparked by interesting condiments, sauces, etc. Simple food is often the most delicious.

Weekends and special occasions: On weekends, special occasions, or when guests are expected, you may wish to include a few extra side dishes for a grand total of four to six dishes; however, the more simple your meals are the more likely you are to cook healthy meals day-in and day-out. We often serve our guests simple but delicious meals consisting of just three or four dishes (plus condiments) and a simple dessert. They like it. You will too once you get the hang of it.

You can be a good cook: If you've never been a good cook, never thought you had time to cook, never enjoyed cooking, or never been able to pull whole meals together from scratch, give our tried and true methods a go. We believe that with our methods, anyone can create simple, successful, healthy, and flavorful meals. Our approach is unique and practical and our recipes and procedures are down-to-earth. They have never failed to please our students, our guests, or us. (See also "The Myth of The Gift: What it takes to be a good cook)

Sample Plates

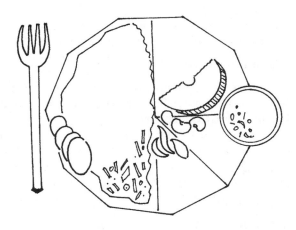

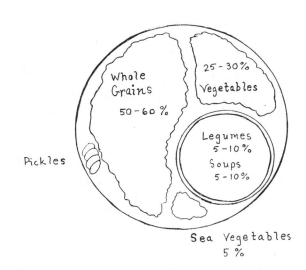

BASIC LUNCH & DINNER FORMATS

EASY 3 DISH FORMAT

Example #1
1. Soup *or* Stew
2. Grain (whole grain, pasta, or bread)
3. Greens *or* Mixed Vegetable Side Dish*

+ *Condiments (pick one or all)*

Seed or Nut Condiment *and/or* Pickles
Roasted or Cooked Sea Vegetable or Sea Flakes
Pungent, Raw Green Garnish

Example #2
1. Sauce or Gravy
2. Grain (whole grain, pasta, or bread)
3. Greens *or* Mixed Vegetable Side Dish

+ *Condiments (pick one or all)*

Seed or Nut Condiment a*nd/or* Pickles
Roasted or Cooked Sea Vegetable or Sea Flakes
Pungent, Raw Green Garnish

Example #3
1. Bean, Tofu, Tempeh or Wheat Meat
2. Grain (whole grain, pasta, or bread)
3. Greens or Mixed Vegetable Side Dish

+ *Condiments (pick one or all)*

Seed or Nut Condiment *and/or* Pickles
Roasted or Cooked Sea Vegetable or Sea Flakes
Pungent, Raw Green Garnish

Example #4
1. Root, Round, or Ground Vegetable
2. Grain (whole grain, pasta, or bread)
3. Greens *or* Mixed Vegetable Side Dish

+ *Condiments (pick one or all)*

Seed or Nut Condiment Pickles
Roasted or Cooked Sea Vegetable or Sea Flakes
Pungent, Raw Green Garnish

Notes:

* If greens are used in the soup, be sure to serve a root, round or ground vegetable side dish.

* If root, round, or ground vegetables are used in the soup, stew, or sauce, serve greens, cabbage, or mixed vegetables (which may also include roots or round vegetables) on the side.

* You may serve two grain dishes in a meal. This is particularly helpful if you have leftover grains that need to be extended. (e.g., porridge *and* mochi waffles; rice *and* bread; polenta *and* bread; pasta *and* bread; tamales *and* rice; or rice *and* a noodle salad.

EASY 4 DISH FORMAT

Add 1-3 of the following dishes not included in the above format of choices.

Tofu, Tempeh, Bean *or* Wheat Meat Dish
Sauce, Spread *or* Gravy
Sea Vegetable Condiment or Side-Dish
A Second Grain Dish
Pressed Salad *or* Pickles
Yogurt, egg, cheese, milk or fish
Soup *or* Stew
Dessert

SAMPLE 4-6 DISH FORMAT:

Soup *or* Stew
Whole Grain or Pasta **and/or** Bread
Green or Mixed Vegetable Dish
Tofu, Tempeh, Bean, or Wheat Meat Dish
(if not used in soup or stew)
+/- Root, Round, Ground or Vine Vegetable
+- Sea vegetable condiment or side dish
Pickle (if not serving Pressed/Marinated Salad)
Seed or Nut Condiment **and/or** dressing
Yogurt, cheese, egg, milk, or fish
Dessert
Grain Coffee or Tea

Or, follow one of the breakfast formats for supper!

BASIC BREAKFAST FORMATS

EASY 2-3-DISH FORMAT

Example #1

1. Hot Cereal or Porridge
2. Greens *or* Mixed Vegetable Side Dish

+ Condiments (pick one or all)

Seed or Nut Condiment *and/or* Pickles
Roasted or Cooked Sea Vegetable or Sea Flakes
Pungent, Raw Green Garnish

Example #2

1. Hot Cereal or Porridge
2. Root, Round, Ground or Vine Vegetable Dish

+ Condiments (pick one or all)

Seed or Nut Condiment *and/or* Pickles
Roasted or Cooked Sea Vegetable or Sea Flakes
Pungent, Raw Green Garnish

Example #3

1. Bread, Noodles, Mochi *or* Dinner Grain
2. Soup, Sauce, Gravy, or Spread
3. Green or Mixed Vegetable Side Dish

+ Condiments (pick one or all)

Seed or Nut Condiment and/or Pickles
Roasted or Cooked Sea Vegetable or Sea Flakes
Pungent, Raw Green Garnish

Example #4

1. Bread, Noodles *or* Mochi
2. Root, Round, Ground or Vine Vegetable Dish
3. Greens or Mixed Vegetable Side Dish

+ Condiments (pick one or all)

Seed or Nut Condiment *and/or* Pickles
Roasted or Cooked Sea Vegetable or Sea Flakes
Pungent, Raw Green Garnish

- **For variety & Simplicity:** A root, round, or ground vegetable may be cooked into grain for breakfast *(e.g. squash, sweet potato, or corn off the cob cooked in with rice, millet porridge, or rolled or whole oats).*

OPTIONAL ADDITIONS TO THE 2-3-DISH FORMAT:

Bread, mochi, rice cakes, rice, arepas, etc.
Plain, unfortified, unsweetened, soy, milk or
  soy yogurt *(preferably warmed or room
  temperature spiced, lightly salted)*
  or yogurt, quark, cheese, milk, or egg

EASY 3-4-DISH FORMAT

If you are very active or eating only 2 meals a day, include the following dishes at breakfast:

1. Thick Porridge or Hot Cereal, Noodles, Mochi, Dinner Grain (Rice, Millet, etc. *or* Bread
2. Root, Round, or Ground Vegetable Soup, *or* Sauce or Spread
3. Greens *or* Mixed Vegetable Side Dish

+ Condiments (pick one or all)

Seed or Nut Condiment *and/or* Pickles
Roasted or Cooked Sea Vegetable or Sea Flakes
Pungent, Raw Green Garnish

Notes:

- **If serving hot cereal/porridge for breakfast:** Avoid serving soup. Both soup and hot cereal contain a lot of liquid; thus, filling up on liquids will prevent you from eating enough substantial food and calories to meet your energy needs. If you want soup with breakfast, serve dinner grain, mochi, bread, noodles, or *very thick* porridge. (We always make our cereal thick enough to pick up with chopsticks.).

- **If you are very active or eating only two meals a day or two meals plus a light snack:** It is helpful to make your breakfast cereal or porridge very thick (thick enough to pick up with chopsticks), regardless of whether you have soup or not. If you make watery cereal it will very difficult to eat enough food at breakfast to maintain your energy until the next meal and throughout the day.

2 MEAL-A-DAY-MENU PLANNER

EVERYDAY BREAKFAST PLAN
Meal should include the following:

* 1 1/3-3 cups Cooked Whole Grain or Pasta
  or 3-8 slices Whole Grain Bread
  or 1 1/2-3 cups Soft Porridge + extra bread or mochi, if needed

* 2-6 tsp. roasted Seed or Nut Condiment
  or 2-3 tsp. Seed or Nut Butter *(preferably diluted with water and tamari, miso, or ume)*
  or 1-2 tsp. flax or sesame oil

* 1/2-1 cup cooked Leafy Greens or Mixed Vegetables *or* Pressed, Marinated, or Raw Salad (*or* *a combination of two of these*)

* 1/2-1 cup Orange or Yellow Vegetables *(may also include a sea vegetable)*
  or 1 cup Vegetable Soup or Stew (made with yellow or orange vegetables)

* 1/2-1 Tbsp. Raw Green Garnish *(parsley, scallions, chives, etc.)*

* *Optional*, 2-3 tsp. Sea Vegetable Flakes
  or 1-3 Tbsp. Sea Vegetable Condiment
  or 1/8-1/2 cup roasted Sea Vegetable

* *Optional*, 1/2-1 tsp. Oil or Ghee *(in cooking or dressing)* or extra seeds or seed/nut butter

* *Optional*, 1/2-1 cup milk, yogurt or kefir, or 3 oz. quark, 1 oz. cheese, *or* 1 egg

Note: Cold pressed or unrefined seed or nut oils may be used at the table, to top cooked grains or vegetables. Nutritionally, flax, sesame, walnut, pumpkin seed oils are richest in essential fatty acids.

These should be stored in the refrigerator in dark bottles and used in a timely fashion to avoid rancidity.

We suggest that you keep a teaspoon on the table and measure what you use so as to avoid overdoing it.

EVERYDAY LUNCH PLAN
Meal should include the following:

* 1 cup Vegetable Soup or Stew
  *(May include Beans, Sea Vegetables **and/or** Tofu, Tempeh, or Wheat Meat)*
  or 1/2-1 cup Sauce, Gravy or Root, Round or Ground Vegetable Dish

* 1 1/3-3 cups cooked Whole or Cracked Grain
  or 3-8 slices Whole Grain Bread or 2-4 Rolls
  or 1 1/2-3 cups pasta + extra bread if needed
  or any two grain dishes combined (rice + bread or tortillas, rice + noodles, etc.)

* 2-6 tsp. roasted seasoned Seed or Nut Condiment *or* 2-3 tsp. Seed or Nut Butter
  or 1-2 tsp. cold pressed vegetable oil

* 1/2-1 cup cooked Leafy Greens or Mixed Vegetables *or* Pressed, Marinated, or Raw Salad (*or* *a combination of two of these*)

* 1/2-1 Tbsp. Raw Green Garnish *(parsley, scallions, chives, etc.)*

* *Optional*, 1/4-3/4 cup Bean, Tofu, Tempeh, or Wheat Meat Side-Dish or Condiment

* *Optional*, 1/2-1 tsp. Oil or Ghee *(in cooking or dressing)* or extra seeds/nuts or "butters"

* *Optional*, 2-3 tsp. Sea Vegetable Flakes
  or 1-3 Tbsp. Sea Vegetable Condiment
  or 1/4-1/3 cup Sea Vegetable Side Dish
  or 1/8-1/2 cup roasted Sea Vegetable

* *Optional*, 1-3 Tbsp. Pickles *(if pressed salad is not served)*

* *Optional*, 1/2-1 cup milk, yogurt, or kefir, 3 oz. quark, 1 oz. cheese, 1 egg *or* 2-3 oz. fish

* ***Optional*, Low-Fat Naturally Sweetened Dessert/Pick 1-3x per week** (+/- *1-3 tsp. seeds/nuts or 1-2 tsp. nut/seed butter)*

2/3-3/4 cup Amasake-, Chestnut-, Grain-, or Vegetable Pudding or Fresh and/or dried Fruit Compote, Sauce, Aspic, or Pudding
or 1-3 small cookies
or 1 slice vegetable or fruit pie
or 1 piece fresh raw fruit

2 MEAL-A-DAY-MENU

PLANNER + SNACK

Use the Breakfast & Lunch Format but add a light snack, taken before 6 p.m.

SNACK

Select 1 item from a single group or select 1 item from 2-3 groups:

Grain Group:

- 2-3 rice cakes
- 1-2 slices of bread, arepas, or tortillas
- 1 steamed bun, dinner roll, or wholegrain bagel *(plain or with a spread)*
- 1 rice ball or mochi waffle, or several pieces of nori-maki sushi
- 1-2 medium to large bowls of popcorn *(hot air popped or cooked with minimal oil and spritzed with umeboshi or apriboshi vinegar, or shoyu or tamari, +/-sea flakes)*
- 1 tortilla roll-up or burrito

Animal Food Group:

- 4-8 oz. raw goat yogurt or milk *(warm or room temperature, with black pepper, chives, ginger, nutmeg, cinnamon)*
- 1/4-1/2 cup raw milk quark (yogurt cheese), cottage cheese, etc.
- 1-1 1/2 oz. raw milk cheese
- 2-4 ounces cooked fish
- 1 cup fish soup or stew

Beverage or Soup Group:

- 1 cup umeboshi kuzu drink
- 1 cup warm soy milk, grain milk, or seed/nut milk *(seasoned with sea salt or miso and ginger, black pepper, cinnamon, or nutmeg)*
- 1 cup vegetable soup or broth

Vegetable Group:

- 1/2-1 cup cooked squash, 1/2-1 sweet potato or yam, or 1 ear of corn
- 1/2-1 cup cooked greens or pressed salad

Dessert Group:

- 3/4-1 cup amasake pudding or fruit-, grain, or chestnut-based dessert, if not eaten with lunch
- 1 piece of vegetable or fruit pie
- 2-3 small cookies
- 1-1 1/2 cups raw tossed salad
- 1-2 pieces fresh fruit

Sample Snack Ideas:

- Yogurt or milk
- Yogurt or soy milk and bread
- Yogurt and cooked greens or salad
- Yogurt cheese, greens & bread or arepas
- Rice ball and soup or tea
- Bean dip, tortillas or bread and raw garnish
- Fruit compote
- Fruit compote and yogurt or quark
- Arepas or tortillas with a spread
- Popcorn and tea or kuzu drink
- Scrambled tofu or quark in a tortilla with greens or salad and mustard
- Amasake pudding and grain coffee
- Rice cakes with spread and salad
- Steamed bun with spread (or filling)
- Squash or sweet corn and yogurt or milk
- Fish and salad or cooked greens
- Filled steamed bun and goat or soy mMilk
- Apple and pear with yogurt

3 MEAL-A-DAY-MENU PLANNER

EVERYDAY BREAKFAST PLAN
Meal should include the following:

* 1 1/2-3 cups Soft Porridge +/- Extra Bread
or 1 1/3-3 cups Cooked Whole Grain or Pasta
or 3-8 slices Whole Grain Bread
or 2-3 buns, rolls, or bagels

* 2-4 tsp. roasted Seed or Nut Condiment
or 1-3 tsp. Seed/Nut Butter (extend by thinning with water and/or miso, ume, or tamari)
or 1-2 tsp. cold pressed oil or ghee

* 1/2-1 cup cooked Greens or Mixed Vegetables
or 1/2-3/4 cup Pressed or Marinated Salad
or Yellow/Orange Vegetable (or *combination*)

* 1/2-1 Tbsp. Raw Green Garnish (*parsley, scallions, chives, etc.*)

* *Optional*, 2-3 tsp. Sea Vegetable Flakes
or 1-3 Tbsp. Sea Vegetable Condiment
or 1/4-1/2 cup Roasted Sea Vegetable

* *Optional*, 1-2 Tbsp. pickles
or 1/2-1 tsp. umeboshi pickled plum paste

* *Optional*, 1/2-1 tsp. Oil or Ghee (*in cooking or dressing)* or extra seeds/nuts or nut butter

* *Optional*, 1/2-1 cup milk, yogurt, or kefir *or* 3 oz. quark,1 oz. cheese, or 1 egg

Note: Cold pressed or unrefined seed or nut oils may be used at the table, to top cooked grains or vegetables. Nutritionally, flax, sesame, walnut, pumpkin seed oils are richest in essential fatty acids.

These should be stored in the refrigerator in dark bottles and used in a timely fashion to avoid rancidity.

We suggest that you keep a teaspoon on the table and measure what you use so as to avoid overdoing it.

EVERYDAY LUNCH & DINNER PLAN

Meal should include the following:

* 1 cup Vegetable Soup or Stew (*May include Beans, Sea Vegetables and/or Tofu, Tempeh, or Wheat Meat)* *or* 1/2-1 cup Sauce, Gravy or Root, Round or Ground Vegetable Dish

* 1 1/3-3 cups cooked Whole or Cracked Grain
or 3-8 Slices Whole Grain Bread or 2-4 Rolls
or 2-3 cups pasta + extra bread if needed
or any two grain dishes combined as desired

* 2-4 tsp. roasted seasoned Seed or Nut Condiment *or* 2-3 tsp. Seed or Nut Butter
or 1-2 tsp. cold pressed oil or ghee

1/2-1 cup cooked Greens or Mixed Vegetables *or* Pressed, Marinated, or Raw Salad or Roots (*or a combination of two of these*)

* 1/2-1 Tbsp. Raw Green Garnish (*parsley, scallions, chives, etc.*)

* *Optional*, 1/4-3/4 cup Bean, Tofu, Tempeh, or Wheat Meat Side-Dish or Condiment

* *Optional,*1/2-1 tsp. oil or ghee (*in cooking or dressing)* *or* extra seeds, nuts or seed/nut butter

* *Optional*, 2-3 tsp. Sea Vegetable Flakes
or 1-3 Tbsp. Sea Vegetable Condiment
or 1/4-1/3 cup Sea Vegetable Side Dish
or 1/8-1/2 cup Roasted Sea Vegetable

* *Optional*, 1-3 Tbsp. Pickle (*if pressed salad is not served*)

* *Optional,* 1/2-1 cup milk, yogurt *or* kefir,
1 oz. cheese, 3 oz. quark, 1 egg, *or* 3 oz. fish

* *Optional*, **Low-Fat Naturally Sweetened Dessert/Pick 1 up to 3-5x per week** (*May include 1-3 tsp. seeds or nuts or 1-2 tsp. nut/seed butter)*

2/3-3/4 cup Amasake-, Chestnut-, Grain-, or Vegetable Pudding *or* Fresh and/or dried Fruit Compote, Sauce, Aspic, or Pudding
or 1-3 small cookies/bars
or 1 slice vegetable or fruit pie
or 1 piece of fresh, raw fruit

EXPLORING THE POSSIBILITIES

Basic Meal Format: *Soup or Stew + Grain + Vegetable Side Dish + Condiments*

Pick a soup or stew...
(Note: Limit to 1 cup per person, at a meal.)
Sweet Root or Round Vegetable Soup
Simmered Vegetable Soup
Oat or Soya "Cream of Vegetable" Soup
Light, Clear Miso or Tamari Soup or Broth
Any Bean Soup
Tempeh or Wheat Meat Stew
Chili Bean Stew (or other bean soup)
Gravy or Sauce
Hungarian Goulash with wheat meat, tofu, or beans
Beef-less (Wheat Meat) Stroganoff
Baked, Stewed or Nishime Root or Round Veggies
Other vegetarian soup or stew
Seasonal Raw Vegetable Soup
Soy Milk or Soy Yogurt (plain, spiced, warmed)

Pick one or two grain dishes ...
(This should comprise at least 50% of a meal's volume.)
Brown Rice
Brown Rice cooked with a second grain
Brown Rice cooked with beans or legumes
Millet cooked with a second grain (or millet slices)
Millet cooked with a bean or legume (or millet slices)
Millet cooked with vegetables (or millet slices)
Polenta (cornmeal) or masa
Buckwheat, Quinoa, Bulgur, or other grain
Whole grain pasta
Corn bread, Arepas, Tamales, or Dumplings
Steamed Buns, unfilled or filled
Pita Breads, Souvlaki-Pita, Tortillas, or Chapatis
Baked Loaf Bread, Dinner Rolls, or Bagels
Whole Grain Dinner Pancakes or Waffles

Pick 1-2 vegetable side dish....
Steamed green or mixed vegetables
Boiled or Blanched Salad
Quick-Boiled Vegetables
Stir Fry or Oil-Free Stir Fry
Lightly Sautéed Greens or Mixed Vegetables
Steamed Greens tossed with pickles
Pressed or Marinated Salad
Seasonal Raw Salad
Baked or Steamed Root/Round/Ground Vegetables*
Sauteed or Stewed Root/Round/Ground Vegetables*

Pick 1-2 condiments or seasonings...
Sesame, flax, walnut, pumpkin, or olive oil
Roasted, Salty Seasoned Seed Condiment
Roasted, Salty Seasoned Nut Condiment
Seed or nut butter (may be mixed with miso or tamari)
Tofu, tempeh, wheat meat, or bean dip, sauce or spread
Light dressing, sauce, or marinade
Vegetable-based sauces, spreads, or gravies
Prepared Mustard and/or Tofu Mayo or Grain Mayo
Soy or grain-based yogurt
Yogurt, kefir, cheese, egg, milk, or fish

Pick a garnish...
Fresh or dried chives or garlic chives
Fresh scallions
Fresh or dried parsley, cilantro or dill weed
Minced celery tops
Grated radish, carrot, beet, or other
Edible flowers
Sunflower, alfalfa, clover or other sprouts

Optional: Pick a pickle or seasoning...
Brown Rice Vinegar or Organic Apple Cider Vinegar
Umeboshi/Apriboshi Vinegar or Paste
Pickled Ginger, Cucumber, Onion, Radish or other
Overnight, Quick 3-Day Pickles, or Salt Bran Pickles
Fat-free or low-fat salad dressing or vinaigrette
Tamari or shoyu mixed with oil and/or vinegar
Miso mixed with water, umeboshi, or rice vinegar

Pick a sea vegetable...
(Use at one to three meals daily)
Dry Roasted, Crumbled Sea Vegetables
Sea flakes, ground, (+/- herbs, seeds, or nuts)
Sea vegetables cooked into
—soup or stew
—bean, tempeh, or vegetable dish
—whole grain, bread, or pasta dish
—side dish with land vegetables
—cooked condiment, sauce, or gravy

Bean, Tofu, Tempeh, or Wheat Meat...
(Use at one or two meals per day)
Baked, broiled, sautéed, or stir fried tofu, tempeh, or seitan
Scrambled Tofu and/or Wheat Meat/Seitan
Tofu, Tempeh, or Bean dip, sauce, spread, gravy, or filling
Tofu, Tempeh, or Wheat Meat (Seitan) cooked in
—casserole, pot pie, tamales, or steamed buns
—vegetarian burger, loaf, cutlets, "meat" balls, etc.
—whole grain, pasta, or bread dish
Soy milk, soy yogurt, etc. (use less often than other products)

To simplify lunch or dinner, use a two dish format such as:

(a) Grain + Leafy Green or Mixed Vegetable Side Dish + Condiments

(b) Soup or Stew + Grain + Vegetable Side Dish + Condiments

(c) Grain + Greens + Sweet Root or Round Vegetable Dish + Condiments

- *For a simple, soothing supper:* Try breakfast for supper: Soft Porridge + Cooked Greens or Mixed Vegetables + Sea Vegetable Condiment + Seed or Nut Condiment + Green Garnish.

MENU PLANNING NOTES

ABOUT FATS, OILS & CONDIMENTS

- **Always have seasoned Seed or Nut Condiments on hand.** They are invaluable for dressing up whole grains, adding minerals, and aiding digestion and assimilation.

- **To keep fat low (15-25% of total calories):** Keep everyday use of nuts, seeds, or nut/seed butters to just one to three dishes in a meal. Dry roast and season seeds and nuts and use as condiments rather than snacks.

- **Figuring the fat:** To use oil and/or ghee consciously and sparingly you will have to do a little bit of elementary math. If you are going to use two teaspoons per person, per day. You could use all or part of this in a single meal or spread out over two or three meals in a day. Thus, if you are cooking a meal for four people (or a day's worth of food for four), you would have eight teaspoons of oil to play with. When making dishes to last for two days, increase the oil accordingly. Cooking for two people, you would have four teaspoons of oil to use (in one or several different dishes) in a single meal or over the course of a whole day. (See Rules of Thumb for Figuring The Fat.)

We typically use one or two teaspoons of oil per person, per day in cooking then we use additional oil at the table, over hot cereal, whole grain, or vegetables. On other days, we

may forego oil in cooking and use raw oil at the table, poured over grains or vegetables. (This is usually flax seed oil or sesame oil, both of which are rich in essential fatty acids.)

- **Try to limit oil to one or two dishes in a meal:** If nuts, seeds or nut/seed butters are used in a dish, use oil very modestly in only one or two dishes for that meal. It is a good idea to have at least one dish in a meal which does not contain oil, nuts, or seeds.

- **Stretch nut or seed butters:** Use sparingly in sauces, light dressing, bean, tempeh, tofu, or wheat meat dishes, soups, stews, or desserts. For use as a spread, dilute nut or seed butters with an equal or greater volume of water then add a pinch of sea salt or a dash of miso, umeboshi, or tamari (Add vinegar and/or herbs or spices for dressings, as desired.)

- **In lieu of high fat spreads:** Use bean or vegetable side dishes as toppings, spreads, or sauces for grains. Also, replace mayonnaise, butter, cream cheese, and cheese spreads with vegetable "butters," Grain Mayo, or spread prepared mustard or quark on bread. Or, try Miso-Tahini, Sunflower-Miso, or Miso-Nut Butter Spreads. (Refer to the condiment section for low-fat spreads.)

- **Use Green Garnishes daily:** Sprinkle parsley, scallions, chives, or arugula over soup, stew, beans, tofu, tempeh, vegetables, casseroles, or hot cereal to lighten them up, add color, and spark the digestive fire.

- **Emphasize low-fat & fat-free desserts:** Focus on fresh fruit or amasake, chestnut, vegetable, grain, or fruit puddings; vegetable or fruit pies; fruit sauces, compotes, or gels; or other oil and dairy-free puddings. Use cookies, cakes, and bars less often and make them oil-free or low in fat.

- **Make desserts in small amounts:** Make only enough to last for just two or three days at a time (and just one serving per day!) This will keep you from over-dosing on dessert.

Figuring the fat.

If we use 2 teaspoons of ghee or oil to make 4 cups of soup to serve 4 (or 2 days for 2) that amounts to 1/2 teaspoon of oil per person/per cup of soup. If we use one teaspoon of in the same soup, each serving contains 1/4 teaspoon.

If we use 1 tablespoon of oil in a stir fry to serve 6 (or 3 meals for 2) the amount of fat per person, per serving amounts to 1/2-3/4 teaspoons.

If the rich soup is served once and the stir fry twice in the same day and other dishes are made without oil then oil use would total 1 1/2-2 teaspoons per person for that day (1/4-1 3/4 tsp. if the soup was made with less oil).

If in one meal we take 1/2 teaspoon of oil in our greens and 1/2 teaspoons of oil in a sea vegetable side dish, we'd each get 1 tsp. of oil in that meal. We'd also take in 1/2-1 1/2 tablespoon of nut or seed condiment per person as well.

If for breakfast we sautéed a bunch of greens in 2 teaspoons of oil/ghee to serve 4 or 2 meals for two. We'd each get 1/2 teaspoon of oil per serving of greens. Having these greens at two meals, we'd each get 1 teaspoon of oil for the day, plus any oil used in other dishes in other meals. If we also used 2-3 teaspoon of oil to pan fry wheat meat cutlets for the two of us for lunch. We'd each take in 1 1/2 teaspoon of oil for that. Thus our total oil intake for the day would be 2-2 1/2 teaspoons. We would also serve seed condiments with these meals and would roughly keep track of how many teaspoons we use at each meal, and for the day.

On a different day, we might cook 3/4 to-1 cup of nuts (12-16 tablespoons) into a pot of rice (4 cups of dry rice). This would serve 4-6 (or 2-3 meals for 2). Thus each serving would contain 2-4 tablespoons of nuts. In this case we would not serve a seed or nut condiments with this rich grain. Instead, we would use sea vegetable flakes, a sea vegetable condiment, beans, or umeboshi paste on the grain. We would also serve oil-free or low-oil side dishes in that meal. In making side dishes for other meals for that day, we would use our daily oil allotment over one or two remaining meals.

Note: Some of your daily oil may be replaced with organic raw butter or ghee if desired.

Put it simply, when cooking for three people in your family, you will probably need to use 3-6 tablespoons of oil per day. (Some of this may be used in cooking and some at the table.) Alternately, you might use all of your daily oil at the table (served with a teaspoon for awareness!) If you cook rich dishes with ghee or oil to last for two days three people, you would use 6-12 teaspoons (2-4 tablespoons) of oil or ghee.

In addition to the oil, we usually figure 2-4 tablespoons of nuts or seeds per person per day. For a family of three, figure roughly 6-9 tablespoons of seed or nut condiment per day. Keeping a rough accounting can help you to create rich and satisfying meals without overloading your system with too much fat.

Seed or nut condiments can be served in the same meal in which oil is used. We usually figure 2-4 teaspoons of seeds, nuts, or seed or nut butter per person, per meal, or slightly more for those who are very active. However, once or twice a week we usually have a slightly richer meal and use slightly more nuts or seeds (say 2-3 tablespoons per person). When using a larger amount of nuts or seeds in a meal or when using nut or seed butters, we are often sparing or avoid the use free oil in the meal. (For special occasion meals or when serving company we may occasionally break this "rule.")

When cooking fancier meals or for company we figure out how many people we will be cooking for, then how much oil and/or nuts or seeds we want to use in the meal. Next we decide which dishes to use this oil allotment in. We do the same for seeds, nuts, or seed or nut butters.

All of this might seem complex, but it really isn't. When you plan ahead and roughly calculate how much food to make for a given number of people and a given number of meals, the oil and nuts or seeds can easily be factored in. This will eventually come naturally. Trust us.

We use the same rules of thumb when planning our special Friday Night Dinners (family style ethnic dinners that we prepare for students and friends to test new recipes for articles and books), for our special Sunday meals, meals for company, and for our everyday meals.

Here's our rule of thumb for figuring the fat in meals:

For most every day meals—

- 1/2-2 tsp. free-fat (oil) per person **plus** 1-2 Tbsp. nuts or seeds or 1/2-1 Tbsp. nut or seed butter, or a combination of nuts or seeds and nut or seed butter, per person

For fancy meals, a couple of times per week—

- Increase nuts or seeds to 3-4 Tbsp. per person with or instead of 1/2-1 tsp. oil per person

- *Or,* use only one concentrated fat in the meal—oil; seeds or nuts; or seed or nut butter *(e.g., 2-3 tsp. oil; or 2-4 Tbsp. nuts or seeds; or 1-2 Tbsp. nut or seed butter per person).*

  Or, 2-3 tsp free-fat (oil) per person *and* 1-2 Tbsp. nuts or seeds or 1/2-1 Tbsp. nut or seed butter per person *or* a combination of nuts or seeds *and* nut or seed butter

For most desserts—

- up to 1-3 tsp. seeds or nuts or 1-2 tsp. nut or seed butter per person

For fancy desserts, infrequently—

- Increase seeds or nuts to 1-2 Tbsp. per person. and/or add 1/2-1 tsp. oil per person to the dessert.

ABOUT BEANS, TOFU, TEMPEH, WHEAT MEAT & SOY MILK

- Use small amounts of tofu, tempeh, wheat meat, or beans daily. They help maintain even energy and blood sugar levels. They can also alleviate sweets craving. And they make vegetarian and vegan meals more filling and satisfying. Beans also have been shown to have pronounced anti-cancer activity.

- Soy milk may be used in cooking or as an occasional snack or a soup replacer in a meal.

- You may occasionally serve two high protein bean products in the same meal, but it is best to use them in small amounts.

- **Don't over do it.** It is unnecessary to serve these concentrated, high protein foods in large volumes. Once a day is usually enough. Twice a day may be necessary for some individuals. However, taking in too much protein, even vegetable protein, can burden your system. Whole grains if eaten in quantity and supplemented with seeds, nuts, vegetables, and miso, and small amounts of dairy products, eggs, or fish will supply ample protein.

ABOUT FOOD VOLUME

The ideal amount of grain and side dishes to eat will vary from person to person, depending on one's metabolism, activity level, and the number of meals taken per day.

When eating low-fat grains and vegetables, it is necessary to eat a relatively large volume of food to meet your nutritional needs. The average person will eat one pound of uncooked/dry grain in a day. (The average person, on a typical diet, eats three to five pounds of food a day.) This is normal and necessary. Our intestines are designed to take in a high-bulk diet: a large volume of fiber rich food is essential for proper intestinal function.

Because grains and vegetables (in the absence of large amounts of fats and oils) are not as calorie or fat-dense as most of the foods eaten on a Standard American Diet, we have to eat a larger volume of these fibrous foods to sustain ourselves. So do not be alarmed if you or the members of your family find it necessary to eat large volumes of this new food. This is *normal* on a low-fat, grain-based diet. You can eat your fill of these foods, even if our aim is to lose weight. It is unnecessary to restrict grains, even if your aim is to lose weight. Even dieters should eat 3-4 slices of bread or 1 1/2-2 cups of rice, pasta, or porridge at every meal.

Look How it Flows

What you will find in the appendix are four weeks' worth of menus to get you started. We have provided a two-meal-a-day menu plan and a three-meal-a-day plan. With simple variations, these menus can even be stretched to serve you for four months. And, for the most part, the same plan can be used in any season, with slight variations in ingredients and cooking methods.

At first the way of Nourishing Life outlined may look overwhelming, but appearances aside, it is really quite simple. We've tried to capture the essence of our daily practice to help you make a vegan, vegetarian, or nearly vegetarian diet easy, healthy, enjoyable, and sustainable. Our aim is to show you how to create a system, one that will make you proficient in the kitchen. Formula recipes or Basic Procedures and a basic meal format simplify meal planning and prep. They have been created to provide maximum flavor, beauty, convenience, and nutrition with minimal effort and expense. They also provide a framework for you to create consistently good food according to your taste, the season, and the availability of local produce. They have served us well and we hope that they will do the same for you.

How much time will I need to invest?

At first it my take more time, energy and concentration to plan and prepare your daily meals; however, with continued repetition of basic recipes, advance planning, practice, and patience, you will become better at cooking and more efficient. Eventually you will spend less time in the kitchen. Just hang in there. And remember, you are providing the greatest nourishment to all who eat your meals. Cooking is like any other skill, the more you do it the more it becomes a part of you, and the easier it becomes. If possible find some friends or family members to join you in the learning process.

Three-a-day plan:

To make three meals per day, you might spend 20-30 minutes every morning and 20-60 minutes every evening in meal preparation. Another scenario might involve spending 45 minutes each morning and 45-60 minutes every other evening. On some days you may find that all of the day's preparations can be done in the morning, with little more than reheating leftovers at lunch or supper. Hands-on-time in the kitchen will vary with your level of skill, the organization of your kitchen, the number of people you are cooking for, and the amount of thought and advance planning you have given. You must also factor in the complexity of the meals you choose. Don't plan a complicated meal at the end of a long work day. Instead, you will want to have planned leftovers or soaked grains ready and waiting when you set food in the door. You will also want to have a repertoire of quick dishes that you can repeatedly mix and match so that dinners do not become a big production.

Two-a-day plan:

If you choose the two-meal-a-day plan, morning is usually the best time to cook and prep. In this case, you will probably need to allot 1-1 1/4 hours of kitchen time every morning to make both meals, including enough for leftover the next day. In the morning, the mid-day meal can be packed in a thermos and lunch box containers for meals away from home. When cooking at home, all or most of the food for the second meal can be cooked first thing in the morning then reheated as needed come lunch time. Alternately, several of the dishes for lunch may be leftover or cooked ahead, with the rest completed one-half to one hour before serving. If you decide to have a light bite or snack in the evening, this may be comprised of leftovers or items which need very little if any "fixing."

Once you have a system down, the usual hour in the kitchen in the morning can often be reduced to 60 minutes every other morning and 30 minutes on alternate days, with perhaps 15-30 minutes every or every other evening to sort, wash, or soak grains or beans, assemble pickles or pressed salad, make a seed condiment, or start grain cooking or amasake fermenting.

If you plan it right, on every other day you will only need to reheat leftovers from the previous day for one or both meals. At most you will need to prepare one or two new dishes on these days, depending upon how your leftovers overlap. For example you may have one new meal every day

Variety is The Way of Nourishing Life

Different foods provide different nutrients and tastes. Choosing a wide variety of foods enriches your diet, and your life. When you limit the variety of foods you eat, the flavors, nutrients, and energetic value of your diet also becomes limited. Thus, it is better to eat a wide variety of grains, beans, and vegetables—even if some are non-organic—than to limit yourself to only organic foods and suffer from a limited food selection.

If you are worried about the possible risks of chemical or pesticide contamination, make grains your main foods; make vegetables secondary; go easy on the fruits; and limit animal products to the highest quality possible. Environmental contaminants become more concentrated as you move up on the food chain. (Fruits are also one of the most heavily sprayed foods, much moreso than vegetables.) If you eat a low-fat, plant based diet, the fiber and antioxidant nutrients naturally present in whole grains, beans, and vegetable foods will protect you against the dangers of possible contamination. For added insurance, be sure to eat some sea vegetables, miso, and/or tamari every day. All of these have been shown to help draw toxins out of the body while at the same time offering rich flavors and a wide range of nutrients.

and one meal of leftovers, or two meals of fresh foods combined with leftovers. Or, you may need to make new greens at breakfast and a new soup or grain for lunch, or a new jar of seed condiment and a big bowl of pressed salad to last for the coming week.

With the two-meal-a-day plan you will avoid having to cook, clean, and wash dishes in the evening when you are tired. You may need to wash and soak a pot of beans or grain, assemble a soup to be cooked first thing in the morning, or put porridge on to cook overnight, but for the most part, you will free up your evenings for rest, relaxation and rejuvenation, perhaps with a very light, early evening snack if you find that you need the energy. Following this meal plan you will have more time in the evening to spend with family, to study, to read, or to exercise. The two-meal-a-day plan also takes the focus off of the evening meal as the main event and shifts the focus to breakfast—which will be your most refreshed time—as a time for the "family meal."

You will want to set aside at least one full hour for each meal when you eat just two meals a day and making breakfast a main meal. Even on a three meal a day plan it is wise to allow at least 45-60 minutes for each meal) This can be your meditation time. While at first, making breakfast the main meal of the day may be unfamiliar, you will be surprised at how early you can awaken, how alert you feel, and how strong your appetite is after skipping dinner or eating very lightly and going to bed on an empty stomach. The quality of your sleep and your thinking will be greatly improved as well.

Special occasions

Fancier weekend, company, or holiday meals may take a little more time to prepare than everyday meals, particularly if you make a few extra side dishes or more time-consuming recipes. However, even these meals can be made speedily once you develop a plan and get into the rhythm of it. And you will!

Extras

If you want fresh bread, you can make two or three double batches of bread with less than 1 1/2-2 hours of hands-on-time on the weekend. This will feed two or three people for an entire week with bread as the main dish (i.e., the only grain) at one of your daily meals. Or, a double batch of bread, to serve as a side dish grain, can be made once a week in about an hour, either on the weekend or during the week. Of course you could buy a loaf of good quality bread once a week then use it judiciously throughout the week. Another alternative would be to make mochi waffles to stand in for bread once or twice a week (and to be your grain for those meals). Condiments, quick desserts, and other extras can usually and fairly easily be squeezed into morning or evening preparations. More complicated desserts are best saved for weekends or special occasions.

How to Make A Meal in One Hour or Less

1. Wash and soak whole grain 4-12 hours in advance. Optional, soak beans or defrost tempeh. If mochi will be your grain, defrost one or more packages (if mochi is frozen).

2. Put the dish that takes the longest on the stove first. (Usually grain but sometimes beans.) If you have leftover whole grain or bread, reheat it by steaming 20 minutes before serving. If beans will be used in the soup or a side dish, cook them earlier in the day, perhaps during breakfast. If tempeh will be used, pressure marinate it the morning or evening before.)

3. Assemble a soup or stew and get it cooking (unless you have leftover soup to reheat or leftovers which can be turned into a quick soup).

4. Make a seasoned, roasted seed or nut condiment (unless you already have one on hand).

5. Chop and cook greens or mixed vegetables for a side dish (unless you have leftovers on hand). If leftover land or sea vegetables are to be served, take them out of the refrigerator 30-90 minutes before serving. Pressed or marinated salad can stand in for or supplement cooked greens, if desired. Leftover or premade pickles can also come in handy.

6. Stir the grain when it is done cooking. Or, start pasta cooking if this will be your grain. If mochi will be your grain, cut it into slices then preheat the waffle iron or oven.

7. Purée the soup if desired; season the soup or stew as needed; then mince a green garnish.

8. If dessert is desired, assemble a fruit compote or make Almost Instant Amasake Pudding. (Or, if you have a leftover dessert, take it out of the refrigerator to take the chill off.)

9. If time permits, wash dishes and clean the kitchen as you go or before eating.

10. Put tea on to cook. Serve up the meal. Enjoy. Wash the dishes, then have dessert and/or tea.

What if I live alone?

Most of the recipes in this book serve four, or two meals for two people. If you live alone, simply reduce recipes as needed to last for just two or three meals and practice the same basic techniques. When cooking for one, it is best to cut most recipes in half, except for bread recipes, so you will be assured the freshest and most nutritious food. (See "Secrets For Meals Made Ahead.") You may also wish to find a nearby friend and set up a cooking exchange. You could split the dishes you make, each cooking for the other on alternate days, or one of you could make the whole grain or bread and condiments while the other makes the soups and/or stews, then you could each make your own green vegetable side dishes. You can also stick to simple meal formats. A small crock pot or two or a couple of thermal cookers can help tremendously if you are constantly on the go.

What if I am cooking for a large family?

If you are cooking for more than two people, increase the basic recipes accordingly so that you still have leftovers. Prep time may be increased slightly when cooking for a large family. (See Secrets For Meals Made Ahead.)

Developing a system

To get started, it may be helpful to use our meal planner. The menus are guidelines only. Prep time will vary depending upon how many you are cooking for, how much you plan ahead, how you use your leftovers, and how efficient you are in the kitchen. Following our basic meal formats, menus, and guidelines can take the guesswork out of meal planning and keep prep and cooking to a minimum. The more you memorize the basic recipes and proportions, the more more smoothly and effortlessly things will go After following several weeks of the outlined plan, or a modification of the plan, in the appendix you might try planning your meals every two to four days or even every evening, rather than weekly. Our recipes are flexible and allow for infinite variations and substitutions, so you can plan for the week, or the day, without having to make up rigid menus or rush off to the store for last minute ingredients.

Using a system

When we plan for the week, we rarely write out fixed or rigid menus—except for our more involved friday night dinners when we are expecting ten or fifteen people and have printed a list of meals for our guests, a month in advance. However, even these may be modified a day or two before hand, according to what is available at the market). When cooking for ourselves, we make a tentative list of some of the dishes or meals we would like to have over the next few days or the coming week. Each evening we recount what we have leftover for the next day and what we need to make to fill in the following day; this helps us to decide what to soak before bed and what to cook overnight, first thing the next morning, or later the next day.

When planning tentative menus several days to a week, we plan for leftovers and include these in the menus. For example, we may plan to have puréed squash soup, rice with millet, sunflower seed condiment, and stir fried vegetables one evening. The next day we would then have the same meal for breakfast or lunch, or we'd use the stir fry with porridge and seed condiment at breakfast then serve the squash soup with rice, seed condiment, and a made-ahead pressed salad or freshly cooked greens for lunch. (Alternatively, these or other types of leftovers may actually be transformed into new dishes the second day.)

Today's meal of refried beans, millet-rice, pumpkin seed condiment, pressed salad, and baked or nishime winter squash might become tomorrow's breakfast: mochi waffles topped with mashed squash and Walnut-Miso or Miso-Tahini and pressed salad or quick-boiled greens. Lunch might become refried bean soup, rice made into rice balls, coated with seed condiment or umeboshi and nori, with leftover pressed salad on the side. Alternatively, some of the leftover rice might become breakfast cereal; the squash might become a quick soup for lunch or a sandwich filler with miso-nut butter; and the beans might become a burrito filler or a waffle topper for supper, with a side of quick-boiled greens at both meals. The possibilities are as endless as your imagination once you commit the basic meal format and some basic recipes to memory.

Sometimes we make bread to last for several days or the entire week. We always make seed condiments to last for one to two weeks at a time. We make soups, stews and/or gravies for two consecutive day, and whole grains, tamales, or noodles for two or three meals or one or two days at a time. We can quickly and easily build meals around these staples. We pick one or two new soups or stews and one or two grain dishes every few days then we make vegetable dishes, spreads, condiments or side dishes as needed to fill in the gaps.

Every day we rotate in some fresh foods to go with our leftovers. The fill-in dishes vary from day-to-day. Some days we may only have to make fresh greens or pressed salad, or perhaps a seed, nut, or sea vegetable condiment or a quick sauce. On other days we may need to cook a new pot of whole grain or pasta or a double batch of steamed buns, or one or two small pots of soup or stew. Or we may have to prepare several of these. Rarely do we have to make everything from scratch on a given day though. There's always something leftover, whether it is yesterdays' stir fry or quick-boiled greens; a cup or two of vegetable soup; a wheat meat side dish; a bowl of noodles; half a loaf of bread and some steamed greens; or a couple of sweet potatoes, some bread, and a few servings of pressed salad.

Whatever we do, we always plan to make enough of a dish so that it can form part of at least two meals. This keeps our prep and cooking time to a minimum, yet provides a steady and consistent supply of nourishing food.

Note: It is best to keep most leftovers for no more than three days. However, condiments, pickles, pressed salad, amasake, and bread are a few exceptions.)

Secrets For Meals Made Ahead
Don't Wait 'til You're Hungry

You're busy. Whether you're single or married, with kids or without, you want to eat healthy meals without spending all of your time in the kitchen. Most people in this situation rely upon convenience foods. The problem with these foods, including instant foods, frozen foods, and canned goods is that they are not fresh or healthful (for us or the planet). They are also very expensive and unnecessary.

It really doesn't require excessive time and energy to put together a healthy diet. In fact, a busy schedule can be just the thing to help you get organized. The secret is in planning and preparing ahead. An ancient Chinese proverb says, "Don't wait until you are thirsty to dig a well;" we say, "don't wait 'til you're hungry to start cooking." Plan ahead: Healthy, varied meals prepared with a minimum of time require a plan, and a system that makes use of leftovers. We never cook for just one meal. Whether we're making rice, pancakes, pasta, or polenta, we always make enough for two or three meals. Ditto for baked or steamed squash or sweet potatoes, soup, stew, stir fry, salad or steamed veggies. This greatly simplifies meal planning and prep and provides variety. And, leftovers need never become boring.

Ways to create variety without spending more time cooking:

- Make one soup but season it light miso one day and dark miso the next. Add a new herb or spice to the leftovers, change the garnish, or serve it with a different grain or vegetable dish the second day.

- Yesterday's unadorned steamed vegetables can be tossed with pickles; rice vinegar and tamari; ume vinegar and toasted seeds or sesame oil; or a dressing of tahini, water, and miso, ume, or tamari.

- Leftover stir fry, baked sweet potato, or steamed winter squash can be quickly transformed into a soup; a sauce for pasta, pizza, or waffles; a bread spread; or filling for burritos or sandwiches.

- The same rice or millet won't taste the same— even after two or three meals in a row—served with different condiments and/or a different combination of side dishes.

- Noodles can be served with beet, carrot, or squash sauce at supper, then the "unsauced" leftovers can be heaped into a bowl and topped with a warm cup of bean or wheat meat stew or scrambled tofu and greens for lunch the next day. Leftover noodles can also be cooked into morning porridge for a creamy texture, used as the base for a casserole or salad, or added to stir fry.

- One day's refried beans might be diluted to make another day's sauce for millet, bread, or polenta; used to fill sandwiches or burritos; or made into a soup with other leftover items.

- Pan fried wheat meat cutlets served one day as a condiment for rice or millet might be used the next day in a stir fry or stove-top-casserole; as a filling for sandwiches; or as the final ingredient in an instant soup made from a bit of leftover beans, squash, casserole, or what have you.

- Ultimately, you can create a whole range of different dishes by combining leftovers, adding new leftover ingredients, or changing the way in which you serve a particular dish. Likewise, several different meals can be created from one meal's leftovers by mixing and matching the dishes.

You could serve millet with squash and parsnip soup, seed condiment, and quick-boiled greens at breakfast or lunch. Serve the same millet with seed condiment, bean soup and sautéed greens or pressed salad for lunch or dinner that evening. Or, serve bean soup with bread and salad for lunch and ladle the same soup over noodles the next day, with a seed condiment and a side of greens.

Staying Ahead of the Game

With a little advance planning and cooking, you will soon be able to put together balanced and varied meals in under 30 minutes. On Sunday, for example, make extra portions of the dishes that you plan to serve that day so that you will have leftovers to use over the next couple of days. While you are in the kitchen, also make several extra dishes to have on hand. You can then serve these dishes in different combinations with different pickles, different condiments, and different garnishes. You can rotate them with new dishes each day and even transform the dishes themselves by adding different seasonings or changing their form.

We don't recommend making a pot of soup, rice or beans to last the week, nor do we suggest cooking vegetables to last for days. While there are some things that keep exceedingly well—breads, seed and sea vegetable condiments, pressed salads, pickles, and salad dressings—most other things don't. Cooked green vegetables lose vital energy and taste within about 24 hours. Cooked root and round vegetables lose their vitality within about one and a half to two days. Cooked whole grains dry out, turn sour, or simply don't have much energy left after two or three days. Ditto for soups, stews, beans, and casseroles. On the other hand, marinated salads can be made to last for a 2-3 days and pressed salads for 3-7 days if you are pressed for time and need something handy. Seed condiments can be made to last for one to two weeks. Some breads will keep for just a week, or two at room temperature; others will keep for several weeks in the refrigerator. Overnight or quick three-day pickles will keep for several weeks while vegetables pickled for a longer time and with more salt will keep for many months.

How Much To Cook

When cooking for two, use the chart below as a guide. Exact amounts will vary with your appetite, activity level, and with the number of meals you have each day. When cooking for one, reduce quantities by one-third to one-half or set up a meal exchange plan with a nearby friend. When cooking for more, increase the quantities accordingly.

Item	Quantity	Serves	Meals or Days	Use within
Rice or millet	4 cups dry = 10-12 cups cooked	4-8	2-4 meals for 2	1-2 1/2 days
Pasta	16 ounces dry = 10 cups cooked	3-6	1-3 meals for 2	2-3 days
Breakfast cereal	1+ cup dry whole grain = 3-5 c. cooked	2	1 meal for 2	1 day
Breakfast cereal	2 cups raw whole = 6-8 cups cooked	4	2 meals for 2	2 days
Breakfast cereal	2-3 cups rolled grain = 4-5 cups cooked	2	1 meal for 2	1-2days
Breakfast cereal	4-5 cups rolled grain = 8-10 cups cooked	4	2 meals for 2	2 days
Bread, whole grain	5-6+ cups flour =16 buns or rolls	4-8	2-4 meals for 2	1 week
Bread, whole grain	5-6+ cups flour = 2 small loaves	4-8	2-4 meals for 2	1-2 weeks
Bean soups/stews	4-4 1/2 cups	4	2 meals for 2	2-3 days
Vegetable soups	4-4 1/2 cups	4	2 meals for 2	2-3 days
Steamed greens	6-10 cups raw = 3-6 cups cooked	4-8	2-3 meals for 2	1-1 1/2 days
Saute or stir fry	6-10 cups raw = 3-6 cups cooked	4-8	2-3 meals for 2	1-1 1/2 days
Cooked squash	1 1/2 lbs/5 cups raw = 4 cups cooked	4-8	2-4 meals for 2	1-3 days
Marinated salads	12-14 cups raw = 6-7 cups marinated	10-12	5-6 meals for 2	2-4 days
Pressed salads	12-14 cups raw= 6-8 cups pressed	10-12	5-6 meals for 2	3-7 days
Sea & land veg. dish	2-3 cups side dish	6-8	3-4 meals for 2	2-3 days
Sea vegetable dish	1 cup salty seasoned condiment	8-16	3-8 meals for 2	1 week
Green garnish, fresh	1/2-3/4 cup chopped = 8-12 Tbsp.	8-12	4-6 meals for 2	1-3 days
Seed condiments	1-1 1/4 cup = 16-20 Tbsp. roasted	16-30	8-15 meals for 2	1-2 weeks
Roasted sea vegetable	2-3 cups packed	6-10	3-5 meals for 2	
Yogurt	16 cups (1 gallon)	16	8 meals for 2	4-10 days

1. Cook grains in quantity

Grains are the core of a sustainable diet and serve as the bulk of every meal. Their naturally sweet taste nourishes the body and provides lasting and stable energy when eaten in sufficient quantity. Always cook a pot of grain to last for two to four meals. For pasta, cook enough to last for two meals. When making breads, make enough to last for three to four meals or up to a week (about 2-4 loaves per week for two adults, depending upon how often you intend to serve it and whether or not it will be used as a side dish grain or as the main dish). You may need to purchase bread, but if you do, make sure that the bread you select is made from whole grains and is sweetener and oil-free.

Leftover whole grain, pasta, or bread can be served at room temperature (for meals away from home) or reheated by steaming (for meals at home. Rice balls are also a delicious way to use leftover rice.) Whole grain, pasta, or bread may be topped with various nut or seed condiments; land vegetable dishes; sea vegetable condiments; bean, tofu, or tempeh spreads; or gravies or sauces. Leftover whole grain or pasta can also be mixed with a new grain (cornmeal, millet, rolled oats or barley flakes) to create a delightful morning cereal or they can be used to fill a pita bread or a burrito; or they can form the base of a casserole or salad. Tossing cooked grains with sauteed, steamed, or marinated vegetables, beans, herbs and/or spices; or pickles is yet another possibility.

The Best Grain Strategy

Don't wait until you run out of grain to get a new pot rinsed and soaked. We even suggest cooking a new grain while you still have leftovers on hand. Just before bed, wash a pot of grain and let it soak overnight, then cook it first thing in the morning or while you are eating breakfast. This way you'll have grain for the next few meals. Another scenario would be to wash the grain first thing in the morning, soak it all day, then cook it before lunch, if you're eating at home, or as soon as you set food in the door if you are out all day.

2. Stock up on stock

Keep a bowl on the kitchen counter and toss in the vegetable scraps that you would not otherwise use. Every three or four days, add water to your vegetable scraps (or egg shells) then cook them for 30-60 minutes (you can do this during a meal for convenience). This creates flavorful

If you use eggs, toss the clean shells into a different bowl. Egg shells can be simmered in water with cider vinegar for one half to one hour then drained. To do this, combine the shells from 4-8 eggs in 5-6 cups of water with 2 teaspoons of apple cider vinegar.

Either of these stocks can be used in place of water to make or thin, bean or vegetable soups, stews, or gravies. Stocks can also help turn leftovers—steamed, stewed, sauteed, stir fried, or baked vegetables; beans; tofu; tempeh; or sea vegetable dishes—into new soups or sauces in a matter of minutes.

Save the water leftover from cooking pasta too. Keep it in jars in the refrigerator. We use it to cooking morning cereal in (for a super creamy taste), or use it to replace water in gravies, sauces, soups, stews, bread, or puddings. It adds a delightful flavor and texture. Leftover water from steaming or blanching vegetables is also good to save and add to your soups and stews.

3. Make enough soups and stews to last for a couple of meals

After grains, soups and stews are the second most important element in meal planning. They are suitable and desirable to use once or twice a day, throughout the year. Serving soup (or stew) daily makes meal planning easy while minimizing food waste. Almost any vegetable, bean, or leftover can be turned into soup; and soups are simple to make. Most can be assembled in under fifteen minutes and take 30-60 minutes to cook.

You can make soups in the evening, or first thing in the morning before sitting down to breakfast. All you need to do is chop up a measured amount of vegetables then add a measured amount of water or stock, herbs, and/or beans. Your soup or stew can then cook for 30-60 minutes while you eat your morning meal, exercise, shower, dress and get ready in the morning, or do dishes. You can season a serving to pack in your thermos for lunch (or several servings to pack into several thermos') and store the rest in stainless steel bowls, ready to reheat at other meals. It's that simple. Soups can also be assembled in the morning, set in the refrigerator, then cooked 30-40 minutes before the meal. If you have a thermal cooker or crock pot, you can cook in one of these for up to eight hours.

You can make two pots of soup at a time for added convenience. If you make each batch to last for two meals then you will have two different soups each day, one for breakfast and one for lunch, or one for lunch and one for supper. (For two people, that means you will want to cook each soup in a four cup batch.)

Instant soups for single meals, can also be made throughout the week using bits of leftovers (leftover sauces, marinades, gravies, leftover water from steaming vegetables, dried vegetables, minced or grated fresh vegetables, etc.)

Having grains and leftover soups (or leftover that can be made into soups) on hand at all times means that a whole meal is rarely more than a 10-30 minutes away!

4. Make vegetable dishes to last for 2-3 meals

Freshly cooked vegetables are a must. Steam, quick-boil, or stir fry fresh leafy greens or mixed vegetables to last for no more than 2-3 meals then rotate them with freshly cooked vegetables.

Yesterday's sautéed or steamed greens can be served at room temperature for breakfast, lunch or dinner (with grain and condiments) or they can be turned into a quick soup.

Baked or nishime cooked winter squash or sweet potato can be cooked into or mashed on top of morning cereal; packed for lunch or a snack; or mashed with light miso for a bread spread, burrito filling, or polenta or pizza sauce. Or it you may combine it with soup stock and/or cooked beans to transform it into a quick soup, stew, or sauce. Tasty instant soups or sauces can be made by simply simmering leftover vegetables with soup stock or water, or puréeing them with a few spoonfuls of sea vegetable condiments, cooked, beans, and/or a few spoonfuls of grain. The soup can be simmered with or without a few pinches of herbs and season with miso, tamari, or shoyu before serving.

Leftover beans and root and round vegetables also make good fillings for rice-wiches, burritos, gyoza, won tons, steamed buns, tamales, or calzones. Cooked vegetables can also be tossed with pickles or sea vegetable condiments for a side dish or they can be mixed with pasta or rice and a light dressing for a salad. Yesterday's raw tossed salads can be pressed or marinated after a light crushing with sea salt, ume vinegar, tamari, salty (minced) pickles, or sea vegetable condiment for a longer lasting dish. Crumbled or mashed tofu or sliced wheat meat can be added to leftover stir fried vegetables, sandwiches, or burritos to jazz them up, fill them out, and fill you up.

Unlike most vegetable dishes, pressed salad. can be made to last for three or four days or for up to a week at a time. These won't lose nutrients or decay as tossed salads and cooked vegetables will. In fact, pressed salads improve as they age. They are easy to make and a real boon to the busy cook. (See the vegetable chapter for our basic pressed salad recipes.) Although they are usually served at room temperature, meal size portions of pressed salads can also be lightly steamed to make a delectable warm slaw in cold weather or for individuals who feel chilly in any weather.

5. Keep garnishes and condiments on hand

Garnishes:

Garnishes add color, freshness, texture, and a light energy to meals, enlivening even the simplest fare. They also enhance digestion by adding trace minerals that assist digestion and spark the digestive fire. Garnishes can even help reserved leftovers by changing the appearance and taste of a dish. For example, the same soup with different garnishes will taste refreshingly new each time.

We mince enough scallions, chives, fresh dill, arugula, parsley, or cilantro to last for two or three days at a time then store them in one or two small glass jars in the refrigerator. Raw garnishes can be sprinkle over a soups or stews; soft breakfast cereal; pasta; or rice, along with a sea vegetable condiment or sea flakes. These garnishes are also tasty on top of bean or gravy topped millet; bread spread with tofu pate; or whatever else you like. Dried chives also make good year round garnishes or soup extenders, particularly when fresh ones are out of season. For pack lunches and meals away from home, you can carry small vials full of dried chives, and/or sea vegetable flakes in your back pack, satchel or brief case.

Sea vegetable flakes (sea cress, nori, dulse, etc.) can be purchased in several varieties or you can grind raw sea vegetable in a hand crank food mill or high powered blender, at home. The flakes can be used to garnish soups, grains, beans, or vegetable dishes. Roasted and crumbled sea vegetables also make a tasty garnish for grains and are a staple in our house. With sea flakes you can enjoy the flavor and nutritional benefits of sea vegetables minus the soaking, chopping, cooking and seasoning. (Please refer to the sea vegetable chapter for instructions.)

Condiments:

Make roasted, salty seasoned seed condiments every one to two weeks—try flax, sesame, sunflower, or pumpkin seeds. Try walnut or pine nut condiment now and then. These condiments are delicious and take 15-20 minutes to make. They can be used at the table in place of salt or butter and really add spark to a meal. We use them every day and often at every meal. Make small amounts that you will use up within one or two weeks because nut and seed condiments spoil quickly and lose their flavor after two weeks. The exact amount you need to make will depend on how much you use at meal, how many times per day you use it, and how many people you are cooking for.) Avoid commercially packaged gomashio or tamari seasoned seeds: they are far less tasty than homemade seed condiments and they are almost always rancid. (As always, fresh is best!) If you do choose to use ghee as a cooking fat or table condiment (to replace oils and/or seed or nut condiment), you can make it once every one to two months. It keeps for months without refrigeration.

Condiments and garnishes are important for taste and digestion. Added at the table for variety, they allow each person to season foods to taste without the harshness of soy sauce or pure salt. Using different condiments or garnishes can also spark up leftovers, providing slightly different tastes to yesterday's fare.

For meals away from home, pack vials with one or two condiments and/or garnishes to liven up simple restaurant fare. Plain boiled rice or pasta, steamed or water sautéed vegetables, baked sweet potato, etc. can all be enhanced by simple homemade nut condiments. Even plain oatmeal can be enlivened with fresh or dried scallions, chives, or parsley and a spoonful of two of homemade seed or nut condiment. A hefty shake of sea vegetable flakes or a handful of crumbled sea vegetable strips can also do the trick. Umeboshi or apriboshi paste can also be used to enhance hot cereal, with perhaps a hint of plain roasted seeds or chopped nuts. The same pickled plum paste can also be used as a fat-free spread for bread!

6. Schedule in prep time then cook while you eat or clean house

Food for later in the day or for the next day can cook while you're eating, doing laundry, studying, stretching, or cleaning the house. While eating supper, you can cook a fresh pot of grain, simmer some soup, bake squash, or stew root vegetables for the next day. Whole grain, porridge, soups, and so on can also cook while you're taking a shower or doing your morning exercises.

If possible set aside 30-60 minutes every morning to prep and cook. In that time you can assemble breakfast and make one or two soups, one or two cooked vegetable dishes, or a pressed salads and/or condiments. You might also transform leftovers into dips, spreads, soups or sauces, or burritos, or wash and soak grains and beans.

Grains and beans are best soaked at least 4-8 hours or overnight before cooking, so you'll need to plan ahead. Wash and soak them just before going to bed or before leaving for work in the morning. You can then start them cooking first thing in the morning, in the afternoon, or upon arriving home in the evening. While they cook you are free to do other things. And every two or three days you might want to turn leftover cooked dinner grain into morning cereal, then soak and cook rice or another grain combination to last for the next day or two.

Soups and pressed salads can be quickly assembled in the morning or evening. Once assembled, soups can be set aside to cook later or simmered for 30-90 minutes. Salads can be mixed and set to press for 3-6 hours, all day, or up to 24 hours. While the soup simmers, just use a timer and a low flame and don't stray too far from the kitchen.

If you are really pressed for time, invest in a crock pot or thermal cooker so that hot cereal can cook while you sleep and bean and vegetable soups, stews, or sauces can brew overnight or while you are out during the day.

7. Stock up on staples

Keep a ready supply of basic staples in your pantry, refrigerator, and freezer. (Grains, beans, tempeh, wheat meat, hearty seasonal vegetables, herbs and spices, oils and seeds, real sea salt, miso, tamari, and so forth. These will help you pull together quick and creative everyday meals as well as fancier weekend or party meals.

Packaged foods, even those from the health food store, do not build sustainable meals. Such foods won't match the taste or nutrition of home cooked food and will end up costing you an arm and a leg if you use them on a regular basis. We have run into many individuals who spend $250-$300 per person, per month, eating out or buying so called "healthy" convenience foods from the natural foods store.

On a grain based diet of home cooked food, with proper planning and preparation, a single person can eat incredibly well on $100-$150 per month, and two can eat well on $200-$225 a month. The cost will be even less if you have a garden and can grow most of your own vegetables. Just one convenience entrée a day can cost you $120 in a month and one meal out each day, at $5-$7 can cost you $150-$210 a month. A muffin here or there or several boxes of cold cereal will also add up quickly. It clearly pays to explore the alternatives. High quality premade foods from your local co-op can be lifesavers in a pinch, but when used frequently they can be a real drain on your pocketbook and your health. We suggest that you keep some "healthy" convenience foods stashed in the cupboards or freezer then save them for emergencies.

If you don't yet have the hang of using leftovers and making efficient use of your kitchen time, some prepared foods can help you make the transition to a healthier way of eating; just don't become dependent on them. You'll find low-fat, dairy-free, vegetarian burritos, tamales, enchiladas, gyoza, burgers, and casseroles in the freezer section of your local health food store. On the dry goods shelves you will find prepared bean dips, refried beans, chili, rice cakes, bottled organic beans, instant bean and miso soup cups, and sauces, all of which may prove useful in a pinch.

When using prepared products, it is a good idea to balance them with at least one homemade dish—lightly cooked greens, pressed, tossed or boiled , or several of these. In this way you will have a nutritious and satisfying meal within minutes.

Convenience foods can always be stretched to make your dollars go farther. Canned refried beans or chili (or your own planned leftover beans) can be turned into a sauce for millet, polenta slices, tortillas, buns, or pasta, or made into soup with the addition of soup stock, herbs, and perhaps leftover bits of cooked land or sea vegetables, all seasoned with miso or tamari. Nevertheless, we still encourage you to make your own convenience foods by always cooking enough food for several meals at a time and creatively mixing and matching the dishes at meals.

Frozen foods lack vitality so it's not a good idea to make huge batches of food for freezing. If you freeze homemade foods, do so infrequently and in small portions. Bare in mind that they *will* lose a great deal of flavor and nutrition and that their textures may be altered. Frozen foods use up a great deal of energy. Frozen foods and the freezers they are shipped, warehoused, sold from, and stored in are all major contributors to pollution and ozone depletion. In our aim to nourish ourselves, we must take into account the effect we have on our environment (and the next seven generations). Modern freezers are not a necessity. They are a luxury. We can choose to use them discriminately or not at all.

Nourishment For Lunch
Tips, Techniques, and New Ideas

Why pack a lunch?

An occasional meal out may be a treat, but eating out on a regular basis is financially and nutritionally unsustainable. If you spend $4-$6 a day on lunch out, and you do this five days a week, in one week you will spend $20-$30. In a month you will spend $80-$120. In one year, you will spend nearly $1,200 for one meal a day for one person! Multiply that by the number of people in your family, then add it to what you spend on coffee, muffins or cookies, other meals out, or premade "convenience foods." Now add that figure to what you spend for your regular groceries. You will be amazed at how much you are spending. (Incidentally, if you've never kept track of your food budget, keeping a log for three months can be a real eye opener.)

Besides being expensive, restaurant fare is produced in large quantities and generally with a lot more waste and less care than home cooking. This food is designed to appeal to the public, not your health and personal needs. A single meal out typically contains more fat and animal products than you need in a week, let alone a meal. Such meals also typically lack sufficient grain and dark green leafy and deep orange vegetables and contain an excess of hidden sugar and preservatives. So what do you do for lunch if you work away from home? The best way to get a good lunch— one that sustains personal, financial, and planetary health— is to make it yourself. With a homemade lunch you will also have more time to relax and enjoy your meal than if you have to hunt for a restaurant, order, wait, then pay before eating your meal and returning to work.

If you work outside your home or must be away for a trip, it is always wise to pack a lunch (unless you are enjoying an occasional meal out with a friend or family member). When traveling by bus, train, or airplane it is just as important (and helpful) to pack your own food. You may even want to bring a little extra, just in case you experience transportation delays, changes in travel schedules, or other such problems. Don't expect to find the kind of healthy food you desire in an airport or train or bus station. Although many airlines now offer special meals, they may not be what you are looking for. They may be too oily; too spicy; too old; too full of sugar, preservatives, and/or animal products you don't want; or they may not contain enough grain. They may be forgotten by the airlines; given to the wrong passenger; or unavailable in the event of last minute flight changes, late arrivals, layovers or other changes. Thus, it pays to be prepared—both in terms of your health and your pocketbook.

With a little advance planning and without investing a huge amount of time, you can put together varied and nutritious box lunches for yourself and your family. If you make your own "convenience food" at home by always cooking enough for several meals, your leftovers will be ready and waiting to jump into your thermos and lunch box. Neither you nor the environment will have to pay for the extra labor, packaging, shipping, and storage costs of pre-packaged, preserved "convenience" foods. And you will be able to trust that your meals are fresh, wholesome, low-fat, grain-based, and vegetable-rich.

Once you get the hang of mixing and matching soups, grains, vegetables and condiments, and transforming yesterday's dishes into lunch box fillers, you'll find that you can come up with endless variations on the basic format. Best of all, you will find that most lunches can be assembled in minutes. Some foods can be packed the night before and others can be assembled, cooked, or gently warmed in the morning.

Munchable, lunchable options

There are a wide variety of pack lunch options beyond the sandwich and salad bar or sandwich, chip, and cookie routine. These options are often more interesting and healthier. We offer several different ideas below to give you a sense of the possibilities. Your choices will vary with the season; what you happen to have on hand; time constraints; and your mood, appetite and health condition. The emphasis should always be on whole grains, or whole grain products, complemented by vegetable, seed, nut and/or bean condiments and side dishes.

The basic lunch pattern=

Soup or Stew + Grain + Vegetable Side Dish(es) + Condiments*

Examples:

- Vegetable Soup + Rice + Stir Fry or Sauteed Vegetables + Seed Condiment +/- Sea Flakes

- Bean Soup + Bread + Pressed Salad +/- Pickles +/- Low-Fat Spread

- Vegetable Soup + Filled Buns + Steamed Greens or Pressed Salad

- Vegetable Soup + Tofu or Tempeh Sandwiches + Boiled Salad or Greens

- Gravy or Sauce + Bread or Noodles + Boiled, Pressed, or Marinated Salad

- Miso Broth + Bread + Steamed Greens + Low-Fat Spread +/- Pickles

- Mashed Squash or Sweet Potato + Chapatis or Loaf Bread + Miso Nut Butter + Pressed or Boiled Salad

Note: When eating only two meals per day, you may want to add an extra vegetable or grain dish, or a bean, tofu, tempeh, or sea vegetable dish (if the soup or stew does not contain them), thereby creating a four dish meal format. (e.g., you might serve a cooked greens dish and a pressed salad with your soup and whole grain, pasta, or bread. Or, you might serve two grain dishes, such as bread and rice, with a soup, stew, or sauce and cooked greens and/or salad. Or, a cream of vegetable soup, whole grain, sautéed greens, and a bean, tofu, or tempeh side dish. Or, a vegetable soup, tempeh or bean filled buns or sandwiches, and pressed salad or cooked greens.

The simplified lunch pattern (for a 2-Meal-A-Day Plan) =

Grain + Vegetable Side Dish + Condiments

Note: If you will be eating a substantial supper, you may want a simple lunch such as this.

Examples:

- Rice + Pressed or Boiled Salad or Stir Fry + Seed or Nut Condiment +/- Sea Vegetable Condiment or side dish

- Noodles or Rice + Seed Condiment + Stir Fry +/- Pickles +/- Sea Vegetable Condiment

- Rice Balls + Boiled or Pressed Salad or Stir Fried Mixed Vegetables +/- pickles

- Tamales, Calzones, or Filled Steamed Buns + Pressed or Boiled Salad

- Bread + Low-Fat Spread + Pressed or Boiled Salad

- Rice & Bean Burritos, Tofu & Veggie Burritos, or other +/- pressed, marinated or or boiled salad

Plan ahead

To get a running start, you might use Sunday night to whip up some extra food to use in pack lunches during the first half of the week. Throughout the week you can then cook extra portions at supper for the following day's lunch. These leftovers, as discussed elsewhere in this book, can be creatively transformed or mixed and matched so that each meal is different and interesting. Please note that food will loses its life and isn't particularly tasty or nutritious after several days, so making food for the entire week on Sunday isn't recommended. (See also Secrets for Meals Made Ahead; Getting Down a System; and In Keeping with the Seasons.)

Soup (or stew)

Soups and stews are easy to make and soothing to the system. We consider these essential and serve one almost every day with lunch (and sometimes with breakfast or supper). We make soups made from vegetables or vegetables combined with beans. We like some some soups chunky and others smooth, some thick and some thin. A gravy or sauce stands in nicely for soup now and then, too. All travel well in a thermos, and at lunch time you can pour them over room temperature noodles or millet slices or dunk pieces of bread into them for a nice warm meal. (Warm your soup in the morning then stow it in a wide mouth thermos. In very hot weather you may occasionally want to serve your soup cool or close to room temperature.

Some good staples in the soup department are Any Bean Soup, Oat or Soya Cream of Vegetable Soup, and Simmered Vegetable Soup. If you have a few basic recipes that you can use again and again with only slight variations, you'll be set. Soups can also be readily made from leftovers combined with pasta water, vegetable steaming liquid, vegetable stock, broth, or gravy.

Grain

Whole or minimally processed grains will provide the fuel you need to carry you through your day, so it's important to make these the *main* dish at lunch. You can pack leftover rice or nori-maki sushi rolls, polenta, millet-vegetable slices, or plain pasta. Or pack tortillas, pita breads, dinner rolls, loaf bread, corn bread, bagels, Chinese-style steamed buns, or calzones. You could also venture into new arenas with Squash-wiches or "Yam"-wiches, a healthy grain and vegetable based alternative to the peanut butter and jelly sandwich.

Most whole grains, noodles, and breads, can be served at room temperature without reheating and will last from breakfast to lunch without refrigeration. Whole grain breads or millet slices can be packed in wax paper, cellophane or brown paper bags, then eaten with warm soup, stew, sauce, or gravy or oil. Others, such as plain noodles, can be carried in a bowl then topped with warm cup of soup, stew, sauce, or gravy or seed condiment come serving time.

To retain the texture of seed or nut condiments, pack them in a small vial or bottle to sprinkle over your grain at lunchtime. If you plan to pack a spread for bread, also pack it separately so as not to have soggy bread come noon time. However, tortillas or pita breads can often be expertly filled with a little practice, and Chinese-style steamed buns can be stuffed with favorite fillings before cooking for a no mess-sandwich alternative (Ditto for calzones.) Unfilled steamed buns are also good split in half and filled with hummus, tofu or tempeh dip, low-fat pesto, marinated and cooked tempeh slices or salad or pickles right at meal time. Or you can simply dunk them into soup or stew during the meal. Burger buns can be used for sandwiches or for bean or tempeh burgers which are perfectly tasty served at room temperature when dining away from home.

SUPER SANDWICH FILLERS

If you like sandwiches, there are a multitude of healthy fillers. Just bare in mind that on a grain based diet, most people will need two sandwiches; two or three steamed buns; three to four Squash-wiches or Yam-wiches; or one burger sandwich with a side of rice, noodles, or corn on the cob or popcorn. The emphasis here is on the bread rather than mountains of filling.

Sandwiches can be filled with bean, tofu, tempeh, or wheat meat spreads, cutlets, or burgers. Pickles, mustard or relishes may be added as well. Or, you may opt to pack spreads separately from bread and vegetables then assemble the sandwiches at lunch time.

Round out a sandwich or two with a cup of soup and cooked greens or mixed vegetables or a pressed, marinated, or tossed salad. If you're making a pita pocket sandwich, you can stuff your vegetables; vegetables with beans; or vegetables and grain right in the pockets.

Here are some tasty sandwich fillers

•Squash-wiches & Yam-wiches

•Tofu Cream Cheese

•Tofu Pesto Spread

•Hummus

•Tempeh Mock Tuna

•Sea Sage & Sunflower Spread

•Garbanzo Butter

•Pan Fried Tempeh Cutlets

•Pan Fried Wheat Meat Cutlets

•Tempeh Bacon

•Tempeh Sausage

•Basic Bean Burgers

•Oven "Fried" Wheat Meat

•Scrambled Tofu with sea vegetable

Vegetables

Leafy green vegetable side dishes are another must for lunch. The options extend far beyond tossed salads. Yesterday's stir fried, sauteed, quick-boiled, or steamed vegetables could be used. Or, try...

•a boiled salad

•a pressed or marinated salad

•a pressed salad and cooked greens

•a mixture of cooked sea and land vegetables

•leftover stir fry or sautéed greens

•a marinated sprout salad

• cooked green or mixed vegetables tossed with beans or seasoned, cooked tempeh or tofu.

Some of these salads may call for a hint of toasted sesame oil, olive oil, flax oil, or diluted tahini, with perhaps some pickles, brown rice vinegar, pickled umeboshi or apriboshi vinegar, or tamari. Another option is a light low-fat or oil-free dressing or sauce. However, most of our salads and vegetable side dishes need no dressing because sea salt, tamari, or ume have heightened their flavors in the cooking process (quick-

boiled vegetables or pressed or marinated salads are prime examples).

In order to simplify lunch preparation, we often make use of leftover vegetable dishes. Most should be eaten within one or two days for optimal flavor and nutrition. Pressed and marinated salads are the exception.

Condiments

Condiments add flavor and variety to the midday meal. They can also add essential nutrients and benefit digestion. Condiments such as tofu, vegetable or bean dips, or soy yogurt can be packed in a small container and spread on bread or whole grain at lunch time. Roasted seasoned seed condiments can also be carried separately to sprinkle over whole grains, noodles, or bread. Still other rich condiments such as toasted sesame oil, herbed oil, or diluted Miso-Tahini Spread can be tossed with plain pasta, cooked veggies, or pressed salad if little or no added fat is used in other lunch dishes. Soup or stew can make a terrific bread spread—just dunk your bread in or pour it over a bowl of plain noodles at lunch time for moisture, richness, and flavor. For colorful garnishes.

Optional, animal products

If you choose to use animal products, use them sparingly as condiments for whole grains, noodles, bread, or vegetables. An occasional hard boiled, pickled, or preserved egg, a tofu and egg salad, or a steamed one-egg omelet could serve as a rice or bread topper. Or tuck a bit of grated cheese into a small jar or pack plain goat yogurt into a thermos cup for a special treat.

Beverages

You may wish to pack bags of non-caffeinated herb tea, a jar of instant grain coffee, or a thermos full of your favorite brew for an after-meal drink or mid-afternoon treat. Tea bags and instant grain coffee will keep for prolonged periods of time in a cupboard or drawer at the office. Though tea is often available in many offices, you may not be able to find exactly what you're looking for unless you bring a supply from home. You can also save money by packing your own. (Refer to the beverage section for interesting tea and grain coffee recipes.) Occasionally you might pack a cup of warm, lightly spiced, miso seasoned soy milk in a thermos cup, to replace soup in a meal or for a late afternoon snack.

The inessential dessert

Desserts and fruits are not essential for a nourishing lunch. If you are eating two large meals per day and skipping supper, lunch time is a nice time for dessert (or you might save dessert for a late afternoon or early evening snack). Simple desserts are best for regular use. Fruit compotes, sauces, or aspics are easy to make and pack into a lunch sack or box. Grain or fruit-based puddings and chestnut or amasake puddings also travel well. Occasionally, you might even pack no-bake cookies, brownies, or bars. (You will need to set aside a fairly good block of time—usually one full hour—to eat your meal, (or more with) and dessert in an unhurried manner. If this is not possible, you might consider having your dessert later in the day or skipping it altogether.

If your sweet tooth cries out for something mid-morning, try eating more grains and vegetables at breakfast and/or adding some squash, sweet potato, or chestnuts to your morning meal. (Including a little bit of nuts, seeds, or nut or seed oil can also help you go the distance.) You could pack a slice of millet, polenta, or corn bread, a steamed bun or bagel, a hunk of winter squash, half a sweet potato, or some amasake beverage for a snack. If the urge to nibble hits you mid-afternoon, it could be that you're not eating enough food in general, or enough grain in particular or fat—at lunch time. If you eat more grain at lunch, chances are you'll be able to hold out 'til dinner time. In general, it is better to avoid snacking and to eat sufficient amounts at meal time. In this way you will avoid spoiling your appetite and give your digestive system a much needed rest between meals.

Some like it hot

While a hot meal is always nice, it is best to completely avoid the use of microwave ovens for cooking or heating your food. Other more traditional, practical and healthful alternatives exist, including the use of a thermos. If you pack a cup of warm soup or stew in a wide mouth thermos, it can be ladled over room temperature noodles or eaten with bread, millet slices, or biscuits. Many other foods can be eaten and enjoyed at room temperature.

Though at home we almost always heat our leftover breads and whole grains by steaming, for meals away from home it is usually necessary to eat them unheated. Salads or leftover cooked greens are also fine at room temperature. In fact, they are more nutritious if not warmed up. Both grain and vegetable dishes will be fine kept out of the refrigerator between breakfast and lunch. Fresh or dried green garnishes can also be kept at room temperature. Bean side-dishes and soups and stews are most easily packed into a thermos. Alternatively, some of the more perishable items (bean, tofu, or tempeh spreads or cutlets for example) may be packed in a small stainless steel lunchbox or bowl with a snap on lid, then stowed alongside or on top of an ice pack in hot weather. Toasted sesame oil, sea vegetable condiments or flakes, or roasted seed condiments can all be packed into tiny vials for travel and don't need any special temperature. If you want a hot drink, don't forget to pack tea bags or instant grain coffee, or brew one of these at home and stow it in a thermos for later in the day.)

Keep emergency rations on hand

You might want to have a stash of emergency rations at the office, for those days when you're short on time and low on leftovers, when you didn't pack enough for lunch or when you must unexpectedly work late. You might want to set aside a special desk drawer just for this purpose.

Good emergency foods include instant, fat-free, bean or veggie soups in a cup; whole grain ramen; instant oatmeal; fat and sweetener-free whole grain crackers and crisp breads; brown rice cakes; a jar of low-fat bean dip; and several spice jars filled with dried chives, seed condiment, and sea vegetable flakes. These keep well in a cool, dry place and may save the day. Tuck a few apples into your briefcase or backpack now and then. Keep them displayed in a bowl on your desk and use them for an occasional treat for yourself or share them with your office mates. A few fat-free naturally sweetened cookies or packages of amasake might also be nice to have on hand and share now and then as well. If you keep your stash stocked, others who have to keep late hours with you may become interested in what you have to eat and may even be won over to your new way of eating.

Other tips

If you keep it simple, as we do, the same lunch formats can be used again and again throughout the year, yet they never become boring because you can use different whole grains, breads, beans, vegetables, seasonings, condiments, and combinations to meet the changing seasons and your varied desires.

Basic equipment for Pack Lunches

Thermos See Tips and Tools section for more on these.

Stainless steel lunch boxes See Tips and Tools section for more on these.

Bowl Pack a small wooden or stainless steel bowl if you want to pour hot soup over room temperature noodles at lunch-time or if your thermos isn't wide enough to accommodate dunking your bread.

Spice jars or tiny bottles Spice jars or tiny bottles are perfect for storing and transporting condiments. Raw or roasted, salted seed condiments*; flax or sesame oil; prepared mustard, reduced fat pesto*, or other spreads*; pungent green garnish minced scallions, chives, dill, or parsley, (fresh or dried); sea vegetable flakes; and/or pickles are all easily stored in small bottles. You could even keep one bottle of a particular condiment in your lunch sack and one at the office. For optimal taste, nutrition, and economy the items marked by an asterisk (*) are best home- made not purchased.

Bags Small brown or wax paper bags work best for packing breads, buns, biscuits, polenta slices, and the like. They will easily fold over to seal your goodies inside. Empty cellophane bags or leftover plastic bread bags can be used as well, particularly for sandwiches, calzones, tamales, savory filled buns, etc.. A large canvas bag, preferably with a hard exterior and handles can be used to consolidate several containers for easy transport.

Eating utensils: A soup spoon and a fork or chopsticks can be wrapped in a cloth napkin and tucked into a purse, tote, or back pack. A butter knife or small frosting spreader is handy for spreads or slicing steamed buns but is not always necessary.

Dry ice bag This is not essential; many meals will travel fine without ice. They are handy in the summer, however, or when you are packing foods for several meals (say for lunch and supper, or lunch and a light afternoon or evening snack). Opt for a leak-proof dry ice bag which can be frozen and refrozen. You can place it on top of or next to your stainless steel lunch box or other containers filled with perishable items. An ice bag is not be necessary for plain cooked grains, breads, cooked greens, or salads (that are free of animal products) since these will last from breakfast to lunch without spoiling. The dry ice bags work well for bean dips and spreads; some types of sandwiches; dishes which contain tofu sauces or dressings; bean or vegetable aspics; fragile oils; or fruit compotes or amasake desserts that will not be eaten within 4-5 hours of leaving home.

Miniature cooler Though not really necessary for the average lunch packer, a mini-cooler can be helpful for longer road trips, airplane travel, or if you will be gone from dawn to dusk and need to pack food for several meals. These come in various hand-held sizes and hold various boxes, bins, old miso tubs full of food, and a dry ice bag.

Chapter 4
Going with the Grain

The Whole Grain and Nothing But

Hop on the Grain Wagon

Today, many health authorities—including the U.S. Senate Select Committee, the National Academy of Sciences, CSPI (Center for Science in the Public Interest), and the National Cancer Institute are encouraging Americans to go with the grain. In fact, the current U.S.D.A. Food Guide Pyramid based on the U.S. Senate Select Committee's Dietary Goals recommends six to eleven servings of grains and grain products daily. This means, six to eleven slices of bread or three to six cups of cooked rice daily or three to four slices of bread or one to two cups of cooked whole grain at each meal, three time a day. When eating a grain-based, vegetable-rich diet and minimizing your use of animal products, sweets, fats, and oils, you'll likely want *and even need* to eat at least this amount of grain in a day. You may even want to eat substantially more than this if you are very active, pregnant, lactating, or involved in competitive sports or other strenuous activities.

At first the recommended volume of grain may seem daunting, but eating this amount of grain will give you the energy you need to sustain your activity throughout the day. Instead of filling up on high-fat foods, water-dense soups, salads, fruits and vegetables, or snacking between meals, you'll want to go for more grain at meal-time. If you must snack, reach for a slice of whole grain bread or polenta, a steamed bun, a bagel or roll, a few brown rice cakes, or a bowl of air popped popcorn. Eating this way will help both your pocket-book and your body. If you cannot eat this amount of grain, it is

likely that you are not active enough. The solution is not to continue to eat lightly, rather, you should get more physical activity to strengthen your body—including your appetite and digestion.

The history of grains

Grain cultivation, which began about 15,000 years ago, is largely responsible for the evolution of human culture. It enabled us to store enough food to last through sparse seasons.

What is a healthy appetite?

Traditional Chinese physicians have judged a patient's health by asking about appetite. A healthy, young male appetite means the desire and capacity to eat about one pound of dry uncooked rice or three pounds of cooked rice per day. Although western physicians do not use the same criteria, your grandmother probably did. In most traditional cultures, a strong (big) appetite has always been a sign of health and vigor... (It is only in modern times—with artificial foods and a highly unnatural way of life—that people have come to view the appetite as something to fear, suppress and control. However, even if you wish to lose weight, you should not fear or suppress your appetite. Instead, you should improve and strengthen and feed it through proper exercise and proper food.)

Whole grains are quite literally the nourishment that created civilization. All major civilizations, including the American experiment, have relied upon grains as the staple food. In some cultures, this is not immediately obvious because this grain is cycled through feed animals rather than directly consumed (though this latter practice is certainly the most inefficient and foolish way to use grains). Grains have been an integral part of the world's major culinary traditions: Far Eastern; Middle Eastern; Northern, Southern, Eastern, and Western European; and Northern, Southern and Central American. And as if the test of time were not convincing enough, recent scientific research confirms that a grain based, vegetable-rich diet promotes optimal health and longevity.

Researchers involved in a landmark study known as the China Health Project have suggested that the relatively low incidence of heart disease, many cancers, and other degenerative diseases in China is due to the abundance of grains and vegetables in the traditional Chinese diet. The China Health Project is an ongoing, collaborative study of the current dietary patterns in rural China, undertaken by the Chinese Academy of Preventive Medicine and Oxford and Cornell Universities. According to this study, the typical Chinese receives 90% of his or her calories from whole grain and vegetable foods; in contrast, the typical American takes less than 10% of his or her calories from such foods. Also, the typical Chinese person consumes three times as much starch and fiber as the typical American as a result of the abundance of plant products in the diet. The average Chinese person also consumes 25% more calories (but one-half to one-third as much fat) when compared to the average American, yet the average Chinese person weighs 20% less.

Going with the Grain

Most Americans don't know how to make grains the central part of a meal. To go with the grain, you need to have more than an occasional cup of hot or cold cereal for breakfast or small dish of rice with dinner. Going with the grain means eating more grain than anything else, with grains appearing at every meal, and in sizeable volumes.

Whole Grains Make Whole Brains

How are we to attain wisdom? Throughout the ages, many philosophers and spiritual leaders have maintained that it is necessary to eat a vegetarian diet in order to support our search for wisdom and enlightenment. Recent research has confirmed this view, showing that children raised on breast milk and grain-based vegetarian diets tend to be significantly more intelligent than those raised on animal foods. One study found that a group of children raised on a macrobiotic diet had a mean I.Q. of 116—16% higher than the average IQ. Also, many of the intellectual giants of human kind, from Plato to Albert Einstein, have eaten and advocated vegetarian diets. If you don't want to starve your brain, build your daily diet around whole grain. Unlike animal foods, whole grains and vegetables are rich in all of the nutrients that are necessary for complete development of the human body and mind.

Eating a nourishing, grain-centered diet requires that you consume nearly a pound of dry whole grain in a day, or even more if you are very active. Your daily grain might include a single grain or it might be comprised of several different grains and grain preparations. The average person will consume one and one-half to two cups of dry rice or millet; or four or six cups (about 10-12 oz.) of uncooked pasta; or three to four cups of flour (before being cooked into bread) etc. in any given day. This translates into four slices of bread; one and one-half to two and a half cups of cooked rice; or two to three cups of cooked hot cereal or pasta at each of three daily meals.

Those who grew up in China, Japan, Korea, Tibet, Pakistan, Africa, India, Eastern Europe, or South or Central America may be used to eating fairly large volumes of grain in a day. But to others, eating the recommended amount of grain may seem impossible. However, we can assure you that eating a substantial quantity of whole grain is possible, enjoyable, and energizing. In fact, it is necessary once you reduce your intake of animal products, high fat snack foods, oils, desserts, and other less nourishing foods.

If at first you can't conceive of it, try, and try again

Though it may seem bizarre to eat such a volume of grain, persevere. If you do, you will be richly rewarded. Within a week or two of eating regular, grain-centered meals, you could be surprised to find that you can go from breakfast to lunch and from lunch to dinner without running out of steam and going for coffee, sweets or junk foods. You may suddenly find that you are more calm, focused, and productive. Your daily tasks may seem easier. You may also find that you no longer want to snack between meals or eat junk food or dessert or, as incomprehensible as it may seem, you may lose the urge to drink coffee. If you are overweight, you might even lose a few pounds while eating more food (and more bread, pasta, and whole grain) than you ever thought possible.

What's the main dish?

In the Nourishment for Life Diet, grain functions as the "main" dish in every meal with everything else serving as a side dish or condiment for the grain. Small portions of well seasoned side dishes enhance the grain and your health.

When planning meals, it helps to prepare foods in the proper proportion: grains should be made in abundance and vegetables and beans, and various condiments should be made and served in proportionately smaller amounts. It also helps to plan ahead by preparing a big pot of whole grain (such as rice or millet) or pasta and/or a large volume of bread, even if you are just cooking for one or two people. You won't want to run out of grain in a meal because it is the "main dish." Leftover grain is never a problem; it can always be re-heated for other meals or transformed into new nourishing dishes.

Chinese restaurant syndrome

Often people complain that they feel hungry soon after eating a large meal at a Chinese restaurant. The same thing can happen when people switch to a vegetarian or vegan diet. Why? Because many people fill up on vegetables, soup, and other side dishes and neglect to eat enough grains. Soups and vegetables are temporarily filling but they won't stick with you even if eat a lot of them. In fact, if you take a second helping of such dishes, you're likely to feel too full to eat much grain and ravenously hungry an hour or two later. For this reason, when serving a meal for yourself, family, or guests, it is inadvisable to serve seconds of soup or stew. Your stomach can only hold so much food and if you fill up on soup or vegetables these will displace more substantial and energizing grain foods. Though you may want a second helping of soup or vegetables, it is important to remember that these are side dishes designed to enhance your enjoyment of and to help you to eat more of the grain. Thus it is best to take seconds of grain *before* taking seconds of vegetables, and to avoid serving seconds of soup any time. Grains are substantial foods and will carry you from one meal to the next, if you eat enough of them. They should comprise 50-60% of the volume at each meal. By eating one or two bites of grain for each mouthful of soup, stew, or side dish, you will be assured of eating at least 50% grain in any given meal. So when desiring seconds, thirds, or fourths, reach for the grain then use your side dishes as condiments. Your body will love you for it.

Licking the snack attack habit

If you are a snacker or meal skipper, chances are that you don't snack or make up for lost meals by eating whole grain pita bread, tortillas, loaf bread, steamed buns, brown rice, millet slices, polenta, or oatmeal. If you are like many Americans, when hunger hits you reach for chips, crackers, pretzels, candy, cookies, fruit juice, coffee, donuts, soda pop, chewing gum, ice cream, dried fruit, or other items which aren't healthy replacements for real meals. Though some may argue that these items are okay in moderation, many of them are nutritional blanks; others are actually quite harmful. Junk food in any quantity is still junk food and will displace more nutritious foods. Eating snack food and dessert items is an expensive habit often cultivated in response to irregular or missed meals, the appeal of advertising, and/or a lack of proper nutrition education.

If you crave sweets or eat late at night, chances are you haven't been eating three meals a day, including a substantial grain-based breakfast. If you have been eating three meals a day, maybe you just haven't been eating enough grain. Eating grain-based meals will help you ward off cravings and binges by helping you to maintain a more even energy level. If you tend to tire easily, this can also be aided by the addition of more wholesome, unrefined grain foods at each and every meal.

The healthiest snack

If you must snack, try plain brown rice cakes the thick, dense, flavorful kind, not the airy, styrofoam-like grocery store variety (we like Lundberg). Try them plain. Or, you might occasionally top them with a low fat vegetable, tofu, tempeh, bean, or vegetable spread or some quark or goat cheese. Other snack options include whole grain bagels, buns, dinner rolls, tortillas, pita bread, rice balls, brown rice sushi, polenta, millet slices, arepas, or corn bread. Or try hot air popcorn misted with umeboshi vinegar or tamari soy sauce. Whatever option you choose, be sure to eat sitting down, in a relaxed environment free of distractions, and chew well to promote good digestion and assimilation.

Grains help you go the distance

If you are involved in vigorous physical activity, whether for work or pleasure, you will surely discover that grain-based meals provide lasting strength and endurance. In fact, grains are among the richest sources of complex carbohydrates, the body's preferred source of fuel. (Whole grains are also rich in protein and vitamins, so they won't leave you empty handed.) Load up on grains and you will be able to go the extra mile.

Eating grain saves you money

Grain based meals are both healthier and more economical than meals based on meats, cheeses, fruits, or even vegetables. And unlike most animal products and fresh produce, whole grains keep for long periods of time. Even healthy whole grain breads keep longer than most other perishables.

Grains are good for the environment

When going with the grain, you lessen your burden on the environment. Grain growing uses less land and less water then either animal or vegetable cultivation and it requires less energy to store grains than other types of food. Eating more whole grains, purchased in bulk, also allows you to minimize the amount of waste (packaging) you contribute to the world. Countless other environmental advantages can be reaped through the adoption of a grain-based diet. You may soon discover them all.

What's a grain anyway?

A grain is a small hard fruit or seed produced by a cereal grass. There is a staggering variety of grain in the world, from numerous types of wheat, corn, and rice to specific species found only in the remote regions of Eastern Europe, Africa, or South America. The Nourishment for Life Diet uses many grains from around the world although those grown on your continent or in your bio-region are preferable to grains imported from far away. Not only are grains from your locality better suited to life in your environment, but they are more ecologically and economically sound choices. Also, many grains grown traditionally in Ethiopia, South America, India, Europe, Africa, China, and other countries are now being grown in many parts of the United States and provide an endlessly rich variety of choices for us.

Foods that fall into the grain category include:

(a) whole grains: brown rice, millet, barley, oat groats, kasha etc.
(b) ground or cracked grains: cracked wheat, cornmeal, polenta, etc.
(c) rolled grains: oatmeal, barley flakes, kamut flakes, etc.
(d) flour products: pasta, various breads, crackers, and many dry cereals
(e) miscellaneous: popcorn*, rice cakes, dry cereal (cold cereal), etc.

* Note: Popped and puffed cereal grains are delicious and certainly a healthier choice than potato or corn chips; however, they are most intelligently used only as occasional snacks, infrequent breakfast treats, or supplementary grains. They are not very calorie or energy dense and cannot be eaten in the quantity necessary to be considered daily staples or main foods. They are also expensive, with the exception of popcorn, being are far more costly than whole grains, rolled grains or flour.

Cereal	Price	Volume	Serves
Natural, preservative-free, sweetener-free, cold cereal	$3-$4	14-16 oz. (8-12 cups)	5-7
Millet, whole	$3-$4	6-8 lbs (15-20 cups, dry)	30-40
Rolled oats	$3-$4	9-12 lbs. (44-52 cups, dry)	44-100

Whole or minimally refined cereal grains such as whole wheat flour or whole grain brown rice are almost always preferable to refined and heavily processed grains like white flour or white rice, although in some cases you may need to make exceptions to this rule. For example, when traveling or dining out it is not always possible to get whole grain products, but any grain is better than no grain at all. You just have to make the wisest choice among the available options. (It is also a good idea to skip deep fried grain products, such as fried corn chips, and choose oil-free or low-fat preparations.)

Cooking the Perfect Pot of Whole Grain

Due to their high fiber content, whole grains are relatively difficult to digest. Although white rice and other polished grains may be easier to digest, they are considerably less nutritious. To help you get the most nutrition and flavor from whole grains such as brown rice, and to offset possible digestive difficulties. Proper handling and cooking are of the utmost importance.

Making whole grains more digestible

Several things can be done to make whole grains more digestible. These include:

1) washing and scrubbing

2) presoaking

3) thorough cooking in general and pressure cooking in particular

4) cooking with a mineral rich, sun dried sea salt

Washing grains: By washing and scrubbing whole grains such as brown rice or millet, you remove some of the tough, indigestible fiber. Washing also removes the dirt, sand, and dust which may have adhered to the grain during the harvest, shipping, or storage. If is often necessary to rinse and drain the grain two to four times before setting it to soak or cook.

Soaking Grains: Presoaking whole grains initiates the sprouting (process, and makes) them more tender, sweet, and digestible. Most whole grains benefit from an overnight soak, or at least 4-8 hours of soaking prior to cooking. You can even soak your grains for as long as 24 hours. Once soaked, the grains should be cooked in their soak water for the recommended time. Soaking is not meant to reduce their cooking time. (See index for recipes).

Now and then, you might want to skip the soaking process altogether and dry roast your rice before cooking it. Roasted, pressure cooked rice is fluffier than soaked, pressure cooked rice and both will be more tender than unsoaked, boiled brown rice. Roasted rice is particularly nice served with stir fried veggies or other Chinese-style dishes.

Cooking grains with sea salt: Cooking grains with the proper amount of high quality sun dried sea salt makes them taste rich and buttery without added fat. This special sea salt also tenderizes the grain and benefits digestion. When appropriately used, sun dried sea salt does not have a sharp taste nor does it make foods taste strongly "salty." Commercial table salt, which may or may not be labeled sea salt, is very different and not recommended. It has a completely different composition, flavor, and effect on the body.

Salt should be added to grains after soaking and just before cooking. It should not be added during the soaking period. If added during soaking, it could hamper the sprouting process.

Salt should never be added to foods at the table. Also, avoid using tamari, shoyu, or soy sauce at the table. These salty seasonings are not designed to be used as table condiments; rather, they are designed to be used in the kitchen by the cook. When added at the table, salt dries out and irritates the mucous membranes, often stimulating excess thirst. It can also cause other more serious imbalances when added to foods at the table. Salt will bring out the sweet and rich tastes in natural foods and will produce a more gentle and nourishing effect when used in cooking.

It is always a good idea to use a mineral-rich sun dried sea salt in cooking grains. If you desire a saltier taste at the table, use well seasoned seed or nut condiments, sea vegetable condiments, seasoned beans, gravies, and sauces, or well seasoned vegetables, all of which are designed to be eaten with your grain.

Commercial salt is kiln dried at 1200° F., or boiled then dried. It is also very dry, and tastes very salty. It has been stripped of its minerals and bleached, making it almost pure sodium chloride. It is usually combined with anticaking agents and dextrose (sugar) as well. This type of salt and other artificially processed salts may be the culprit in causing people to associate salt with water retention. In contrast, true sun-dried sea salt is very moist, has a gentle taste, contains less sodium chloride, and has a more balanced mineral profile than its refined cousin. In fact, true macrobiotic quality sea salt contains over 83 different trace minerals in addition to sodium, and chloride. These minerals are essentially absent from commercially processed sea salts but they are necessary for the production of digestive enzymes and dozens of metabolic processes.

From the traditional Chinese medicine perspective, salt has a downward energy and a moistening and tenderizing action. Thus, it softens hard foods, makes food go down through the digestive system, and helps to produce sufficient saliva and digestive juices to properly break down and digest foods.

So salt is not a villain, though poor quality salt is not your best medicine.

Grains under pressure

Pressure cooking whole grains seals in nutrients and moisture and improves the flavor and digestibility of the grain. If you do not have a pressure cooker, a pot with a heavy lid (such as an enamel lined cast-iron pot) will work well. Such a pot heats the grain from all sides and does not allow the steam to escape as in most boiling pots. (A sturdy stainless steel pot can be used. Ideally, it should have a double thick bottom for even heat distribution and to prevent burning.)

Pressure cooked grain is suitable year round. Although some people prefer to make boiled brown rice more often than pressure cooked grain in warmer weather, this is certainly not necessary. We all need the strengthening and nourishing quality of pressure cooked whole grains, regardless of the weather. Indeed, if used often, boiled whole grain can lead to vague hunger pangs because it provides much less energy than more calorie and nutrient dense pressure cooked grain. The exceptions here are rolled grains—rolled oats, etc.—which should not be pressure cooked, or cracked grains—cornmeal, polenta, etc.—which should not be pressure cooked unless combined with a much larger volume of whole grain such as rice. These grains are suitable for boiling; however, on a grain based diet cracked or rolled grains are not usually served at every meal and are often served along with a second grain dish to provide ample calories, or else cooked very thick.

Does pressure cooking reduce the cooking time for grain?

Not really. We do not pressure cook grains in order to save time. Rather, we pressure cook grains in order to make them more concentrated and digestible. It takes nearly as long to pressure cook whole grain as it does to boil them. For example, a pot of boiled brown rice takes one hour to cook. A pot of pressure cooked brown rice takes 45-60 minutes. Millet takes 30 minutes to cook at a simmer or 20-25 minutes to pressure cook. Although you won't really save time by pressure cooking grain, this way of cooking does dramatically improve the flavor and texture of grain.

The sweet taste of grain

Grains have a naturally sweet taste and become even sweeter when properly prepared. And the more you chew them, the sweeter they get. This takes practice and awareness because grains don't dance on your tongue the way sugar does, but the more you chew them the more their flavor grows on you. You may even learn to enjoy them with no adornments. When breads, pancakes, pasta, and other flour products are prepared with whole grain flour, good quality sea salt, and care, they too will taste surprisingly rich, moist, sweet, and delicious when eaten plain or with minimal toppings.

Sticky is right

When properly cooked, whole grains are moist, tender, and slightly sticky, but they have a definite taste and body. Pressure cooked rice or millet does not separate into dry kernels as its boiled counterpart does, nor is it fluffy. This is to be expected. While the slightly sticky texture of well cooked whole grain may be unfamiliar to you, particularly if you are used to hard-boiled, dry rice, you may soon come to prefer this softer grain and the improved digestion and energy it provides.

The long and short of it

We prefer short and medium grain brown rice for daily use. They produce a nuttier and slightly buttery taste and a softer, stickier texture than long grain brown rice.

Long grain brown rice is dryer, harder, and easily falls apart. It is less well suited to a low-fat grain-based diet because it falls apart so easily, is less calorie and energy dense, and tends to need more added fat and toppings to be tasty. People always seem to want to put something on it to moisten it (soy sauce or lots of butter, oil, fish, greasy chicken, etc), or to cook it with a lot of strong flavored spices, herbs, fruits, or nuts (or in chicken or beef broth). Long grain rice appears more in pilaf form and in diets where larger amounts of animal foods, nuts, seeds, and/or fruits predominate. It is also much more difficult to pick up with chopsticks than short grain rice.

Sweet brown rice produces an even stickier, sweeter and denser dish than either short or medium varieties and is particularly good for those who are very active, growing, pregnant or lactating. It is especially nice in cool or cold weather though it can be used at other times as well. (When cooking sweet brown rice, we suggest cooking it with an equal volume of millet or short grain brown rice; cooked solo it is a bit too dense, sticky, and heavy. The exception here is sweet rice that has been made into mochi then sliced and baked until lightly crisped in a waffle iron or oven, a process which counters its overly gooey and sticky qualities.)

Getting the ratio right

The texture of your cooked grain will depend as much upon the amount of liquid used, the length of soaking and cooking, and the cooking method as it does upon the grain itself. In general, the less water you use in cooking, the harder the grain will be; the more water, the softer and more digestible the finished product will be since the grain must absorb the additional water while cooking. However, grain cooked with too much water will be watery and less flavorful while grain cooked with too little water will be hard, dry, less digestible, and undercooked. Because breakfast grain (porridge or congee) is generally cooked with more water, it will be creamier in taste and softer in texture than dinner grain. You should be cautious to avoid using too much water for breakfast porridge though, because it will be almost impossible to eat enough cereal to meet your energy needs if you make your cereal like soup. If you are very active or only eating two meals a day, you may need to eat dinner grain rather than porridge or supplement your porridge with bread at breakfast.

We recommend a basic ratio of water to grain to salt which you can memorize in a short time. This will make it easy for you to cook with any grain and to produce consistent and tasty results every time. As a general rule, boiled grain requires more water than pressure cooked grain. (However, some grains, such as millet, are often cooked with nearly the same amount of water whether boiled or pressure cooked. This will be indicated in the basic recipes that follow.)

To each his own

With practice, you can turn out interesting and exciting daily meals based on whole grains, without the repetition and monotony characteristic of grain dishes commonly served in American cuisine. It is important to realize that each grain has its own unique taste and characteristics. Amaranth will never cook up like rice, no matter what you do to it. It's just not the same kind of grain. Millet won't cook up just like rice either. Millet has a character all its own. The more you cook and eat grains, the more you will come to appreciate each grain and to know its particular flavor and disposition.

Making the most of millet

While we're on the subject of millet, we have encountered many people who like rice, but claim to have no great fondness for millet. Often they say that millet is "too dry" or "too bland." They expect it to be like rice and are sorely disappointed when they discover that it is not. Millet is a different grain entirely. But it is a wonderful grain. When soaked and properly cooked with sufficient sea salt, millet yields a creamy and extraordinarily buttery tasting dish. It is smooth and creamy like polenta and very delicious.

Properly cooked millet can be served with a rice paddle or ice cream scooper; packed into a 12-ounce bowl and inverted over each serving plate; conveniently pressed into pans, allowed to firm up, then sliced like bread or polenta and served with seed or nut condiments, sauces, gravies; or simply eaten out of hand. Millet slices make an easy to reheat, excellent no-bake bread or meatloaf alternative.

Serving your daily grain

It is not necessary or desirable to cook butter, oil, sautéed vegetables, or spices into your daily whole grains. Daily whole grains should be simple and contain few ingredients. They are best and most versatile when cooked and served plain and accompanied by a variety of condiments or side dishes.

When selecting condiments to serve with your grain, try one rich topping and/or eat your grain with bites of other more highly seasoned foods. In Chinese, Japanese, and Ethiopian cuisines, the bread, pasta, or rice are used as utensils or backdrops for other more rich and colorful dishes. Every dish in the meal needn't be sauced, dressed, or embellished with overly salt, spicy, oily, or sweet toppings to be enjoyable. You will appreciate the subtle taste of grains as you eat more of them and chew them more thoroughly.

Condiments help

Nut and seed condiments make the perfect topping for daily grains. These are made from dry roasted seeds or nuts and seasoned with tamari, shoyu, umeboshi vinegar, or sea salt. These seasoned nuts and seeds are usually ground to a coarse powder after roasting, making them more digestible and making it possible to distribute them more evenly and to make a little bit go a long way. Being both salty and rich, these condiments are needed in only minute amounts—about 2-4 teaspoons per person in a given meal. They make a suitable replacement for both the salt shaker and the butter dish at the table. These may be used as frequently as you like and are one of the most nutritious and versatile condiments for grains. Their wonderful flavor will encourage you to eat more grain than you ever thought possible. Flax, sesame, or walnut oil are other options for topping grains; these can stand in for whole or ground, roasted seed or nut condiments. (Just be sure to use a teaspoon at the table to avoid over-use of oil.) Occasionally, nut or seed butters can stand in for the dry seed or nut condiments, but they should be diluted with water and a salty seasoning such as miso or tamari then used in various sauces, gravies, or dressings.

Whole grain portions & proportions

Rice and other grains more than double and sometimes triple in volume when cooked. Pressure cooked rice generally increases to two and one-half times its dry size. Thus, four cups of uncooked brown rice usually yields ten cups when cooked with five cups of water.

A good rule of thumb is: 1/2 to 1 cup of raw/dry whole grain per person per meal. (People who are not accustomed to eating much grain may eat less.) If bread, pasta, masa or some other grain product will accompany the whole grain in a given meal, figure 1/3-1/2 cup of dry whole grain per person. If cracked or rolled grains are used in a meal, double the amount of dry grain listed above to be on the safe side; cracked and rolled grains such as rolled oats, bulgur wheat, polenta, and cornmeal are less dense than whole grains such as brown rice or millet.

When eating a grain-based diet, you will want to prepare at least one pound of dry grain (2 1/3 cups dry whole grain such as rice or millet; 4 3/4 cups rolled grain such as rolled oats; or 4 cups flour) per person, per day. In our house, when the two of us are eating just two meals a day, two pounds of dry rice (4-5 cups) lasts for just 2-2 1/2 meals! When eating three meals a day, we usually find that two pounds (4-5 cups) of dry rice or millet lasts for 2 1/2-3 meals. Thus, a family of five would need to cook four or five pounds (9-12 cups) of dry whole grain in a day if whole grain will be the only grain served. (If bread or noodles are served at a meal, we go through less whole grain in a day; in this case the bread or pasta are eaten in large amounts instead of, or in addition to, whole grain.)

It is advisable to always cook enough grain to last for two to four meals (or one to two days) at a time so that you will have leftovers for pack lunches, fast suppers, or simple breakfasts. Cooking grains in quantity will save you time and energy in the kitchen and is one of surest ways to take the hassle out of meal planning. Since whole grains take longer to cook than most other dishes, having cooked grain on hand will mean that a whole meal is rarely more than 15-45 minutes away, depending on what other leftovers you happen to have on hand.

At times, you might even want to have two different cooked grain dishes on hand. This adds for variety to a meal or a day's worth of meals. For example, you might make a new pot of plain rice while you still have a bowl of rice cooked with millet. This way you can serve one grain at lunch and have a different one at supper. Various hot cereals, noodles, dumplings, breads and buns may be served along with a whole grain to extend it or they may be served instead of a whole grain. Though we usually prefer to serve whole grain at least once or twice a day, we sometimes like to have bread or pasta at one of our daily meals. We go through stages with this, sometimes making a big batch of bread on weekends to last for the week so we can have it as "the" grain for one meal each day; and sometimes going for several weeks or a couple of months without making or eating much bread. Likewise, sometimes we enjoy pasta or tamales once or twice a week, while at other times we may go for several weeks without eating pasta or even several months without eating tamales. This is highly individual, but it is best to serve some whole (uncracked, unground) grain every day because whole grains are so strengthening, centering, and integrating and eating them helps us to develop these attributes as well. If you plant a whole grain it will sprout and grow into more food. If you plant whole wheat flour or oatmeal it will not grow. Whole grains are also one of the most ecological, economical, and shelf stable foods.

Things to Cook into Your Pot of Rice or Millet for Added Variety

For best results, don't add too many different things to the grain pot or you'll end up with a real mish-mash of too many flavors vying for attention. We suggest adding just one additional grain and/or one type of bean, nut, seed, or vegetable. For a still fancier effect, try adding one vegetable and one nut or seed to a single grain. See examples below.

Note: Precook items with an (*) before adding them to the rice pot. Add nuts, seeds, dried vegetables, and/or additional grains to the pot of rice or millet before soaking. Add sea salt; if desired, also add precooked or soaked, drained beans or fresh raw vegetables just before cooking your grain.

Add a second grain:

Millet
Whole wheat berries
Rye berries
Spelt berries
Kamut berries
Amaranth
Quinoa
Ivory Teff
Chestnuts, dried
Hato mugi (Job's tears)
Wild rice
Wehani rice
Sweet brown rice
Black Thai sweet rice
Medium grain brown rice
Barley, pearl or pot variety
Polenta
Sprouted wheat berries
Sprouted rye berries
Bulgur wheat (cracked wheat)
Posole, blue*
Posole, yellow*

or add a seed or nut:

Poppy seeds
Flax seeds
Sunflower seeds
Toasted brown sesame seeds
Toasted black sesame seeds
Walnuts, chopped
Almonds, chopped
Hazelnuts, chopped
Lotus seeds (very low in fat)
Pine nuts (pignolias)
Peanuts, raw
Caraway seeds

or add a bean or legume:

Black turtle beans
Garbanzo beans
Whole dried peas
Azuki beans
Small red beans
Kidney beans
Chestnuts, dried
Lentils, brown or green
Black soybeans*
Yellow soybeans*
Pinto beans
Black eyed peas
White kidney beans
Navy beans
Lima beans*
Cubed tofu

or add a vegetable:

Corn of the cob
Winter squash, cubed
Carrot, diced
Turnip, cubed
Sweet potato, diced
Cauliflower, cut
Fresh green peas
Red or green bell peppers, diced
Dried sweet corn
Sun dried tomato, chopped
Lotus root, diced
Kelp or kombu sea vegetable

Favorite Seasonal Whole Grain Combinations

Spring Favorites

Millet with Chestnuts or Chickpeas
Sweet Rice with Millet & beans
Millet with Poppy Seeds +/- Herbs
Brown Rice or Millet with Polenta
Brown Rice with Sunflower Seeds
Brown Rice with Lentils
Brown Rice with Whole Dried Peas
Brown Rice with Chestnuts or Chickpeas
Brown Rice with Sprouted Rye Berries
Brown Rice with Sprouted Wheat
Brown Rice with Millet & Chickpeas
Brown Rice with Hato Mugi

Year Round favorites

Millet
Millet with Hato Mugi
Millet with Fresh or Dried Chestnuts
Millet with Brown Rice & Beans
Millet with Amaranth
Millet with Quinoa
Brown Rice with Millet
Sweet Brown Rice with Millet
Brown Rice (Short or Medium Grain)
Brown Rice, Millet & Azuki or Black soybeans
Brown Rice, Millet & Chickpeas, or Black Beans
Brown Rice with Amaranth
Brown Rice with Dried Chestnuts
Brown Rice with Beans
Brown Rice with Hato Mugi or Pearled Barley
Brown Rice with Roasted Seeds

Summer Favorites

Millet with Sweet Corn
Millet with Fresh Green Peas
Millet with Polenta
Polenta with Brown Rice
Brown Rice with Quinoa
Brown Rice with Sprouted Rye
Brown Rice with Sweet Corn

Fall Favorites

Millet or Rice with Sweet Corn
Millet with Squash or Sweet Potato
Millet with Turnips or Cauliflower
Brown Rice with Polenta
Brown Rice with Millet
Brown Rice with Wheat or Spelt Berries
Brown Rice with Quinoa
Sweet Rice with Brown Rice & Black Beans

Winter favorites

Millet with Turnips or Winter Squash
Sweet Rice, Millet & Chestnuts
Millet with Walnuts or Peanuts
Brown Rice with Wild or Wehani Rice
Brown Rice, Sweet Rice & Squash
Brown Rice with Posole
Sweet Rice, Millet & Beans
Rice with Peanuts or Walnuts
Brown & Sweet Rice with Azuki Beans
Sweet Rice, Millet & Walnuts or Almonds
Sweet Rice, Millet & Black soybeans

Note that the brown rice referred to here is short or medium grain brown rice.

COOKING GRAINS BY THE BOOK

Basic Ratios and Cooking Times

Hard Shelled Grains (brown rice, sweet brown rice, barley, wheat berries, etc)

Cooking method:	Grain:	Water:	Sea salt:	Cooking time:
Boiling	1 cup grain	1 3/4-2 cups water	1/8 tsp.	50-60 minutes
Pressure cooking	1 cup grain	1 1/4-1 1/3 cup water	1/8 tsp.	45-60 minutes*

*Note: Cooking times may vary with the amount of pressure and temperature used

*Note: Add proper amount of sea salt to grain after soaking, but before cooking.

Soft Shelled Grains (millet, quinoa, amaranth, teff, buckwheat, cornmeal, etc.)

Cooking method:	Grain:	Water:	Sea salt:	Cooking time:
Boiling	1 cup grain	2 cups water	1/8 tsp.	30-35 minutes
Pressure cooking	1 cup grain	1 1/3-2 cups water	1/8 tsp.	20-30 minutes

*Caution: if pressure cooking cornmeal and other small grains, you must cook them with a larger volume of millet or rice, or use the covered bowl-within-a-pot method so that you do not clog the pressure valves.

Hard Shelled Grain + Soft Shelled Grain

Cooking method:	Grain:	Water:	Sea salt:	Cooking time:
Boiling	see above	see above	see above	as per longest cooking grain
Pressure cooking	see above	see above	see above	as per longest cooking grain

When adding beans to grain

Beans or chestnuts:	Water:	Sea salt:
1 cup dry unsoaked chestnuts	1 1/2-2 cups additional water	1/4 tsp. additional sea salt
1 cup dry unsoaked beans	1 1/2-2 cups additional water	1/4 tsp. additional sea salt
(soak beans; drain then add to grain)	no extra water is needed	(add above volume extra salt)
1 cup precooked beans	no extra water is needed	1/4 tsp. additional sea salt

Note: When adding uncooked beans to a pot of grain; first soak the beans, drain, then add to the grain pot just before cooking. (Azuki beans or lentils, however, may be soaked directly with the dry grain without discarding the soak water. In this case, add 2 cups of water to the grain for each cup of dry, unsoaked beans.)

When adding vegetables, nuts, or seeds to grain:

• No extra water is needed for vegetables, seeds, or nuts. (Treat lotus seeds and chestnuts like a grain: add them to the grain in soaking, with an additional 2 cups of water per cup dry lotus seeds or chestnuts.)

• Add vegetables to the pot just before cooking.

• Add raw seeds or nuts when soaking grain, or stir roasted seeds or nuts into just cooked grain.

Soaking Times

Item:	length of soaking time recommended
Hard shelled grains	several hours, all day, or overnight (especially for barley)
Soft shelled grains	several hours (not required for buckwheat or polenta)
Beans, dry, uncooked	several hours, preferably overnight, varies with kind
Precooked beans	none (add these just before cooking grain)
Chestnuts, dried	several hours or overnight, unless using fresh-frozen, peeled variety
Nuts or seeds	preferably several hours or overnight (see notes above)

• **Special notes:** Cook the grain in its soak water.

Tips for Washing, Soaking, and Cooking Whole Grains

Washing & scrubbing

Rinse and scrub whole grains in the cooking pot or a large bowl. To do this, add cool or cold water to cover grains. Rub them between your hands using a back and forth motion then pour through a strainer. (Use a fine mesh strainer for millet or quinoa.) Repeat several times until the water is nearly clear. Do not rinse cracked or rolled grains such as bulgur wheat, cornmeal, polenta, or oatmeal. Do not rinse buckwheat/kasha—it gets soggy— or tiny seed grains such as teff or amaranth which are too difficult to wash due to their small size.

Soaking

Soak all grains (except bulgur or cracked wheat) directly in the pot you intend to cook them in. To do this, after washing, scrubbing and draining the grain as described above, add the recommended amount of water. When adding dried beans, sort to remove any stones then rinse, drain, and soak in a separate bowl with additional water. When adding seeds or nuts, soak them with the grain (unless you want to dry roast them and stir them into the grain after it is cooked). For best results and optimal digestion and assimilation, soak grain for several hours, all day, or overnight—particularly when using brown rice, barley; wheat, rye, or spelt berries, millet, teff, amaranth, or quinoa. Soak quinoa when combining and cooking it with other grains. (Do not soak bulgur wheat or cracked wheat as these absorb too much water. Soaking buckwheat/kasha is optional.)

Whole Grain Classifications

Hard Shelled Grains:

Medium grain brown rice
Short grain brown rice
Sweet brown rice
Barley, pearled or pot variety
Wild or wehani rice
Long grain brown rice
Whole wheat berries
Whole spelt berries
Whole rye berries
Whole kamut berries

Soft Shelled Grains:

Millet
Amaranth
Teff
Quinoa
Kasha (roasted buckwheat)
White buckwheat
Chinese pearl barley
(a.k.a. Jobs's tears/hato mugi)

Cracked Grains:

Polenta
Cornmeal
Bulgur wheat
Spelt bulgur
Cracked wheat
Riz cous (cracked rice)

Adding sea salt

Add sea salt just before cooking for best results. If you wish to add a strip of kelp or kombu sea vegetable (to further tenderize your grain), add this before soaking. (A 4 to 6-inch strip will suffice.)

Grains Combinations

Pearled or pot barley, Chinese pearl barley (hato mugi or Job's Tears), wild rice, wehani rice; or whole wheat, rye, spelt, or kamut berries should be combined with three to four parts short or medium grain brown rice for best results (and often for economy as well). These grains also need lengthy soaking— from four to twelve hours— for optimal flavor and digestion. Whole grain berries may also be sprouted for several days prior to being cooked with brown rice (e.g., 1 cup of dry wheat berries produces 4 cups of sprouts which can be combined with 3 cups of brown rice). Amaranth, quinoa, or teff should be combined with two to three parts short grain brown rice, medium grain brown rice, millet, or rolled oat (for economy, optimal flavor, and maximum digestibility).

Mixing two grains

You can combine two different grains in the same pot: you might try two hard shelled grains; two soft shelled grains; or one hard and one soft shelled grain. Whichever option you choose, always cook the grain as per the time recommended for the longest cooking grain.

Adding beans, nuts, or seeds to grain

Soak dried beans separately then drain and add to your grain before cooking or, precook beans then stir them into warm grain just after it has finished cooking. Figure 1/4-1/3 cup dry beans or chestnuts per each cup of dry rice or millet (1 cup dry beans per 3-4 cups whole grain). Dried chestnuts, nuts, or seeds can be added to your grain when soaking.

If using nuts or seeds, figure 2-4 Tbsp. nuts or seeds per cup dry whole grain (1/2-3/4 cup nuts or seeds 4 cups of dry whole grain). We usually prefer to add raw seeds or nuts to the grain pot when soaking, though we occasionally dry roast then stir them into cooked, warm grain before serving. This retains a nuttier texture. Or you can stir raw seeds into the grain after cooking.

Don't pressure cook rolled/cracked grains or buckwheat

Rolled grains, cracked grains, and buckwheat (kasha) should not be pressure cooked as they can clog the pressure cooker valves. Boil these grains with brown rice or millet or boil them alone and mix them with warm, freshly cooked or leftover (resteamed) brown rice or polenta. Cracked grains such as polenta or cornmeal can be pressure cooked, but only if combined with a much larger volume of millet or brown rice.

Cooking grain

Add sea salt to pot of soaked grains and place over medium to medium-high heat. Allow about 10-15 minutes for the pot to come to boil or pressure. Start counting the cooking time, only after the grain has come to either a full boil or to full pressure. (Set a timer if needed) a larger or fuller pot of grain will take longer to come to boil or pressure than a smaller, less full pot. The type of stove you have can also affect the amount of time it takes to come to boil or pressure. (If you are pressure cooking a small amount of grain, refer to the bowl-within-a-pot/pressure cooker method.)

No-fuss, no-stir technique

Do not stir the grain before or during cooking. Not only is it unnecessary, but stirring the grain as it cooks or comes to boil will cause the starches to separate, preventing steam from rising up and cooking the grain evenly. Stirring grain as it cooks leads to sticky grain and burned pots. Simply cover the pot, bring it to boil, reduce the heat to low or medium-low, and let it cook. Do not stir, and do not lift the lid or steam will escape. The boiling water will do all the stirring necessary leaving you free to do other things while your grain cooks. (Polenta is the exception to this rule— it is a coarse flour or meal which requires stirring if it is cooked on its own. Cooked with brown rice, millet, or rolled oats, however, it needs no stirring.)

Using a heat deflector/flame tamer:

Slipping a heat deflector under the pot before turning it to low will keep your grain from burning on the bottom.

If you are using a gas stove, slip the heat deflector/flame tamer under the pot once it has come to a full boil or full pressure (with loud hissing).

When using an electric stove, preheat the deflector on a separate burner over medium heat while your grain comes to boil or pressure on a different burner. Transfer your boiling or hissing pot to the deflector and turn the heat to low or medium-low. Electric stoves take a long time to heat so it is crucial to preheat the flame deflector to keep the pot from losing pressure or temperature. Gas stoves respond much more quickly, are easier to use, and produce the best tasting food. If you have an electric stove, you will have to learn to adapt to its nuances.

After cooking

If possible, let the grain pot sit undisturbed for 10-15 minutes after cooking. During this time, the steam in the pot will lift any stuck grain off the bottom then your grain will then be ready to stir and serve. Grain cooks differently depending on where it is in the pot. (Some parts are in direct contact with heat, others are not. It is vitally important to stir the cooked grain before serving; this will evenly distribute the moisture and the crust. Use a large wooden rice paddle to mix the grain well, mixing from top to bottom and mixing the sides into the middle. Stir in any crust (unless it is black). A golden brown crust is very tasty and strengthening.

Removing grain from the pot

This is important. Grain left in the cooking pot too long will keep cooking and will turn mushy and solidify into one big lump as it cools. Transfer cooked grain to a glass, stainless steel, pottery, pyrex, or ceramic dish and cover loosely with a bamboo sushi mat to keep warm and allow air to circulate. Your grain will stay warm this way for one-half to one hour. (Don't cover grain with a lid or it will keep cooking. Storing it with a lid will also invite mold and cause the grain to sour rapidly so we recommend storing it covered with a bamboo sushi mat.) Instead of washing the pot straightaway, you can use the unwashed pot to soak and cook tomorrow's breakfast cereal in if it is the appropriate size,-not too large. This means one less pot to wash and makes for a tasty breakfast.

Storing leftover grain

Cooked grain may be stored at room temperature in a bowl, covered with a bamboo mat, for 24-48 hours. If you have a cold box (a cupboard with an air vent to the out-doors found in many old houses), cooked grain may be placed on a shelf in such a box. Otherwise, your cooked grain can be kept on the counter, in a corner, and away from direct sunlight. Grain is tastiest if not refrigerated. When refrigerated, it becomes dry and is sapped of its vital energy. Freezing definitely is not recommended. When frozen, cooked whole grain explodes and become watery and tasteless. If beans or vegetables are cooked into grain, use it within 24-36 hours or refrigerate it in a bowl with a plate on top. Grain dishes made with sautéed ingredients should be used within 24 hours or refrigerated.

Serving leftover grain

Reheat leftover grain by steaming it in an uncovered bowl on top of a steamer tray or vegetable steamer basket or in a stainless steel bowl placed within a pot. Heat only as much grain as you think you will use up within a meal or within a day. Heating up the whole batch at once wastes energy and will cause leftover grain to lose flavor and/or to sour prematurely. Even dry millet or rice are revived when resteamed for 15-30 minutes (this can be done while other leftovers heat up or fresh foods cook).

When taking a pack lunch, store and serve leftover cooked grain at room temperature. Avoid using a microwave oven to cook or heat any food, whether fresh or leftover. Microwave ovens rob foods of their vital energy. See Chapter 2 for uses for leftover grain and for steaming and reheating tips.

Rice To Water Ratio for Pressure Cooking:	
Brown Rice:	Water
2 cups:	3 cups water
3 cups:	4 cups water
4 cups:	5-5 1/2 cups water
5 cups:	6-6 1/2 cups water
6 cups:	7 1/2 cups water

Note:

- The above ratios may be used for brown rice cooked with a second grain: rice with hato mugi; rice with sweet rice; rice with amaranth, etc.

- As you increase the amount of rice, or rice with a second grain, the amount of water needed for each cup of grain goes down.

- Figure 1 1/4-1 1/3 cup water per cup of brown rice, more for batches of less than 3 cups rice.

- Figure 2 cups water per cup millet, pollenta, quinoa , or pearled or pot barley.

- Remember that a pressure cooker should be at least half-full when cooking grain. Thus, you will need to cook at least 3 cups of brown rice in a 3 1/2-4 quart pressure cooker, if you cook the grain directly in the pot. Smaller batches should be cooked with the bowl-within-a-pot method.

Basic Procedure, Pressure Cooked or Boiled Brown Rice (Year Round)***

Prep: 5 minutes
Soaking: from 3-24 hours
Cooking: 45-60 minutes

Serving size: 1 1/2-3 cups per person
Serves: 4-8 (or 2-4 meals for 2)

When soaked several hours or overnight, pressure cooked brown rice has a sweet, rich flavor and is far easier to digest than unsoaked and/or boiled rice. While it may sound troublesome, it only takes a little advance planning to soak your grain. This is best done before you run out of cooked grain. Soak the rice before bed, then cook it first thing in the morning or later in the day, or soak it first thing in the morning and cook it in the afternoon or evening. We always make enough to last for 2-4 meals at a time.

Rules of thumb:

Amount of uncooked whole grain per person:
   1/2-1 cup dry grain per person, per meal
Water to grain ratio (to pressure cook):
   1 1/4-1 1/3 cups water per cup of dry grain
Water to grain ratio (to boil): 1 1/2-1 3/4 cups water per cup of dry grain
Grain to salt ratio: 1/8 tsp. sea salt per cup of dry grain

4 cups short or medium grain brown rice (or combination of the two grains)

5 cups water to pressure cook (7 cups water to boil)

1/2 tsp. sun dried sea salt

1. Wash, scrub and drain whole grains. (If desired, save rinse water in a basin for house plants or the garden.) Transfer grain to a pressure cooker or a heavy pot if not already there. Add cooking water as per recommended proportions. Allow grain to soak, either uncovered or covered with a bamboo sushi mat, at room temperature, for 4-24 hours.

2. Do not pour or drain off soak water. Add sea salt. Cover the pot and cook.

   To pressure cook: Bring to pressure over medium heat. When the pot begins to hiss loudly, slip a heat deflector under the pot, reduce heat to medium-low, and cook 45-60 minutes. If you omit the heat deflector, use a low heat.

   To boil: Bring covered pot to a boil over medium heat without stirring. Use a heat deflector as above. (If using an electric stove, see Hints.) Simmer on low for 50-60 minutes. Do not remove the lid or stir during cooking.

3. When cooking time has elapsed turn off heat. If using a pressure cooker, allow about 15 minutes for the pressure to come down naturally; if you can't wait, run the pressure cooker under cold water or stick it in a basin of cold water to bring the pressure down quickly. If boiling, allow 10-15 minutes of resting time before stirring. (In this time, the steam will condense in the pot and lift any stuck grain off the bottom.)

4. Stir thoroughly with a wooden or bamboo rice paddle, mixing from top to bottom and incorporating the rice from the sides into the middle. Stir in any brown crust from the bottom of the pot. (The crust is very tasty, unless it is black!) Transfer grain to a glass, wood, or ceramic serving bowl. Cover with a bamboo sushi mat.

Serving suggestions: Serve with soup or stew, a green or mixed vegetable side dish or dishes, and condiments. (Serve rice from an ice cream scoop, a rice paddle, or pack servings into a 10-12 ounce bowl and invert over each plate.)

Storage: Store leftovers at room temperature, covered with a bamboo mat. There is no need to refrigerate leftover rice. It will not spoil if cooked with sea salt stored in a glass, pottery, or wooden bowl, covered loosely, and kept out of direct sunlight.

Note: Grain cooked in animal fat, dairy products, meat broths, or with sugers will spoil quickly. Refrigeration will negatively alter the taste, texture, and value of the grain. Use leftovers within 2 1/2 days for optimal flavor and nutrition.

Steam heat leftovers using the uncovered bowl-within-a-pot method. For meals eaten away from home, serve leftover grain at room temperature. ❏

Variations on the Basic Rice

Cook any of the variations listed below using the same basic ratio of salt to water to grain

Rice with a Second Grain (Year Round)***

Prep: 5 minutes
Soaking: from 3-24 hours
Cooking: 45-60 minutes

Serving size: 1-3 cups per average person
Serves: 4-8 (or 2-4 meals for 2)

3 cups short or medium grain brown rice

1 cup other whole grain (hard shelled or soft-shelled grain—see suggestions below)

5-5 1/3 cups water to pressure cook (7 cups water to boil)

1/2 tsp. sun dried sea salt

1. Replace 1 cup of short or medium grain brown rice in the basic recipe with an equal volume of a second whole grain. We also enjoy a 50:50 ratio of sweet rice with millet or sweet rice with short or medium grain brown rice.

2. Follow the instructions as given in the basic recipe: (Use 2 cups water per cup of dry millet, barley, or wheat, spelt, or rye berries; these are a bit dryer than rice.)

Special notes:

• Rinse millet and quinoa in a fine mesh strainer but do not rinse other small seed grains such as teff or amaranth. Add the seed grains to the rice after washing it. Add the amount of water called for in the basic recipe. Soak, and cook as above.

Favorites:

• Rice & Millet
• Rice & Sweet Rice
• Hato Mugi (Job's Tears) & Rice
• Sweet Rice & Millet
• Rice & Chestnuts
• Rice & Rye
• Rice & Wheat Berries
• Rice & Spelt
• Rice & Kamut
• Polenta-Rice
• Rice & Amaranth
• Rice with Quinoa
• Rice & Teff

Essene Rice (Spring, Summer)***

1. For a sweet and chewy rice that tastes like Essene bread, sprout 1 cup of dry wheat, rye, kamut, or spelt berries in a quart jar covered with a screen or mesh lid. (This will yield 4 cups sprouts.)

2. Soak berries overnight in a quart jar filled with water to cover.

3. Cover jar with a screen or mesh lid and store at room temperature on the counter or in the cupboard, placed on its side and tilted at an angle to allow for drainage. (A pyrex loaf/bread pan is ideal for this. The jar may be tilted across the width of the bread pan for the entire sprouting process.) Store for three days, rinsing berries two or three times per day.

4. Wash and sort 3-4 cups short or medium grain brown rice. Soak in appropriate amount of water for 4-8 hours before cooking. If using 3 cups of rice, use 5 cups of water to pressure cook or 7 cups to boil. If using 4 cups of rice, use 6 2/3 cups of water to pressure cook or 7-8 cups to boil.

5. Add the sprouts and salt before pressure cooking or add sprouts during the last 4 hours of soaking.

6. Cook as per Basic Procedure, Rice, above.

Posole Rice (Fall, Winter, Spring)***

1. Start with 1 cup whole dried corn (red, yellow, blue, or white posole). Soak, cook, rinse and drain according to Basic Procedure, for Posole.

2. Wash 3-4 cups of short or medium grain brown rice. Soak as per basic procedure. Add cooked mashed, drained posole when soaking (or add cooked posole just before cooking rice). No additional water is needed. Add an extra 1/8 tsp. of sea salt per cup dry posole that you started with.

3. Cook as per Basic Procedure, Rice, above.

Roasted Rice (Year Round)

1. Rinse and drain short or medium grain brown rice.

2. Dry roast in one or two batches in a wok or cast iron skillet, stirring constantly over medium heat until the grains start to pop, smell nutty, and turn golden. Do not allow grains to turn dark or burn.

3. When the rice is almost done roasting, bring the cooking water and salt to boil in a pressure cooker. Immediately add the warm, roasted rice; seal the pot; then pressure cook as per Basic Procedure, Brown Rice.

Note: If using the bowl-within-a-pot method, get the pot and bowl ready; add the roasted rice and sea salt to the small stainless steel bowl; pour the boiling water over the grain; seal the pot, then pressure cook as per Basic Procedure but with a slighly higher flame. Roasted rice may be simmered in a pot with a heavy lid, but it is not nearly as tasty as when pressure cooked. ❏

Beans-In-Rice (Year Round)***

Prep: 5 minutes
Soaking: from 3-24 hours
Cooking: 45-60 minutes

Serving size: 1-1 1/2 cups per average person
Serves: 4-8 (or 2-4 meals for 2)

4 cups short or medium grain brown rice

5 cups water to pressure cook; 7 cups water to boil

3/4-1 tsp. sun dried sea salt

1 cup dry beans:

(Chickpeas or garbanzo beans; small red, kidney, navy, pinto, azuki/aduki, black turtle beans; lentils; whole dried green peas; dried chestnuts, lotus seeds; or other)

3 cups water to soak beans (this will be discarded)

1. Wash and soak rice as per Basic Procedure, Rice. If using dried chestnuts or lotus seeds, add to washed grain then add 2 cups of water per cup of dried lotus seeds or chestnuts.

2. In a separate bowl, wash and soak 3/4-1 cup dry beans in 2-3 cups of water. (Note: Dried chestnuts and louts seeds may be treated like beans, except that we don't discard their soak water.)

3. After soaking time has elapsed (4-12 hours), drain beans and add to uncooked rice. (No additional water will be needed.)

4. Add salt and cook as per Basic Procedure, Rice.

Note: If using precooked beans, figure 2-3 cups cooked beans per 3-4 cups dry rice. Add to rice with sea salt just before cooking. Add sea salt (the same amount as recommended for uncooked beans: 1/4-1/2 tsp. sea salt per cup dry beans or per 2-3 cups precooked beans. Cook as per Basic Procedure, Rice

Variation:

• **Soybeans-in Rice:** Soak and precook black or yellow soybeans separately then add to rice with sea salt just before cooking.

Alternatively, dry roast black soybeans in a cast iron skillet until the skins split, turn brown, and smell nutty. Do this in a 300° F oven, or stir constantly on top of the stove over medium heat. Soak the roasted beans with short grain brown rice or brown rice with sweet rice. Add an additional 2 cups water per cup dry beans. Add sea salt (1/8 tsp. for each cup of rice plus 1/4-1/2 tsp. per cup of dry beans). Cook as per Basic Procedure, Rice.

Favorites:

- **Chickpeas-in-Rice**
- **Whole Dried Green Peas-in-Rice**
- **Rice with Black Soybeans**
- **Azuki Beans-in-Rice**
- **Rice with Chestnuts**
- **Lotus Seed-in-Rice**
- **Rice with Lentils**
- **Rice with Wheat Meat:** Dice and add 1/4 cup wheat meat (seitan) per cup of dry rice before cooking rice.
- **Sesame & Seitan Rice:** For 4 cups of uncooked brown rice, stir 1/2 cup of dry roasted sesame seeds into the pot after the Rice with Wheat Meat has cooked. ❏

Sweet Rice, with Rice & Beans or Sweet Rice, Millet & Beans (Fall, Winter, Spring)***

- Short or medium grain brown rice; rice + sweet rice or sweet rice + millet. (Try 50% brown rice with 50% sweet brown rice or millet, or three parts brown rice with one part sweet rice or millet).

- **Sweet Rice, Millet & Chickpeas**
- **Sweet Rice, Millet & Green Peas**
- **Sweet Rice, Rice & Black Soybeans** (See notes for soybeans in rice above)
- **Rice, Hato Mugi, & Black Soybeans** (See notes for soybeans in rice above)

- **Sweet Rice, Rice & Azuki Beans**
- **Sweet Rice, Millet & Chestnuts**
- **Sweet Rice, Brown Rice & Chestnuts**
- **Sweet Rice, Millet & Lotus Seeds** ❏

Nutty or Seeded Rice (Year Round)***

Add 2-4 Tbsp. seeds or nuts per cup of dry short or medium grain brown rice, sweet rice + rice, or sweet rice + millet. (e.g., 1/3-3/4 cup seeds or nuts per 3 cups dry grain, or 1/2-1 cup seeds or nuts per 4 cups dry grain.)

Try raw flax, poppy, pumpkin, sunflower, or chia seeds, or chopped raw almonds, walnuts, or hazelnuts, or whole raw peanuts or pine nuts.

Or, lightly dry roast sesame, flax, or poppy seeds and add to grain after it has soaked but before it has cooked. Or, stir the roasted seeds or nuts into the warm grain after it has cooked.

Serving suggestions: Omit nut or seed condiments at the table when serving grain which contains nuts or seeds. (Lotus seeds or chestnuts are the exception: they are very low in fat (more like beans) and we usually serve them with a seed or nut condiment.) Serve oil-free or low-fat side dishes and condiments. You might try serving a sea vegetable condiment or a baked, nishime, or kinpira root or round vegetable dish and/or a sea vegetable condiment or side dish. Be sure to serve your grain with sautéed greens or a pressed, marinated, or boiled salad. A vegetable soup would also make a nice addition (with or instead of a root or green vegetable dish).

Favorites:

- **Rice with Pine Nuts**
- **Peanuts-in-Rice**
- **Poppy Seed Rice**
- **Sunflower Rice**
- **Sweet Rice, Millet & Walnuts**
- **Sweet Rice, Millet & Peanuts**
- **Sweet Rice, Rice & Almonds** ❏

Vegetable Rice (Year Round)***

- Add 2 cups diced winter squash, sweet potato, or fresh corn off the cob to the grain pot just before cooking. (If using corn, cut corn off cobs then cook the bare corn cobs and corn silk to make a stock; cool it; then use this as part of the soaking/cooking water. Remove the cobs after cooking and before stirring.).

- **Rice with Fresh Sweet Corn** (Summer, Fall)
- **Rice with Dried Sweet Corn** (Winter, Spring)
- **Rice with Winter Squash** (Fall, Winter)
- **Sweet Rice, Millet & Squash** (Fall, Winter)
- **Sweet Rice, Millet & Sweet Potato** (Fall, Winter)

Pressure Cooking a Small Batch of Whole Grain

- A pressure cooker works best when at least half full. If you want to cook just one or two cups of dry whole grain, use the *uncovered-bowl-within-a-pot method* below. Alternatively, use an Ohsawa Pot, a special ceramic insert with a lid designed specifically for pressure cooking.

1. Wash and drain grain as per Basic Procedure. In a small stainless steel bowl (or ceramic Ohsawa pot), soak whole grain in the cooking water. Be sure that the bowl allows room for expansion during cooking. Soak several hours or overnight, if possible.

2. Add sea salt to soaked grain. Fill a pressure cooker with about 1/2-1 inch of water. Place the bowl in the bottom of the pot. The water level should rise to one-third to one-half the height of the bowl. If it comes up higher, remove the bowl and pour off some of the surrounding water in the pot.

3. Do not cover the stainless steel bowl. Cover the Ohsawa pot with its special lid. Seal the pressure cooker and bring it to full pressure. Cook without a heat deflector, over medium or medium-high heat for 45-60 minutes.

4. When pressure comes down, remove the bowl from the pot, stir well and serve.

TROUBLESHOOTING: Problems with your grain?

- **The grain burned on the bottom:**

(a) You didn't use a heat deflector

(b) the heat was not turned down after the pot came to boil or pressure or heat was too high

(c) not enough water was used

(d) the grain was cooked too long (perhaps you lost track of time?)

- **The grain was undercooked, hard and dry:**

(a) Not enough water was used with the grain, or, if dry chestnuts, millet, or barley were added, not enough extra water was added

(b) the pot did not come to a full boil or full pressure, with loud hissing before you turned the heat down

(c) temperature was turned too low after it came to boil or pressure

(e) the grain was not cooked long enough

(d) you did not adequately stir the grain from top to bottom after it finished cooking.

- **The grain was soggy:**

(a) You stirred the grain while it was coming to boil or during cooking

(b) too much water was used*

(c) you left the lid on for too long after cooking or you let the rice cool in the pot

(d) see above notes for undercooked grain.

- **The grain was bland:**

(a) You forgot to add the sea salt

(b) you didn't use enough sea salt for the grain or for the added beans, seeds, or nuts.

- **The pot lost pressure:**

(a) The pot was not brought to full pressure

(b) the heat was turned down too soon or too low after full pressure was reached

(c) the heat deflector was not preheated (with electric stove)

(d) the temperature was turned down too low during cooking. ❏

Basic Procedure, Boiled or Pressure Cooked Millet (Year Round)***

Prep: 5 minutes
Soaking: 3-12 hours or overnight

Cooking: 20-35 minutes
Serving size: 1-3 cups per person

Millet is moist, tender and delicious when soaked and properly cooked. The grains should not be fluffy or distinct, rather, they will be soft and smooth like polenta.

Serves: 3-6 (or 2-3 meals for 2)

3 cups of millet
  (or mixed grain combination below)
5-6 cups water to pressure cook *(6 cups to boil)*
1/3 tsp. sun dried sea salt

Serves 5-8 (or 2 1/2-4 meals for 2)

4 cups millet
  (or mixed grain combination below)
6-8 cups water *(8 cups to boil)*
1/2 tsp. sea salt

1. Rinse millet in a bowl, scrub with your hands, drain with a fine mesh strainer and repeat several times. Put the millet in a stainless steel pressure cooker with the appropriate amount of water. If boiling, put millet n a heavy glass, enamel-lined cast iron, or stainless steel pot with a heavy, tight fitting lid.)

2. Soak 4-6 hours or overnight, uncovered or covered with a bamboo sushi mat on the counter. (Omit soaking in emergencies when pressed for time, you forgot to soak, etc.)

3. Do not throw off soak water. Add the sea salt.

   To pressure cook: Cover and seal the pot. Bring to pressure over medium heat. When the pot hisses loudly, slip a heat deflector underneath the pot, reduce heat to medium-low and cook 20-30 minutes.

   To boil: Cover pot, bring to a boil over medium heat without stirring, slip a heat deflector under the pot, reduce heat to low and simmer 30-35 minutes. Do not stir or remove lid during cooking.

4. When cooking time has elapsed, let pressure come down naturally. (This takes 10-15 minutes.) If you boiled the grain, let it cool 10-15 minutes before stirring. During this waiting period, the steam will lift any stuck grain off the bottom of the pot, eliminating the need to scrub the pot.

5. Stir well and mash millet against the sides of the pot using a wooden rice paddle. Transfer to a glass, wood, pottery, or ceramic serving bowl and cover loosely with a bamboo sushi mat.

Serving suggestions: Serve with rice paddle or a wet ice cream scoop, or pack each serving into an 8-12 ounce bowl then invert over each serving plate. Some good toppings for millet include: seasoned seed or nut condiment or flax or sesame oil and/or sea vegetable condiments; baked, stewed, or refried beans; pesto, vegetable sauces or gravies. Nice garnishes include dried or fresh chives, garlic chives, fresh dill, parsley, or edible flowers added to individual servings at the table.

For Millet "Polenta" Slices: Pack warm grain into a round, square, or oblong cake pan, pie plate, or bread tin. Smooth it out with a wet spatula. Allow it to firm up briefly, 15 minutes or up to several hours. Slice like cornbread, pie, meatloaf or bread. Serve warm or at room temperature with soup or stew, a vegetable side dish or dishes, and condiments.

Storage: Store leftovers on the counter at room temperature covered with a bamboo mat. Reheat by steaming in an uncovered bowl or using the bowl-within-a-pot method. Steam heat slices or squares on a plate on top of a rack/tray. Use leftovers within 2 1/2 days for optimal taste and nutrition. Small amounts of leftovers can be cubed and cooked into breakfast cereal. ❑

Variations on the Basic Millet

Use the basic proportions of water and salt to grain listed in Basic Procedure, Millet above. Soak and cook as above. Any combination which includes beans, seeds, or nuts, will be more flavorful and digestible if pressure cooked rather than boiled. Any combination may be served soft, in scoops, or by the slice.

Millet with a Second Grain (Year Round) ***

Replace 1 cup of millet in the basic recipe with 1 cup of another grain: brown rice, Chinese hato mugi barley (Job's Tears); amaranth; teff; quinoa; or polenta or cornmeal. Add a four to six inch strip of kelp or kombu to the pot if desired. Do not rinse rolled or cracked grains (polenta or cornmeal) or tiny seed grains such as amaranth or teff. Wash quinoa to remove the bitter saponin coating it contains. For a nice mock cornbread, try Millet & Polenta.

Favorites:

- **Millet, Amaranth & Kelp**
- **Millet & Quinoa**
- **Millet & Polenta** (or coarse cornmeal)
- Also see **Millet & Sweet Rice**. ❏

Topping Suggestions for Millet with a Second Grain: Millet combinations are especially good with a seasoned seed or nut condiment or flax or sesame oil and/or a sea vegetable condiment or side dish. Or try Mochi-zy Chickpea Sauce, refried beans, and/or other side dishes.

Basic Beans-In-Millet (Year Round)***

Prep: 5 minutes
Soaking: 3-12 hours or overnight
Cooking: 20-35 minutes

Serving size: 1-3 cups per person
Serves: 5-8 (or 2-4 meals for 2)

4 cups millet

6-7 cups water to pressure cook *(8 cups if boiling)*

1 cup dry, uncooked beans
   (lentils; chickpeas; azuki, small red, anasazi, kidney, black turtle or navy beans; whole dried green peas; dried or steam-peeled fresh-frozen chestnuts; or lotus seeds)

3 cups water to soak (this will be drained off before cooking)

3/4-1 tsp. sun dried, mineral rich sea salt

1. Wash and soak millet as per Basic Procedure, Millet, above.

2. In a separate bowl, wash and soak 3/4-1 cup dry beans in 2-3 cups of water.

3. After soaking 4-12 hours, drain beans and add to uncooked millet. (No additional water will be needed.) Add salt and cook as per Basic Procedure, Millet. The finished product can be pressed into loaf pans, sliced, and served with a gravy, refried beans, or seed condiment; or it can be served from an ice cream scoop or packed into 8-12 oz. bowls and inverted over individual serving plates.

Note: If using precooked beans, figure 2-3 cups cooked beans per 3-4 cups dry millet. Add them to millet and sea salt before cooking. (1/2 tsp. sea salt per cup dry beans or per 2-3 cups precooked beans.) Cook as per Basic Procedure, Rice.

Favorites:

- **Millet with Lentils**
- **Millet with Chickpeas**
- **Millet with Chestnuts**
- **Millet with Whole Dried Peas**
- **Millet & Whole Lotus Seeds** ❏

Millet & Lentil Meat-less Loaf (Fall, Winter)

Prep: 5 minutes
Soaking: 3-12 hours or overnight
Cooking: 20-35 minutes

Serving size: 1-3 cups per person;
Serves: 3-6 (or 2-3 meals for 2)
or more as a side dish grain

2 cups millet

1 cup lentils

6" piece kelp or kombu sea vegetable

5 cups water to pressure cook (6 cups to boil)

1 small onion, minced.

2 fresh or dried shiitake mushrooms

1/2-3/4- tsp. sea salt

1. Wash and drain millet. Soak as per Basic Procedure, Millet, but add the kelp or kombu now. If using dried shiitake, add it now.

2. Do not drain off the soak water. Remove sea vegetable and cut into 1/2-1" pieces. Add mushrooms, onions, and 1 tsp. salt before cooking. (If using fresh mushrooms, cut into thin strips before cooking. If using dried mushrooms, cook them whole then remove and chop them after cooking then add them back to the rice). Cook as per Basic Procedure, Millet.

3. After cooking time has elapsed, stir grain well then pack into loaf pans.

Serving suggestions: Slice and serve with Tamari Thyme gravy, Mock Poultry Gravy, Sunflower or Walnut Condiment, or flax or toasted sesame oil. Sprinkle with minced fresh chives or dried chives and serve with a green or mixed vegetable side dish and soup, stew, or a root vegetable dish and/or pickles.

Storage: Store at room temperature for 1-2 days as per Basic Rice or Millet. ❏

Millet-Chickpea Loaf (Any Season)

Prep: 5 minutes
Soaking: 8-12 hours or overnight
Cooking: 35 minutes

Serving size: 1-3 cups per person
Serves: 4-8 as a side dish grain with bread or rice

1 cup millet

5 1/2 cups water to pressure cook (6 1/2 cups if boiling)

4" piece kelp or kombu sea vegetable

2 cups dry chickpeas (garbanzo beans)

6 cups water

1/2-3/4 tsp. sea salt

1. Wash and soak millet as per Basic Procedure, Millet.

2. In a separate bowl, soak dry chickpeas in water all day or overnight.

3. Drain chickpeas and discard their soak water. Do not drain the water from millet. Add soaked beans and salt to the millet before cooking. Cook as per Basic Procedure, Millet.

4. When done, stir, and pack into loaf pans.

Serving suggestions: Slice and serve with Beet Sauce Italiano, Mock Poultry Gravy, Tamari Thyme Gravy, Seed Condiment, or Miso Vegetable Condiment. Also serve with a green or mixed vegetable side dish. Optional additions include soup or stew; a root/round vegetable dish; and/or pickles.

Storage: Store at room temperature for 1-2 days as per Basic Rice or Millet. ❏

Topping suggestions for Millet & Bean Slices

- Seed or nut condiment or nut or seed oil
- Seed or nut condiment + a land or sea vegetable dish
- Beet Sauce Italiano
- Parsnip White Sauce
- Tamari-Thyme Gravy
- Mock Poultry Gravy
- Squash Butter
- Nishime or Kinpira-Style Vegetables
- Leek or Scallion Miso Condiment or Carrot Top Miso Condiment
- Sea Vegetable Side Dish or Sea Vegetable Condiment
- Diluted Miso-Tahini

Nutty Millet or Super-Seeded Millet (Year Round)***

For 3-4 cups of dry millet, add 1/2 cup seeds or nuts before soaking. Pick one: lightly dry roasted sesame or pumpkin seeds, raw sunflower, poppy, or flax seeds, peanuts, pine nuts, or chopped walnuts or hazelnuts. Add the usual amount of salt plus 1/8-1/4 tsp. salt per 1/2 cup dry nuts or seeds.

Favorites:

- Millet with Walnuts
- Millet with Hazelnuts
- Millet with Poppy Seeds
- Millet with Flax Seeds
- Nishime or kinpira vegetable stew
- Mochi-zy Chickpea Sauce
- Stir Fried Vegetables

Basic Vegetable-Millet/Millet & Vegetable "Polenta" (Year Round)***

Prep: 5 minutes
Soaking: 8-12 hours or overnight
Cooking: 25-35 minutes
Serving size: 1-3 cups per person
Serves: 4-6 (or 2-3 meals for 2), or 6-8 as a side dish grain

Use 1/2-1 cup vegetables per cup dry millet in this recipe. Use a single vegetable, or one of the following vegetables combined with onion. This dish makes a great cornbread alternative when pressed into pans and sliced. This is finger food at its best (like cornbread), though you can eat it with a fork or chopsticks, depending on the toppings you select.

3 cups millet

3 cups diced winter squash with skins left on
(*kabocha, buttercup, butternut are best*)
or sweet potato (red garnet, jewel, or white sweet potato peeled or unpeeled)
or turnip; cauliflower; or corn off the cob

4 1/2-6 cups water to pressure cook (6 cups to boil)

3/4-1 tsp. sea salt

1. Wash and soak millet as per Basic Procedure, Millet. (No additional water is needed for the vegetables.)

2. Dice vegetables into 1-inch pieces and add to the grain. If using sweet corn, cut it off the cob and add to the pot, Also add the bare cobs to the pot for extra flavor. Add sea salt and cook as per Basic Procedure, Millet.

3. Remove corn cobs if they have been cooked with grain. Stir grain well and serve from a rice paddle or ice cream scoop or, pack into bowls then invert over serving plates or, or pack into 9-inch square or round cake pans or loaf pans then cut into bread-like slices.

Serving suggestions: Serve with soup or stew and stir fried vegetables, or quick-boiled vegetables, or pressed or marinated salad. Top servings with thick stew, Miso Vegetable Condiment; refried or soupy beans, or a seasoned seed or nut condiment.

Storage: Store at room temperature for 1-2 1/2 days as per Basic Rice or Millet.

Variation:

• **Millet with Fresh Green Peas (Summer):**
Cook millet above without vegetables. Mix 2-3 cups of raw shelled green peas into cooked millet (made from 3-4 cups dry grain) while the grain is still warm. ❏

Favorites:

• Millet & (Winter) Squash Squares or Millet & Squash Mounds

• Millet & Sweet Potato Mash, Squares, or Mounds

• Millet & Sweet Corn Slices or Mounds

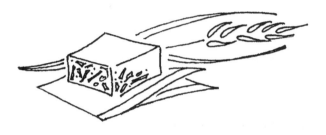

Topping Options for Millet & Vegetable Mounds or Squares:

• Nut or seed condiment

• Tamari-Thyme;, Soy-Sage Gravy, or Mock Poultry Gravy

• Seitan Stroganoff

• Hungarian Goulash

• Stir Fried Vegetables

• Tempeh, tofu, or wheat meat side dish

• Onion Butter

• Refried, baked, or stewed beans

• Sea vegetable side dish or condiment + seed or nut condiment

•Miso Vegetable Condiment

Millet & Turnip "Mashed Potatoes"***
(Fall, Winter, Spring)

Prep: 5 minutes
Soaking: 8-12 hours or overnight
Cooking: 25-35 minutes

Serving size: 1-3 cups per person
Serves: 3-6 (or 2-3 meals for 2); or 6-8 as a side dish grain

3 cups millet

2 cups cubed cauliflower **or** turnip (1" pieces)

1 cup minced onion **or** additional cauliflower or turnip

6 cups water to pressure cook (8 cups to boil)

1/3-3/4 tsp. sea salt

1. Wash, drain, and soak millet as per Basic Procedure, Millet.

2. Add sea salt and chopped vegetables, cook as per Basic Procedure, Millet.

3. When done, mash with a potato masher or beat with an electric mixer. Add a bit more water as needed to produce a creamy texture.

Serving suggestions: Serve with Mock Poultry Gravy, Tamari Thyme Gravy, Stroganoff, or other brown gravy; and a side of cooked greens and pickles, or a pressed or marinated salad. A tempeh, tofu, or wheat meat dish is optional.

Storage: Store at room temperature for 1-2 1/2 days as per Basic Rice or Millet.

Basic Procedure, Kasha, Bulgur, or Quinoa (Any Season)

Prep: 5 minutes
Soaking: 0-8 hours or overnight
Cooking: 20-30 minutes

Serving size: 1-3 cups per person
Serves: 3-6 (or 2-3 meals for 2); or 6-8 as a side dish grain

3 cups quinoa, bulgur wheat, or kasha or white buckwheat

6 cups water

1/3-1/2 tsp. sea salt

1. Rinse quinoa but do not rinse kasha, white buckwheat, or bulgur. Add water. Soaking is optional. (Do not soak bulgur!)

2. Add sea salt. Cover, bring to boil, reduce heat to low and simmer without stirring. It is helpful to use a heat deflector to keep the grain from burning on the bottom. (Do not pressure cook these grains alone. Quinoa or bulgur may be pressure cooked only if combined with 3-4 parts brown rice or millet.)

3. Cook 20 minutes for quinoa, bulgur or quinoa combined with bulgur; cook 25-30 minutes of for kasha or white buckwheat.

4. When done, let sit 10 minutes, stir and serve with a rice paddle or ice cream scoop.

Serving suggestions: Serve with soup, stew and/or a root or round vegetable dish and a greens dish. Top with a gravy, sauce, or seed or nut condiment and/or sea flakes or a sea vegetable dish. Pickles are optional. ❏

Variation:

• **Bulghur & Quinoa**

• **Kasha & Quinoa**

Basic Procedure, Polenta (Cornmeal Mush): (Year Round)***

Prep: 5 minutes
Soaking: none
Cooking: 30 minutes
Serving size: 1 1/2-2 cups per person, 2-3 cups for very active people, *or* less if served with bread, pasta, or rice

Polenta is a snap to make and a treat to eat. Golden scoops, slices, or squares of cornmeal mush can be topped with almost anything—stir fried vegetables, refried beans, seed or nut condiment, or a hearty gravy, stroganoff or goulash. Make plenty; leftovers are just as tasty the second day and perfect for pack lunches.

Serves 3-6 (or 1 1/2-3 meals for 2)

3 cups of polenta (coarse cornmeal)

6-8 cups water

1/2-3/4 tsp. sun dried sea salt

Serves 5-8 (or 2 1/2-4 meals for 2)

4 cups of polenta (coarse cornmeal)

8-10 cups water

1/2-1 tsp. sun dried sea salt

1. Combine all ingredients in a 3-4 quart pot. Bring to a boil over medium heat. Stir with a wire wisk as it comes to boil. Reduce heat to low and continue stir ring with a whisk or large wooden spoon or rice paddle. Stir about 10 minutes until it thickens.

2. Slip a heat deflector under the pot, cover, reduce heat to low, and simmer 20 minutes, until stiff.

   Note: If using an electric stove, heat the flame deflector on one burner, over medium heat, while the pot comes to boil over a different burner. When polenta becomes thick, transfer to the burner with the warm deflector and reduce heat to low. Cook as above. A heat deflector keeps the grain from burning on the bottom and allows you to cook without stirring it for the entire time.

3. Turn off heat. Let the pot sit for 10 minutes with the heat off and the lid on.

4. Stir well using a wooden rice paddle, mashing it against the sides of the pot. Transfer to round, square or oblong cake pan(s). Allow to cool 15 minutes or several hours. Alternatively, serve while still warm using an ice cream scoop dipped in cold water or by packing warm polenta into 10-ounce bowls and turning onto each plate.

Serving suggestions: Cut into slices (or see notes above for serving warm polenta). Serve with condiments, a soup, stew, or root/round vegetable dish; and cooked greens or pressed or marinated salad. Note serving and suggestions for millet and rice above.

Storage: Store at room temperature for up to 48 hours, covered with a bamboo mat. Reheat leftovers by steaming slices on a plate on a rack, by covering and warming an entire panful in the oven, or by pan frying or grilling slices. Small amounts of leftovers can also be cut into small cubes and cooked in with morning oatmeal, rice, or millet. (See breakfast chapter for Cereals from Leftovers.)

Variations:

- **Polenta the Italian way:** Combine polenta with an equal volume of water. Add salt, and bring to boil over medium heat stirring constantly. Reduce heat slightly. Continue to stir, adding remaining water a little at a time. Stir and cook 30 minutes until thick, smooth, and mushy. Serve soft or press into a dish and cool.

- **Double Corn Polenta:** Add 1-2 cups corn off the cob just before cooking polenta.

- **Polenta with Peas:** Stir in 2 cups shelled fresh green peas after cooking.

- **Polenta-n-Beans:** Stir 2 cups of cooked, drained beans into polenta after it has cooked. (Try black turtle, kidney or small red beans, or whole dried peas.)

- **Nutty Polenta:** Stir in 1/3 cup raw seeds or chopped nuts before cooking, or add dry roasted seeds or roasted, chopped nuts after polenta has cooked. ❏

Stretching Leftover Whole Grain with New Grain (Year Round)

Prep: 5 minutes
Soaking: none
Cooking: 20-30 minutes
Serving size: 1 1/2-2 cups cooked grain per person *or* 2-3+ cups per active person

If you find you don't have enough leftover grain for a meal, you can serve what whole grain you do have with bread, pasta, or dumplings, or you can stretch it. Stretching leftover grain is particularly handy when unexpected company arrives. It takes about 30 minutes to perform this feat and it is best to cook only enough for a meal or for a day since it won't keep as long as grain that is entirely newly made.

Note: Figure about 1/2-1 cup of dry grain per person. Use the larger volume for big-eaters or very active folks.

1 cup soft shelled grain (one variety): millet, quinoa, roasted buckwheat (kasha) *or* bulgur wheat

2 cups water

1/8-1/4 tsp. sun dried sea salt

1-2 cups leftover dinner grain (rice, barley, millet, or a mixed grain combination)

1. Place uncooked grain in a saucepan with water. Add salt.

2. Cover and bring to boil over medium heat. Do not stir. Slip a heat deflector under the pot. Reduce heat to low and simmer, covered, without stirring, for 20-30 minutes.

3. Stir precooked grain into freshly made grain using a wooden rice paddle. Transfer to a serving bowl and cover with a bamboo sushi mat.

Serving suggestions: Serve with a rice paddle or ice cream scooper. Top with the condiments of your choice and accompany with soup or stew and a green vegetable dish.

Variation:

- In place of leftover cooked grain above, stir leftover cooked noodles into fresh grain. ❏

Minute Made Mochi-Waffles (Year Round)***

Prep: 10 minutes
Yield: 4, 6 x 6" waffles or 8, 3 x 3" waffles
Cooking: 8-12 minutes for each 1-2 waffles
Serves: 2 average eaters
Serving size: 6 oz. uncooked mochi/1/2 pkg per person *or* 8-9 oz. (1/2-3/4 pkg.) per active person

These marvelous waffles require no messy mixing or blending of batter, and contains no oil, eggs, leavening agents, or sweeteners. And they won't stick to the griddle like most. Anyone, even a kid, can make these quick, convenient and healthy waffles. They're not just for breakfast; we also make them for lunch or dinner. (Even for breakfast we serve our waffles with vegetable toppings.) They make the perfect stand in for rice, bread, or pasta. For a quick meal, mochi waffles can't be beat.

*** Increase mochi to 1 1/2-2, 12 ounce packages if feeding two active individuals.*

1, 12 ounce packages thawed mochi
   (plain, pizza, garlic-sesame, basil-garlic, or cinnamon-raisin flavor)*

Notes: Rather than make all the waffles before a meal, we plug the iron in at the dining table then make small to medium sized waffles, one at a time. While we eat our first waffle, the next one cooks, and so on throughout the meal. These are best fresh from the griddle; they dry out quickly.

1. Cut each package of thawed mochi into 8 squares then cut each piece into a thin slab, like a very thin piece of bread.

2. Place 2-4 thin mochi slices into a non-stick Belgian or standard waffle iron, covering the bottom of the iron or just the middle section for smaller waffles. (You'll need to bake in several batches.) The exact number of waffles will depend upon the size of your waffle iron.

3. Press the lid down, and continue to press lightly until the mochi softens and spreads out. Put a jar on top to weight the lid down. (Be patient, it takes a few minutes to melt). Bake until golden brown and crispy, about 8-12 minutes. Exact time will depend upon the size of the iron, temperature, and thickness. Check several times. They're done when they firm up and easily peel away from the iron and appear slightly crispy, like dark toast.

4. Remove waffle with a fork or chopstick. Put 2-4 pieces of mochi in so your next waffle will be ready when you are. Bake as above. Repeat until mochi is used up or you are full.

Serving suggestions: Serve as you would biscuits, tortillas, dinner rolls or other bread.

For breakfast or lunch: Serve with a sweet vegetable topping spread, or stew. (Onion Butter, Squash Butter, mashed yams or sweet potatoes or baked or nishime squash with Walnut Condiment, Walnut-Miso, or Miso-Tahini and a side of steamed or quick-boiled greens and pickles or boiled or pressed salad.

For lunch or supper: Millet Butter; Refried beans; Garbanzo Butter; Hummus; Chickpea Natto; Tofu Sour Cream; or Seitan Stroganoff, with a side of greens. Or, dunk waffles into hearty bowls of lentil or pea soup then top with cooked greens or salad. Try Tofu "Sour Cream" or quark cheese on waffles. (See variations for using sweetened mochi).

Leftover tips: Leftover mochi waffles can be diced and added to soups, like croutons; added to morning porridge; or re-crisped in the oven, toaster oven, or on a stove top grill.

Variations:

- **Sweet dessert waffles (use Cinnamon Raisin Flavored Mochi):** Try applesauce, fruit compote, stewed fruit, or diluted rice malt, barley malt, or maple syrup thickened with arrowroot or kuzu. For a more nourishing and gentle effect, top with cooked mashed squash, yam, or sweet potato puréed and mixed with light miso and sesame tahini, peanut butter, or chopped, roasted nuts).

Garlic Toast:

- Brush garlic flavored mochi with olive oil or corn oil before or after cooking. ❑

Mochi Croutons, Triangles, and "Bread"-Sticks (Year Round)

Prep: 10-12 minutes
Cooking: 8-14 minutes

Serves: (12 oz. package) 2-3 as a main dish grain *or* 5-8 as an appetizer with dip *or* more as garnish

You can make golden, crispy, "bread sticks," crunchy croutons, and puffy biscuits without a batter and with no added fat, flour, leaveners, or sweeteners. All you have to do is thaw a block of mochi then cut it into 1-inch, 2-inch, or 3-inch cubes, triangles, pencil long sticks or other fun shapes and bake until puffy and/or crunchy. For parties and potlucks, pair mochi sticks with Hummus Tahini dip, Herbed Tofu "Cream Cheese," or Peanut Butter & Squash Paté. Bake the mochi right before you plan to serve it (it will dry out if baked too far in advance.

1 12 oz. package mochi *(plain, basil-garlic, garlic sesame or other variety)*

1. Cut mochi into 3/4-1-inch cubes or triangles for croutons; 1/3-1/2-inch wide x 3-5-inch long sticks or pencils for bread sticks, and/or 3-inch x 3-inch cubes or triangles for biscuits.

2. Arrange on an unoiled baking sheet or cookie sheet, allowing some room for expansion. Bake in preheated 400° F oven until crispy, puffy, and slightly golden, about 8-12 minutes depending upon oven, placement of oven rack, and size of pieces. Check periodically.

Serving suggestions: Serve immediately. Serve sticks or biscuits with bean dip, tofu pate, or a vegetable spread. Drop croutons into or on top of a soup, stew, or salad just before serving.

Storage: Leftovers baked mochi will dry out quickly, but need not be thrown away. Simmer pieces in a soup or stew for several minutes before serving; cook them into your morning cereal; or dunk them into some sort of sauce or gravy to soften. ❏

Variation:

• **Mochi biscuits:** If you like a chewier biscuit-like product—cut mochi into 2-4 inch blocks before baking, that way the mochi will form pockets on the inside and will be more doughy, like a buttermilk biscuit. You can break open the baked mochi puffs and stuff them with your favorite dip. Try Herbed Tofu Cream Cheese, Tofu Pesto Paté, Tempeh "Tuna," Mocheeze-y Chickpea sauce, Refried Beans, quark, goat cheese, or mashed squash or sweet potato with Whipped Miso Nut Butter, Walnut Condiment, or ghee.

• Use Cinnamon-Raisin mochi or other sweetened variety of mochi. Bake as above then top with applesauce, apple butter, or chestnut purée or serve with a stewed fruit compote or diluted rice meat & tahini syrup for dessert.

Basic Procedure, Posole (Whole Dried Corn) (Fall, Winter, Spring)***

Prep: 15 minutes
Cooking: 1 hour
Yield: 2-2 1/2 cups

We use posole most in late fall and throughout the winter and spring when fresh corn is out of season. Posole, or whole dried corn, requires special processing to be tender, tasty and digestible. You will need to seek out a reliable source for Cal which is powdered lime. (Hint: don't use the gardening variety!) We usually find it in Latin American grocery stores. This white powder softens the corn and removes the outer inedible husk or hull. Alternatives to Cal include wood ash and volcanic ash or baking soda as a last resort. The key to good posole is thorough and lengthy soaking, cooking, and rinsing.

*****Note:** Baking soda is the least desirable softening agent. Using cal or volcanic ash adds more calcium and other minerals.

1 cup whole dried corn (posole)—red, yellow, blue, or white

3 cups water

1 1/2 Tbsp. Cal (lime powder) *or* 2 Tbsp. wood ash or volcanic ash or 2 tbsp. baking soda*

1. Rinse posole and place in a pressure cooker. Soak, uncovered, all day or overnight in above volume of water.

2. Add Cal, wood ash, volcanic ash, or baking soda (Wood ash may be saved from burning wood in a fireplace without any newspaper or other chemically treated paper.)

3. Seal pressure cooker. Bring it to full pressure then reduce heat to medium-low. Cook 1 hour at a low-hiss. (Posole can also be cooked for an hour on medium, in a covered-bowl-within-a-pot.)

4. When pressure comes down, pour posole and cooking water into a colander. Run cold water over it, stirring the corn in a circle with your hands. Continue rinsing for several minutes until the hulls come off the corn and fall through the holes of the colander. Corn should be tender; test it by eating a piece.

Serving suggestions: Add cooked posole to soups, stews, bean casseroles, or to whole grain before cooking. It will need further cooking once added to one of these dishes. Alternatively, grind cooked posole in a Foley food mill or hand meat grinder and use it to make fresh corn tortillas or masa dough for tamales. ❏

Uses for whole dried corn/posole:

- **Posole Rice:** Add precooked posole to a pot of soaked short or medium grain brown rice before cooking.

- **Millet & Posole:** Add precooked posole to the millet pot before cooking.

- **Posole & Whole Oat Porridge:** Add precooked posole to whole oats before cooking overnight.

- **Posole Con Frijoles (Dried corn with beans):** Add precooked posole to a baked bean dish, bean soup, stew, chili, etc. (Add posole to uncooked beans or to cooked beans that will undergo additional cooking in soup or stew.)

- **Sweet Corn Amasake Pudding:** Combine precooked posole with sweet brown or white rice before cooking. Cook, cool and incubate as per Basic Amasake Procedure then purée and cook briefly. Suggested ratio: 1 cup uncooked posole (about 2-3 cups cooked) + 2-4 cups uncooked sweet brown rice. For soaking/cooking, figure 2 cups water per each cup of precooked posole and dry grain. Use 1/4-1/2 cup koji per cup dry grain.

This naturally sweet pudding can be served as is, spooned over seasonal cooked fruit, or used to replace the sweetener and most of the oil in any cookie, cake, muffin, or pastry recipe.

Uses for Leftover Whole Grain (rice, millet, buckwheat, polenta, etc.)

Reheat by steaming in a bowl, then top with any of the following:

Choose one of these

seed or nut condiment
low-fat gravy
stir fried or sauteed vegetables
refried beans or cooked tempeh or seitan
scrambled tofu
goulash or stroganoff
flax, walnut, or sesame oil

Top freely with these

fresh or dried spices or herbs
fresh or dried pungent garnishes
minced pickles
sea vegetable flakes
cooked sea vegetable condiment
steamed vegetables
pressed salad
your taste buds

Turn leftover grain into breakfast cereal

with leftover cubed bread
with leftover pasta
with suribachi scrapings
 (from making seed/nut condiments)
with dry soft shelled grain (buckwheat or millet)

with leftover pasta water
with dry rolled grain (i.e., oatmeal)

Stuff into a whole grain pita pocket or fold burrito-style in tortillas after mixing with

sauteed or steamed vegetables
cooked beans, tofu, tempeh, or wheat meat
chopped pickles or relish

baked or simmered vegetables
fresh or dried herbs or spices
vinegar, tamari, ume paste and/or mustard

Toss into salads

with beans, tofu or tempeh
with cooked vegetables
with cooked sea vegetables
with vinegar, ume, or tamari
with a small amount of seeds

with minced pickles
with minced fresh herbs
with dried herbs or spices
with a low fat dressing or marinade
with chopped tempeh "sausage' or sauteéed
wheat meat

Press into a pie plate for a no-fuss savory pie crust
Stuff into burritos with refried beans and condiments
Stir fry with vegetables and/or wheat meat and seasonings

Other ideas....

*Mix with just cooked buckwheat, millet, or rice
*Knead into bread dough or mix into biscuit, cookie, or muffin batter
*Add to a soup—puréed as a thickener or left in chunks or cubes (millet)
*Make a rice pudding
*Add to a casserole or a bean loaf
*Add to salad dressing, puréed with herbs and seasonings

Rice Balls: (Any Season)***

Prep: 15-20 minutes
Yield: 4 rice balls

Serves: 1-2 (or 1-2 meals for 1)
Serving size: 2 rice balls per average person *or* 3-4 per each active individual or person with a large appetite; *or* 1 per person as a light evening snack

Rice balls are to the Japanese what sandwiches are to Americans. They are easy to carry, can be eaten without utensils, and can be made from leftovers. The traditional rice ball is made from plain brown rice wrapped in sushi nori (a type of seaweed processed into sheets) or rolled in green nori flakes, although you can just as easily skip the seaweed and roll your rice balls in a coating of crushed roasted, seasoned seeds or nuts. You can also use a two grain combination (rice with a second grain) for added variety. To make the balls hold together, pressure cooking the rice is almost essential.

Note: Fresh rice is easiest to form into balls. Leftover rice is best be steamed in a bowl to moisten and freshen it before making balls, or you may simply wet your hands a lot during the shaping process.

Rule of thumb: ~2/3-3/4 cup of cooked grain (brown rice or rice combination) per ball.

Grain:

2 2/3-3 cups pressure cooked brown rice *or* brown rice combined with a second grain *(e.g., Millet & Rice; Rice with sweet corn; Rice with Polenta; or Rice & Hato Mugi)*

Traditional coating or wrapper:

4 sheets toasted sushi nori, each sheet cut into 4 squares *(see variation below)*
Additional nori as needed

Filling:

2 tsp. umeboshi or apriboshi paste *or* 2 tsp. white, yellow, or mellow miso *or* 2 tsp. prepared mustard mixed with miso or ume
2-4 tsp. seasoned, ground seed or nut condiment, **or** nut or seed butter

1. If using untoasted sheet nori, place nori sheets on oven rack in a 300-350° F oven and roast for several minutes until green. Or wave sheets one at a time, back and forth, across a gas flame being careful not get them too close or to catch them on fire. Split each nori sheet into quarters by folding sheet in half, then in half again, then tearing or cutting with scissors to make four squares. Arrange squares on a dry cutting block, counter top, or plate. Fill a small bowl with water.

2. **To form balls:** Divide cooked rice into four portions, roughly 2/3-3/4 cup each. Wet your hands and form rice into a ball with cupped hands. Make a flattened burger shape. Cup the rice ball (burger) in your left hand, cup your right hand across the top of the ball, then turn the ball about twenty times, pressing and squeezing as you go to firmly pack the rice. Wet your hands periodically as needed. Turn the ball over and repeat the process, pressing and squeezing. This firmly compacts the rice to keep it from falling apart during transit or consumption.

3. **To fill balls:** With your thumb, make a small hole in each rice ball, halfway through the center. Fill hole with about 1/2 tsp. ume or apriboshi paste or omit hole and spread paste on one side of ball. Alternately, spread 3/4 tsp. nut or seed butter on four of the nori squares or on each rice ball. (Or, mix the nut/seed butter with the ume, apriboshi, miso, and/or mustard then tuck about 1 tsp. of mixture into the hole of each ball or spread it on one side of each ball.)

4. **To wrap balls:** Set four squares of nori aside. Place the other 4 sheets of nori on work surface. Sprinkle each with 1/2-1 tsp. seed or nut condiment (omit this if nut or seed butter were used above). Place one rice ball (burger) in the center of each of the four squares. Place the remaining 4 sheets of nori on top of the rice balls at an angle to make a star shape. Lightly dampen your finger with water; dab the corners of the nori then tuck the top corners down and the bottom corners up to completely cover the rice. Do not make the nori too wet or the balls will become soggy. Roll the balls in your hands briefly to seal the nori edges, covering any holes with small pieces of additional nori.

Storage: Store balls at room temperature, in a bowl covered with a bamboo mat or in a brown paper or wax paper bag folded over to seal. Use within three days.

Serving suggestions: Serve at room temperature with pressed or marinated salad and/or cooked green or mixed vegetables. Vegetable or bean soup is optional. Serve rice balls without side dishes for a snack. ❏

Variations:

- **Rice Balls with Sea Flakes:** Omit the nori sheets and the seed or nut condiment. Roll the formed and filled balls in dulse or nori sea flakes.

- **Nutty Rice Balls:** Omit umeboshi, apriboshi, miso or mustard and the nori. Place 3-4 Tbsp. ground, seasoned, nut or seed condiment on a plate. Roll the formed, unfilled rice balls in the seasoned seed condiment.

- Prepare rice balls as above but use rice cooked with nuts or seeds. Omit nut or seed condiment. Use umeboshi or miso as above then wrap in nori or roll balls in sea flakes.

Making Rice Balls:

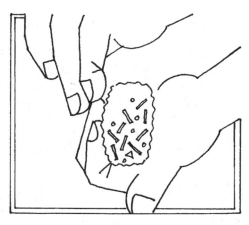

Step #1

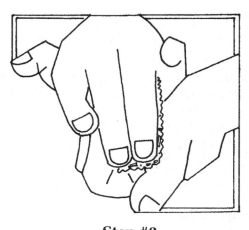

Step #2

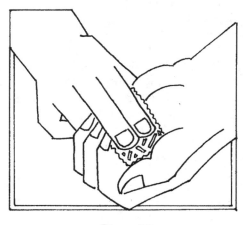

Step #3

The Breads of Life

In western civilizations, bread has historically been the staple food, the staff of life, for a vast majority of the population. Although it is tempting to say that bread is to the west what rice is to the east, bread has long been a staple food for many people in the northern regions of Asia. In fact, bread appears in some form in almost every major culture on Earth. In China, wheat has long been cultivated in northern regions and steamed bread is a staple food for the northern Chinese.

Western Bread, Eastern Bread

In the west, bread is most often baked in the form of large loaves then cut into individual slices By contrast, in Asia bread is more often made in the form of small buns, such as Chinese steamed bread, or flat loaves, similar to the Indian chapati or the Middle Eastern pita bread.

There are a number of reasons we prefer the Asian style of bread making over the European and American methods. First of all, baking bread in loaves is a relatively energy intensive enterprise. It generally requires heating an oven—essentially a large box—to a high temperature for a prolonged period of time. In contrast, Chinese-style steamed breads require less energy and less cooking time. Although pita-style "loaves" and some flat breads require an oven, they take far less time to bake than large loaves. For this reason, they can be a good compromise between the energy intensive baked loaves and quick-stove top steamed buns. When you do make baked loaf breads, it pays to make and bake several batches at once to utilize valuable resources (yours and mama earth's). Quick baked breads (i.e., those that cook in thirty minutes or less are another option. The most ecologically sound way to prepare bread, however, is to steam cook it Chinese-style or to make tortillas or chapatis on a griddle.

Baked bread is generally rather dry, so people tend to want to moisten it with oily, fatty, or sugar laden spreads. This makes it harder to digest and increases its mucous-forming potential. Breads cooked by steaming, rather than baking, come out moist and tender, hence they do not cry out for oily, greasy, or sticky sweet spreads. Their high moisture content also makes them much easier to digest than hard, dry baked breads. You won't believe how moist and delicious bread can be until you try making whole grain steamed buns.

To avoid the gastronomical hazards which so often result from eating bread, we recommend steam-heating your daily bread (that includes baked breads) to moisten it and chewing your bread thoroughly. Bolting down any food will create indigestion and bread is no exception. To further enhance digestion, avoid adding oils, fats, dairy products or sweeteners to your daily bread or bread dough (save oil for use in special occasion breads). If you buy some or all of your bread, you'll have to scout around for good local brands that meet these standards. When serving your bread, instead of using high-fat spreads, try serving our breads with soups, stews, gravies or other dishes that serve as moistening dunks for the "staff of life." Low fat spreads are also a nice alternative to digestively disastrous fat laden toppings. Above all, relish your daily bread with passion. If you love it and chew it well, it can not fail to be superb nourishment for life.

The Whole-Grain Truth

Generally speaking, whole grain flours are more nutritious and preferable to polished varieties. However, whole wheat has an exceptionally coarse and indigestible bran coating, and quite a lot of it. This coating has a cooling, laxative effect, making whole wheat valuable for some and quite a problem for others.

One hundred percent whole wheat or whole grain bread is valuable for people who have a tendency toward constipation. It is also appropriate for people with good digestion and regular elimination. On the other hand, individuals with poor digestive capacities and a tendency to diarrhea often do better with wheat bread if it is made with a combination of whole wheat or whole spelt flour and a small amount of unbleached— meaning slightly refined— wheat or spelt flour that has had some of the bran removed. A good proportion might be 50% whole grain flour with 50% unbleached flour or perhaps 75% of whole grain and 25% refined flour. Once a person's condition improves, it is usually possible and always desirable to reduce then eventually eliminate the refined flour from one's daily bread. Whole grain flour in rich is so many nutrients that we need for health and that are so lacking form the modern diet of refined and overly processed food.

(Unbeknownst to many, whole grains are a rich source of protein, iron, vitamins, and minerals.)

Bread made from either spelt flour or hard white wheat flour (not refined red wheat, but a different type of wheat altogether) is an exception. Whole spelt behaves much like wheat, but is much more nutritious and easier to digest than whole grain hard red wheats from which most whole wheat flour is made. Whole grain hard white wheat is also more nourishing and less laxative in action than the hard red wheats. Hard white wheat has been used in Asia for decades, particularly for noodle making, and it is now being grown in America. Whole grain hard white wheat flour produces a whole grain bread with a similar taste, texture, and appearance of refined flours. This feature makes it appealing to many Americans who are accustomed to a softer, whiter and lighter bread but want a more nutritious product. You may have to hunt around to find this flour (or order it through the mail), but it is worth the effort. Many health food stores are now carrying what were once specialty flours but are now becoming more common fare. Experiment with these varieties of flour and the others listed in our basic bread recipe to see what works for you.

What's a Serving of Bread Anyway?

According to American dieticians, nutritionists and food-exchange charts on serving goals:

- 1 slice of bread, 1 bagel *or* one english muffin half (1-1 1/2 oz. each)
- 1 small dinner roll, 1 medium sized pancake, *or* 1 average flour tortilla (1-1 1/2 oz. each)
- 1/2 cup of cooked whole grain: rice, pasta, millet, oatmeal etc.
- 2 average rice cakes (1-1 1/2 oz. each) *or* 1 1/2 very dense cakes
- 1 oz. fat-free crackers
- 1-1 1/2 corn tortillas (5-6")
- 1-1 1/2 ounce uncooked mochi

Current U.S.D.A. recommendations: 6-11 grain servings per day; 3-4 servings per meal

Nourishment For Life recommendations: 8-20 U.S.D.A grain servings per day; 3-7 per meal, depending upon your activity level, digestive ability, and the number of meals you eat daily.

Note: On a grain based diet, it is desirable to eat more than the U.S.D.A. minimum 6 daily grain servings, even for women, children and dieters. It is often necessary to eat more than the U.S.D.A's 11 servings of grain per day if one is very active. When you reduce your use of high fat, calorie dense foods— particularly animal foods such as meat, fish, poultry, eggs and dairy foods— and reduce the use of oils, nuts and seeds, something has to take their place. That something is extra servings of both vegetables and whole grains.

Our Daily Bread:

Besides being delicious and nutritious, bread is versatile. You can serve it for breakfast, lunch, dinner, or a snack. It can be the solo grain in a meal or served alongside brown rice, pasta, polenta, millet, kasha, or oatmeal. You can dunk bread into a cup of soup or stew, use it like a utensil to scoop up cooked vegetables or beans, or you use it like a sponge to sop up yummy cooking juices and gravies. Breads can serve as wrappers for all sorts of fillings or breads can be spread with pesto or bean, tofu, or vegetable patés.

Bread often serves as the only grain in one of our daily meals although we sometimes serve our bread as a side dish, with rice, pasta, or millet and two or three other side dishes. By no means is it necessary to eat bread every day. But why deprive yourself? (There are far worse things to indulge in.) If you like bread, buy or make the best quality product you can, chew it well, and relish every bite.

But I've Never Made Bread!

Anyone can make bread! If you can open an envelope you can make your own bread— really. (It needn't be difficult or time consuming.)Approach it as an adventure, commit yourself to success, visualize the outcome, and practice. The more you make it, the better and faster you'll be at turning out nourishing bread. Learn from your mistakes and remember, bread makers aren't born, they are made!

Secrets for Fast & Fail-Proof Bread Making:

If the idea of making your own bread conjures up hours of work, fear not, our one-rise method will give you speedy and reliable results. We think bread making should be easy and unintimidating. If it's just too frustrating, trying, or time consuming, you're liable to give up at the start. (Simple = Sustainable.)

We have one basic recipe for bread dough (you'll learn it by rote in no time) which we use to make well over a dozen different variety of breads by changing the shape, cooking time, cooking method, or types of flour used or by adding herbs, spices, or seeds the possibilities are endless. Change several factors and you'll never run out of interesting and tasty breads to nourish you for life. (We also offer you three different rising methods—Rapid-Rise, Standard-Rise, and Slow-Rise. You can select the one that fits with your experience level, your time constraints and your needs. Each has its merits. And all produce tasty bread.)

We urge you to test our simple bread making techniques. Once you have, you will find that, even with the most hectic schedule, you can make your own bread once or twice a week. It only takes 20 minutes to mix and shape the dough, 15-30 minutes to wait for it to rise (if Rapid-Rise Yeast is used) or 30-60 minutes (if you've made your dough ahead of time and are waiting for the second rise). During this "waiting period" you can prep other foods for the next meal or the next day, then 15-30 minutes to steam or bake. It nearly makes itself from here one out!

Dough #1: Rapid-Rise Yeast Bread

If you've never made bread in your life, had repeated failures with yeasted breads, or are crunched for time, this is the place to start.

Rapid-Rise or Quick-Rise Yeast, a special strain of yeasts selected for their rapid rising ability, allows you to make and rise your bread in a fraction of the time required for other breads. With this yeast, you use slightly hotter water (125-130 F) than with Active Dry Yeast and mix the yeast right into the flour. You do not "proof" the yeast or make a sponge. With this method you also do not need to let the dough rise twice. Rapid-Rise Dough can be mixed and shaped in under 20 minutes then left to rise for 15-30 minutes, in a warm place, until it doubles in size. Then it's ready to be cooked. You will not need to work more than 30 minutes in the kitchen.

Rapid-Rise Bread can also be made with Active Dry Yeast (without any sugar, honey, molasses, oil, or other sweeteners or fats). When using Active Dry Yeast you will need to allow 30-60 minutes for the dough to rise once (using the one-rise method).

One drawback of the Rapid-Rise method is that the finished bread will dry out more quickly than bread made from other longer rising methods. But if you're going to eat your bread within several days, or if you don't mind steaming it to remoisten it before a meal, this won't be a problem. Another more serious disadvantage to this method is that Quick-Rising does not allow the yeast microbes to predigest much of the bread's starches. This means that the resulting bread will not be as digestible as the Standard or Slow-Rise Bread. Though this may not pose a problem in all cases or at all times, if you have a history of digestive problems (gas, bloating, indigestion, heartburn, food allergies, etc.) or you simply want the most nutritious bread under the sun, it is advisable to use the other methods more often.

Dough #2: Standard-Rise Bread

Most cookbooks make this method sound far more complicated than it has to be. We've simplified the process. However, the Standard Rise Method is more time consuming than the Rapid-Rise Method. The longer rising time makes this bread a bit more moist and digestible and improves the keeping quality of bread (it doesn't dry out as soon, thus it doesn't need to be steam warmed as soon or as often as Rapid-Rise Yeast Bread) because the yeasts have time to predigest some of the grain for you. This bread also has a better texture than Rapid-Rise Bread.

We use the same basic bread recipe for both Active Dry Yeast and Rapid-Rise Yeast, with a few modifications. We use the same proportions of flour, salt, water and yeast. (Make sure flour etc. is room temperature). The main difference is that with The Standard Rise Method we use a slightly cooler water (100 F). We also give the bread two risings rather than one—once in a bowl covered with plate or upside-down bowl, at room temperature in a warm place, and once in bread pans, on cookie sheets, or on oiled plates (for steamed buns), also in a warm place. The first rising takes 1-1 1/2 hours, the second rising 30-60 minutes. You needn't tend the bread, just stay close to the kitchen so that you can see when it has nearly doubled in size and preheat the oven or steamers before baking, steaming, or boiling the dough.

Dough #3: Slow-Rise Yeast Bread

This method produces the "Rolls Royce" of breads, the most digestible, most nutritious and best textured breads. The bread dough is allowed to rise slowly— for a long time —8-10 hours or overnight. This allows the yeasts to predigest most of the starches in the grains (flour) and it also provides a culture of beneficial bacteria much like that found in yogurt or unpasteurized miso. This is especially important for those eating a purely vegetarian diet and desiring maximum nutrition. Long, slow fermentation breaks down the phytates in whole grains, thus improving their nutritional profile and increasing the amount of absorbable mineral in our grains. (Phytates are naturally occurring substances found in whole grains which can reduce the nutrients available to us. For this reason, we favor slow-rise yeast breads, naturally leavened, desem or sourdough breads and whole grains which have been soaked prior to simmering or pressure cooking. These processes add to the nutritional value of grains.) Eating breads prepared in one of these manners significantly lightens the load on your digestive organs, adds nutrients which enhance your digestive tract, and makes for a sweeter tasting bread with a more moist texture and excellent keeping quality.

For the Slow-Rise Method we use the same basic recipe as the other methods except that we use much less yeast (usually one-fourth to one-eight the normal amount) and allow the bread to rise for 8-12 hours before baking or steaming. The flour and other ingredients should be at room temperature. The water should be heated to about 100° F and Active-Dry Yeast should be used.

This bread dough is risen at room temperature, in a bowl covered with an oiled plate or upside down bowl, all day or overnight (8-10 hours), then punched down (gently), shaped, then allowed to rise for about 30-60 minutes or until it has doubled, in a warm place, before baking, steaming, or boiling as per the particular recipe you use.

Bread Machines vs. Hand-Made Bread

Though bread machines are in vogue, they do have disadvantages. First, bread mixers usually take as much time to clean as is supposedly "saved" by using them. Secondly, bread machines are expensive. Once you add the cost of the machine—usually around $300—to the cost of the ingredients for each loaf of bread it becomes very high. Even if you can get 300 loaves out of the machine before it breaks down and needs expensive repairs, you'll still have to add one dollar to the cost of supplies for each of those loaves.

Thirdly, a bread machine doesn't allow you to have direct contact with the dough. This matters because you may need to add additional flour to the dough. The exact amount of flour needed in a recipe for kneaded bread doughs is always a range. Different flours differ in moisture content and even the same type of flour can vary greatly in its absorption ability, from batch to batch, depending upon the day's temperature and humidity, how finely it was ground, and what you mix it with. Only your hands can tell you if the dough is too wet.

Fourth, with your hands you can make an incredibly wide assortment of sizes and shapes not available with a machine. By hand, you can shape dough into twists, wreaths, braids, Parker House or clover leaf rolls, buns, baguettes, peasant loaves, bread sticks, bagels, pita, pizza, and so on.

Finally, a bread machine is, by design, very energy inefficient and you cannot make several loaves or batches at a time. Most machines make just one small loaf. By hand, however, you can easily make two or three double batches, in several stages or all at once, in the same bowl. You could even bake or steam all of these batches at once, using less energy than is needed to run a single bread machine. With a conventional oven, you can also bake bread along while other foods to maximize your energy use.

If you still think a machine is a time saver, consider that you can mix, shape, and rise, one to three double batches of bread dough in just 30-50 minutes. Making bread by hand is both satisfying and sustaining.

Bread Making Made Easy

One Basic Dough Makes Over 16 Styles of Bread

Bread making was never so simple. With our Basic Bread Dough you can make all of these breads, plain or fancy.

- Steamed Buns
- Freeform French Bread
- Baguettes
- Sandwich Bread
- Dinner Rolls (of various sizes and shapes)
- Pita Pocket Breads
- Souvlaki Pita Breads (pita without the pocket)
- Pizza Dough
- Calzones & Savory Turnovers
- Bagels
- Focaccia
- Bread Sticks
- Turkish Sesame Rounds
- Wreath Breads
- Soft Pretzels
- Burger Buns & Hot Dog Buns
- Cinnamon Rolls & Danishes (special occasion treats)

One Basic Dough Also Makes Dozens of Flavors

By combining different types of flour or adding dried or fresh herbs, spices, seeds, chopped nuts, or grated vegetables or vegetable purees you can make dozens of different doughs hat can be formed and cooked into almost any shape. For most breads, spelt or whole wheat bread flour must comprise at least 75% of the total amount of flour in a recipe. for specific proportions of various flours.

- Spelt Dough
- Whole Wheat Dough
- Millet Dough
- Barley Dough
- Kamut Dough
- Buckwheat Dough
- Chestnut Dough
- Rye Dough
- Yellow or Blue Cornmeal Dough
- Oat Dough
- Golden Amaranth Dough
- Super Soy Dough
- Quinoa Dough
- Herbed Dough
- Dough with Fresh Corn
- Potato Dough
- Nutty Dough or Super Seeded Dough
- Fruited Holiday Dough

Breads For Health— Plain and Fancy

Breads for everyday use should be made from few and simple ingredients: minimally refined whole grain (or part unbleached) flour, water, sun dried sea salt, and baker's yeast or natural desem or sourdough starter. They should be made without oil, butter, or other fats and without milk, yogurt, cheese, sweeteners (such as honey, molasses, malt, sugar, etc.) conditioners, or other artificial leaveners, or preservatives. Baking soda and baking powder should be used sparingly as they do not break down the phytates in whole grains and they destroy many of the B vitamins found in the grains. Yeast or sourdough/desem leavening makes breads are far more nutritious and more digestible.

You may be able to find a bakery in your area that makes desem, sourdough bread or yeasted whole grain breads free of oil and sweeteners (a rare find these days) the old-fashioned way—in a brick oven. This is good bread to buy, especially if you're crunched for time. However, buying bread when you eat it frequently as part of a grain based diet cost more than you think. Most good quality breads cost $3-4 per loaf; chapatis and tortillas usually cost $2 for a meal-size volume; most bagels cost $.40-.50 each; most "health food" muffins, pastries, and cookies cost $.40-$1.50 each; and most cakes sell for $2-$3 per slice. These prices might not seem high, until you add them up. If you buy two to three bagels a day (enough for one meal for one person) in one month it comes to $30.00 for one person, $60 for two people, or $90 for three people. That adds up to $720-$1,080 in bagels per year for one to three people. Cookies, pastries, chips or crackers can cost even more. If you buy a lot of bread, you'll have to work many hours to be able to afford it. By comparison, home made bread won't cost an arm and a leg, so you won't have to sell your soul for your daily bread. (Who doesn't want to have their bread, and it it too?)

Basic Breads

Easiest Everyday Breads

Steamed Buns (plain, unfilled, and/or herbed)
Sandwich Loaf Breads
Freeform French & Peasant Loaves
Baguettes
Burger & Hot Dog Buns
Mochi Waffles & "Bread" Sticks
Souvlaki-Pita Breads
Dinner Rolls
Steamed Buns (with filling)

More Involved Breads

Pizza
Corn or Millet Batter Breads
Focaccia
Flat Breads & Chapatis (unleavened)
Tortillas (leavened or unleavened)
Pancakes & Waffles (from batter)**
Bagels
Soft Pretzels
Crepés & Doilies
English Muffins*
Muffins (low-fat or fat-free)
Unleavened Rice Breads

Party & Gift Breads, for Very Infrequent Use

Bread Sticks
Crackers
Braids or Wreath Breads
Cinnamon Buns and Cinnamon Rolls
Sweetened Steamed Buns

Note: When eating out, the breads available may contain refined flour or some sweeteners. This is not a problem if your daily bread and other fare is healthy and sugar-free. It is best to be flexible and make the most of whatever situation you are in. Go for the grain, whatever it is!

Quick & Easy Daily Bread

As mentioned, daily bread should be quite simple. Steamed buns (filled or unfilled) or quick breads— tortillas, chapatis, flat breads, pita, arepas, pizza, skillet bread, calzones, and tamales—are preferable to most long-baked loaf breads for regular use. For festive or fancy meals or when you have a little more time to invest, you may wish to add herbs, spices, seeds, or a savory filling. These quick cooking breads save time and fuel and tend to be easier on the digestive system than are long baked, hard, dry preparations. However, sweetened breads— whether quick-cooked or not, are less healthful, particularly if they contain a fair amount of oil, butter, nuts, or seeds. These should be used very infrequently.

Basic Bread Making Tools

Before you head into the kitchen, review the basic tools listed below. These will simplify the task of bread making and can be found in kitchen or ethnic shops or even thrift stores or garage sales.

Measuring cups and spoons: Accuracy in measuring is of the utmost importance in cooking, particularly if you want to produce good results. Measure, measure, and measure!

Mixing bowls: Invest in one or two extra-large, 12-18 quart stainless steel mixing bowls. These are a must for easy bread making and cleanup; the bread can be kneaded right in the bowl. Glass or pyrex bowls are too heavy and awkward for kneaded bread dough because they can't be spun as you mix and knead; though they work for batter bread, pancakes, waffles and other such things.

Mixing spoons: A large, sturdy, long handled stainless steel spoon is important for mixing the water into the flour before kneading. A wooden handled spoon can easily break when you're mixing dough for kneaded breads.

Pastry Cloth: If you don't want to mess with flouring your counter top or butcher block, invest in a pastry cloth. They only cost a couple of dollars and eliminate the mess. You simply turn or roll the dough out onto the cloth, shape it, then put it in the appropriate pan for baking.

Thermometers: see Basic Tools.

Baking Pans: see Basic Tools.

Bamboo steamer trays (2 sets) + 4 heat-proof plates: see Basic Tools.

Cooling racks & bread baskets: see Basic Tools.

Towels (cotton, linen, white): see Basic Tools.

Essential Bread Making Ingredients

Flour: Like other foods, your flour should come from as local a source as possible and preferably organically grown. Flour should also be fresh because once ground, the polyunsaturated fats in the grain break down (oxidize) quickly when exposed to light and air. Therefore, buy flour in small amounts that can be used up within three months. Store in a cool, dry place away from sunlight, moisture or the heat of the kitchen. Four may also be stored in a paper bag, wrapped in a plastic bag, in the freezer or refrigerator to prolong its shelf life and retain more of its nutrients.

The best flour is that which is ground just before or close to the time of use. Millet, amaranth, and quinoa can be ground to a fine flour in an Osterizer mini-blender container. You'll need patience to process it in small batches to produce a fine and powdery flour needed for good bread. For most grains, however, a proper flour grinder is essential. Most grains are just too hard to grind in a blender and cannot be turned into flour without a flour mill. For best nutrition, invest in a home flour mill so you can grind your flour fresh. (Get a flour mill which uses a low temperature, to avoid spoiling the flour. If the temperature is too high your flour will get cooked as it is being ground and this will destroy many of the vital nutrients.

You can make delicious breads from spelt or whole wheat bread flour combined with a second flour. (Whole wheat pastry flour does not work for bread doughs, however; it lacks the gluten necessary to give bread its shape and rising powder.) Some favorite additions include:

These may be used to replace 1/3 to 1/2 of the flour in kneaded or quick breads:

(1/2-1 cup of one of these per batch of Basic Bread Dough or more for quick-batter breads)

Buckwheat flour— produces a hearty, slightly sweet, dark, and moist bread

Barley flour— adds a moist, cake-y crumb and texture

Kamut flour—creates a super moist dough with a pasta-like taste and texture

Rye flour— makes the dough a bit sticky, dark, very moist and sweet

These may be used to replace 1/4 to 1/3 of the flour in kneaded or quick breads:

(1/4-1/2 cup of one of these per batch of Basic Bread Dough or more in quick breads)

Millet flour— adds a golden color and a rich and buttery cornbread-like taste and texture

Corn meal—adds a golden color, slightly coarse texture, hearty and slightly rich flavor

Corn flour—add a golden color and a velvety smooth texture

Oat flour—adds a moist, cake-like crumb and a velvety smooth texture

Soy flour—adds a rich taste and smooth, silky texture

Amaranth flour—adds a buttery, rich flavor and moist texture

Chestnut flour—adds a slight pink hue, sweet taste, and added moisture

Sweet rice flour—adds a sweet taste and sticky texture

Quinoa flour—adds a nutty taste, coarse texture, and slightly bitter but pleasant taste

Notes on Gluten Flour: We add a small amount of gluten flour (not more than 1 Tbsp. per total cup of flour) to our loaf breads, buns, and other doughs. The gluten flour lightens up whole grain breads and helps them hold their shape as they rise. It gives them a more moist and spongy texture much like what other bakers achieve with less nutritious white flour. We do not use gluten flour in cookies, cakes, batter breads, or pie crusts where too much gluten flour would produce too tough a texture.

Sea salt: You can taste and feel the difference in using natural sun dried sea salt. Look for it in the macrobiotic section of your local co-op or health food store. If you can't find it there, you may want to order it by mail. (See Resources.)

Sea salt is crucial in bread making. It controls the proper yeast growth, and keeps the dough from rising too much or too fast. Salt also strengthens the gluten strands in the dough, making a stronger dough with better rising and holding power, It also wards off spoilage, maintains the proper acid-alkaline balance, aids digestion and assimilation, and makes breads more flavorful and enjoyable. (Salt-free bread is usually tasteless and harder to digest. Many find unsalted breads totally unpalatable.)

Pure water: Pure water is best for drinking, cooking, and baking. Your food (including bread) will taste much better when made from pure well water, spring water, or purified water. City water is usually highly contaminated with heavy metals (lead, mercury, cadmium, etc.), chlorine, fluoride, microbes, pesticides and other chemicals. All of these can affect the taste and the rising quality of your baked goods. They are also injurious to your health and can contribute to the creation of cancer, osteoporosis, heart disease and premature degeneration.

Other liquids: Water left over from cooking pasta may be used in place of all or some of the water in any bread (however, we prefer to use pasta water to cook our morning porridge). Bear in mind, however, that some varieties of pasta may leave too strong a flavor in the water and may overpower some types of bread. It is best to avoid using (dairy) milk or yogurt in baking. Using them in baking is unnecessary, can easily lead to over-use and wastes these precious foods. (If you use them it is best to use them as table condiments, sparingly and consciously, rather than in cooking.) In actuality, these foods are not necessary for health and usually contribute to excess fat on the frame, in your arteries, and around your internal organs. Other alternatives exist which will not compromise your health or the flavor of your baked goods.

For pancakes, waffles, and corn breads, biscuits and other batters, plain, unsweetened soy, almond, sunflower, or rice milk will do the trick. These are a bit too rich and expensive for use in everyday breads though. Occasionally, however, they make excellent replacements for goat or cow's milk, or even buttermilk (just add a tablespoon of brown rice vinegar or cider per cup of soy milk for the latter). For a slightly sweeter taste in main-dish breads, you may wish to use carrot juice for some of the liquid or puree sweet corn, when in season, with the water or soy milk in the recipe. (You can do this when modifying someone else's corn bread, loaf bread, pancake, or waffle recipe that calls for sweetener. You can also replace sweeteners in "savory" bread recipes with plain water.) For dessert breads (sweet rolls, raisin-bread, sweet buns, etc.) water can be replaced with commercial amasake nectar, thinned homemade amasake, sweetened rice or nut milk, or apple juice, however, these are best left out of daily breads or those that will be served as part of meal, with vegetables, beans, and the like. Adding sweeteners to main-dish breads is a surefire recipe for gas and indigestion. By replacing 25% of the flour in a savory or dessert bread recipe with chestnut flour you can also add a very sweet taste without side-effects.

Oil: Though most conventional and commercial breads contain oil, margarine, or shortening, these are unnecessary when using the simple techniques outlined in this chapter. You will also discover that shelf life is longer for oil-free breads. Margarine, hydrogenated vegetable oils and vegetable shortening are artificial and should be avoided at all costs! Corn oil is far healthier and more digestible than artificial fats and gives a rich and buttery taste to baked goods. Even butter and ghee are nutritionally superior to margarine, vegetable shortening, and the like. (Used every now and then— and sparingly— in whole grain corn bread, biscuits, or for cooking pancakes, they can be a real treat and a part of a nourishing diet. Just be sure to make the other dishes in the meal oil-free or low in fat if you use these in a particular dish or meal.)

Copious quantities of vegetable oils are not healthful and should therefore be used sparingly. When adding fats or oils to bread, small quantities are sufficient. A reasonable amount is one or two tablespoons of fat per three to four cups flour, or one tablespoon oil for every two cups of flour when making pie crusts (see index for "Spanokopita" for our Basic Pie Crust).

If used, butter, ghee, or other rich items are often more satisfying when added at the table rather than to the dough. You may find spreads unnecessary or only need them in trace amounts if you use soup, stew, or cooking juices from tempeh, beans, or vegetables to dunk your bread in. Bread may also be used as a utensil, as is done in Middle-Eastern, Mexican, Ethiopian, and other cuisines, to pick up beans, dips, sauteed vegetables, or other tasty morsels. Countless other low-fat spreads also exist.

Corn oil imparts the most buttery taste of all oils. Light sesame or sunflower oil will add a rich, slightly buttery flavor. Olive oil is very strong and best for pizza, focaccia, or garlic bread. Quality is key. Avoid commercial "salad oil" which has been heavily bleached and processed at very high temperatures which create harmful byproducts (free radicals). These poor quality oils are usually rancid, tasteless, and a serious detriment to health. Butter and ghee are far superior to highly processed oils and margarines; actually, they are also more heat stable than any vegetable, seed or nut oils and are good for oiling pans. Mild tasting oils— light sesame, safflower, or nut oils—also work particularly well for greasing baking pans or the plates that will hold raw dough for steamed bun making. The most heat stable of the oils are olive and sesame, both of which contain natural substances which slow down and retard the spoilage of the oil.

Rapid-Rise Yeast:: Look for "Rapid-Rise Yeast" in your local grocery store or health food store, either in the refrigerator section or on the baking aisle. Rapid-rise yeast comes in small envelopes, usually in packs of three, each 1/4 oz. in weight and comes in more economical sized jars. Be sure the label says Rapid-Rise Yeast. This is crucial for the best and fastest results. Check the pull date—you'll want yeast that has not extended it's shelf life. At home, store it in the refrigerator. (No sugar, honey, malt, or other sweeteners are needed to start the yeast.)

Note: When using Rapid-Rise Yeast, make the dough stickier than if you were using regular baking yeast. Active Dry Yeast comes in similar packages and jars but has a different name. This yeast needs just one rising but it usually takes 30-90 minutes to rise, rather than 15-30 minutes. for the benefits and drawbacks of Rapid-Rise Yeast.

Active Dry Yeast: This is available in envelopes (1/4 oz. each, sold in sets of three envelopes) and in 4-oz. jars, in the same places that you would find Rapid Rise Yeast. It should be stored in the same way and used before the expiration date for best results. (No sugar, honey, malt or other sweeteners are needed to start the yeast.)

Desem or natural leaven starter: See *FRESH: From a Vegetarian Kitchen* by Meredith McCarty for more on this.

Yeast Feeding Myths

Contrary to popular belief, sweeteners are not needed to activate the yeast to make the dough rise. When making any yeasted bread or batter breads, whether using Rapid-Rise yeast or Active Dry yeast, sweeteners (sugar, honey, molasses, fruit concentrate, or others) are totally unnecessary and can be eliminated. Bread will rise without it. We guarantee it!

You'll find that your breads last longer without molding and will be far more digestible if sweeteners and fruits are left out (and if little or no oil is used in the dough). You may want to add sweeteners to the dough or batter when you want a special occasion dessert-bread with a sweeter taste but otherwise, sweeteners are best left out of your daily breads.

To make a whole grain bread a bit lighter, you needn't resort to using bleached, white flour. Instead, add a very small amount of gluten flour to your dough— replacing 1 tablespoon of whole grain flour with 1 tablespoon gluten flour or vital wheat gluten flour for each cup of flour in your recipe. If your recipe calls for 2 1/2-3 cups of flour, replace 2-2 1/2 tablespoons of this flour with 2-2 1/2 tablespoons of gluten flour. This will make your bread spongier and higher rising.

Has Yeast Gotten a Bum Rap?

Yeast has gotten a bad rap in many circles, and has been implicated as a causative factor in candidiasis (a common problem of systemic yeast overgrowth) and food allergies. This condition is usually due to a high stress lifestyle, the taking of antibiotics, irregular or missed meals, ingestion of highly processed, refined or spoiled (old) foods, too much raw and/or cold foods and beverages, and an excess of sweets and oily foods. Yeast is often blamed as the cause of such problems, yet it is highly unlikely that the removal of yeast, in and of itself would be sufficient to produce health for an individual or that it would be a major "causal" factor. Yeast is not a problem for a healthy body. In fact, yeasts— including candidiasis— live in nature, and naturally inhabit the human body, even if you don't have "candidiasis" overgrowth. It is only when these microbes are given room to thrive— when we have created the perfect breeding ground for them— and when they crowd out more beneficial microbes that disease sets in.

Many people believe that either wheat or yeast, or both, are the cause of may of their health complaints. But it is actually more complex than this. People have been eating wheat and yeast for centuries, without the modern plague of food allergies and yeast "sensitivities." It is only when we are weak that we have problems with otherwise nutritious foods. Most of today's commercial breads contain yeast in combination with sweeteners, oils, poor quality salt, preservatives, additives, refined flour, rancid flour, and other ingredients which may aggravate or undermine one's health. However, bread can be made without sweeteners and oil or fat. Bread can also be made from high quality, nutritious, freshly ground flour. And, what the bread is eaten with should not be overlooked. Many people habitually top their bread with high fat spreads such as butter, margarine, nut and seed butters; egg-, chicken, or tuna salad; mayonnaise; cheese; meats; rich tofu spreads. It could be that the fat—not the bread, wheat, or yeast— is what is sapping your energy and devitalizing you. Or it could be a combination of factors (rancid flour, fats, sugars and/or dairy products in the bread, plus fatty toppings and/or cold drinks taken with the bread), coupled with an irregular eating pattern, too frequent or late night eating, snacking and other unhealthy practices, all of which overwork the digestive organs and impair their proper functioning.

Furthermore, the kind of yeast used to make bread is not the same as that which plagues those with systemic candidiasis. Candida or candidiasis is not a condition of "baker's yeast" overgrowth! Baker's yeast is any of various fungi of the genus saccharomyces. It reproduces by budding, is capable of fermenting carbohydrates, and is totally unrelated to the candida albicans "yeast" microbe. Baker's yeast is sensitive to temperature, so much so that it is "killed" at temperatures over 140° F. Baking temperatures typically reach 350-400° F so the yeast which has fermented the starches in your bread does it's job then dies in the oven. Once ingested, baker's yeast will not come back to life and repopulate the intestines. (Candidiasis is a condition in which the body's mineral balance and intestinal microflora have been disturbed by irregular or skipped meals, poor food selection, stress, overwork, use of medications and/or coffee or drugs, and resulting nutritional deficiencies.) So the fear of "yeast" may be chalked up to a fad in which many of people's health problems are mistakenly pinned on a harmless (and in fact, helpful) food whose effects are largely misunderstood.

Baker's Yeast & Natural Leaven: What's the difference?

A natural leaven or desem starter does not contain commercial yeast of any sort. Instead, it is a collection of wild airborne yeasts. (These yeast are free for the taking and cost you nothing.) When a natural leaven starter is used to make bread, a longer period of time is needed for rising than with commercial yeast. This longer fermentation allows the wild yeasts to predigest more of the starches in the flour and to break down the phytates (anti-nutritive substances found in whole grains). This makes the bread more digestible and nutritious because it adds more beneficial bacteria. Bread made with such a starter can contain viable vitamin B-12, due to the long fermentation by bacteria. Vitamin B-12 is particularly important for vegetarians and vegans. Though some people buy supplements, fermented foods can contain sufficient amounts for health.

Equally good results can be achieved by allowing your bread to slow-rise for 8-10 hours at room temperature before baking. (see Slow-Rise Bread.)

Notes on Sourdough & Desem starters:

Sourdough or desem starters take more time to tend and use than regular baker's or rapid-rise yeast. A starter must be fed every week or it will die and it should be used weekly since it grows with each feeding. Desem or naturally leavened bread needs two risings, each taking two to four hours. These breads take more time, attention, and practice to perfect. So, if you want to make bread but don't have the time, energy or desire (yet) to make and keep a starter, our Rapid-Rise, Standard-Rise, and Low-Rise Doughs can meet your need for fresh, wholesome bread.

Can I use a desem/naturally leavened starter with these recipes?

If you choose to make a natural leaven starter (which is just a collection of air born yeasts) you can use our basic recipes, though you'll need to modify the proportions of flour to water, the rising time, and the cooking time and temperature. (For example, if you want to make Chinese-style steamed buns with our starter you will need to make the dough a bit more dry so that it will hold its shape on the second rise (on oiled plates). To learn how to make good naturally leavened breads, we suggest reading Meredith McCarty's *FRESH: From a Vegetarian Kitchen*, or her video, *Quick Whole Grain Sourdough Breads* or see *The Do of Cooking* by Cornellia Aihara (GOMF Press).

Say Goodbye to Baking Soda & Baking Powder

Yeast is a natural, whether you are making loaf breads, biscuits, corn bread, quick breads, pancakes, waffles, muffins, cookies, or cakes. It can meet all of your leavening needs, eliminating the need for less healthful alternatives such as baking soda and baking powder.

Whole grains and whole grain flour are incredibly nutritious and essential for health, but they must be prepared in ways that make them more digestible. (This is one of the reasons why we soak whole grains, and even some rolled grains prior to cooking.) Live yeast (e.g., Rapid Rise Yeast, Active Dry Yeast, or a desem or sourdough starter) as an ingredient in baked flour products breaks down some of the anti-nutritive substances in grains, making their nutrients or energy more available. The yeast makes whole grain baked goods more digestible and nutritious— something neither baking soda nor baking powder can do.

Baking soda and baking powder are best reserved for rare occasions. Baking powder contains bicarbonate of soda and tartaric acid, two chemicals which offer no nutritional value. They retard digestion, destroy many of the B vitamins in whole grain breads, and often lead to acid heartburn, flatulence, and poor assimilation as well. Neither baking powder nor baking soda offer the nutritional benefits of live yeast (or of desem or sourdough starters). Additionally, the chemicals in baking soda and baking powder burden the eliminative organs, which have to work harder to throw them off. From the western analytic view, baking soda has been shown to decrease pancreatic juices which are crucial for digestion of protein, fats, and carbohydrates.

Baking soda, which contains bicarbonate of soda, is often used as an internal remedy for acid indigestion because it reduces stomach acids! Eaten at a meal, baking soda leavened products can reduce the effectiveness of your digestive enzymes when you need them the most! (Why do people use antacids? To counter and reduce stomach acids— after a meal. But we don't want to reduce the effectiveness of our stomach acids in the midst of a meal. Instead, we want to eat in a way that promotes proper digestion and functioning of our internal organs.

Baking powder is no better than baking soda. Phosphates and aluminum are used in at least half of the baking powders manufactured in the U. S. Not only has aluminum been linked to Alzheimer's disease, but the phosphates contained in these products are also used by many non-food industries to make things like chemical fertilizers, soft drinks, laundry detergent, dish/body soaps (not very appetizing?!). Non-aluminum varieties are best avoided as well; they do not aid digestion and have the disadvantages mentioned above.

Pancakes, waffles, crepés, biscuits, batter breads and occasional use items such as cookies, cakes, and pastries can all be made with yeast as a leavener and some of these can be made unleavened now and then too! (Read on for tips and guidelines to help you convert replace baking soda or baking powder with rapid-rise or active dry yeast.)

Using Yeast—How & How Much To Use

Figure a 1/4 oz. packet of Rapid-Rise Yeast or Active Dry Yeast per 3-4 1/2 cups of flour for bread batters or dough. When making Slow-Rise Bread (allowing 8-12 hours for rising) you may reduce the amount of Active Dry Yeast to 14-1/2 teaspoon per 3-4 1/2 cups of flour. When making very Slow-Rise Bread (allowing 24-36 hours for three risings, punching the dough down twice) you may reduce the mount of yeast to 1/4 teaspoon Active Dry Yeast per 3-4 1/2 cups flour.

When making a double batch of bread, you do not need to double the yeast. (If you double a recipe that calls for 1 teaspoon of yeast, use just 1 1/2 teaspoons in the double recipe.)

Regardless of how you make and rise your dough you do not need to add sweeteners to the batter or dough nor must you proof the yeast before it goes into the batter or dough. However, there is a special way to add the yeast, in order to achieve satisfying results. The following recipes will take you through the process, step-by-step.

Best Rising Places for Breads and Batters

(a) a sunny windowsill or counter top in warm weather;

(b) near a radiator;

(c) on top of a heating pad on low setting

(d) a gas oven with just the pilot light on (no hotter than 100° F.)

(e) an electric oven with just the light on

(f) an oven heated briefly to 140° F., then turned off

(g) *For steamed bun making only:* Fill a 4-6 quart wide pot with 2-inches of water, cover, and bring to boil. Turn off heat. Remove the lid and place the bamboo steamer trays on top (each tray should contain an oiled heat-proof dinner plate with dinner roll or burger bun sized dough balls), stacking one or more trays on top of each other. Cover the top tray with a bamboo lid. Allow to rise over the steam until doubled in bulk (15-30 minutes with Rapid-Rise Dough, 30-90 minutes for Standard or Slow-Rise Dough which has been risen in a bowl for the first rising.) Cook as per Basic Steamed Bun Procedure.

Tips for storing bread & baked goods

It is best to allow breads to cool thoroughly before wrapping and storing them. Stored properly, most breads will keep for a week or two, in or out of the refrigerator. Sourdough or desem breads will last even longer, often for four to six weeks without drying out or molding.

All breads can be steam heated to re-create that just-baked or steamed taste, freshness, and moist texture. Even breads and biscuits that you would normally call stale (dry) and might have beenthrown out will taste fresh, moist and delicious when resteamed on a bamboo tray or rack, wrapped in a kitchen towel. (See notes below and steaming tips, Uses For Leftover & Old Breads.)

Breads, biscuits, batter breads, unfilled buns, arepas, rolls, etc.: Store in brown paper bags (open or folded over on top), cellophane bags, waxed paper bags, a bread box, or wrapped first in a dry, white cotton/linen towel and placed in a bowl or basket. Plastic wrap and plastic bags trap moisture and invite mold so they are not advisable for most breads though they can be used for short term storage now and then. Cellulose bags are a healthier alternative to plastic. Keep bags of unfilled steamed buns or other bread in a cool dry place or the refrigerator for a week or so (some will last longer and most can be revived by steam even if they dry out like hockey pucks). Sourdough breads will last for four to six weeks without spoiling. Any bread may be reheated, remoistened, and freshened by steaming 5-25 minutes (wrapped in a towel). Exact steaming time depends upon the moistness/dryness of the bread, the thickness of the slices or pieces and distance from the steam. (Fairly fresh sandwich bread may need five to seven minutes of steaming while thick, slightly dried out slabs of French bread, or dinner rolls or buns may need ten to twenty minutes to become soft and warmed throughout.)

Pancakes and waffles: Store in a bowl, with a plate on top or cover with a bamboo sushi mat and kept at room temperature and eaten within 24-hours. Pancakes and waffles may be kept in wax paper bags and steamed briefly to reheat.

Filled breads: (steamed buns, turnovers or fruit or vegetable breads) Store in cellophane, waxed paper bags, or brown paper bags or use leftover plastic bags if the filling is drippy or messy. Store in the refrigerator if they will not be eaten with 24 hours (or contain beans, tofu, or animal products). Herbed breads do not need refrigeration. Refrigerate breads which contain fruits or vegetables if they will not be eaten within three days. Reheat these breads by steaming, as desired.

Make Bread For The Week in 1-1 1/2 hours with our One-Rise Method

(Note: If using either the Standard or Slow-Rise Method, hands on time will be the same as with the Quick-Rise Method, but you will need to allow more time for rising and checking.)

If you choose to have bread as the only grain in one of your daily meals, as we often do, you will need to make a fairly large quantities

When making bread on a grain based diet, you will need about 3/4-1 cup of flour per person when bread is served as the only grain in a meal. Figure 1-1 1/2 cups of flour per active male, growing teenager, competitive female athlete, or pregnant, lactating woman when bread is the only grain served at a meal. Of course, you could stretch your bread, making it go farther by serving it with a second grain such as rice, millet, polenta or pasta.

In one week, two people can go through four single or two double batches of bread (each batch comprised of 2 1/2-4 cups of flour) when bread is eaten as the only grain in one of your daily meals.

For convenience, you can make one double batch of bread about 6 or 7 cups of flour) twice a week or two double batches (about 12 to 14 cups of flour) once a week. This will give you enough bread to feed two people at five or six meals where bread is the only grain. This can be done in under an hour. If you're cooking for a large family, you may wish to make three or four double batches of bread at one time or two double batches twice a week. Even if you live alone, it is not unreasonable to make one or two double batches of bread once a week. It's easier and less expensive than making or buying muffins, cookies, crackers, rice cakes, or other snack foods. Bread is also more nutritious and digestible than chips and other hard, dry, crunchy, and/or deep fried "fast foods" or snack foods.

Bread making doesn't require much hands-on time. In fact, one person can make and shape a double batch of dough in 20 minutes or two double batches in an hour or less, from start to finish!

Here's How:

1) Make a double batch of dough. Shape it, then set it to rise while you make another double batch of bread.

2) While the second double batch rises, the first one cooks.

3) While the second batch cooks you can clean up the kitchen, make a pressed salad or stir fry or assemble a soup for the next day or two. If you're really feeling ambitious, you could prepare still another batch of bread while the second batch rises and the first one cooks.

Or, make a double or triple batch of dough in one bowl. Make it the night before, let it rise all night, then punch it down and shape it in the morning, put it in pans or on sheets, then leave it to rise while you get ready in the morning. In one half to one hour it should be ready to bake or steam. It can even cook while you're eating breakfast, then you'll have warm bread for your lunch box (to serve with a thermos cup of soup and leftover salad or cooked veggies).

Notes on Making Multiple Slow Rise Doughs: If you opt for our more nutritious Slow-Rise Method, you can still make one, two or three double batches in short order. Just mix the doughs in the evening, allow them to rise in oiled, covered bowls, at room temperature then gently "punch" the dough down in the morning, shape the breads, set them to rise then cook while you shower, dress, stretch, cook, eat breakfast, assemble pack lunches, do other morning activities.

Make 2 double batches of Rapid-Rise Bread in 1-1 1/2 hours, from start to finish

Example # 1:

1 double batch steamed buns + 1 double batch pita, souvlaki pita, baguettes, or freeform loaves; or 2-3 double batches loaf bread, made all at once in one large mixing bowl & cooked all at once

15-20 minutes	**1)** Make a double batch Basic Rapid Rise Dough then shape as for buns.
15-20 minutes	**2)** Let bread rise while you make a second double batch of dough; shape as for pita pockets, souvlaki-pita, free form loaves, or baguettes.
15 minutes	**3)** Steam cook the first batch; meanwhile, let the second batch of Basic Rapid Rise Dough (with a different flour combination) rise. Clean the dishes
15 minutes	**4)** Bake the second batch of dough; cool the first then prep something else for the next day.

Total time elapsed: 1-1 1/2 hours

Example # 2:

1-2 double batches freeform or sandwich loaves + 1 single or double batch corn or millet batter bread, or dinner rolls or arepas

15-20 minutes	**1)** Make a double batch Basic Rapid Rise Dough then shape as for freeform or sandwich loaf bread.
15-30 minutes	**2)** Let bread rise while you make a single or double batch of corn or millet batter bread, dinner rolls, or arepas. (Arepas need no rising.)
15-20 minutes	**3)** Bake the first batch; meanwhile, let the second batch rise and clean up the dishes and prep something for the next day (soup, salad, or stew).
15-30 minutes	**4)** Put the second batch in the oven as soon as its risen enough; take the first batch out and let it cool.

Total time elapsed: 1-1 1/2 hours

Make 3 double batches of bread in 1 3/4-2 hours, from start to finish

Example #3:

1 double batch steamed buns + 1 double batch souvlaki-pita or pita pocket bread + 1 double batch flat breads, tamales, arepas, Souvlaki-pita, steamed buns, freeform/loaf breads, or baguettes

15-20 minutes	**1)** Make a double batch of unfilled Basic Rapid-Rise Dough as steamed buns.
15-20 minutes	**2)** While the buns rise, make a double batch of similar dough, using a different flour combination: Shape as for souvlaki-pita or pita pockets.
15-20 minutes	**3)** Put buns on to steam. While the buns steam and second bread rises, make a third batch of bread—unleavened flat breads*, arepas*, unfilled tamales, more pita, buns, or free-form french or baguette loaves. Use yet another flour combination if you like.
15-35 minutes	**4)** First batch of buns will be done about the time the second batch is ready to bake. Bake third batch of bread immediately, if they need no rising*; if they need to rise, wash up the dishes in the meantime. Transfer buns to a cooling rack; check the second batch of dough.
15-30 minutes	**5)** Bake or steam the last batch of dough.

Total time elapsed: 1 1/4 hour-2 hours

Bread Toppings & Spreads

Wait—before you reach for the butter dish (or peanut butter jar) ask yourself if you really need it. Is there something else in the meal that you can use to moisten and en-rich your bread?

You may desire a little bit of butter or ghee or grated cheese, but for optimal health you'll want to cut way back on or even eliminate the use of these high fat animal products. Often rich spreads are unnecessary, or needed in only minute amounts, if you are serving a soup or stew which contains tofu, soy milk or yogurt, or sauteed tempeh or wheat meat. Likewise, other side-dishes which contain oil, tahini, nut butter or tofu, tempeh, eggs, nuts, seeds, or butter or ghee may be used to top your bread.

For starters, serve your soup or stew along with the rest of the meal and try dunking your slices of bread, bagels, buns, rolls, biscuits, pancakes, tortillas or pita into a savory cupful as you eat your meal. You can also use bread to scoop up cooked, pressed or marinated vegetables, beans, wheat meat, tempeh or salads. Gravies also make wonderful bread toppings or sopping liquids for dunking. You'll be amazed at how easy it is to cut back on the amount of fat and oil you eat by doing this. If eggs or (soy or dairy) yogurt are served in a meal, these too can be used as condiments for your bread instead of using a spread.

If you want a spread (such as when your soup is light and low-fat or animal-free), try one of the following. Some are rich, others are light, but all are tasty and sure to please.

Very low-fat bread spreads & toppings

- Millet Butter
- Garbanzo or Chickpea Butter
- Onion Butter
- Refried Beans
- Squash Butter
- Baked Beans
- Parsnip Butter
- Pressed or Marinated salad
- Mock Poultry Gravy
- Stir Fried Vegetables
- Herbed Gravy
- Any low-fat bean dip, sauce, or spread
- Parsnip White Sauce
- Prepared mustard (any natural variety or brand)
- Umeboshi paste or light miso
- Lightly oiled or dressed vegetables
- Any vegetarian soup or stew
- Vegetable pickles
- Hungarian Goulash
- Glazed Vegetables
- Seitan Stroganoff
- Pressed Salad +/- flax or sesame oil

Rich Spreads Richer Dips & Spreads

(Use sparingly, now & then)

- Sesame tahini (diluted)
- Sea-Sage & Sunflower Spread
- Whipped Miso Nut Butter
- Herbed Tofu "Cream Cheese"
- Dairy-Free/Low-Fat Pesto
- Tofu Tartar Sauce
- Soy yogurt or goat yogurt cheese
- Hummus, (garbanzo bean dip)
- Soup or stew with tempeh or seitan
- Tempeh Mock Tuna Salad
- Garlic & White Miso with Corn Oil
- Tofu Pesto Pate
- Olive oil (brushed on)
- Tofu Ricotta or Sour Cream
- Ground seed condiment
- Natto "Cream Cheese"
- Raw or cultured Butter
- Ghee
- Grated raw milk cheese
- Quark or herbed quark spread

Kneading Tips & Techniques

Proper kneading is essential. Some bread requires a fair amount of kneading, about ten minutes (loaf breads, bagels, pizza, dinner rolls, and other shaped and risen breads), unlike unleavened flat breads such as chapatis, tortillas and arepas—masa corn cakes. Kneading is not used for wet batter breads (pancakes, waffles, cookies, etc).

By stretching the dough and the fibers in all directions, kneading develops the gluten which gives breads their rising and holding power and helps maintain their shape. With the technique outlined below, the gluten is developed quickly, easily, and efficiently without a lot of elbow grease. This technique is less messy than other methods of kneading because the bread is mixed and kneaded in the same bowl rather than being mixed in a bowl then dumped on to a floured cutting board for kneading.

A large 12-18 quart stainless steel bowl is essential. Follow the basic instructions as per All-Purpose, Rapid-Rise, Standard-Rise or Slow-Rise Dough. Stir the flour, yeast, and warm liquids with a large, sturdy stainless steel spoon, adding additional flour a little at a time, measuring it out as you go, until a dough begins to form. When it becomes too difficult to mix with a spoon, use your hands— but not your fingers. Pretend you have no fingers and that your hand is a flexible spatula.

If you are right handed, hold the bowl with your left hand and knead with the right. Slightly cup your right hand to scoop the dough toward you then push the dough away, fold the dough in on itself, toward the center of the bowl. Push it away using the heel of your hand. Repeat once then give the bowl a quarter turn (clockwise) with your left hand. Repeat this kneading process adding just a little more flour, about 1/4 cupful or less at a time as needed to create a smooth dough that pulls away from the sides of the bowl and form a smooth and supple ball.

Be careful not to add too much flour. The dough will dry a bit as you work it. A dough that is too dry will not rise. The finished dough should spring back to the touch when you poke it, without sticking to your finger. It should be ear-lobe consistency (pinch your earlobe) or soft and smooth like a baby's bottom.

Basic Bread Recipes

Basic Procedure, All-Purpose Bread Dough***

Yield: 6 burger buns *or* 8 steamed buns, bagels, calzones or turnovers *or* 6-8 Souvlaki-pita, pita pockets, or dinner rolls *or* 1 standard sandwich loaf or freeform French or Italian loaf *or* 2 baguettes *or* 6-8 mini-pizzas or 2 medium thick crust (10 to 12) or 1 large (16") thick crust pizza. **Serves:** 3-4 as the only grain in a meal *or* 6-8 accompanied by noodles, rice, or other grain.

This recipe can be endlessly varied by using different flour combinations; mixing in herbs, spices or seeds; changing the shape or using a different cooking technique. Making a double batches of any bread is convenient and time and energy efficient. If you have several mouths to feed or want to set yourself up with plenty of bread for the week, make two double batches of bread (the same or two different types).

Note: A large stainless steel mixing bowl is most appropriate for mixing and kneading any kind of bread. One or two double batches of bread can be mixed all at once in the same bowl!

Basic Ingredients:

2 1/2-3 1/2 cups spelt flour *or* finely ground whole wheat bread flour *(red or hard white wheat flour or combination of flours, see notes below)**

2 Tbsp. gluten flour or vital wheat gluten flour (or substitute other flour)

1/4 oz. pkg. *or* 2 1/4 tsp. Rapid-Rise or Active Dry Yeast (use less for Slow-Rise Bread)**

1 1/3 cups water

1 tsp. sun dried sea salt

Slightly more flour only as/if needed

+/- Flour to dust pans and/or oil for pans (depending upon type of bread) ❏

Rapid-Rise Dough:

Prep: 20 minutes
Rising: 15-30 minutes
Cooking: 15-90 minutes (depending on shape and cooking method)

1. Reserve 1 cup of spelt or wheat flour. In a large stainless steel mixing bowl, mix remaining 2 1/2 cups flour with gluten flour and Rapid-Rise Yeast or Active Dry Yeast. Stir briefly.

2. In a saucepan with a metal stem thermometer, heat water and salt until hot to the touch— 125-130° F, but no hotter. If too hot, cool to the proper temperature.

3. Mix warm water into flour with a large metal mixing spoon to form a soft dough. Knead right in the mixing bowl, about 10 minutes or until smooth and supple. (See Basic Kneading Tips and Techniques.) Add remaining 1 cup flour a little at a time only as needed to make an elastic, soft and slightly sticky dough that pulls away from the sides of the bowl and forms a smooth ball. It should be earlobe consistency and should spring back to the touch. If you need to add a bit more flour, do so cautiously! A dry dough will not rise. It is better a bit too sticky than too dry!

4. Oil your hands to keep dough from sticking to them, as needed. Shape the dough as called for in any of the basic bread recipes listed in this chapter. Place shaped dough on oiled plates, in oiled bread bans, or on floured baking pans as directed in each recipe.

5. Let rise 15-30 minutes, or until almost doubled in bulk, in a warm place. (see Best Rising Places). Do not allow dough to over-rise and become too stretched out. Preheat the oven before the dough has doubled in bulk. (Remove bread from oven before preheating if it is in there.)

6. Bake or steam as directed in each recipe. (Rapid-Rise bread doesn't require a second rising.) ❏

Standard Rise Dough:

Prep: 20 minutes
Rising: First rise 1-2 hours + Second rise ~30-60 minutes
Cooking: 15-90 minutes (depending on shape and cooking method)

1. Heat liquid to lukewarm, 100-110° F (no hotter). Cool to the proper temperature if needed. Add Active Dry Yeast.

2. Flour should be at room temperature; not ice cold from the refrigerator. Reserve 1 cup of spelt or wheat flour. In a large stainless steel mixing bowl, mix remaining 2 1/2 cups flour with gluten flour. Stir briefly with a spoon. Add wet ingredients to dry ingredients then mix and knead as above.

3. Oil a mixing bowl, one which allows room for the dough to double in size. Place dough in bowl. Oil the bottom of a dinner plate and place this over the bowl of dough. (We use a 3-quart pyrex or glass bowl for a single batch.) Cover bowl with a dinner plate or divide the dough in half if making a double batch, then cover each bowl. Or, place a double or triple batch of dough in a 8-16 quart stainless steel bowl then cover with another 8-16-quart bowl that fits on top of or inside the rim of the bottom bowl, or lay a cooling rack over the bread bowl and cover with a damp towel.

4. Place in a warm place and allow dough to rise until doubled in size, about 1-2 hours or as needed.

5. Gently punch down dough and knead a couple of turns in the bowl. Shape the dough as desired or as per recipe instructions.

6. Arrange dough on oiled heat-proof plates (for steamed buns), or in oiled pans or on well floured cookie sheets. Allow it to rise until almost doubled in size, about 1/2-1 1/2 hours. Do not allow dough to over-rise or it will bubble, tear and the resulting bread will taste "yeasty" and/or it will fall. (Check it often.)

7. Bake, boil or steam cook as per recipe instructions. ❏

Slow-Rise Method:

Prep: 20 minutes
Rising: First rise: 8-10 hours or overnight +
Second rise: 1/2-1 hour, or as needed
Cooking: 15-90 minutes (depending on shape and cooking method

1. Allow all ingredients to come to room temperature for 1/2-1 hour before starting.

2. Reserve 1 cup of spelt or wheat flour. In a large stainless steel mixing bowl, mix remaining 2 1/2 cups flour with gluten flour (or spelt flour if you are wheat sensitive). Add Active Dry Yeast— but reduce the amount to 1/4-1/2 tsp. per 3-4 cups flour. Stir briefly with a spoon.

3. Heat liquid to 100-110° F (no hotter). Cool to the proper temperature if needed. Mix and knead as for Basic Bread Dough.

4. Allow dough to rise in a large bowl covered with a plate, all day or overnight, at room temperature or in an oven with a pilot light on.

5. In the morning, or after 8-10 hours, punch down risen dough, shape, and place in oiled bread pans, on floured baking sheets (for freeform breads), or on oiled heat-proof dinner plates (for steamed buns).

6. Allow dough to rise in a warm place until almost doubled in size, about 1/2-1 hour. Do not allow dough to over-rise or it will tear and the bread will taste "yeasty" and/or it will fall. (Check it often.)

7. Bake or steam as per the recipe you are following. ❏

Variations On The Basic Dough:

- **Tips for steamed bun, pizza, souvlaki pita, pita, calzone, loaf bread, and dinner rolls:** The dough should be a bit more sticky for these than for doughs which will be baked freeform on a floured cookie sheet (such as French, Italian, or Peasant style round loaves). Breads which are not baked in a container (pan with sides) must be a bit firmer to hole their shape when rising and baking.)

- **Light Wheat or Light Spelt Bread:** Use unbleached wheat or unbleached spelt flour for 1/3-1/2 of the total flour (to replace 1-1 1/4 cups whole grain flour). Do this if you suffer from weak digestion with a tendency to chronic diarrhea or loose stools or for special occasions.

- **For the wheat sensitive individual:** Use spelt flour in the basic recipe then replace gluten flour with additional spelt flour. Spelt is more moist than wheat flour so you may need to add more flour to the basic dough to produce a smooth, supple and firm enough dough.

- **Mixed grain breads:** Replace 1/2-1 cup of spelt or wheat flour with a one of the following flours— brown rice, sweet brown rice, buckwheat, barley, kamut, rye, corn, or millet flour, millet meal, or yellow or blue cornmeal. Or, replace 1/2 cup spelt or wheat flour with a specialty flour (chestnut, amaranth, chickpea, soy, quinoa or teff). For best results, do not use these for more than 25-30% of the total flour in a bread dough recipe (not more than 1/4-1/2 cup per 2 1/2-3 cups of total flour).

Notes:

- When using more than one kind of flour, add the flour you will use the least of first and always reserve an extra 1/2 cup of wheat or spelt flour (for a single batch of dough). Different flours have different moisture contents. Depending upon the type and how finely it is ground, you may need to add slightly more flour than is called for in the recipe.

- Whole grain millet, amaranth, or quinoa may be ground in a blender by whizzing the dry grain, 1/2 cup at a time until it becomes fine and powdery like flour.

- We don't recommend grinding buckwheat groats into flour. Good buckwheat flour contains the hull and cannot be ground without a flour mill.

- If you can afford it, a home flour mill is a healthful investment and can turn any whole grain or bean into flour. Freshly milled flour is tastier and more nutritious than purchased flour since most purchased flours are allowed to sit on shelves for days, weeks, or months.

Favorite flour combinations (see notes above):

These amounts apply to a single batch of dough; double amounts for a double batch.

- **Buckwheat Bread:** Use buckwheat for 1/2-3/4 cup flour in the basic recipe

- **Millet Bread:** Use millet flour or millet meal for 1/2-3/4 cup flour in the basic recipe

- **Rye Bread:** Use rye flour or millet meal for 1/2-1 cup flour in the basic recipe

- **Super Soy Bread:** Use soy flour for 1/4-1/3 cup flour in the basic recipe

- **Golden Amaranth Bread:** Use amaranth flour for 1/4-1/2 cup flour in basic recipe

- **Chestnut Bread:** Use chestnut flour for 1/4-1/2 cup flour in the basic recipe

- **Kamut Bread:** Use kamut flour for 1 cup flour in the basic recipe

- **Oat Bread:** Use oat flour for 1/4-1/2 cup flour in the basic recipe

- **Corn Bread Dough:** Use cornmeal or corn flour for 1/2 cup flour in the basic recipe

- **Oatmeal Rye Bread:** Use 1/2 cup oat flour + 1/2 cup rye flour in the basic recipe

- **Sweet Rice Bread:** Use sweet rice flour for 1/4-1/2 cup flour in the basic recipe

- **Barley & Sunflower or Flax Seed Bread:** Replace 1 cup spelt or wheat flour with barley flour in the basic recipe then add 1/3 cup raw whole or powdered raw sunflower or flax seeds.

Vegetable Breads:

For a single batch of dough (wheat, barley millet, kamut, or spelt) try one of the following—

- **Double Corn Dough:** Add 1 cup fresh sweet corn, cut off the cob, to the dough or puree sweet corn with the warm liquids before adding to the flour. (Extra flour may be needed.)

- **Squash or Sweet Potato Bread:** Add 1 cup cooked and mashed winter squash or peeled, cooked sweet potato to the water in the basic recipe or add to warmed water or soy milk then prepare as for Basic Rapid-Rise Dough. (Puree vegetables and room temperature liquids for Slow-Rise Dough). Add a little more flour only as needed.

- **Potato Bread:** Use leftover potato cooking water for water in the basic dough, if desired. Puree 1 cup cooked, peeled, diced potato with the liquids before heating (for Rapid or Standard Rise Breads) or add 1 cup mashed potato to the mixing bowl after adding liquid to the flour and yeast. Prepare as above.

- **Sun Dried Tomato, Onion, or Pepper Bread:** Soak 1/4 cup dried flaked bell pepper, onion or garlic flakes, or minced sundried tomato in hot water to just barley cover. Drain and add veggie bits to dough. Use the remaining liquid as part of the total liquid or save it for soup.

More variations on the Basic Dough:

- **Risen Rice Bread:** Mix 1 cup of cooked wild rice, brown rice, bulgur, or millet into the basic flour mixture above (wheat, spelt, barley, soy or kamut dough) in step #3 before adding warm (or cool) liquid. Knead a bit more to evenly distribute the cooked grain. You may or may not need to add the reserved 1/2 cup of flour when kneading the dough.

- **Super Seeded Bread:** In step #1 or when kneading dough, add 1/4 cup seeds, chopped nuts, or ground nut or seed meal per single batch of dough. (We generally prefer to grind the seeds or nuts into a meal; this makes a lighter bread). Try lightly roasted sesame or flax seeds, unroasted sunflower or chia seeds, or minced or ground walnuts, almonds or hazelnuts. Or add 1-3 Tbsp. cumin, fennel, mustard, caraway, or anise seeds per single batch of dough.

- **Herbed Bread:** Add 2-2 1/2 tsp. dried *or* 2-4 Tbsp. freshly minced herbs per single batch.

  *3/4 tsp. dried basil + 1/2 tsp. dried oregano + 1/2 tsp. dried thyme + 1-2 Tbsp. dried onion

  **or* 1 Tbsp. dried parsley + 1/2 tsp. each dried rosemary & thyme + 1/4 tsp. sage

  **or* sage + thyme + marjoram or oregano

  **or* rosemary + sage or thyme

  **or* thyme + garlic +/- dill weed

  **or* sauteed onion + garlic +/- oregano or thyme

  **or* 1/2 tsp. each of dried sage + thyme + rosemary + savory + celery salt

Special Occasion, Sweet Dessert Doughs

Use for steamed buns, bread sticks loaves or bagels. Prepare a basic bread dough. The best flour combinations for these are the spelt, wheat, barley, corn, millet, or buckwheat variety. **Try one or more of the following:**

1. Use commercial amazake (milky consistency), thinned homemade amasake, sweetened almond milk or rice milk, or carrot or apple juice to replace water in the basic dough.

2. If desired, mix 1/2-1 cup of raisins or minced dried fruit into the liquids when heating or puree the dried fruit with the liquids before heating it and adding to flour.

3. Add 2-4 tsp. cinnamon; or 1/2 tsp. each of cinnamon plus cardomom or nutmeg; or 1-2 tsp. cinnamon + 1/2 tsp. dried ginger powder; or use some other ground sweet spice powder.

4. Add 1/4 cup finely chopped nuts or seeds to the flour mixture or add 1-2 Tbsp. corn oil or 2-4 Tbsp. peanut, almond, or hazelnut butter to the liquids.

- **Note:** Be very cautious in adding flour beyond the initial 2 1/2-3 cups in the basic recipe. You may or may not need more than this with the added fruit. The consistency of the dough should be similar to regular breads. It should be slightly sticky or it won't rise.

The following sweet doughs are good for special occasions. They can be made into steamed buns, Souvlaki-Pita rounds, sandwich-style loaves, freeform loaves, mini-loaves, or bagels.

- **Carrot "Cake" Dough:** Prepare as above for Sweet Dough but add 1 cup finely grated carrots with nuts and spice before kneading.

- **Pumpkin Spice Dough:** Prepare as above for Sweet Dough but puree 1 cup cooked, mashed squash, pumpkin or peeled sweet potato with the sweet liquid before or after heating. (Try using our buckwheat, rye, hard white wheat, or spelt dough for this.) Add the spices and ground nuts to flour mixture. This version can be made with nuts or without. Raisins would be nice in this dough.

- **Cinnamon-Raisin Bread:** Prepare as above for Sweet Dough. Use chestnut flour for 1/2 cup of the total flour if desired.

Bread Making Chinese Style

The art of Chinese cooking goes back to antiquity. Four thousand years back in fact. Chinese culture is believed to be the oldest civilization in the world and the Chinese fathered many inventions. Believed to be among the earliest users of fire, they invented the suspension bridge, the abicus, the noodle, and steamed breads.

Early Chinese cookery was shaped by many forces. The ancient Chinese society had a substantial leisure class with time and money to spare to satisfy their gustatory desires. Also, the dieticians of the Imperial Court were, as early as 1115 B.C., among some of the earliest professionals to study the effects of foods and food preparations on people and their wisdom was incorporated into Chinese cuisine in its early development. Like other cuisines, Chinese cuisine was also shaped by the day to day realities of famines, floods, and overpopulation. Out of necessity the Chinese became domestic economists. They learned to be resourceful. Large livestock such as cattle were used as work animals because work animals could be fed uncultivated grass and straw and did not need grazing land. This allowed the Chinese to feed larger numbers of people on a smaller amount of land than if beef were used as a staple food. Pigs and fowl were raised for food, but they could be raised sustainably because they needed relatively little land to range and grains and vegetables still served as the core of the Chinese diet.

Economic necessity led the Chinese to be courageous in their selection and preparation of foods. They had to comb both land and sea in search of new ways to feed their masses. And they put everything to use. In fact, the Chinese were among the first environmentalists and believers in the "waste nothing" philosophy. They were able to take this philosophy and transform it into a truly imaginative and inspired cuisine in which the smallest bits of foods were transformed into artistic and exotic delights.

Not content with relegating cooking to menial task, the Chinese evolved cooking into one of the highest art forms, taking simple foods and creating endless ways to use them. Chinese cookery is said to include over 80,000 dishes, with over 200 different ways to cook pork alone. So ingenious and artful are the Chinese that they could prepare tofu a different way every day for weeks and never tire of it.

A scarcity of fuel required the Chinese to develop techniques to make use of limited resources. Stir frying and other quick stove-top preparations came out of this thrifty tradition. It was also discovered that less wood or charcoal could be used to steam rice than to bake bread, so rice and other whole grains became dietary mainstays. Later, it was discovered that bread too could be steamed— and in a fraction of the time required for conventional baking.

Compared to conventional baked breads, steamed buns offer many extraordinary benefits: they come out softer, moister and easier to digest with no added fat, and they take minutes, rather than hours, to prepare. Most baked loaf breads take 1-1 1/2 hours to bake at 350-400 °F. Most quick batter breads take 35-50 minutes at these temperatures. In contrast, steamed breads can be cooked in 15-20 minutes, stacked several tiers deep on bamboo steamer trays. Even more amazing is the fact that several different varieties may be cooked at once, using the same burner, pot, and steam, and therefore a lot less fuel than is required for standard bread, muffin, and cookie baking.

Steamed buns are incredibly versatile. They are equally at home in Chinese, Italian, German, English, American, or Middle Eastern Meals. They can be made to stand in for any bread you'd normally serve with meals. Whether plain— like a soft dinner roll or kaiser roll— or filled— like a sandwich, calzone, or pastry— this bread can hold it's own.

Plain, unfilled steamed buns can stand in for bagels, English muffins, corn bread, biscuits, dinner rolls, bread sticks or loaf breads. They make excellent burger and hot dog buns and due to their spongy texture, steamed buns make the perfect soup and gravy soppers too. They're marvelous dunked into hearty soups and stews or used to scoop up stir fried, steamed, or marinated salads, or baked, stewed or refried bean dishes, and tofu spreads.

Steamed buns can be stuffed with a variety of savory or sweet fillings to make interesting side dishes, main dishes, snacks, or desserts. And with a hint of filling, a steamed bun can easily be transported, and eaten out of hand, making a convenient sandwich alternative for kids, busy students, moms, executives, and other folks on the go!

For finicky kids, the peanut butter and jelly-filled bun is always a hit. And for squash or sweet potato lovers, these delectable vegetables can be teamed up with nut or seed butter for a luscious and creamy spread or filling. Steamed buns can also be filled with all sorts of sweet treats for a no-bake alternative to cake, cup cakes, or danish pastries.

If you want a Mexican inspired meal, try a corn meal bun or a or refried bean filled bun. For an Italian meal, there's the garlic bun, the pesto bun, the herbed bun, or the pizza bun. For a Middle Eastern style meal you can have a plain barley, rye, or wheat bun or for a taste of the exotic, fill your buns with hummus or babaganouj. Fillings can also include basic vegetarian staples such as tofu, tempeh, or wheat meat (gluten) used singly or in combination with land or sea vegetables. The possibilities are as endless as the world's cuisines are varied. Steamed breads can be enjoyed year round, at breakfast, lunch or supper; and their ingredients may be varied to fit any occasion and everyone's tastes.

Steamed buns are also quick and yeasty to make. With a little advance planning you can have piping hot buns on the table in just about an hour from start to finish. And buns store well, so they can be made in quantities to last for several days or for the entire week. Buns can also be eaten sandwich-style at room temperature or gently steam-heated for that moist, fresh-made taste.

In our house, this marvelous, age-old bread making method has virtually replaced loaf bread and rolls. In the late spring and throughout the summer, we generally shun baked loaf breads; instead, we cook up one or two double batches of steamed buns each week and often serve the buns at one of our daily meals, as the only grain or as a side dish grain to complement rice or millet. (In the fall and winter, we gravitate more toward baked breads since we often use the oven to make other things but even in these seasons steamed buns are a favorite.) Below you will find some of our favorite combinations of filled and unfilled steamed buns.

Basic Procedure, Steamed Buns (Year Round) ***

Prep: 15-20 minutes
Rising: 15-30 minutes for Rapid-Rise Dough; longer for Standard or Slow-Rise Dough
Cooking: 15-20 minutes + 10 to rest

Yield: 8 steamed buns (or 6 larger steamed burger buns)
Serving size: 2-3 buns per person as the grain in a meal *or* 1 per person served with rice, millet, or pasta
Serves: 3-4 (or 1 1/2- meals for 2) as the grain in a meal *or* 8 accompanied by rice, millet, or pasta

This is, By far the most moist, tender, digestible and quick cooking bread. Though they can be made throughout the year, they are the bread of choice in warm weather when you don't want to heat up the kitchen or yourself with a hot oven.

Stacking 10-1/2 or 12 inch bamboo steamer trays are needed for this preparation. You can cook between one batch (8 buns) and three batches (24 buns) at one time, using one pot, one burner, and just 15-20 minutes worth of kitchen fuel. If you don't have bamboo steamer trays, you may improvise using one or more roasting pans with racks inside, though this is not as efficient or effective.

1 recipe Basic All Purpose Dough (from ~2 1/2-
   3+ cups of flour)
   (Try buckwheat, barley, millet, cornmeal, fresh corn, kamut, spelt, amaranth or herb dough)
Light sesame or olive oil, or other mild oil for
   dinner plates

1. Oil two 9-inch heat proof plates for each batch of dough.

2. (If using Standard or Slow-Rise Dough, rise is as per Basic Procedure before proceeding). Form Dough into a uniform 8" log. Using a ruler and knife, cut into 8 equal pieces and even them out as needed. Place one piece of dough in the palm of your left hand. Fold the top edge toward the center (like closing the petals of a flower). Give the dough a quarter turn, then pull an overlapping piece of dough toward the center again. Repeat this until dough is smooth and round and all the sides have been tucked in. Place the ball seam side down in your left hand. Cup your right hand over the dough and roll it gently between your palms to make a smooth ball or burger shape. Seams should disappear quickly as you fold the dough in on itself; if they don't, the dough is too dry. Dry buns may be a bit heavy. Proceed onward but be more cautious about adding flour next time.

3. Arrange 4 balls of dough on each oiled plate, seam-side down, leaving 1 to 2 inches between each ball for rising. Put each plate on a 10 1/2 inch bamboo steamer tray, stack trays, cover with a lid. Let rise in a warm place 15-30 minutes for Rapid-Rise Dough, or until doubled in size. Rise longer for Standard-Rise or Slow-Rise Dough.

4. Heat 2-inches of water to boiling in a wok or a wide, deep stainless steel pot, (preferably a 4-6 quart pot) which allows 2-4 inches between the water and the bottom of the steamer tray. The pot's diameter should match that of the steamer trays for thorough and even cooking. (If you do not have a wok or a proper sized pot, look for a round electric fry pan with a 10 1/2 or 12 inch diameter.) Stack steamer trays on top of each other, 2 trays for a single batch; 4 trays for a double; and 6 for a triple.

Note: If you have been rising over steam, simply turn the burner to high to cook. Use the bamboo cover when rising and cooking.

5. Once the pot comes to a full boil with steam rising, turn heat to medium and cook over rapidly boiling water. Steam over rapidly boiling water, 15 minutes for a single batch, (20 minutes for a double or triple batch.)

6. Immediately turn off the heat, but don't peek! Allow buns to rest, covered and undisturbed over the warm pot for 10 minutes.

7. Use a small butter knife to separate the buns. Remove from plates with a spatula. Transfer to a cooling rack or a towel-lined basket. Buns left on the plates too long will become soggy.

Storage: When cooled, store in paper, cellophane, or wax paper bags. Refrigerate filled buns. Unfilled buns may be kept in or out of the refrigerator. Serve leftovers warm or at room temperature. Reheat, remoisten and freshen leftover or dry buns by steaming over rapidly boiling water, wrapped in a cotton-linen towel. Use within 1 week.

Serving suggestions: Serve with a green or mixed vegetable side dish and a soup, stew, sauce, gravy and/or a colorful root, ground or round vegetable dish. If the buns do not contain beans, tofu, tempeh, or wheat meat, add one of these to a side dish if you like.

Note: If you don't have a pot with a diameter to match the bamboo steamer trays: you may use a wok or a purchase 12" steamers to fit over a round 12" electric skillet or inside an electric wok or 10" steamers to fit over a 10" round, electric skillet.

Filling Steamed Buns:

Figure 1-3 Tbsp. (no more!) sweet or savory filling per bun. For very rich fillings such as pesto or a buttery garlic filling, figure 1-2 teaspoons filling per bun.

1. After step #2 above, flatten each ball of dough, one at a time, into a 4-5" round in the palm of your hand.

2. Spoon filling into the center of each. Immediately pull edges up over the filling to form a semi-circle or half-moon then pinch shut. Tuck edges toward the center to form a ball then turn the ball over so the seams are on the bottom. Roll it gently between the palm of your cupped hands. Keep the seam side down and don't push too hard.

3. Place each bun seam-side down on well oiled plates. Rise and cook on plates as above.

Favorite Fillings:

Use wheat, spelt, barley, kamut, or corn dough for each.

- **Mocheese Buns:** Fill each bun with 1-2 Tbsp. Mocheese filling. (Very gooey and cheesey

treat, minus all the fat and the cheese.) Try it for breakfast or lunch with a side of steamed greens or boiled salad and/or a cup of creamless cream of vegetable soup.

- **Inside Out Bagel Bun:** Use wheat, spelt, buckwheat, kamut, corn, or millet dough. Figure 1-3 Tbsp. Herbed Tofu Cream Cheese, Tofu Spread, or any other tofu dip or spread per bun. (This is like a bagel, except the outside is on the inside. Serve if for breakfast, lunch or supper with cooked, pressed or marinated salad, perhaps with a cup of soup made from colorful orange, yellow, or red vegetables.)

- **Garlic Buns:** This fills 8 buns: In a suribachi or mortar, mix 4-8 cloves fresh, minced garlic + 1 Tbsp. white, yellow, mellow, or sweet miso + 2 1/2-3 Tbsp. corn or olive oil. Use about 1 tsp. filling per bun. This variation on traditional garlic bread makes a nice accompaniment to a hearty bean or vegetable soup and salad meal. It is also tasty served with lasagna, spaghetti, or brown rice with a pressed, marinated or cooked vegetable side dish.

- **Pesto Buns:** Figure about 1-2 tsp. pesto per bun. Great for pack lunches or supper, with a hearty bean or veggie soup and cooked mixed vegetables or pressed or marinated salad. Or try it with pasta, red sauce, and cooked greens or mixed vegetables.

- **Refried Bean Filled Buns:** Use any of the basic bread doughs. Fill each bun with 1-3 Tbsp. cooked, mashed, seasoned beans such as Refried Beans (Serve with cream of vegetable soup and boiled, quick-boiled, or pressed or marinated salad.)

- **Hummus Buns:** Use 1-3 Tbsp. Hummus, per bun. Great for a summer meal, with salad or cooked greens, and a light vegetable broth or creamless cream of veggie soup.)

- **Chili Bean Buns:** Use a super thick chili to fill wheat, corn, barley, spelt, or millet dough. Serve with a smooth and creamy squash, corn, tomato, or carrot soup and a side of pressed, marinated, par-boiled or sauteed vegetables.

- **Spinach & Tofu "Cheese" Filled Buns:** for Spanokopita. Figure 2-3 Tbsp. filling per bun.

(Serve with a colorful cream of vegetable soup or root vegetable side dish for breakfast, lunch, or supper. For a fancier meal, serve with vegetable soup, pickles, and a side of rice or tabouli.)

- **Scrambled Tofu Buns:** See Scrambled Tofu. Serve these buns for breakfast, lunch or supper, with quick-boiled or steamed green or mixed vegetables and pickles. Add a colorful puréed winter squash, carrot, corn or mixed root veggie soup or a Nishime-style vegetable side dish.

- **Chinaman's Purse:** Serve these buns with roasted or plain pressure cooked rice, a light miso broth, stir fried or quick-boiled veggies, and pickles. For a simple pack lunch, have buns and a leafy green or mixed vegetable side dish and soup.

- **Tempeh or Wheat Meat Chorizo:** Serve these buns as per Scrambled Tofu Buns above.

- **Sea Veggie Buns:** Use any of the basic bread doughs mentioned above. Figure 2-3 Tbsp. filling made from sauteed land and sea vegetables. Examples include: Sea Palm Saute, or Sea, Sage & Sunflower Spread. Serve with a baked or stewed beans, veggie soup or root/round vegetable dish, a greens dish, and a side of rice.)

- **Sweet Potato or Squash Buns:** Mash baked, simmered, or steamed winter squash or sweet potato with sweet light miso and nut or seed butter. Figure 1 tsp. sweet miso and 2 tsp. nut/seed butter per sweet potato or cup of cooked squash. Add a few spoonfuls of water as needed to make a thick, spreadable paste. Tuck 3 Tbsp. filling into each uncooked bun. Serve with tea or grain coffee and/or a green or mixed vegetable dish—pressed or marinated salad is great for breakfast, lunch or a light supper. Add a cup of bean soup or some other bean dish for a more substantial meal.

- **Squash & Corn Buns:** Combine mashed winter squash with corn off the cob. If desired, add lightly sauteed, seasoned tofu, tempeh, or shredded wheat meat and a hint of herbs or spices.

Dessert Filled Buns:

(For dessert or occasional light supper, brunch, or party fare.)

- **The Danish, Jelly Roll, or Jelly Doughnut Alternative:** Use wheat, spelt, barley, kamut, corn, or millet dough. Fill each uncooked bun with 2 tsp. diluted peanut, almond, hazelnut, sunflower or sesame butter plus 2 heaping tsp. fruit sweetened preserves —apricot, peach, strawberry, blueberry, raspberry, boysenberry, or other. Good for a special Sunday breakfast when you want the comfort foods of yore. Serve with grain coffee or herb tea.)

- **Peanut Buttery & Jelly Bun:** See Danish Alternative above.

- **Honey Buns:** Whip 3-4 Tbsp. honey or rice malt syrup with 3-4 Tbsp. peanut, almond, hazelnut or sunflower butter or sesame tahini and 3 Tbsp. water or apple juice to make a frosting consistency. You can also add 1/4-1/2 tsp. cinnamon. Divide filling between 8 pieces of raw steamed bun dough. (See serving suggestions above.)

- Steamed Cinnamon Raisin Buns: Use sweetened wheat, spelt, barley, kamut, rice flour or millet dough). Use one of the following fillings and divide spread between 8 buns:

  #1: Mix 1/3 cup of dry roasted, chopped walnuts + 1/2 cup minced raisins + 1 tsp. cinnamon + 1/8 tsp. sea salt or 2 tsp. light miso + dash apple juice or honey into a paste;

  #2: Mix 3-4 Tbsp. peanut or sunflower butter + 1 Tbsp. white, yellow or mellow miso + 1/2-1 tsp. cinnamon + 1/2 cup chopped raisins + 1 Tbsp. arrowroot powder + 1-2 Tbsp. apple juice or as needed to make a smooth paste.

- **Chestnut Cream Filled Buns:** Use wheat, spelt, barley, kamut, or rice flour dough made with water or apple juice for the liquid. Figure 2-3 Tbsp. Raisin Glazed Chestnuts, Maple Chestnut Pudding, or Chestnut Apple Compote, per bun.

- **Fruit Filled Buns:** Figure 2- 3 Tbsp. filling per bun. Try Apple Compote, Anise Pears, Apples & Anise, Caraway Apple Sauce, Rosehip & Apple Sauce/Compote, apple butter, or other stewed fruit concoction. ❏

Basic Procedure, Baguettes, French, Italian & Peasant Loaves (Fall, Winter, Early Spring) ***

Prep: 20 minutes
Yield: 1 medium or 2 small French/Italian loaves or 2-4 small baguettes
Rising: 15-30 minutes for Rapid-Rise Dough *or* 1/2-1 1/4 hour for Standard or Slow-Rise Dough
Serves: 3-4 (or 1-2 meals for 2) more if accompanied by rice, millet or pasta
Cooking: 20-35 minutes

These breads will be done baking in 20-35 minutes— one-half to one-third the time required for sandwich loaves! Freeform breads have a wonderful crust and stay incredibly moist on the inside, even after several days. These are great for dunking into hearty soups and stews. We always make a double or quadruple batch.

1 batch of Basic All-Purpose Dough, *(Try Chestnut, barley, rye, kamut, spelt, soy, millet, wheat, herbed or seeded dough)*

Flour to dust pans ~1/2-3/4 cup corn meal, barley, spelt, or other flour (no oil necessary)

1. Liberally flour a 12 or 14 x 9" stainless steel cookie sheet or oil and flour 2-4 baguette pans.

2. If using Standard-Rise or Slow-Rise Dough, allow the dough to rise once in a covered bowl before punching down and shaping. (for Basic Procedure.) If using Rapid-Rise Dough, form dough immediately after mixing.

   For French or Italian Loaves: Form dough into one large ball or two smaller balls. Form each into a 10-inch log, flatten, then roll up lengthwise to form a log. Cut an 8" long slash down the center or cut 3-4 diagonal slits. Make each cut 1/3 inch deep.

   For Peasant Loaves: Form dough into one or two balls or globes. Flatten slightly on top. Arrange on a single floured baking pan/cookie sheet. Cut an "x" slit on top.

   For Baguettes: Form into 2-4 pieces. Flatten each then roll into logs to fit 2-4 oiled and floured baguette pans. Cut 3-5 diagonal slits across the width of each.

3. Rise in a warm place until almost doubled in size, 15-30 minutes for Rapid-Rise Dough, or 1/2-1 hour for Standard-Rise or Slow Rise Dough. Watch dough and do not allow it to over-rise and tear. Preheat oven before the dough has doubled in size. If rising bread in the oven, take it out before preheating the oven.

4. Mist bread and the inside of the oven (avoid the light bulb) with a spray bottle of water before baking. Mist bread and the inside of the oven 2-3 times while baking to form a golden crust.

   Full-size French, Italian or Peasant Loaves: Bake at 400° F for 20-25 minutes then turn heat to 350° F and bake for another 10-15 minutes or until firm, slightly golden brown and hollow sounding when tapped on the bottom.

   Baguettes or Mini Loaves: Bake 20-25 minutes or until golden at 350° F.

5. Transfer to metal racks to cool. Save the roasted flour from cookie sheets. Keep it in a bowl to cook with rolled oats for breakfast. Allow bread to cool several hours or overnight before slicing, if possible. If serving warm from the oven, slice what you think you will use within a day or two. Store unwashed bread pans in the oven, broiler compartment or cupboard until your next baking venture. Store bread in brown paper bags. Reheat by steaming as desired.

Variations:

- **Garlic Bread:** Here, the garlic filling is baked inside the raw dough. Use 1 recipe Buttery Garlic Filling, per single batch of dough. Divide a single batch of dough in half. Flatten each piece of dough into a 12 x 6" oblong. Spread filling down the center of each oblong, roll up jelly roll style into a semi-flat loaf, rise, then bake on floured cookie sheets at 350-400 F° for 20-30 minutes. Slice as needed, serve, and resteam leftovers as needed.

- **Quick Garlic Bread:** Cut a 1-1 1/2 pound loaf of premade whole grain bread into slices. Place on aluminum foil. Spread Buttery Garlic Filling between the slices. Wrap foil over the bread and heat in a 300° F oven for 20-30 minutes before serving. Rewarm leftovers. ❏

Basic Procedure, Souvlaki-Pita Breads (Year Round)***

Prep: 20 minutes
Rising: 15-30 minutes for Rapid-Rise; 1/2-1 1/4 hours for Standard or Slow-Rise Dough
Cooking: 18-20 minutes

Yield: 6 large thick pita-like rounds
Serves: 3-4 as the grain in a meal (or 1 1/2-2 meals for 2) with rice serves 6
Serving size: 1 1/2-3 per person, or 1 round per person served with another grain

** Double recipe as desired for convenient leftovers.

These breads are round like pita pockets but they are far thicker and have no pocket. They're great for sopping up hearty soups, stews, or side dishes or topped with a tofu pate or a hint of butter or ghee. If you wish to make a traditional Greek gyros sandwich, you'll have to roll the dough much thinner than we do so that it can be folded over a filling after baking. The coating of flour on the bread is reminiscent of cinnamon-sugar doughnuts A nice crust forms around the outside of these breads if they sit for 1-2 hours before serving. Leftovers keep well and can be eaten at room temperature or briefly steamed if they become dry.

**Even if you've never been a rye bread fan, these breads made with part rye may win you over.

1 recipe Basic All Purpose Bread Dough, *(Try rye** or barley, chestnut, kamut, wheat, spelt or herbed dough)*

Barley, spelt, kamut, rye, or other flour to dust cookie sheets liberally (about 1/2-2/3 cup)

1. Dust two cookie sheets liberally with flour. Do not oil the pans, the flour is sufficient and will make a lovely and tasty coating for the bread.

2. If using Standard-Rise or Slow-Rise Dough, allow the dough to rise once in a covered bowl before punching down and shaping. If using Rapid-Rise Dough, form dough immediately after mixing. Roll dough into a 6 inch uniform log. Cut into 6 equal size pieces; roll each into a ball. Dip each ball of dough into a shallow bowl of flour then flatten in a tortilla press. Or, roll into 6-inch rounds with a lightly floured rolling pin. Put 3 rounds on each cookie sheet.

3. Let rise in a warm place until almost doubled in size, 15-30 minutes for Rapid Rise Dough, or 1/2-1 hour for Standard or Slow-Rise Dough. See Best Rising Places. In warm weather, the bread will rise nicely right on the counter top.

4. Preheat oven to 400° F.

5. Bake 18-20 minutes or until barely golden on top and hollow when tapped on the bottom.

6. Transfer bread to a bowl, casserole dish, or clay pot lined with a clean cotton or linen kitchen towel. Wrap towel around bread. Cover pot with a lid, if desired. (Scrape the flour from the pans into a bowl; set aside to cook into morning cereal. See Roasty-Toasty Oats.) Baking pans don't need to be washed. For best results, let bread sit 1-3 hours. It will stay fairly warm wrapped and covered, though it can be heated, wrapped in a towel inside a heat proof dish in a 225° F oven.

Storage and serving tips: Store cooled leftovers wrapped in a towel or in a brown or cellophane bag in a cool, dry place. Serve at room temperature and dunk into a hearty soup or stew. Briefly re-steam two to five day old bread for a softer, moister texture.

Note: Traditional Greek Gyros sandwiches are served with a topping of grilled lamb or meat, yogurt, tomato slices and/or cucumbers or pickled vegetables. This bread is folded over the filling to form a half moon. For Veggie Gyros: Fill with Pressure Marinated Tempeh, or Pan Fried Wheat Meat Cutlets, Quick Pickled Onion Rings, sprouts and/or tomato+ Tofu Sour Cream" or Tartar Sauce. Serve with rice, soup and steamed broccoli. ❏

Basic Procedure, Sandwich Loaf Bread

Prep: 15-20 minutes
Rising: 15-30 minutes for Rapid-Rise Dough *or* 1/2-1 1/4 hours for Standard or Slow-Rise Dough

Yield: 2 loaves; 14-16 slices per loaf
Serves: 5-8 as the only grain in a meal (or 3-4 meals for 2)
Serves more with rice, millet, or pasta

** Make 2-3 double batches (i.e., 4-6 loaves) for maximum efficiency.

When baking loaves of bread, try to fill up the oven with several pans of bread— and maybe corn bread, sweet potatoes, winter squash, or a casserole. Loaf bread made without oil or sweeteners will keep a week or two without spoilage, and without freezing. As a regular practice, steam rather than toast your bread to warm it— this will minimize the nutrient loss, add moisture, and bring back that moist, fresh-made taste and texture.

(If you make more bread than you can eat, give the gift of bread. It is a healthful alternative to one of cookies, cakes, and candies.)

1 double recipe Basic All-Purpose Bread
    Dough, (from 5-6 cups flour)
*(Try wheat, spelt, barley, chestnut, rye, soy,
    kamut, herbed or seeded bread)*

Oil for pans

Corn meal, wheat, spelt, oatmeal, or cracked wheat to dust pan(s) liberally

1. Oil bread pans liberally. Dust with flour, oatmeal, or cracked wheat or spelt bulghur.

2. If using Standard-Rise or Slow-Rise Dough, allow the dough to rise once in a covered bowl before punching down and shaping. If using Rapid-Rise Dough, form immediately after mixing. Form dough into a smooth ball and cut in half with a sharp knife. Flatten each piece then roll into a log shape. Roll the dough back and forth on a cutting board to smooth out any seams. Push on and tuck in the ends to make uniform logs to fit your bread pans. Place seam-side down in two oiled 9 x 2" stainless steel or glass loaf pans.

Alternately, shape the dough into two round peasant loaves and place each one in an oiled and floured 3 or 4-quart enamel lined cast iron pot (e.g., a Creuset pot) or stainless steel dutch oven pots with lids. (The lid allows the bread to steam-bake to retain moisture.)

3. With a sharp knife cut three diagonal slits across the width of each loaf or make one slit down the center, 1/4 inch deep, or cut an "x" across the top of a round loaf to allow room for bread to rise without tearing. Rise in a warm place until almost doubled, 15-30 minutes for Rapid-Rise or 1/2-1 1/4 hours for Standard or Slow-Rise Dough.

4. If dough has been rising in the oven, remove it before preheating the oven to 400° F.

    For steam-baking in a casserole dish, cover bread with a lid before baking. Mist the bread and the inside of the oven with a spray bottle full of water before and during baking to develop a nice crust. Bake at 400° F for 20 minutes, reduce heat to 350° F and bake 45-60 minutes.

5. To test for doneness, remove one bread pan from the oven, turn it upside down and tap it. If it sounds hollow, it's done; if not, return it to the oven and bake a bit longer. It should be slightly golden and firm to the touch, a skewer inserted into the center should come out clean. Don't overbake!

6. Turn finished loaves onto a cooling rack. For best results, allow bread to cool for 4-24 hours before slicing. Bread will retain its moisture longer if cooled to the core before slicing. If you can't wait, that's okay! Try to cut only the amount of bread you think will be eaten at a meal, lest the rest dry out prematurely.

Storage: Store cooled bread in paper bags.

Note: For a moist and almost invisible crust, place a pan filled with 1 inch of water in the bottom of the oven before baking (and leave it in while the bread bakes) to create steam in the oven. ❏

Basic Procedure, Pita Pocket Breads (Year Round) ***

Prep: 20 minutes
Rising: 15-30 minutes for Rapid-Rise Dough; 1/2-1 1/4 hour for Standard or Slow-Rise
Cooking: 3-5 minutes or 6-8 served with a second grain dish
Yield: 6 extra large or 8 average pita pockets
Serves: 2-4 as the grain in a meal (or 1 1/2-2 meals for 2)
Serving size: 2-4 per person or 1 per person w/other grain

Far surpassing the flavor and quality of store bought varieties, these lovely tortilla-like breads usually puff up as they bake then collapse to form pockets. The pockets can be folded taco-style around various fillings or sliced in half and stuffed with sandwich fillings. Traditionally, they are not filled, rather, they are used as a utensil, to scoop up morsels of side dishes such as cooked beans or tofu, cooked vegetables or salad, and pickles or relish.

1 recipe All-Purpose Bread Dough, (from 2 1/2-
    3+ cups whole grain flour)
    *(Try whole wheat, spelt, kamut, rye, buck-
    wheat, chestnut, or barley dough)*

1. If using Standard-Rise or Slow-Rise Dough, allow the dough to rise once in a covered bowl before punching down and shaping. If using Rapid-Rise Dough, form immediately after mixing. Divide into 6-8 equal pieces. Form into balls.

2. Place dough on a pastry cloth and flatten into an 8-inch round, 1/8-1/4" thick, with a lightly floured rolling pin. Or, roll out dough on a lightly floured cutting board or chopping block. Alternatively, dip each ball into a shallow bowl of flour then flatten in a tortilla press.

3. Allow to rise until almost doubled in size, on top of the counter or in a warm place (not in the oven, though), 15-30 minutes for Rapid-Rise Dough, or 1/2-1 1/4 hours for Standard or Slow-Rise Dough, on an extra set of well oiled cookie sheets. While the dough rises, heat 1-2 dry, unoiled cookie sheets or a pizza stone on the floor of the oven, not the racks, on the hottest setting (usually 500° F). The secret to turning out great pita is a piping hot oven and a baking sheet placed right on the floor of the oven.) The pans don't need to be oiled but must be very

hot so the dough will puff up and bake quickly once it hits the hot sheets and enters the oven.

4. Quickly place 3-4 risen pita rounds on each unoiled, preheated cookie sheet or pizza stone. Immediately return trays to the floor of the oven. Bake 3-4 minutes or until bread puffs up and starts to brown. Flip with a metal spatula and cook several minutes more until lightly golden and puffy. Do not over-bake these or you will end up with crackers. Transfer baked pita to a large bowl or ceramic pot lined with a white cotton-linen towel. Fold the towel over to cover the bread. Repeat above procedure to cook any remaining dough.

Serving & Storage suggestions: Serve warm or at room temperature. Store cooled leftovers in a paper or cellophane bag or a towel lined glass, ceramic, pottery, or wood bowl (or plastic bags as a last resort). Store in a bread box or cool dry place. Serve at room temperature or steam briefly, 2-6 minutes to moisten. Don't steam too long or pita will turn mushy. Use within 5-7 days for best results.

Pita Topping Filling Ideas:

- **Classic Pita Bread Topping:** Hummus dip + cucumbers, lettuce, tomato, sprouts

- Scrambled tofu with vegetables. Serve with greens, pickles or relish, and chives or scallions

- Tempeh "Tuna" or Tofu & Egg Salad+ steamed leafy or mixed vegetables +/- pickles

- Tofu "Cream Cheese" + Kale, Carrots, Caraway & Kraut or pressed salad or steamed greens

- Oven Fried Mock Chicken + steamed, marinated, pressed or parboiled salad + pickles

- Steamed Omelet + stir fried, steamed, or quick boiled green or mixed veggies or pressed salad

- Refried Beans + steamed greens + parsley, scallions or chives +/- Tofu "Sour Cream"

- Noodles tossed with Beet Red Sauce and seasoned, precooked, minced tempeh or wheat meat

- Pan Fried Seitan or Tempeh cutlets + Tofu Tartar Sauce + pickles + sprouts +/- steamed greens ❑

Basic Procedure, Bagels

Prep: 30 minutes
Rising: 15-30 minutes for Rapid-Rise Dough
or 1/2-1 1/4 hours for Standard or Slow-Rise Dough
Boiling: 10-15 minutes total for batch
Baking: 20-30 minutes

Yield: 6-8 bagels
Serves: 3-4 (or 1 1/2-2 meals for 2)
Serving size: 2-4 per person

Bagels take a little more time and attention than steamed buns or baked breads, but for those who grew up on bagels with lox and cream cheese as I did, they're well worth the added effort every now and again. For added variety and fun, try different combinations of flour or knead herbs, spices, seeds, fresh sweet corn, or dried veggies (minced onion, garlic, bell pepper flakes, tomatoes bits) into the dough. Try steam warmed bagels for a moist texture. Instead of cream cheese, try Tempeh Mock Tuna, Tofu "Cream Cheese," Tofu Pesto, Refried Beans, Hummus, or Garbanzo Butter. Or top with sautéed or stir fried veggies, or pressed salad or pickles with sesame butter. We also like to dip our bagels in cups of pea soup. Bagels also make excellent teething bisquits for babies to suck.

1 recipe Basic All-Purpose Bread Dough. *(Try spelt, kamut, barley, chestnut, millet, buckwheat, fresh corn, poppy seed, or herb)*

For Boiling:

~1 1/2-2 quarts water + 1/2 Tbsp. sea salt
Flour to dust baking sheets

1. If using Standard-Rise or Slow-Rise Dough, allow the dough to rise once in a covered bowl before punching down and shaping. (see for Basic Procedure.) If using Rapid-Rise Dough, form immediately after mixing.

2. Form dough into an 8 inch long cylinder. Cut into 8 equal pieces. Form each into a smooth ball after folding the dough in on itself to eliminate any seams. Poke your thumb through the center of each piece of dough then twirl it on your finger. Spin it around your finger to even out the hole. Repeat until all of the dough has been shaped.

3. Place uncooked bagels on a lightly floured cookie sheet and allow to rise 20-30 minutes until doubled in bulk. Meanwhile, boil salted water in a 4-6 quart pot and preheat oven to 375 or 400° F. (See notes below).

4. Drop bagels, three at a time, into boiling salted water. Keep water on high and cook bagels uncovered, cook for 3-5 minutes or until they float to the top of the pot. Turn bagels with a large slotted spoon or a skimmer once during the boiling process. Remove each bagel with tongs or a skimmer spoon and transfer to a dry baking sheet. Repeat until all the dough is used. (Save and refrigerate the cooking water to cook morning porridge in.)

5. If desired, glaze bagels before baking. Bake at 375° F for 25-30 minutes or 400° F for 20 minutes, until firm to the touch. (Experiment to find the texture you like best.) Cool on racks.

Storage: Store in brown paper or cellophane bags. Store at room temperature or refrigerate bagels that contain fruit or vegetables. Serve as is or steam heat to remoisten and warm. Or, slice and toast lightly.

Variations:

Try these flavors:

- Savory Herb & Onion; Caraway-Rye; Garlic; Buckwheat Sunflower; Sun Dried Tomato & Chives; Tomato-Garlic; Chestnut-Raisin; Amaranth; Yellow or Blue Corn; Fresh Corn; Jalapeno Pepper; etc.

- For a sweet treat try:

- Carrot Raisin; Cinnamon Raisin; Pumpkin-Spice; Chestnut-Raisin-Cinnamon; Pumpkin Spice; or Mocha flavor. ❏

Basic Procedure, Dinner Rolls (Fall, Winter, Early Spring)***

Prep: 15 minutes
Rising: 15-30 minutes for Quick-Rise; 1/2-1 1/4 hours for Standard or Slow-Rise Dough
Cooking: 20-35 minutes**

Yield: 8 medium dinner rolls
Serves: 3-8 (or 2-3 meals for 2) as the only grain served, more if accompanied by a second grain
Serving size: 2-3 rolls per person *or* 1 per person if served with a second grain in the meal

You may either steam-bake these rolls or bake them uncovered for quick rolls or in open pans. Steam-baked, in a covered casserole dish, these rolls are far moister than if baked uncovered. If you don't have one or two heavy lidded oven-proof pots in which to steam-bake, use cookie sheets, cake pans, oblong baking pans or cast iron skillets. Because these contain no oil, they may dry out more quickly than most rolls, but don't despair or throw them away. Instead, steam heat meal-size amounts in a cotton towel on a bamboo tray for that moist, tender, fresh from the oven taste. You'll be amazed at how they come back to life, even after five days!

1 recipe Basic All Purpose Bread Dough.
(Try kamut, millet, barley & oat, poppy seed, sunflower & spelt, herb, or wheat)
Oil to coat pan
Cornmeal, millet meal or oatmeal to dust pans

1. **For Steam-Baked Rolls:** Oil a 4-quart enamel-lined cast iron pot (Le Creuset) or heavy stainless steel or cast iron dutch oven casserole dish. Dust with flour. Alternately, oil a 9 inch stainless steel cake pan with sides, a 14 x 9 x 2 inch oblong pan, or a 9 to 10 inch cast iron skillet.

   For Quick Rolls: liberally dust two medium sized cookie sheets with flour; do not oil.

2. If using Standard-Rise or Slow-Rise Dough, allow the dough to rise once in a covered bowl before punching down and shaping. If using Rapid-Rise Dough, form immediately after mixing.

3. Form dough into a ball then an 8-inch log. Using a ruler as a guide, cut into 8 equal pieces. Even them out as needed. Fold the dough in on itself to eliminate seams and roll each piece into a ball after.

4. Arrange the balls on prepared baking dishes, figure 8 balls per 10 inch baking pot, cake pan, or iron skillet, or arrange more rolls on a floured cookie sheet or oiled oblong pan. Balls may touch each other or not.

5. Cover the pot(s) loosely with a damp towel. If using cake pans or sheets, cover with a large upside down bowl if possible. Let rise until almost doubled in size, 15-30 minutes for Rapid-Rise Dough or longer for Standard or Slow-Rise Dough. For oven rise method, be sure to remove pan from the oven before preheating!

6. Preheat oven to 400° F.

   Steam-Baked Rolls (or rolls in a pan with sides): Cover the pot of rolls with a lid and place in oven (or bake uncovered on a skillet, cake pan, etc.). Bake 15 minutes then reduce heat to 350° F and bake for 15-25 minutes or until rolls sound hollow when tapped on the bottom.

   Quick Rolls (on cookie sheets): Bake uncovered, for 15-20 minutes in a 350-400° F oven.

7. Remove bread from the oven and immediately transfer to a cooling rack or towel-lined bowl, pot, or basket or let rolls sit in the covered pot for 30 minutes to stay warm for serving. Invert pan over a wire rack or towel lined bowl or pot.

Cleanup tips: Instead of washing the casserole pot, set it aside to soak and cook morning cereal in the crumbs tin the bottom of the pot will add flavor. If a cookie sheet was used, scrape the flour coating into a bowl. Save and cook this into morning cereal.

Storage: Store cooled bread in paper or cellophane bags. Refer to storage and reheating tips.

Variations:

- **Richer Rolls:** Per batch of dough (2 1/2-3 cups flour) add 1-2 Tbsp. butter, ghee, corn, sunflower, or safflower oil to the water when heating it to make the basic dough.

- **Super Seeded Dinner Rolls:** Omit oil from dough; glaze raw dough with glaze then sprinkle the top of each section with poppy, sunflower, sesame, cumin, or flax seeds before rising. Bake as above.

- **Clover Leaf Rolls:** Oil a muffin tin. Divide dough into 8 balls and divide each of these balls into 3 sections. Roll each piece into a ball. Place 3 balls, touching, in each oiled muffin tin. Rise and bake according to instructions above.

- **Buttermilk-like Rolls:** In the basic recipe replace the water with plain soy milk + 1 Tbsp. cider or rice vinegar to replace the water; add 1 Tbsp. corn oil or butter or ghee to the liquids if desired. Prepare as usual.

Basic Procedure, Burger or Hot Dog Buns***

Prep: 15 minutes
Rising: 1 5-30 minutes for Quick-Rise *or* 1/2-1 1/4 hours for Standard or Slow-Rise Dough
Cooking: 20-35 minutes**

Yield: 6 medium sized burger or hot dog buns
Serves: 3-6 (or 1-3 meals for 2) as the only grain or more if accompanied by a second grain
Serving size: 1-2 1/2 buns per person

It's hard to find a good commercial bun that's free of sweeteners, dairy products, and oil, and made from whole grains. These buns fit the bill. They are easy enough to make and keep for a week at room temperature or in the refrigerator. We like to serve them with Lentil, Tempeh, or Wheat Meat Burgers, Grain Mayo, Mustard, Pickles and pressed salad or cooked greens. They are equally good without a filling, dunked in bean soup or topped with squash butter.

1 recipe Basic All Purpose Bread Dough
(Try wheat, spelt, or kamut dough or poppy, sesame or sunflower seed, onion, or herb dough)
Corn meal, millet meal or oatmeal to dust pans

1. Flour a cookie sheets. It is not necessary to oil the sheets.

2. If using Standard-Rise or Slow-Rise Dough, allow the dough to rise once in a covered bowl before punching down and shaping. (see Basic Procedure.) If using Rapid-Rise Dough, form immediately after mixing.

3. Form dough into a 6" uniform log, with a ruler and knife, cut into 6 equal pieces. Even them out as needed.

   For Burger Buns: Fold the dough in on itself to eliminate seams and roll each piece into a ball after. Flatten each ball so that it looks like a burger.

   For Hot Dog Buns: Flatten each piece into an oblong shape then roll it into a log.

4. Arrange buns on floured sheets, with 1-2" between each for expansion. Let rise until almost doubled in size, 15-30 minutes for Rapid-Rise Dough or 1/2-1 1/4 hours for Standard or Slow-Rise Dough. Using oven rise method, be sure to remove pans from the oven before preheating.

5. Preheat oven to 400° F. Bake 20-25 minutes or until firm to the touch, golden, and hollow sounding when tapped on the bottom.

6. Remove bread from the oven and transfer to a cooling rack. Cool or serve immediately.

Cleanup tips: Instead of washing the baking pans, scrape the flour coating into a bowl. Save and cook this into morning cereal.

Storage: Store cooled bread in paper or cellophane bags. Refer to storage and reheating tips in Chapter 2. ❏

HAVE YOUR PIZZA & EAT IT TOO!

Pizza has become an American obsession. It's easy. It's tasty. It could be healthy. The problem is, most pizzas are piled high with more cheese, meat, and olives than anyone really needs. Take two slices of your typical pizza and you can easily pack away more fat than anyone needs for an entire week!

Most pizzas are made with a refined white flour crust with added sugar, dough conditioners, and oil. Most are also sorely deficient in the vegetable department. When was the last time you had a pizza that was topped with a wide assortment of fresh seasonal vegetables? Save for the tomato sauce—which is usually made from canned, processed, out-of-season tomatoes (which are actually a fruit anyway)— most pizzas don't have much to boast in the vegetable department.

All of pizzas common shortcoming can be fixed, if you make your own pizza and make it with fresh and wholesome ingredients. Made properly, pizza can be part of a nutritious and balanced meal. And before you say "It's too much trouble," take a look at our easy pizza making process. You really can make simple, tasty, low-fat pizzas, we promise!

Tips for making or ordering a healthier pizza

- **Don't skimp on the crust**— it's one of the most nutritious parts. Think of the crust as the foundation and build the rest of meal on top of that using fresh, low-fat toppings. You'll want to think of this as the main event. Don't be bashful, you can eat a lot of it without getting fat.

- **Fiber up**—Whole grain pizza crusts are tastier and far more nutritious than their more refined counterparts.

  Eating out? Ask for a whole wheat crust. Many chain pizza joints do offer these and some are actually quite good. In some pizza places you can also buy unbaked wheat crusts to take home.

  Dining in? Use our basic dough recipe or one of the variations. Make a wheat, spelt, kamut, cornmeal, millet, super-soy, or barley crust. If you're really in a pinch for time but want a pizza— try a quick pizza crust comprised of already made whole grain pita pockets, Souvlaki-pita rounds, whole grain english muffins, or French or Italian loaves (split lengthwise).

- **Go easy on the cheesey**— it's high in fat, super-concentrated, and one of the most over-used items on pizzas and difficult to digest. You really don't need much of it or any at all

  Eating out? Ask for half as much cheese on your pizza; better yet ask for it without the cheese. If you skip the cheese, you might want to ask for roasted vegetables and/or pesto on your pizza. Some Italian restaurants offer seafood pizzas and other unique options. Don't be afraid to order a-la-carte to create your own combinations. Another option: ask for a 1-1 1/2 oz. portion (4-6 Tbsp. grated cheese) on the side. Add this to your warm pizza at the table where a little bit goes a lot farther. (Animal foods are best used in only small amounts—too much can easily overwhelm your digestive system. It is best to save these foods for occasional use, just a few times a week, month, or year and in very small amounts. It is also important to strive to use the highest quality animal products available.)

  Dining in? Instead of using that tired old cheese, try new and exciting options. Use tofu, tempeh, wheat meat, or any of our unusual sauces—for example, Onion Butter, Beet Sauce Italiano, Squash Sauce, or "Mocheese."

- **Pick a Theme:** Try Mexican, Italian, Mediterranean, Chinese, Japanese, Indian, or Ethiopian pizza. Use animal products sparingly, if at all. Cook and add a bit of ground or chopped vegetarian "sausage" or smoked tofu, or seasoned wheat meat or tempeh. And don't forget the herbs—they can do wonders to jazz up your pizza and spark the digestive fires. Try basil, oregano, thyme, marjoram, garlic, cumin, sage, pepper, etc.

In place of cheese: Try a mixture of crumbled or puréed tofu mixed with light, yellow, or mellow miso. Add a bit of nutritional yeast flakes or grated uncooked, plain mochi. (Mochi melts like cheese if you moisten it with a bit of water and it tastes kind of like cheese too.) See Squash & Sauerkraut Pizza, Pizza Bianca, Mocheese filling/topping,or Mochi Pizza Pie, for ideas. Other topping options include smoked tofu, Tofu Cream Cheese or Tofu Pesto, (which, by the way, don't need a base of tomato sauce to taste good!) You can spread them directly on the dough then add sliced vegetables as desired.

- **Try tomato sauce alternatives when tomatoes aren't in season:** Instead of tomato sauce, try caramelized onions, puréed red beans, Beet Sauce Italiano, Velvety Beet & Squash Bisque, pureed winter squash or carrot, Onion Butter, Parsnip White Sauce, or pesto for a change of taste. Save the tomato sauce for tomato season or a special treat.

- **Go heavy on the veggies**—This is what's lacking on most pizzas; feel free to use these freely on top of your pizza whether dining at home or eating out.

  Eating out? Order a vegetarian pizza or cheese-less vegan pizza. Ask for a wide variety of veggies or pick your favorites. They'll let you. Order pesto on your pizza, without the cheese, then add broccoli, sun dried tomatoes or roasted red peppers and/or olives. Limit high fat toppings (cheese, meats, nuts, etc.) and load up on low-fat ones. Order a salad or sprouts on the side.

  At home? Try the ethnic theme idea mentioned above. Some good pizza veggies include: onions, scallions, leeks, broccoli, cauliflower, various mushrooms, red, yellow or green bell peppers, roasted red peppers or garlic, bean sprouts, asparagus, carrots, corn off the cob, and winter squash. Pick a few and cut them into bite sized pieces. Parboil, stew, roast or saute the tough ones before tossing them onto the pizza.

  Add herbs: Try whole cloves of garlic, fresh or dried chives, garlic chives, dill, basil, oregano, thyme, marjoram, sauteed fresh chili peppers, or scallions. Some can be sprinkled on at the table, others are best cooked right on the pie. Garlic becomes very mild when baked.

Here are some theme ideas to get you started:

- **Mexican:** Add some yellow or blue corn meal to the dough. Top with thinned low-fat refried beans. Add fresh or roasted bell peppers or chili pepper strips, minced or whole garlic cloves, seasoned tofu, pre-cooked tempeh, or shredded or ground wheat meat. At the table, sprinkle with fresh parsley, scallions, or fresh or dried chives and steamed veggies or salad.

- **Chinese:** Top prebaked barley, wheat, soy, or spelt dough with parboiled or lightly stir fried onions, mushrooms, cabbage, broccoli, carrots and/or sunchokes, plus cubed tofu, seasoned tempeh, or vegetarian sausage. Add plenty of garlic. Bake. Serve with Kim Chee if you like.

- **Indian:** Top a wheat, barley, or spelt dough with curried and lightly cooked veggies. At the table, add a dollup or two of Tofu "Sour Cream" or plain soy or goat yogurt and chutney.

- **Italian:**

  #1: Top pizza with a thin coating of Pesto Presto or Tofu Pesto. Add shredded wheat meat, homemade seitan sausage or sliced vegetarian sausage links, red and yellow bell pepper strips and broccoli.

  #2: Try Pizza Bianca, or Beet Sauce Italiano, with a topping of vegetarian sausage and olives.

  #3: Skip the tomato sauce then brush the crust with olive oil or pesto then top with fresh or dried herbs, exotic mushrooms and/or olives. Bake. Serve with roasted veggies or salad.

Basic Procedure, Pizza Dough

Prep: 15-20 minutes
Rising: 15-30 minutes for Rapid-Rise Dough; 1/2-1 1/4 hours for Standard or Slow-Rise Dough
Cooking: 15-25 minutes, depending on size

Yield: 6-8 mini-pizzas, or 2 thick or 3 thin 9-10 inch crusts, or 1 12 inch deep dish + 1 6 inch deep dish or one thick crust 16 inch pizza or one thin 16 inch + several sticks
Serves: 3-4 avg. folks or 2 large appetites

Pizza isn't time consuming to make. Simply make and roll out the dough; while it's rising on the cookie sheets or pizza pans, ready the toppings. Handy toppings can be found in most refrigerators —leftover thick soups, stews and sauces; cooked beans, tempeh or wheat meat, tofu, bean dips or patés; pickles, relish, fresh veggies, herb garnishes, etc. Check the pantry for dried veggies, spices, etc.

Here's the basic procedure; vary the dough and toppings as you like. To recreate the taste of brick oven baked pizza like the kind you get it pizza parlors, pick up a pizza stone at your local kitchen shop or bake your pizza in cast iron skills.

1 recipe Basic Bread Dough
   (Try chestnut, kamut, barley, millet, whole wheat, spelt, or yellow corn)
Flour or corn meal to dust pans **or** olive, canola or sesame oil and flour for deep dish pans

Toppings: (Pick several as desired)

Sauce—1/4 cup of sauce per mini pizza, 3/4-1 cup per medium pizza, **or** 1-1 1/2 cup per large pizza

Fresh veggies—1/4 cup veggies per mini pizza, 1-2 cups per large pizza

Tofu, tempeh, or wheat meat—1-3 oz. per small pizza, 3-5 oz. per medium, or 5-8 oz. per large

Optional, garlic—1-2 whole cloves per small pizza, 2-3 per medium, or 2-6 per large pizza

Optional, parsley, scallions, chives, onions, peppers, mushrooms, basil, oregano, dill— use freely

Optional, pickles *(kraut, ginger, onion, etc.)*— 1/2-1 Tbsp. per mini-pizza or 3-8 Tbsp. per large pizza

Optional, olives 1 Tbsp. per mini-pizza **or** 1/2 cup per larger pizza

Optional, Cheese— grate and add at the table— about 2-5 Tbsp. goat cheese per person

1. If using Standard-Rise or Slow-Rise Dough, allow the dough to rise once in a covered bowl before punching down and shaping. (see Basic Procedure.) If using Rapid-Rise Dough, form immediately after mixing.

2. Liberally flour cookie sheets or pizza pans with wheat or spelt flour or corn meal (for a crunchy and traditional pizza taste). For deep dish pizza, oil and use square or round cast iron skillets for the best crust, or use oblong glass or steel baking pans with sides (14 x 9 x 2" or 9 x 9 x 2") if the others are unavailable.

3. Divide dough into the desired number of pieces. Roll or stretch dough to fit pizza pans. For a deep dish, stretch dough up the sides of your pizza pans, cake pans, or cast iron skillets. Spread sauce and/or toppings on right away. Leave a one-half inch edge of the crust when adding toppings. Allow to rise in a warm place, 15-30 minutes, or until almost doubled in size or rise the dough while you fix the toppings. Check often so it doesn't over-rise and tear.

4. Remove crusts from the oven, if they are rising there, before preheating oven to 450° F. Place pizza pans in the hot oven. Bake 10-15 minutes for mini-pizzas or 15-25 minutes for larger pizzas, or until the bottom is crisp and browned. Be careful not to overcook it.

Serving suggestions: Serve warm with pressed, marinated, boiled, or tossed seasonal salad. Very infrequently, and if you are in good health, you may wish to sprinkle a small amount of grated or crumbled cheese on top of your pizza at the table. ❏

Favorite Pizza Combos Super Squash & Sauerkraut Pizza (Any Season)***

Prep: 20 minutes
Cooking: 15-20 minutes, depending on size
Rising: 15-30 minutes for Rapid-Rise Dough; 1/2-1 1/4 hours for Standard or Slow-Rise Dough

Yield: 6-8 mini pizzas or 2 9-12" crusts or 1 16" deep dish pizza pie
Serves: 2 large appetites 2 1/2-3 average folks or 4 light eaters

This pizza is always a hit. You can vary the sauce—using squash, onion and beet; beet and carrot; carrot and tomato; or winter squash with fresh tomato in the fall. You can make it a little different each time with the vegetarian toppings (with or without cheese). A thick puree of winter squash and sauerkraut also makes a good calzone filling, alone or with sliced wheat meat.

1 recipe Basic Bread Dough
  (Try chestnut, barley, kamut, soy, spelt, whole wheat or corn)

Sweet Squash Sauce: (See variations below)

1 cup white or yellow onion, diced

2 cups cubed winter squash (or 1 cup each squash and tomato) *(kabocha, buttercup, hokaido, butternut, sweet dumpling, or delicatta)*

1/8-1/4 tsp. sea salt

1/2 cup water, or as needed

3 Tbsp. nutritional yeast flakes or powder (not brewers yeast!)

1 Tbsp. light or yellow miso

1 Tbsp. arrowroot powder

Optional, 1 tsp. each dried basil and oregano

1/2 tsp. dried thyme *or* 2 Tbsp. fresh minced herbs

Optional, 2-3 cloves minced fresh garlic

Toppings:

1/2-2/3 cup natural sauerkraut, drained *or* 1/2 cup black olives, minced finely

Optional, 1 cup shredded plain or spiced wheat meat or seasoned, crumbled tempeh or cubed tofu*

Optional, 3 oz. grated raw goat or cow's milk cheese (~3/4 cup), sprinkled on at the table

Optional, black pepper and/or fresh or dried chives or minced parsley, added at the table

1. If using Standard-Rise or Slow-Rise Dough, allow the dough to rise once in a covered bowl before punching down and shaping. (see Basic Procedure.) If using Rapid-Rise Dough, form immediately after mixing. Fill pans as per Basic Procedure.

2. Combine onions and squash in a saucepan with salt and water. Cover, bring to boil, reduce heat and simmer on low for 25 minutes or until soft. Remove the skin if using sweet dumpling or delicatta squash. Puree with other sauce ingredients in a blender or foley food mill. Add water a little at a time as needed to make 3 cups of sauce, thin with water if too thick.

3. Spoon sauce over crust, leaving a half inch margin around the edges. (Reserve any leftover sauce to dilute and use as a soup tomorrow.) Spoon on sauerkraut or olives. Add shredded, crumbled, or minced wheat meat/seitan, seasoned tempeh, or tofu, if desired.

4. Bake as per Basic Procedure, Pizza.

5. Sprinkle on grated cheese at the table if desired. Serve with salad or steamed vegetables.

Variations:

- Omit nutritional yeast. Combine carrots, onions, mushrooms, and a small piece of peeled beets for sauce. Season with tamari or dark miso. See Beet-Sauce Italiano.

- See index for "bacon" or "sausage-style" tempeh or buy plain, BBQ-, sausage-, or chicken-style wheat meat or use crumbled vegetarian burgers, cutlets, or "sausage" in above recipe.

- Purée leftover steamed or baked squash with tomato and seasonings as above. ❏

Pizza Bianca (Pizza with White Sauce) (Any Season)***

Prep: 20 minutes
Cooking (entire pizza): 15-20 minutes
Cooking (sauce & toppings): 30-40 minutes
Rising (dough): 15-30 minutes for Rapid-Rise crusts; 1/2-1 1/4 hours for Standard-Rise Dough

Yield: 6-8 mini pizzas with 8 inch crust or two medium pizzas with thick 9-12 inch or one large 14-16 inch thick crust
Serves: 2 active folks or 4 light eaters

Pizzas don't need tomato sauce to taste or be authentic. In fact, white sauce is a common pizza topper in Italy. This sauce is made from sauteed and slow simmered onions which turn smooth, delectably sweet and delightfully buttery. We top the onion sauce with chopped walnuts, hazelnuts and/or olives, with or without wheat wheat, or tempeh; or we use vegetarian sausage and olives. (These combinations also make great fillings for calzones.)

Crust:

1 recipe Basic All Purpose Dough (from 2 1/2-3+ cups flour)

(Try spelt, whole wheat, soy, kamut, barley, or chestnut)

Caramelized Onion Sauce: (yield: ~ 2 cups thick sauce)

1-1 1/2 tsp. sunflower or light or dark sesame oil, *or* ghee

4 packed cups white onions, minced or cut in thin crescents, preferably sweet varieties

1/4 tsp. sea salt

Optional, 3 cloves fresh garlic, minced finely

1 Tbsp. water

Toppings:

2 tsp. dried, ground or crushed rosemary, basil, thyme or oregano *or* 2 Tbsp. fresh, minced herbs

1/4 cup chopped raw walnuts or hazlenuts, or peanuts

1-1 1/4 cup shredded, grated or minced wheat meat *(regular, sausage-or chicken-style)* or sliced or crumbled vegetarian sausage/links *or* Pressure Marinated Tempeh, *or* smoked tofu, thinly sliced

Optional, 1/2 cup chopped black olives

Fresh or dried chives and/or black pepper for garnishing at the table

1. If using Standard or Slow-Rise Dough, allow dough to rise once in a bowl as per Basic Procedure. Shape Rapid-Rise Dough immediately after mixing.

2. **Sauce:** A cast iron skillet or wok works best. Heat oil or ghee, over medium heat. Add onion and salt immediately, and if desired, garlic. Saute and stir for 5-8 minutes or until onions are soft. Add a tablespoon of water, cover with a lid, reduce heat to low, and cook for 15-20 minutes until dark and syrupy. Stir periodically to prevent burning.

3. **Topping pizza:** Spoon onion sauce over dough. Sprinkle with herbs. Add nuts and olives; nuts and wheat meat, tempeh, smoked tofu, or veggie sausage; or use nuts, olives, and a vegetarian product.

4. Allow to rise until almost doubled in size, about 15-30 minutes, or more if needed. Preheat oven.

5. Bake as per Basic Pizza Procedure. Slice and add a fresh garnish at the table.

Serving suggestions: Serve with steamed vegetables or pressed, marinated, or boiled salad. Optional, light vegetable soup or miso soup broth.

Variations:

- Use leeks in place of onions or use part onions and part mushrooms—try crimini, shiitake, or regular button mushrooms.

- **Caramelized Onion, "Sausage" & Cheese Pizza:** Bake pizza with olives and herbs and tempeh, tofu, or wheat meat. If desired, sprinkle servings with a small volume of grated raw milk cheese at the table (~2-3 oz. ~1/2-2/3 cup cheese per large pizza). ❏

Basic Procedure, Calzones (Fall, Winter, Spring)

Prep (dough + filling): 20 minutes
Rising: 15-30 minutes for Rapid-Rise Dough; 1/2-1 1/4 hours for Standard or Slow-Rise Dough
Baking: 20-25 minutes

Yield: 8 filled savory pastries
Serving size: 1 per person *with rice* or 2 per person if no other grain is served

A calzone is basically a pizza turned outside-in. A golden crust surrounds a tasty filling. It's roughly equivalent to the English Cornish pasty, the Indian samosa, the American pot pie, or the filled Chinese steamed bun. Experiment with different types of fillings, and be sure to make a few extra calzones to stash in lunch boxes or to reheat for supper tomorrow. Serve with soup or broth and salad or cooked greens. For dinner you might want to add a side of rice as well.

Though calzones traditionally contain cheese, ours don't. Interesting, tasty calzones can be made with our basic bun fillings below, or adapt a filling from your favorite pot pie, tamale, baked bean, or chili recipe, or prepare one of the stews in this book, made very thick. Expand your horizons try Mexican, Chinese, Thai, Spanish, Hungarian, or American-inspired fillings.

Crust: 1 recipe Basic All-Purpose Rapid Rise Bread Dough

(Try wheat, barley, spelt, kamut, chestnut, millet, or soy dough)

Filling: ~2-3 cups filling (~1/4-1/3 cup per calzone)

see suggestions below, pick 1 filling or make a variety at once

Flour *(wheat, spelt, barley, or kamut flour)* to dust baking sheets

1. If using Standard-Rise or Slow-Rise Dough, allow the dough to rise once in a covered bowl before punching down and shaping. (see Basic Procedure.) If using Rapid-Rise Dough, form immediately after mixing. Form dough into an 8" uniform log. Mark off with a ruler and cut into 8 equal pieces. Form each piece into a ball. Roll each ball on a pastry cloth or floured work surface (into a 6-8 inch round) with a lightly floured rolling pin, or dip each ball of dough into flour then flatten with a tortilla press.

2. Put 1/4-1/3 cup of filling in the center of each circle. Cup dough in the palm of your hand then pull the sides up and over the filling to form a half moon or leave dough on the counter top and fold the dough in half to cover the filling. (Hint: Don't add too much filling or they won't close properly.) Pinch the edges with your fingers then set them on two un-oiled but well floured cookie sheets. Press the edges with the tines of a fork to seal completely.

3. Allow to rise until doubled in size, 15-30 minutes for Rapid-Rise Dough or 1/2-1 1/4 hours for Standard or Slow-Rise Dough. (see Best Rising Places.)

4. If calzones are rising in the oven, remove them from the oven before preheating the oven to 375° F. Bake 20-30 minutes, until lightly golden and hollow sounding when tapped.

Serving suggestions: Warm or at room temperature like a sandwich, with a cup of light soup or broth. Add a side of steamed, sauteed, or parboiled greens or pressed or marinated salad. If serving just one calzone per person, add a side of rice or polenta. Calzones can be made ahead and heated on plates, wrapped in a cotton or linen towel 10-12 minutes before meal-time, or warmed in the oven.

Storage: Refrigerate leftovers in brown paper bags, cellophane bags, or wax paper bags if they will not be eaten within 12-24 hours. They will keep in a cold box or at room temperature in a lunch box between breakfast and lunch. If the weather is hot, you may want to pack along a dry ice bag. ❑

Calzone Fillings:

Note: these same fillings can be used for pot pies, savory turnovers, or pizza toppers. In smaller volumes many are suitable for tamales, won tons, ravioli and steamed buns.

Rule of thumb for filling: 1/4-1/3 cup filling per calzone or large turnover

Cheesey Fillings:
- **Spanokopita Filling**
- **Mocheese**
- **Mocheese,** mixed with mashed squash, sweet potato, or corn off the cob
- **Tofu Herbed "Cream Cheese" Spread** mixed with, parboiled, chopped asparagus
- **Tofu Pesto Spread,**
- **Tofu Ricotta,** chopped sun dried tomato and dried onion flakes

Meaty Fillings:
- **Tempeh Chorizo** with Beet Sauce Italiano, Tomato Sauce, or Squash Purée
- **Bulgar & Sundried Tomato** (tamale filling)
- **Hungarian Goulash**
- **Chinaman's Purse** filling
- **Thick Chili Bean Stew,** (Cook recipe with half as much water or less)
- Sauteed or stewed wheat meat with cubed vegetables

Very Veggie Fillings:
- **Mashed Sweet Potato or Squash** with Whipped Miso-Tahini or Walnut Miso
- **Slow Simmered Squash, Parsnip & Carrot,**
- **Dulse with Sunchokes**
- **Squash & Corn Dinner Pudding,** mixed with a dash of sesame tahini
- **Sea Palm or Ocean Ribbon Saute,** and cubed tofu

Other ideas:

Ground wheat meat with lightly sautéed onions, mushrooms, and herbs or spices

Sautéed land and sea vegetables

Mashed beans with wheat meat, tofu or tempeh

Beet-based red sauce and/or cubed or crumbled pressure marinated tempeh or grated wheat meat

Beet Sauce Italiano or tomato sauce + sautéed veggies + seasoned tempeh or tofu

Thick stew (leftover)

Scrambled tofu with land and sea vegetables (onion, nori or alaria, mushrooms, chives, etc.)

Dessert Turnovers:

- Anise Pears
- Caraway Apple Sauce
- Rosehip & Apple Compote
- Cranberry Apple Sauce
- Raisin Glazed Chestnuts
- Maple Chestnut Pudding
- Creamy Dreamy Chestnut Pudding
- Chestnut-Apple Compote
- Any fruit pie filling
- Any stewed fruit
- Mashed winter squash with white miso and chopped roasted walnuts or nut butter+/- spices

Uses For Leftover & Old Breads, Biscuits &, Muffins

Dry bread can be revived in a variety of tasty ways: On top of a metal steamer basket for 2-4 minutes, atop a bamboo steamer tray for 10-20 minutes or until moist throughout. The same method even works for adding moisture and a cake-like texture to corn bread, millet bread, muffins, biscuits, and even cookies.

1. Resteam leftover sliced or whole baked goods on a steamer tray or basket, wrapped in a white, cotton/linen towel, until tender. Serve as you normally would (with soup or stew, grain, vegetable side dish, and other condiments).

2. Cube dry bread or corn bread and let it dry on the counter overnight on a cookie sheet or gently toast in the oven at 140° F. for a few hours. Toss in salads or soups, use to make stuffing, bread pudding, or use it to top casseroles. See Chick-n-Pea Sourdough Dressing, Easiest Ever Bread Cube Dressing, or Basic Bread Pudding.

3. Cube leftover bread, biscuits, or muffins and cook in to morning cereal (with millet or rolled oats, or leftover cooked oatmeal, millet, buckwheat, rice, or other leftover dinner grains. For specific recipes, see Breakfast Cereals From Leftover Grain.

4. Cube old bread, biscuits, muffins or cookies and use to stuff cored baked apples, perhaps with a few raisins, a pinch of cinnamon, and a few teaspoonfuls of juice to mix.

5. Cube old bread, brush lightly with olive oil and sprinkle with Italian herbs. Toast on a cookie sheet in the oven or toaster oven until lightly browned. Use as croutons over soup or salad.

6. Cut old bread into finger long pieces, toast in oven and serve with dips instead of crackers.

7. Grate dry bread. Use bread crumbs for stuffing, pate, or casserole topping.

8. Add crumbled old bread to sautéed onions, garlic, mushrooms, celery, ground or minced   w h e a t meat or cooked lentils. Add a small volume of chopped walnuts, sunflower seeds, or sesame or sunflower butter. Add Italian herbs and a dash of tamari, shoyu or dark miso. Cook until mushrooms are wilted and watery. Use as a stuffing for mushroom caps, tiny pumpkins, tomatoes, or onions. Alternately, purée in a blender or food processor for "mock liver" pate! (Shiitake mushrooms are especially nice—but add just a few, they're potent.)

9. Crumble and mix old cookies, sweet muffins, or corn bread with a dash tahini, oil or ground nuts. Add apple juice as needed to make a crumble crust. Press into an oiled pie plates and top with pumpkin, yam, sweet potato, apple or other pie filling.

10. Steam old cookies and serve with tea or apple sauce.

11. Use crumbled cookies, cakes, muffins, or corn bread as an apple pie or fruit cobbler topping.

12. Crumble old corn bread; use as bottom crust for a bean or bean and squash pie/casserole. ❑

Batter Breads, Pancakes, Crepés & Flat Breads

Steam-Baked Millet Batter Bread or Corn Batter Bread ***

Prep: 20 minutes
Rising: 15-30 minutes for Rapid Rise; or 8-10 hours for Slow-Rise Method 2-3 hours for Standard Rise Batter
Baking: 30-40 minutes

Yield: 10-12" diameter x 1 3/4" deep round pan
or 1 12 x 9 x 2 pan
Serves: 4-5 (or 2 meals for 2); or 3 very active or more served with rice

This corn bread variation always takes the cake. It's egg-and dairy-free and low in fat. Steam-baking in a covered casserole dish makes this bread moist with a cakey crumb. For best results, use a heavy 4-quart stainless steel or cast iron Dutch oven pot or an enamel-lined cast iron pot, with a tight fitting lid. If you don't have such a pot, you can bake the bread in an uncovered 12 x 9 x 2-inch pan; however, the texture will not be as moist. Leftovers keep for a week and can be moistened, warmed, and freshened with brief steaming. Really dry leftovers can be cubed and cooked into morning cereal.

2 1/2 cups blue or yellow corn meal, *or* millet meal*

1 1/4 cups spelt or barley flour, or whole wheat bread flour (not pastry flour)

1/4 cup arrowroot powder

1/4 oz. pkg. *or* 2 1/4 tsp. Rapid Rise Yeast*

2 1/2 cups plain, unsweetened soy milk or rice milk

1 tsp. sun dried sea salt

1 1/2-2 Tbsp. raw butter or ghee *or* unrefined corn or sesame oil

1. Liberally grease a large cast iron, enamel-lined cast iron (Creuset) or stainless steel dutch oven pot with vegetable oil. (We use a pastry brush.) The round pot or pan must be deep to allow the batter room to double in size. If you do not have a deep pot as described above, use an oblong 12 x 9 x 2 glass or stainless steel baking pan; some glass varieties come with lids.

2. In a mixing bowl combine corn or millet meal, flour, arrowroot, and Rapid Rise Yeast. Stir briefly with a spoon.

3. In a saucepan, combine water, salt, and butter ghee, or oil. Stick a metal stem thermometer in the pot. Heat to 125° F until hot to the touch but not scalding. If the water gets hotter than this, cool to the proper temperature. Stir liquids into dry mixture. Mix only enough to yield an oatmeal textured batter. Pour into baking pot/pan, cover loosely with a lid, cookie sheet, or plate, and set in a warm place for 15-30 minutes or until doubled in size. (see Best Rising Places.) Do not let the batter over-rise or it will over-stretch, turn sour, taste yeasty, and collapse after baking.

4. *If rising bread in the oven, take it out before preheating.* Preheat oven to 350° F.

   Cover pot with a lid. Note: bread may be baked uncovered, but it will be drier. Bake 30-40 minutes, until crust is golden and bread is firm and pulls away from the side of the pan. A tooth-pick inserted in the center should come out clean.

5. Remove pot from oven. If possible, leave to cool the lid on for 15-20 minutes to allow the steam to lift the bread off the bottom of the baking pot or pan.

6. **To serve:** Run a knife around the sides to loosen then invert over a plate or wire rack. Cut into 8-9 wedges and transfer to a platter or towel lined bowl. Or, allow uncut bread to cool several hours or overnight, at room temperature, in the baking pan.***

Serving suggestions: Serve with a bean or colorful root or round vegetable soup or a hearty bean, tempeh, or wheat meat stew, with quick-boiled greens or mixed vegetables or a pressed, marinated, or tossed or boiled salad. This bread's great for dunking and doesn't need a spread. (Squash Butter, Millet Butter, or plain soy yogurt do make a tasty spreads, however.)

Storage: Leftovers keep well and resteam well.

***Note:** Don't wash the casserole dish used to bake this bread; instead, set it aside and use it to cook your next morning's cereal in. You'll save on dish washing and water use and have a wonderful tasty morning cereal enhanced by the crumbs or bits of bread stuck to the bottom or sides of the pot.

Variations:

- To make millet meal, grind millet to a coarse meal in an Osterizer mini-blend container, coffee spice mill, or flour mill. Grind 1/2-cup at a time to produce a uniform consistency.

- To use active dry yeast see Standard or Slow-Rise instructions below.

- **Standard Rise Batter Bread:** Replace Rapid-Rise Yeast with Active Dry yeast. Use warm liquid as above. Let rise once in a covered bowl (1/2-2 hours in a warm place), stir, pour into oiled baking pan and let rise about 1/2-1 hour, in a warm place, or until doubled in size. Bake as above.

- **Slow-Rise Batter Bread:** Replace Rapid-Rise Yeast with Active Dry Yeast and reduce the amount of yeast to 1/4-1/2 tsp. Use 100° F liquid. Cover the bowl of batter with a dinner plate and allow it to rise at room temperature, on the counter, for 6-9 hours or overnight. Stir risen batter then pour into oiled baking pan and allow to rise for 1/2-1 hour in a warm place, or until almost doubled in size— do not allow it to over-rise and tear—then bake as above.

- **Chestnut Corn Bread:** Use 1/2 cup chestnut flour to replace 1/2 cup of millet or corn meal.

- **Double Corn Bread:** In the late summer and early fall, shave the fresh corn off 1 cob and add it to batter when mixing.

- **Dessert Corn Bread or Corn Cake:** For a holiday cake-like treat, replace water with amazake rice nectar, almond milk, or Rice Dream Beverage (plain, almond, original, or vanilla flavor). Add 1/2 cup raisins or currants and 1 1/2 tsp. cinnamon. Replace corn meal with corn flour (for a finer texture). Replace spelt flour with barley flour or whole wheat pastry flour. Be sure to bake this in a covered casserole dish so that it is moist and cakey. If this cannot be done, you may need to steam the freshly baked cake for 10-15 minutes before serving to moisten it. (Resteam leftovers, wrapped in a white, cotton-linen towel before serving.) ❏

Basic Procedure, All Purpose (Dinner) Pancakes (Year Round) ***

Prep: 15 minutes
Rising: 15-30 minutes for Rapid-Rise Batter **or** 2-4 hours for Standard Rise Batter **or** 8-10 hours or overnight for Slow-Rise Batter
Cooking: 45-60 minutes, less with a large griddle

Yield: 14-16 6" pancakes
Serves: 3-4 (or 1 1/2 meals for 2)
Serving size: 4-5 med. cakes per person

These egg-, dairy-, oil- and sweetener-free, pancakes are far more nutritious and digestible than standard versions. Using yeast rather than baking powder or baking soda makes it more nutritious. Though most folks serve pancakes for breakfast (decked with sticky, sweet fruits and syrups), they are far more healthful served as a savory breakfast, lunch, or supper with with soup, stew, gravy, or spread with a green or mixed vegetable side dish. Plan for leftovers; they are just as tasty the second time around.

Our favorite pancakes: Buckwheat, Chestnut, Blue Corn, or Oatmeal.

Rule of Thumb: Figure 3/4-1 cup flour per average person; 1-1/2 cups flour for very active individuals or if you are only eating two meals a day.

1 1/2 cups buckwheat flour *(see variations)*

1 1/2 cups spelt or finely ground whole wheat bread flour

1/4 cup arrowroot powder (acts as an egg replacer and binder)

1/4 oz. pkg. Rapid-Rise Yeast (2 1/2 tsp.)

3 1/2 cups plain, unsweetened, plain soy milk or rice, nut- or seed-milk

3/4 tsp. sun dried sea salt

For oiling the pan: 1-4 tsp. ghee or light sesame oil for the entire recipe

1. Mix flours and Rapid-Rise Yeast in a 4-quart heat-proof pyrex or stainless steel bowl.

2. Combine soy milk and salt in a saucepan. Insert a metal stem thermometer. Heat over medium-low, to 125-130° F but no hotter. Let it cool to the proper temperature if it gets too hot.

3. Stir warm liquids into dry ingredients. Mix briefly with a fork or whisk until thoroughly blended. Batter will thicken as it rises, so don't worry if it looks thin.

4. Cover bowl with a plate and set in a warm place for 20-30 minutes until it bubbles and doubles in size. (See Best Rising Places.) When risen, batter should still be pourable. If too thick, add water or soy milk, a few tablespoons at a time, and stir.

5. Heat a cast iron skillet or griddle over medium heat until a drop of water sizzles and dances on the surface. With a metal spatula or pancake flipper, spread 1/4 tsp. oil or ghee in the skillet.

6. Drop 1/3 cup batter on the hot griddle for each cake. Tilt the skillet slightly. Don't make cakes too thin or they won't rise properly. When they start to firm up around the edges and bubbles, flip and cook the other side.

7. Transfer to a bowl or plate, cover with an upside-down plate, then repeat the process with the remaining batter. You will not need to re-oil the skillet every time when you use a cast iron skillet and use the spatula to spread the oil or ghee. (We re-oil every five or six pancakes.) Make sure the heat is not too high or the cakes will burn.

Serving suggestions: Top with a vegetable, bean or tofu spread or sauce, or dunk in soup, stews, or gravy and serve with a green or mixed vegetable side dish. (Try Onion Butter, Squash Butter, or yam purée). Or used like tortillas to scoop up vegetables, beans, tofu, or tempeh side dishes. For a special treat, spread a thin coating of butter or ghee over your hot cakes and sprinkle with chives or sea flakes.

Storage: Store leftovers in wax paper bag(s) or a plate covered bowl. Reheat by steaming for just a few minutes on a plate wrapped in a kitchen towel. Refrigerate. Use within 1-3 days.

Variations:

- **Barley Pancakes:** Use barley flour to replace spelt or buckwheat flour.

- **Chestnut Pancakes:** Use 1/2 cup chestnut flour with 2 1/2 cups spelt or whole wheat flour.

- **Millet or Corn Pancakes:** Replace buckwheat flour with corn or millet flour.

- **Oatmeal Pancakes:** Use 1 cup rolled oats with 2 cups spelt or whole wheat flour.

- **Fresh Corn Pancakes:** In summer or fall add 1 cup of corn off the cob to batter in step # 3.

- **Standard Rise Method:** Replace Rapid-Rise Yeast with Active Dry yeast. Use warm liquid as above. Let rise once in a covered bowl (1/2-2 hours in a warm place), stir, then let rise about 1/2-1 hour, in a warm place, or until doubled in size. Cook as above.

- **Slow-Rise Method:** Replace Rapid-Rise Yeast with Active Dry Yeast but reduce the yeast to 1/2 tsp. for a single batch. Use room temperature rather than warm liquid. Cover the bowl of batter with dinner plate. Allow to rise at room temperature, on the counter, for 6-8 hours or overnight. Stir then allow to rise for 1/2-1 hour in a warm place, or until almost doubled in size. (Do not allow it to over-rise and tear.) Cook as above. ❏

Quick Crepés & Doilies (Any Season)

Prep: 10-12 minutes to mix
Yield: 16 (5-6" size) to 24 (4" size)
Cooking: 1/2 hour hands on, more for a double batch
Serves: 2 as a main dish grain *or* 8-12 with rice or other grain

A cross between a crepe and a pancake, these quick egg-less breads are perfect for wrapping up stir-fried vegetables, mashed beans or squash, or pressed salad. The batter takes just a minute to whip up. If you've got two bodies in the kitchen, whip up a double or triple batch with two skillets on the stove. Plan on a fair amount of cooking time since pouring, cooking, and flipping these paper thin crepés will take your undivided attention for 30-40 minutes. (Leftover doilies can be re-warmed on a bamboo steamer.) You can make these wheat free and create many variations by using different flour combinations.

Rule of Thumb: *As the solo grain in a meal figure 1 cup flour per person or 1 1/4-1 1/2 per very active person. To serve as a side-dish grain with rice, millet, or noodles, figure 1/4 - 1/2 cup flour per person.*

Note: A cast iron skillet or griddle works best for this preparation.

2 cups whole grain flour
   (e.g., buckwheat, brown rice, spelt, hard white wheat, or barley flour)

2 cup water

1/2 tsp. sun dried sea salt

~ 1-3 tsp. light sesame oil or ghee for the skillet

1. In a 4-cup measuring cup (one with a spout), combine flour, water and salt. Whisk with a fork until thoroughly mixed. Batter should be the consistency of thin, watery pancake batter.

2. Lightly coat a cast iron or stainless steel skillet with 1/4 tsp. ghee or oil. (Ghee works best.) Heat over medium flame until almost smoking. Pan only needs to be lightly oiled a few times during each batch (1/2 tsp. oil every 4-5 pancakes).

3. Pour a few teaspoons of batter into the center of the skillet, a little at a time. Immediately pour more batter around this in a spiral to make a 4-6" pancake. Lift and gently tilt pan to spread the batter and to keep the pancake thin. (Each pancake will have about 1 1/2-2 Tbsp. batter.)

4. Place a lid on skillet and cook 1-2 minutes until surface bubbles and sides begin to firm. Flip pancake and cook the other side, covered, about 2 minutes. Transfer to a plate.

5. Repeat with remaining batter. Stack cooked pancakes on a plate, on top of each other.

Serving suggestions: Serve with stir-fried or quick-boiled vegetables or a pressed or marinated salad with scrambled tofu or baked or stewed beans. Add a serving of squash, carrot, parsnip, corn, or other root vegetables as a side dish or soup, to round out the meal.

Storage: Refrigerate leftovers in a bowl covered with a saucer or plate, or in wax paper or cellophane bags. Serve at room temperature or reheat briefly by steaming on a plate.

Favorites:

• **Brown Rice Doilies:** 100% brown rice flour.

• **Buckwheat Doilies:** 100% buckwheat flour.

• **Spelt or Wheat Doilies:** 100% spelt, hard white wheat, or whole wheat pastry flour.

• **Mixed Grain Doilies:** 75% spelt or finely ground whole wheat flour + 25% corn flour (not corn meal), barley, buckwheat, millet, or teff flour. ❑

Basic Procedure, Flat Bread & Tortillas

Prep: 30 minutes
Yield: 16-20, 6 inch flat breads *or* 2, 9 x 13-inch sheets of crackers
Serves: 5-7 (or 2-3 meals for 2) *or* more if accompanied by rice or other grain

This simple dough can be used to make chapati, thick or thin flour tortillas, or crackers. You can even make the dough in advance, refrigerate it for several days, then roll a little out each day for fresh flat bread. These are thicker and don't bend as easily as the tortillas one finds in most grocery and health food stores. (Note if you have a lot of patience with a hot griddle, or an electric tortilla maker, you can make thin, bendable tortillas like the ones found in most supermarkets and health food stores. These thin breads are more suitable for thins such as burritos, and squash roll-ups.) We dunk thick flat breads into hearty bean stews or top them with refried beans, Tofu "Sour Cream," or quark and pressed salad or steamed greens. These tortillas travel well in lunch boxes, back packs, and airplane carry on bags.

4 cups spelt flour or whole wheat bread flour

2 cups other flour: *buckwheat, rye, kamut, barley, or millet flour or yellow or blue corn meal*

1 tsp. sea salt

2 cups boiling water or plain, unflavored soy milk

2 Tbsp. ghee or sesame, olive, or corn oil (or replace with additional water)

Additional flour to roll out dough

1. Place 2 cookie sheets in a 400° F oven to preheat for about 10-15 minutes while making the dough. This eliminates the need to oil the sheets—the dough will not stick if pans are piping hot.

2. In a large mixing bowl, combine wheat or spelt flour with the second flour.

3. In a sauce pan, combine water or soy milk and salt. Add oil if desired. Bring to boil then immediately pour the hot liquid over the flour. First stir with a sturdy mixing spoon

then with your hands. Form into a ball by kneading briefly, right in the mixing bowl, until smooth. If too wet add flour a tablespoon at a time as needed. If too dry, add water a tablespoon at a time.

4. Roll entire ball of dough into an 8-12 inch uniform log then cut in half. Form each half into an 8-12 inch log. (smaller for a fewer number of thick flat breads, longer for a greater amount of thin flat breads.) With a ruler and sharp knife, cut into 1 inch pieces (16-24 total pieces) and place in a bowl covered with a damp kitchen towel to keep dough from drying out.

5. Take each piece of dough out of the bowl and roll into a ball. Dip each ball into a small bowl of flour and lightly coat to prevent sticking.

6. On a pastry cloth or work surface, roll each ball into a 5-6 inch circle—not too thin or they'll dry out as they bake in the oven. Alternately, flatten floured balls of dough in a tortilla press. Repeat with other pieces. (See notes below for cooking thin flat breads on top of the stove.)

7. **For baked flat breads:** Remove one hot sheet from the oven and place 6 flattened rounds of dough on the piping hot, preheated cookie sheet. Immediately place sheet in the oven (preferably on a rack in the middle of the oven).Fill the second cookie sheet. Bake both sheets for 3-4 minutes, then flip breads. Repeat until well browned, flipping about 3-4 times during cooking. Bake until firm and lightly browned, about 10-12 minutes total. Breads may puff up as they bake.

8. Transfer to a basket or bowl lined and covered with a clean white kitchen towel.

Serving suggestions: Serve warm or room temperature with soup, stew, or a root, round, or ground vegetable dish and cooked, pressed, or marinated vegetables. A raw green garnish, pickles, beans, tofu, tempeh, and other items are optional. You can also serve flat breads and rice in the same meal.

Storage: see bread storage and reheating/steaming tips.

Variations:

- Use above dough to make two thick 9 or 10 inch single pie crusts, two 9-10 inch pies with thin top and bottom crust, or eight smaller pot pies (with top and bottom crusts).

- **Crackers:** Roll dough into a long sheet; cut into 2-4 inch squares before baking or roll into thin circles. Bake until golden around the edges. Store in a paper bags or cookie tins.

- **Griddle Flat Breads:** Divide dough into 24 pieces. Cook very thin, flattened pieces of dough, one at a time (or two at a time if space permits) on a very hot griddle or cast iron skillet. Flip every 2-3 minutes until browned and slightly puffy then transfer to a towel lined bowl.

- **Chestnut Flat Breads:** Use 1 cup chestnut flour and 5 cups wheat or spelt flour.

- **Fresh Corn Flat Breads:** Purée 2 cups fresh sweet corn with the water before heating it then proceed with basic recipe. Use all spelt or whole wheat bread flour or part barley flour.

- **Greek Turnovers:** Use the above wheat or spelt dough filled with tofu and spinach, kale, or collards. (See Spanokopita filling). Divide dough and filling into 16-20 portions. Place filling on the center of each circle then fold the sides in three places toward the center and pinch on top to form a triangle. Bake on oiled or floured cookie sheets at 350° F for about 20 minutes. Serve warm or at room temperature. ❑

Easiest Ever Bread Cube Dressing (Fall & Winter)

Prep: 15-20 minutes
Drying (bread cubes): 6-8 hours or all day **
Cooking (oat sauce): 30 minutes
Baking (dressing): 50 minutes

Yield: 3 loaf pans of stuffing
Serves: 6 as the only grain *or* 12-14 w/ rice or millet
Serving size: 1-2 scoops per person

** *Reduce recipe by 1/2 if desired*

This richly seasoned holiday side dish will get rave reviews and many requests for the recipe. It's so tasty and easy to make that you may want to serve it beyond Thanksgiving. It's great for any winter evening, with winter squash soup, tempeh or wheat meat cutlets, rice or Millet "Mashed Potatoes," and greens, and gravy. For best results dry the bread yourself. Rather than put the stuffing inside a bird, we bake it in loaf pans. Use fresh herbs if possible and don't forget the nutritional yeast for a rich taste without fat.

Note: *Brewer's Yeast will not work in this recipe. Use only nutritional yeast!)*

Bread:

16 cups cubed whole wheat, spelt, rye, or chestnut loaf bread *or* steamed buns, sourdough or yeasted variety, (8 cups when dry)

Oat-Cream:

1 cup rolled oats

1/2-2/3 cup nutritional yeast flakes*

7 cups water or water + vegetable soup stock

Other ingredients:

1 Tbsp. ghee *or* toasted or light sesame oil

1 1/2 cups white or yellow onion, minced finely

1 cup celery *or* 1/2 cup celery root, minced

Optional, 1 cup button mushrooms, minced *or* 4 fresh or dried/soaked shiitake, minced

2-2 1/2-3 tsp. sea salt

1 cup minced fresh herbs *(combination of sage, thyme, marjoram, rosemary, and parsley)*

(Or 2 Tbsp. rubbed sage + 1 Tbsp. dried, powdered thyme + 1 Tbsp. dried oregano + 1/2 tsp. powdered cumin + 1/2 tsp. black pepper)

Butter, ghee or sesame oil for loaf pans

1. Cut fresh or stale bread into 1/2-inch cubes. If dry and hard to cut, wrap in a cotton towel and steam for 15 minutes, then slice.

2. Put bread cubes on unoiled cookie sheets. Bake at 140 ° F for 6 hours or until crisp, dry, and reduced in size. (This may be done 1-5 days ahead then stored in a sealed glass jar.)

3. In a 4-quart saucepan, combine Oat Cream ingredients. Cover and bring to boil, do not stir, simply reduce heat to low and simmer, covered, 30-40 minutes. Go to step #3 now.

4. Sauté onions in oil or ghee over medium heat. Add mushrooms and a pinch of salt. Stir a few seconds, add celery, continue to stir, add the rest of the salt and fresh or dried herbs. Stir, and cook several minutes until vegetables wilt and soften, remove from heat and set aside.

5. Turn off oat mixture when cooking time has elapsed. Stir with a strong wooden spoon. Purée in a blender to make smooth and milky.

6. In a large mixing bowl, combine bread cubes, sautéed vegetables and oat-sauce and stir to distribute ingredients.

7. Spoon into 3 lightly oiled stainless steel or glass bread pans. (Shallow pans will not work well.) Cover tightly with foil or a lid. Bake at 350° F for 40-50 minutes. If made in advance, simply reheat in a covered dish before serving. Remove foil.

Serving suggestions: Top with gravy if desired. Serve with tempeh, wheat meat or tofu; Millet "Mashed Potatoes" or rice; and cooked, pressed, or marinated salad or greens. Add a soup, sweet potato or squash dish if desired, and/or relishes.

Storage: Leftovers keep for several days, refrigerated, and can be easily reheated using the covered-bowl-within-a-pot method.

Use Your Noodle

Pasta past and present

The idea of noodles is as old as the cuisine of China, the birth place of pasta. In fact, it is believed that Marco Polo introduced this Chinese delight to Italy where it quickly became a favorite food. Since then, pasta's worldwide popularity has continued to grow. Thomas Jefferson dabbled in pasta cookery during his stint as ambassador to France and even shipped home "macaroni" and a pasta making machine. Today, in America, the National Pasta Association predicts that pasta consumption will reach 30 pounds per capita by the year 2000. How much do you eat in a year?

Pasta is health food

Pasta is the perfect fitness staple—along with brown rice, millet, oats, and whole grain bread. Whether you want to lose weight, gain weight or simply maintain a trim physique, pasta provides more energy for your money than many other foods. Pasta is low in fat, high in complex carbohydrates, and rich in vitamins, minerals and fiber— if you pick varieties made from whole or minimally refined grains. (Skip "enriched" white flour pasta, unless you're eating out and that's all they have.)

For years pasta took a bum rap for being high in calories when it's really not. Pasta won't make you fat. Topping your pasta with heavy, fat-laden sauces will, however. Puddles of butter or cream sauce, mountains of cheese, or rich meat sauces not only accumulate on your hips, thighs, and abdomen, but also in your arteries and lungs. What can you do? Lighten the load on your body by lightening up your pasta with low fat sauces and toppings. You'll be able to eat more pasta, have more energy, and be healthier. Not only that, eliminating all the cheese, meat, and cream sauces will unmask a world of culinary possibility and taste sensations. You may be surprised to find that you like some of the new pastabilities more than your old favorites!

Pasta is good-for-you-fast food

Pasta is the ultimate fast food. It can be cooked in minutes and costs a lot less than most "prepared" or "fast foods" both in terms of your health and your pocketbook.

Pasta is the perfect food when you forget to plan ahead, get home late, have unexpected dinner guests, are pressed for time, or just want a change of pace. If you're cupboards are stocked with several varieties of pasta, a grain-based meal is never more than a few minutes away. In the time it takes to boil a pot of pasta you can steam, quick-boil, sauté or stir fry some greens and reheat leftover soup (for a pasta sauce), scramble tofu for a topping, or whip up a quick sauce such as Miso Tahini or Walnut-Miso. (Also see Sesame Buttered Noodles.) Or you can use one of the simplest pasta toppers, a seasoned, ground seed or nut condiment.

Saucing pasta

If you still want the occasional butter or ghee on your pasta, you can occasionally indulge—just do so more moderately using these rich items less often and in smaller amounts.

About tomatoes and tomato sauce

Tomatoes have a very cooling effect on the body and can wreak havoc on your belly. When eaten either too frequently or out of season, they can cause indigestion, acid heartburn, gas, burping, bloating, or a feeling of heaviness. They can also aggravate arthritis, psoriasis, autoimmune disorders, edema, and allergies.

Tomato sauce should be used infrequently during the heat of summer. Instead of tomato sauce, you might try beet, squash, carrot, parsnip, mushroom, broccoli, and other vegetable sauces on your pasta. You can also sauce your pasta with soups and stews; stir fried or sautéed or stir fried vegetables; low fat pesto, or Tofu Ricotta; stroganoff or goulash. Or try a sea vegetable condiment (or flakes) or side dish, or buttery tasting Flax Seed Condiment. You could also try some buttery tasting flax, walnut, or olive oil and garlic or a light tahini or tofu sauce. A whole new world of pasta toppings awaits you. The recipes listed in this chapter and the sauces in the condiment chapter are merely a spring-board for experimentation.

Souping it up with pasta

One of our favorite ways to serve pasta is to top large individual serving bowls of cooked pasta with a cup of leftover or freshly made soup or stew. These might be vegetable-based soups (creamy winter squash, parsnip, carrot, beet, or cream of broccoli); bean and vegetable-based soups (chili, minestrone, or whole or split pea soup); or stews made with wheat meat or tempeh (Stuffed Cabbage Leaves, Wheat Meat Stew, Hungarian Goulash, or Seitan Stroganoff).

Butter up to those noodles

"Buttered" noodles are another favorite though we butter our noodles with dairy-free "butter," and buttery tasting condiments. We top individual bowls of plain noodles with a few teaspoons of diluted Miso-Tahini, Walnut-Miso Spread, seed condiment, or a light sauce made of toasted sesame oil, tamari or ume vinegar, and a few pinches of dried, powdered herbs or spices. At the table we also sprinkle fresh or dried chives, scallions, or parsley over our noodles, often with sea vegetable flakes or a cooked sea vegetable condiment or side dish. We also spoon lightly steamed, sautéed, quick-boiled or stir fried vegetables over our noodles. You could also top your pasta with a few ounces of warm vegetarian sausage and stir fried vegetables or you could top your noodles with an occasional steamed or poached egg and a sprinkle of scallions, arugula, or chives. The simplest noodles become a gustatory delight, served with soup and a colorful green vegetable side dish.

Leftover pasta does good

Pasta can be cooked in quantities large enough to last for two meals or two days at a time. (See leftover ideas and storage tips.) It makes packing lunches or assembling quick suppers a snap.

Leftover pasta can be transported in a covered bowl for lunch and served at room temperature (it will keep from breakfast to lunch without refrigeration), topped with a thermos cup full of warm soup or stew and a small cup of leftover steamed veggies. Or top it with a seed condiment or seed oil and sautéed or stir fried vegetables or boiled salad. Last night's pasta can also be turned into a salad or tossed with a wide array of other leftovers at the table—cooked, pressed or marinated salads, cooked beans, marinated or sautéed tofu, cooked and seasoned tempeh, wheat meat or sea vegetables, various sauces, dips, dressings, roasted seeds, herbs, seasoned vinegars, tamari or shoyu, or pickles.

For meals eaten at home, you can steam warm leftover noodles in a bowl on top of a metal steamer basket or bamboo steamer tray before topping, tossing, or saucing. In 10-12 minutes your pasta will taste fresh as new.

More pastabilities

Leftover pasta can also be used in casseroles, as a soup extender, or for making noodle pudding. Even the leftover pasta cooking and rinsing water can be strained off, saved and used We use it to replace water to soak and cook breakfast cereal in or as a soup stock or soup extender. It can also be used to thicken sauces, gravies, or stir fried vegetables or as the liquid in biscuit, bread, or pancake batter.

Pasta for breakfast? You bet

You can even add leftover pasta to your breakfast cereal pot for a super creamy morning meal. This is a great way to use leftover noodles, especially if you don't have enough for a whole meal. Or, for a fun and filling morning meal, scramble tofu with roasted, crumbled alaria, kelp, nori or dulse and onions then serve it over plain or sesame buttered noodles, with a side of steamed greens or boiled salad, sauerkraut or radish pickles, and a squash or carrot soup or side dish. Or, for an uncommonly good breakfast, try pasta sauced with puréed squash soup (or sesame or flax oil and dulse flakes) served with cooked land and sea vegetables on the side.

New fangled pastas

Tired of spaghetti? Try the dazzling array of dried pastas available in health food stores, Italian markets, Chinese grocery stores, and gourmet shops. You might also want to sample freshly made Italian specialty pastas for a treat now and then.

Skip the super refined flour and go for the high protein, high flavor, and mineral rich types— such as whole wheat, hard white wheat, spelt, kamut, barley, millet, rye, rice, corn, amaranth, buckwheat, soba, Jerusalem artichoke, hard white wheat, lupini, quinoa, soya, green pea, or other exotic grain and bean pastas. Beware, some whole grain pastas are a bit tough and chewy and some bean pastas have an unusual texture. Whole wheat or brown rice udon and somen noodles— once made only in China, Japan, and Korea—are some of the most moist and tender whole grain pastas and are now being made in America and Canada. Kamut pasta is also very much like refined white pasta in taste and texture, but is far more nutritious. You will have to experiment to find the pastas that please you and your family. (The health food store or co-op may be your best bet for egg-free, preservative-free, and whole grain or minimally refined pastas. Our mail order section offers a wide array of tasty pastas that can be delivered to your door.)

Many types of noodles are interchangeable. If a recipe calls for macaroni or elbows, for example, feel free to use spirals, conchiglie (medium or large shells), or rotini or rotelle (corkscrews). If the recipe calls for spaghetti, try soba, udon, somen, fetuccini (flat ribbons 1/4-inch wide), linguini (flat ribbons 1/8-inch wide), fusilli (twisted spaghetti), mafalda (flat ribbons), udon, or rotini or rotelle. You might also want to experiment with unusual pasta shapes—such as rigatoni (ridged short pasta tubes), capellini (angel hair), farfalle (butterflies or bow ties), fusili, tortellini and tortelloni (little stuffed rings), ruote (wagon wheels), and ziti (long tubular pasta).

Another option is couscous, a quick cooking pasta that looks like cracked wheat. Many people mistake it for a whole grain but couscous is actually made from semolina wheat flour. It cooks up to a fluffy consistency in minutes. Unlike most pastas, couscous needs no rinsing and can be made into a pilaf or tasty porridge then topped with a hearty sauce, stew, seed condiment, or stir fry, or it can be added to a soup. Couscous holds up well under almost any bean, vegetable, tempeh, tofu, wheat meat, or sea vegetable side dish. Although most of the couscous on the market is made from refined flour, you can find whole grain couscous in your local health food store and some ethnic markets.

WHAT'S THE PASTA PLUS?

Pasta is:

1. high in complex carbohydrates (the body's main source of fuel)

2. high in fiber (if you pick whole grain varieties)

3. easy to digest

4. low in fat (so it is less likely to be stored as fat on your frame)

5. sugar-free (so it won't leave you with the low blood sugar blues)

6. quick and easy to fix

7. inexpensive when compared to many other fast to fix foods

8. readily available in your local health food store, grocery store, or restaurant

9. a good source of vitamins and minerals (especially the whole grain varieties)

10. very versatile. You can sauce it; soup it; toss it in a salad, stir fry, casserole, pudding, or lunch box; serve it with Chinese, Italian, Greek, Mexican, Moroccan, or Japanese type meals.

Money Saving Tips

- Because a pound of pasta usually serves just three or four people (or one and one-half to two meals for two), it can add up if you eat a lot of it. The following hints may help lessen the strain on your pocketbook.

- Though it may not be obvious due to the size of the package, dried pasta is usually less expensive than fresh or frozen pasta. Fresh or frozen pasta often sells for $6-8 per pound.

- Dried whole grain pastas in bulk bins at co-ops and health food stores usually go for $2-4 per pound, but watch out for Japanese imports which can sell for $8 a pound. (Look for American-made versions of Japanese udon, soba, and somen; these are less expensive.)

- If you have the time and inclination to make your own pasta, you can make a month's worth of pasta in one or two afternoons for only pennies (or dimes) per pound. (We've not ventured into this area much, except for making the occasional ravioli, won tons, and gyoza.)

- Serve pasta as a side dish grain, along with cooked rice, millet, or whole grain bread to make your pasta supply last longer.

- Buy pasta by the case or in 10 pound boxes at wholesale through a buying club.

PASTA YIELDS & RECOMMENDED SERVING SIZES:

	Dry	Cooked
How much will it make?		
	2 cups dry noodles	3 cups cooked
	8 oz. dry whole grain variety	~4-5 cups cooked pasta
	16 oz. (1 lb.) dry pasta	~10 cups cooked pasta

How many will it serve?

Rule of thumb:

per average person: 3-4 oz. dry pasta *or* 1 1/2-2+ cups cooked pasta
per person on a two-meal a day plan: 4-7 oz. dry pasta *or* 2-3 1/2 cups cooked pasta
per very active person: 6-8 oz. dry pasta *or* 2 1/2-4 cups cooked pasta

Notes:
**If pasta is to be served with rice, bread, won tons, gyoza, or dumplings figure less per person.

**If using fresh pasta, which is perishable and expands less in cooking, you may need twice as much (about 6-12 oz. fresh pasta per average person or 12-16 oz. per active person). This will depend upon the variety you choose.

**Make enough pasta to last for two meals so that you will have leftovers for the next day. Leftovers can be to steamed or served at room temperature.

Quick & Easy Pasta Meals

Pasta meals are simple meals. Pasta can be the only grain in the meal or it can be served in smaller portions with a side of pita, foccacia, steamed buns, loaf bread, or any other kind of bread. Here are some basic formats to make meal planning easier.

Example #1: The Souper Noodle Bowl

Pasta, any variety

Vegetarian vegetable soup

Steamed, stir fried, or sautéed vegetables

Sautéed or simmered tempeh, tofu, or wheat meat, sea vegetables, or a steamed egg

Pungent green garnish—minced scallions, chives, parsley, arugula, or cilantro

+/- Sea vegetable flakes (if not used already)

1. Place pasta in individual serving bowls. Ladle soup or stew on top of pasta. Top with a green garnish and/or sea vegetable flakes.

2. Serve the cooked vegetables and tempeh, tofu, wheat meat, sea vegetable, or egg either on top of the soup-sauced pasta or serve it on the side then spoon it on as you eat.

Example #2: The Dragon Bowl

Optional, light soup broth or vegetable soup

Pasta

Vegetable sauce *(beet, carrot, squash, parsnip, etc.)* **or** gravy

Steamed, stir fried or sautéed veggies **or** pressed salad

Stir fried tofu, wheat meat, cooked, seasoned tempeh or tempeh "sausage"**or** a steamed or poached egg or flax or sesame oil

+/- Sea vegetable flakes, condiments, and a vegetable side dish

Pungent green garnish—minced scallions, chives, parsley, or arugula

1. Place in individual serving bowls.

2. Ladle sauce or gravy. Top with tofu, tempeh, wheat meat, egg, or oil and a garnish.

3. Serve green or mixed vegetables on the side or on top of your noodle bowl.

Example #3: Veggie Noodle Bowl

Vegetarian soup or light broth

Pasta

Light Miso-Tahini, Walnut-Miso or Miso-Sunflower Sauce, *or* low fat pesto, Tofu Sauce, ground Seed or Nut Condiment, *or* flax or toasted sesame oil +/- tamari or light miso, *or* butter or ghee

Pungent green garnish—minced scallions, chives or parsley, and/or black pepper

+/- Sea vegetable flakes or cooked sea vegetable condiment

Steamed, stir fried or sautéed veggies or pressed salad

1. Serve soup on the side.

2. Place pasta in individual serving bowls. Spoon on a bit of butter/ghee, oil or other sauce.

3. Sprinkle on a green garnish and/or a hint of spice and/or sea vegetable condiment. Serve veggies on the side or toss them on over pasta.

Note: See index for Macaroni & Sea, Macaroni & Cheese-less Casserole, or Chick-n-Pea Sourdough/Noodle Casserole.

Favorite Pasta Toppers

Fat-Free Garnishes

(Use with any of the toppings listed below)

- Dried or fresh minced chives or scallions
- Chopped parsley, cilantro, dill, or arugula
- Edible flowers
- Black pepper
- Dulse, Dried Onion & Sea Cress Sprinkles
- Dulse flakes, sea cress flakes
- Grated ginger juice (squeezed from finely grated ginger)
- Minced miso garlic pickles, sauerkraut, or other vegetable pickles

Low-Fat & Oil-Free Sauces and Soupy Pasta Toppings

(Serve with steamed, quick-boiled, pressed, marinated or stir fried vegetables +/- pickles)

- Puréed Squash Soup or Beet Sauce Italiano
- Seitan Stroganoff,
- Mock Poultry Gravy
- Tamari-Thyme Gravy
- Creamy Green Garlic Sauce
- Whole Dried Pea Soup
- Onion Butter with dry roasted, chopped nuts or seasoned nut condiment
- Any-Bean Soup, plain or puréed
- Creamy Tomato Soup or Sauce
- Stir Fried Vegetables
- Stir Fried Vegetables with Tempeh or Wheat Meat

Mock Cream & Sauces

(Serve with steamed, parboiled, pressed, marinated or stir fried vegetables +/- pickles)

- Hummus Dip, thinned
- Parsnip White Sauce
- Herbed Tofu "Cream Cheese"
- Tofu Sauce
- Pesto-Presto
- Tofu Pesto
- Sesame Buttered Sauce
- Squash Sauce
- Sweet Squash Soup, +/- tahini

Simple savory topping combinations

(Serve with soup and steamed, boiled, pressed, raw or marinated or stir fried vegetables)

- Walnut or Pine Nut Condiment

- Pumpkin, Sesame, Sunflower, or Flax Seed Condiment

- Alaria Condiment +/- flax or sesame oil or seed or nut condiment

- Sea vegetable flakes + tamari + flax or sesame oil or olive oil

- Sesame or flax oil + juice from grated ginger root + ume or tamari + fresh or dried chives or scallions

- Olive oil + minced vegetable pickles or sea vegetable condiment + fresh or dried chives

- Sea Sage & Sunflower Spread + fresh or dried chives, scallions or parsley

- Tahini + umeboshi vinegar or light miso + water, (heated, tossed with chives)

- Natural teriyaki, Szechuan or plum sauce (with steamed or stir fried vegetables)

Pasta Sauces from Leftovers:

(Serve with steamed, parboiled, salad or stir fried vegetables +/- pickles)

- Cubed Tempeh "Sausage" Cutlets +/- beet, carrot, squash or tomato sauce

- Cubed Tempeh "Bacon" +/- beet, carrot, squash or tomato sauce

- Puréed baked squash + light miso +/- chopped, roasted walnuts or tahini

- Stir fried, quick boiled, steamed or sautéed vegetables + seed condiment +/- sea vegetable condiment, side dish or flakes

- Minced vegetable pickles + cooked sea vegetable + olive or other oil

- Light miso broth with stir fried veggies and tempeh or seasoned tofu cutlets

- Puréed steamed veggies with herbs and/or soup stock

- Leftover cooked wheat meat, tempeh, or tofu + Szechuan, teriayki, or plum sauce (tossed with leftover boiled, pressed or marinated salad or steamed vegetables)

Rich toppings

(Serve with soup and steamed, boiled, pressed, marinated, or raw salad, or stir fried vegetables +/-pickles)

- Flax, pumpkin, sunflower or sesame oil

- Steamed, poached, or scrambled egg

- Quark, yogurt cheese, or grated cheese

- Scrambled egg with tofu

Basic Procedure, No Fuss Pasta Cooking (Year Round)***

Prep: 5 minutes
Cooking: 15-18 minutes boil & soak method
or 5-10 minutes simmering

Serves: 4-6 (or 2-3 meals for 2)
Servings size: 1 1/2-3 cups per person

The boil and soak method requires minimum attention, keeps pasta from boiling over, and saves energy. We generally cook enough pasta to last for two meals.

1 lb. (16 oz.) dry pasta (any variety)

12-16 cups water

1/4-1/2 tsp. sea salt (only if the pasta is salt-free)

1. Combine water and salt in a 3-4 quart pot. Cover and bring to a rapid boil.

2. Add pasta and return to a rolling boil. Shock pasta by splashing it with 1 cup of cold water. Return to a boil again, stir briefly, then turn off the heat.

3. Allow pasta to sit in the pot, covered, for 10-15 minutes or until tender and cooked through. Pastas vary in their cooking time—some cook quickly while others cook more slowly—so check several times. The inside and outside should be the same color and texture. You may need to taste it to be sure.

   Note: Don't let it soak too long or it will absorb too much water and turn to mush.

4. Put a large colander inside a very large stainless steel mixing bowl in the sink. Pour the pasta and cooking water into the colander.

5. Lift the colander from the bowl and allow water to drain into the bowl. Pour 2-4 cups of cold water over pasta and toss it gently, allowing the water to drain into the bowl. Light rinsing keeps the pasta from sticking together.

Note: If you need to reheat the pasta before serving, steam it briefly in a bowl on a rack or in a colander above boiling water.

Note: *DON'T THROW OUT THE STARCHY PASTA WATER!* Refrigerate it in jars for later use. (See leftover tips below.)

Serving suggestions: Serve pasta in large individual serving bowls, topped with a warm soup, stew, sauce or gravy, low-fat pesto, or a few ounces of sautéed tofu, tempeh "sausage" or wheat meat. Also add a side of cooked green leafy or mixed vegetables or pressed or marinated salad. Soup and sea vegetable dishes are optional. To make pasta go further, serve it with a side of bread or rice.

Variation:

- **Boil & Shock Method:** Bring pasta to boil as above. Continue to cook on medium heat. Each time pasta comes to rolling boil, stir briefly then shock by adding 1/2 cup cold water to the pot. Return to boil. Repeat 4-5 times or until pasta is done.

Leftover tips:

- Pour pasta water into one or more jars and cover and refrigerate when cooled. Use it as your liquid for making breakfast cereal, or in soups, stews, or in baking.

- Refrigerate leftover pasta stored in a covered bowl. Resteam the leftovers for supper or serve at room temperature. Pack it for lunch then serve with a piping hot cup of soup (stored in a thermos), condiments, and a salad or cooked vegetable side dish.

- See "Uses for Leftover Pasta," for more ideas

- **To reheat leftover pasta:** Put pasta in a heat proof bowl on top of a steamer tray or basket (stainless steel works well) and surround with 1-inch of water. Cover the pot, but not the bowl. Steam 10 minutes or until warmed. ❑

Uses for Leftover Pasta

If you've got a lot of pasta

- **Make a casserole**
  with beans, vegetables, and herbs or spices with land and sea vegetables
  with vegetables and chopped or ground wheat meat or vegetarian sausage +/- herbs or spices
  with a thick puréed soup, land or sea vegetables, and herbs or spices
  with a thick chili or bean sauce +/- herbs or spices

- **Make a pasta salad**
  with vegetables and herbs or spices
  with vegetables and beans, tofu, or tempeh +/- herbs or spices
  with vegetables and cooked wheat meat +/- herbs or spices
  with a tahini dressing or low-fat or oil-free dressing or marinade

- **Stir fry it**
  with vegetables and herbs or spices
  with vegetables and tofu, tempeh, or wheat meat (seitan) +/- herbs or spices
  with vegetables, herbs, and a whisked egg and/or tofu

- **Make noodle pudding for dessert**
  with soy milk, amasake, almond milk or oat-cream and fresh or dried fruit, and/or spices
  with apple juice, ground nuts or seeds or nut/seed butter and/or dried fruit, and spices

If you've got a smaller amount of pasta:

- **Add it to**
  a soup or stew
  other leftovers and liquids for a fast soup

- **Cook it into breakfast cereal**
  with leftover cooked rice, millet or other grain
  with dry rolled oats
  with dry buckwheat or washed, drained millet
  with dry rolled oats and leftover cubed bread
  with pasta water and any of the above

- **Stir it into warm rice, millet, or buckwheat**
  to extend your grain for another meal

- **Toss it with**
  leftover steamed or stir fried veggies
  leftover pressed or marinated salad
  leftover sea vegetable side-dish
  a marinade or low-fat dressing + herbs or spices

Sesame Buttered Noodles (Any Season)***

Prep: 15 minutes
Cooking: 8-12 minutes

Serving size:~ 1 1/2-3 cups noodles per person
Serves: 2 (or 2 meals for 1)

***If serving two very active individuals, you may need to cook 12 ounces of dry pasta. Increase sesame tahini sauce by one half.**

It only takes a hint of sesame tahini to add a rich and buttery taste—reminiscent of butter, cheese, or cream sauce—to noodles. This quick-to-fix dish is sure to become a family favorite. Round out the meal with a side of boiled salad, steamed leafy greens or quick boiled veggies and a side of steamed or nishime cooked carrots, winter squash and onions, corn on the cob, or a cup of creamy vegetable soup. Add a dash of sauerkraut or colorful red or white radish pickles for extra special spark.

Pasta

8-12 oz. dry spelt, kamut, wheat, or other noodles *(try spaghetti, rotini, rotelle, udon, soba,*
or giant macaroni shells)

Water to cook pasta (about 8 cups)

1/4 tsp. sea salt for water (omit if pasta is a salted variety—Japanese pasta usually is)

Sauce

1 1/2-2 Tbsp. sesame tahini or sesame butter

1/2 cup water

1/4 tsp. sea salt *or* 2-4 tsp. white, yellow, or mellow miso

Topping

1/4-1/3 cup minced fresh chives, scallions, or parsley *or* 3 Tbsp. dried chives

Optional, 1/2 recipe (1 1/2 cups) Scrambled Tofu *or* Tofu & Wheat Meat
or 1/3-1/2 recipe (1/2-3/4 cup) Crumbled Tempeh "Bacon" or "Sausage,

1. Cook, drain, and rinse noodles as in Basic Pasta Procedure, Noodles. Set noodles aside. (Save the cooking water for making soup, breakfast cereal, bread, or pancakes.)

2. Combine sauce ingredients in a suribachi, blender, or Osterizer container and blend until smooth. Pour sauce into a small saucepan and simmer and stir over low heat for 1-3 minutes to thicken.

3. Pour over drained noodles and toss with cooking chopsticks (metal spoons can cause breakage) or a pasta fork until coated. Garnish with parsley, scallions, or chives in the kitchen or at the table. Toss again if desired.

Serving suggestions: Put 1 1/2-2 cups of Sesame Buttered Noodles into each of two large, individual serving bowl then arrange a small cup of cooked greens or mixed vegetables around the sides of each bowl. If desired, add a tablespoon of pickles and/or top with 2/3 cup Scrambled Tofu, Scrambled Tofu-n-Wheat Meat, or a few tablespoons of homemade Tempeh "Bacon" or Tempeh "Sausage." Also serve with a cup of colorful vegetable soup or nishime cooked or steamed carrots, squash or mixed root vegetables or corn on the cob (in season). Add a side of bread as needed. ❏

Macaroni & Cheese-less Casserole

Prep: 20 minutes
Soaking (for beans): overnight or 24 hours
Cooking: 1 hour (beans); 1 hour (casserole)

Serves: 6-8 accompanied by bread *or* 4 as a main dish
Serving size: 1-2 cups per person

Who needs macaroni & cheese when you can have macaroni and squash? It is nutritious, delicious, and low in fat. We like to serve it with mushroom or onion broth, bread, and a side of pressed salad or steamed vegetables and pickles.

Dry Beans *(Or, use 1 1/2 -2 cups of previously cooked soy beans and skip to step #3):*

3/4 cup dry yellow soybeans

2 cups water + fresh water for cooking

4-5" piece kelp or kombu sea vegetable

Squash sauce

1/2 cup onion, minced

1-2 cloves garlic, minced

4 cups cubed winter squash, with skins left on *(1/2 medium butternut or kabocha squash)*

1/2-1 tsp. sea salt

1/2" water, to cover bottom of pot

Seasoning

1-2 tsp. dried Italian herb blend

Optional, 1 tsp. cumin *or* 3 cloves of minced garlic

Optional, 3-4 Tbsp. nutritional yeast flakes

2 heaping Tbsp. light, yellow, or mellow miso

1 cup bean stock from cooking soybeans

1 cup grated, plain, uncooked mochi

Noodles

1 pound dry spelt, kamut, or wheat noodles *(e.g., elbows, rotini, rotelle, macaroni, udon, spaghetti, or other)*

1. Wash, sort, soak and cook beans as per Basic Bean Procedure. (Pressure cook 1 hour using the covered-bowl-within-a-pot method. Drain beans and reserve liquid for this dish and for use as soup stock.

   Note: If you do not have a pressure cooker, use garbanzo, cannelloni, or navy beans. Prepare as per Basic Procedure, Beans.

2. Arrange drained, cooked beans in the bottom of a pressure cooker. Layer squash sauce ingredients on top. Pressure cook 1 hour, until very soft. Or, layer ingredients in a 3 quart saucepan, cover, bring to boil, reduce heat to low and simmer, covered, for 1 hour.

3. Cook pasta as per Basic Procedure. Drain and rinse. Reserve and refrigerate cooking water for tomorrow's hot cereal or soup.

4. Preheat oven to 350° F. Purée squash-bean sauce in a blender or Foley food mill. Pour sauce into a large mixing bowl. Add herbs, miso, 1 cup bean stock, and grated mochi or flour. Stir gently with pasta. Turn into a large oiled casserole dish or 2 oiled loaf pans. If making the dish ahead, cover the pans and refrigerate for up to 12 hours before baking.

5. Bake, covered for 1 hour, just before serving. This dish tastes even better the second day.

Storage: Refrigerate leftovers and reheat using covered-bowl-within-a-pot method.

Variations:

• Replace soybeans with 3 cups cooked garbanzo or white beans.

• Use 3 cups soft tofu in place of soybeans, adding it to cooked squash in step #2. ❏

Cheese-less Chestnut Lasagna
(Fall, Winter, Early Spring)

Prep: 45-60 minutes
Soaking: 4 hours or overnight (chestnuts)
Cooking: 45 minutes (for chestnuts) + 5-8 minutes (for noodles) + 40-50 minutes to bake

Serves: 10-12 accompanied by rice or bread
Servings size: 1 slice per person with bread or rice

Halve recipe to serve 5-6 (or 2-3 meals for 2).

This is comfort food at its best. Most lasagnas are loaded with fat, largely due to the mountains of cheese (or meat and cheese) called for in most recipes. This lasagna is vegetarian, dairy free, and very low in fat. And what's more, it's so tasty we bet you won't miss all that fat. Tofu, wheat meat, mochi, and chestnuts lend a rich and hearty flavor. Serve with a "cream-less", cream of vegetable soup or light broth, bread or rice, and a salad or cooked greens. Feel free to experiment with the herbs and spices, especially if you like a lot of garlic.

Filling

1 cup dried chestnuts*

2 cups water (increase to 3 cups if boiling)

2 cups grated or shredded wheat meat
(omit herbs if using spiced wheat meat)
or 12 oz. crumbled Pressure Marinated Tempeh **or** veggie burgers*

1 Tbsp. ghee or sesame or olive oil

2 cups minced onion

1 cup packed, very finely grated carrot

1 1/2 tsp. dried basil **or** 1 1/2-2 Tbsp. fresh, minced basil

1 1/2 tsp. dried oregano **or** 1 1/2-2 Tbsp. fresh, minced oregano

1 tsp. dried thyme **or** 1 Tbsp. fresh thyme

2-3 cloves minced garlic

1 1/2 lb. soft tofu, drained

2 Tbsp. white, yellow, mellow, chickpea, millet, or sweet miso

2 Tbsp. arrowroot powder or kuzu

Sauce

2 cups grated mochi (uncooked, thawed, plain variety or garlic sesame flavor)

1/2 cup nutritional yeast flakes or powder (do not use baker's or brewer's yeast!)

1 cup water + 2-3 Tbsp. if needed

2 Tbsp. mellow, yellow, or sweet white miso

Noodles

3/4 pound whole grain lasagna noodles

3 quarts water + dash sea salt

Garnish

Fresh or dried chives or chopped fresh parsley, scallions, chives, or arugula

Optional, black pepper

1. Soak dried chestnuts in a small stainless steel bowl at room temperature for 4-12 hours. (Do not throw off the soak water.)

2. Pressure cook 45 minutes using the covered-bowl-within-a-pot method. Or, put chestnuts directly in a 2-quart pot, adding an extra cup of water. Cover, bring to boil, reduce heat to low and simmer 1 hour or until tender, adding a small amount of water as needed to

prevent chestnuts from boiling dry.

2. Sauté onion and carrot in oil until soft and translucent around the edges. Add ground wheat meat, tempeh, or veggie burgers. Cook 3-5 minutes over medium heat until browned.

3. In a mixing bowl, combine cooked chestnuts, chestnut cooking water, vegetables, herbs, and tempeh or wheat meat. Crumble and mix with a fork to evenly distribute seasonings.

4. Boil noodles in a large pot until firm but pliable—al dente (just barely tender). Drain pasta (reserve pasta water for other uses). Rinse under cold water, drain, and set aside.

4. Meanwhile, mash tofu through a Foley food mill or in a food processor. Add light miso and arrowroot or kuzu.

5. Preheat oven to 350° F. Lightly oil a 9 x 13 x 2 inch oblong pan and one 9 x 9 square pan.

6. Place a layer of noodles on the bottom of each pans. Cover with a layer of wheat meat or tempeh and chestnut filling. Spread evenly. Top with a layer of noodles, then tofu mixture, then another layer of noodles.

7. Grate mochi with a cheese grater. Mix with nutritional yeast, water, and light miso. Pour evenly over lasagna then cover casserole dish with a lid or foil.

8. Bake for 40 minutes. Remove cover and bake for an additional 10 minutes until slightly golden and sticky looking on top.

Serving suggestions: Serve warm with a light soup, bread or rice, and cooked green or mixed vegetables or a pressed, marinated or boiled salad and pickles.

Storage: Refrigerate leftovers and reheat small portions using the covered-bowl-within-a-pot method. Reheat larger portions in a covered dish in the oven.

Variations:

• Chestnuts may be replaced with small red beans or azuki beans if you cannot find dried or fresh-frozen, steam peeled chestnuts. The taste will not be the same, but it will still be tasty. ❑

WON TONS, GYOZA & RAVIOLI AS EASY AS 1-2-3

You don't have to be mad about Chinese or Japanese food to like won tons or gyoza. Whether you call them; won tons, pot stickers, gyoza, filled dumplings, or turnovers; these bite sized morsels have been popular for centuries throughout China and Japan. Similar creations show up in most other culinary traditions: ravioli in Italy, pirogies and piroshkies in Poland, pasties in England, samosas in India, and the ever popular turnover pastries here in America. In fact, won tons can be served ravioli style and similar fillings can be used for one or the other of the two!

The Asian wrappers tend to be made without the high fat and cholesterol-laden butter characteristic of many of the other filled pastries from around the world. The Chinese and Japanese wrappers are usually made with refined flour and eggs and filled with a meat or seafood. Italian ravioli and Russian pirogies tend to be equally as heavy on the meat and cheese fillings and the wrappers are often made with eggs and white flour. However, the wrappers for any of these can just as easily be made egg-less and the fillings meatless!

You needn't buy those artificial white flour based won ton wrappers, nor must you buy a pasta maker to make good ravioli. We've pared it down to one basic dough, one which is rich in nutrients and fiber and is fat free. Not only that, this dough can be used to make won tons, gyoza, ravioli, baked turnovers, and pirogies. And it is easier to make than you might think. An added bonus to making these delicacies at home, besides the nutritional bonus, is that they can be filled with almost anything: crumbled tofu, seasoned tempeh, or veggie burgers; mashed, sautéed, or refried beans; stir fried, marinated, or minced veggies; fruits and nuts; and almost any leftovers you happen to have on hand, from sweet to savory and everything in between!

Both won tons and ravioli (and their cousins the gyoza and pirogies) can be made ahead in quantity and easily reheated or eaten at room temperature, making the perfect homemade fast food for kids, busy moms, students, or anyone on the go. And if you're looking for the ideal party, pack lunch, supper or snack food, or a low-fat dessert, these filled pouches are just the thing to share with friends and family.

They're delicious, nutritious, and inexpensive to make. And once you get the hang of it, you can turn out several dozen in under an hour. They can be steamed, boiled, or even baked to create a variety of tastes and textures for use in any season. If you use a set of stacking bamboo steamer trays, you can cook several batches at once, using one pot, one burner, and steam!

Whether you serve them for an appetizer, a luncheon dish, a tea time snack, or breakfast, brunch, or dessert, these tasty tid-bits are sure to be as big a hit in your home as they are in ours. They can be served tossed in soups, raw or parboiled salads, covered with a ladle full of gravy, pasta sauce, puréed beet, parsnip, broccoli, or squash sauce, and bread, or as a side dish to accompany rice, stir fried, steamed or sautéed vegetables, and soup. Serve them solo as a party appetizer or with spicy, sour, or pungent sauces, or natural relishes. Or, for a real treat, try fruit filled dessert won tons to round out your next dinner party or family get together (these too can be baked, steamed, or boiled). Once made they'll last for several days in the refrigerator.

Suggested portions for won tons, gyoza, and ravioli

For a main dish (like ravioli): 6-8 small won tons, gyoza, or ravioli per person with bread, depending on the number of other side dishes; figure slightly more for a very active person

As a condiment with rice or noodles: 2-4 won tons, gyoza, or ravioli per person

As an appetizer: 2-5 small won tons or turnovers per person

For dessert: 2-3 small won tons or turnovers per person

**As a side dish serve won tons, ravioli, or gyoza with soup, whole grain, and a green or mixed vegetable two vegetable side dishes.

Note: Won ton and gyoza wrappers, ravioli, and turnovers aren't difficult to make. We use the same dough to make all of these. You may choose to make a small batch such as this, or a larger batch. Our egg-less dough makes delicious wrappers that are far better than the ones sold in most stores. Ours are made from whole grain flour and contain no preservatives, additives, sugar, or refined flour. The same dough can also be used to make pasta, either cut by hand, or put though a pasta machine.

Basic Procedure, Whole Grain Pasta, Gyoza, Won Ton & Ravioli Dough***

Prep: 20-30 minutes
Cooking: 20-30 minutes

Yield: 36-40 ravioli, wonton, or turnover wrappers
Serves: 8-10 as an appetizer or side dish
2-3 as a main dish *or* 9-18 with bread or rice
Serving size: 12-20 as dessert

Rule of Thumb: 3/4-1 cup flour per person as a main dish; 1-1 1/2 cups per active person; less for a side dish or appetizer or if accompanied by rice, millet, noodles, or bread.

You can vary the dough by using different flour combinations. Chestnut dough (made from spelt and chestnut flour) is a real favorite for both sweet and savory dough, though kamut flour also works well singly or in combination with wheat or spelt. The dough can be made a day in advance then stored in the refrigerator in a covered bowl. When using made-ahead dough, be sure to take it out of the refrigerator to allow it to soften at room temperature for 8 hours before you roll it out and fill it. Be sure to make extras which can be served over the course of a few days.

2- 1/2 cups spelt or kamut flour* (see variations below)

1/2 tsp. sea salt

3/4 cup water + 2 Tbsp. additional water

Filling options (pick 1 or 2):

Tofu Ricotta, Tofu Cream Cheese, or Tofu Pesto Paté

Spanokopita Filling

Scrambled Tofu with Nori

Refried Beans

Meaty Burdock & Walnut Filling

Mustard-n- Black Bean Filling

See also Fillings For Steamed Buns

See also Fillings For Calzones

See also Fillings for Tamales

See also bean, tofu, or tempeh dips and spreads

Making & filling the dough

1. Boil water and salt. Mix in flour and quickly form into a dough. Let rest 10 minutes then roll into an 18-inch long rope.

2. Cut into 36 pieces using a ruler as a guide. Roll into balls and cover with a damp cloth to keep dough from drying out. Dip each ball, one at a time, into flour to lightly coat. Roll each ball out flat using a rolling pin, or a tortilla press, to make a 3-4 inch circle of dough.

3. Spoon 1-2 tsp. filling into the center of each circle. Fold dough in half then seal and crimp edges with the tines of a fork or pinch between your thumb and forefinger as you'd crimp a pie crust.

4. Follow one of the cooking instructions below (baking, boiling, steaming, or pan-frying).

Variations in the dough

- **Barley or kamut won ton or ravioli dough:** Replace half of the spelt flour with barley or kamut flour, or experiment with other combinations.

- **Chestnut won ton or ravioli dough:** Replace 1/4 cup of spelt flour with chestnut flour. (This is good for sweet or savory preparations! Chestnuts add a subtle sweetness to the dough.)*

- **For dessert turnovers:** Use apple juice, rice milk beverage, amasake concentrate or shake, or almond milk to replace the water above then fill the dough with thick stewed fruit, fruit compote, mashed squash, yam, or sweet potato, thick chestnut purée, or cooked chestnuts, raisins and cinnamon.

- **Basic Pasta:** Use the above dough to make fetuccini, lasagna, or other noodles. Either roll out and cut the dough by hand or use a pasta machine.

Cooking & serving won tons, gyoza & ravioli

Note: Pick just one of the following cooking methods

To boil

1. Boil 2 quarts lightly salted water.

2. Drop ravioli or won tons, 6-8 at a time, into boiling, salted water. Loosen them from bottom with a large spoon. Boil 10 minutes, turning once, in a covered pot, with a lid ajar.

3. Remove and drain, then cook the rest of ravioli in the same manner.

4. If made ahead, reheat by steaming on a plate on top of a metal steamer or bamboo steam tray, or in a covered casserole dish in the oven at 350°F.

To steam (any season:

1. Place filled won tons on each of two oiled 9-inch heat proof plates. Put plates on 10-inch bamboo steamer trays, which come in sets of two, and stack. Top with a lid. Or, place on plates on top of metal steamer baskets, then cover the pot or pots with a lid.

2. Fill a wide pot with 2-inches water, or use a large wok. (If using a wok, the steamer will fit inside). If using a metal steamer basket, water should not touch the bottom of the baskets.

3. Place bamboo trays on top of pot. Steam over medium-high heat, covered, for 30 minutes. Won tons may be cooked up to a day in advance then gently re-steamed 10 minutes before serving. Cook in several batches if you have only one metal steamer basket.

To bake (for fall and winter)

1. Bake at 350°F, in a lightly oiled square or round casserole dish with a lid, for 30 minutes for a glazed appearance. (**Note:** If making dessert won tons and turnovers, dust the turnovers with flour after filling and bake on a well floured cookie sheet for 18-20 minutes.)

To pan fry (use this less often and only if filling is low-fat or fat-free)

1. Lightly pan fry in a shallow cast iron skillet or wok which has been lightly oiled with ghee, light sesame, sunflower, or safflower oil.

2. Cook 6-8 filled won tons over medium heat until browned, covered with a lid. (You may be able to fit more in if the pan is large. Flip them over and cook the other side until browned. Remove to a paper towel or plate when done. Serve warm with a pungent or spicy sauce, mustard, grated horseradish, or pickles and side dishes.

Serving suggestions: Serve with a green vegetable side dish, soup or sauce, and whole grain or bread as needed.

- **Ravioli or pasta style:** Top with Parsnip White Sauce, Tomato Sauce, Beet Sauce Italiano, puréed squash sauce, etc. or a few drops of olive oil and fresh or dried chives; toss into a soup; or serve with bread, soup and salad or cooked greens.

- **Won-ton or gyoza style:** Serve with a soup, stir fried, steamed, or parboiled veggies and noodles or brown rice.

- **Dessert style won-tons and tiny turnovers:** Serve with tea or grain coffee. Fill dough with cooked fresh and/or dried fruit or chestnuts (see index for fruit compotes and sauces). Steam or dust with flour and bake.

- **Appetizer style:** Serve as is or with prepared mustard, black bean sauce, grated horseradish mixed with tamari or umeboshi vinegar, or other relishes.

Storage: Refrigerate leftovers and resteam before serving.

Leftover tips: Serve leftovers at room temperature, in packed lunches, or reheat and serve with soup, rice, and stir fry, steamed greens, or pressed salad. ❏

A Few Sample Won Ton and Ravioli Fillings

"Meaty" Burdock-n-Walnut Filled Won Tons/Gyoza/or Ravioli

Prep (filling only): 30 minutes
Cooking: 15-30 minutes
Yield: filling for 36 ravioli or wontons *or* 10 tamales

Serves: 12-18 with rice or noodles, soup and vegetables
Serving size: 2-3 per person

Burdock root and walnuts add a rich and meaty taste to these vegetarian ravioli or won ton filling. Burdock is available in most Oriental markets and many health food stores across the country. These filled pouches can be served as a side dish with brown rice or noodles, soup, and steamed or stir fried vegetables. They'd also be tasty served ravioli-style with Parsnip White Sauce, Beet Sauce Italiano, or a hearty tomato soup or sauce in the summer or early fall.

Dough

1 recipe Won Ton/Ravioli Dough

Filling

1 cup finely grated burdock root, (first washed and scrubbed with a vegetable brush)

1/8 tsp. sea salt

1 cup minced onion

2 cloves minced garlic

2 tsp. light or toasted sesame or sunflower oil

1/2 cup water

1/2 cup walnuts

1-2 Tbsp. barley miso

2 Tbsp. dried Italian herb blend (*basil, oregano, thyme, marjoram, etc.*) *or* chili powder

1. Dry roast walnuts in a skillet in the oven (See condiments.) Remove and crush to a powder in a suribachi (a ceramic mortar and pestle with ridges on the inside).

2. Heat oil in skillet. Sauté onion and garlic with a pinch sea salt until translucent. Add burdock and 1 pinch of salt. Sauté 2-3 minutes. Add water and bring to boil. Reduce heat to medium low and simmer 5-10 minutes, until water is gone.

3. Combine burdock with other ingredients.

4. Fill each won ton wrapper with 1 heaping tsp. of filling. Seal edges and cook as per Basic Won Tons or Ravioli Procedure.

Serving suggestions: Serve warm or room temperature as an appetizer; serve ravioli-style with a sauce, bread and greens; or serve as a side dish with brown rice or millet, cooked leafy green or mixed vegetables, condiments and soup or a colorful root, round, or ground vegetable dish.

Storage: Refrigerate leftovers and resteam before serving.

Variations: Use this filling for tamales. It looks so much like meat you won't believe it. It tastes pretty meaty too!

Wheat Meat or Tofu Filling For Won Tons, Ravioli, & Gyoza

Prep: 20-30 minutes
Cooking: 15-30 minutes

Yield: filling for 36 ravioli or wontons *or* 10 tamales
Serves: 12-18 with rice or noodles or 3 as main dish "ravioli" with vegetable sauce

For a meaty filling without the meat, try wheat meat (seitan). If you don't have wheat meat on hand, try tofu. It works well too. This simple filling can be varied endlessly. You can also use it to fill tamales or steamed buns.

Wrapper

1 recipe Basic Won Ton or Ravioli Dough

Filling

1-3 tsp. olive, sunflower, or toasted sesame oil

1/2 medium onion, minced

1 pinch sea salt

1 stalk celery, minced

2 cloves minced garlic

1 cup minced or ground wheat meat (or substitute mashed tofu)

1-2 tsp. tamari soy sauce or to taste (use a total of 1 Tbsp. tamari or shoyu with tofu)

Optional, 1 Tbsp. sesame tahini dissolved in 1 Tbsp. water

1/2 tsp. dried sage, powder

1/4 tsp. dried thyme

1/8 tsp. dried marjoram

1 Tbsp. minced parsley

1. Sauté onion in oil in a 2-quart saucepan or cast iron skillet with a pinch of salt. When translucent, add celery, garlic, and herbs.

2. Sauté over medium heat 5-8 minutes. Add tofu or wheat meat then herbs. Continue to stir.

   Add tamari soy sauce and diluted tahini. Toss in parsley and stir.

3. Spoon 1-1/2 tsp. filling into each won ton and steam or boil as per Basic Procedure Won Tons or Ravioli.

Variation

- If using a highly seasoned wheat meat—such as Sausage Style, Curry, BBQ, or Italian flavored, omit herbs and spices above or just add parsley.

- Replace wheat meat or tofu with 1 packed cup cooked, drained beans such as navy, kidney, garbanzo, or azuki. Mash beans before adding to the pot in step #2. ❑

Sweet Potato Filling for Ravioli, Won Tons & Tiny Turnovers:

Prep (filling): 20-30 minutes
Cooking (sweet potatoes): 1-1 1/2 hours
Cooking (won tons): 15-30 minutes for won tons

Yield: filling for 36 ravioli, wontons, or turnovers
Serves: 12-18 with rice or noodles
Serving size: 2-3 per person

1 large or 2 medium white sweet potatoes **or** red garnet or jewel "yams"

1-3 tsp. light, yellow, or mellow miso

Optional, 1/2 tsp. pumpkin pie spice, dried ginger, or cinnamon

1 Tbsp. peanut or sunflower butter

2-4 Tbsp. water

1. Scrub sweet potatoes. Bake as per Basic Procedure.

2. Peel sweet potatoes or yams. Mash with miso, spice, nut butter, and water as needed to make a smooth paste.

3. Spoon 1-2 tsp. filling into each piece of won ton dough. Seal edges and cook as per Basic Won Tons or Ravioli Procedure. Use any left-over filling in soups, stews, or sandwiches.

Serving suggestions: Serve with a cup of soup, brown rice, millet, or kasha, and cooked greens or pressed salad and condiments. Or, serve as a dessert with fruit sauce.

Storage: Refrigerate leftovers and briefly steam or pan fry before serving or serve at room temperature in a pack lunch.

Variation:

• **Sweet Potato Dessert Won Tons:** Use apple juice, vanilla soy milk, or amasake nectar in place of water in mashing the filling. Add 1/4 cup raisins if desired. ❑

HOLY TAMALES!

The origins of the tamale

Tamales are a traditional Mexican dish born of the union of Spanish and Native American cuisines. In many parts of Mexico, vendors sell the most common version of the dish— a spicy filling of fried chopped meat and crushed red peppers encased in corn dough, wrapped in fresh or dried corn husks, and steamed. Yet this most common version is not the only version. Mexican corn dough may be stuffed with spicy, mild, or sweet filling of any ethnicity. In fact, natural foods stores often carry tamales filled with spicy tofu, sunflower seeds, peanut butter, yams, or vegetarian meat alternatives.

What is masa?

Masa and *masa harina* are both low in fat and high in fiber and complex carbohydrates. *Unlike cornmeal products*, masa products provide substantial amounts of calcium, a result of cooking the dry corn in lime, with wood ash, or with the ash that remains from burning corn stalks after a harvest. The special processing in lime or ash significantly increases the bio-availability of the niacin (vitamin B-3) in corn, thus-making the corn more nutritious than when it started. In fact, masa is far more nutritious, digestible, and assimilable than cornmeal.

Tamale making methods, old & new

The corn dough for tamales is prepared in a unique fashion peculiar to Native Americans. First dry corn is cooked in water mixed with a measured amount of lime or wood ash. The mixture is then thoroughly washed and ground until it becomes a pliable dough. This dough, is dried into a flour called masa harina. Simply adding water reconstitutes the masa into a dough and a dash of sea salt brings out its flavor. Although the traditional practice was to incorporate a relatively large amount of lard or vegetable oil into the dough—a process which is highly unnecessary—our method requires little or no added fat, thus producing a dish which is much lower in fat and heart healthy.

Tamale fillings go international

In Mexico and New Mexico, tamale fillings don't change much from season to season. Chorizo (a spicy sausage filling) is used even in the extreme, firey heat of summer. But you needn't use meat or spicy fillings. Almost any filling will do. The same fillings that are tucked into steamed bun dough, won tons, gyoza, or ravioli can also be used to fill tamales.

Tempeh or wheat meat make perfect substitutes for meat and poultry-based fillings. Try our Tempeh Chorizo, the Chinaman's Purse filling, or our Meaty Burdock and Walnut filling. Refried or baked beans also make good fillings, used alone or with crumbled Pressure-Marinated Tempeh or minced wheat meat. Another option for a meaty taste and texture is tofu that has been frozen, thawed, pressed to remove most of the liquid, then seasoned with miso or tamari and herbs or spices.

For a cheesy taste, we like Mocheeze (a cheesy-like, non-dairy filling we make by mashing tofu with sweet light or white miso, corn oil, and grated, uncooked mochi). For Mediterranean tamales, hummus tahini (chickpea dip) can be used as a filling, alone or mixed with a dash of minced fresh or dried bell pepper and/or sun dried tomato or minced parsley or chives.

Other favorite fillings include our Bulgur & Sundried Tomato Filling or a mixture of mashed, baked, steamed or nishime cooked sweet potato or winter squash mixed with nut butter and light miso. (See index for Squash-Wiches). Winter squash may sound wintery, but this highly storable vegetable keeps for months, particularly if you select some of more hearty varieties such as kabocha or buttercup. Thus, these squashes can be used throughout most of the year. Our Spanokopita filling would also be delightful. You could even make peanut butter and jelly filled tamales for a real sweet treat.

Do you eat the husk?

Each tamale is made from a piece of masa dough that is spread thinly over a corn husk (or a square of parchment paper), topped with a tablespoon or two of filling, folded like a package, bundled shut, then steamed over boiling water to cook both the filling and the dough. The corn husk (or parchment paper) is used as a wrapper only. Removing it before taking your first bite will save you from an embarrassing or unpleasant experience. When storing and reheating tamales, it is imperative that you leave them in the corn husks or parchment paper wrapper to retain moisture and flavor.

Risk-free wrappers

Currently all of the dried corn husks available in the U.S come from Mexico. Some have been detained by the FDA due to mold, mildew, and pesticide contamination, a problem which has led the natural foods companies which make tamales to switch to wrapping their tamales in parchment paper. Many brands of parchment paper are bleached with dioxin, although several eco-friendly companies now make dioxin-free parchment paper.

In the summer, you can wrap tamales in fresh corn husks saved from fresh corn cobs. However, you must use the fresh husks within several days as they do not keep as well as dried husks. Of course you could dry fresh husks in the summer sun or a food dehydrator, until they resemble straw, then store in a sealed bag or canister, in a cool dry place. Once dried they will last almost indefinitely. In our experience, corn husks have the best flavor and cost next to nothing.

Storing tamales

Once made, tamales may be refrigerated in a covered container and stored for 2-3 days. (Vegetable fillings do not keep as well as bean, tofu, or grain-based fillings.) Because tamales are so easy to make, we think it is far better to make them fresh when you want them rather than making and freezing a huge batch. However, we would rather see you use high quality homemade frozen tamales as emergency rations than store bought convenience foods, so if you must freeze anything, freeze extra tamales to use in a pinch—when you're short on time and need a hearty dish to round out a simple meal of rice and vegetables. Made ahead frozen tamales can save you the expense of eating out in restaurants.

How to freeze tamales

Whether you freeze cooked or uncooked tamales, freeze them in the corn husks or paper wrapping, placed in "ziploc" freezer bags, in meal-size portions. To prevent freezer burn, suck the air out with a straw as you seal the bag. The tamales will keep for several months, though the flavor will not be as good as when eaten fresh, particularly if little or no fat is used in the dough or filling. (Don't forget to label the bags with the date and type of filling.)

Defrosting & reheating tamales

Frozen tamales may be defrosted overnight, in the refrigerator, then heated, or they may be taken directly from freezer to warmer.

Heat in one of several ways:

(a) on a bamboo or metal steamer basket

(b) on a plate on a metal or bamboo steamer

(c) wrapped in foil or a covered casserole dish in the oven (conventional or toaster oven)

Note: Do not remove the paper wrapping or corn husk until serving and then remove them one at a time, as you eat each tamale. They will be ready to serve within 15-30 minutes. (Heat less for thawed tamales, more for frozen tamales. Stove top steaming is faster than oven heating.)

Do you have to warm tamales?

Yes and no. When dining away from home, previously unfrozen, leftover tamales may be packed in a lunch and eaten at room temperature, like a sandwich, dunked in a warm cup of soup; however, they don't taste nearly as delicious cold as warm. For this reason, tamales are best reserved for meals eaten at home, where an oven, toaster oven, or steamer is available.

Try it; you'll like it.

Tamales are delicious for breakfast, lunch, dinner or dessert. They are fun, delicious, nutritious, inexpensive homemade convenience food suitable for road trips, pic-nics, pot-lucks, and dinner parties.

How to serve a tamale

Although tamales can serve as the only grain in a meal (to replace rice, bread, pasta, or millet), we prefer to serve them in the traditional way, as a side dish grain, accompanied by brown rice or tortillas. This also makes your tamales go farther. Just be sure to make enough.

To serve tamales (masa) as the only grain in a meal, you'll need about 3/4-1 cup of dry masa per person (or 1-1 1/2 cups masa per person for an average male or very active teen, heavy laborer, or pregnant or lactating woman). That works out to about 3-4 tamales per person or 4-5 for more active people. If tamales are served as a side dish or main dish, with rice or tortillas, figure 1-2 tamales per person. Either way, we serve tamales with a green leafy or mixed vegetable side dish and soup or a root, round, ground, or sea vegetable dish as well. The exact number per person will vary with the size of the tamales and the the size and number of side dishes your serve them with.

Tamale making is easy as 1-2-3

The basic steps for making tamales are simple and the possibilities unlimited. Tamales don't take a long time to assemble, roughly 30-60 minutes, depending upon the size of the batch and complexity of fillings. You can reduce the prep time even more if you enlist the aid of a friend, child, or spouse. Once filled, your job is done; the wrapped corn bundles can steam away while you do other things. While the tamales cook, you can make side dishes to be used over the course of two to three meals or a day or two.

Arepas & Masa Balls

We often use the basic masa dough to make arepas (baked corn cakes) or steamed masa balls (something like a dumpling). Both can be made in a jiffy and used to stand in for or to supplement rice, millet, noodles, or bread in a meal.

Arepas and steamed corn dumplings make especially nice alternatives to corn bread, biscuits, or muffins with the benefit that no added fat is needed in the dough. Arepas are tasty for breakfast or a light snack. They are particularly delicious dunked into a hearty soup, stew, or gravy, or halved and dabbed with a garlic flavored corn oil, flax oil, or pesto. Or, mix fresh or dried herbs, spices, and/or dried vegetables directly into the uncooked masa dough, as is commonly done in Italian Foccacia bread or herbed bread loaves. These herbed masa cakes could be steamed, boiled, or baked for use as a side dish.

Keeping the fat low

Low-fat and easy to digest fillings are the norm rather than the exception in our house. Tamales are a traditional grain-based dish with just a hint of filling—usually one or two tablespoon per tamale, depending upon size. What you get is a hefty serving of complex carbohydrate rich corn dough stuffed with a condiment sized portion of slightly rich vegetarian products such as tempeh, tofu, beans, or wheat meat, with vegetables, and perhaps a hint of nuts, seeds, oil or other rich additions. In this way, satisfaction comes without sacrifice to your health or mama earth.

Tamales for dessert?

If you're hankering for a dessert or special Sunday brunch food that's low in fat and filled with wholesome ingredients, try making sweet tamales! That's right, corn dough can be filled with sweet starchy vegetables such as squash or sweet potato and a hint of cinnamon, nutmeg, ginger or anise, heightened with sweet miso or a dash of barley malt, rice syrup, or mashed chestnuts. Alternately, dessert tamales can be filled stewed fresh or dried fruits and spices; pureed or chopped chestnuts mixed with chopped nuts, seeds, or diluted nut or seed butter. Or you might mix fruits, spices, and nuts right into the dough for a scrumptious muffin-alternative. (If you plan to have a tamale for dessert, you may want to eat a little bit less grain in the meal than you normally would because a tamale is more filling than fruit compote or fruit sauce.)

Get into the tamale routine

If you're ready to dive into tamale making, then by all means "go for it!" For starters you might mix up a single filling for the whole batch of tamales, then experiment with several different fillings later. Feel free to unleash your creativity. Almost anything goes, though low-fat fillings are best. If you want to really get the hang of it, we suggest making a batch of tamales (with one or two different fillings) once a week for a month. You'll become proficient and the recipe will stick in your head the more you make it.

Basic Masa Dough & Tamale Making Procedure (Year Round)***

Prep: 30-60 minutes
Cooking: 45-60 minutes
Yield: 18-22 tamales, depending on size
Serves: 9-22 as a side dish with rice **or** 3-5 as a main dish grain
Serving size: 2-4 per person

Masa Harina is available in the ethnic section of most grocery stores, Latin American markets, and many health food stores. Masa is high in calcium, fiber, and complex carbohydrates. The kind found in health food stores is often organic, usually preservative and additive-free, and is made from whole, unrefined corn. Thus, it is more nutritious than the degerminated, enriched varieties sold in most grocery stores. Masa comes in a yellow and a blue corn variety.

(Please note: Corn meal will not work as a substitute for masa.)

4 cups Masa (a.k.a. Masa Harina)

3 1/2-4 cups water, or slightly more as needed *(you may need an additional 1/2-1 cup water)*

1/2 tsp. sea salt

Optional, 4 tsp. corn oil, or light sesame or olive oil

18-24 pieces of parchment paper, cut in 8" x 12" oblong or 9" x 9" squares or 16-22 corn husks

Preparing the wrappers:

1. **If using corn husks:** Steam to soften or immerse in water and soak for several hours or overnight. Remove them from the water and shake off moisture before using. If you inadvertently soak too many, dry the remainder in a slow oven, on a cookie sheet, or in the sun or a dehydrator.

    If using parchment paper: Parchment paper comes rolled up in a box, similar to aluminum foil. The box is 12-inches wide. Cut off pieces at 6 1/2-inch intervals to make oblongs 6 1/2-by 12 inches.

Making the filling:

1. Make one or two different fillings then measure the volume. Figure out how many tamales it will fill. You will need 2 level tablespoons filling per tamale.

To make dough:

1. Bring the water and sea alt to a low boil. After turning off the heat, add oil if desired.

2. In a large mixing bowl, blend masa flour and water. Use a sturdy spoon to mix. If dough becomes stiff or dry, add additional water one to two tablespoons at a time until you have achieved a frosting like consistency. Set aside.

To fill dough:

1. **If using parchment:** Arrange a piece of parchment paper on the work surface with the short end toward you. Spread 1/4-1/3 cup (4-level to heaping tablespoons) of masa dough over the slickest side of the parchment paper. Spread dough lengthwise with a frosting knife or spatula to make a 4 1/2 wide by 5- 6-inch long rectangle. (You will need to dip the knife into a bowl of cold water periodically to prevent sticking.)

2. Arrange 2 Tbsp. filling in a line down the middle of the masa. Leave 1/2 inch of the dough uncovered on the short ends and about 1-inch on each of the long sides.

3. Lift the right side of the paper and dough over the center of the filling then pull the paper back slightly. Fold the other long side of paper and dough over to the opposite side to completely cover the filling and the first fold. The paper should cover the length of the tamale. Fold the other long side of paper over to cover. (Make the masa dough meet when folding; that is, avoid overlapping the first edge of the paper before the dough is sealed, otherwise you will end up with separate "flaps" of cooked masa.)

   Note: When folding the paper, don't fold too tight. Leave a little bit of room for expansion during cooking.

4. You should have a long package, 2-inches wide by about 5-6-inches long. Fold the short

sides of the paper toward the center to close and seal package and keep the paper shut.

5. Place seam side down on a bamboo or metal steamer basket. You may be stack several layers of tamales on the trays.   then arrange tamales seam side down on a steamer tray(s).

If using corn husks:

1. Use 1 large husk or overlap two husks. Spread the masa over the corn husk leaving to make a 4-4 1/2 by 5-inch oblong. Leave 1-inch of uncovered husk on one side and 2-3 inches on both the top and bottom of the husk. Spread masa with a knife, bringing it close to the edge of the husk on the fourth side.

2. Fold this side of the husk over the masa and filling to the opposite side, overlapping the 1-inch border. (Make the masa dough meet when folding; that is, avoid overlapping the husk otherwise you will end up with separate "flaps" of cooked masa.)

3. Fold the remaining ends of the husk over the tamale to hold the leaves in place and make a sealed packet, Place seam side down on a bamboo or metal steamer basket. You may be stack several layers of tamales on the trays.

To cook:

1. Put one or more stacking bamboo steamer trays above a wok filled with 1-2 inches of water (water should not touch the tamales but may cover the bottom inch of the bamboo tray) or on top of a pot whose diameter matches the sides of the bamboo trays above 2-3-inches of water. Or, put a metal steamer basket or colander in a wide 3-4 quart stock pot above 2-3 inches of water (water should not touch the bottom of the colander or basket).

2. Cover the pot or bamboo steamer with a lid. Bring water to a full boil over medium-high heat then, reduce heat to medium and cook 35-45 minutes.

Note: The water must be boiling with steam rising for the entire cooking time. Check periodically. If water level gets low, replenish with boiling water as needed to maintain steam.

3. Transfer warm trays to the table. (Place bamboo or metal steamers on or in a bowl to avoid burning your table top) or transfer tamales to a heat-proof bowl or casserole dish, cover, and place on a table.

Serving suggestions: Serve warm, with rice or tortillas; a soup or root vegetable dish; and a green or mixed vegetable side dish. Let each diner unwrap the tamales as they eat them, one by one.

Note: If tamales contain beans, tofu, or tempeh, it is generally best to avoid serving side dishes which contain beans, tofu, or tempeh. Miso, tamari, or shoyu, however, may be used in any side dish. Likewise, if the tamales contain oil, seeds, or nuts, make the side dishes low in fat or oil.

Serve super sweet or fruit-filled tamales with warm goat milk, yogurt, kefir, or tea or grain coffee, as a dessert, snack, or special occasion breakfast or brunch treat. Squash or sweet potato filled tamales can, however, be served in the context of a meal, with greens and soup, beans, or other side dishes.)

Storage: Refrigerate leftovers (wrapped in corn husks or parchment paper) and placed in a covered bowl or wax paper, cellophane, cellulose, or old plastic bags.

Leftover tips: Resteam tamales for 15-20 minutes before serving, or cover and warm (fresh or frozen) tamales in a 300° F oven for 20-30 minutes.

Steamed Unfilled Tamales or Masa Balls (Year Round)***

Prep: 15-20 minutes
Yield: 12-18 unfilled tamales *or* 12-48 balls
Cooking: 30-40 minutes
Serves: 4-12 (or several meals for 2)
Serving size: 2-4 unfilled tamales *or* 4-8 masa balls per person, or as needed

Unfilled tamales and masa balls make perfect biscuit, bread or pasta alternatives. You can dunk them in soup or dab them with a mixture of white miso and water with corn oil or tahini. You might also try them with a hearty helping of bean soup, refried or soupy black or red beans, or vegetable sauce made from green peas, parsnips, winter squash, or beets and carrots. They can even be used like pasta, with a sauce. Masa balls are at home with almost any bean or vegetable combination.

1 recipe Basic Masa Dough, *(made without oil)*

To make unfilled tamales:

1. Follow basic procedure to make masa dough.

2. Divide the dough into 1/4-1/3 cup portions and roll each into an elongated cigar-shape.

3. Wrap each in a corn husk or square of parchment paper as per basic procedure.

4. Cook as per Basic Tamale Procedure above. steaming for 30-40 minutes.

To make masa balls/dumplings:

1. Follow Basic Procedure, Tamale Dough then use a spoon to scoop u p 2-3 Tbsp. of masa dough. Roll each piece into a ball.

2. Cook parchment paper or corn husk wrapped dough as per Basic Tamales above. Alternatively, arrange masa balls on one or more oiled heat-proof dinner plates, on top of bamboo trays or metal steamers, or improvise and place plates on top of tin cans (with the tops and bottoms cut out). (We use 9-inch dinner plates with 10-10 1/2" bamboo steamers.) Put a lid on the pot or bamboo tray.

3. Cook as per Basic Procedure, Tamales. *Alternatively*, cook masa balls like dumplings or ravioli, dropping 4 balls at a time into a time in a pot of boiling salted water. Boil 5-6 minutes or until tender. Remove to a plate and repeat with remaining dough.

Serving suggestions: Serve warm. Dunk in soup, stew, or gravy or arrange in shallow bowls and top a sauce or a few drops of a spicy oil or Miso-Tahini Spread. Or use tofu dip, pesto, or refried beans as a topping. Garnish any of these masa balls with a sprinkle of fresh or dried chives or fresh minced parsley and/or black pepper.

Storage: Store leftovers wrapped in a bowl covered with a bamboo mat or in a towel-lined bowl, at room temperature, or in a bowl, covered loosely with a mat or plate in the refrigerator. Steam leftovers (in a towel or on a plate0 for 10-20 minutes before serving. Use within 2-4 days for best results.

Arepas (Baked Corn-Cakes) (Any Season)***

Prep: 20 minutes
Yield: 20-24 cakes (look like small biscuits)
Cooking: 15-25 minutes
Serves: 3-5 (or 2 meals for 2) as the only grain in a meal or 8-12 as a side-grain
Serving size: 3-6 per person, *or* 1-2 per person served with rice or other grain

Arepas, are made from the same dough as are tamales, but they have no filling and are quicker to make. They are crispy on the outside and moist on the inside (if baked) and resemble little biscuits. If steamed, they are moist and tender. The dough contains no oil or leavener. These little cake perfect for dunking into soups, stews, gravy, or flax or sesame oil. They are also good with pesto, grated cheese, miso-tahini, or quark and sea vegetable flakes. (If oil is added to the dough, serve plain or with fat-free toppings.)

1 Recipe Basic Masa Dough (from 4 cups masa)
Optional, add 1 Tbsp. corn, olive, or light sesame oil to the water when heating

1. Prepare dough as per Basic Masa Dough. Mix ingredients in a bowl, with your hands, to make a smooth dough that resembles silly putty. Add water if needed. Form into a smooth ball. If possible, let dough sit for 40-50 minutes before shaping. The dough needs time to soak up the water.

2. Place 1-2 unoiled cookie sheets in an oven at 400° F and preheat for 15 minutes.

3. Form dough into a brick and divide in half. Form each half into an 8-12-log. Mark dough in 1-inch increments with a ruler and vegetable knife. Cut dough into 1-inch pieces. Shape each into a ball then flatten into a 4-5-inch burger shape or square disk about 1/4-1/3-inch thick. Or use a stainless steel 1/4 cup measuring cup to scoop out uniform pieces then form each into a smooth ball then into a round disk, 13-inch thick, with smooth sides.

4. Remove cookie sheets from the oven one at a time. Arrange arepas on hot sheets and bake in 400° F oven. When dough puffs up slightly and develops a thin crust with cracks in it—about 15-18 minutes—flip with a spatula and cook other side for another 10-15 minutes. Transfer to a basket or bowl lined with a clean white, cotton or linen towel and cover.

Serving suggestions: Serve as you would biscuits, bread, or rolls. They can be served as the solo grain in the meal or alongside rice or millet.

Storage: Store in a wax or brown paper bag. Use within about 5 days. Eat at room temperature or resteam leftovers to moisten, before serving.

Variations:

- **Steamed Arepas:** Arrange cakes on oiled, heat-proof dinner plates and stacking bamboo trays then steam for 30-40 minutes.

- **Boiled Masa Dumplings:** In step #3 above, form dough into 20-30 balls. Instead of baking, steam on oiled plates in bamboo steamer trays for 30 minutes. Serve with red or black beans or drop 2-3 masa dumplings into each serving bowl of a chili or stew just before serving.

- **Bagel Textured Arepas:** Boil 2 quarts of water with 1-2 tsp. sea salt in a wide pot. Drop 4-5 arepas into boiling, salted water at a time. Boil 5-6 minutes or until they float to the top and puff up a bit. Remove and cook remaining arepas. When done bake as above for 15-20 minutes.

Meatless Bulgar Filled Tamales (Fall, Winter, Spring)

Prep: 15 minutes
Cooking: 1 hour steaming, once filled
Yield: 9-10 tamales
Serves: 3-4, or 1 1/2-2 meals for 2
Serving size: 2 1/2-4 tamales per person as a main dish *or* 1 per person with rice

This is one of our favorite tamale fillings. It has a rich almost meaty taste, reminiscent of Sloppy Joes. We like to make these for a Sunday dinner, served with a hearty vegetable-bean soup and a side of sauteed greens. We always make a double batch then eat the remainder over the next day or two.

1/2 recipe Basic Masa Dough, or use a full batch of dough and double the filling recipe below

Filling for 9 tamales:

1/2 cup bulgur wheat or spelt bulgur, uncooked

4 sun dried tomato halves, minced (or substitute dried carrot pieces)

1 Tbsp. dried bell pepper

1 Tbsp. dried onion

1 cup boiling water

1-2 Tbsp. barley or brown rice miso

1 Tbsp. arrowroot

16-20 corn husks or parchment paper or 18-20 (6 11/2 x 12") pieces of parchment paper

1. In a medium size mixing bowl, combine bulgur, tomato bits, dried pepper and onion. Add boiling water. Stir; cover with a saucer or dinner plate; let sit 15 minutes.

2. Add miso. Stir. Add arrowroot and stir again. With a tablespoon, evenly divide filling into 9-10 portions (2 Tbsp. each) and arrange on a plate.

3. Fill as per Basic Procedure, Tamales, Cook as per Basic Tamale Procedure.

Serving suggestions: Peel corn husks or paper from each tamale as you eat it. These are delicious drizzled with flax or sesame oil at the table. Serve with greens and a soup, stew, or root vegetable dish. (The tamales will dry out if you cut up the whole batch.)

Storage: Refrigerate leftovers and use within about 3 days. (Or, freeze uncooked tamales, wrapped in paper or husks, inside airtight bags.) Resteam leftovers to heat.

Variation:
- Substitute minced dried mushrooms for dried tomatoes.

Tofu "Cheese" Filled Tamales (Year Round)

For a cheese-y filling without the cheese, try a mixture of grated mochi, mashed tofu, sweet white miso, and corn oil. We call it Mocheese.)Other cheesey options include our tofu-based dips and spreads. For a low-fat meal, serve with oil-free cooked leafy greens or mixed vegetables with a cup of vegetable soup.

2 Tbsp. tofu dip or spread per tamale—

See Mocheese filling, Herbed Tofu Cream Cheese, *or* Scrambled Tofu

1. Fill and steam using Basic Tamale Procedure. Steam 45 minutes.

Serving suggestions: Serve with a vegetable soup; a boiled, pressed or marinated salad or steamed mixed vegetables; a side of rice; and pickles or other condiments.

Squash-n-Peanut Butter Filled Tamales (Fall, Winter, Spring)

Prep: 15 minutes
Cooking: 1/2-1 hour (for squash) + 1 hour (for tamales)
Yield: 18-20 tamales
Serves: 5-8 (or 3-4 meals for 2)
Serving size: 3-5 per person *or* 1-2 per person if served with a side of rice

Peanut butter and squash combine to create a taste like Reese's Peanut Butter Cups if you get a really sweet squash. Stick to the varieties below. Winter squash isn't just for winter, in fact, it's sweet, succulent and juicy when steamed on top of the stove and just the thing to whet a summer appetite. In winter we bake it for an even sweeter taste, or we crock pot cook it in any season. Peanut butter adds a rich flavor for stick to the roof of your mouth fun!

Plan on making a little extra filling for use as a sandwich stuffer or bread spread too! Most Oriental grocery stores stock kabocha squash year round though we've also found them in grovery stores or kept them from fall or winter shopping trips at the local farmer's market. Look for the other varieties in co-ops, health food stores, and farmers' markets. Sweet potatoes or yams can also stand in for the squash.

1 recipe Basic Masa Dough,
2 1/2-3 cups baked, steamed, or nishime cooked sweet winter squash, yams or sweet potatoes, mashed
    (Kabocha, buttercup, hokaido, sweet dumpling, or red garnet or jewel or white sweet potatoes)
1 Tbsp. tsp. light, yellow, mellow, millet, or sweet miso
3-4 Tbsp. natural peanut butter (chunky) or sunflower butter

1. In a suribachi, mash tender cooked squash or sweet potato with miso and nut butter. (If red garnet or jewel "yams" or white sweet potatoes are used, peel first. We leave the skins on the squash; they are tasty.) Add a few spoonfuls of water as needed to make a smooth purée.

2. Figure 2 Tbsp. filling per tamale. Prepare using Basic Tamale Procedure.

Serving suggestions: For lunch or supper, serve with a bean or wheat meat soup or stew; a marinated, pressed or boiled salad or steamed mixed vegetables and pickles. Serve a side of rice if desired, or, serve squash filled tamales for breakfast or lunch with a side of pressed or marinated salad or quick-boiled greens and pickles. Use leftover squash filling to make a quick soup, stew, or sandwich filling. This squash filling makes a fabulous waffle topping!

Storage: Refrigerate leftovers and use within about 3 days. Resteam leftovers to heat.

Unfilled, Flavored Tamales:

Mix any of the following into the basic masa dough with additional sea salt. Skip the filling, them steam cook as per Basic Tamale Procedure.

Note: When making unfilled tamales, add more salt—or miso or umeboshi—to the dough for flavoring.

- Corn off the cob +/- sun dried tomato bits and garlic and red pepper + umeboshi or apriboshi
- Cooked and chopped chestnuts + cinnamon
- Cooked, drained black or red beans + ground garlic, cumin, and mustard or red pepper
- Fresh or dried, minced red, yellow, and green bell peppers + sea salt
- Sun dried tomatoes + garlic + basil or oregano + olive oil + sea salt
- Chopped walnuts + rubbed sage + dark miso or sea salt
- Red pepper powder (ancho, anaheim, or chipotle) + chopped, dry roasted walnuts + minced scallions or dried chives + umeboshi or apriboshi vinegar or paste
- Poppy seeds + dried onion flakes + dill

Huminta Tamales (Fall, Winter, Spring)

Prep: 30 minutes
Yield: 18-20 tamales
Cooking: 45 minutes
Serves: 4-5 (or 2-3 meals for 2) or more as a side dish with rice
Serving size: 2-5 per person *or* 1t per person accompanied by rice or tortillas

This Bolivian dish is made from sweet winter squash, anise seed, and corn (or quinoa). Our version combines this South American dish with the Central and North American tamale. The sweet flavor of these tamales combined well with refried beans or bean soup and a colorful boiled, pressed or marinated salad or lightly sauteed greens with dulse and sweet onions. Leftovers are great for breakfast with a cup of warm cinnamon or ginger spiced soy, rice, or goat milk.

4 1/2 cups masa harina

1 1/2 tsp. powdered or ground anise seed

1/2 tsp. sea salt *or* 1 Tbsp. white, yellow, sweet or mellow miso

3 cups water

2 cups cooked and mashed or pureed winter squash or sweet potato

> *(Kabocha, buttercup or butternu squash, hokaido pumpkin, or red garnet or jewel "yam")*

2 Tbsp. corn or hazelnut oil *or* 3 Tbsp. peanut or hazelnut butter *or* 4 Tbsp. chopped raw walnuts or hazelnuts

18--24 corn husks *or* 6 1/2-12-inch pieces of parchment paper

1. Prepare corn husks or cut parchment paper as per Basic Tamales Procedure.

2. In a large mixing bowl, combine masa harina and anise.

3. In a saucepan, heat salt and water. Add squash or sweet potato and puree (in a blender or by hand) or mash until smooth. Stir in nut butter, oil, or chopped nuts.

4. Pour liquid mixture over masa and anise mixture. Mix and knead briefly, first with a spoon then your hands, until smooth.

5. Form dough as per Basic Procedure, Tamales, excluding filling. Wrap in a single corn husk or two overlapping husks.

6. Steam 45 minutes as per Basic Tamales Procedure.

Serving suggestions: Serve with a green vegetable side dish, with or without soup, stew, beans, or sea vegetable side dishes. Or serve for breakfast, lunch or a snack with warm soy or goat milk.

Storage: Refrigerate leftovers and use within about 3 days. Resteam leftovers to heat.

Variation:

- **Double Corn Tamales:** Replace anise with ground, 1 1/2 tsp. powdered cumin, 1/4 tsp. mild red pepper powder and 1-2 tsp. garlic powder. Replace squash or sweet potato with cooked, unpuréed sweet corn (cut off the cob). Increase the water to a total of 4 cups or as needed to make a smooth dough. If desired, add 4 Tbsp. chopped sun dried tomatoes or dried bell pepper flakes to dough.

- **For a sweet dessert or muffin-like tamale:** Prepare as above but substitute commercial amazake nectar or shake for the water (or homemade amasake concentrate. Omit nuts from the dough if using amazake which contains nuts or seeds.

Tamales p. 206

Chestnut Magic

The festive Chestnut

"Chestnuts roasting on an open fire, Jack Frost nipping at your nose...."

While many folks have heard this familiar line in a popular holiday song, just as many may be unfamiliar with the chestnut, its colorful history, and the variety of its culinary uses.

Chestnut trees once covered the North American continent and formed a significant part of the Native American diet. The early settlers of North America learned from the natives to gather and roast or dry these precious nuts in the fall, and they have formed some part of American holiday cooking ever since. As the settlements of Europeans moved westward over America, blight and over-harvesting of chestnut wood destroyed the once plentiful stands of American chestnut trees. Yet one legacy of the chestnut remains besides their appearance in some holiday meals — as you hop off the subways in New York city you stand a good chance of being met by street vendors selling small paper bags bursting with the smoky fragrance, nutty flesh, and sweet flavor of freshly roasted chestnuts.

Chestnuts 'round the world

Although Americans tend to associate chestnuts with the holidays, on other continents the chestnut is in common usage year round. Chestnuts are commonly used in Italian cuisine, and they form an important staple food in some regions of Italy, where chestnuts are dried and ground to a flour, then used as a staple food. In China, the chestnut tree is still going strong, and the fruit of those trees is dried and used extensively in Chinese cooking. Italian and Chinese markets are very good sources of these sweet nuts.

Chestnuts as medicine

In Oriental medicine, the chestnut is classified a Spleen and Kidney tonic. It is revered for its ability to activate and tonify the Blood, expels Cold, remove Stagnant Blood, strengthen the Tendons, and nourish the Middle Burner organs (stomach, spleen, and liver). Its energy is warming and its taste is sweet yet it has none of the drawbacks of fruit, thus it can be used as a frequent part of anyone's diet, throughout the year. Energetically, on the spectrum of foods, the chestnut falls somewhere between grains and beans.

Chestnuts make a comeback

Recently, several American entrepreneurs have set about the task of reintroducing the chestnut tree and its fruit to this continent. Orchards of chestnuts are being established once again in Washington state and Texas. The individuals involved in this effort are hoping to see the chestnut become a common food on American tables, as they once were.

Chestnut, the low fat nut

If you have never tried this unique nut, you are in for a treat! Unlike most other nuts, the chestnut is sweet in taste. This is because it has a nutrient profile more like that of grains than of nuts. Whereas nuts and seeds typically derive 70-80% of their calories from fat, chestnuts contain a mere 8-9% fat. Over 80% of the chestnut's calories come from sweet-tasting complex carbohydrates, with the remainder coming from protein. The naturally sweet taste of chestnuts can satisfy even the most unwieldy sweet tooth, without the negative effects associated with sugar, honey, fructose, and other concentrated sweeteners.

The versatile chestnut

For a low-fat, high complex carbohydrate diet the culinary versatility of the chestnut is outstanding. They make incredibly rich and satisfying soups, stews, and side dishes when cooked with sweet vegetables, whole grains, vegetables and beans, or vegetables and wheat meat, tofu, or tempeh. When chestnuts are cooked alone then puréed, they make a delightful sauce for cooked root or round vegetables, grain loaves, or cake, pies, or cooked fruit. When combined with other ingredients, chestnuts can form the base for elegant patés, pies, puddings and pastry fillings. Their sweet taste and moist texture makes them an ideal ingredient for simple, low-fat desserts.

Buy dry

Roasting and peeling fresh chestnuts is not practical for wide or frequent culinary use; one can easily spend an entire hour peeling one or two cups worth of these fruity-nuts. Dry roasting fresh chestnuts and painstakingly peeling them from their shell, one is likely to find a good number that are moldy and/or dried out, and to end up with sore fingers to boot! For the best results, we recommend purchasing dried or fresh-frozen, steam-peeled chestnuts which are ready to use. They are predictably sweet, tender and flavorful. Skip the bottled chestnuts, they will cost a fortune and are a waste of packaging. Dried chestnuts need no roasting or peeling.

Baking & Cooking with Dried Chestnuts

Both dried and fresh-frozen, steam-peeled chestnuts are delicious in bean and vegetable soups, stews, sauces, gravies, stuffings or pates. They are also tasty when soaked and cooked with whole grains such as millet or brown rice or used to make delectably sweet dessert fillings, pastries, puddings and baked goods without sugar. Their sweet taste makes them the perfect sweetener, particularly when cooked and puréed. Puréed cooked chestnuts have a high moisture content and smooth texture which, when used in baking, may enable you to greatly reduce the amount of oil, butter, or shortening in your favorite cookie, cake, muffin, brownie, or pastry dough recipe.

Where to buy chestnuts

Dried chestnuts may be found in Oriental grocery stores, Italian or specialty foods stores, or by mail (see index). They must be soaked for several hours or overnight prior to cooking and one should take care to save the soak water for cooking since much of the sweet taste will be in this liquid. Once soaked, they should be cooked like beans, simmered for about 1-1 1/2 hours or pressure cooked for 20-40 minutes alone or combined with whole grains, beans, or fruits.

Storing dried chestnuts

Dried chestnuts can get buggy, particularly if stored for prolonged periods of time or in warm weather. Keep your supply in the freezer or to a minimum in warm weather. If you don't have a large freezer to accommodate your stash, either buy your chestnuts in smaller quantities or do what we do. Store your five or ten -pound bag in a large bucket on the back porch in fall and winter months. The cold will keep larvae from hatching or infesting other foods—if there are any in the chestnuts. Even if you find some little bugs, you can still wash the chestnuts in a strainer before soaking them. At the very least you'll get some added nutrition from these little critters. Alternatively, buggy dried chestnuts can be dry roasted in the oven, on a cookie sheet, at 200-225 degrees for several hours to kill the larvae and keep them from infesting all of the grains in your pantry. They will smelly nutty and sweet when roasted. Cool them fully then place them in jars; they will keep for a long time.

Using fresh-frozen, steam-peeled chestnuts

While these are not nearly as ecological as dried chestnuts, they do present a convenient option for many folks since they need no soaking and cook up more quickly than dried or fresh varieties. Fresh-frozen, steam-peeled chestnuts are available by mail (see the Resource section) or in the freezer section of many health food stores. Fresh-frozen chestnuts must be kept in the freezer—a disadvantage for long time storage or for those who possess only a small freezer. Fresh-frozen chestnuts require 1/2-1 hour of simmering or 15-20 minutes of pressure cooking, though there's no harm if they cook longer, such as in savory stews, pies, casseroles, or in a pot of brown rice.

As a general rule, dried or steam-peeled chestnuts should be cooked until soft *before* they are added to puddings, batters, doughs or short cooking dishes, or prior to puréeing. When making stuffings, casseroles, and baked or simmered fruit or grain based desserts, use steam-peeled chestnuts or lightly cooked dried chestnuts before adding. Cook chestnuts in their soak liquid and simmer the excess cooking liquid into the chestnuts, for maximum flavor and nutrition. Or, leftover chestnut cooking liquid can be added to a pot of soup, stew, or breakfast cereal prior to cooking.

Using Chestnut Flour

Chestnut flour is a real treat, though it is a bit pricey. It has a fine texture and a sweet and fruity taste. In baking it adds a rich taste and moist texture even when little or no oil is added to batter or dough; however, it must be combined with a larger volume of wheat, spelt or other gluten containing flour since it does not contain gluten and therefore offers none of the binding qualities necessary for breads and other baked goods. (The flour also makes wonderful puddings, though it does need some arrowroot powder or kuzu root starch for thickening.)

You may use chestnut flour to replace up to one-fourth of the flour in savory breads, dinner roll, tortilla, cookie, muffin, biscuit, or cake recipes. Due to the sweet taste and moisture content of chestnuts, one can usually reduce the amount of sweetener and fat in baked goods when chestnut flour or chestnut purée is used. The flour can also be used to coat diced apples or pears when making pie fillings. Chestnut flour can be purchased by mail (see Resources) and should be

stored under refrigeration, in the freezer, or in a bag or jar in a cool cupboard or pantry.

Ideas for using steam peeled fresh-frozen chestnuts

- Dice and add to cookie and muffin dough (See Desserts)
- Add to fruit pie fillings or stewed fruit, before cooking
- Add to stews, casseroles or bean dishes (See Soups & Stews)
- Add to stuffings or nut/grain loaves
- Add to sweet root and vegetable dishes
- Add to bean and vegetable soups and sauces (See Soups & Stews)
- Mix with beans and cook to make pates and dips
- Cook with polenta, millet, rice, or breakfast cereal (See Breakfasts)
- Cook in apple juice for a super sweet treat or as a dessert sweetener (See Desserts)
- Added to steamed puddings and fruit cakes

Ideas for using dried chestnuts

- Soak, cook until tender, then add to any of the above dishes
- Soak, then added to brown rice or millet before cooking (see Grains)
- Soak, then cooked with beans (See Beans)
- Soak, cook, then mix into pumpkin, squash or sweet potato pie fillings
- Cook with dried and/or fresh fruits for a quick dessert, sauce, or filling (See Desserts)
- Cook with winter squash, sweet potato, or parsnip as a side dish for dinner.

Cook dried or fresh-frozen steam-peeled chestnuts, puree, then:

- Add to cookies, cakes, brownies or pastries to replace most of the oil, butter, or shortening
- Add to baked goods to replace all or part of the sweetener
- Purée with raisins to use as a dessert sweetener
- Use as a base for cake frosting or icing with added flavorings and a small amount of raw butter or nut or seed butter
- Serve over crépes, waffles, pancakes, cake, or stewed fruit
- Use as a sauce for grain, bean, nut or millet loaves
- Mix into pumpkin or sweet potato pies
- Serve over pumpkin, sweet potato or apple
- Use to fill pastry dough
- Serve over winter squash or brussel sprouts

Ideas for using chestnut flour:

- Use to make puddings and custards (See Desserts)
- Add to cookie, cake, and muffin recipes (See Desserts)
- Add to pancake or biscuit batter (See Breads)
- Use in pastry dough
- Add to tortilla, chapati, loaf bread, dinner roll, biscuit or bagel dough (See Breads)
- Use to dust cut pieces of sweet vegetables or fruits before baking
- Mix with juice and use as a pastry filling
- Mix into fruit cake batter

Basic Boiled or Pressure Cooked Chestnuts (Year Round) ***

Prep: 5 minutes
Yield: 2 cups cooked chestnuts
Cooking: 20-60 minutes

The chestnut can be considered a grain, though in some instances it can stand in for beans or even fruits. No matter how you use it, the basic cooking procedure below can be used. You can soak and cook chestnuts with beans for soups, stews, or baked beans. You can soak and cook them with rice or millet for breakfast, lunch, or dinner grain. You can soak and cook them with dried and/or fresh fruit for desserts. Or, you can soak and cook them solo for a simply scrumptious dessert.

1 cup dried chestnuts
2 cups water

1. Combine water and chestnuts in a small (16-24 oz.) stainless steel bowl. Soak several hours or overnight. (Do not throw off the soak water; you will cook the chestnuts in it).

2. **To pressure cook:** Place the bowl inside a stainless steel pressure cooker. Cover the bowl with a small heat-proof saucer. Seal the pressure cooker and bring to pressure over medium heat. When pot hisses loudly, reduce heat to medium and cook for 20-30 minutes. When cooking a larger volume of chestnuts, you may omit the bowl and place the chestnuts and their soak water right in the bottom of the pot. The bowl is used here to allow you to cook a small volume and to prevent burning.

   To boil: Add an additional cup of water. Bring to boil in a pot with a tight fitting lid. Reduce heat to low and simmer 45-60 minutes or until tender. Check periodically to be sure chestnuts do not boil dry.

3. When done, allow pressure to come down then open the lid and remove the plate, then the bowl of chestnuts. They should be tender at this point. If boiling, simply remove chestnuts from the cooking pot after cooking away or saving the excess liquid. Use chestnut liquid in the same dish or in a different dish.

Variations & Uses:

- Add cooked chestnuts to a sweet squash, bean, or wheat meat soup or stew.

- Add to a casserole, pot pie, stir fry, lasagna, stuffing, or other dish.

- Chop chestnuts before adding to any cookie, cake, waffle batter, or bread dough.

- Mash chestnuts with a few pinches of cinnamon or dried ginger then use as a filling for buns, won tons, tamales or pastry.

- Eat cooked chestnuts, as is, for a simple and healthful dessert.

- **Sweeter chestnuts:** Soak and cook dried chestnuts in apple juice rather than water. This is especially good when making a sweet pudding, dessert sauce, sweetener for baked goods, or for a quick and easy dessert. (You can eliminate all other sweeteners and just add some raisins if you like.)

- **Chestnut Purée:** Purée cooked chestnuts with their cooking liquid. Use as a sauce for desserts, as a dessert sweetener or oil replacer in baked goods, or as a base for frostings.

- **Chestnut Cream Cake Frosting:** Cook chestnuts in apple juice. Purée, adding additional apple juice as needed for the desired consistency. Add a small volume of butter or nut or seed butter, vanilla or almond extract and other spices if desired. Add a hint of carob powder or grain coffee powder if desired. Chill then use to frost a special occasion dessert.

- **Chestnuts & Beans:** Prepare as above but use half dried beans and half chestnuts (e.g., azuki, kidney, black turtle or small red beans). Add a 3-4-inch strip of kelp or kombu sea vegetable before soaking or cooking. Cook the beans and chestnuts then add fresh seasonal vegetables once the beans and chestnuts are tender. Add dried ginger or ginger juice if desired, simmer until vegetables are tender, then season with sea salt, miso or tamari. For soup you will want to add additional water.

Chapter 5
Harmony in the Soup Pot:
Soups & Stews

Harmony in the Pot: Soups & Stew

The wisdom of "old wives" is evident in the classic folk remedy for colds and flus: homemade chicken soup. Good soup is nourishing, strengthening, and easy to digest. It is simple and inexpensive to make, suitable any time of year and infinitely variable. Unfortunately, this wonderful food has virtually disappeared from the American dining table. It has been replaced, in most cases, by nutrient-robbed expensive or fast foods. Even the classic chicken soup has been replaced by canned soup or by antibiotics, over the counter cold remedies and drugs with high cost, questionable value and unacceptable side effects.

Soups are good medicine

With the cost of health care rising, and the health of Americans definitely on the decline, it is time to bring back to the table the culinary wisdom of yore. Having soup twice a day, or at least once a day, helps to regulate digestive functions. If you have a large appetite and need to lose weight, a warm cup of soup in a meal can be just the thing to fill you up and slow you down. If, on the other hand, you tend to have a weak appetite, a cup of warm soup can bring it back to life.

Difficult to digest foods such as beans and hearty vegetables are made more digestible when prepared as soup or stew and eaten warm. The soft, semi-liquid form of soups and stews helps lighten the load on your digestive organs while at the same time providing essential vitamins and minerals. Indeed, soups are one of the most soothing and nutritious foods imaginable.

Soups are inexpensive

Serving soups daily can greatly reduce your food bills. Various vegetable scraps can be made into nourishing, tasty stocks for mere pennies. And expensive items, such as sea vegetables and shiitake mushrooms, can be made to go a long way when added to a soup or stew.

Serving soups on a daily basis can minimize food waste

Almost anything can be turned into soup or stew. Soups are a truly planet-friendly food. You can stretch small volumes of leftovers, with other fresh or leftover items to create fast and fabulous soups. Some of the best soups and stews are comprised of leftovers—bits of bean dip; a quarter cup of vegetable or bean soup; fish; yesterday's casserole, root stew or baked squash; small portions of tofu or wheat meat dishes; wheat meat or bean cooking juices; a spoonful of stir fry; or leftover gravy. You will be amazed at what you can create with a handful of this or a tablespoon of that and a bit of water or stock. Things that you used to throw out or stuff into an already full belly can be transformed into wonderful soups. Even leftover soup can be turned into a totally new and different soup.

Soups are infinitely variable

Some soups are chunky and thick, others are smooth and creamy. Different stocks and seasonings also add variety. In fact, you can create endless variety from the same basic recipe simply by using different stocks or seasonings, different beans or vegetables, or by pureeing the soup instead of leaving it chunky.

Soups are easy to make

Most soups and stews can be assembled in under 15 minutes and require little or no attention while they cook. In fact, most need only cook for one-half to one hour. They can also be cooked totally unattended for several hours in a thermal cooker, or all day or night in a crock pot. And they rarely need stirring so they won't take much time out of your morning, afternoon or evening routine. Although beans need to be pre-cooked before they are added to vegetables, even this can be done without much effort.

Entire meals can be built around a cup of soup or stew

Round out a cup of soup or stew with a hefty serving of whole grain, pasta, or bread and a small serving of cooked, pressed, or marinated leafy green or mixed vegetables. Garnish the soup (with parsley, chives, or scallions); add a condiment or two for your grain or vegetables, and you've got a full and satisfying meal.

Soups can simplify meal planning and preparation

Having soups on hand means that a whole meal is rarely more than 30-45 minutes away. In many cases, if you've planned ahead, you'll have a completely nourishing meal in 15-20 minutes! And leftover soups and stews need not be boring if you make only enough to last for two meals. Add a pinch of a new herb; change the garnish; serve a different type of whole grain or pasta or bread on the side; or have different greens, and you have a whole new meal.

Soups are good anytime

Contrary to what you might think, soups are more than just cold weather fare. They are suitable throughout the year, no matter what the weather, hot, cold, damp, or dry. By relying on the season's produce and various beans, stocks, herbs, spices, and seasonings, you can create delicious soups and stews to suit the season and your condition.

Getting Down A Soup System

You can assemble a soup first thing in the morning—before hopping in the shower or sitting down to breakfast–then cook it while you are getting ready or eating, or refrigerate it in a small pot then put it on to cook as soon as you arrive home in the evening. Or cook all day, until supper in a crock pot or thermal cooker so it will be ready to eat when you set foot in the door. Or, assemble it before bed and let it stew all night (in one of these slow-cookers). In the morning, it will ready to packed in a thermos and for lunch. Soups comprised of leftovers can be assembled at night for easy reheating the next day.

Soups are simple to make. All you do is chop a measured amount of vegetables; add them to a measured amount of water or soup stock, with or without cooked beans, tempeh, tofu, or wheat meat, and seasonings; cover the pot; bring it to a boil; reduce the heat to low, and simmer for 30-60 minutes or cook for up to 8 hours in a thermal cooker or crock pot. See Tips, Tools & Techniques. for adapting your favorite recipe for the thermal cooker.. Either way, while your soup cooks you are free to do other things.

For added convenience, make two soups or stews at a time, each to last for two days. This way you will have two different soups each day, one for lunch and one for dinner. You can also make "instant" soups from leftovers that you have on hand, with or without minced, grated, or dried vegetables and various seasonings.

Come serving time, just add miso, tamari or shoyu to season the amount of soup that will be served at a single meal or packed into a thermos. Added variety comes when you season meal-size portions of soup with different salty seasonings—light, red, or dark miso; tamari; shoyu; or natural soy sauce at different meals, change the garnish—scallions, parsley, dried or fresh chives, celery tops, sea vegetable flakes, finely grated carrot, croutons, or sauerkraut. To retain flavor and nutritional value, reheat individual portions of soup as needed, rather than heating up the entire pot. We store the unseasoned, left-over soup in meal size portions, in heat-proof bowls for ease of clean-up and convenient reheating.

Keep a variety ingredients on hand for fast soup making

Fresh vegetables: Seasonal, locally grown fresh vegetables make up the bulk of nourishing soups and stews. Hearty root, round and grouns vegetables are best. Examples include onions or leeks, carrots, rutabaga, winter squash, parsnips, jerusalem artichokes, burdock root, daikon radish, beets and turnips. Such vegetables are the most nutritious, storable, colorful, and weather hearty. Tender and watery vegetables (those which spoil quickly and have short growing seasons), do not hold up to rough weather, and are less densely nutritious. Examples include tomatoes, spinach, zucchini, fresh corn, asparagus, etc. These are fine to use in their season but do not make good staple foods.

Dried vegetables: These "soup helpers" are invaluable for soup and stew making. They can be stored for long periods of time and used year round. Keep on hand a few jars full of minced dried onions, bell pepper flakes, dried chives and parsley, sun dried tomato halves or bits (dry, not packed in oil), shiitake and other mushrooms, etc. They are especially handy for making soups from leftovers, stretching half portions of already made soup or stew, or adding color or texture to soups made from scratch. When you're making a soup and find that you are low on fresh vegetables, dried vegetables can round it out and add interest. They are also wonderful added to stir fry, sauces, breads, chili beans, gravies, stuffings, fillings, or casseroles.

You can purchase dried vegetables in many health food stores and co-op or invest in a food dehydrator to save money and provide a wide variety of convenient foods. You can dry the excess bounty of your summer garden or your neighbor's and/or make the most of summer over-stocks and low prices at your local farmers' market or co-op, using a home food dehydrator.

Fresh and/or dried herbs & spices: A variety of fresh and dried herbs can be used throughout the year to add flavor, benefit digestion, and improve overall health. Fresh herbs can even be grown in a little pot on a windowsil. Certain herbs or spices may be more or less appropriate for your condition. From an ecological perspective, it is best to emphasize herbs grown in your local region, bio-region, or continent; although herbs from other countries with similar climates may also be used. (Since these products are dried, they do not require extensive energy in storage and last for prolonged periods of time they are fairly ecological.) For Americans, it is best to emphasize European herbs and spices as well as those from North and South America. Examples include: basil, oregano, thyme, marjoram, bay leaf, rosemary, savory, fennel, cumin, mustard, poppy seed, anise, caraway, cumin, garlic, and mild red peppers and chili peppers. Although ginger root does not grow in America, you may wish to use it from time to time, for medicinal purposes.

Tips For Quick & Efficient Soup Making:

1. Arrange all of the ingredients you need on the counter.

2. Cut all of the vegetables and arrange each kind in a separate bowl.

3. Measure out the herbs, spices, and other ingredients, arranging them in small cups.

4. If items must be cooked in stages (such as beans), put them on to cook while you do other things (eat a breakfast, shower, dress, wash dishes, prep side dishes, eat supper, etc). Set a timer then come back later to add the already chopped and measured vegetables and herbs to the soup.

5. Always make soups to last for two days (that is two meals) at a time. Once for today and once for tomorrow. (To do this you will need to measure and to memorize the basic proportions or refer to the recipes).

6. Serve just one cup of soup per person then portion out the leftovers in a ready-to-heat stainless steel bowl; cover with a saucer; refrigerate; then reheat the next day using the covered-bowl-within-a-pot method. (This will save on dishwashing and time and will assure that you have leftovers for another meal. Just like you planned it!).

Vegetable Volume Guide:

Per person or per 8 oz. cup soup or stew, figure:

Light Brothy Soup: 2 Tbsp. dried or fresh, minced or grated vegetables

Simmered soup: 1/4-1/2 cup fresh vegetables, cut as desired

Simmered, thick soup or hearty vegetable stew: 3/4-1 cup fresh vegetables, cut as desired

Simmered, thick, pureed soup: 3/4-1 1/4 cups fresh vegetables, cut as desired

Simmered soup or stew with beans, tempeh, or wheat meat: 1/3-1/2 cup cut vegetables, cut as desired

Seasoning Guide

Per person or per 8-10 oz. cup soup or stew, figure:

1/4-1/3 tsp. sun dried sea salt

or 1-3 tsp. light or dark miso, tamari, shoyu, or natural soy sauce

or 1/8 tsp. sea salt + 1/2-3/4 tsp. miso, tamari, shoyu, or natural soy sauce

Herb Guide

Figure per 4 servings soup or stew:

+/- 1-2 cloves minced garlic

1-2 tsp. dried, powdered herbs *or* 1-3 Tbsp. fresh, minced herbs*

(* Add fresh herbs during the last 10 minutes of cooking to preserve their flavors)

How to season a soup or stew:

If little or no sea salt has been used in cooking...

(1) Dissolve a little miso, tamari, shoyu, or soy sauce into a large ladle-full of warm soup then stir this into the portion or portions to be served;

(2) Stir, taste, and adjust seasoning as needed.

How to serve a soup or stew:

1) Ladle soup or stew into individual serving bowls (just 8-10 ounces per person);

2) top with a light garnish (fresh or dried chives; minced scallions; parsley; dill; arugula; cilantro; dulse or sea cress sea vegetable flakes; or finely grated carrot, beet, or other vegetable);

3) serve with a large portion of cooked whole grain, pasta, or bread (or two grain dishes);

4) add a green or mixed vegetable side dish;

5) include condiments of your choice and;

6) add a bean, tofu, tempeh, or wheat meat side dish, if desired and if the soup or stew does not contain any of these;

7) chew well and enjoy!

To reheat leftover soup or stew, see Table of Contents for page reference for bowl-within-a-pot method.

Seasonings for Soups & Stews

Light, yellow, mellow, or sweet miso: Light colored misos are aged less than one year (usually six to nine months). They add a "creamy" or "dairy-like" taste to soups, sauces, spreads, and other dishes, without added fat or cholesterol. In some dishes, they even taste like chicken stock. In general, you should add miso just before serving a soup or stew so that both its flavor and digestion enhancing enzymes remain intact or if miso is added to the entire pot, don't let the soup boil when reheating leftovers.

Dark miso: Dark colored misos are aged two to three years, or longer. They can replicate the taste of beef bouillon in almost any preparation. Add dark miso to soup, stew, or gravy just before serving (see notes above for light miso). Dark miso has a richer flavor and tastes a bit saltier than light miso; thus, it can often be used in smaller amounts than sweet, white, yellow or mellow misos.

Red miso or rice miso: These misos, azuki bean, peanut, and 1-2 year rice misos, have a taste somewhere in between the briefly aged, sweet, light miso and the hearty, dark, long aged misos.

Miso the ultimate digestive aid

If you want to see just how good miso is at aiding digestion, stir a teaspoon of unpasteurized miso into a bowl of hot cereal. It will begin to digest the starches in your cereal as you sit. The cereal will become progressively thinner and milky after only 10 to 20 minutes. This is the digestive process in action. However, miso can only do this and provide you with beneficial enzymes if it is "live." This means that it must be unpasteurized, and added to a dish after cooking is complete or at the end of cooking and kept under a boil. (Unpasteurized miso is sold under refrigeration in health food stores. It can also be ordered by mail. See resources.)

Fantastic Foods...Miso:

Studies done in Japan by the National Cancer Center have shown that people who eat miso soup daily are 33 percent less likely to contract stomach cancer and have 19 percent less cancer at other sites than those who never eat miso soup. Also, those who never eat miso soup have a 43 percent higher death rate from coronary artery disease, and a higher mortality rate from all other causes combined.

Miso is a delicious seasoning for any soup. .

Miso Protects Your Health:

Free radicals and lipid peroxidation are involved in immune system suppression and development of a wide range of degenerative diseases, including cancer. Miso has been shown in several previous studies out of Japan to be protective against a wide range of degenerative diseases.

Researchers at Okayama University Medical School in Japan have shown that the protective effect of miso is due to its being an antioxidant that scavenges free radicals and inhibits lipid peroxidation. the researchers point out that the soybeans in miso have antioxidant properties. These properties appear to be enhanced by the natural fermentation process involved in making miso. Miso is a delicious seasoning with culinary uses.

Taking Stock

Flavorful stocks can be made from vegetable scraps, pasta cooking water, shiitake mushrooms, and/or various herbs and dried roots. Thy are inexpensive, delicious, nutritious, and easy to make. Some will be ready to use in under and hour while others may need to simmer a bit longer. All of the stocks from the recipes below are versatile, though some may need to be diluted in certain soups.

Shoyu, tamari, and natural soy sauce:

These are particularly good in bean soups, stews, and gravies. Shoyu, tamari, and soy sauce do not do well in delicate creamy-style soups—such as cream of corn, zucchini, parsnip, potato, winter squash, or sweet potato—where their strong tastes overpower and discolor the soups. Light or red misos are better for this purpose. Tamari and shoyu are typically used to replace sea salt, commercial soy sauce, and beef-type boullion in soups and stews, though dark miso can be used for the same purpose and with equally good results.

Traditional tamari is the thick liquid poured off after making miso. It is thicker, richer and has a more robust flavor than shoyu. It is also wheat-free. Shoyu and natural soy sauce are made from soybeans mixed with wheat and koji and fermented. Both of these are thinner than tamari and sometimes contain mirin (a sweet cooking rice wine) or a small amount of alcohol, used as a preservative. (Mirin is better than alcohol.) Purchase unpasteurized varieties of these seasonings, if possible. These are usually made by smaller manufacturers for local consumption.

Sun dried sea salt: This may be used in place of miso, tamari or shoyu. However, if this is used, it should be added to the soup during cooking, rather than just before serving, to allow it to dissolve into, mingle with and add flavor to the soup or stew. You may wish to use a small amount of sea salt in cooking and a little miso or tamari or shoyu to your soup just before serving. The sea salt you use should not be kiln dried. Rather, it should be true sun-dried, mineral-rich sea salt, free of preservatives, additives, bleaches, and anticaking agents. (See Mail Order Resources for quality sea salt and sea minerals.)

Note: Good quality miso, tamari, soy sauce, or shoyu soy sauce should not contain any sugar, malt extracts, MSG, dyes, or artificial colorings or flavorings. They should be naturally aged and come from a reputable natural foods company. You can find such products in your local health food store, in the natural foods section in some large grocery stores, or through quality mail order sources. (See appendix).

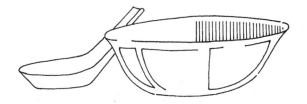

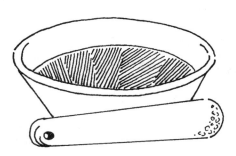

Suribachi

Basic Soup Stocks

Note: Making stocks is a great way to get the most out of your vegetables before the remains hit the compost bin.

Basic Procedure, Vegetable Stock (Year Round)***

Prep: several days of collecting vegetable scraps
Yield: variable
Cooking: 30-60 minutes, unattended

One batch of concentrated soup stock can provide the foundation for several soups or stews and will last three to seven days. Dilute your stock with water, particularly if it is very dark or strong flavored or you want to stretch it. Also remember that fresh is best; so make stock in manageable volumes. (We usually start with 6 cups of water and 2 cups of scraps for a single batch.) The basic stock outlined below adds a rich taste to any soup, though it's flavor may be too strong for delicate soups such as creamless cream of vegetable soups.

Use a combination of any of the following:

onion skins, ends and outer peeling

carrot, parsnip, daikon, rutabaga and turnip ends

squash, pumpkin and sweet potato skins

garlic skins and peelings

broccoli stalks that are woody

shiitake mushroom stems

green onion, shallot and leek trimmings/ends

cabbage, cauliflower and lettuce cores

cauliflower leaves and trimmings

celery and lettuce leaves and hearts

green bean ends, green pea pods, pods, etc.

bare corn cobs and/or corn silk

other miscellaneous vegetable trimmings

Note: Don't add highly perishable, soggy or wet vegetable bits (such as tomatoes or pumpkin pulp), or moldy scraps to the scrap bowl; these will invite mold and spoil the whole lot!

2-3 packed cups vegetable scraps
5-8 cups water

1. Set a stainless steel, glass, or ceramic (not plastic) bowl on the counter. Fill with vegetable scraps, peels, skins and cuttings you might normally throw out. Leave the bowl uncovered or cover with a bamboo sushi mat. (Heavier covers will make the scraps mold). There is no need to refrigerate this, except in very hot weather when you would want to refrigerate the bowl of scraps with a sushi mat on top. (Do not to add sopping wet scraps or mold will develop.)

2. Measure out the desired number of cups of scraps then place in a pot. The exact measurement is not crucial; you can make a quart of stock from a single cup of scraps. If you have more scraps than you can use, just toss some out. Cover scraps by 2 to 3" of water to make a concentrated stock. Too much water may produce more stock than can be used up within a week. (You can always dilute a strong or dark stock.) Cover and bring to boil. Reduce heat to low and simmer 1/2-1 hour.

3. Pour through a colander with a bowl underneath to catch stock. Compost or discard scraps.

Storage: Store cooled stock in jars in the refrigerator and use up within a week. It is inadvisable to freeze soup stock as this leads to a loss of both taste and nutritional value.

Usage: Use this stock, alone or diluted half and half with water, as the base for any bean or vegetable soup or gravy. You can also use it to thin soups or to add to leftovers to make quick new soups. If you make more stock than can be used within 4-7 days, toss it in the garden, or down the drain. ❏

Basic Procedure, Sea Vegetable Stock or Broth (Year Round)

Prep: 5 minutes
Cooking: 15-30 minute
Yield: 1 quart (~4-5 cups)
Serves: 4 (or 2 meals for 2)

Seasoned with miso or tamari and garnished with scallions, this broth makes a satisfying clear soup. Enhanced with various vegetables and/or leftovers it forms a nutritious base for a heartier soup.

4-5 cups pure water

4-5" strip kelp, kombu, sea palm, or ocean ribbons, whole, or dry roasted and crumbled

Optional, 2 fresh or dried, soaked, shiitake mushrooms or other variety
  or 1/3-1/2 cup chopped, fresh crimini, porcini, or other exotic mushrooms

Seasonings & garnish:

4 tsp. to 3 Tbsp. light or dark miso or shoyu or tamari

Scallions, chives, or parsley, minced finely

Optional, squeeze of ginger juice (from freshly grated ginger root)

1. If using dried mushrooms, soak in 1 cup of the liquid for 30 minutes. (Use hot liquid to speed the soaking or simply crumble dried mushroom into pot and proceed with next step.)

2. Combine ingredients in a 2-quart pot. Bring to a boil over medium heat, cover, reduce heat to low, and simmer, 15-30 minutes.

3. Remove sea vegetable and mushrooms. Cut finely and add back to the pot or set aside for use in some other dish.

4. Use this broth as a base for any soup, or season and garnish each cup with the recommended ingredients, as desired. (For ginger juice, finely grate 2-3 tsp. ginger root with a special ginger grater or the finest setting of an all-purpose grater then squeeze the juice into the bowls and discard the pulp.)

Serving suggestions: Serve seasoned broth alongside rice, bread, or noodles; with stir fried vegetables or boiled salad; pickles; and condiments. Or ladle seasoned broth over individual bowls of noodles, top with a cubes of tofu, and serve with greens and a root vegetable dish. You can also use unseasoned broth as the base for heartier and thicker soups, stews, or gravies.

Variations (pick 1):

- Add 1-4 Tbsp. dried vegetables (onions, carrots, daikon radish, or other) in step #1.

- Add 1-2 cups of bean sprouts in step #2 above.

- Follow steps #1 and #2, then add 1-2 cups very finely cut or minced vegetables —onions or scallions, daikon, radish, carrots, button mushrooms, mung bean sprouts, or a mixture of several of these. Cover and bring to a boil, turn heat to low and simmer for 10-12 minutes. Season, garnish, and serve.

- Follow steps # 1 and #2, then place 1 minced scallion and a few cubes of tofu in each serving bowl. Ladle seasoned broth into bowls. ❏

Creamy Soups without Cream

Basic Procedure, Sweet Squash Soup (Year Round)***

Prep: 10-15 minutes
Cooking: 40-45 minutes to simmer or 15-20 at pressure
Serves: 4 (or 2 meals for 2)
Serving size: 8 oz. per person

We never tire of this delectably sweet and creamy soup and use it year round. The sweet taste comes from onions and sweet winter squash. You can puree it, as we usually do, or serve it chunky. Make it thicker in cold weather and thinner in warm weather. It's great seasoned with sea salt in cooking or with light, yellow, mellow, or sweet miso just before serving. Leftovers make a great pasta topping, too.

Rule of thumb: 1-1 1/4 cup raw vegetables per person for thick, puréed soup; 3/4 cup vegetables per person for thinner, puréed soup; or 1/2-3/4 vegetables cup per person for a chunky soup.

1/2-1 cup onion, cut finely (or additional squash, carrot, parsnip, or rutabaga)

3-4 1/2 cups sweet winter squash, cut in 1/2-1" cubes, skins left on

*(kabocha or buttercup squash, delicatta or sweet dumpling squash, hokaido pumpkin **or** half parsnips, carrots, beets, or rutabaga and half squash **or** squash + onion)*

~3 cups water or pasta water, or more as needed

Optional, 1 bay leaf or a 4" piece kelp or kombu sea vegetable

1 tsp. sea salt *or* 1 1/2-2 Tbsp. light miso (1-2 tsp. per cup)

Optional, 1/4-1/2 tsp. dried, powdered cinnamon, nutmeg, allspice, or anise powder

Garnish: Minced fresh or dried parsley, chives, dulse flakes, or other

1. Wash vegetables but leave skins on unless they are terribly bruised, blemished, or waxed. Discard the seeds from squash or pumpkin. Cube or dice squash in 1/2-1 inch pieces. Slice or dice onions.

2. Combine vegetables in a 32-ounce measuring cup. Add water to the 4-cup line plus an extra 1/2-1 cup water. Add salt now , or if using miso add it just before serving.

3. Cover, bring to a boil, reduce heat to low, and simmer 30-40 minutes, until tender. Add powder spice now when pureeing, if desired.

4. Remove bay leaf or sea vegetable. Purée half the soup in a foley food mill, blender, or food processor, or mash. Or purée entire soup for a creamier texture. Add water as needed to yield 4-4 1/2 cups of soup. If salt was not used, dissolve light miso into a ladleful of soup; add back to the soup pot (or to the portion you plan to serve right away); stir; taste; then adjust seasoning as needed.

Serving suggestions: Ladle 1 cup of soup into each bowl. Garnish and serve with whole grain or bread; condiments; greens. For pasta sauce, ladle over individual bowls of pasta and serve with above side dishes. Top with wheat meat balls, seitan "sausage" or tempeh.

Storage: Store the rest in a small heat-proof bowl, covered with a plate, in the refrigerator.

Favorite combinations:

- Squash + onion, puréed or unpuréed (Year Round)
- Winter squash + onion + parsnip or carrot, puréed or unpuréed—(Fall, Winter, Spring)
- Puréed squash + onion + rutabaga (Fall, Winter, Spring)
- Puréed winter Squash or carrot + onion + peeled beets (Year Round)
- Winter squash + fresh tomato + onion (Summer & Fall), unpuréed

Variations:

- Omit herbs or spices. Before serving, add 1/2-1 tsp. ginger juice to the whole pot or 1/4 tsp.

ginger juice for each cup of soup.

- In step #2, add water to the 3 cup line. Cook as above; add 1 cup of plain, unsweetened soy milk, when puréeing. Add additional water if needed to produce 4-5 total cups of soup. ❏

Velvety Beet-Squash Bisque (or Mock "Tomato Soup")***

Prep: 15-20 minutes
Cooking: 1 hour
Serves: 4 (or 2 meals for 2)
Serving size: 8 ounces per person

Halve recipe to serve 4 (or 2 meals for 2).

This sweet soup makes a marvelous starter to any meal. Like tomato sauce, it can be ladled over heaping bowls of noodles, millet loaf, or polenta. We also use it to replace tomato sauce in chili, minestrone, tomato-based soups, and pizza and pasta sauces. Not only is it extremely versatile, it also has several distinct advantages over tomato sauce. It doesn't taste acidic or create heartburn and it won't aggravate arthritis. Good beets are also available nearly year round.

1/2 large white onion, cubed

4-6" piece kelp or kombu seaweed

1 bay leaf

Optional, 1-2 cloves garlic, minced

1-2 small beets, (~1-1 1/2 cups) washed, peeled, cubed

1/2 large kabocha or buttercup squash, or hokaido pumpkin, cubed (~3 cups)

2 1/2-3 cups water or part vegetable stock and part water

1/2 tsp. sea sea salt

Optional, 1 1/2 tsp. dried *or* 1-1 1/2 Tbsp. fresh, minced herbs *(thyme, basil, oregano, or mixed Italian herb blend)*

Seasoning & Garnish:

Tamari, shoyu, natural soy sauce or dark miso, ~1 tsp. per bowl

Fresh or dried chives or fresh, green onions, chives, cilantro, or parsley, chopped

Optional, organic sauerkraut for garnish *or* 1/2 to 1 tsp. brown rice vinegar per bowl

Optional, 1 Tbsp. Tofu "Sour Cream," Pesto Presto or "Tofu Pesto" per bowl (See index)

1. Combine all ingredients except seasoning and garnishes in a 3-4 quart pot. Cover; bring to a boil; reduce heat and simmer, 35-45 minutes until tender. Or, pressure cook 20 minutes.

2. Purée mixture in a blender until smooth. (Season the entire batch with miso, tamari, or shoyu when blending if all of the soup will be served at once, otherwise hold the seasoning until serving time). Add water a little at a time to thin slightly, if needed.

3. Ladle one cup of soup, a little at a time, into each bowl. If unseasoned, season each cup with 1 tsp. tamari, shoyu, or dark miso, or to taste. If desired, add 1/2-1 tsp. brown rice vinegar to each bowl before serving or top bowls with 1-2 tsp. naturally aged sauerkraut.

Serving suggestions: Garnish and serve with grain; a green vegetable side dish; and tempeh or wheat meat if desired. We often combine second day leftovers with ground wheat meat, or cubed Pressure Marinated Tempeh and serve it as a stew with bread or rice or ladled over individual bowls of noodles.

Storage: Refrigerate and reheat using the covered-bowl-within-a-pot method.

Variation: Replace all or part of the winter squash with carrot. ❏

Basic Procedure Oat-Cream of Vegetable Soup (Any Season)***

Prep: 15 minutes or less!
Cooking: 25-30 minutes
Serves: 4 (or 2 meals for 2)
Serving size: 8 ounces per person

We make this soup almost every week using whatever vegetables are in season. It is most flavorful and attractive if you use just one vegetable combined with onions or leeks. If you toss in too many different kinds of vegetables, you'll have a dingy grey soup with too many competing flavors. Occasionally, however, we combine onions with two root or round vegetables that have compatible flavors (such as parsnip and carrots or carrot and sweet potatoes). Sweet vegetables are especially tasty and strengthening when prepared in this way.

3 cups tightly packed, finely chopped, in season vegetables (see suggestions below)

Optional, 1-2 cloves minced garlic

1/2 large onion, minced **or** 1 leek, washed and chopped

1/4 cup rolled oats

2 1/2-3 cups water or pasta water, or slightly more as needed

1 tsp. sea salt or use 1/2 tsp. sea salt in cooking and adjust with light miso before serving

Garnish:
Fresh, chopped parsley, dill, or arugula; minced red, yellow or green bell pepper; or grated carrot, beet, or radish, uncut edible flowers; or ground cinnamon or nutmeg (for sweet soups)

1. In a 32-ounce measuring cup, layer ingredients in the order listed. Add liquid to the 4-cup line then add an extra 1/2-1 cup of liquid to allow for evaporation. Add salt (1/4 tsp. per cup) or wait to season with miso before serving. Or, use half the amount of salt in cooking then adjust with miso before serving. When using dried spices or herbs, add before cooking.

2. Empty the cup into a 2-3 quart pot. Cover and bring to boil. Reduce heat to low and simmer, covered, 20-30 minutes, or until tender. Time will depend on type of vegetable used.

3. Purée in a blender, foley food mill, or food processor until smooth. Add water as needed to yield 4-4 1/2 total cups soup or use water to thin soup if it is if too thick. Stir and taste. Adjust with miso if needed. (If sea salt was omitted, use 1-2 tsp. miso per cup of soup.)

Serving suggestions: Ladle 8 ounces of soup into each bowl. Garnish and serve with whole grain, pasta, or bread, a vegetable side dish and condiments. (If soup is made from a green vegetable, serve a colorful root, round, or ground vegetable dish on the side, otherwise serve with cooked, pressed or marinated leafy greens or mixed vegetables.)

Storage: Portion leftovers into a heat-proof bowl, cover and refrigerate. Reheat the next day using the covered-bowl-within-a-pot method (heat only what will be eaten at a particular meal). Use within 2 days.

Variations:

- **For a richer taste:** Sauté onion or leek in 1-2 tsp. light sesame or sunflower oil until tender and translucent around the edges then add ingredients in step #1 above, or add oil directly to the soup pot in step #2.

- **Spice it up & spark your digestive fires:** Add 1/4-1/2 tsp. dried, ground cinnamon, nutmeg or ginger powder in step #1 for carrot, parsnip, or winter squash soup or add 1-2 tsp. juice from finely grated, squeezed ginger root to the pot or 1/4 tsp. per bowl before serving.

Favorite Cream of Veggie Soups:

- Cream of.... Broccoli; Brussel Sprout ; Kale Zucchini; Summer Squash; Corn; Cucumber; Celery; Asparagus ; Leek; or Parsnip Soup ❑

Basic Procedure, Soya-Cream of Vegetable Soup (Year Round)***

Prep: 5-10 minutes
Cooking: 20-30 minutes
Serves: 4 (or 2 meals for 2)
Serving size: 8 oz. per person

Here's another handy basic recipe to have up your sleeve. It is creamy, rich tasting, very low-fat soup that's sure to soothe your tummy. It's a snap to make and can be made with almost any seasonal vegetable. In the hottest part of the summer we sometimes serve this soup close to room temperature (not ice cold or straight from the refrigerator though! (Cutting vegetables in tiny pieces makes them cook up more quickly; this is especially important in warm weather.)

1/2 cup onion, diced or cut in thin rounds, or 1 cup cleaned, minced leek or scallion

3-3 1/2 cups finely cut, packed, seasonal vegetables (*1-2 types of vegetables*)

3-4 Tbsp. soy flour (see variations below)

1 tsp. sea salt (*or omit and season with light miso just before serving*)

2 cups water or pasta water or more as needed to make 4-5 cups of soup

Optional, herbs or spices: 1/2 tsp. powdered cinnamon, nutmeg, allspice, cardamom, or 1/2 tsp. dried dill weed, and/or 2 cloves minced garlic

Garnish: Fresh or dried chives, minced dill, parsley; a pinch of cinnamon, nutmeg, or ginger; grated carrot, beet or radish; or finely grated vegetables; sea vegetable flakes, croutons, *

1. Combine solid ingredients in a 32 oz. measuring cup then add liquid to the 4 cup line.plus an extra 1/2 cup liquid. Pour contents into a small stainless steel bowl. Place the bowl in a 2-3 quart saucepan surrounded by 1-inch of water, then top .with a heat proof saucer Cover the pot and bring to boil over medium heat then reduce heat to medium and cook 25-40 minutes. Cook less for finely cut summer vegetables. (This double-boiler-type method keeps the soy from curdling.)

2. Purée in a blender or foley food mill. Add water as needed to yield 4 1/2 total cups soup. If sea salt was not used in cooking, season each cup with about 1-1 1/2 tsp. of sweet, light miso. (Miso may be added while the soup is in the blender..) If too thin, dissolve 2-3 tsp. arrowroot or kuzu root powder in 2 Tbsp. cold water, add to the soup, and stir to thicken over a low heat.

Serving suggestions: Ladle 1 cup of soup into each bowl; garnish; serve with grain and a vegetable side dish and condiments. (Serve a deep orange vegetable side dish if the soup is made from a green vegetable, otherwise serve with leafy green or mixed vegetables.)

Storage: Place leftovers into a ready-to-heat stainless steel bowl, cover with a saucer; when cool refrigerate. Heat meal size portions using the covered-bowl-within-a-pot method.

Variations:

- **Use sweet spices**—cinnamon, nutmeg, or allspice—with deep orange or yellow vegetables.

- **For added richness**: Saute onion in 1 tsp. light sesame or sunflower oil before combining and adding all other ingredients in step # 1. (Omit if using soy milk for soy flour).

- **"Cheesy" Soya Cream of Vegetable Soup:** In step # 1 above, add 3 Tbsp. nutritional yeast flakes (not the same as brewers yeast!)

- **Creamy Soy Milk Soup:** Omit soy flour above; use 2 cups water in the recipe. Cook; purée; then add 1 cup plain soy, almond, or peanut milk and additional water to yield 4-5 cups soup; add 2-3 tsp. arrowroot or kudzu root powder dissolved in 2-3 Tbsp. cold liquid. Add miso if sea salt was not used in cooking then simmer several minutes to thicken.

Favorites:

- Cream of Zucchini; Summer Squash; Corn; Asparagus; Cucumber; Parsnip; or Parsnip & Carrot; Potato-Leek Soup; Winter Squash; or Rutabaga Soup ❏

Basic Procedure, Simmered Vegetable Soup (Any Season) ***

Prep: 5-10 minute
Cooking: 20-40 minutes, depending upon thickness

Serves: 4 (or 2 meals for 2)
Serving size: 8 oz. per person

Soup making doesn't get much simpler. Once you follow the recipe a few times, you will master this technique and will be able to make great soups at whim. Use the measuring cup method below and you'll always make just the right amount of soup. We use this method for most of our soups, and we always make enough to last for two meals.

Note: This soup can be made without oil; however, sautéing the vegetables brings out a rich taste, and when combined with miso or tamari this technique produces a more strengthening soup.

Optional, 4-6" strip or 1 small handful of sea vegetable, scissor cut; soaked then chopped finely; or crumbled after dry roasting; *(kelp, kombu, alaria, sea palm or ocean ribbons)*

Optional, 1-1 1/2 tsp. sesame or olive oil

1/8 tsp. sea salt

1 1/2-2 1/2 cups cut seasonal vegetables, 2-3 kinds, diced, roll-cut, or cut in quarter or half moons *(onions, scallions or leeks; dried or fresh mushrooms, carrots, daikon, turnip, carrot, rutabaga, parsnip, winter squash, summer squash, tomato, sweet corn, etc.)*

Water, or corn silk tea/stock, or vegetable stock to yield 4-5 total cups of soup

Miso, shoyu or tamari (1-2 tsp. per cup)

Optional, 1 tsp. dried basil, oregano, thyme, marjoram or 1/8 tsp. mild red pepper powder

Optional, 1 clove garlic, minced finely

Optional, 1 bay leaf

Garnish: fresh or dried chives, scallions, arugula, parsley, or other

1. Soak sea vegetable in water to just cover for 30 minutes or 4-8 hours. Chop finely. If using alaria, simmer 20-30 minutes in water to cover, before combining with land vegetables and other soup ingredients. Alaria needs longer cooking than most other sea vegetables.

2. Chop land vegetables. Use less vegetables for a thinner soup, more for a thicker soup. Sauté onion or leek (or some other vegetable if no onions or leeks are used) in a pot with oil and sea salt and stir until tender. Add other vegetables, one kind at a time and stir briefly after each addition. Combine all ingredients in a 32-ounce (4 cup) measuring cup. Add water or clear stock to fill to the 4-cup line; add an additional 1/2-1 cup water and/or herbs if desired.

3. Pour contents into a small sauce pan. Cover; bring to a boil over medium heat; reduce heat to low, and simmer, covered, 20-40 minutes or until tender. Cooking time will vary with the type of vegetables used and with the size of the cut. (Small pieces cook faster.)

4. Add a bit more water if needed to produce 4-5 cups of soup. Remove the amount of soup you plan to serve at once, setting the rest aside. Season meal size portions with miso or tamari.

Serving suggestions: Garnish and serve with grain; a green or mixed vegetable side dish; and condiments.

Storage: Store remaining soup in a glass jar, covered glass bowl, or small stainless steel bowl. Refrigerate when cooled. Heat using the covered-bowl-within-a-pot method.

Variation:

• Add 1 tsp. sea salt in step #2 above then omit adding miso, tamari, or shoyu.

Favorite Combinations:

Fall/Winter:

- Carrots + onions + parsnips or jerusalem artichokes + winter squash

- Turnip + carrot + onion/leek + alaria or kelp

- Turnip + leek + mushrooms + sea palm or alaria

- Winter squash + brussel sprouts + onions + sauerkraut (+/- sea vegetable)

- Winter squash + onion + parsnip + rutabaga (+/- sea vegetable)

Summer/Fall:

- Corn + carrot + onion/leek (+/- sea vegetable)

- Cauliflower + corn + onion/leek + carrot (+/- sea vegetable)

- Tomato + zucchini + onion/leek +/- baby turnip +/- sea vegetable

- Daikon or turnip + onion + carrot + alaria

Spring/Summer:

- Asparagus + onion or leek + and carrot

- Daikon or turnip + onions or leeks + shiitake or crimini mushroom + sea vegetable

- Summer squash + carrot + onions or scallions (+/- sea vegetable) ❑

Daikon, Onion, Alaria Miso Soup (Any Season) ***

Prep: 5-10 minutes
Serves: 4 (or 2 meals for 2)
Cooking: 40-50 minutes
Serving size: 8 oz. per person

This soup is always a favorite We use the measuring cup method below and always make just the right amount to serve two meals for the two of us so we can enjoy it two days in a row. It can be made without oil; however, sautéing brings out a rich taste and when combined with miso or tamari produces a more strengthening soup.

1 small handful of alaria or wakame

Water to cover

1-2 tsp. ghee or sesame oil

1/8 tsp. sea salt

1/2-3/4 cup onion, cut in cubes, crescents or half-moons

1 1/2-1 3/4 cups daikon radish or turnip cut in thin quarter or half-moons

Water, or corn silk tea/stock, or vegetable stock to yield 4-4 1/2 total cups of soup

Season to taste with miso, shoyu, or tamari before serving (1-2 tsp. per cup)

Optional, 1 clove garlic, minced finely

Optional, 1 bay leaf

Garnish: Fresh or dried chives, scallions, arugula, parsley, or other

1. Soak sea vegetable in water to just cover for 30 minutes or several hours. Chop finely then simmer 20-30 minutes, in water to cover. Skip the precooking if using wakame. Alari needs longer cooking than Japanese wakame because it is not parboiled by the harvesters.

2. Chop other vegetables. Use less vegetables for a thinner soup, more for thicker soup. Sauté onion or leek with oil and sea salt. Stir until tender. Add daikon, radish, or turnip, stir until tender then combine vegetables with cooked alaria in a 32-ounce measuring cup. Add water or soup stock to fill to the 4-cup line. Add an extra 1/2-1 cup water to allow for evaporation. Add herbs if desired.

3. Pour into a small sauce pan. Cover, bring to a boil over medium heat, r educe heat to low, and simmer, covered, 20-40 minutes or until tender. Exact time will vary with the type of vegetables used and with the size of the cut.

4. Add more water if needed to produce 4 cups soup. Remove the amount of soup you plan to serve at once; set the rest aside. Season meal size portions with miso or tamari.

Serving suggestions: Garnish and serve with grain; greens; and condiments.

Storage: Store in a glass jar, covered glass bowl, or small stainless steel bowl. Refrigerate. ❏

Fresh Corn, Squash & Tomato Soup (Summer & Early Fall)

Prep: 10 minutes
Cooking: 1-1 1/2 hours
Serves: 6 (or 3 meals for 2)
Serving size: 8 ounces per person

It's hard to believe that so few ingredients could taste so good, but they do.

Optional, 1 bay leaf
3/4 cup white onion, diced 1/4" pieces
3 medium tomatoes (2 1/2-3 cups) diced
1 ear fresh sweet corn (1 cup), cut off the cob
1 3/4 cups starchy, sweet winter squash, cut in 1/2" dice, skins left on but scrubbed (*kabocha, buttercup, hokaido, sweet mama, delicatta, or other*)
3/4 tsp. sea salt
1 1/2 cup water

Seasoning & garnish:

Light miso (1 Tbsp. for entire batch, or to taste, *or* 1/2-1 tsp. per cup)
Fresh or dried minced parsley or arugula

1. Layer ingredients (except seasoning and garnish) in a 4-quart pot in the order listed. Cover and bring to a boil. Reduce heat and simmer, covered, for 1 hour or until very soft.

2. Add water as needed to produce 6-7 total cups of soup. If serving only part of the soup, remove and season only the portion you plan to use immediately.

Serving suggestions: Garnish. serve with grain; a pressed, marinated or boiled salad or stir fry; and condiments. Add a bean or wheat meat side dish made if desired.

Storage: Refrigerate leftovers in a glass or stainless steel bowl or jar. Reheat using the covered-bowl-within-a-pot method ❏

Dulse & Sunchoke Chowder (Fall, Winter, Spring)

Prep: 10 minutes
Cooking: 45-60 minutes
Serving size: 8-10 ounces per person
Serves: 4-5 (or 2-2 1/2 meals for 2)

This is our vegetarian rendition of New England Clam Chowder—a favorite in the fall, winter, and spring. We've taken great liberties with the original recipe. Jerusalem artichokes/sunchokes stand in for potatoes, and dulse adds that unique briny flavor of the sea, with the benefit of being even more nutritious than the original.

2 tsp. sesame oil *or* olive oil

1/3-1/2 cup dry dulse sea vegetable, scissor cut, torn, or crumbled

2-3 cloves minced garlic

1/2-1 medium onion, minced *or* 1/2-1 leek** cut in thin half-moons

1/2 tsp. sea salt

3 cups well scrubbed sunchokes (jerusalem artichokes) cut in 1/2-1" cubes or dice**

Optional, 2 stalks celery, minced finely

3 cups water, vegetable soup stock, pasta water, or a combination of several

3 Tbsp. soy flour

1 tsp. dried, powdered sage or cumin

1/2 tsp. dried, powdered cumin

Optional, 1/8 tsp. celery seed

1/8-1/4 tsp. ground black or red pepper

Note: Sunchokes are very sandy so scrub them well with a bristle vegetable scrub brush. You may need to wash them before and again after cutting as there tends to be hiden sand in the crevices. Leeks are also sandy and should be split down the center then run under cold water; run water and your fingers between each leaf.)

Seasoning & garnish:

Dark or light miso, tamari, or shoyu to taste (about 1-2 tsp. per cup of soup)

Dried or fresh chives, parsley, scallions, or other

1. In a 2-3 quart pot, sauté onion or leek in oil for 3-5 minutes or until tender and translucent. Add garlic, stir and add dulse, cut sunchokes, and sea salt. Stir until slightly wilted then add remaining ingredients. Cover; bring to boil over medium-low heat; slip a heat deflector under the pot; reduce heat to low heat and simmer for 45-60 minutes or 2-3 hours on a very low in the winter. Or, combine ingredients, after sautéing, and cook 6-10 hours or all day on low in a thermal cooker.

2. Remove and purée half of soup in a blender or mash in the pot with a potato masher. If too thick, dilute to desired consistency.

3. Season the entire pot and serve. Or, if serving less than four or five people, season meal size portions. (Start with a little miso, tamari, or shoyu, taste, then adjust as needed.)

Serving suggestions: Serve with whole grain (millet-rice, rice & barley, or rice with black beans) or arepas or steamed buns; and pressed salad or sautéed or quick-boiled greens, and condiments. (It is great for dunking bread in!)

Storage: Refrigerate unused portions in ready to heat bowls covered with saucers. Reheat using the covered-bowl-within-a-pot-method.

Variations:

- Omit the soy flour and soy milk. Pulverize 3 Tbsp. rolled oats in the blender and add to the liquids in step #1, or purée 1/3-1/2 cup leftover cooked rice, oatmeal or barley with a portion of the liquids before serving.

- If you use fish in your diet, you may want to add 1/2-3/4 cup of shrimp, dried fish, or salmon to the soup or use a fish bone stock to replace the liquid above. ❏

Basic Procedure, Tempeh or Wheat Meat Stew (Fall, Winter, Spring) ***

Prep : 15 minutes
Cooking: 35-55 minutes
Serves: 4 (or 2 meals for 2)
Serving size: 8-10 ounces

This is another basic every-day method which can simplify meal planning. You can come up with a different stew each week. Create variety by using different combinations of vegetables and herbs, spices and seasonings to suit the season and your fancy. This strengthening stew has a rich and meaty taste that is sure to satisfy.

Quick tip: Assemble and cook stew in the morning or assemble in a small covered saucepan and refrigerate it until one half to one hour before dinner. Simmer 30-40 minutes while getting dinner resteaming leftover cooked whole grain or bread, or cooking up batch of fresh noodles, polenta, or millet. Take leftover pressed salad out of the refrigerator or quickly steam or saute some greens. Dinner will be ready in no time flat! Or, cook your stew for 2-6 hours in a thermal cooker or all day in a crock pot. Season it when you get home!

1 bay leaf

1-1 1/4 cup wheat meat/seitan, or Pressure Marinated Tempeh, cut into 1/2" cubes

   (homemade, original-, hearty-, or chicken-style wheat meat, or any variety of tempeh)

2 cups seasonal root, round, and/or ground vegetables, cut in 1/2-1" dice, cubes, diagonals, or irregular wedges*

   (onions or leeks + 1-3 colorful vegetables e.g., carrot, parsnip, winter squash, burdock, rutabaga, turnip, jerusalem artichoke, quartered brussel sprouts, corn off the cob)

2 1/2-3 cups water or part vegetable soup stock, or as needed to fill to the 4-5 cup line

Optional, 1-2 small fresh or dried shiitake mushrooms, cut finely or crumbled

Optional, 1 1/2 tsp. dried herbs or 1 Tbsp. fresh herbs, minced(*thyme, basil, oregano, marjoram, rosemary, sage, cumin, Italian blend, etc.*)

Optional, 2 cloves minced garlic

Dark miso or tamari or shoyu, to taste (1/2-2 tsp. per cup soup)

Garnish: fresh or dried parsley, scallions, chives, cilantro, arugula and/or black pepper

1. Layer ingredients in a 32-oz. measuring cup with wheat meat or tempeh on the bottom, followed by root or round vegetables, then onions and herbs or spices. Add liquid to the 4-cup line, plus 1/2-1 cup. Pour ingredients into a small sauce pan. Cover and bring to boil over medium heat. Reduce heat to low and simmer, without stirring, for 35-45 minutes, or until vegetables are tender. (Do not boil hard or wheat meat will toughen and the flavor will be lost from the vegetables.) Or, cook in a thermal cooker or crock pot.

2. To serve two, ladle half of the soup into a small stainless steel bowl and set aside. Add a bit more water if needed to make 2-2 1/2 cups of soup. Season remaining two portions. To serve four, season entire batch at once.

Serving suggestions: Ladle into cups. Garnish and serve with grain and greens. Or spoon over two large bowls of noodles, garnish, and serve with a side of cooked leafy green or mixed vegetables.

Storage: Allow the extra bowlful of unseasoned soup to cool. Cover with a heat proof saucer and refrigerate when cooled. Reheat leftovers using the covered-bowl-within-a-pot method.

Variations:

- For a thick as gravy stew, layer ingredients in a 2-3 quart pot in the order listed then add just enough water to cover the bottom of the pot with 1-inch of water or stock. Cook as above until tender. Dissolve 2-3 tsp. arrowroot or kuzu in 1/2 cup cold water or stock, add miso, tamari or shoyu, then add to the stew and stir to thicken. Serves 4.

- Sauté tempeh in 1-2 tsp. olive or toasted or light sesame oil in the soup pot before combining with other ingredients in step #1. ❏

Favorite vegetable combinations:

Fall & winter:

- Squash + corn + onions+/- shiitake mushroom
- Parsnip or rutabaga + carrot + onion or leek
- Mushrooms + squash +/- sun dried tomato
- Squash + parsnip or carrot + leek or onion
- Sunchokes + carrots or squash + onion or leek
- Rutabaga + carrot + parsnip/turnip + onion

Summer & fall:

- Onion/leek + tomato + squash or zucchini
- Onion + tomato + baby turnip + carrot
- Onions or leeks + bell pepper + carrots
- Corn + bell pepper + carrot + onion/leek

Spring:

- Dried tomato & mushroom + carrot + daikon
- Onion or leek + dried bell pepper + dried sweet corn or precooked posole
- Onions or leek + sunchokes + carrot/ rutabaga
- Onion + burdock + carrots + celery
- Onion + mushroom + celery + dried bell pepper + carrot

Year Round:

- Winter squash + carrot + onion
- Winter squash + onion + burdock root
- Carrot + burdock root + leek or onion
- Turnip or baby turnip + carrot + leeks or onion
- Shiitake mushroom + onion +/- burdock +/ dried bell pepper
- Dried or fresh onions + dried or fresh carrots and/or other dried or fresh vegetables
- Sunchokes (jerusalem artichokes) + onion or leek (+/- carrot) ❏

Basic Procedure, Beefless Bean Stew or Chili (Year Round)***

Prep: 1-20 minutes
Soaking (beans): 6-8 hours or overnight
Cooking (beans): 1/2-1 1/2 hours
Cooking (stew): 1-2 hours or all day in crock pot

Serves: 4 (or 2 meals for 2)
Serving size: 8 ounces per person

Consider adding this to your everyday recipe repertoire; it's easy to make and so delicious! We make it throughout the year. Even if you make it every week, it can be a little different each time—with a different kind of tempeh or wheat meat, herbs or spices, and various seasonal vegetables. We like it mild, though you can spice it up. It's great served with steamed buns, corn bread, millet squares, or arepas and a side of sautéed greens or pressed salad.

Beans: (or use 1 1/2 cups precooked beans and skip step #1)

1/2 cup dry beans

(pinto, kidney, azuki, small red, black turtle, anasazi, chickpea, lentil, or other)

2 cups water for soaking + fresh water for cooking

4-6" piece kelp, kombu, alaria, or a few strips sea palm or ocean ribbons sea vegetable

Other ingredients:

Optional, 2 tsp. toasted sesame oil or olive oil

1 cup minced wheat meat or 1/2 of an 8 oz. block Pressure Marinated Tempeh, cubed

1 1/2-2 cups seasonal vegetables, cut in 1/4-inch dice or minced: pick 2-4 varieties—

(onion , leeks or scallions + winter squash, carrot , rutabaga, burdock root, parsnip, jerusalem artichoke, turnip, celery, summer corn, bell pepper, or other)

Optional, 2-3 Tbsp. dried bell pepper flakes or sun dried tomato or 1/2 fresh bell pepper, minced

Optional, 1-2 cloves garlic, minced

1 bay leaf

2 tsp. dried herbs or 1-2 Tbsp. fresh, minced herbs (pick 1 herb or several)

(cumin, thyme, basil, oregano, marjoram, sage, rosemary, Italian blend, or other)

or 1/4-1/2 tsp. mild red pepper powder (ancho, anaheim, or chipotle)

Bean cooking juices, water, vegetable stock, or a combination as needed to yield 4-5 cups stew.

Seasoning & garnish

Barley, red, or brown rice miso; tamari; or shoyu (about 1-2 tsp. per cup).

Fresh or dried scallions, chives, arugula, cilantro, or alfalfa or clover sprouts.

1. Sort, rinse, soak and cook beans as per Basic Bean Procedure. (If using black soy beans, soak 12-24 hours then drain, and pressure cook 1 hour. Skip precooking if using lentils, split peas, or previously cooked beans.

2. Layer ingredients (except for seasoning and garnish, onions on top, in a 32-oz measuring cup. Add liquid to the 4-cup line. Invert over a 2-3 quart pot and add 1/2 cup additional liquid. Or, sauté vegetables, herbs or spices and wheat meat or tempeh in oil before combining with liquid and beans. Cover pot and bring to boil. Slip a heat deflector under the pot; reduce heat to low, and simmer 1-2 hours. Or, cook in a thermal cooker or crock pot.

3. Add more water as needed to yield 4 1/2-5 cups thick stew. Season meal size portions with miso, shoyu, or tamari. If wheat meat broth or salty tempeh is used, use less miso, tamari, or shoyu. Taste, adjust as needed, ladle into cups.

Serving suggestions: Garnish and serve with grain and cooked greens or salad..

Storage: Store leftovers in a stainless steel bowl; covered with a heat-proof saucer; Refrigerate. Heat as per covered-bowl-in-a-pot method.

Variations:

- **Summer-n-Fall Stew** (Occasional Use): Reduce water or stock to 1 cup; use 1-1 1/2 cups diced fresh tomato or 3/4 cup tomato purée, 1 grated carrot or 1 cup corn off the cob, 1/2 chopped onion, and a dash of fresh or dried bell pepper for vegetables above.

- **Chili:** Use 2 tsp. dried thyme and/or oregano + 2-3 cloves minced garlic + + 1/2-1 tsp. dried, powdered cumin + 1-2 Tbsp. chili powder or 1/4-1/2 tsp. red pepper powder

Favorite vegetable combinations:

Fall, Winter & Spring:

- Carrot + parsnip + onion + burdock root +/- fresh bell pepper or dried bell pepper flakes

- Winter squash + onion or leek + celery +/- burdock root

- Onion + carrot + sun dried tomato + dried bell pepper

- Onion + rutabaga + carrot or parsnip +/- burdock root

- Onions + mushrooms + burdock root

- See also Basic Procedure, Tempeh or Wheat Meat Stew, for more combinations.

Summer:

- Onion + winter squash or carrot + bell pepper + dried sweet corn

- Onion + tomato + grated carrot + bell pepper. ❏

Savory Tomato Soup or Sauce (Summer & Early Fall)

Prep: 15 minutes
Cooking: 8 hours or 8-10 hours in a crock pot
Yield: 5+ cups thick sauce; or 8-10 cups soup
Serves: 6-8 as soup, with leftovers

Use this recipe to make an all-purpose tomato soup or sauce in the summer and fall. It can be thinned and served as a soup or combined with wheat meat, tofu, Pressure Marinated Tempeh, and/or sauteed mushrooms and your favorite seasonings for use as a topping over polenta, pasta, pizza, millet slices, or Mexican food. Use low-acid yellow tomatoes for a yellow hue.

Special note: Tomatoes have a cold energy and are not suitable for year round use in all climates. We suggest moderate use in the summer and early fall when fresh tomatoes and in season. (In the off-seasons, replace tomato sauce with Beet & Squash Bisque, Beet Sauce Italiano, Sweet Squash Soup, or use a few sun dried tomatoes now and again.

2 tsp. light sesame, toasted sesame, or olive or sunflower oil

2 onions, diced

3 pinches sea salt

2 lb. Roma tomatoes (or other variety such as low-acid yellow tomatoes), chopped finely

4 carrots, grated or minced

6-inch piece kelp or alaria sea vegetable, cut in 1/2 inch pieces with scissors

2 tsp. sea salt

6 cloves minced garlic

2 bay leaves

Optional, 1 Tbsp. dried or 3 Tbsp. fresh Italian herbs (basil + oregano + thyme + marjoram)

Water, as needed to thin

Seasoning & garnish:

1-2 Tbsp. dark miso; tamari; or shoyu, or to taste

Fresh arugula, chives, garlic chives, parsley, and/or black pepper

1. Sauté onions in oil with a few pinches of sea salt to draw out additional moisture. When wilted and translucent around the edges, add garlic. Stir, add tomatoes and additional sea salt; cover; reduce heat to low and simmer 30 minutes.

2. Add carrot, bay leaf and sea vegetable. Slip a heat deflector under the pot. Simmer, covered, on low heat all day (or for 8 hours). Add herbs during the last 2 hours of cooking if desired.

3. Add water or soup stock to thin as desired. Leave all or part of the mixture thick to use as a sauce for pasta, millet slices or other dishes. Stir well and dissolve miso or tamari into just the portion you plan to serve at one meal. (When serving as a soup, thin only a portion of the soup with water or stock as needed.)

Serving suggestions: Garnish and serve as a soup with whole grain, pasta and/or bread; with a green vegetable side dish; and a condiments. Or, use on top of pizzas or in calzones, pot pies, lasagna, sloppy joes, BBQ sauce, etc. (See index for some of these recipes).

Storage: Store in a glass jar or covered bowl in the refrigerator. Reheat portions using the covered-bowl-within-a-pot method. You can also serve over pasta, with or without leftover bits of minced and sauteed tempeh, wheat meat, or vegetarian sausage.

Variations:

• **Crock Pot Tomato Sauce:** Layer ingredients in a crock pot and cook 8-10 hours on low.

• Add cooked wheat meat balls, diced wheat meat, or chopped vegetarian sausage links to a portion of the sauce then spread on pizza dough with "Mocheese," or serve as pasta sauce. ❏

Basic Procedure Any Bean Soup (Year Round)***

Prep: 15 minutes
Soaking: 6-8 hours or overnight
Cooking: 1/2-1 hour for beans, 1/2 hour for soup
Serves: 4 (or 2 meals for 2)
Serving size: 8 ounces per person

This is the basic formula for most of our bean soups. Any seasonal vegetables can be used, but simple combinations are often the best. We favor a combination of two to three colorful vegetables. Especially good to emphasize are hearty root, round and ground vegetables, particularly deep orange varieties. For quick cooking, cut the vegetables in small pieces in warm weather and in larger chunks in cold weather. Even without herbs or spices, these soups are tasty.

Beans: (or use 1-1 1/2 cups precooked beans and skip steps #1 and #2)

1/2-2/3 cup dry beans, legumes, or raw peanuts—use 1 type of bean or a combination of two varieties*
(*lentils, azuki, small red, kidney, pinto, garbanzo, black turtle beans, or other*)

1 1/2 cups water to soak + fresh water to cook

4-6" piece kelp or kombu sea vegetable or a few pieces sea palm or ocean ribbons

Vegetables & other additions:

1-2 cups fresh seasonal vegetables: 1-3 kinds, cut into 1/4-1" cubes or thin slivers or 1/2-3/4 cup dried vegetables, *or* part fresh and part dried vegetables, minced or diced
(*onions, leeks, or scallions + carrots, parsnips, rutabaga, turnip, winter squash, bell pepper, corn, burdock root, jerusalem artichoke, dried or fresh mushrooms, etc.*)

1/4 tsp. sea salt

1-2 cups water or part vegetable soup stock or more as needed

Optional, 1-2 tsp. dried herbs or 1-2 Tbsp. freshly minced herbs, or to taste

(*basil, oregano, thyme, marjoram, cumin, Italian blend, 5-spice blend, or other*)
Optional, 1-2 cloves fresh garlic, minced

Seasoning & garnish:

Light or dark miso; tamari; or shoyu to taste (~1-2 tsp. per cup of soup)

Fresh or dried scallions, chives, parsley or arugula +/- ginger juice or black pepper

1. Wash, sort, and soak beans, then cook as per Basic Bean Procedure. If using red or brown lentils you may skip the soaking, or if using precooked beans, go to step #2.

2. In a measuring cup, combine cut vegetables, salt, beans, bean cooking liquid and water to make 4-5 total cups soup or stew. Add herbs or dried powdered spices as desired. Empty measuring cup into a 2 quart pot. Cover pot, bring to boil, reduce heat to low and simmer 1/2-1 hour until vegetables are tender.

3. If to thick, add a bit more water or vegetable stock as needed. Season just the amount of soup you plan to serve at a meal (1 cup per person)— with tamari, shoyu, or light or dark miso.

Serving suggestions: Ladle soup into cups, garnish each and serve with whole grain (millet-rice; millet & amaranth; millet with sweet rice; barley-rice; etc.). Add a steamed, stir fried, or parboiled greens dish or pressed salad; and condiments.

Storage: Refrigerate in ready-to-heat portions; reheat using covered-bowl-within-a-pot method.

Variations:

- **Crock pot cooking:** Assemble cooked beans and other ingredients in a crock pot. Cook 8-10 hours on low. Season and serve as above. (This is not as tasty as the stove top method.)

- Omit miso, tamari or shoyu above; instead, add an additional 1 tsp. sea salt in step #2.

- Add 1-2 tsp. olive or toasted sesame oil in step #2, or saute onions in oil before step #2.

- If using red or yellow beans with orange or yellow vegetables, you may wish to purée the soup before serving; however, this is not essential. If soup has too many colors, purée-ing will result in an unappetizing grey color.)❑

Try a two bean combination:

- Azuki beans + chickpea/garbanzo beans

- Small red beans + chickpea/garbanzo beans

- Kidney beans + chickpea/garbanzo beans

- Azuki beans + black turtle beans

- Kidney beans + black turtle beans

- Pinto or anasazi beans + kidney beans.

- Pinto or anasazi beans + black turtle beans.

Favorite Basic Bean Soups: (All are suitable for year round use unless otherwise noted.)

- **Lentil or Chickpea Soup with Squash & Sauerkraut: (Fall, Winter, Spring) ***

Use onions, winter squash (with skins left on), and 1/2 cup sauerkraut in the above recipe. If adding sauerkraut, reduce the amount of miso or tamari used.

Season with light miso if chickpeas are used, otherwise use dark miso. This is good without spices or herbs, though you can add thyme and garlic; cinnamon; or dill and paprika.

- Serve with whole grain combination (millet-rice, sweet rice with millet, barley-rice, etc; a seed condiment; and quick boiled, sauteed, or stir fried vegetables.

- **Lentil, Mushroom & Burdock Soup Black Bean-Mushroom & Burdock Soup (Any Season):**

This combination is good with onions, carrots or red bell pepper in addition to the lentils or black beans, mushrooms and burdock root. Spice it with thyme, oregano, basil or marjoram, cumin or sage and/or 1/4 tsp. red pepper powder and 2 cloves garlic. (Figure just 1 shiitake or 1/8-1/4 cup crimini or button mushrooms per cup of soup.)

See serving suggestions above. In addition to grain, serve with Kale-Carrots-Caraway & Kraut or sautéed greens or mixed vegetables.

- **Basic Bean & Leek Soup (Any Season):*** Use azuki, small red beans, lentils, or black turtle beans + leeks. Use garlic and/or dried cumin or in cooking or add ginger juice just before serving. Another nice spice option is roasted, ground cumin, fennel, mustard seeds.

Purée all or half of the soup if desired. (See Spiced Bean Soup.)

This soup is good with any whole grain or bread, condiments, and a mixed vegetable side dish or greens and a nishime or kinpira root vegetable dish and/or pickles.

- **Red Bean & Parsnip Soup (Fall, Winter, Spring):*** Use small red or azuki beans and parsnips in the basic recipe. Add onions if desired; also add cinnamon or ginger juice for a sweeter taste.

This soup goes well with rice or a two grain combination, seed condiment, and stir fried or quick-boiled vegetables or pressed or marinated salad. Add a sea vegetable condiment if you want another side dish.

- **Sweet Bean & Squash Soup (Fall, Winter, Spring):***

Use azuki, chickpea, lentils, or anasazi beans with winter squash and onions in the basic Any Bean Soup Recipe.

Add cinnamon, nutmeg, or pumpkin pie spice in cooking or fresh squeezed ginger juice before serving.

If desired, purée all or half of cooked soup. For the sweetest tasting soup, season with light, sweet , or red miso. Serve as for Red Bean & Parsnip Soup above, or serve with bread, a spread, and greens.

- **Red or Black Bean Soup (Summer):** Add carrots, sweet corn, onions and/or celery to the beans. (Use posole or dried sweet corn in the winter and spring). Add Italian herbs or fresh chili peppers and/or powdered cumin and garlic.

Top servings with a dollup of Tofu Pesto,, Pesto Presto,], or Tofu Sour Cream or yogurt,if desired. (See index for recipes.)

This soup would be great with tamales, arepas, millet slices, polenta, steamed corn buns, or corn bread; a pressed, marinated, or boiled salad; and condiments.

- **Peanut Miso Soup (Late Summer, Fall, Winter):** Use peanuts to replace beans (pressure cook or boil as for beans) in the basic recipe. Add onions or leeks, winter squash, and burdock *or* try sunchokes, onions and carrots.

Spice it with 1 tsp. powdered cumin, 2 cloves minced garlic and/or 1/8 tsp. red pepper powder. Or, add ginger juice just before serving.

This soup goes well with cooked whole grain (try millet and sweet rice, millet with chestnuts, or brown and wild rice topped with a seasoned seeds or sea vegetable condiment); and raw, pressed, marinated, or boiled salad. Pan fried seitan or tempeh cutlets are also a nice addition.

- **Red Lentil-Beet Soup/Sauce (Summer, Fall):** Use red lentils with carrots, onions, beets. (Do not precook the red lentils; instead, cut the vegetables in thin slices and combine all of the main ingredients together to cook. Season with one or more of the following: basil, oregano, thyme, marjoram, and/or garlic. Purée all or half of the soup before serving.

This may be used either as a sauce for pasta or millet loaf or as a soup, topped with sauteed wheat meat and/or a dollup of Tofu Mock Sour Cream, Tofu Pesto, or soy or goat yogurt.

For Sloppy Joe sauces, add ground sausage-style wheat meat and dried bell pepper flakes, simmer, and serve over whole grain buns with a side of minced dill pickles and steamed broccoli or quick boiled-greens.

- **Basic Bean & Bur-dog Soup (Year Round):***** Scrub burdock root with a vegetable brush but do not peel. Measure 1 cup burdock root, cut into 1/2-1" round logs (like little hot dogs) and cook with soaked, dried beans—azuki, lentil, or black turtle beans.

If starting with precooked beans, slice burdock into thin rounds or half-moons before combining with other ingredients. When beans are tender, add 1 cup cut onions or leek, sea salt, 1-2 cloves garlic and/or 1 tsp. dried, powdered cumin or sage (or add ginger juice just before serving). For a richer taste, add 2 tsp. flax or sesame oil with vegetables.

Cook as per Basic Procedure, Any Bean Soup. Season with dark miso, tamari, or shoyu. .

Burdock root grows wild in many places and can be purchased in Asian markets and many health food stores. Burdock root has a woodsy taste and wonderful medicinal properties. It suitable for year round use.

- **Three Sisters Soup (Late Summer, Fall):**

Use anasazi, black turtle, pinto, or kidney beans in the Basic Any Bean Soup Recipe. Add onions, fresh corn and winter squash; and/or celery sautéed in 1 tsp. of sesame, sunflower, or safflower oil. Add thyme and/or cumin, garlic and 1/2-1 fresh, mild, fresh chili pepper (ancho, Anaheim, or chipotle) or 1/8-1/4 tsp. powdered red chili. Optional, add diced wheat meat. Season with miso.

Serve with polenta; millet; millet-polenta; sweet-rice millet and chestnuts; millet rice; corn bread; arepas; or tamales. Add a cooked greens dish and/or pressed salad, and condiments. ❏

Perfect Pea Soup (Fall, Winter, Spring)***

Prep: 10-15 minutes
Soaking: 6-10 hours for whole dried peas
Cooking: 1-2 hours; or all day or overnight in a crock pot
Serves: 4-5 (or 2-2 1/2 meals for 2)
Serving size: 8 ounces per person

Whole dried peas are far more flavorful than split peas, though they be soaked then pressure cooked before adding vegetables. They will not block a pressure cooker if brought to pressure over a medium (rather than high) heat or pressure cook them in a covered stainless steel bowl.

Dried peas:

1/2 cup whole dried green peas

2 cups water to soak + fresh water for cooking

4" piece kelp, kombu, or alaria sea vegetable

Vegetable & seasonings:

1 small onion, minced or diced *or* 1/2 medium sized leek, washed well and cut finely

Optional, 1-2 cloves garlic, minced

1-1 1/2 cups seasonal vegetables, cut in 1/4-1/2" dice (try 2-3 varieties)

(carrot, parsnip, rutabaga, sunchoke, burdock, celery, cauliflower etc.)

Optional, 1/4 cup well scrubbed, minced burdock root *or* 2 Tbsp. dried burdock root

1/4 tsp. sea salt

2-3 cups water and/or bean or vegetable stock

1 1/2-2 tsp. dried herbs, one or several) or 1-2 Tbsp. fresh herbs

(thyme, marjoram, oregano, basil, Italian herb blend, savory, or other)

Optional, 2-3 Tbsp. nutritional yeast flakes or powder (not brewers yeast)

Optional, 1/2-2/3 cup minced seitan/wheat-meat or vegetarian sausage

Seasoning & garnish:

Light miso, tamari, or shoyu, to taste (1-1 1/2 tsp. per 8 oz. serving of soup)

Dried or fresh chives, garlic chives, arugula, parsley, scallions, or other

1. Wash, sort and soak whole dried peas, then pressure cook as per Basic Procedure, Beans. (Whole dried peas are best pressure cooked in a covered bowl.) If using fresh burdock root, add to the dry beans before pressure cooking.

2. Combine ingredients in a 32-ounce measuring cup. Add water to the 4 cup line plus an extra half cup water. Omit or reduce herbs or spices if using herbed or spiced wheat meat or "sausage." Add nutritional yeast for a rich, smokey flavor. **Note:** If you intend to purée the soup, do not add wheat meat or sausage until after puréeing then cook an additional 15-20 minutes on low. Pour contents into a 2-3 quart pot. Cover, bring to boil; slip a heat deflector under the pot; reduce heat to low and simmer 45 minutes or 1-2 hours. Or, cook 8-9 hours on low in a crock pot.

3. If desired, purée or mash half of soup for a creamy texture. If too thick, add water or soup stock to make 4-5 cups soup. Season meal size portions to taste with miso, tamari, or shoyu.

Serving suggestions: Garnish and serve with whole grain or bread, greens and condiments. When pureed, this soup also makes a tasty topping for individual bowls of noodles.

Variations:

• **Smokey Pea Soup:** Add 1/2-1 tsp. liquid smoke (hickory smoke seasoning) in step #2.

• **Split Pea Soup:** Omit whole dried peas. Combine 1 cup split peas with 4 cups water and sea vegetable. Soaking is optional; omit pressure cooking. Simmer 1 hour or until tender then add remaining ingredients. Cook 30 minutes. (If using burdock, chop finely and simmer with the peas, water, and sea vegetable before adding other ingredients.) Season and serve as above.

Favorite vegetable-pea soup combinations:

- Rutabaga + onion + burdock (Fall, Winter, Early Spring)
- Carrot + onion +/- celery or burdock (Any Season)
- Sunchokes + onion or leeks +/- celery (Fall, Winter, Spring)
- Potato + onion or leek + celery +/- carrot (Any Season)
- Onions or leeks + cauliflower +/- corn + celery (Summer, Early Fall) ❏

Kidney Bean & Walnut Chili (Fall, Winter, Spring)***

Prep: 20 minutes
Soaking: 4-8 hours or overnight for beans
Cooking: 45-90 minutes for beans

Serves: 4 (or 2 meals for 2)
Serving size: 1 cup per person

This hearty vegetarian chili tastes incredibly meaty. The secret is the walnuts. The tomato-red color comes from red kidney beans rather than tomatoes. The seasoning is quite mild, so feel free to fire it up as you like!

Beans: (or start with 1 2/3 cups cooked kidney beans and skip to step #2)

2/3-3/4 cup dry kidney beans
Water to cover 1" over beans for soaking (~1 1/2 cups)
4-6" piece kombu or kelp sea weed
Fresh water for cooking beans

Other ingredients:

2 tsp. ghee or sesame or olive oil
1/8 tsp. sea salt
1 large onion (1 1/2 cups), minced
2-3 cloves garlic, minced

1 bay leaf
1-2 Tbsp. chili powder *or* 1/4-1/2 tsp. ancho, anaheim or chipotle pepper powder, or more to taste
1 tsp. powdered cumin
1/2 cup walnuts, coarsely chopped or ground in a suribachi or mortar and pestle
1/4 tsp. sea salt
Additional water as needed to yield 4-4 1/2 total cups of chili

Seasoning & garnishes:

1-3 Tbsp. red miso, brown rice, or barley miso or tamari
Minced scallions, chives, garlic chives, or dried chives
Optional, black pepper or red pepper, if desired, added at the table

1. Wash, sort and soak beans then cook as per Basic Procedure, Beans.

2. In a 2-3 quart pot, sauté onions in oil. Add 1/8 tsp. sea salt to draw out additional moisture. Stir until browned, about 10 minutes. Add garlic and spices; layer nuts, bay leaf, salt, cooked beans, bean liquid and water in a 32-ounce measuring cup, filled to the 4-cup line. Empty into soup pot. Cover; bring to a boil; slip a heat deflector underneath; reduce heat to low; simmer, 2-3 hours or cook 3-6 hours in a thermal cooker or 8 hours in a crockpot.

3. Chili should be wet slightly soupy. Add a bit of water to thin if needed. Season to taste with miso, tamari, or shoyu. If too salty, add a few teaspoons of cider vinegar.

Serving suggestion: Ladle out 1 cup of chili per person. Serve with brown rice or millet and/or corn bread, steamed corn buns, or tortillas; and boiled or pressed salad. If desired, also serve baked, steamed, or nishime cooked winter squash (in the fall, winter, or spring) or with steamed or pressure cooked corn on the cob in the summer. (We like to spread umeboshi paste diluted white miso or our corn for a rich and buttery taste.). ❏

Spiced Red or Black Bean Soup
(Fall, Winter, Spring)

Prep: 15-20 minutes
Soaking: 6-12 hours
Cooking: 1 1/2-2 1/2 hours
Serves: 4 (or 2 meals for 2)
Serving size: 8 ounces per person

The simple soup has gotten rave reviews from guests. Roasted mustard, fennel and cumin seeds create a rich and full bodied soup that's not too spicy. Don't let the simplicity of this recipe fool you. You can vary the recipe endlessly using different varieties of beans and/or vegetables. Served chunky or pureed it's sure to be a hit. Leftovers improve with age, so be sure make a little extra for tomorrow. In the summertime you might add in some fresh or leftover cooked corn, green beans, or celery.

Beans: (or 2 cups cooked beans + 1 cup water)

3/4 cups dry aduki or small red beans

2 cups water for soaking + fresh water for cooking

6" piece kelp or kombu sea vegetable

Vegetables & spices:

~1-1 1/2+ cups water or part soup stock

1/4 tsp. sea salt

1 1/2 tsp. whole, brown mustard seeds

3/4-1 tsp. whole cumin seeds

3/4 tsp. whole fennel seeds

Seasoning & garnish:

1-1 1/2 Tbsp. barley miso, black soy bean miso, tamari, or shoyu, or to taste

Fresh or dried chives, parsley, scallions or other

Optional, Tofu "Sour Cream" or "Tofu Ricotta" to top each bowl (See index for recipes)

1. Wash, sort and soak beans, then cook as per Basic Procedure, Beans. (Skip to step #3 if using precooked beans.)

2. Dry roast whole spices in a cast iron skillet or wok, stirring over medium heat until fragrant (about 4 minutes). Transfer to a suribachi or electric coffee-spice mill; grind to a powder.

3. In a 32-ounce measuring cup combine ground spices, sea salt, cooked beans, bean cooking liquid and/or water to produce 4 1/2-5 total cups soup. Chop sea vegetable; add to soup.

4. Pour into a 2-quart saucepan. Bring to boil, cover; reduce heat to low and simmer; 45-60 minutes or up to several hours with a heat deflector under the pot or cook several hours in a thermal cooker or combine and cook ingredients 6-8 hours, in a crock pot on low.)

5. Soup should be fairly thick. Season meal size volume of soup to taste with miso.

Serving suggestions: Garnish and serve with grain, greens, and condiments. Add a deep orange or yellow vegetable side dish if desired (squash, carrot, parsnip, rutabaga, sweet corn, or some combination).

Storage: Refrigerate leftovers and reheat using the covered-bowl-within-a-pot method.

Variations:

- Add 1 diced onion and/or 1 cup diced carrot, parsnip and/or burdock root in step #3.

- Add 1 tsp. sesame oil in step #3 above.

- Add 1/2 cup minced or sliced wheat meat or Pressure Marinated Tempeh, or vegetarian "sausage" in step #3 above then reduce miso, tamari or shoyu when seasoning soup. ❏

Sweet Chestnut & Bean Soup (Any Season) ***

Prep: 15 minutes
Cooking: 1 1/2-3 hours
Serves: 4 (or 2 meals for 2)
Serving size: 1 cup per person

This is a real favorite. It's nourishing, grounding and satisfies a sweet tooth. Its one of our all-time favorites, in any season. Dried chestnuts add a smokey taste reminiscent of baked beans.

Beans & chestnuts:

1/2 cup dry black soy beans, kidney beans, or azuki beans

1 1/2 cups water to soak + fresh water to cook

~1/3 cup dried chestnuts or fresh, frozen, peeled chestnuts

1 cup water

4-5" piece kelp or kombu sea vegetable

Vegetables & other ingredients:

1-1 1/2 cups winter squash or carrot cut in 1/2-3/4" cubes, skins left on

(*kabocha, buttercup, hokaido, delicatta, sweet dumpling, or butternut squash or carrot)*

1/2 medium onion, diced, *or* 1/2 cup sliced leeks or scallions

1/4 tsp. sea salt

~1 1/2 cups water or water and part vegetable

Seasoning & garnish:

Miso (~ 1-2 tsp. per cup of soup) *(sweet light, chickpea, millet, brown rice or barley miso)*

Dried chives, scallions, parsley, or arugula

Optional, cinnamon, nutmeg, ginger juice, or black pepper

1. Sort, wash, and soak, beans as per Basic Procedure, Bean. (Soak black soy beans for 8-12 hours, if used.) Soak dried chestnuts if a separate bowl. (Do not discard chestnut soak water.) Steam-peeled, fresh-frozen chestnuts, do not need to be soaked.

2. Drain beans. Combine with chestnuts, chestnut soak water, kelp or kombu sea vegetable and additional water to cover 1-inch over beans. Cover, bring to a boil, reduce heat to low and simmer 1-1 1/2 hours or pressure cook 40 minutes. (Black soy beans need to be pressure cooked; otherwise they take 3-4 hours to soften and would need extra water.)

3. When beans are tender, add vegetables, salt and stock or water. Cover, bring to boil, reduce heat to low, and simmer 45-60 minutes, with a heat deflector under the pot.

4. Add additional water as needed to produce 4-5 total cups of soup. Season portion you plan to serve immediately with miso.

Serving suggestions: Ladle 1 cup soup into each bowl. Garnish and serve with whole grain (millet and amaranth; sweet rice and millet; barley-rice; or millet-rice)l and sautéed or stir fried vegetables or pressed or marinated salad, and a seed or nut condiment. Add a bit of ginger juice (see below) and/or cinnamon or nutmeg at the table, if desired.

Storage: Refrigerate leftovers in ready-to-heat stainless steel bowls and cover with a saucer. Use the bowl-within-a-pot method to reheat.

- **To make ginger juice:** Finely grate fresh ginger root with a ginger grater or the smallest holes of a standard grater. Hold the grated ginger in your fist and squeeze the juice into the pot or individual bowls. You will need to grate about 1 tablespoon (about 1-inch of root) of ginger to produce nearly 2 teaspoons of juice. (Figure 1/2-1 tsp. ginger juice per serving of soup, or as desired.) ❏

Uncooked Vegetable Soups

Aunt Ruthie's Gazpacho (Infrequent Use, Summer, Early Fall)

Prep: 10-15 minutes
Marinating: 1-3 hours or overnight
Serves: 4 (or 2 meals for 2)
Serving size: 1 cup per person

Gazpacho is a traditional Spanish dish, one which grew out of a hot and arid climate. It's quite popular in New Mexico. This is a version given to us by my (Rachel's) Aunt Ruth, who lives in New Mexico. In hot, dry weather, nothing satisfying a thirst quite like this thick salad in a soup bowl. If you live in a cold damp climate, you would do best to avoid indulging in this very cooling dish. Pray for a heat wave, then you'll have need of this beat the heat remedy.

1-2 clove garlic

3 ripe tomatoes

1 small cucumber, quartered

1/2 small onion, sliced

1/2 green pepper, seeded and sliced

1 Tbsp. olive oil

2 Tbsp. wine vinegar or brown rice vinegar

1/2-2/3 cup water

1/2-1 tsp. sea salt

1. Put all ingredients into a blender put all ingredients. Cover and blend until the vegetables are well mixed. Don't over-blend.

2. Chill. Remove from refrigerator 20 minutes before serving. Serves: 4 (or 2 meals for 2)

Serving suggestions: Serve with whole grain, pasta, or bread, and cooked, pressed, or marinated greens. Add a side of baked beans, or a tempeh or wheat meat dish as desired.

Storage: Refrigerate. Use within 3 days. ❏

Raw Sweet Corn Soup (Infrequent Use, Late Summer & Early Fall)

Prep: 15 minutes
Serves: 8 (or 4 with leftovers)
Marinating: 2 hours or overnight
Serving size: 1 cup per person

Here's a cooling, thirst quenching summer soup that will satisfy your sweet tooth. It's quick to fix and needs almost no cooking. Fresh picked sweet corn from your local farmers' market, a road-side stand, or your back yard will yield the best results. Corn that is several days old is far less than pleasing. Be sure to stash some in a safe place for the next day's lunch!

6-8 ears of fresh sweet corn

1 cup onion, Walla Walla Sweets are best

3 Tbsp. dried bell pepper flakes

4-6 cups water as needed

2 Tbsp. white, yellow, mellow, chickpea or sweet miso, or to taste

Garnish:

Fresh parsley, arugula, dill weed, or chives.

Optional, dulse sea vegetable flakes for garnish

1. Cut corn off the cobs and set aside. Place cobs and water in a pot. Cover and bring to boil, reduce heat to medium-low and simmer 10 minutes. Allow to cool 10 minutes.

2. Strain stock from cobs; discard cobs. Blend stock and remaining ingredients in blender until smooth. Add water as needed to yield 8 cups of soup. Add sweet, light miso and purée again; taste; add more miso if desired. Refrigerate in a covered bowl for 2 hours before serving, to marry flavors.

Serving suggestions: Remove a meal size volume rom the refrigerator 20 minutes before serving. Serve with rice, foccacia, steamed buns, or tortillas; a green vegetable side dish (sauteed greens, stir fry, or boiled salad) and condiments. Add a side of pan fried wheat meat or tempeh cutlets if desired. ❏

Leftovers Transformed:
Old Soups Make New Meals

You can get very creative turning leftovers into new soups. You can also use leftovers to extend day-old soups. This is great fun and absolutely transforming leftovers into something new and tasty. You might combine a bit of cooked beans or a seaweed side dish with some leftover vegetables and soup stock, pasta water, or vegetable cooking water. Or, you might combine leftover root or round vegetables with onions or scallions and stock, water, and/or gravy. Small amounts of beans, dip, or other assorted leftovers can also be added. The most flavorful soups are simple, without too many ingredients. Too many ingredients can compete and create sensory and digestive overload.

Small bits, even a few tablespoons-worth of one, two, or three foods and/or cooking juices make perfect soup starters. Herbs or spices can also added just before simmering a leftovers soup if your like. Figure just a few tiny pinches of one to three different herbs per cup of soup. Examples include basil, oregano, thyme, sage, marjoram, garlic, cumin, ginger, ground fennel or mustard. Just to get your started, here's a sampling of ingredients that can be used to create fabulous soups from leftovers. Almost any cooked land vegetable dish that is more than three days old is best composted, not eaten!)

Basic Procedure, Measuring Cup Method, Soups From Leftovers***

Prep: 5 minutes
Cooking: 10-15 minutes in a saucepan *or* 20-30 minutes in a covered-bowl-within-a-pot
Serves: 2 (or 2 meals for 1 person)
Servings size: 1 cup per person

1-1 1/2 cups assorted leftover (cooked) vegetables and/or cooked beans

+/- 1-2 Tbsp. dried, grated or finely minced fresh vegetables

Water, stock, gravy, leftover soup or a combination of several to yield 2-2 1/2 total cups of soup

Optional, few pinches sea salt

Light or dark miso, shoyu, or tamari, to taste before serving

Few pinches herbs or spices as desired

Garnish of choice: fresh or dried pungent green garnish (parsley, scallions, or chives); sea vegetables flakes; croutons; or other

1. If using leftover vegetables that are in large pieces, cut them into bite-sized pieces. Combine leftovers in a 16-ounce (2 cup) measuring cup. Add dried or grated vegetables and or herbs or spices as needed or desired. Add liquids to fill to the 2 cup line. Add an extra 1/4-1/3 cup liquid to allow for evaporation in cooking.

2. **To cook directly in a pot:** Pour ingredients into a small sauce pan with a tight fitting lid. Cover, bring to a boil, reduce heat to low, and simmer 10-15 minutes, or until tender.

   To cook in a bowl: Pour ingredients into a small stainless steel bowl. Cover with a heat proof saucer, place the saucer in a pot filled with 1/2-1 inch of water (enough to come up to one-third of the height of the bowl). Cover pot with a lid; bring to boil; reduce heat to medium and heat for 15-25 minutes to avoid having to stir and prevents sticking or soy milk or tofu from curdling.)

3. If desired, purée all or part of the soup. Add a bit more water or stock as needed to make 2 cups of soup. Taste. Adjust seasoning as needed with a few teaspoons of miso, tamari, or shoyu, added a little at a time. Ladle into bowls; garnish and serve.

Solids: Select several of the following...

Grains:j
Leftover breakfast cereal or rice, puréed or unpuréed
Leftover polenta, cubed, diced or puréed
Small volumes of leftover noodles, dumplings, won tons, or ravioli
A few teaspoons (dry) rolled oats

Land & Sea Vegetables:
Yesterday's steamed greens, stir fry, sauté, or baked root or round vegetables
Leftover sea vegetable condiment
Last night's casserole
Pieces of kelp or kombu leftover from cooking beans or tempeh
Dried, minced vegetables (bell pepper, onion, chives, carrot, tomato, etc.)
Grated fresh vegetables
Minced raw vegetables
Sliced fresh shiitake or crimini mushrooms
Dried vegetables

Beans or vegetarian meat alternative:
Leftover cooked tempeh, crumbled, diced, or sliced
Leftover cooked wheat meat/seitan or veggie cutlets or burgers
Whole or mashed cooked beans
Leftover bean dip or spread or refried beans
Minced tofu

Liquid:
Water from steaming vegetables or making boiled salad
Juices from cooking wheat meat or tempeh
Pasta water
Corn silk tea or corn cob tea
Bean cooking stock or juice
Leftover pickle juice
Leftover soup, stew, sauce, or gravy
Soy milk, diluted with water or stock

<table>
<tr><td>

Cooking Tips:

- For a thicker soup, use more solids and less liquid.

- For a thinner soup, use a smaller amount of solids and more liquid.

- For a moderate thickness, use nearly equal volumes of solids to liquids. Adjust thickness as needed before serving.

- For a creamy texture, purée all or part of the soup before serving.

- Avoid puréing a soup which contains items with many different colors. (Purée chickpeas red beans with winter squash or carrots. Don't purée black beans with squash, beets, or broccoli. It will result in an ugly soup)

- When adding uncooked items to cooked ones, layer uncooked items on the bottom of the pot or simmer uncooked ingredients in a small volume of water before adding leftovers.

</td></tr>
</table>

Examples: *Follow above instructions unless otherwise noted. Each recipe serve 2.*

Leftover Squash or Sweet Potato Soup (Any Season)***

1-1 1/2 cups leftover baked, steamed, or nishime cooked winter squash or sweet potato

Water, plain soy milk, or stock as needed to yield 2-1/2 cups of soup

Seasoning & garnish:

Light yellow or mellow miso

Grated or ground nutmeg, cinnamon, or parsley

1. Mash squash into a measuring cup. Add liquid as needed to yield 2-2 1/2 cups thick soup. Purée in a blender for a smoother consistency. Pour into a small stainless steel bowl; cover with a saucer; heat for 20 minutes with covered-bowl-within-a-pot method.

2. Season, garnish, and serve.

Serving suggestions: Serve with grain, greens, condiments, and a bean, tempeh, or wheat meat dish if desired. ❏

Soup from Leftover Root & Round Vegetables (Any Season)***

1 1/4 cups leftover baked, simmered, nishime cooked, or sauteed vegetables

(squash, carrot, parsnip, rutabaga, onion, sunchoke, sweet potato, turnip, or a combination of several)

3/4-1 or more cups stock, water, gravy, pasta or vegetable cooking water, or combination

Few pinches of sea salt

Optional, few pinches basil, thyme and/or marjoram

Seasoning & garnish:

Miso or tamari to taste before serving as needed

Fresh or dried herbs, sea vegetables, or sprouts

1. Prepare as per Basic Procedure, Soup From Leftovers. Add the extra liquid as needed. Purée if desired.

2. Season as needed; garnish; and serve. A bean, tempeh, or wheat meat dish is optional.

Serving suggestions: Serve with grain, a greens dish, and condiments. ❏

Quick & "Cheeze-y" Chickpea Soup (Any Season)***

1 cup leftover cooked chickpeas (garbanzo beans)

2 Tbsp. nutritional yeast flakes

3 Tbsp. carrot, grated on smallest holes of standard grater

1 Tbsp. dried onion flakes and/or bell pepper flakes

1 Tbsp. dried chives

Water, bean or vegetable stock, or part plain soy milk, as needed to yield 2-2 1/2 cups

1 pinch each of celery seed, ground black pepper, rosemary or thyme, and garlic powder

Seasoning & garnish:

Light miso, added to taste (about 1 tsp. per serving)

Fresh or dried parsley, arugula, or cilantro

1. Prepare as per Basic Procedure, Soup From Leftovers (cook 20-30 minutes).

2. Season, garnish, and serve.

Serving suggestions: Serve with grain, greens, condiments, and/or root or round veggies. ❏

Leftover Beans & Root Soup (Any Season)***

1/2-2/3 cups leftover cooked beans, chopped Pressure Marinated Tempeh, or wheat meat or bean soup, stew or sauce

1/2-2/3 cups leftover cooked, diced root or round vegetables

(leftover cooked squash, carrots, parsnips, onions, or a combination of several)

Water or stock as needed to yield 2-2 1/2 cups soup

Seasoning & garnish:

Light or dark miso, tamari, or shoyu as needed, just before serving

Chives, scallions, parsley, arugula, or other

1. Prepare as per Basic Procedure, Soup From Leftovers (cook 20-30 minutes).

2. Season; garnish; and serve.

Serving suggestions: Serve with grain, a greens dish, and condiments. ❏

Leftover Greens, Cabbage or Boiled Salad Soup ***

1 1/4 cups packed leftover cooked cabbage, kale, bok choy, collards, mixed greens or boiled salad

3/4 -1 cup stock, water and stock, gravy, water, pasta or vegetable cooking water

a few pinches of sea salt

Seasoning & garnish:

Miso or tamari to taste

Fresh or dried herbs, sprouts, or grated root vegetable

1. Prepare as per Basic Procedure, Soup From Leftovers.

2. Season, garnish, and serve.

Serving suggestions: Serve with grain, a root, round, or ground vegetable dish, and condiments. A bean, tempeh, or wheat meat dish is optional. ❏

Fresh & Leftover Sweet Veggie Soup (Year Round)***

1/2 small onion **or** 1/2 cup squash, carrot, parsnip, rutabaga, or other, finely minced

3/4 -1 1/4 cup leftover nishime, kinpira, or baked squash, root stew or assorted cooked sweet root, round, or ground vegetables

1 cup water, pasta water, stock and/or soy milk as needed to make 2 1/2 cups soup

Few pinches of sea salt

+/- 2 pinches cinnamon, nutmeg or cumin

Seasoning & garnish:

Miso or tamari to season

Fresh or dried herbs, sea vegetable flakes and/or cinnamon, nutmeg, or allspice

1. Combine ingredients as per Soup From Leftovers, with the raw vegetables on the bottom of the pot or bowl. Simmer 20-30 minutes until tender, in a saucepan or using covered-bowl-within-a pot method.

2. Taste, season, garnish and serve. ❏

Stretch-A-Bean Soup (Year Round)***

3/4-1 cup leftover bean soup, bean stew, or cooked beans

1/2 cup leftover cooked Tempeh "Sausage" or minced wheat meat

Water, cooking juices, and/or stock as needed to make 2 1/4 cups soup

Seasoning & garnish:

Miso or tamari, as needed, before serving

Scallions, chives, parsley, or other

1. Combine ingredients and cook as per Basic Procedure, Soup From Leftovers, simmer 15 minutes or heat in a covered bowl-within-a-pot for 30 minutes.

2. Season as desired, garnish, and serve.

Almost Instant Refried Bean Soup (Year Round)

Prep: 10-15 minutes
Cooking: 20-25 minutes
Serves: 4 (or 2 meals for 2)
Serving size: 1 cup per person

1 tsp. ghee or olive oil or sesame oil

1/4 cup dried bell pepper or 2/3-1 cup fresh minced bell pepper

1/4 tsp. sea salt

3 Tbsp. dried onion **or** 1/2 cup fresh, minced

1 tsp. cumin powder

1-2 cloves garlic, minced **or** 1/2 tsp. powder

2-3 cups refried beans (homemade or bought))

Water to produce 4 1/2 cups soup

Seasoning & garnish:

Dark miso, tamari, or shoyu, to taste

Minced parsley, scallions, chives, or cilantro

1. In a 2-3 quart saucepan, sauté vegetable in oil with salt. Add spices or herbs. Cook until tender, about 3-5 minutes.

2. Combine ingredients in a 32-ounce measuring cup to produce 4 1/2 cups of soup. Simmer 20 minutes in a pot or covered bowl-in-a-pot..

3. Season to taste with miso or tamari; garnish.

Serving Suggestions: Serve with whole grain or bread, greens or a mixed vegetables, and condiments. Corn or winter squash make nice side dishes.

Variation: Omit oil. Use dried vegetables rather than fresh. Combine ingredients in a 32-ounce measuring cup, pour into pot and simmer, or cook in a covered-bowl-within-a-pot, for 20 minutes. ❏

Creamed Sopa de Leftovers
(Any Season)***

Prep: 10 minutes
Cooking: 15 minutes
Serves: 2 (or 2 meals for 1)
Serving size: 8-10 ounces per person

This recipe guaranteed to produce fabulous soups in minutes. Following this procedure ensures you won't make more soup than you'll eat in 1-2 meals. (You don't want to make leftovers out of "leftovers," as the taste and nutritional value are lost the older your leftovers.)

1-1 1/4 cups leftover cooked cabbage, greens, cauliflower, broccoli, carrots, cut as needed

Optional, 3-4 Tbsp. leftover cooked beans, oatmeal, rice or potato

3/4 -1 cup soup stock, water, or pasta water

2 pinches sea salt

Optional 3-4 pinches herbs or spices of choice *(basil, oregano and thyme or cumin; thyme and garlic or marjoram; or other)*

Optional, 1 Tbsp. sauerkraut or minced pickles

Seasoning & garnish:

Miso or tamari soy sauce to taste (about 1 tsp. per cup of soup)

Fresh, minced parsley, dill, arugula, fresh or dried chives, or sea flakes

1. Combine ingredients as per Measuring Cup Method, Soups From Leftovers. Simmer on low for 10-15 minutes, or until tender, or heat for 25 minutes using the covered-bowl-within-a-pot method

2. For a creamy texture, purée half of soup in a blender or foley food mill. Season, garnish, and serve. ❏

Soup and Stew   p. 246

Chapter 6
Vegetables from the Land & Sea

Vegetables from Land

Though grains provide the primary nourishment in a centered and ecological diet, vegetables round out the diet, adding beauty, texture, taste, and further nourishment. Vegetables are also the healthy component lacking most in the typical American diet. Surveys by the National Cancer Institute have shown that the average American eats only 1.8 servings of vegetables in a day, if you include potatoes, lettuce and tomatoes as vegetables. However, if you exclude potatoes, tomatoes (actually a fruit), and lettuce, the average American eats less than one full serving of vegetables on a typical day, leaving the diet robbed of vital nutrients.

Raw vs. Cooked

When eating a vegetarian or primarily vegetarian diet it is wise to be sparing in the use of raw vegetables. Vegetables are cooling and the digestive fire is warm, and too much of the former will weaken the latter. Also, many of the most nutritious vegetables really need to be cooked in order to be rendered digestible and usable . Unbeknownst to most people, many vegetables contain thyroid inhibiting substances which can only be inactivated by proper and thorough cooking (or by pickling in a salty solution). Cruciferous and cabbage family vegetables are a case in point--broccoli, cauliflower, turnips, rutabaga, kale, collards, Brussel sprouts, etc. If eaten raw they can cause severe gas pains, indigestion, diarrhea, a lowering of body temperature, cold limbs, and many symptoms of hypothyroidism.

Getting Your Daily Vegetables

Vegetables can be served at every meal, from breakfast to supper. They can be chosen, prepared, seasoned, and combined to suit the meal, the dinners, and the season. It is important to create harmony between our internal and external environment. We can do this by eating locally grown produce. This practice is life supporting and life sustaining and deeply satisfying.

Types of Vegetables

Root, round, ground, and dark green leafy vegetables are well suited as daily dietary staples. Green and orange are the basic colors of life, and these are the sorts of vegetables with the most vitality. From the western perspective, these vegetables are rich in beta carotene, vitamin C, folic acid, calcium, iron, and other vital nutrients. By making dark green and deep orange and yellow vegetables daily staples, we incorporate their vibrancy, vitality, and superior adaptation to the immediate environment. From an energetic perspective, when we eat abundantly of these foods, we take on the root-ed-ness of roots, the grounded of ground vegetables, the centered-ness of round vegetables and the light and inspirational quality of upward growing leafy greens.

Balance & Variety

Several different colors, tastes, textures and varieties should be included at each meal or within a day to create balance and enjoyment. Different types of vegetables offer different nutritional benefits, hence eating a wide variety of different vegetables will give you a variety of nutrients.

Meet the Nightshades: Potatoes, Tomatoes, Eggplants

Potatoes, tomatoes, and green peppers are the only "vegetables" that some people in America ever eat. However, these foods have some serious nutritional drawbacks that should be, but aren't, common knowledge. All are members of the deadly nightshade family. Ranchers have noticed that cattle which graze on the vines of nightshade plants have higher rates of rickets, a gross bone abnormality resulting from disturbed calcium metabolism.

It is fairly well known that potatoes with green sprouts are poisonous and should not be eaten. In fact, the potato vine is poisonous, and although it is common to think of potatoes as a root vegetable, they are not really roots—they do not grow downward, like roots do, but horizontally—rather they are enlargements of the underground portion of the potato vine.

Note: Sweet potatoes are not in the same family as regular potatoes. Sweet potatoes and what are commonly call "yams" (red garnet or jewel yams) are members of the morning-glory family. Thus they do not have the detrimental effects common to potatoes and other nightshade vegetables.

Exposure to light activates the poison in and the sprouting of the potato. Thus, there is legitimate question about the safety of the potato as a food, and it is, therefore, wise to eat them infrequently rather than use them as dietary staples. Moreover, potatoes do not contain the same nutrients as whole grains nor do they contain the variety of nutrients available in dark green, deep orange or yellow vegetables. You may be surprised to discover that once you start eating a grain-based diet and taste the many grains available, potatoes lose most of their appeal.

There are similar reasons to avoid over-use of tomatoes. The tomato vine is as poisonous as the potato vine. From the perspective of Oriental medicine, these fruits have a very cold energy. Since the fire of life and the digestive fire are warm, an excess of tomatoes in the diet can damage this fire, as the phrase implies. Further, tomatoes are not nearly as nutritious as hearty green leafy or root and round vegetables. Taken fresh, in minor amounts and in season, they will do no harm; however, it is best to consider them as condiments rather than vegetables. Besides, out of season tomatoes are virtually tasteless and can never compare to their fresh picked counterparts. Classically, potatoes, tomatoes, and eggplants have been used in cuisines rich in poultry, meat, cheese and eggs. Thus, the cooling nightshades balance the extremely constipating and stagnating effects of animal foods. On a vegetarian or near vegetarian diet, eating too many emptying, cooling, draining foods can empty us and weaken us.

Replacing Potatoes

In most recipes for soups, stews, mashed potatoes, casseroles, or turnovers, potatoes can be replaced with onion, daikon radish, turnip, rutabaga, winter squash, Jerusalem artichokes, or judicious amounts of burdock root. These vegetables can give a similar texture, flavor, and in some cases a close-enough appearance to fool and please you and your guests. In other recipes pasta, brown rice, or other grain foods can fit the bill. For a mashed potato alternative, try our Millet Mashed Potatoes, made with millet and turnips or millet and cauliflower. Or try our Sautéed Dulse & Sunchokes.

Eggplants, like tomatoes, have a very cooling energy and are best used infrequently. Medicinally, eggplant may be used to clear pathological heat and to remove stagnant blood; however, when eaten in excess they can cool the body too much, causing depletion. Watch for their season then use them judiciously, and don't let them crowd out more nutritious vegetables such as cabbages and dark green leafy, deep orange and yellow vegetables.

Tomatoes—To Eat or Not to Eat, That Is the Question

The tomato, a vine vegetable, is nice to use judiciously while it is abundant in summer and fall, but is best avoided in the winter and spring when it is not in season and when its overly cooling effects can dampen the digestive fire. Tomato sauce can easily be replaced with puréed winter squash sauce, Beet Sauce Italiano, a carrot marinara, Parsnip White Sauce, or a colorful red bean sauce. Dried tomatoes can also be used now and then for a treat; these are less damp and often easier to digest than fresh tomatoes.

Seasonal Vegetables

As the seasons change, new vegetables may dominate in your kitchen. As the weather turns and you lose one vegetable you will always gain another, or several others, to take its place.

Seasonal variations in produce provide us with an incredible variety of nourishing foods. On a typical day, in any season, you could eat as many as ten different varieties of vegetables. In a given week you could eat 15 different types of vegetables, or more! Over the course of a year, as many as 80 different vegetables may grace your table. Some precious vegetables are available for only a month or two; others for three, four, or six months. Still others may be readily available throughout most of the year, either fresh or stored in traditional ways (via a root cellar, a cold, dry room, or by drying). Though a particular vegetable may only be available during a certain season, each season offers flora and fauna that exemplify the energy of all four seasons. Learning to eat what is in-season where you live will not only lead to culinary creativity, but also greater health.

Note: Available and in-season here refers not to the artificial availability due to our modern agriculture and agri-business, but to true availability via a garden, fresh local farms, farmers' markets, and other outlets which support them.

Springing to Life

In the spring, produce is young, fragile, and full of spunky energy. It radiates hope. Vegetables such as spinach, dandelion, arugula, sprouts, leeks, spring onions, and young tender greens abound. Many of these vegetables have a bitter flavor which helps us to clean out any stagnation that may have accumulated over the long, cold, sedentary winter. These are the most appropriate foods for harmonizing with the climate of spring. Parsnips, celery, burdock root, and Jerusalsem artichokes can also be considered spring food as they may be wintered over and picked in early spring.

Voluptuous Summer Produce

When summer's greenery abounds, enjoy it to the fullest. Summertime produce is more flowery, fruity, leafy and juicy than the tender leaves of spring. It displays the open, outward, and upward movement of the season. This produce has an opening, relaxing, and calming effect. Romaine, red leaf lettuce, asparagus, green peas, string beans, zucchini, arugula, cucumbers, celery, bell peppers, baby turnips, sweet corn, chives, and garlic chives, and tomatoes are just some examples of cooling summer produce. Eating the abundant summer vegetables enables us to adapt to the hot weather. It is important to note that while these vegetables are wonderful nourishment for the summer season, if they are eaten to excess or in cooler seasons such as autumn and winter, they can cool the body too much and lead to energetic (and very physical) imbalances. Mustard greens, cabbages, kale and collards are more hardy and strengthening and are still appropriate in this season and grow well in many regions.

Autumn Harvest

Autumn brings many deep orange root and round vegetables (squashes, pumpkins, rutabaga, parsnips, carrots, turnips, sunchokes, onions, and cabbages) to ripeness and to the farmers' market. All of these vegetables have a somewhat round shape. Round and root vegetables have gathered energy within themselves to guard against the cooler days of the season. Burdock root is an excellent strengthening vegetable to include frequently in this season. By eating these vegetables in the autumn, we become more centered, harmonize with the condensing energy of autumn, and improve our own ability to adapt to the cooling climate.

Winter Sustenance

Many Americans believe that it is impossible to have fresh produce in the winter without importing vegetables from the south. This is unfortunate. There are many vegetables that can be harvested in the fall and simply stored, without refrigeration, throughout the winter and well into spring. There are also a good number of hardy, cabbage family green leafy vegetables (collards, kale, black cabbage, Brussel sprouts, parsnips, sunchokes, etc.) that can be left in the fields and harvested all winter long even in very cold climates. Burdock root may be stored through the winter and used often to root and fortify you in this season. Where there is a will to eat fresh, locally grown vegetables year round, there is a way to accomplish it.

Frozen and Canned Vegetables

Frozen and canned vegetables are "wrecked" foods. They are generally very difficult to digest and have no place in a healthy diet. Further, the processing and storage of frozen and canned vegetables is an ecological disaster. Packaged foods, vegetarian or otherwise, present us with waste we cannot easily dispose of and further contribute to our mounting pollution problems. Keeping foods frozen wastes countless resources and contributes to global warming and ozone depletion by letting chloro-fluorocarbons and other harmful pollutants into the atmosphere. (Thus, we believe that the freezer is best used on a limited scale, if at all) Incredible variety is available in every season without relying on canned, frozen, or boxed produce. If you eat fresh vegetables, you'll be healthier and better nourished and you'll make less waste. Dried vegetables, however, are an acceptable alternative in any season.

Emphasizing the Most Nutritious Vegetables

Dark green leafy vegetables: These include cabbages, kale, collards, mustard, daikon, and turnip greens, bok choy, bok toy, romaine and oak leaf lettuce, wild greens, arugula, Brussel sprouts, broccoli, and other leafy and cruciferous vegetables. Each of these comes in many varieties. For example, there is the Chinese cabbage, nappa cabbage, savoy, red cabbage, hard green cabbage, Tuscan black cabbage, and so on. Cabbages store well and are particularly well suited to cold weather. You can get these year round in many places. Lettuce and spring greens are best eaten only in the spring, summer, and early fall when they are abundant in your area.

It is beneficial to consume one to two cooked cups of leafy greens daily (this may include cooked cabbage family vegetables and/or pressed or marinated salad). These are best spread out over two or three meals rather than consumed all in one sitting where too large a volume would dampen the digestive fire and interfere with digestion.

Greens may be prepared alone or in combination with other seasonal vegetables in the form of a parboiled salad, quick-boiled vegetables, or sautéed, stir fried, or steamed. If your digestive system is strong, you may want to take a portion of your daily greens as pressed or marinated salad. Heartier greens, such as Brussel sprouts, broccoli, cabbage, and kale can also be used in creamy-style soups, sauces, and stews.

Green leafy vegetables offer a light, upward energy. Your mother probably told you to "eat your spinach so you'll grow up to be big and strong like Popeye." Though spinach may not be the most nutritious green, your mother had the right idea. Greens help to enliven and inspire us with their cool, crisp, and vibrant life energy. They can add spring to our every step, every day and in every season.

Root vegetables: These may include carrots, parsnips, rutabaga, turnip, daikon, burdock root, beets, celeriac, Jerusalem artichoke, small red radishes, and more. Each type of root also comes in many varieties, from large winter radishes and turnips to the tiny round baby turnips, or long slender icicle radishes. There are fall and winter parsnips as well as sweeter varieties that have been left in the ground to winter over and are picked in the spring. Hearty root and round vegetables provide nutrients which complement but are not found in green leafy vegetables. Many root vegetables can be harvested year round and some can be stored for months at a time.

Health authorities recommend that we eat deep orange or yellow vegetables each day. Soups, stews, steamed, and stir fried dishes are some of the simplest and tastiest ways to prepare these hearty vegetables. If you make a daily soup and/or stew you will find that it is not difficult to take in at least one-half to one cup of these vegetables each day. Root vegetables can also be grated on the smallest hole of your grater (the hole that is usually reserved for Parmesan cheese or horseradish) and added to pressed or marinated cabbage or lettuce-based salads or served as a salad or relish on their own. (For a very sweet and satisfying relish, finely grate carrots, carrots and beets, carrots and daikon radish, or beets with horseradish, then add a few drops of tamari soy sauce or umeboshi vinegar for every half cup of grated vegetables.)

Literally and figuratively, root vegetables provide us with stability and a sense of root-edness; and help us to keep our feet firmly planted on the ground. They are practical, down to earth nourishment that we need for a balanced life. Thus we use them daily throughout the year.

Round, ground and vine vegetables: Round and vine vegetables include countless varieties of winter squashes, cucumbers, summer squashes, zucchini, onions, bell peppers, etc. For example, there are tiny pickling cukes, long English cucumbers, and various sizes, shapes, and flavors in between. In the winter squash family, one may select from kabocha, buttercup, butternut, sweet dumpling, sweet mama, delicatta, acorn, hubbard, honey delight, and countless others. (Kabocha, buttercup, and Hokkaido are some of the best keepers and some of our favorites.) These are available from late summer through early spring and some varieties keep amazingly for months at a time. There are also dozens of different types of onions: Vadalia, Spanish, Walla Walla Sweets, leeks, scallions, etc. These can be used year round according to local availability. (The harder ones keep for months).

Round, ground, or vine vegetables can be combined with other vegetables for added color, variety, and taste in soups and stews; steamed, quick-boiled, sautéed or stir fried dishes; pressed and marinated salads; and simmered or baked casseroles and side dishes. Many round and vine vegetables can be used to make sauces, spreads, or fillings for pizza, pasta, polenta, sandwiches, pot pies or turnovers.

Round vegetables center and stabilize us. Power and strength radiate out from the center of a bicycle wheel, from the center of a round vegetables, and from the center of a human body. Our center, called "Hara" in Japanese and "Dan Tien" in Chinese, can be likened to the center of a bicycle wheel. If the center is not strong or is out of "true" (proper alignment), then the entire bicycle, or organism in this case, will veer mercilously off course. We can strengthen our center and align ourselves by eating some round vegetables every day and in every season.

Garnishes: Garnishes aren't meant for decoration alone. They are also delicious, nutritious and can benefit digestion.

Raw and pungent garnishes add a light and moving energy to meals and a spark that can ignite and stimulate digestive fire and function. They can add pleasant aromas, vibrant colors, and palate pleasing tastes and a light upward moving energy. Unlike most other vegetables, pungent green garnishes are generally eaten by the teaspoonful or tablespoon rather than by the cupful. Their flavors tend to be more pungent and warm, (i.e., hotter than than other vegetables). Some examples include fresh parsley, scallions, chives, garlic chives, sorrel, arugula, cilantro, edible flowers, dill weed, and alfalfa, sunflower, or clover sprouts. Dried chives can even be used as a table condiment or garnish when fresh ones are unavailable. These garnishes can be sprinkled over soups and stews, breakfast porridge, or vegetable, tempeh, tofu or bean side dishes. Fresh or dried herbs and other garnishes can also be mixed into breads or casseroles to liven them up and add valuable trace minerals.

Dried vegetables: Some common dried vegetables include sun-dried tomatoes, bell pepper flakes, dried sweet corn, shiitake and other mushrooms, onion flakes, chives, and home-dried winter squash, and daikon. A wide variety of dried vegetables can be used as "soup helpers," stew extenders, or seasonings for grain, bean, tempeh, seitan, or tofu-based dishes.

Dried vegetables require no preservatives, additives, refrigeration, freezing, canning, or salting to extend their shelf life. Therefore, they are far more ecological than canned or frozen produce. They take up only one-sixth to one-twelfth the space of fresh vegetables and are incredibly convenient and are far more efficiently and ecologically stored than their frozen or canned counterparts.

How to use kale, collards & other leafy greens:

- Chop, cook, and use instead of spinach in savory pies, pot pies, pastry, casseroles, soups, sautés and appetizers
- Stir fry, steam, sauté, blanch, or quick-boil
- Use in boiled salads
- Simmer in soup
- Chop— then steam with other colorful vegetables
- Parboil these greens whole, chop, then add to a stir fry or sauté
- Blanch or boil, chop, then add to pita pocket sandwiches or tortilla roll-ups
- Cook and stuff in sandwiches with beans, scrambled tofu, tempeh paté, or bean dip
- Serve with scrambled tofu or refried beans and rice, tortillas, toast, or buns
- Use as a wrapper for wheat meat, tempeh, or beans—(See Hungarian Stuffed Cabbage Leaves)

To Get Your 5-10 Vegetables-A-Day:

- Eat vegetables at every meal *(including breakfast)*
- Have 1 cup of vegetable-rich soup or stew each day, served at one or two meals
- Use raw garnishes daily *(parsley, chives, scallions, arugula, etc.)*
- Find creative ways to add new vegetables to your diet!
- Make vegetable-rich desserts now and then *(using carrots, winter squash, parsnips, sweet potatoes, yams, sweet corn, etc.)*

Recommended Number of Daily Vegetable Servings:

- 3 servings dark green leafies and/or cabbage family vegetables *(~1 1/2 cups total)*
- 2-3 daily servings of deep orange or yellow vegetables *(~1-1 1/2 cups cooked)*
- 1-2 daily servings of various seasonal root, round, ground, flowering, or vine vegetables *(~ 1/2-1 cups)*
- 1-3 servings of raw, pungent green garnishes *(~1-6 Tbsp. total per day)*

Note: Some of your daily servings may be included in vegetable soups, stews, sauces, salads, pickles, etc.

Can't get the kids (or yourself) to eat enough vegetables?

For starters, try serving sweet vegetables for breakfast. Who could resist syrupy leftovers of baked or mashed winter squash, sweet potato, or corn on the cob? Or, make sweet vegetable desserts. *Here are some ideas to get you and your family started on the vegetable bandwagon:*

- **Vegetable Muesli:** (A concoction made from rolled grain, soy, nut, or goat or cow's milk or yogurt plus vegetables or sweet vegetables with fruit).

- **Squash Topped Breakfast Cereal:** Top hot cereal with mashed squash then a sprinkle of roasted nut or seed condiment, a dab of ghee, or a small cup of raw goat yogurt or plain, unflavored, warm soy-, rice- or goat-milk.

- **Squash-wiches or "Yam"-wiches:** Serve for breakfast, lunch or dinner. Might sound strange but we've never had a failure with this one! Serve several of these per person, with a small serving of pressed or marinated salad or quick-boiled greens. Add a small cup of warmed, plain soymilk or soy or goat yogurt (with a hint of pepper or ginger) if desired.

- Try a low-fat **Pumpkin, Squash, or Sweet Potato Pie** in a thick whole grain crust, served with with warm soy or grain milk or yogurt, cooked leafy greens or salad, and bread or rice for a tasty and nutritious breakfast.

- **Nutty Squash & Millet Porridge:** Serve with last night's steamed greens or boiled salad.

- **Corny Millet or Oatmeal:** Serve with a side of boiled greens or stir fry, a savory seed condiment, and toasty bits of roasted dulse.

- **Millet & Squash or Millet & Corn Slices:** These make a tasty no-bake bread or muffin alternative served with pressed, marinated, or boiled salad and a savory sprinkle.

- **Buckwheat Pancakes:** Top them with squash or yam purée, squash sauce or Onion Butter and a hint of soy yogurt or roasted, chopped nuts or seasoned, roasted pumpkin seeds.

- Serve leftover **Baked Squash or Sweet Potato** as an after school snack or light supper with a cup of warm, spiced soy-, nut-, rice or goat milk (in place of cookies and milk). (Pack "milk" in a warm thermos for a day at work or school).

- **Corny Baking:** Add corn off the cob to burritos, tamales, or enchiladas, or casseroles, or to waffle, pancake, muffin, cookie, steamed bun or bread dough. The sky's the limit.

- Add sweet corn to salads, sautées, sandwiches, scrambles, sea vegetable dishes, dips, spreads, sauces, soups and stews. bread douch, beans, or burritos.

- **Squash Topped Pizza or Pizza Bianca**

- **Yesterday's stir fry:** Roll it in a tortilla with beans, tempeh, or wheat meat and/or pickles or serve it over steam warmed noodles, bread, or hot cereal with a savory seed condiment.

- **Vegetables-in-Rice or Millet & Vegetable Polenta:** Sweet corn, peas, turnip, sweet potatoes or squash cooked into a pot of grain.

- **Onion Butter it up:** Try sweet onion butter on top of bread, waffles, or whole grains.

- **Beet Sauce Italiano:** Serve over noodles or polenta with wheatmeat balls or tempeh.

- **Spanokopita:** A delectable mixture of greens and cheesy tofu in a whole grain pie crust.

- **Parsnip White Sauce:** Serve this ladled over buckwheat mounds, pasta, or biscuits.

- **Creamy Green Garlic Sauce, Cauliflower Cream Sauce:** Ladle it over pasta or polenta.

- **Macaroni & Cheese-less Casserole:** A reformed version of a classic dish.

- **Mochi Waffles** topped with Walnut-Miso or Miso-Tahini spread and mashed squash or sweet potato and a side of pressed salad or quick-boiled greens.

Procedure Oriented Cookery

The same vegetable may be prepared in countless ways, so things needn't become boring. By emphasizing technique over ingredients, you will be able can make use of whatever vegetables you happen to have on hand. You don't need a special recipe for collard greens, brussel sprouts or turnip tops. Recipes that work with broccoli or cauliflower will usually work with cabbage , kale, or most other dark green leafy vegetables. Likewise, recipes that call for winter squash are usually equally as tasty when prepared with sweet potatoes, parsnips or carrots.

If you learn how to make our basic creamy soup without the cream, you can make the soup with asparagus, broccoli, corn, brussel sprouts, parsnips, or whatever happens to be in season and on hand. If you learn how to make nishime root vegetable dishes, you will find that almost any roots will do, be they Jerusalem artichokes, carrots, turnips, onions, rutabaga, daikon, winter squash, or a combination of several of these. The same goes for other basic techniques in this book. Learn the techniques and you are a liberated person not bound by "recipes."

Though it may initially be helpful to follow the recipes exactly, in no time you'll be able to make appropriate substitutions which will still lead to predictably good results—if the basic principles and procedures are understood and utilized and the basic proportions are recipes are memorized.

There is no one best way to prepare vegetables. Each technique offers benefits and may be more or less appropriate for a particular food, meal, or season. Each vegetable will taste and look different, depending on how it is cut and prepared. Take a carrot, cut it in matchsticks, and it is well suited for a quick stir fry, sauté, or kinpira dish. Cut it into large chunks and it will be at home in a stew or casserole. Grate it and it will blend into a pressed, marinated or tossed salad. Take an onion, cut and pickle it, and it will have a pungent, salty, and sweet taste. Finely cut and sauté the onion, and it will taste slightly sweet and even richer. Bake a whole, uncut onion until it is soft and syrupy and it will become almost as sweet as an apple. Cut, lightly sauté, then long simmer a pot full of onions and they reduce themselves to a thick, caramelized, golden brown and very sweet "butter" resembling apple

butter. Similarly, parsnips, winter squash, leafy greens, and other vegetables can each be prepared in various ways to create a surprising array of flavors and textures.

Some preparation are appropriate for use in a particular seasons, others are suitable for use in several seasons or all seasons. Learning which techniques are suited to which season allows you to create truly nourishing food. Just as we wear a thick coat in one season and a lighter coat in another, it is wise to use more light preparations in warmer seasons and more warming preparations in colder ones. The same vegetables or cooking techniques, used day after day or to the exclusion of others can produce a monotonous diet out of sync with your environment.

We need different types of vegetables and different vegetable preparations to be well nourished: some cooked, some raw, some pressed, some pickled some long cooked, some quickly and briefly cooked; some upward growing leafies, some downward growing roots; and some in between vegetables. Only by incorporating many foods and different techniques can we really have a varied and healthy diet.

Although we eat winter squashes throughout much of the year, we do not bake them in all seasons. In the winter we bake them more often while in the spring or summer we usually steam or nishime cook them or use them in soup. Actually, in all seasons we simmer them in soups and stews. We use shorter cooking times for vegetables in warm weather and slightly longer times in cold weather. We bake some of our vegetables in the late fall and throughout winter. and we bake little if any vegetables in the summer. However, we do not recommend baking or pressure cooking every dish in a meal. We need some contrast, diversity, polarity, and variety. The same vegetable can and should be cut and prepared in ways that harmonize with the energy of each season, with the other dishes in a meal, and with your particular needs. Your condition must also be factored in when deciding how to cook your daily vegetables. For some individuals, baking should be avoided almost entirely; for others, salads may need to be avoided almost entirely.

Nutrient Comparison:
Green leafy vegetables (kale) vs. citrus fruit (orange)

As the chart below shows, kale and other green leafy vegetables such as collard, mustard, turnip, bok choy and other greens are far more nutrient dense than fruits. We emphasize the daily use of green leafy vegetables and discourage the use of fruits, because fruits are not as nutritious as hearty vegetables and are far more labor and resource intensive to grow and store than are vegetables.

You can see from the comparison below that eating fewer vegetables in favor of more fruits could leave you undernourished. (Fruits and vegetables do not stack up the same nutritionally.) It takes only a small amount of hardy vegetables to meet your minimum daily nutrient needs.

Note: A 100 gram serving is roughly 3 1/2 ounces by weight.

Nutrient	Kale (100 g)*	Orange (100 g)	Factor	What this means:
Calories	38	49	8	kale has 2/10 less
Protein	4.2 g	1.0 g	4	kale has 4x more
Calcium	179 mg	41 mg	4	kale has 4x more
Phosphorus	73 mg	20 mg	~4	kale has 4x more
Iron	2.2 mg	0.4 mg	~6	kale has 6x more
Potassium	378 mg	200 mg	~2	kale has 2x more
Vitamin A	8900 I.U.	200 I.U.	45	kale has 45x more
Vitamin C	125 mg	50 mg	2.5	kale has 2 1/2x more

* These numbers are for uncooked kale. Kale in a pressed salad, a common preparation that we use and advocate, may include even more nutrients since such salads concentrate the nutrients of vegetables by reducing their size. The values are nearly identical for cooked kale if the cooking lasts less than eight minutes at boiling temperature, which is also a common technique that we use and advocate. Finally, even if the cooking lasts longer than ten minutes at boiling, less than half of the water soluble vitamins such as vitamin C will be destroyed. Since kale is twice as high in this nutrient as an orange, you can still get as much vitamin C from cooked kale as from an equal volume of orange. Besides that, the kale contains ample amounts of calcium and iron, nutrients which are totally lacking in the orange. It also has more folacin and fiber.

Vitamin C without fruit? You bet !

The China Health Project, conducted by researchers from Cornell University and Oxford University, determined that the average American gets only 73 mg of vitamin C a day, usually from citrus fruits, tomatoes or potatoes. (The U.S. RDA for vitamin C is only 60 mg.) In contrast, the average Chinese person eats considerably more vegetables and large volumes of grains supplemented with cooked leafy greens and animal foods, and takes in at least twice as much vitamin C as an American—at least 140 mg of vitamin C per day, and possibly more if we take into account that the Chinese tend to replenish their soil and, as a result, to produce more mineral and vitamin rich vegetables. The Chinese eat fresh, locally grown vegetables, very few tomatoes or potatoes, and very little fruit.

- 1 cup of soup or stew *(with vegetables or vegetables + beans, tofu, tempeh, or seitan)*

- 1/2 cup thick, puréed vegetable soup or sauce

- 1/2 cup pressed, marinated or tossed salad

- 1/2 cup cooked greens, or root, round, ground, or mixed vegetables

- 1 cup tossed or cut, raw leafy or watery vegetables *(watery salad greens, lettuce, watercress, Mesclun greens etc.)*

- 1-2 Tbsp. raw, pungent green garnishes, fresh herbs, scallions, parsley, sprouts, etc.

Seasoning & Cooking Vegetables

When used, herbs and spices should enhance the vegetables and stimulate your appetite and digestion; they should not overpower the dish though. (We use herbs or spices daily.)

You will find that heavy sauces aren't needed to disguise vegetables when you start with fresh vegetables and prepare them properly.

Adding a small amount of sun dried sea salt or tamari in cooking, tenderizes vegetables and brings out the natural oils, sweetness and the flavors of each morsel. Shoyu, tamari, apriboshi or umeboshi paste or vinegar, or light or dark miso can also be added near the end of cooking, or as a dressing after cooking is complete. These seasonings are best added sparingly to foods by the cook. Occasionally, sauces, dressings or other table condiments may be desired; however, raw salt, soy sauce, tamari, and shoyu should never be added at the table (when used this way they can easily be used to excess and lead to imbalance). A little bit of such strong seasoning will go further and taste better when added to a pot of vegetables than when used to douse and drown your food at the table. When used properly, the taste of these seasonings is delicious and delicate, not overwhelmingly salty.

Vegetables don't need buckets of dressing! Try some alternatives...

- Eat un-dressed vegetables with seasoned beans, tofu or tempeh and rice, bread or pasta. Top the grain with a seed or nut condiment or grated raw milk cheese, or raw goat yogurt, if desired.

- Serve plain steamed or quick-boiled vegetables drizzled with toasted sesame oil or flax oil.

- Toss a serving bowl full of steamed or parboiled vegetables or pressed salad with a few teaspoons of unrefined sunflower, flax, walnuts, or sesame oil or a sprinkle of roasted pumpkin or sunflower seeds.

- Toss lightly cooked vegetables with a shake of brown rice vinegar, used singly or in combination with umeboshi or apriboshi vinegar.

- Toss a bowl of steamed vegetables with a hint of oil and tamari, shoyu, or ume or apriboshi vinegar. If desired, add a sprinkle of rice vinegar and/or dry roasted seeds or chopped nuts.

- Toss lightly steamed or parboiled vegetables with sauerkraut, or minced pickled ginger, onion, cucumber or red or white radish.

- Toss parboiled vegetables with sautéed sea vegetables or leftover pressed or tossed salad.

- Sauté vegetables with garlic or ginger and/or sesame or olive oil and sea salt, umeboshi or apriboshi vinegar, or tamari or shoyu.

- Spoon a serving of seasoned tofu, tempeh, wheat meat or sea vegetables over cooked, pressed, or marinated vegetables.

- Dilute prepared mustard with water, tamari, ume, or light miso +/- a dash of nut or seed oil. Toss over cooked leafy green or mixed vegetables.

- Try nishime cooking root, round and ground vegetables for a rich flavor without added fat.

- Top steamed vegetables or boiled salad with a dollup of Hummus, Refried Beans, Tofu Pesto, Tofu Cream Cheese, Tofu Ricotta, Tofu Mayo or goat cheese, quark, yogurt, or bean dip or spread.

Methods of Preparing Vegetables

Though there are numerous ways to prepare vegetables, it is best to emphasize those that are energy and fuel efficient, that preserve the most nutrients, that produce the best flavored and most easily digested food, and that require very little time. Listed below are the preparations we use most frequently throughout the year. Also listed are preparations which we call "seasonal" or "occasional use" preparations. Some of these take more time and energy to assemble and cook. Others are not appropriate for use in all seasons. Of course, you may choose to use the occasional use preparations several times a week, every few days, or more or less often. We have emphasized what we find easiest, most energy and time efficient, and most enjoyable in our daily practice. We incorporate seasonal and occasional use preparations into our weekly cooking, we just don't use them as often as the everyday methods.

Basic everyday techniques:
Stewing & soup making
Steaming
Stir frying
Boiling and parboiling (boiled/blanched salad)
Quick-boiling
Sautéeing (with and without oil)
Nishime waterless cooking
Pressing, marinating, and pickling
Raw salad

Seasonal or occasional use techniques:
Pan-frying
Baking
Pressure cooking
Pressure steaming
Casserole cooking (stove top or oven)
Grilling
Barbequing
Broiling

Best limited or avoided: Deep fry (tempura, french fries, fried chips, etc.). Good quality deep fry or tempura may be used occasionally. When used, fried foods should be of the highest quality, eaten moderately, and served with salty and/or pungent condiments or relishes to aid digestion.

Note: If your digestion is strong you may wish to serve pressed or marinated salad once a day in place of or in addition to a serving of cooked leafy greens; however, these salads can be problematic for some individuals. If consumed in too large a volume or at the exclusion of cooked greens, pressed salads can weaken even strong digestive systems It is a good idea for everyone to eat some pickles every day, particularly in meals or on days where no pressed or marinated salad is served.

- **Seasonal considerations:** Baked vegetables are more appropriate in fall, winter, and early spring than in warmer months. Tossed raw salads are more suited to the heat of summer than to the cool or cold fall, winter, or early spring. Grilled vegetables are appropriate in late summer. Baked casseroles are appropriate in cold weather.

- **Health considerations:** When using cooking methods that require fats (oils or nut or seed butters), use these sparingly then omit or reduce the amount of fat that you add to other dishes in the same meal. Eliminate fat-laden salad dressings (dress vegetables in the kitchen instead) and ban the butter dish. (Seasonal cooking is also a health issue.)

- **Energy/fuel use considerations**: Baking is more fuel intensive than stove top cooking methods such as steaming, simmering, sautéeing, or stir frying. For this reason, it is a good idea to fill up the oven with as many other dishes as possible when you do bake so as not to waste fuel. A toaster oven is a good option if you like to bake small volumes of vegetables but still want to minimize your fuel/energy use.

- **Time considerations:** Pressed or marinated salads are a practical and efficient preparation. They can be made in large batches to last for three to five days at a time, providing a ready made vegetable dish for daily breakfast, pack lunches, or dinners. This simplifies meal planning and preparation. Quick-boiling and stir frying are other quick and easy methods that can be used daily. All of these are highly nutritious as well.

Greens

Basic Procedure, Steamed or Mixed Vegetables (Year Round)***

Prep: 5-10 minutes
Yield: varies with type

Cooking: 5-10 minutes, depending on type/size
Serving size: 1/2-3/4 cup per person

Steamed vegetables have a light, crisp taste. The key to steaming is to boil the water *before* you add the vegetables. Avoid overcooking by watching and checking often and promptly removing greens from the pot when done. This method works well for broccoli, cauliflower, cabbage, finely cut onions or thin slices of root or round vegetables. However, hard leafy greens such as kale, collards, and mustard greens will be sweeter and more digestible when parboiled, quick-boiled and/or stir fried, or sautéed.

Use one or several different seasonal vegetables. Try lightly cooked leafies such as bok choy, nappa cabbage, savoy or Brussel sprout halves, broccoli, asparagus, or a two or three colorful vegetables, including roots or round vegetables.

Basic Rule of Thumb: 10-12 cups packed, raw vegetables, yields 4-5 cups cooked vegetables and serves 4-6 (or 2-3 meals for 2)

Hint: Cut vegetables in small pieces for quick and even cooking. Try florets, strips, squares, rings, thin rounds, half or quarter-moons, matchsticks, etc. Green leaves may be cut or cooked whole. Waste as little as possible: mince or slice cabbage and cauliflower cores; peel and slice broccoli stalks, finely chop and use scallion and leek roots and shoots.

Leafy greens (Use 1-2 varieties):

Nappa, savoy, hard, or Tuscan Black cabbage, Chinese or American broccoli, cauliflower, quartered Brussel sprouts, bok choy, tot soy, or other greens, whole or cut

+/- Root, round, and/or vine vegetables (Use 1-3 as desired):

Onions, scallions, or leeks

Daikon or red radish, turnip, carrot, rutabaga, Jerusalem artichoke, green beans, pea pods, snap peas, mung bean sprouts, zucchini, summer squash, crimini or fresh shiitake mushrooms, corn off the cob, etc.

1. Add 1 to 2 inches of cold water to a 2-4 quart pot. Insert a metal steamer basket or place a Chinese bamboo or wooden steamer on top of the pot or a wok. Arrange cut vegetables in mounds on a steamer basket. If desired, sprinkle with a pinch of sea salt. If several types of vegetables are used, layer the longest cooking ones on the bottom. Greens may be cooked whole then sliced after cooking if desired.

2. Cover the pot, bring to boil over medium-high heat then reduce heat to medium (enough to maintain steam). Steam 5-10 minutes or until crisp-tender. Cooking time depends upon the type and size of vegetables and the distance between the vegetables and the boiling water.

   If you do not have a steamer tray or basket, steam directly in a pot: Bring 1/2-inch of lightly salted water to boil in a 2-4 quart pot. Add washed greens or layers of mixed vegetables directly to the bottom of the pot, cover and return to boil. Reduce heat to medium. Steam-simmer 6-10 minutes or until leaves and stems turn vibrant green and tender.

3. *Immediately* remove tender vegetables from the cooking pot and transfer to a serving bowl to prevent over-cooking. If desired, cover loosely with a bamboo mat. (Steaming water may be used as soup stock or to make a sauce or gravy. If the water has been used several times and/or is discolored from use with stacking bamboo steamer trays, do not save it, simply discard it.) If greens were cooked whole, chop the leaves and stems finely then toss with other vegetables.

4. If desired, toss with a dash of tamari, shoyu, or umeboshi vinegar, brown rice vinegar or apple cider vinegar and/or oil or toasted seeds. (See Easy as 1-2-3 Dressing.) Or, toss vegetables with sauerkraut or other pickles (chopped) or leftover pressed salad or let diners sprinkle on a few drops of herb or spice seasoned oil or oil-free dressing at the table.

Serving suggestions: Serve while still warm or at room temperature with grain; soup or stew; and condiments. Also serve a bean or sea vegetable dish if desired.

Storage: Store leftovers in a glass, ceramic, or stainless steel bowl at room temperature, covered with a bamboo mat and use within 12 hours or cover with a plate and refrigerate. Take meal size portions out of the refrigerator 20-40 minutes before serving. Use within 24 hours. ❏

Favorite Steamed Vegetable Combinations (Use local, in-season vegetables):

- Quartered Brussel sprouts + carrot and/or daikon rounds
- Quartered Brussel sprouts + red cabbage strips
- Cauliflower or broccoli + red or green cabbage +/- carrot
- Cauliflower + green beans +/- onion or red radish slices
- Chinese greens + carrots or rutabaga matchsticks or red radish slices
- Cabbage, broccoli, or asparagus + red or white onion rings +/- carrot slices
- Daikon radish + zucchini slices
- Red cabbage + carrot + celery or onion
- Cauliflower or broccoli + corn off the cob +/- red or yellow bell pepper strips
- Red radish or turnips + any greens + celery
- Kale + scallions + carrots or corn
- Cauliflower + green beans +/- red radish
- Cabbage or tender greens + pea pods + onions or leeks.

Steamed Greens & Onion (Year Round)**

Prep: 10 minutes
Cooking: 5-10 minutes

Serves: 4-8 (or 2-4 meals for 2) depending on greens)
Serving size: 1/2-3/4 cup per person

Optional, 2-3 pinches sea salt, added to the water or sprinkled over vegetables before cooking (this creates a sweeter dish)

1/2-1 red or white onion, cut in thin rings or crescents or 4 scallions, cut in 1" logs

1 bunch leafy greens, cut into 1/4-1/2" strips or 2" squares with most of stems minced finely *(roughly 6-8 packed cups— black cabbage, Chinese greens, etc.)*

1-2 cups carrot, radish, rutabaga, green beans or other, cut in thin strips, rounds or slices

1. Steam as per Basic Procedure above. ❏

Steamed Turnips with Tops (Spring, Summer, Fall)***

Prep: 5 minutes
Cooking: 4-8 minutes
Serves: 4-6 (or 2-3 meals for 2)

Serving size: 1/2-3/4 cup per person

Optional, 2-3 pinches sea salt, added to the water or sprinkled over vegetables before cooking

1 bunch turnips with tops, (tops cut in thin rounds) greens cut finely, placed on top of turnip slices in the pot

Optional, 1/2 medium onion, cut in thin rounds

1. Steam as per Basic Procedure above. ❏

Steamed Corn on the Cob
(Late Summer, Fall)***

Prep: 4 minutes
Cooking: 5-10 minutes
Serves: 4-6 (or 2-3 meals for 2)
Serving size: 1/2-1 cob per person

4 ears corn on the cob, cut in half

2-3 pinches sea salt (or spread corn with ume paste or diluted light miso when serving)

1. Steam as per Basic Procedure above. ❏

Steamed Brussel Sprouts
with cabbage, daikon, or carrots

Prep: 5-10 minutes
Cooking: 8-10 minutes

Serves: 4-6 (or 2-3 meals for 2)
Serving size: 1/2-3/4 cup per person

3 cups Brussel sprouts, quartered

2-3 cups diced red cabbage, carrot or daikon, cut in rounds or quarter-rounds

1. Steam as per Basic Procedure above. ❏

Kale, Carrots, Caraway & Kraut
(Any Season)***

Prep: 10-15 minutes
Cooking: 10 minutes
Serves: 6-8 (or 4-5 with leftovers)
Serving size: 1/2-3/4 cup per person

Reduce recipe by one half to serve 4-6 (or 2-3 meals for 2).

This favorite fall and winter dish is colorful, flavorful, and fat-free. Caraway has traditionally been used in cooking as a carminative—a digestive aid which eliminates flatulence. It also adds a wonderful taste and aroma. Though most associate its use with rye bread, caraway can also heighten the flavor of cabbage family vegetables. Follow the basic recipe here the first time or two

then try rutabaga in place of carrots. This dish goes well with almost any type of whole grain with an orange vegetable side dish and/or a bean soup. Or, serve it with whole grain bread or mochi and a tofu dip or tahini spread.

1 medium-sized bunch kale *or* 8 cups tightly packed, including stems, cut in strips

1 1/2 cups carrots cut into thin matchsticks

1/4" water to cover the bottom of a pot (use more water if steaming on a rack or boiling)

2 pinches sea salt

1 cup natural sauerkraut, drained

1 Tbsp. caraway seeds

1. Steam cut greens with stems on the bottom, directly in the bottom of pot. Or, boil whole leaves in an uncovered pot until tender. Steam cut carrots on a tray or layer over the greens. Cook 6-8 minutes or crisp-tender.

2. Rinse vegetables with cold water and drain in a colander. Toss with caraway and sauerkraut. Serve right away or allow vegetables to sit at room temperature for 1/2-1 hour. See serving suggestions above.

Storage: Store leftovers at room temperature for up to 24 hours in a bowl covered with a bamboo sushi mat. In hot weather, cover with a saucer or lid and refrigerate. Remove from refrigerator 1/2-1 hour before serving. Use within 24 hours.

Variations:

• Omit carrots and replace with rutabaga cut into matchsticks. (Fall, winter, spring)

• Replace carrots with thinly cut daikon or red radish, or baby turnip rounds. (Any season)

• Omit sauerkraut. Replace with 1/2-1 cup homemade Overnight Onion Ring Pickles, or Quick Pickled Onions, or Umeboshi Pickled Onions. Replace caraway with 2 Tbsp. toasted sesame, sunflower, or pumpkin seeds.

• **Steamed Greens with Pickled Pink Radishes:** Steam greens and toss with pickled pink radish or turnip slices (pickled with umeboshi or apriboshi). Figure about 1/4-1/3 cup chopped pickles per 2 cups steamed vegetables. ❏

Basic Procedure, Quick Boiled Vegetables (Year Round Technique)***

Prep: 5-10 minutes
Cooking: 10-12 minutes

Serves: 4-8 (or 2-4 meals for 2)
Serving size: 1/2-3/4 cup per person

This technique yields tender and tasty vegetables in no time flat and with little or no added fat. It's quicker than a boiled salad and more digestible than a tossed salad. In contrast to steaming, this method uses less water and cooks all or nearly all the water into the vegetables for optimal flavor without dressing. As with stir frying, it is important to cut all the vegetables and arrange them in separate bowls before you start cooking. (**Note:** We always make enough to last for two to three meals at a time.)

Basic Rule of Thumb:

1/3-1/2 cup water, pasta water or stock, or more as needed to cover bottom of pot by 1/3"

1/8 tsp. sea salt

1-2 tsp. tamari, shoyu, or umeboshi vinegar **or** an additional 1/8-1/4 tsp. sea salt

Optional, 1-3 cloves garlic, minced finely **and/or** 1-2 tsp. dried, rubbed sage **or** 1/8 tsp. mild red pepper powder *(ancho, Anaheim, or chipotle)*

10 cups vegetables, cut finely

See Basic Stir Fried Vegetables, page 266 for suggested vegetables

Try 1/2-1 cup onions, scallions, or leeks + greens +/- root, round or vine vegetables

Optional, seed or nut oil, added at the table

1. Wash vegetables and cut into thin pieces. If broccoli or cauliflower are used, cut into florets then peel and finely chop stems and cores; discard only the woody part—the bottom 1-3 inches. If using root or round vegetables, grate or cut into matchsticks, thin rounds, half moons, quarter moons or diagonal slivers. Cut scallions in 1 to 2-inch logs. Finely mince the stems from leafy greens then cut leaves into strips. Cut cabbage or bok choy into strips or 1-2 inch squares. Arrange each kind of vegetable in a separate dish.

   Note: Measure the volume of your soup cups and bowls then use the same bowls each time you make this dish. If you know how much each holds, you will know how much to prepare for a given number of people which will help in planning and preparation.

2. Combine salty seasoning and measured amount of water in a saucepan (use only enough water to just cover the bottom 1/4-1/3 inch of the pot). Add sea salt.

3. Add the vegetables that take the longest to cook first or cook in the order listed in each recipe. For example, first toss onions or leeks into the pot. Stir and simmer over medium heat for 1-2 minutes until almost tender. Add stems from greens and/or mushrooms. Continue to stir and turn vegetables (about 1-2 minutes) using a large slotted spoon or skimmer. Add any root or round vegetables now (carrots, daikon, turnip, sunchoke or rutabaga, etc.). Stir and toss so that vegetables keep getting immersed in the hot water.

4. Layer green leafy vegetables or cabbage on top. Cover and simmer over medium heat for 4-6 minutes or cook uncovered and continue to stir and turn until tender and vibrant green. Cooking time will vary with the size and depth of the pot and the vegetables used.

5. Remove lid, stir, and cook away liquid, about 3-6 minutes. Lift vegetables out of the cooking pot using a slotted spoon. If a small amount of liquid remains in the pot, add this to the serving bowl or reserve liquid for use in soups, stews, or gravies. Cover vegetables with a bamboo mat and serve warm or at room temperature. Or, for a clear sauce, dilute 1 tsp. arrowroot in 3 Tbsp. cold water, add to cooking water and stir to thicken. Pour sauce over the cooked vegetables.

6. If desired sprinkle 1 tsp. oil over each serving at the table.

Storage: Store at room temperature and use within 24 hours, or refrigerate in a covered bowl then remove from the refrigerator 1/2-1 hour before serving. Use within 24 hours. ❑

Quick-Boiled Greens & Onions (Year Round)***

Prep: 3-5 minutes
Cooking: 6-10 minutes

Serves: 4-8 (or 2-3 meals for 2)
Serving size: 1/2-3/4 cup per person

1/3-1/2 cup water, pasta water, or soup stock, or just enough to cover bottom of pot

1/8-1/4 tsp. sea salt

2 cloves finely minced garlic,

Optional, 1-1 1/4 tsp. dried, rubbed sage *or* 1/4 tsp. ancho, anaheim or chipotle pepper powder

1 cup onion or leek, cut in thin crescents or rounds *or* 4 scallions cut in 2" logs

6-9 cups finely cut cabbage, mustard, turnip, or collard greens or other greens, including stems

Optional, 1-1 1/2 cups rutabaga, carrot, or sunchoke cut in thin matchsticks or slivers

Optional, 1-2 tsp. tamari or ume or apriboshi vinegar

1. Cook as per Quick-Boiled Vegetable Procedure above. ❏

Quick-Boiled Turnips with Tops (Late Spring, Summer, Fall)***

Prep: 3-5 minutes
Cooking: 6-10 minutes

Serves: 4-6 (or 2-3 meals for 2)
Serving size: 1/2-3/4 cup per person

1/3-1/2 cup water, or enough to cover bottom of pot by 1/4-1/3"

1/8-1/4 tsp. sea salt *and/or* 1 tsp. tamari, shoyu, or ume vinegar

Optional, 2 cloves minced garlic *and/or* 1/8 tsp. red chili powder *(ancho, Anaheim, or chipotle)*

1 medium onion or leeks, cut in thin crescents

1 bunch baby turnips with tops—tops cut finely, turnip roots cut into thin rounds or half-moons

1. Cook as per Quick—Boiled Vegetable Procedure above. ❏

Quick-Boiled Vegetable Medley (Fall, Winter, Spring)***

Prep: 3-5 minutes
Cooking: 7-10 minutes

Serves: 4-8 (or 2-3 meals for 2)
Serving size: 1/2-3/4 cup per person

1/3-1/2 cup water or soup stock, or enough to cover bottom of pot by 1/4-1/3"

1/8-1/4 tsp. sea salt

Optional, 2 cloves minced garlic

Optional, 1/8-1/4 tsp. mild red pepper powder *(ancho, Anaheim, or chipotle)* *or* 1 tsp. rubbed sage

1 medium onion, cut in thin crescents *or* 1 cup scallions with stems, cut into 1" lengths

1 cup red radish, daikon, rutabaga, *or* Jerusalem artichokes cut in thin rounds, matchsticks, or slivers

6-7 packed cups nappa, savoy or Tuscan Black Cabbage, or bok choy, kale, collards, purple cabbage, or other leafy greens *or* a combination of several types of greens

Optional, 1 cup bean sprouts

1. Cook as per Quick-Boiled Vegetable Procedure above. ❏

Quick-Boiled Vegetable Medley #2

Prep: 3-5 minutes
Cooking: 7-10 minutes

Serves: 6-8 (or 3-4 meals for 2)
Serving size: 1/2-3/4 cup per person

1/3-1/2 cup water or enough to cover bottom of pot by 1/4-1/3"

1/8-1/4 tsp. sea salt (reduce if desired)

Optional, 1 tsp. corn, sunflower, or toasted sesame oil

Optional, 2 cloves minced garlic
and/or 2 tsp. rubbed sage or dried thyme

1 cup cut onion, scallion, or leeks

1 cup crimini or button mushrooms
or 3 fresh shiitake mushrooms, cut finely

1 cup pea pods, daikon, or rutabaga cut in thin rounds, matchsticks, or slivers

1 cup red radish, cut in thin slices +/-1 cup radish tops, cut finely

4-5 packed cups Chinese broccoli, or other dark green leafy vegetables (or part greens, part purple cabbage)

+/- 1 cup bean sprouts

Optional, 1-2 tsp. tamari, shoyu, or umeboshi or apriboshi vinegar

1. Cook as per Quick-Boiled Vegetable Procedure above. ❏

Parboiled Whole Greens (Year Round)***

Prep: 10 minutes
Cooking: 2-10 minutes

Serves: 4-8 (or 2-4 meals for 2)
Serving size: 1/2-3/4 cup per person

Cooking green leaves whole, in an open pot brings out a delectably sweet flavor and vibrant green hue adding a cool, crisp refreshing energy to meals. We use this method throughout the year to parboil hard leafy greens such as kale or collards before adding them to a stir fry or sauté.

Note: Most greens will reduce in size by one-half to one-fourth of their original size.

2-3" water

1/4 tsp. sea salt

1 medium bunch **or** 6-8 packed cups dark green leafy vegetables or cabbage, (*Kale, collards, mustard or turnip greens, bok choy, tot soy, choy sum, Tuscan Black Cabbage, etc.*)

Optional, Easy As 1-2-3 Dressing

1. Wash greens thoroughly to remove all sand. Leave the leaves whole to retain more flavor and nutrients. Also leave stems intact.

2. Add water to cover 2 to 3 inches over the bottom of a 3-4 quart pot. Add sea salt, cover and bring to boil over medium heat.

3. Dip vegetables into boiling water and press down with a large slotted spoon to immerse. Leave off the lid. Cook over medium heat in boiling water until tender. Remove soft type greens (bok choy, nappa cabbage, etc.) after 15-30 seconds and hard greens (kale, collards, mustard greens, etc.) after 6-10 minutes or when tender and vibrant green. Stems should yield when pinched.

4. Drain in a colander. If desired, rinse vegetables briefly with cold water to stop the cooking.

5. Chop leaves into thin strips or 1 to 2-inch squares. Chop stems finely. Serve plain. Or toss with pickles (sauerkraut or sliced onion, radish, turnip, or cucumber pickles), ume and rice vinegar, tamari and rice vinegar, or any of the above plus a hint of toasted sesame oil or dry roasted seeds. Or toss greens with leftover pressed salad, seasoned tempeh or a sea vegetable side dish.

Serving suggestions: Serve with grain, soup and/or beans, and/or a colorful root or round vegetable side dish, and condiments. Add a teaspoon of flax or sesame oil to each serving at the table if desired.

Storage: Store at room temperature covered with a bamboo mat or refrigerate. Serve at room temperature. Use within 24 hours. Serve at room temperature without reheating. ❏

Basic Procedure, Simple Sautéed Greens (Year Round)***

Prep: 10 minutes
Cooking: 8-15 minutes

Yield: ~4 cups cooked vegetables, varies with type
Serves: 4-8 or (2-4 meals for 2)
Serving size: 1/2-3/4 cup per person

The most nutritious vegetables need the most thorough cooking to be digestible. Hard leafy greens are no exception. Parboiling breaks down the tough cellulose fibers and inactivates bitter substances which normally protect hardy vegetables from being eaten by predators or destroyed by rough weather. Sautéing in oil with a salty seasoning seals in the nutrients and flavors, aids digestion, and produces a rich, sweet taste. Adding a dash of herbs or spices further aids digestion and enhances the flavor of this quick to fix side-dish. Leftovers are even sweeter the next day.

Rule of Thumb: 1 med. to lg. bunch of greens (12-16 cups raw) yields 3-4 cups of cooked vegetables and serves 4-8 (or 2-4 meals for 2)

4-6 cups water

1/8-1/4 tsp. sea salt

1 medium to large bunch kale, collards, or mustard greens *or* 2-3 bunches daikon greens or turnip tops *(about 1 pound)*

2-3 tsp. light or toasted sesame oil *or* olive oil

1 medium onion, spring onion, or leek, cut in thin crescents or half moons *or* 1 cup scallions cut in 2" logs (use the green and white parts)

1-3 cloves garlic, minced *or* 1 tsp. finely minced ginger root

Optional, 1/8 tsp. mild red pepper powder *(ancho, Anaheim, or chipotle), black pepper* *or* 1 tsp. powdered, rubbed sage

1 Tbsp. umeboshi or apriboshi vinegar, shoyu, or tamari *or* 1/4-1/3 tsp. sea salt added in step #5

1. Wash greens under running water or by dipping in a basin of water to remove sand.

2. Parboil whole greens as per Basic Procedure Parboiled Greens above, cooking *uncovered* for 5-10 minutes, or until tender and vibrant green. Stems should yield when pinched. Meanwhile, chop raw vegetables, arranging each kind in a separate bowl.

3. Remove greens from pot with a slotted spoon. Drain, cut stems finely, and cut leaves into thin strips or 1/2 to 2-inch squares. Toss together. (Discard leftover cooking water from boiling hard leafy greens; it contains antinutritive substances which we have deliberately removed in cooking.)

4. Measure oil and add to a cast iron skillet, wok, or stainless steel pan. Turn to medium-high heat, add finely cut onions, leeks, or scallions. Add sea salt to draw out moisture. Stir then add minced garlic and/or other herbs or spices. Sauté and stir over medium heat for 2-3 minutes or until tender and translucent.

5. Add chopped stems (if adding root vegetables or mushrooms, add before the stems and stir for several minutes). Stir 2 minutes then add cut leaves and tamari, shoyu, or ume or apriboshi. Stir 2-4 minutes, until tender. Remove from heat and transfer to a serving bowl.

Serving suggestions: Serve warm or at room temperature with whole grain, pasta, or bread; a soup, stew, or root/round vegetable dish; and condiments. If desired, add a bean or sea vegetable dish and/or omit soup or roots.

Storage: Store at room temperature, covered with a bamboo mat or in the refrigerator. Serve at room temperature or briefly steamed in a covered bowl. Use within 24 hours.

Variations:

• ***In step #3, after onions are tender, add one of the following vegetables then sauté for several minutes before adding stems then leaves:***

1/2-1 medium rutabaga, carrot, turnip, daikon or beet, grated or cut in thin matchsticks

2 fresh or dried (soaked) shiitake mushrooms, cut in thin strips

Add extra sea salt in step #2 above then omit tamari, shoyu, or umeboshi in step #4.

* **Note: If using tender greens like Chinese broccoli, tot soy, choy sum, or bok choy, omit parboiling.** Start with 3/4-1 pound of greens. Cut finely. Sauté onions, scallions or leeks as per instructions above. Add herbs or spices and root vegetables if desired. Next add stems and sauté briefly. Then add leaves and sauté for several minutes until tender. Add seasoning. If necessary add 1/4-1/3 cup water, then cover and steam briefly until tender. ❏

Buttery Cabbage & Onion Sauté (Fall, Winter, Early Spring)***

Prep: 10 minutes
Cooking: 15 minutes

Serves: 6-8 (or 3-4 meals for 2)
Serving size: 1/2-3/4 cup per person

This is an adaptation of a classic Hungarian dish, fried cabbage. (It tastes even better the second day so make extras.) We enjoy serving this dish over our morning porridge with a seed condiment and roasted dulse, or serving it with soup or stew and rice or noodles for lunch. Leftovers can also be stuffed in pita pockets or rolled in tortillas with other leftovers or transformed into an almost instant cabbage soup. (See index for Soups From Leftovers.)

2-3 tsp. corn oil **or** light or toasted sesame oil

1 medium or 1/2 large onion, minced finely or cut in thin crescents or half moons

8 packed cups hard cabbage (green or red), cut in thin strips or 1" cubes

1/8 tsp. sea salt

Optional, 1 tsp. ground paprika **and/or** 1/4 tsp. ground black pepper **or** 2 tsp. caraway or anise seeds **or** 2 Tbsp. poppy seeds

1/4 cup water

1-2 tsp. tamari, shoyu **or** umeboshi *or* apriboshi pickled plum vinegar

* **Note:** A stainless steel or carbon steel wok or cast iron skillet works best for this.

1. Heat a cast iron skillet or wok over medium-high heat. Add oil and allow to warm briefly.

2. Add onions with a few pinches of sea salt. Sauté and stir continuously for 4-5 minutes until onions soften and turn translucent around the edges. Add herbs or spices and stir. Add finely cut cabbage and remaining sea salt. Stir over medium heat until cabbage begins to soften and brown. Turn heat to high and add just enough water to barely cover the bottom of the pot. Cover and bring to boil then reduce heat to medium-low and cook 5 minutes.

3. Add tamari, shoyu, umeboshi or apriboshi vinegar, or omit these and use a total of 1/2 tsp. sea salt in step #1. (Cook for a slightly shorter time in the spring leaving the vegetables a bit crisp; cook a bit longer in the fall and winter.) Remove lid and stir. All or most of the liquid should be absorbed.

4. Transfer cabbage and any remaining cooking juices to a serving bowl and cover with a bamboo mat. Do not put a lid on the cabbage or leave it in the cooking pot or it will overcook.

Serving suggestions: See notes above.

Storage: Store at room temperature covered with a bamboo mat or refrigerate. Use within 24 hours. Serve leftovers at room temperature.

Variations:

• Try half purple cabbage, half green cabbage. Or, use half cabbage, half kale or collard greens (stems cut finely and added with onions).

• Use red onion in place of white onion, or add 2-3 cups of mung bean sprouts on top of cabbage in step #2. Cook as above. ❏

Basic Procedure, Stir Fried Vegetables (Year Round)***

Prep: 10-15 minutes
Cooking: 8-12 minutes
Serves: 4-8 (or 2-4 meals for 2)
Serving size: 1/2-3/4 cup per person

Stir frying is similar to the French sauté method. Vegetables are cooked quickly, in a small amount of oil, with high heat and continuous stirring. The combination of oil, heat, and salty seasonings creates a rich and strengthening dish suitable for frequent use throughout the year. (We use far less oil than is commonly used with no loss of flavor or enjoyment. Cooking time will be a bit longer when using less oil.)

You can use this technique with whatever vegetables are in season. Use cabbage or dark green leafies as the base, then add other colorful root, round, ground, and vine vegetables as desired. The trick is to wash and cut all of the vegetables and arrange them in small bowls, according to kind, before you start cooking. Cook the hard and hardiest vegetables first. You won't need to use a measuring cup after the first time if you use the same bowls each time and have measured and memorized how much each hold. Just count up the total volume.

We always make stir fry to last for two or three meals. Leftovers are often richer and sweeter the second day and are great for breakfast (on top of hot cereal with a seed condiment) or with soup and whole grain, pasta, or bread for lunch, or dinner.

Note: Leafy green vegetables will usually reduce to one-half to one-fourth their original size, so be sure to cut enough. The recipe below may be halved if needed.

Rule of Thumb:

2-6 tsp. light or toasted sesame oil **or** olive

Optional, 1-3 cloves minced garlic

Optional, 1 tsp. finely minced ginger root

10-12 packed cups cut seasonal vegetables

1/8-1/4 tsp. sea salt

2-3 tsp. tamari or shoyu **or** 1/4-1/2 tsp. sea salt

1/4-1/2 cup water, pasta water, or soup stock

Base (largest volume): 1-3 types of greens, cut in thin strips or 1-2" squares or shredded

(red or green cabbage, kale, collard or mustard greens, Chinese greens, bok choy, cauliflower, broccoli, turnip tops, asparagus, etc.)

Additional vegetables: 1-4 varieties cut in thin rounds, slivers, matchsticks, or half moons—preferably including onions, scallions, spring onions, or leeks

(onions, scallions, or leeks, carrot, rutabaga, daikon, red radish or Jerusalem artichoke, mushrooms, pea pods, celery, green beans, zucchini, red, yellow, or green bell pepper, bean sprouts, etc.)

1. Wash and drain vegetables to remove sand. Cut finely and arrange by kind in separate bowls. (Hardy greens such as kale, collard, or mustard greens are best parboiled, whole (uncut) for 6-8 minutes before cutting and adding to a stir fry. (If parboiled, the greens will shrink to one-third to one-fourth their original size, so you will need a smaller volume of parboiled greens than if raw vegetables are used.)

2. Heat oil in a wok or cast iron skillet. Add onions, scallions, or leeks first, then ginger and/or garlic. Stir fry 1-2 minutes over medium-high heat. Add sea salt to draw out additional moisture. Add each vegetable one kind at a time, adding the longest cooking vegetables first (or add vegetables in the order listed in each recipe). Stir 1-2 minutes before adding the next kind of vegetable, then the next. Continue to stir, raise heat and add leafy greens or watery, quick cooking, light vegetables. (The exception: add mushrooms and stems from greens right after the onions, leeks, or scallions.)

3. Dissolve tamari or shoyu in above volume of water and add to wok. If using very watery vegetables (bok choy, nappa, tot soy, and/or lettuce), omit the extra water. Stir and toss over medium heat until tender. Or, cover pan and steam 4-5 minutes or until crisp-tender.

4. Immediately transfer vegetables and juices to a serving bowl and cover with a bamboo mat. They will stay warm for almost half an hour.

Serving suggestions: Serve warm or close to room temperature with whole grain, pasta or bread and condiments, with or without soup or stew.

Storage: Store at room temperature, covered with a bamboo mat and use within 12 hours or cover and refrigerate. Remove meal-size portions from refrigerator 30-90 minutes before serving or warm in a covered-bowl-on-a-rack for 3-5 minutes before serving.

Variations:

• **Stir Fried Vegetables with Glaze:** Dissolve 2 tsp. arrowroot powder or kuzu root in 1/2 cup cold water + 1 Tbsp. tamari or shoyu. Set aside. Prepare vegetables as above in steps #1 and #2. After stir frying briefly, add 1/3 cup water to the wok or skillet, cover and steam briefly. Heat the sauce in a small saucepan and stir to thicken. Pour over nearly tender vegetables then stir to coat. Turn off heat and transfer vegetables to a serving dish. Serve as above. ❏

Stir Fried Vegetable Medley #1 (Year Round)

Prep: 10-12 minutes
Cooking: 5-10 minutes
Serves: 6-8 (or 3-4 meals for 2)
Serving size: 1/2-3/4 cup per person

1 Tbsp. toasted or light sesame or olive oil

Optional, 2 coin-sized slices ginger, minced finely

2 cloves garlic, minced finely

1-1 1/2 cups onions or leeks, cut in thin half moons or crescents **or** 1-2" scallion logs

1/8 tsp. sea salt

1 cup carrots, cut in thin diagonal half-moons

1 cup daikon or turnip, cut in thin quarter-moons or oblongs, or sunchokes cut in quarter-sized rounds

2 cups mung bean sprouts

5-6 cups cabbage, bok choy, or Chinese greens, leaves cut in 1-2" squares or thin strips, core minced

Sauce:

1/2 cup water or pasta water

1-1 1/2 Tbsp. tamari or shoyu or umeboshi or apriboshi vinegar **or** 1/4-1/2 tsp. sea salt

1. Stir fry as per Basic Procedure above.

Variations:

• **Use other types of vegetables:** collards, kale, or asparagus for the base; thin slices of rutabaga, turnip, or jerusalem artichoke cut in rounds or pea pods; and/or mushrooms in above recipe. ❏

Stir Fried Asparagus Medley (Late Spring & Early Summer)

Prep: 10 minutes
Cooking: 5-10 minutes

Serves: 6-8 (or 3-4 meals for 2)
Serving size: 1/2-3/4 cup per person

2-3 tsp. olive or toasted or light sesame oil

2-3 cloves minced garlic

1 tsp. finely grated or minced ginger root

1 medium onion, cut in thin crescents **or** 1 cup scallions cut in 2" long pieces

1/8 tsp. sea salt

1 large, fresh shiitake mushroom **or** 2 dried shiitake, cut thin (if using dried mushrooms, soak then chop and use the soak water in the sauce below)

1 carrot, cut in thin matchsticks

1 bunch asparagus, cut in diagonal 1-2" pieces (tough parts of stems discarded)

Optional, 1 cup mung bean sprouts

Sauce:

1/3 cup water
1/2-1 Tbsp. tamari or shoyu

1. Stir fry as per Basic Procedure above. ❏

Stir Fried Chinese Vegetables with Sauce (Any Season)

Prep: 10 minutes
Cooking: 5-12 minutes

Serves: 4-8 (or 2-4 meals for 2)
Serving size: 1/2-3/4 cup per person

1/2-1 Tbsp. sesame, pumpkin **or** sunflower oil

2 cloves garlic, minced

1 medium onion, cut in thin crescents or half-moons **or** 4-5 scallions cut in 1" logs

1 cup button or crimini mushrooms, cut finely- **or** 2-3 fresh or soaked, dried shiitake

1 stalk celery, cut finely

1 carrot, cut in thin, diagonal half-moons

1/2 bunch Chinese broccoli or collard greens, cut in 1" squares (~4 cups)

2 cups hard green or red cabbage, in 1" squares

2 cups mung bean sprouts or pea pods

1/2 cup water

1/4 tsp. sea salt

Optional, 1/8-1/4 tsp. ancho, Anaheim, or chipotle red pepper, powder

Glaze:

1-1 1/2 Tbsp. tamari or shoyu

1/4 cup water

2 tsp. arrowroot

1. Stir fry as per Basic Procedure, adding vegetables one kind at a time in the order listed. When all vegetables have been added, turn to high heat, add 1/2 cup water, cover, and steam 7 minutes.

2. In a separate pan, dissolve arrowroot in cold water or soup stock with tamari or shoyu. Heat and stir until thick.

3. Pour sauce over vegetables, stir to coat and remove from heat. Transfer to a serving bowl and cover with a bamboo mat.

Serving Suggestion: Serve with whole grain, soup, and condiments. Add a bean, tofu, wheat meat, or tempeh dish if desired. ❑

Favorite Stir Fry Combinations
Use Onions, scallions or leeks and...

- celery + cabbage or bok choy
- red radish +/- celery + romaine lettuce or Mesclun greens
- sunchokes + cabbage or broccoli
- carrots + daikon radish or turnip + cabbage or dark green leafy vegetables + bean sprouts
- +/- mushroom + carrot + sunchoke + kale or collards + cabbage + bean sprouts
- mushrooms + carrots, turnips or red radish + cabbage or greens +/- pea pods
- shiitake mushroom + carrot + radish + celery + red cabbage or collards
- mushrooms + rutabaga + sunchokes + asparagus + cabbage
- carrot or rutabaga + cabbage + broccoli or cauliflower +/- bean sprouts
- carrot and/or turnip or red radish + kale or collards + savory or purple cabbage
- carrot or red radish + cauliflower + green beans or pea pods
- mushrooms + celery + red bell pepper or carrot + broccoli, kale, or cauliflower
- **See also Stir Fry with Tempeh, Tofu, or Wheat Meat. ❑**

Basic Procedure, Boiled Salads
(Year Round) ***

Prep: 20 minutes
Cooking: 10-15 minutes total, depending upon volume
Serving: size: 1/2-3/4 cup per person

This method of salad making, "Ohitashi" in Japanese, uses minimal cooking to produce maximum flavor and vibrant color. By cooking each type of vegetable separately, the unique tastes and colors of each are maintained.

You will need a 3-4 quart pot, (or a 2-quart pot for half a recipe), a stainless steel colander, a large slotted spoon or skimmer, and several platters or bowls. Before you start cooking, each type of vegetable should be washed, cut in thin pieces, and placed in a separate bowl. Each will be cooked separately (in the same water), but all of them will be combined before serving. Leftover cooking water can be saved to use as a soup extender or stock. Boiled salads may be enjoyed year round, particularly in cooler weather when raw salads are not appropriate.

We suggest a combination of 3-6 different types of vegetables for a colorful presentation. Some of our favorite vegetables to use are:

- Onions, scallions, or leeks, cut in thin crescents, rings, or half moons or 1/2-1" lengths

- Carrot, rutabaga, daikon, red radish, cut thin rounds, matchsticks, or quarter or half moons

- Fresh sweet corn, cut off cob

- Cabbage, kale, collard or mustard greens, cut in paper thin strips or squares

- Bok choy, tot soy, choy sum or other Chinese greens, cut in paper thin strips or squares

- Cauliflower and/or broccoli, cut in florets, stems peeled, cores cut into small pieces

- Jerusalem artichoke, scrubbed well, cut into 1/4" thick rounds or half-moon slices

- Green beans, pea pods, or snap beans, cut in 1" lengths

- Zucchini or summer squash, cut in 1/8-1/4" rounds, half or quarter moons

- Asparagus, cut into 1" lengths

- Red leaf or romaine lettuce, arugula, or other salad greens, (leaves cooked whole)

- Celery, minced or cut in thin diagonal slices

Rule of thumb: 10-12 cups cut, raw vegetables + 1 1/2 quarts water + 1/2 tsp. sea salt yields 4-5 cups cooked vegetables (to serve 4-8 or 2-4 meals for 2)

1. Bring salted water to boil in a large pot. Cook vegetables one kind at a time with the mildest tasting vegetables first, so that each retains its distinct flavor. Cook purple cabbage, red radish or vegetables that bleed last. Cook greens in 2-3 batches if needed,

2. Drop the first batch of vegetables into rapidly boiling water (2-4 cups of vegetables at a time). Cook *without a lid* for 1/2-2 minutes, until barely tender but still crisp.

3. Remove immediately with a large slotted spoon or skimmer basket and transfer to a strainer or colander. Run under cold water to stop the cooking and allow to drain. Wring out if necessary. (Cook lettuce leaves whole—dip into boiling water remove immediately, and cut after rinsing and draining.)

4. Allow the water to return to a boil then repeat above procedure with another kind of vegetable. Repeat until all the vegetables are cooked rinsed and drained. Arrange vegetables attractively on a platter or in a bowl. Drain again to remove excess water.

5. Toss the entire salad with a light marinade or dressing (see easy as 1-2-3 Dressing) or with sauerkraut or some other minced vegetable pickles. Or toss with a dash of umeboshi and/or brown rice vinegar. Or, let each diner add a low-fat or oil-free dressing, a drizzle of seasoned oil, or toasted seeds at the table. Or serve the salad plain to complement richer or more highly seasoned dishes in the meal.

Serving suggestions: Serve with whole grain, pasta, or bread, soup, stew, or a bean, tofu, tempeh or wheat meat dish and condiments as desired.

Storage: Store at room temperature 4-12 hours, covered with a bamboo mat. Refrigerate leftovers that will not be served in this time. Do not reheat before serving; remove from the refrigerator and allow to come to room temperature 1/2-1 hour before serving. ❏

Boiled Salad #1 (Summer & Fall)***

Prep: 15-20 minutes
Cooking: 10-15 minutes depending upon volume

Serves: 6-8 (or 3-4 meals for 2)
Serving size: 1/2-3/4 cup per person

1-1 1/2 quarts water + 1/2 tsp. sea salt

1/2 medium bunch kale, collard greens **or** 1/4 head cabbage cut finely (about 6 cups)

1/2-1 medium red or white onion cut in thin crescents or half-moons

1-2 carrots cut in thin rounds, quarter or half-moons, diagonals, or matchsticks

1/4 small head cauliflower, cut in florets, core mined finely, or additional greens

Optional, 2-3 handfuls green beans or snap peas cut in 1" slices

4 red radishes **or** 3" piece daikon radish, cut in thin rounds or half-moons

1. Cook as per Basic Boiled Salad Procedure above. ❏

Boiled Salad #2 (Any Season)***

Prep: 15-20 minutes
Cooking: 10-15 minutes

Serves: 6-8 depending on volume (or 3-4 meals for 2)
Serving size: 1/2-3/4 cup per person

1 1/2 quarts water + 1/2 tsp. sea salt

1 onion, cut in thin rings or half moons
    or 1 cup scallions cut in 1/2-inch lengths

1 bunch bok choy, tot soy, or Chinese mustard greens, cut finely (7-8 cups)

1 cup daikon radish or red radish, cut in thin quarter moon slices

1 rutabaga, carrot, or zucchini (depending upon season), cut in matchsticks or thin rounds

1. Cook as per Basic Boiled Salad Procedure. ❏

Boiled Salad #3 (Fall & Winter)

Prep: 15-20 minutes
Cooking: 10-15 minutes

Serving size: 1/2-3/4 cup per person
Serves: 5-7 (or 3 meals for 2) depending upon volume

1 1/2 quarts water + 1/2 tsp. sea salt

1/2-1 cup onions or leeks, cut in thin slivers **or** scallions (with green part), cut in 1" logs

1-1 1/2 cups rutabaga or carrot, cut in matchstick pieces

1 cup Brussel sprouts cut in thin rounds, or dark green leafy vegetables, cut finely

4 cups green cabbage, cut in thin strips

2 cups purple cabbage, cut finely

1. Cook as per Basic Boiled Salad Procedure. ❏

Other favorite boiled salad combinations:

- Kale or collards + green or red cabbage + carrot or rutabaga + onion, scallions, or leeks

- Kale, collards, cabbage or bok choy + onions + sunchokes +/- carrots +/- mushrooms

- Chinese greens + onion, scallions or leeks + red radish

- Broccoli + romaine, escarole, endive, or oak leaf lettuce + scallions or onions + carrot

- Romaine or red leaf lettuce + red radish slices + scallions

- Greens + cauliflower + onions, scallions, or leeks + carrot

- Cauliflower or broccoli + carrots or rutabaga + onions, scallions, or leeks + purple cabbage

- Broccoli + cauliflower + onions or scallions + sweet corn

- Cabbage + onions, scallions or leeks + yellow summer squash + carrots + snap peas

- Onions or leeks + broccoli and/or cauliflower + sweet corn + red radish + carrot

- Cauliflower + onions + green peas + daikon

- Dark greens + red and/or yellow bell pepper + onions + carrots +/- red radish+/- cauliflower ❏

Basic Procedure, Pressed & Marinated Salad (Year Round)***

Prep: 15-20 minutes
Pressing: 6-24 hours for hardy cabbage-based salads
Marinating: 1/2 hour -8 hours with tender greens
Serving size: 1/2-3/4 cup per person

Although the idea of a pressed salad may sound strange to Americans, they have been long-time staples in many parts of Europe and Asia. Not only are these salads tasty, but they also have several advantages over tossed salads.

Pressed salads are made from more hearty and densely nutritious vegetables than are most tossed salads. Examples include various American and Chinese cabbages, wild salad greens such as Mesclun blends and/or dark green lettuce with onions, scallions or leeks, and carrot, radish, celery, and/or cucumber, or lettuce mixed with arugula, endive, radiccio, dandelion, mustard greens, or edible flowers.

By pressing or marinating we concentrate the nutrients contained in the vegetables by tenderizing and reducing them in size. Thus, you get more nutrients per bite and need eat only a small portion. Moreover, pressed and marinated salads are incredibly convenient. These salads won't become tasteless after a day or two the way tossed lettuce salads do; instead they improve with age. Sunday night's pressed salad won't taste "old" and empty in Tuesday, Wednesday, or Thursday's lunch.

We make these salads year round even in the winter with whatever is in season. Marinated salads made from tender greens keep for 2-3 days. Pressed salads made primarily from cabbage will keep for up to a week. Having salads on hand will greatly simplify meal preparations. They are particularly handy for pack lunches or traveling and keep well in a lunch box, quart jars in an ice chest, or a covered bowl or jar in the refrigerator.

These salads offer the crispy, crunchy texture of raw vegetables with the ease of digestion that comes with cooked vegetables. (Actually they fall somewhere in between cooked and raw vegetables.) They also add beneficial digestive-enhancing flora and B-12 due to fermentation.

Finally, and perhaps most importantly, with today's emphasis on low fat meals, pressed and marinated salads need no added dressing. They make their own dressing as they marinate in their own juices. An undressed pressed salad is just the thing to serve on the side of an otherwise rich meal, to keep the fat-low and the flavor high. For lighter meals, individual servings of pressed or marinated salads can be sprinkled with a half teaspoon of toasted sesame, walnut, olive, or herb infused oil or a couple of teaspoons of unsalted, roasted pumpkin or sunflower seeds.

It is a good idea to serve pickles and/or pressed or marinated salads daily; they add a crisp taste and fresh energy to the diet. Pressed or marinated salads can be served instead of cooked leafy greens in a meal, or alongside a cooked green or mixed vegetable side dish. (Pickles, however, are served with a cooked greens dish, never instead of greens. We omit pickles from a meal if a pressed or marinated salad will be served.)

Pressed or marinated, what's the difference?

For either salad the vegetables should be cut very finely, shredded, torn, or grated, then crushed and kneaded with a salty seasoning. The addition of herbs and/or spices adds interest as well as a variety of trace minerals that help us to produce enzymes for digestion and metabolism.

A pressed salad is crushed then pressed into the bottom of a bowl, or ceramic crock and covered with a plate and topped with a heavy weight or contained in a plastic pickle press with a screw down press lid. These salads are pressed several hours, all day, overnight, or up to 24 hours before serving. Pressed salads usually contain cabbage and other hardy, difficult to digest vegetables.

Note: It is a little known fact that cabbage family vegetables contain sulfur-type substances which, when taken raw—uncooked, unpickled, or unpressed—have been shown to inhibit the functioning of the thyroid gland, thereby decreasing metabolism and lowering one's metabolic rate. Thus, proper preparation of these vegetables is essential for your health.)

Marinated salads are made in the same fashion as pressed salads but pressed for a shorter duration or with little or no weight. Dark green types of lettuce, escarole, endive, dandelion, radiccio, other tender salad greens, and/or Mesclun greens (a mix of 10, 15, or 20 wild salad greens) are typically used in combination as the base.

Note: Salty seasonings called for in these recipes—sea salt, shoyu, tamari, umeboshi or apriboshi vinegar or paste—are crucial. They break down the vegetable's outer cell wall and draw out excess water, thereby concentrating the nutrients and making the vegetables more digestible and flavorful. The salads will not turn out without the salty seasonings. Store the salads in their brine: this acts as a natural preservative. Listed below are the basic proportions, a detailed procedure, and several variations.

Basic Rules of Thumb: *12-14 cups tightly packed, finely cut and/or grated vegetables yields 6-7 cups pressed salad and serves 8-10 (or 4-5 meals for 2) 1/2-3/4 cup per person*

Salty Seasoning per every 4-5 cups tightly packed, cut and/or grated vegetables: *add 1 Tbsp. tamari, shoyu, or umeboshi or apriboshi vinegar or 3/4 tsp. sun dried sea salt*

Herbs or Spices per 4-5 cups packed, cut or grated vegetables: Add -1-2 pinches spice *(mild red chili pepper powder, chipotle, ancho, or Anaheim)* **or** 1/2-1 tsp. dried herbs (dill weed, basil, oregano, thyme, mustard powder, etc.) **or** 2 Tbsp. fresh minced herbs **and/or** 1 clove garlic

Vegetables

Base: 9-10 cups leafy salad greens or cabbages; one or several varieties

(nappa, savoy, Chinese or hard cabbage, bok choy, tot soy, romaine; red leaf lettuce, Mesclun greens and/or a small portion of purple cabbage, turnip greens* and/or mustard greens*, arugula* or endive*)

Note: If using hot or strong greens such as arugula, endive, turnip or mustard greens, or radiccio, combine them with a much larger volume of mild greens such as lettuce or cabbage.

Additional vegetables:

2-5 cups (1-4 different varieties) finely cut or grated (onions, leeks, or scallions, red, green, or yellow bell peppers, carrots, cucumber, red radish or daikon, parsley, rutabaga, celery, red cabbage, or other seasonal vegetables)

1. Roll up your sleeves. Wash vegetables thoroughly to remove sand. Scrub root and round vegetables with a vegetable scrub brush but do not peel. Shake off excess water. Spin dry lettuce or pat dry with a kitchen towel.

2. Finely mince, shred or chop cabbage and/or greens. Hard cabbage may be grated with a special cabbage-grater (a wooden box with a sliding top and stainless steel blade). Cut softer Chinese cabbage in to 1-2 inch squares. Grate root or round vegetables or cut in thin matchsticks. Mince onions or cut into crescents or half moons. Cut leeks into rounds, scallions with tops in 1-inch lengths, celery or bell peppers in thin slivers, and cucumbers or radishes in thin rounds or half-moons. Tear or cut greens or lettuce into bite-sized pieces, mince cabbage cores.

3. Measure vegetables by packing batches into a 32-ounce (4-cup) measuring cup as you chop or grate. Be fairly exact so that you know how much salty seasoning and/or vinegar to add.

4. Combine vegetables in a large stainless steel mixing bowl. Add salty seasoning. Add vinegar if desired. Knead vigorously, crushing the vegetables between your hands or pound with a suricogi (wooden pestle) in a suribachi, until wilted, watery, and reduced in size by about one-half, about 8-12 minutes or less if you will be using a plastic salad or pickle press. (With a plastic salad/pickle press, knead vegetables just until they begin to soften and shrink.) Add herbs or spices after crushing and kneeding.

5. **Using a pickle press or salad press:** Press vegetables into the bottom of the container a and screw the top down tightly. (Look for one in an Asian market or our mail order section.) After 2-3 hours, tighten the lid to maintain pressure on the shrinking vegetables. If possible, check several times during pressing and screwing the lid down more as needed.

Creating a homemade press: Press vegetables into the bottom of a ceramic crock or a 3 to 4 quart bowl. Cover with a small saucer which fits inside the rim of the bowl and allows 1/2-inch clearance between the edge of the plate and the sides of the bowl. The plate should press directly on the vegetables, covering most of them while allowing room for the plate to be pressed down as the vegetables shrink. Push down on the plate briefly to compact the vegetables. Put a heavy jug of water or some other weight on top of the plate.

For either method: Brine should rise up over the vegetables within 1-2 hours. If not, the vegetables should be crushed and mixed more thoroughly or a heavier weight must be applied. Press for 4-6 hours, overnight or up to 24 hours at room temperature. Lengthier pressing makes hearty cabbage salads more digestible, particularly in colder months. Press lettuce or tender greens for 1-6 hours or simply allow to marinate at room temperature or in the refrigerator without a weight.

6. Drain meal-size portions of salad before serving or tossing with oil or seeds.

Storage: After pressing for desired amount of time, remove the weight or lid and transfer salad and brine to a wide-mouth glass jar or a glass bowl covered with a plate. Refrigerate. Flavors will improve as the salad sits 12-24. The salad will still be good even if it smells a bit sour. Use lettuce-based salads within 2-4 days. Use cabbage and hard leafy green based salads within 3-6 days. (They will start to turn into a pickle if left to sit longer, though they won't last as long as pickles unless a good deal more salt is added.) Extend small portions by mixing with leftover steamed, stir fried, or parboiled vegetables.

Serving suggestions: Serve 1/2-3/4 cup salad per person at a meal with bread, pasta, or whole grain, plus a cup of soup, stew, or a hearty vegetable and/or bean side dish, and condiments. (You may wish to serve pressed or marinated salad *and* cooked greens in the same meal. In this case, serve smaller portions of each.) No dressing is needed. If desired and if the rest of the meal is oil-free or low-in fat, drizzle 1 tsp. flax, sesame, or olive oil over individual portions of salad or serve salads plain and eat them with other richer side dishes. Or toss salad in a large bowl with roasted seeds (1 Tbsp. seeds per 11/2-2 cups salad).

Digestion suggestion: If you suffer from poor digestion be sure to make your salad with herbs or spices (Don't use so much spice that it burns your mouth, however.) If your digestion is particularly weak, steam meal-sized salads in ramekins or custard cups on a steamer tray or rack for 3-8 minutes. Remove, add a 1/2-1 tsp. toasted sesame oil or flax oil for a wonderful, warm, digestible slaw!

Note: Sample salads below start with 12-14 cups packed, raw vegetables, yield 6-8 cups pressed salad, and serve 6-8 (or 3-5 meals for 2). ❑

Pressed Salad #1 (Fall, Winter, Spring, Summer)

Vegetables:

10-11 packed cups napa, savoy, Chinese, or hard green cabbage, shredded or finely minced (Napa cabbage may be cut in 1" squares)

1 1/2 packed cups carrots, grated on the smallest setting or cut in paper-thin matchsticks

1/2-1 packed cup onion or leek, minced or cut in thin rounds *or* scallions cut in 1" sticks

Optional, 1/2 cup packed celery, daikon, red cabbage, or red radish, cut paper thin

Salty seasoning:

2 1/2 tsp. sea salt *or* 1 tsp. sea salt + 1 1/2-2 Tbsp. umeboshi or apriboshi vinegar *or* 1 Tbsp. umeboshi vinegar + 2 Tbsp. tamari or shoyu

Herbs & spice:

Optional, 2-3 cloves garlic, minced + 1/8 tsp. mild red pepper powder *or* 2-3 tsp. dried dill *or* 3-8 Tbsp. fresh dill

Optional garnish: fresh sprouts such as alfalfa, cabbage, clover, onion, radish, or sunflower

1. Prepare as per Basic Pressed Salad above, pressing for 6-24 hours. ❑

Pressed Salad #2 (Summer, Fall)

Vegetables:

9-10 cup tightly packed, shredded or finely cut cabbage combined with mixed hardy leafy greens—mustard greens, arugula, bok choy, tot soy, choy sum, endive, or romaine

6 scallions **or** 1 cup Walla Walla Sweet or Vadalia onions, cut finely or minced

2 cups kirby or other pickling cucumbers, cut in thin quarter-moons or half-rounds

Optional, 1 red bell pepper, minced finely (seeds removed and discarded)

Optional, 1/2 cup minced celery **and/or** 1 cup very finely grated carrot or red cabbage

Salty seasoning:

2 Tbsp. tamari soy sauce + 1 Tbsp. umeboshi or apriboshi vinegar
   or 3-4 Tbsp. umeboshi vinegar
   or 3 Tbsp. tamari **or** 2-2 1/2 tsp. sea salt
   +/- 2 Tbsp. brown rice vinegar

Herbs and spice:

2 cloves garlic, minced finely

Optional, 1 Tbsp. dried dill weed **or** 2-8 Tbsp. fresh dill, minced (Great with ume or apriboshi)

1. Prepare as per Basic Procedure. Pressed or Marinated Salad. Press or marinate for 4-8 hours before serving. ❏

Pressed Salad #3 (Spring, Summer, Fall)

Vegetables:

7-8 cups packed hard green or nappa or savoy cabbage, shredded or cut in 1" squares

1-2 cups packed arugula, mustard greens, turnip tops, endive, or other pungent greens

2 cups packed carrots or purple cabbage, or a bit of both, grated on very small setting

3 small pickling cucumbers, cut in thin quarter-moon slices **or** 1/2 large cucumber

6-8 small red radishes **or** 4" piece daikon radish, cut in thin rounds or grated

1-2 handfuls parsley or chives washed (well) and minced finely

Salty seasoning:

2-2 1/2 tsp. sea salt
   or 1 tsp. sea salt + 1-1 1/2 Tbsp. umeboshi or apriboshi vinegar
   or 3 Tbsp. tamari or shoyu +/- 2 Tbsp. brown rice vinegar
   or 3 Tbsp. umeboshi or apriboshi vinegar
   or 3-4 tsp. umeboshi or apriboshi paste

Herbs & spice:

Optional, 2 cloves garlic minced

2-3 tsp. dried dill weed **or** 1-3 Tbsp. fresh dill weed (good with umeboshi or apriboshi)
   or basil + oregano or 1/4 tsp. chipotle, ancho **or** Anaheim chili pepper powder

1. Prepare as per Basic Pressed or Marinated Salad above. Press for 4-8 hours or marinate for 1-6 hours without a weight. ❏

Marinated Salad #1 (Summer, Fall)

Vegetables:

9-10 cups packed romaine, red leaf or oak leaf lettuce, shredded or finely minced

3 cups packed arugula, mustard greens, turnip tops, endive, Meslcun greens, or other

1 1/2 packed cups carrots or purple cabbage, or a bit of both, grated on the smallest setting

1 1/2 cups small pickling cucumbers or red radish, cut in thin quarter-moon slices

Optional, 1/2 cup scallions, leeks, or Walla Walla or Vadalia onions, cut finely

1-2 handfuls parsley or chives washed and minced finely

2 cloves minced garlic **+/-** 1/4 tsp. mild red pepper powder (*ancho, Anaheim or chipotle)*

Salty Seasoning:

2 tsp. sea salt **or** 1 tsp. sea salt + 1 Tbsp. umeboshi or apriboshi vinegar
or 3 Tbsp. tamari or shoyu +/- 2 Tbsp. apple cider vinegar or brown rice vinegar
or 3 Tbsp. umeboshi or apriboshi vinegar
or 3 tsp. ume or apriboshi paste

1. Prepare as per Basic Pressed or Marinated Salad above, with or without a weight. May be served within 8 hours. ❏

Marinated Salad #2 (Summer & Fall)

Experiment with different vegetables. Thin red radish or kirby cucumber slices also make a nice addition (in place of carrots). Make a big batch like this so you will have salad for several days served at one or two daily meals. Keep the sprouts separate and serve them on the side as a garnish, about 1/4 cup per person.

Vegetables:

10-12 cups packed Chinese cabbage or mixed Chinese greens, cut paper thin **or** a mixture of lettuce and Chinese greens such as bok choy, bok toy, or tot soy or Mesclun greens

2 cups spring onions or scallions, cut finely, stems and all

4 cups very finely grated carrot

Optional, 2 cloves minced garlic

1/8-1/4 tsp. ancho, Anaheim **or** chipotle red pepper powder **or** 1 Tbsp. dried **or** 3 Tbsp. fresh minced dill

Salty seasoning:

3 Tbsp. tamari or shoyu (**or** use umeboshi vinegar and omit rice vinegar)

3 Tbsp. brown rice vinegar

Garnish:

3-4 cups alfalfa, clover or sunflower sprouts, added before serving

1. Prepare as per Basic Pressed or Marinated Salad above, with or without a weight. ❏

Marinated Salad #3
(Mustard Green Salad)

1 cup pickling cucumbers, washed and cut in thin rounds

1 cup Spanish, Walla Walla Sweet, or Vadalia onions *or* 1 bunch scallions, cut in thin crescents

1 1/2 medium to large head romaine or oak leaf lettuce, washed and torn into tiny pieces

1 bunch Chinese or Mizuna mustard greens chopped finely, leaves & stems

Optional, 2 cloves minced garlic

Optional, 2-3 tsp. dried dill weed *or* 2-3 Tbsp. fresh, minced dill

Salty seasoning:

3 Tbsp. tamari or shoyu *or* 2 tsp. sea salt

3 Tbsp. rice vinegar *or* 1 1/2 Tbsp. apple cider vinegar

1. Prepare as for Basic pressed or Marinated Salad above. May be served within 2-6 hours. ❏

Marinated Salad #4
(Lettuce, Radish & Green Salad)

6 packed cups, washed, finely cut beet greens (left from making soup with the roots) or other summery greens

6 cups washed, packed, sliced or torn romaine or oak leaf lettuce

1-1 1/2 bunch red radishes, washed well and cut in thin rounds

Radish greens (tops) from 1-2 bunches, washed well and cut in thin strips

1 cup scallions (greens and white part), onion tops, or parsley, minced finely

Optional, 1 carrot grated very finely

1 Tbsp. dried dill weed *or* 1/4 tsp. mild red pepper powder
(*chipotle, Anaheim, or ancho*)

Optional, 2-3 cloves minced garlic

Salty seasoning:

1 1/2 tsp. sea salt
   or 1 1/2 Tbsp. umeboshi vinegar
   or 1 1/2 Tbsp. tamari + 2 tsp. apple cider vinegar or brown rice vinegar

1. Prepare as per Basic Pressed or Marinated Salad Procedure, above, pressing for 1-6 hours before serving. ❏

Pressed Salad with Broccoli & Mustard

Prep: 20 minutes
Cooking: 5 minutes for broccoli

Serves: 10-12 (or 5-6 meals for 2)
Serving size: 1/2-3/4 cup per person

Crushing vegetables with salt draws out tasty vegetable juices so that they produce their own non-fat dressing and are more digestible. Pressed salads are tasty served in their own juices, but in this recipe the vegetables are taken out of their juices and complemented with parboiled broccoli and a tangy mustard sauce. This is great for the holidays and potlucks. Vary the parboiled vegetables according to season.

6 tightly packed cups Chinese cabbage mixed
    fall salad greens, chopped finely

1 1/2 cups leeks, washed and chopped finely

2 cups celery, cut into thin slivers

1 cup carrots, grated

1 3/4 tsp. sea salt

3 cups broccoli florets

2 Tbsp. prepared natural mustard
    (stoneground or dijon)

1 Tbsp. brown rice vinegar

1. Mix the first five ingredients and knead as per Pressed Salad Procedure. Allow to sit for -8 hours or overnight with or without a weight. A weight helps tenderize the vegetables.

2. Before serving, parboil broccoli in lightly salted water until it turns bright green, about 3-5 minutes, then run under cold water to stop the cooking then drain.

3. Drain brine off wilted salad vegetables. Do not rinse. Toss salad with broccoli.

4. Mix prepared mustard with rice vinegar and toss with the pressed and cooked vegetables.

Serving suggestions: Serve with grain, soup or stew, and condiments. At Thanksgiving serve with Millet Mashed Potatoes, Gravy, Tempeh or Wheat Meat Cutlets, Stuffing and pumpkin or apple pie or chestnut pudding.

Storage: Refrigerate in a covered bowl. Use within 1-3 days. ❏

Basic Procedure, Glazed Vegetables (Any Season)***

Prep: 10 minutes
Cooking: 8-9 minutes

Serves: 4-6 (or 2-3 meals for 2)
Serving size: 1/2-2/3 cup per person

For a rich taste, without oil, try glazed. Simmering and glazing in a clear sauce transforms the simplest vegetables into a real taste treat.

Soup stock, pasta water, or pure water to just
    cover the bottom of the pot or wok

Optional, 2 cloves minced garlic

4 scallions, cut in 1-2" logs **or** 1 cup onion or
    leek, cut in thin half moons or rounds

4 cups chopped broccoli or cauliflower, cut in
    florets, tender part of stalk peeled, minced
    or 6 packed cups, cut cabbage, cauliflower
    collards or chinese greens, including stems

Sauce:

1/2-2/3 cup cold or room temperature water,
    soup stock, or pasta cooking water

1 1/2 tsp. arrowroot powder or kuzu

1-1 1/2 tsp. tamari, shoyu, **or** umeboshi or apri-
    boshi vinegar

1 Tbsp. natural prepared mustard **or** 1-2 tsp.
    dry, powdered yellow mustard

1. Cut flowering vegetables into florets; leafy greens into 1-2 inch squares, cabbage into strips, and onions in half moons or crescents. Peel broccoli stalks then cut into thin slices cut collard stems finely. Finely chop cabbage or cauliflower cores. (You may wish to cut some vegetables into large pieces and some into small or thin slices depending upon kind.)

2. Add water to just barely cover the bottom of a wide and shallow skillet or wok (about 1/2 inches of liquid.) Bring to boil, add scallions, leeks or onions first. Add a pinch of sea salt and the garlic. Stir until tender. Add any vegetable stems first then broccoli, cauliflower, or greens. Stir, cover, and simmer over medium heat until almost tender, about 2-3 minutes.

3. Meanwhile, in a separate saucepan combine sauce ingredients and stir to dissolve. Heat and stir to thicken.

4. Pour sauce over crisp-tender vegetables and stir until sauce thickens even more. Transfer immediately to a glass, stainless steel, wood or ceramic bowl. Cover with a bamboo mat. Do not leave vegetables in the pot or they will overcook and become soggy.

Serving suggestions: Serve with whole grain, pasta, or bread and soup and/or a bean, tofu, or tempeh dish, and/or a deep orange or yellow vegetable dish. These vegetables are also tasty served over hot morning cereal with seed condiment, sea vegetable, and a green garnish.

Storage: Refrigerate leftovers, then serve close to room temperature. Use within 24 hours.

Variations:

• Use above procedure and proportions for any seasonal vegetables. Try a combination of two or three colorful vegetables. Add the harder longer-cooking vegetables before the greens or other tender vegetables. When using carrots, celery, rutabaga, daikon or red radish, cut into matchsticks, thin slivers, rounds, or crescents.

• Omit mustard then add 1 tsp. dried herbs basil, oregano, or sage. to the sauce mixture.

• **Quick Soup:** Mix 1-1 1/4 cups of soup stock or water with 1-1 1/4 cups leftover glazed vegetables, with or without 2-3 Tbsp. sea vegetable condiment or crumbled, roasted sea vegetable. Simmer briefly then season with miso or tamari to taste. Garnish with minced parsley, scallions, chives or dill. Serve with whole grain, pasta, or bread, an orange vegetable side dish, and condiments. ❏

Root, Round, Ground & Vine Vegetables

Basic Procedure, Nishime Style Vegetables (Fall and Winter)***

Prep: 10-15 minutes
Cooking: 30-40 minutes
Serving size: 1/2-1 cup per person

Nishime, or waterless cooking, is a wonderful Japanese technique. Chunks of hearty root, round, and/or ground vegetables are layered in a pot with just enough water to barely cover the bottom of the pot then cooked at a low temperature for a long time to produce a tender, rich, sweet tasting dish. We always cook enough to last for two meals. Leftovers can be warmed briefly and served as is, or transformed into a succulent soup, stew, sauce, or pot pie filling.

Rule of thumb: 3/4-1 cup uncooked vegetables per person, per meal

Optional, 4-6" piece kelp or kombu (whole or scissor cut into 1" pieces) *or* 1-2 bay leaves

4-6 cups colorful root, round and/or ground vegetables, 1-5 varieties, cut in 1-2" cubes or roll cut in irregular wedges *(onions, carrots, parsnips, rutabaga, turnip, Jerusalem artichoke, sweet winter squash, daikon, sweet potato or burdock root)*

Water to just cover the bottom of the pot

1/8 tsp. sea salt

Optional, 1/4-2/3 tsp. powdered herbs or spices, less for some spices *(e.g. powdered cinnamon, nutmeg, ginger, allspice, anise, or sage)*

Optional, 1-2 tsp tamari or shoyu
   or reduce sea salt, omit tamari or shoyu, then add 2-3 tsp. light, yellow, mellow, or sweet miso dissolved in 1-2 Tbsp. water during the last few minutes of cooking)

Note: Use a pot with a heavy lid, preferably cast iron or enamel lined cast iron. A stainless steel pot with a tight fitting lid will also do.

1. Scrub vegetables with a vegetable scrub brush but do not peel. Cut into 2-inch chunks or roll cut in irregular wedges. (For cutting techniques, see index or chapter #1.)

2. With kitchen shears, cut kelp or kombu sea vegetable into 1-inch pieces or leave whole. Arrange it or bay leaf on the bottom of a pot. Top with cut onions if used, then add other root or round vegetables arranged in layers. (If burdock root is used, combine it with a larger volume of sweet vegetables.) Add salt, herbs or spice if desired, and water to just barely cover the bottom of the pot. (If miso will be used, dissolve this in 1-2 Tbsp. water and add during the last few minutes of cooking.) Do not stir this dish.

3. Cover the pot, bring to boil over medium heat, reduce heat to low and simmer, without stirring, 30-40 minutes or until tender and juicy.

4. Remove kelp or kombu, slice finely, then add back to the pot if it was not cut before cooking. Add tamari, shoyu, or light miso dissolved in water if desired. Remove the lid, stir gently, and cook away excess liquid. *Or,* to create a sauce, dissolve 1-2 tsp. arrowroot in a dash of cold water then add to the pot and stir to thicken.

5. Transfer to a serving bowl and cover loosely with a bamboo mat.

Serving suggestions: Serve warm or at room temperature with whole grain or porridge, cooked greens or salad; and condiments. A soup, beans, or wheat meat side dish may be added to the above items for lunch or supper.

Storage: Store leftovers in a cold box covered with a bamboo mat or refrigerate in a covered stainless steel, glass, or ceramic bowl.

Leftover tip: Reheat leftovers in covered-bowl-within-a-pot method or in an uncovered bowl atop a steamer tray, or simply remove from the refrigerator and allow to come to room temperature 30-90 minutes before serving. Or, turn leftovers into a soup or stew with added water or stock and/or leftover cooked beans, wheat meat, tempeh, gravy, or other dishes. Or use as a filling for Squash-wiches or pot pie. ❏

Nishime Carrots, Nishime Parsnips, or Nishime Carrots & Parsnips

Prep: 10-15 minutes
Cooking: 30-40 minutes
Serves: 4-6 (or 2-3 meals for 2)
Serving size: 1/2-3/4 cup per person

4- 6" piece kelp, or kombu sea vegetable

Optional, 1/2-1 medium onion, cut in 1" chunks

4-5 medium sized parsnips or carrots, roll cut into irregular wedges *(about 6 cups total)* *or* use half of each

1/8-1/4 tsp. sea salt
  or 1/8 tsp. sea salt + 2-3 tsp. sweet/white/yellow or mellow miso

1/2 tsp. cinnamon, nutmeg, allspice or pumpkin pie spice

Water to just cover bottom of pot

1. Prepare as per Basic Nishime Vegetables.

Example #2: Nishime Winter Medley

Prep: 10-15 minutes
Cooking: 30-40 minutes
Serves: 4-6 (or 2-3 meals for 2)
Serving size: 1/2-3/4 cup per person

4-6" piece kelp or kombu

1 small to medium onion, cut in 1" cubes or wedges

2-3 small Jerusalem artichokes, washed, cut in 1-2" wedges

1 small carrot, cut in irregular wedges

1 small parsnip or turnip cut in irregular wedges

1/2 cup burdock root, scrubbed, cut in 1/4-1/2" rounds or quarter-moons

1/4 tsp. sea salt *or* 1-1 1/2 tsp. tamari per 5-6 cups packed vegetables

Water to just cover the bottom of pot

1/2 tsp. dried, ground cumin, sage, rosemary or thyme

1. Prepare as per Basic Nishime Vegetable Procedure above.❏

Example #3: Nishime Squash, with Parsnips & Onions (Fall, Winter, Spring)

Prep: 10-15 minutes
Cooking: 30-40 minutes

Serves: 4-8 (or 2-3 meals for 2)
Serving size: 1/2-3/4 cup per person
4-6" piece kelp or kombu

1 onion, cut in 1" cubes or wedges

2 1/2 cups parsnips, roll cut into 2" chunks

3-4 cups winter squash
  (buttercup, kabocha, butternut, dumpling, or delicatta), cut in 2" cubes

1/2 cup water or as needed to cover bottom 1/3" of pot

1/4-1/3 tsp. sea salt **or** 1 Tbsp. white miso dissolved in 2 Tbsp. water

1/2-2/3 tsp. cinnamon or pumpkin pie spice

Sauce:

1-2 tsp. arrowroot **or** 1 tsp. kuzu dissolved in 1/4 cup cold water

1. Prepare as per Basic Nishime Vegetable Procedure above. When done, dissolve arrowroot (or arrowroot and light miso) in water. Add to the pot and stir gently to thicken.

Serving suggestions: Serve with whole grain, condiments, and pressed salad or sautéed greens; and pickles. Optional: a side of beans.

Variations:

- **Squash-Parsnip & Mochi Melt:** Before cooking the above dish, sprinkle 1 cup grated, uncooked mochi over the top of the vegetables. Use white miso instead of salt for a sweeter taste. Cook as above but do not use arrowroot or kuzu.

- **Daikon Rounds with Tamari (Any Season):**

- **Turnip, Onion, Carrot Nishime with Rosemary with Tamari (Any Season):** Use baby carrots with tiny turnips, and pearl onions in summer and fall.

- **Nishime Rutabaga, Onion, Turnip and Carrot with Thyme & Tamari (Fall, Winter, Spring).** ❏

Basic Procedure, Whole Baked Vegetables (Fall & Winter)***

Prep: 5-10 minutes
Cooking: 1-2 hours or 8-9 hours in a crock pot
Serving size: 1/2-1 cup per person

As hearty root, round and ground vegetables bake, their natural sugars carmelize giving them a rich, syrupy, and very sweet taste without added sugar or fat. Some hearty root, round and ground vegetables can be baked whole in uncovered pans, others are best stew cut or baked in a covered dish. Any can be cooked all day or overnight in a crock pot. Be sure to cook extra for the next day's breakfast, pack lunch, or dinner. If you opt for oven baking, fill the oven with a few loaves of bread, a casserole, baked beans, or a pie to maximize energy use and kitchen prep.

1. Wash and scrub squashes, yam/sweet potatoes, garlic bulbs, onions, or white potatoes, leaving the skins on. It is not necessary to poke fork holes in the tops of the vegetables. For vegetables which will be baked uncovered, you may lightly coat the skins with sunflower, safflower, walnut, or light sesame oil if desired. This will seal in moisture and produce a richer taste.

2. **To bake in the oven:** Arrange whole vegetables on a baking pan with sides (to catch the juices). Do not add water. Bake uncovered for 1-1 1/2 hours in a preheated 375-400° F. oven until tender and syrupy.

   To bake in a crock pot (year round): Arrange washed vegetables in a crock pot. Add 1/2 cup water to the pot (for 4-6 sweet potatoes, yams, or potatoes or 2-4 small winter squash). Cover and cook on high heat for 1 hour then reduce heat to low and cook 8-9 hours.

Serving suggestions: Serve plain, with whole grain or bread, a green or mixed vegetable side dish, and condiments. A bean or light vegetable soup is optional. If desired top vegetables with a sprinkle of chopped roasted nuts or seeds, Tofu Sour Cream, Tofu Ricotta, or a dash of soy yogurt mixed with miso and/or chives or parsley. (See also Squash-wiches, or Yam-wiches.)

Basic Baked Sweet Potatoes & Yams

Note: Red garnet and jewel "yams" are actually not true yams, but are sweet potatoes, contrary to popular advertising and store labeling!

Prep: under 5 minutes.
Cooking: 1 1/2-2 hours *or* 6-8 hours in a crock pot

Serves: 2-4 (or 1-2 meals for 2)
Serving size: 1/2-1 cup per person,
or 1/2-1 medium or 1 small sweet potato per person

Properly prepared, sweet potatoes and yams are chock full of flavor even with nothing on them. We like 'em for breakfast, lunch or supper with whole grain, hot cereal or bread, a seed or nut condiment and salad or cooked greens. They can satisfy a sweet tooth in the most natural and healthy way.

2 large (10-12 oz.) sized or 4 medium sized red garnet or jewel "yams" or white sweet potatoes

Optional, oil to coat skins before baking

Optional, 2 tsp. light, yellow or mellow miso (added after mashing, before serving)

1. Prepare as per Basic Procedure, Whole Baked Vegetables above. Bake 1 1/2-2 hours.

Serving suggestions: Serve with morning porridge, millet, rice, a mixed grain combination or bread with condiments and a side of pressed or marinated salad or cooked leafy greens. ❏

Basic Baked Potatoes

Prep: under 5 minutes.

Cooking: 1 1/2-2 hours or 8 hours in a crock pot

Serves: 2-4 (or 1-2 meals for 2)

Serving size: 1/2-1 cup per person

or 1/2-1 medium or 4 tiny potatoes per person

When baked for a long time, potatoes become very tender and sweet. Top them with a hint of soy yogurt or pesto, hummus, or Tofu Cream

Cheese, Tofu Ricotta and chives, thick pea soup, or Stroganoff. Leftover potatoes can also be peeled and puréed to make a creamy soup thickener, sliced for potato salad, mashed for use in breads, eaten out of your hand as a snack, or sliced and used to replace chips, with dip.

2 extra large or 4-5 medium sized baking potatoes *(russet, yukon gold, red, etc.)*
or 8-10 small to medium potatoes

1. Prepare as per Basic Procedure, Whole Baked Vegetables above. Bake large potatoes 2 hours at 400° F until tender; bake medium potatoes 1 1/2-2 hours; bake extra small potatoes for about 1 hour.

Serving suggestion: Serve with soup, stew, gravy, or a bean dish, plus cooked, pressed salad, condiments and bread or rice. ❏

Basic Baked Onions (Late Fall, Winter)

Prep: 10 minutes. or less
Cooking: 1 1/2 -2 hours

Serves: 4 (or 2 meals for 2)
Serving size: 1/2-1 cup per person

These onions take on an apple-like flavor when baked for a long time. You won't believe it until you try it! Leftovers can be turned into soup or stew with water or stock and light miso.

4 large white or 8 small white onions with skins left on
(preferably Walla Walla Sweets, Vadalia or other sweet variety)

1. Prepare as per Basic Procedure, Whole Baked Vegetables. Bake 1 1/2-2 hours (more for large onions, less for smaller ones.) Bake until tender and syrupy and a knife inserts easily.

Serving suggestion: Serve with a bean or orange vegetable soup, stew or side dish; greens or salad; and rice, millet, pasta, polenta, or buckwheat plus condiments. ❏

Baked Garlic (Fall, Winter, Spring)

Prep: under 10 minutes.
Cooking: 1-2 hours

Serves: 3-6 (or 2-3 meals for 2)
Serving size: 2-5 large cloves per person

Bake these when you've already got the oven fired up and nearly filled. Baked garlic becomes soft, sweet, and mild. You'll be amazed to find that you can eat three, four or even eight whole garlic cloves. The taste is very rich, almost like butter, and it makes a wonderful spread on bread or rice.

1-2 whole heads of elephant garlic, unpeeled

1. Bake 1-2 hours or until soft enough that garlic cloves can be squeezed from their skins.

2. Transfer to a small bowl. If desired, drizzle with a dash of olive oil. Squeeze cloves from skin and spread on bread or use to top rice, millet, or pasta, or purée with tofu, seasoned tempeh, or beans to make dips and patés. Refrigerate leftovers. ❏

Basic Procedure, Steamed Winter Squash (Year Round)***

Prep: under 10 minutes.
Cooking: 20-30 minutes
Serves: 4-6 (or 2-3 meals for 2, depending on size)
Serving size: 1/2-1 cup per person

You won't believe how sweet squash can be until you try this. (The sea salt makes a world of difference!) Steaming rather than baking cut squash greatly reduces the cooking time and is more appropriate for Spring and Summer. .

Note: *The skins are completely edible and loaded with vitamins and flavor. Give them a try. So many people throw them out without a taste! Just cut off any rough or bruised spots.*

1 small or 1/3-1/2 medium winter squash,
    about 1 1/2 lbs; 4-6 cups cut
    (*kabocha, buttercup, butternut , honey
    delight or sweet mama squash*) **or** 1-2 sweet
    dumpling **or** delicatta squash

1. Halve squash with a sturdy vegetable knife. Scoop the seeds and pulp out of only the part you plan to cook right away. (Leaving the seeds in the rest of the squash will help it keep without spoiling.)

2. Cut into melon like crescents, triangles, or 1-2 inch cubes for quick cooking in spring time. Arrange, skin side down, one layer deep on bamboo steam trays or a metal steamer basket.

3. Steam on a metal steamer basket in a 2-4 quart pot over 1-2 inches of water or on 1-2 large bamboo steamer trays over a wide pot or inside a wok, covered with a lid. Steam 20-30 minutes over steam or until tender. Check the water level during cooking and add more boiling water to pot if needed.

4. Immediately remove from the cooking pot to prevent over-cooking. Transfer to serving bowls and cover with a bamboo mat.

Serving suggestions: Serve warm or at room temperature with hot cereal, bread, or whole grain, greens, condiments and/or pickles.

Storage: Refrigerate leftovers in a covered bowl. Use within 1-3 days.❏

Basic Procedure, Casserole Baked Vegetables (Fall & Winter)***

Prep: 5-10 minutes
Cooking: 1 1/2-2 hours

Serves: 4-6 (or 2-3 meals for 2)
Serving size: 1/2-2/3 cup per person

Here's a nice wintery way to prepare hearty root and round vegetables. Baking stew cut chunks of vegetables in a covered dish brings out a rich sweet taste. While you're at it, whip up a few loaves of bread, and a casserole or pot of baked beans. It helps to maximize your time and the oven's energy. Instead of making a thick or rich soup to go with your meal, try a light miso or tamari broth, also serve a whole grain rice or sweet rice combination, greens, and a toasty nut or seed condiment. (Leftover vegetables make great soups, sauces, or stews when combined with water or stock and seasoned with miso.)

Rule of Thumb:

4-6 cups of cut hearty root, round and/or ground vegetables—

2-4 different varieties, preferably including onions and one or several of the following: *carrots, red garnet or jewel "yams" or white sweet potatoes, parsnips, jerusalem artichoke, rutabaga, turnip, burdock root, lotus root, etc.*

1/4 tsp. sea salt *or* 2 tsp. white, yellow, or mellow miso per 5-6 cups cut vegetables

Optional, 1 bay leaf *or* 4" strip kelp or kombu

1-2 whole cloves of garlic
  and/or 3 penny slices of fresh ginger root *or* 1/2 tsp. ground cinnamon, nutmeg, or allspice or dried herbs *(dill, basil, thyme, or other)*, depending upon the vegetables used

Boiling water to just cover the bottom of the dish by 1/4"

1. Preheat oven to 375-400° F. Cut vegetables into 1-1 1/2 inch chunks or rolling cuts. If desired, lightly oil the bottom of the e dish.

2. Put a bay leaf or a strip of seaweed on the bottom. Add 1-2 whole garlic cloves or penny-size slices of ginger root to the bottom of the casserole dish or sprinkle sweet spices or dried herbs over the top of the vegetables. Layer cut vegetables in the dish, beginning with onions, if using, according to kind.

3. Add sea salt and boiling water to just cover the bottom of the pan by 1/4 inch. Cover immediately and transfer to the middle or lower shelf in a preheated oven.)

4. Bake 1 1/2-2 hours (depending on size of pieces), until tender and juicy. Stir gently when done cooking.

Serving suggestions: See notes above.

Leftover tips:

- Refrigerate leftovers in a covered dish or jar. Serve at room temperature or heat in a bowl on a steamer basket or using the covered-bowl-within-a-pot method. Or turn leftovers into a spread, sauce; or soup (chunky or puréed) with stock or water and light miso to taste. (See index for leftover vegetable suggestions.) ❑

Basic Onion, Sweet Potato & Carrot Casserole (Fall, Winter)

Prep: 10 minutes
Cooking: 1 1/2-2 hours

Serves: 4-6 (or 2-3 meals for 2)
Serving size: 1/2-3/4 cup per person

Optional, 1 bay leaf or 4" piece kelp or kombu sea vegetable

1 medium onion, cubed

2 medium red garnet, jewel "yams" (sweet potatoes) *or* white sweet potatoes, cut in 1-2" cubes or wedges

2-3 carrots or parsnips, cut in 1-2" diagonal wedges

1/4 tsp. sea salt *or* 1-2 tsp. white, yellow, or mellow miso per 4-5 cups cut veggies

1/2 tsp. cinnamon, nutmeg, or anise powder

Water to just cover bottom of casserole dish

1. Prepare as per Basic Procedure, Casserole Baked Vegetables above. ❑

Basic Baked Onion, Carrots, & Sunchoke Casserole (Fall, Winter)

Prep: 10 minutes
Serves: 4–6 (or 2-3 meals for 2)

Cooking: 1 1/2-2 hours
Serving size: 1/2-3/4 cup per person

Optional, 1 bay leaf *or* 4" piece kelp or kombu sea vegetable (scissor cut seaweed into 1" pieces)

Optional, 2 cloves garlic whole or cut

1 medium onion, cubed

3 medium sized nobs of Jerusalem artichoke, cut in 1-2" cubes (about 3 cups)

2-3 medium carrots, cut in 1-2" diagonal wedges

1/4 tsp. sea salt per 4-5 cups cut veggies

Optional, 1/2 tsp. dried, powdered thyme, sage, or cumin

Water to just cover bottom of casserole dish

1. Prepare as per Basic Procedure, Casserole Baked Vegetables above.

Variations:

- Use just one vegetable in the above recipes— winter squash, parsnips, sweet potatoes, yams or carrots.

- **Mix two types of vegetables in the above recipes:** winter squash + onion; winter squash + carrots or tomatoes; parsnips + rutabaga; parsnips + carrot; or sunchokes with onions and dulse.

- **See Nishime Vegetables for more ideas.** ❏

Squash & Corn Dinner Pudding (Late Summer, Fall)

Prep: 10-15 minutes
Cooking: 45 minutes

Serves: 4-8 (or 2-4 meals for 2)
Serving size: 1/2-3/4 cup per person

This sweet dinner pudding is a fall weather favorite. Serving up sweet tasting vegetables on a daily basis can help to even out your energy level while at the same time satisfying your sweet tooth. Leftovers are fabulous on waffles, in Squash-wiches, or over morning cereal..

4 cups cubed winter squash, skins left on (*kabocha, buttercup, delicatta, sweet dumpling, or Hokkaido pumpkin*)

1/4 inch water to cover bottom of pot

1/8-1/4 tsp. sea salt

3-4 ears of corn (3-4 cups fresh corn off the cob)

2-3 Tbsp. water

Optional, 1 Tbsp. arrowroot or kuzu dissolved in 2 Tbsp. cold water

1. Arrange squash in a 1 1/2-2-quart pot. Add water and salt. Cover, bring to boil, reduce heat to low and simmer 20-30 minutes, or until soft without stirring.

2. Mash squash in the pot with a potato masher. Add corn off the cob plus 2 Tbsp. water. Cover again, bring to boil, reduce heat to low and simmer 15 minutes.

3. If too watery, dissolve 1 Tbsp. arrowroot in 2 Tbsp. cold water, add and stir over low heat to thicken. Or, spoon cooked vegetables into an 8 or 9-inch casserole dish and bake uncovered for 30-40 minutes at 350° F. for a thicker and even sweeter dish. Transfer to a serving bowl and cover loosely with a bamboo sushi mat.

Serving suggestions: Serve with whole grain or chapatis or tortillas and a green or mixed vegetable side dish. Add a bean or tempeh side dish, stew, or soup and/or pickles. Add a seed or nut condiment if desired.

Storage: Cover and refrigerate. Serve at room temperature or briefly heat in a covered bowl-within-a-pot or in a dish in the oven. ❏

Basic Procedure, Baked Squash Halves (Fall, Winter, Early Spring)***

Prep: 5 minutes
Cooking: 1-1 1/2 hours on the stove
or 8-9 hours in a crock pot

Serves: 4-8 (or 2-4 meals for 2)
Serving size: 1/2-1 cup per person

Baked squash halves are very sweet and rich tasting without added fat if you buy a sweet variety. Rub it with sea salt or miso and bake it cut-side down. The sweetest varieties are listed below. (We don't bother with acorn or danish squashes; they are usually very starchy and not nearly as sweet as the others.) Don't be afraid to cook extras, they can be used in a myriad of ways, at breakfast, lunch, dinner, or even for dessert. Though most people throw the skin out, we don't—they are usually very tasty and always nutritious.

1 (3-4 lb.) medium to large kabocha, sweet
  mama, or honey delight squash *or* 3 (1-1
  1/4 lb. each) sweet dumpling, delicatta,
  small butternut or blue hubbard squash

1/8 tsp. sea salt per squash half *or* 1 tsp. light
  miso per small half, (2 tsp. for a large one)

1. Wash and scrub squash; cut off any moldy or overly rough spots. Halve with a sturdy vegetable knife. With a spoon, remove and discard seeds and pulp from only the portion you plan to use immediately. If desired, rub a few pinches of sea salt into the cleaned flesh or spread a very thin layer of light miso over the cut side to bring out a rich and buttery taste.

2. **To bake in the oven:** Place squash, cut side down on a lightly oiled cookie sheet or baking pan with sides (to catch juices) or in glass or stainless steel pie or cake pans. They must be placed cut side down or they will dry out and become mealy. If desired, brush cut side and outer skin with a dash of oil to seal in moisture and to add a richer flavor.

3. Do not cover or add water to the dish. Bake at 375-400° F for 1-1 1/2 hours or until very soft, syrupy and sweet smelling. Cooking time will vary with the size of the squash, height of oven shelf, etc.

   To bake in a crock pot: Place squash halves cut side down in a crock pot/slow cooker. Add about 1/2 cup water for 2-4 small, 2 medium, or 1 large winter squash. Cover and cook on high heat for 1 hour then reduce heat to low and cook 8-9 hours (all day or overnight.)

4. Remove squash from oven or crock pot. Cut into wedges or cubes before serving.

Serving suggestions: Serve with whole grain, bread, or pasta and cooked greens or pressed or marinated salad. Add beans, soup, plain soy yogurt or warm, spiced soy milk if desired.

Storage: Cover and refrigerate leftovers in glass, stainless steel, or pyrex dishes with a saucer, plate, or lid on top. Use within 1-3 days. Serve leftovers at room temperature by removing from the refrigerator at least 30-60 minutes before serving. (They'll last from breakfast to lunch time unrefrigerated.) Or, resteam briefly in a covered bowl on top of a steamer rack.

Leftover tip

- Leftovers can be packed, as is, for school or work—as a snack or lunch component.

- See also **Soups from Leftovers**

- See also **Squash/Yam-Wiches**

- See also **Squash Sauced Pizza**

- See also **Pumpkin, Sweet Potato, or Squash Pie**

- See also **Uses For Leftover Sweet Vegetables**

- **Mashed Squash:** Mash squash, with or without skin. Add water a little at a time to create a smooth consistency. Per 3-4 cups purée, add 1-2 tsp. light miso and 1/4 tsp. cinnamon or allspice. If desired add 4 Tbsp. nut or seed butter or sprinkle with 2-4 Tbsp. chopped, dry roasted nuts. ❏

Carrot & Parsnip Kinpira
(Fall, Winter, Spring)***

Prep: 10 minutes
Cooking: 40 minutes
Serves: 4-8 (or 2-4 meals for 2)
Serving size: 1/2-2/3 cup per person

Kinpira is a strengthening Japanese cooking technique in which root vegetables are cut into thin matchsticks and sautéed for a long time over a low heat. The resulting flavor is quite unlike baked, steamed, or stir fried vegetables. These juicy, rich, sweet-tasting vegetables are perfect at dinner or breakfast.

2-3 tsp. ghee or sesame oil

Vegetables, cut in pencil shavings or matchsticks,

3 cups carrots

3 cups parsnips

2 pinches sea salt

Optional, 1/2 tsp. cinnamon, ground pumpkin pie spice, or allspice

1/4-1/3 cup water, or enough to just cover the bottom of the skillet

1/4 tsp. sea salt *or* 1 Tbsp. tamari or shoyu *or* 1 Tbsp. light/sweet miso dissolved in 1 Tbsp. water

Optional, garnishes:

3 Tbsp. minced parsley

1-2 Tbsp. dry roasted poppy seeds or sesame seeds

1. Wash vegetables. Cut into 1 1/2-2 inch long matchstick pieces.

2. Add oil to a 9 to 10 inch cast iron, carbon steel, or stainless steel skillet or wok. Sauté carrots with a pinch of salt. Stir over a medium heat 3-4 minutes; add parsnips and a pinch of salt. Continue to stir over medium heat for 2-3 minutes then add a dash of water to just barely cover the bottom of the skillet. Add spices if desired and add remaining salt (or wait to season with tamari or miso in the last 10 minutes of cooking).

3. Cover pot, turn up heat and bring to a boil. Don't peek, just listen for boiling and watch for steam rising. Reduce heat to low and simmer, covered, 30 minutes. (Do not stir vegetables as they cook or they will turn to mush. Do not lift the lid or the moisture will steam off and they will burn on the bottom!)

4. If additional salt was not added earlier, add tamari or thinned white miso when vegetables are tender. Cook with the lid ajar for several minutes to evaporate any remaining liquid. Stir gently so as not to break up vegetables. If desired, sprinkle minced parsley and/or toasted seeds. Transfer to a serving dish. Cover loosely with a bamboo sushi mat.

Serving suggestions: Serve warm or near room temperature with a light miso or tamari seasoned soup or broth, rice or millet, cooked greens or pressed salad, and condiments.

Storage: If leftovers will be used within 8 hours, cover with a bamboo mat and store on the counter or in a cold box; otherwise, refrigerate in a covered bowl. Serve close to room temperature or warm briefly using covered-bowl-within-a-pot method. Leftovers keep well and are just as delicious the next day as a side dish or turned into a quick soup, stew, or filling for Squash-Wiches, burritos, or won tons.

Variation:

- **Burdock & Carrot Kinpira:** Use burdock root in place of parsnips. Scrub burdock root well but do not peel. Cut in pencil shavings and sauté until fragrant, 3-4 minutes, before adding carrots. Cook as above. Use tamari or shoyu, (not light miso) as the seasoning. Omit sweet spices. I desired, add 1/8 tsp. mild red pepper powder. Before serving, top with toasted sesame seeds or parsley if desired.

- Try carrots & jerusalem artichokes in the above recipe. ❏

Basic Procedure, Pressure-Steamed Vegetables (Year Round)

Prep: 4-5 minutes
Cooking: 15-45 minutes

Serves: 3-8
Serving size: 1/2-1 medium potato per person, or 3-4 tiny potatoes,

We don't use this method often, but now and then we use it for white potatoes, sweet potatoes (commonly called "yams") or beets. These vegetables can be cooked in a quantity to last for two or three days then refrigerated for quick and convenient meals in hot or cold weather. Pressure-steaming renders these vegetables more tender than baking and less soggy than boiling. This technique is particularly well suited for spring and summer when baking is less desirable. This method cooks hearty vegetables to perfection in a relatively short period of time while retaining their nutrients and flavor. After cooking, these vegetables can be chopped, sliced, or diced and added to soups, salads or casseroles or topped with bean dips, sauces or herbed Tofu Sour Cream.

3-4 red garnet, jewel or white sweet potatoes
    or 4 large, 6 medium *or* 16 tiny red or
    white potatoes *or* 4-6 medium-sized beets

Water to cover the bottom of a pressure cooker
    by 1-2"

Optional, pinch sea salt

1. Wash and scrub vegetables. Leave the skins intact. Remove any sprouts from potatoes with a paring knife.

2. Put 1-2 inches of water in bottom of a pressure cooker. Add sea salt if desired. Place a metal steamer basket in your pressure cooker and arrange whole vegetables on the basket. Seal the pressure cooker; bring to pressure over medium heat. Reduce to medium-low and cook 20-30 minutes for large potatoes, 15-20 minutes for medium sized potatoes or beets, or 10-15 minutes for small potatoes or beets.

3. Turn off heat and wait for pressure to come down or run the pot under cold water to make the pressure come down faster.

4. Remove vegetables from pot and test with a fork. If the center does not yield when poked with a fork, cook for several minutes more. Vegetables should be tender but not soggy and should retain their shape. Serve piping hot.

Serving suggestions: Slice beets into silver dollar rounds; cut potatoes or yams in half or in rounds. Serve with whole grain or bread, cooked leafy greens or pressed salad, and condiments.

Top with Tofu Sour Cream, Tofu Pesto, Tofu Cream Cheese, Hummus, or seed condiment, with or without minced fresh or dried chives, garlic chives, dill weed, or sea vegetable flakes. Or, top white or red potatoes with Seitan Stroganoff, Hungarian Goulash, thick pea soup, or Sea Sage & Sunflower Spread. Beets may also be sliced finely and tossed with cooked sea vegetables, beans, seasoned tempeh or tofu, or with a light dressing or marinade.

Storage: Store leftovers in the refrigerator. Serve room temperature or lightly and briefly resteam vegetables on a basket before serving.

- For more toppings, see Pasta and Bread Toppers and Spreads.

- Purée leftover potatoes and use in soups, stews, sauces, or bread making.

Variations:

- **Pressure-Steamed Corn (Summer & Fall):** Arrange whole or halved corn cobs on a steamer basket over 1 inch of water in a pressure cooker. Bring to pressure, reduce heat; and cook for 10 minutes. Run the pot under cold water to release pressure, remove from cooker and serve warm. Spread lightly with umeboshi paste or thinned white miso if desired. (Cut leftover corn off the cob and add to soup, stew, salad, beans, breakfast cereal, batters, or sea vegetable dishes.) ❏

Uses for leftover cooked greens or mixed vegetables:

To save time and energy, always cook extra vegetables to have on hand for a couple of meals. Here are a few ideas for using up leftover steamed or parboiled veggies.

- Toss with sauerkraut or other pickles—1 Tbsp. pickles per cup cooked vegetables.

- Toss with a leftover cooked sea vegetable side dish. Serve at room temperature.

- Toss with Easy As 1-2-3 Dressing or a splash of brown rice vinegar.

- Toss leftover steamed veggies with leftover pressed or marinated salad. Optional, add 2 tsp. roasted pumpkin or sunflower seeds per cup of vegetables.

- Toss with leftover cooked beans, pasta, and a light marinade or dressing.

- Top each portion with 1/2 tsp. toasted or spiced sesame oil at the table. Also add 1-2 Tbsp. quick pickled cabbage, onion, or other pickled vegetables, minced finely.

- Toss with leftover cooked rice or pasta, cubed tofu, seasoned tempeh, or wheat meat. Add a dash of umeboshi vinegar, brown rice vinegar, minced garlic, and a hint of olive oil.

- Toss with raw salad vegetables, cooked beans, brown rice, or pasta, and a light dressing.

- Toss with a light vinaigrette, mustard dressing, Tofu Sour Cream, Tofu Pesto, or yogurt cheese. Serve with rice, pasta or bread and soup.

- Toss with tofu or bean dip and roll in a whole grain tortilla or pita pocket. Top with sprouts, chives, parsley, or nori flakes. Try a topping of soy yogurt if beans are used.

- Transform into a new and exciting soup, (puréed or unpuréed.) See Soups from Leftovers.

- Reheat leftover steamed vegetables in a shallow bowl or custard cup(s) on a rack or trivet, in a pan filled with 1/2-1 inch of water. Cover pot and steam 1-3 minutes or until barely warm. Turn off and let set another minute or two before serving.

- Mince or chop vegetables and add to leftover soup (puréed beet-squash, parsnip, winter squash, carrot, creamy corn, asparagus, broccoli, or bean soup.) Add 1 clove of minced garlic, a few pinches of basil, oregano and/or thyme, marjoram or add ginger juice (from freshly grated ginger) or chili powder.

- Serve leftover steamed veggies with a gravy over rice, pasta, polenta, or with bread or buns.

- Spoon onto bread or a tortilla after lightly spreading with diluted peanut, sunflower or sesame butter and a thin layer of prepared mustard (optional) and/or dash sauerkraut or minced dill pickles.

- Serve on rice, millet, bread or noodles topped with pesto, hummus, tofu or tempeh paté, or some other sauce or dip.

- Spoon over breakfast cereal with a seed condiment or sesame or flax oil and roasted sea vegetable.

- Serve on top of bread spread with Miso Tahini or Sunflower Miso spread.

- Spread veggies on a tortilla with scrambled tofu and a spoonful of sauerkraut. Roll up burrito style.

Uses for leftover cooked winter squash & sweet potatoes:

- Take out of refrigerator, let come to room temperature and serve with morning porridge, a seed or nut condiment, and roasted dulse.

- Serve as is, as a side dish at any meal, as a snack or as dessert instead of fruit, cookies, cake, or pastry. (They do this in Asia!)

- Mash and spread on bread or tortillas with a thin layer of diluted nut or seed butter or Miso-Nut Butter.

- Mash then add dash of light miso and a few pinches of dried ginger powder or juice (from freshly grated and squeezed ginger root). Steam to warm and serve "mashed potato" style with a sprinkle of dry roasted chopped walnuts.

- Steam heat, mash, then spread on chapatis or tortillas and roll into burritos. Top with a dollup of Tofu "Sour Cream" or soy yogurt mixed with chives.

- Mash or purée in a blender. Add to leftover cooked beans, tempeh, or wheat meat. Add a small amount of miso or tamari and water for sweet baked beans.

- Mash with a dash of tahini, light miso and water, pour over noodles, top with grated mochi, bread or crumbs cracker crumb. Bake in a covered dish for a macaroni and cheese-less casserole.

- Chop or purée and add to chili. Or, add to baked beans and stock for a sweet and tasty soup or stew.

- Mash or purée. Add to a leftover bean or vegetable soup. Add grated ginger root and a pinch of cumin, cinnamon or nutmeg. Simmer, garnish, and serve.

- Blend with water, amasake, or almond or rice milk. Add to muffin, cookie, quick bread, or cake batter in place of most of the oil or shortening. Or, use in place of banana in banana bread recipes.

- Blend with amasake or apple juice and a pinch of cinnamon. Heat and serve as a pudding, custard, or as a sauce for whole grain pancakes or waffles to replace maple or fruit syrup. Sprinkle with a few teaspoons of chopped roasted walnuts or hazelnuts.

- Mash and mix with a dash of light miso. Spoon over morning porridge or spread on waffles, tortillas or bread. A chopped, roasted and seasoned nut or seed condiment can also be added.

- For pie filling, mash and mix with amasake, apple juice, or rice milk. Add cinnamon, dried ginger, or allspice, and a dash of light miso. Add a few teaspoons of tahini. Spoon into a whole grain pie crust and bake. (For a main dish pie, use water or plain unsweetened soy milk with light miso and spice.)

- Mix puréed squash or sweet potato with miso and leftover cooked beans and spices. Pour into a pie crust. Bake 30 minutes for a savory, mildly sweet main dish pie.

- For a quick soup, blend with stock or water. Add leftover cooked beans, tempeh, or wheat meat. Season with light miso before serving. (See Formulas for Soups From Leftovers.)

- Make Squash or Yam-wiches!

- Purée and use as a pizza sauce!

- Blend with cooked chestnuts, raisin purée, or apple sauce for a lusciously, sweet pudding.

Scrumptious Squash-Wiches
& Yam-Wiches (Any season)**

Prep: 15 minutes
Cooking: none with leftover squash or sweet potato

Serves: 2 (or 2 meals for 1)
Serving size: 2-3 roll-ups *or* 3-4 bread slices per person
or 3-4 rollups *or* 4-6 slices bread if very active

** *Increase this recipe as needed.*

Though the combination may sound bizzare, everyone loves these sweet sandwiches. They taste a bit like Reese's Peanut Butter Cups if you get a super sweet squash with a deep orange flesh (or a white, red garnet, or jewel yam or sweet potato.) They taste even better than peanut butter and jelly sandwiches and are better for you. This is a great way to use leftover cooked squash or squash fresh from the oven, crock pot, or steamer tray. Chapatis or tortillas are best for these sandwiches, but thick slices of whole grain bread also do. We love to serve these for breakfast, lunch, or dinner almost any time of year.

1-1 1/2 cups steamed, baked, or nishime
cooked winter squash
or 2 medium yams or sweet potatoes
(1 medium delicatta or sweet dumpling squash; 1/2 medium or 1 small butternut, buttercup or kabocha squash or Hokkaido pumpkin; or 2 red garnet, jewel, or white sweet potatoes/yams

2-4 Tbsp. Miso-Sunflower, Miso-Tahini, Miso-Nut Butter Spread *or* diluted lightly salted, natural peanut or sunflower butter

6-8 large whole wheat or spelt chapatis or soft tortillas (8-10 to serve 2 very active folks) or 6-8 slices whole grain bread (8-12 slices to serve 2 very active folks)

1. Take all ingredients out of the refrigerator 30-40 minutes before serving and allow to come to room temperature. Sandwiches can be made the night before then refrigerated or made in the morning and stored at room temperature between breakfast and lunch, or assembled right at the table at meal time.

2. If using loaf bread that is a bit dry, try wrapping it in a white kitchen towel and steam for several minutes on a metal or bamboo steamer to moisten. Do not steam chapatis or tortillas or they will turn to mush. Squash, yams, or sweet potatoes may be cut into chunks, cubes or slices for easy mashing or puréed in a suribachi with a dash of water. Arrange all ingredients on the table and let each person build his/her own sandwiches.

For roll ups: Spread about 1-1 1/2 tsp. Sunflower-Miso, Miso-Tahini, or Miso-Nut Butter Spread or nut or seed butter over the center of each tortilla or chapati. Top with about 1/4-1/3 cup cooked squash or 1/4-1/3 of a yam or sweet potato. Flatten with the back of a fork or butter knife. Fold the bottom edge of the tortilla over the filling, fold the right side into the center, fold the left side in, then fold the top edge down to make a small oblong pouch, like a burrito. Don't try to stuff too much filling inside. Repeat with the rest of the tortillas.

For sandwiches: Spread 1 tsp. Miso-Nut Butter or nut/seed butter on each piece of bread. Top with 1/3-1/2 cup squash, yam, or sweet potato then top with a second slice of bread.

Serving suggestion: Serve sandwiches or roll-ups at room temperature with pressed/marinated salad or steamed greens. (Sandwiches and salad or cooked greens will keep out of the refrigerator between breakfast and lunch.) If very active, heat a small cup of warm soy milk, rice milk, or almond milk after adding a pinch of sea salt or 1/2-1 tsp. light miso and pinch or two of cinnamon, nutmeg, ginger, or black pepper to aid digestion. For packed lunches, warm the "milk" and transport in a thermos. Or, serve with a small cup of plain, unsweetened soy yogurt or goat milk, kefir, or liquid yogurt (at room temperature.) ❏

Sunflower-Miso, Miso-Tahini, or Miso-Nut Butter Spread (Year Round):

Prep: 5 minutes
Yield: 2/3-3/4 cup

Serves: 5-6 (or 2-3 meals for 2)
Serving size: 1-2 Tbsp. per person, depending on meal

This delectable spread is a favorite in Squash-wiches and Yam-wiches although it is equally delicious spread on waffles with mashed squash or sweet potato. Small portions can also be diluted for use as a coating for steamed veggies or boiled salad.

1/3 cup sunflower, sesame, or peanut butter or lightly roasted tahini

1 Tbsp. sweet white, yellow, or mellow rice or barley miso

4-6 Tbsp. water, or more as needed to make a smooth paste

1. In a suribachi or bowl, mix to make a smooth frosting consistency.

2. Transfer to a wide mouth jar or small crock. It will thicken as it sits.

Note: This spread is also good on top of millet slices or bread, topped with minced parsley, scallions, chives or sea vegetables flakes. ❏

Variation:

• **Walnut-Miso Spread:** In a Suribachi mash 1 cup dry roasted walnuts with 2 Tbsp. dark miso or 3 Tbsp. sweet light miso and 1/-1/3-1/2 cup water. Blend until smooth. Add more water to produce desired consistency.

Note: This spread is great in the above sandwiches or on mochi waffles with mashed squash or sweet potato. You can also dilute a portion of this to use as a dressing for boiled salad or steamed vegetables.

Vegetables From The Seven Seas

Who needs them, who eats them?

Unglamorous as they may sound, seaweeds are good food. These vegetables from the sea are virtually free of calories, low in fat, high in protein, and contain 10 to 20 times the minerals found in land vegetables. Research has demonstrated their ability to cleanse and detoxify the body, safely drawing wastes and impurities out of our tissues so that they can be excreted from the body.

Uncommonly common fare

If the thought of eating sea vegetables leaves you queasy, you may be surprised to find out that you have probably been unwittingly consuming minute amounts of these vegetables for years in many common prepared foods. Many store bought varieties of ice cream, pudding, soup, sauce, dressing mixes and packaged desserts contain some form of seaweed—often caragheen or caragheenan. The extract from these and some other varieties of sea weed help to thicken many processed foods, though the manufacturers don't always list these on the label! Oriental restaurants use sea vegetables in everything from soup and stir fried vegetable dishes to sushi rolls and sashimi plates.

You don't have to be afraid of sea weeds. They don't have to taste slimy. Some are more sweet than salty, Some are more chewy, others are crispy. (They vary widely in flavor; so if you don't like one, try another, and another.) And sea vegetables have a myriad of uses. At first it might seem strange to eat these foods and their tastes may be unfamiliar, but if you give them a try, and start out gradually, within a short time you will likely become a fan of these vegetables from the seven seas.

A rainbow of colors and flavors

Sea vegetables can be used to add flavor and minerals to everything from salads to desserts, depending on the variety. Agar agar, a Japanese sea vegetable, is essentially tasteless, and is often mixed with fresh fruit and juices to create natural jell-o or aspic-type desserts, called "kanten." Some varieties taste like caviar when cooked, others lend a hearty poultry- or meat-like taste to soups and stocks, still others taste a bit like bacon bits or potato chips when oven roasted or lightly pan fried. Powdered sea vegetable flakes often look and taste like herbs and come in shaker bottles, though they can also be made at home. Sea vegetable flakes can be sprinkled over soups, salads, rice, millet, pasta, or bean dishes. In this way, they can be used to replace the salt shaker at the table. Though they may taste salty, sea vegetables are not really that high in sodium; this is because their salty taste comes from a wide range of minerals that are necessary for health.

Small is beautiful, local is logical

We also encourage the purchase and use of sea vegetables from small-scale, family-owned and run operations which have demonstrated a commitment to the safest and most sustainable harvesting practices we know of. We have listed the names and addresses of some of these sea vegetable harvesters in our resource section at the end of this book.

Many consumers are unaware of the benefits that sea vegetables offer, or of the price savings available to those who purchase American and Canadian grown and harvested sea weeds over Japanese varieties. (This is a recommendation for Americans and Canadians of course. If you live in other countries, we urge you to seek out more local sources of sea vegetables.) Others are unsure of how to best introduce these unfamiliar foods to their families

WHY EAT SEA VEGETABLES?

1. **Sea vegetables are rich sources of trace minerals:** Sea vegetables add beneficial trace minerals not found as abundantly in land vegetables. They contain calcium, iron, potassium, iodine, magnesium, as well as a wide range of other trace minerals which are required in only minute amounts, but are often lacking in our diets. Processed and refined foods have been robbed of their natural minerals and many of our land vegetable crops have been commercially grown in mineral-depleted soils. Minerals are necessary for all essential bodily functions, yet mineral deficiencies are common in this country and can cause the body to degenerate prematurely, leading to a variety of diseases. Eating sea vegetables can protect us from such problems. The iodine contained in sea vegetables, for example, can prevent goitre, an enlargement of the thyroid gland due to lack of sufficient iodine.

   It is not necessary to eat sea vegetables in as large a volume as land vegetables—they are highly concentrated. Small amounts are quite beneficial—used as condiments, side dishes and seasonings for soups, stews, salads, beans, grains and other dishes.

2. **Sea vegetables are low in fat and calories:** Besides being very nutritious, sea vegetables are virtually free of calories, making them appealing to those concerned about their weight. What other food can boast such nutritional benefits for so few calories?

3. **Sea vegetables have a cleansing effect on the body:** The abundance of trace minerals found in sea vegetables help alkalinize the blood and purify the system by eliminating or counterbalancing the acidifying effects of our modern lifestyles and environment. Interestingly, the natural Ph of our blood is close to that of sea water: healthy blood is on the salty side and rich in minerals. However, due to the effects of our modern diet-which includes highly processed, preserved and rancid, chemical and sugar laden foods, an excess of poor quality fats, and a deficiency of vitamins and minerals- our blood streams have become polluted and overly acidic. We can begin to turn this around by eating a highly nourishing diet of whole grains, fresh seasonal land vegetables and beans, and by eating more sea vegetables, whose minerals have an alkalizing effect on our blood and can begin to neutralize the effects of years of abuse.

4. **Sea vegetables help to detoxify the body:** Scientific studies at McGill University in Montreal have shown that the alginic acid in sea vegetables binds with toxins in the body (including heavy metals, radioactive particles and other pollutants) through a process called chelation, which allows us to excrete these impurities through normal channels of elimination (sweat, urination, and bowel movements). In this way, sea vegetables act as a stabilizing force against the damages that have come with rampant industrialization and the resultant pollution and degradation of our planet and her food. We are, in fact, a part of (not apart from) nature.

5. **Sea vegetables have anti-tumor effects:** Not only do sea vegetables dissolve fatty or cholesterol deposits in the human body, they've also been shown to have anti-tumor effects. Several laboratory studies, including one done at the Harvard School of Public Health, found that animals fed 5% of their diet in kelp (a sea vegetable also referred to as kombu) showed resistance to laboratory induced cancers. In addition, animals that had cancerous tumors and were fed kelp showed complete tumor regression.

   The ability of sea vegetables to soften hardness and dissolve tumors makes sense in light of the fact that they actually grow and feed on rocks and shells on the ocean floor. Note what happens when you put salt on ice; it melts! When you rub salt into vegetables (as when making pickles or a pressed or marinated salad) they soften, shrink, and even reduce in size as the outer cells and plant fibers are broken down and moisture is drawn out. People often marinate meat with sea salt, tamari, or shoyu (soy sauce) to tenderize it prior to cooking. And salt is used to soften hard water in many parts of the country.

6. **Sea vegetables enhance the flavor of other foods:** The tenderizing ability of sea vegetables softens foods, making them more digestible and flavorful. (This is particularly true of beans, legumes, and hearty root and round vegetables.) Unlike MSG (a chemically formulated flavor enhancer), sea vegetables add flavor and have beneficial side effects rather than harmful ones.

7. **Sea vegetables taste great:** Sea vegetables come in a wide variety of colors, textures and tastes, enhancing the flavor and presentation of whatever you cook or serve them with. When oven roasted in strips, crushed or ground into flakes, or soaked, seasoned and cooked, sea vegetables can stand in for the salt shaker at the table. They are particularly pleasing spooned over cooked millet, rice, hot cereal, noodles, or added to bean, grain or vegetable salads. Although it might sound strange, you may even come to crave sea vegetables once you add them to your diet.

8. **Sea vegetables are versatile:** Sea vegetables are simple to use and go well with almost any dish. They can be added to everything from soups or hot cereals to desserts, depending on the variety.

9. **Sea vegetables are an ecological food:** Sea vegetables can be stored almost indefinitely if kept in a cool, dry place. They do not require refrigeration until they are cooked in a liquid medium. (Dry roasted sea vegetables do not need refrigeration.)

10. **Sea vegetables are a completely natural food:** Support your local planet. These ancient plants have nourished life for longer than humans have been on the earth. Many traditional cultures have prized these foods and revered them for their nutritional benefits, particularly for pregnant, lactating and nursing mothers and children. They are part of our native ecosystem and are ripe for the picking.

General Notes About Using Sea Vegetables:

Sea vegetables add beneficial trace minerals not found as abundantly in land vegetables. Because they are so concentrated, however, we need only eat them in small volumes (10 pounds of wet seaweed becomes a single pound when dried.). When soaked your sea veggies will expand again, so start with a small amount or follow a recipe if you are unsure of how much to use.

Sea vegetables should be prepared with a small amount of oil or ghee (clarified butter) or served with seed, nuts, nut or seed butter (or a dish containing one of the aforementioned products) to facilitate mineral absorption and metabolism.

We suggest that you follow recipes when first using sea vegetables. Most sea vegetables double or triple in size when soaked; still others hardly increase at all. Some varieties have a more salty or fishy taste; some cook up quickly; others need no cooking and may simply be soaked and added to salads or soups; still others require more lengthy soaking and cooking to render them tender and tasty. Once you get the hang of it, you'll be able to create your own recipes, but for a taste of success, start with recipes that others have used and enjoyed.

Why Buy American Sea Vegetables?

1. **Cost!** Sea vegetables harvested in this country are often one-half to one-third the price of imported Japanese sea vegetables. A two-ounce package of Japanese wakame typically sells for $3.55 ($28 per pound). Another Japanese variety called arame usually sells for at least $25 per pound. Hijiki can cost upwards of $42 a pound! In contrast, one can find American varieties for $16-$22 per pound (see resources at the end of this book).

2. **Purity!** Sea vegetables have a unique ability to excrete pollutants and metals from the human body and sea vegetables will not grow abundantly where pollution is high, why take chances? Small American companies are usually your best bet for clean sea vegetables as they tend to harvest more reasonable volumes and to be more concerned with quality than with turning a fast profit.

   Japanese macrobiotic sea vegetables--from reputable companies, such as those listed in our resource section, are another option though they are not as economical as local varieties. These sea vegetables are also pure and clean and we use these infrequently. However, we cannot be as sure of the sea vegetables found in Korean, Japanese and Korean markets; some of these have been dyed and many come from the Sea of Japan, one of the most polluted bodies of water. Thus, we avoid buying from these latter sources).

3. **Reputation!** The small sea vegetable companies in America are built on a dedicated following, word of mouth, and repeat customers. Their good reputation comes from sincere business practices. Take Larch Hansen who runs the Maine Seaweed Company and has been harvesting the same waters and plant beds for 16 years. He knows what he's doing. Unlike many sea vegetable harvesters who use toxic paints on their boats, spray their drying fields with herbicides, and use harvesting practices that expose sea vegetables to toxic pollutants, Larch harvests in such a way that the sea vegetables continue to regenerate year after year. He considers his boat a floating salad bowl and refuses to use toxic paints, opting for natural oils instead. He also refuses to harvest out of season, with drag nets, or spray his drying fields with herbicides.

4. **Ecology.** Location is everything. When you buy locally grown and harvested foods you save money and natural resources. In this way, you can avoid heavy shipping, packaging and advertising costs; support small, local companies; have direct contact with your food source; and promote small scale, sustainable farming operations. We need to do more of this with all of our food.

5. **Taste!** American sea vegetables come in varieties unavailable in Japan. Thus, they offer new tastes and new culinary applications.

To Rinse or Not To Rinse:

There is no need to rinse the sea vegetable before roasting, soaking, or cooking. They have been cleaned and sorted by the harvesters, and in some cases rinsed. One need only soak the sea vegetable in recipes which call for this step. You should sort shallow water sea vegetables, such as dulse and nori because they often contain little shells, and occasional stones, which can crack a tooth or at least give you a good scare. (You can toss the little shells into the soup stock scrap bowl.)

If you've tried one, you've not tried 'em all

Sea vegetables are nutritious and come in an array of colors, shapes and textures as well as tastes. They are rich sources of calcium, iron, potassium, iodine, magnesium and other essential trace minerals. They also offer numerous health-protective benefits.

Sea Vegetables To Use:

Note: We recommend sea vegetables from the North American Continent. If you live on another continent, please seek out varieties from that are native to your area. Sea vegetables grow all around the world. Some may have the same name but a different flavor when gathered from different coastal waters.

Alaria (or Pacific Coast Wakame)

Bladderwrack (Fucus)

Dulse

Canadian Kombu

Caragheen

Kelp (or Canadian Kombu)

Longicruris Kelp

Digitata Kelp

Sugar Kelp

Ocean Ribbons

Wild Nori

Sea Palm & Sea Palm Fronds

Sea Cress/Sea Lettuce

Note:

- Other varieties exist in America as well, though these are the most common.

- Both the alaria and wild nori from California will taste different from alaria or wild nori from Maine. Just like land vegetables, sea vegetables come in many varieties— each with different tastes and characteristics, all of which depend upon the climate in which they are grown—so despite having the same "family" or name, sea vegetables will undoubtedly vary in taste.

- **Substituting Sea Vegetables:** As you experiment with sea vegetables you will begin to note their subtle taste differences and properties. You will also find that it is easy to use one type of sea vegetable for another in cooking. We urge you to make substitutions in recipes that call for sea vegetables from far away places, replacing them with more local varieties.

- If you live in America, use sea palm or ocean ribbons (American Seaweeds) to replace arame or hijiki (Japanese varieties); use kelp to replace kombu; and use alaria to replace wakame.

Shopping For Sea Vegetables:

We like to buy our sea vegetables directly from suppliers in California and Maine to avoid excess packaging and high prices. Don't be afraid to buy several pounds at a time; they last indefinitely when kept in air-tight containers.

Check our resource list for sources near you. Bear in mind that price is not the only criteria for selecting these foods. Cheap seaweeds can be found in Asian markets but they are often of low quality and not very ecological because of the distance they've traveled. Cheap seaweeds may be dyed or contain artificial ingredients.

You won't find arame, hijiki or "sheet" nori growing here in North America. If you're going to eat ecologically, you'll have to learn to use the sea plants that grow in your area or at least on your continent. It just doesn't make sense to use Japanese sea vegetables as staples when you can get some from native waters. Let the Japanese eat Japanese sea vegetables!

Unfortunately, you cannot make nori sushi rolls from American wild nori, which comes in thick folded bunches, not in sheets. Japanese nori has been processed to form it into paper thin sheets that are well suited for sushi making. We do not know of any American source of sheet nori at this time. Wild nori is in short supply anyway—so we use it as it is and don't try to turn it into something it's not. If you want to buy sushi nori, and we sometimes do, look for the less expensive bulk packs of 50-sheets. (The sheet nori sold in small packages is usually very pricey.)

Methods of Preparing Sea Vegetables:

No doubt there are many ways to prepare sea vegetables. On a daily basis we prefer cooking methods that involve the least amount of preparation. There is nothing wrong with the seasonal or occasional use preparations, we simply prefer to save them (as they are slightly more involved) for parties, potlucks, weekends or when company will be coming.

Everyday sea vegetable preparations simply represent the methods we use most often throughout the year. They're also the ones that we think will be easiest for you to use on a day-in, day-out basis. You will surely discover many different ways to use sea vegetables, particularly if you are open to trying new foods, new combinations, and new methods. We hope that you will try many of our sea vegetable recipes and that you will become as fond of these ancient vegetable foods from the sea as we are. Please refer to our table of contents and seasonal menu section, for sea vegetable recipes and ideas beyond the ones found in this chapter.

•**Time considerations:** For everyday meals, it is almost effortless to add a strip of sea vegetable to the things you normally make—a pot of rice, beans, or bean soup. For daily use, it's also a snap to fill a skillet with some sort of sea vegetable then to dry roast it in the oven. This can then be used as a table condiment—crumbled over breakfast cereal or dinner grain or crushed and made into a condiment (alone or combined with roasted seeds, nuts, dried and powdered vegetables, herbs, spices, or several of these). Cooked and seasoned sea vegetable condiments or side dishes can be made on weekends to last for several days. They can also be made during the week if time permits.

•**Financial considerations:** Most of the everyday sea vegetable preparations listed above require relatively small volumes of sea vegetables, so they don't cost too much. However, some of the seasonal or occasional use preparations, particularly those served as side dishes, require larger amounts of sea vegetable, making such dishes cost prohibitive for daily use by some individuals..

•**Seasonal considerations:** Some preparations (such as casseroles or other baked preparations) are most appropriate for cold weather while sea vegetable salads are more suited for warm weather. Some preparations, however, can be used in any season. Examples include: as fillings for steamed buns, tamales, or won tons; cooked or tossed with leafy greens or mixed (land) vegetables; added to a stove top casserole, or soup, stew, or beans; or prepared as a condiment for whole grain or bread.

Basic everyday

Sea vegetable preparations:
Dry roasting
Cooking with beans
Cooking with tempeh
Cooking with whole grains
Cooking in soups & stews
Cooking with breakfast cereal
Cooking with land vegetables
Preparing as a special condiment

Seasonal or occasional use

Sea vegetable preparations:
Adding to sautés or stir fry
Adding to casseroles
Adding to salads
Preparing as a side dish*
Adding to stuffings & fillings*
Cooking with greens
Scrambling with tofu
Added to dressings or spreads

Notes:

* e.g., used as a filling with squashes, tomatoes, bell peppers, steamed buns, calzones, etc.
* e.g., sautéed or cooked with onions and other land vegetables.

What counts as a serving of sea vegetables:

- 1/2-2 tsp. sea vegetable powder/granules
- 1-4 tsp. sea vegetable flakes (*plain or combined with vegetable or herb powders*)
- 1/3-1/2 cup loosely packed, dry roasted sea vegetable
- 1/8-1/3 cup coarsely crumbled sea vegetables
- 1-3 Tbsp. (well seasoned) sea vegetable condiment
- 1/4-2/3 cup sea vegetable side dish (*prepared with land vegetables +/- beans*)
- 4-8 inch strip of sea vegetable strip (*cooked into a pot of rice, porridge, soup, stew, or beans*)
- 1-2 sheets sushi nori

Recommended Daily Sea Vegetable Intake:

- 1-3 servings daily for children and adults

Everyday Methods of Sea Vegetable Cookery:

Cooking sea vegetables with beans: Add a 4-inch strip of kelp or kombu sea vegetable to the pot when cooking any dried beans. This helps to tenderize and make beans more digestible. This little bit won't overpower the great taste of beans, it will only enhance and improve their flavors. Once the beans are tender you may chop or mash the sea vegetable right in with the beans or remove it and add it to a soup, stew, or casserole, or serve it atop rice or noodles. Sea vegetables such as sea palm or ocean ribbons may also added to bean soups. They are especially delicious in quick cooking lentil and pea soups. (See index for Any Bean Soup, Bean Cooking, Whole Dried Green Pea Soup or Pressure Marinated Tempeh.)

Dry roasting sea vegetables: Dry roast sea vegetables in the oven, a process which takes just minutes to assemble. It's done in 20-30 minutes, or overnight in a gas stove with just the pilot light on. The sea vegetables can be roasted while you do other things, such as cook, clean, eat, study, or sleep! Favorites for this are dulse, sea palm, wild nori, and ocean ribbons. (Some brands of dulse may be too tough to eat this way and may need to be used in cooked dishes only.) Once roasted, sea vegetables can be crumbled, like bacon bits, over soups or hot breakfast cereal, brown rice, millet, with spoonful or two of seed or nut condiment or an occasional steamed or poached egg, or dab of butter or ghee.

Leftover roasted sea vegetables keep well so we always roast enough to last for several days or the entire week. (Roasted or unroasted, they will keep indefinitely.) Alaria and other sea vegetables may also be dry roasted before adding to soups, stews, casseroles, sautés, tofu scrambles, or other dishes, a process which facilitates faster cooking and adds a rich smokey flavor.

You can also grind dry roasted sea vegetables to make a powder. This powder can be mixed with plain, or tamari or umeboshi seasoned, seeds or nuts or with dried parsley, chives, or onion granules). This makes a great table sprinkle for grain, bean, or vegetable dishes. Unroasted sea vegetable flakes can be used in the same way, as a table condiment. (See Dulse, Dried Onion and Sea Cress Sprinkles.)

Cooking sea vegetables with whole grain: Instead of roasting and serving sea vegetables over morning cereal or dinner grain, sometimes we cook a dry 4-6 inch strip of kelp or kombu in with a pot of (3-4 cups dry) whole grain for dinner or with 1-1/2 cups of dry whole grain for breakfast porridge. The sea vegetable tenderizes the grains—whole oat groats, brown rice, millet, a combination of two of these, or millet and amaranth. It also makes your grain very creamy. Once the grain is cooked, just stir in the sea vegetable; it dissolves right into the grain and may go unnoticed by friends and family members. Alternately, you may remove it, chop it, then add it back at the table.

Sea vegetables in soups and stews: You can add a little piece of sea vegetable to vegetable or bean soups, stews, or baked or nishime cooked root vegetable dishes. Since sea vegetables swell up with soaking and cooking you only need a small piece (about 3-4 inches in length). A little bit goes a long way! (See vegetable and soup chapters). Dulse & Sunchoke Chowder is always a hit with lovers of seafood.

Sea vegetable condiments: Sea vegetables can be sautéed, slow simmered, pressure cooked, or pan-fried to make marvelous condiments for whole grain or pasta. Some of our favorites include Sea Palm Sauté, Ocean Ribbon Sauté, Nori Condiment, and Alaria Mock" Caviar" Condiment. Herbed Sea Vegetable "Chips," are also tasty, eaten in the context of a whole meal, with whole grains, rather than as a snack on their own. Most sea vegetable condiments can be made to last for several days or a week at a time.

Uncooked sea vegetables can be pulverized in a blender or meat grinder then mixed with dried onions, garlic powder, or dried chives and used as a topping for soups or whole grains. You can also purchase sea vegetable flakes for this purpose, a particularly good idea if you are pressed for time or new to this way of cooking. These condiments can be served solo or even on top grains along with salted seed or nut condiments.

Sea vegetable side dishes: When prepared as a side dish, rather than a condiment, sea vegetables may be served in larger volumes (1/4-1/2 cup per person). In such a dish, the sea vegetable is usually combined with an equal or larger volume of land vegetables and sautéed, simmered, or stewed until tender. Root, round and ground vegetables such as onions, carrots, parsnips, burdock, and sunchokes are favorite additions for sea vegetable side dishes. Greens also pair up well with sea vegetables. Try Kale, Sea Palm & Shoyu with Mushrooms; Dulse & Sunchokes; Sea Palm with Carrots; Sea Palm with Sweet Corn; Ocean Ribbons in Peanut Sauce; or Sea Palm in Sesame Sauce.

Occasional Use Methods of Sea Vegetable Cookery:

Sea vegetables in casseroles: Sea vegetables can add a rich and savory taste to casseroles. Favorites include: a tuna tasting, fish-free dish that we call Macaroni & Sea or Macaroni & Sunchoke Casserole, and Nishime Root Vegetable Stews.

Sea vegetable salads: You can add sea vegetables to raw or parboiled salads. While most varieties must be soaked and cooked first, dulse may be snipped with scissors, soaked briefly in water to just cover, then tossed with parboiled vegetables and a light dressing or marinade. Sea palm, ocean ribbons, alaria and kelp should be soaked, chopped, then simmered in their soak water before being tossed with other ingredients such as vegetables, pasta, rice or cooked beans, and dressing. For more richness or crunch, add roasted chopped nuts or seeds or baked, grilled, or broiled Tempeh "Bacon," mock sausage, seitan/wheat meat or smoked tofu cubes.

Try our Tempeh Mock "Tuna" Salad spread. It is one you definitely won't want to miss. It will satisfy past and present tuna lovers and has won over vegetarians and non vegetarians alike. It is one of the best introductions to sea vegetables and tempeh.

Sea vegetables with greens: Sea vegetables can be soaked, chopped and added to quick-boiled, sautéed, or stir fried greens or mixed vegetables or soaked, chopped, simmered, then tossed with steamed vegetables or boiled salad. A small volume of dulse can also be soaked or roasted then used in salad dressings.

Sea vegetable broths and stocks: Sea vegetables may be simmered, alone or in combination with dried mushrooms and/or to make a light, clear broth or stock. In such a preparation the kelp or kombu are simmered in water for 15-30 minutes then removed from the pot and reserved for use in another dish. The broth is then seasoned with miso, tamari, or shoyu or it is used as the base for a light mixed vegetable soup or hearty bean soup.

Basic Procedure, Oven Roasted Sea Vegetables (Year Round)***

Prep: 3-4 minutes
Cooking: 30-40 minutes or overnight

Serves: 6-10 as a topping for grain (or 3-5 meals for 2)
Serving size: 1/3-1/2 cups per person

Sea vegetables are easy to roast. They add a nice crunch as well as a savory and slightly salty flavor when crumbled over hot cereal or dinner grains. Roast them half an hour before serving to retain their crispy texture or roast them ahead then store them in the oven or an airtight glass jar. Once roasted they keep well, so don't hesitate to roast a few cupfuls at a time. We like to roast them overnight while we sleep (with just the pilot light on in the gas stove). That way we wake up to crispy sea weed—just in time for breakfast!

Dulse, wild nori, ocean ribbons, or sea palm are tasty crumbled into the bottom of your cereal bowl (or over the top) before spooning on other condiments.

Note: You can cut the cooking time for many sea vegetable dishes by dry roasting them before adding them to soups, stews, stir fried dishes, sautés, and the like) Please sort the sea vegetables well. Dulse often contains small shells, sea urchins, or pebbles.

3-3 1/2 cups dry sea vegetable

(*dulse, alaria, digitata kelp, kombu, ocean ribbons, sea palm, wild nori, or other variety*)*

1. Sort sea vegetables, particularly dulse, and remove any shells or tiny mollusks or stones (add these to your soup stock scrap bowl.)

2. Place dry seaweed in a cast iron skillet or on a cookie sheet. Dry roast in the oven at 200-225°F. for 20-40 minutes or until crispy, while you get ready in the morning. They won't burn if left in longer at this low temperature. Or, place the skillet or panful of sea vegetables in a gas oven with just the pilot light on before bed, then leave it all day or overnight. It will be roasted within 12 hours and may be stored there almost indefinitely. Take out what you need then put the skillet back in the oven.

Storage: Store leftovers in an airtight jar for later use or keep them in a skillet in the oven, with the pilot light on. Be sure to take this pan of sea vegetables out of the oven before baking, broiling or preheating the oven.

Serving suggestions:

- **Note:** Whole or roasted kelp, alaria and kombu are generally too hardy and tough to be eaten as a dry condiment over grains or with porridge. These are best cooked into various dishes. Dulse from Maine is also very tough and best cooked or soaked and added to salads or dressings. Dulse from Canada, however, is tender enough to be roasted and eaten out of hand or crumbled over hot cereal, dinner grain, or squash dishes.

- **Morning sea veggies:** Place the skillet on the table and crumble a handful over your morning porridge or into the bottom or your cereal bowl before adding your soft grain. Stir. Top with the condiments of your choice—a seasoned and ground seed or nut condiment or a teaspoon or two of flax or sesame oil, or an occasional poached egg or dab of raw butter or ghee. Serve any of these combinations with a side of steamed, stir-fried, or quick-boiled greens or leftover pressed or marinated salad, along with a sprinkle of parsley, chives, scallions and/or black pepper or ginger.

- **Supper sea veggies:** Use dry roasted sea vegetables as a condiment for dinner grain.

- Grind roasted sea vegetable in a suribachi and/or mix with an equal volume of powdered onion granules, dried parsley or chives, or ground, roasted, seasoned seeds or nuts if desired. Use as a salt shaker alternative at the table—sprinkled over soups, stews, casseroles, rice, millet, vegetables or eggs.

- Crumble a small amount into a soup or stew or use in a sauté or casserole dish..

- Use roasted sea vegetables in any recipe for sea vegetable condiments. You may need to use less of them because they will be more concentrated after roasting. ❏

Dulse, Dried Onion & Sea Cress Sprinkles (Any Season)

Prep: 10 minutes
Cooking: None
Serving size: 1-3 tsp. per person.

This herb-like condiment makes a delicious topping for soups, stews, cooked vegetables, morning cereal, or brown rice, millet, or noodles. It adds trace minerals, color, and flavor to simple dishes. We keep it in a jar on the table, and serve it by the teaspoonful, with or without a seasoned seed or nut condiment such as Walnut Condiment, Tamari Roasted Pumpkin Seeds, or Buttery Flax Seed Sprinkle. You may want to double the recipe, spoon it into small spice jars, then share it with friend or take it with you when you travel or dine out.

1/2 cup dulse flakes

1/2 cup sea cress flakes or ao-nori flakes

1/2 cup dried onion granules or onion powder

1. Mix all ingredients in a bowl then transfer to small jars or spice bottles.

Serving suggestions: Serve by the 1/2 tsp. to 4 tsp. per person over dinner grain, hot cereal, gravy topped grain or cooked vegetables or sprinkle a few pinches over soup or stew.

Storage: Kept in a sealed jar this condiment will last almost indefinitely away from direct sunlight. We keep a bottle on the table.

Variations:

• Mix dulse flakes with onion granules or onion powder.

• Mix sea cress flakes with onion granules or onion powder.

• **Grind your own sea flakes:** Start with raw, unroasted sea vegetables. Pulverize in a blender, Corona Mill, or other high powered grinder.

• **Note:** Dulse flakes and sea cress sea vegetable flakes can be found in the bulk herb section of some health food stores or in the macrobiotic section or by mail order. (See resources at the end of this book.) ❑

Basic Procedure, Sea Palm or Ocean Ribbon Sauté(Year Round) ***

Prep: 15-20 minutes
Soaking: 1-8 hours
Cooking: 40-50 minutes

Serves: 4 (or 2 meals for 2)
Serving size: 1/4-1/2 cup per person

** *Reduce recipe by one-half to serve 4 (or 2 meals for 2).*

Here's a simple sea vegetable dish that's sure to be a hit—even with the new-to-sea vegetables-crowd. It makes an especially nice condiment for pressure cooked brown rice or rice with amaranth, quinoa, beans, nuts, or seeds. Leftovers keep for several days and are great, served at room temperature or turned into a soup with other leftovers.

1-1 1/3 cup dry ocean ribbons **or** sea palm
   (*becomes ~2 cups when soaked*)

3-4 cups water to soak

2-3 tsp. ghee or sesame or olive oil

2 packed cup onions, preferably white, Walla Walla Sweets or Vadalia onions, cut in thin crescents

1/8 tsp. sea salt

2-3 cloves garlic, minced

Optional, 1 tsp. finely minced ginger root

1 1/2 tsp. tamari or shoyu

1. Soak sea vegetable in water, in a bowl or jar topped with a glass of water or smaller jar to keep the vegetables submerged in the soak water. You won't need much water if you have a weighted object pressing on the sea vegetables. Soak 1-8 hours before bed, first thing in the morning, or before doing other things in the kitchen.

2. Remove sea vegetable from soak water, chop into 1/2-inch lengths (save soak water).

3. Chop vegetables. Sauté onions in oil in a large wok or cast iron skillet. Add sea salt to draw out additional moisture. Add garlic and/or ginger. Sauté until onions are translucent around the edges, stirring often. If desired add mushrooms and stir to soften, or add carrots.

4. Slowly add soak water and tamari or shoyu. Cover, bring to boil, reduce heat to low, and simmer, covered, for 30 minutes or until sea and land vegetables are very tender.

5. Remove lid, cook away most of the remaining liquid. Transfer to a serving bowl and cover with a bamboo sushi mat if desired.

Serving suggestions: Serve with soup, grain, and a green vegetable side dish. If the grain does not have nuts or seeds, add a seasoned seed or nut condiment on the grain.

Storage: Refrigerate leftovers. Take out 20-60 minutes before a meal to serve at room temperature. Use within 2-4 days.

Leftover tips:

• Toss a small amount of this dish with leftover steamed greens or boiled salad.

• Toss with plain noodles plus steamed cauliflower and/or broccoli.

• Stuff in won tons, ravioli, steamed buns, or add to a steamed omelet, stir fry, or salad.

• Combine a portion with leftover root, round or ground vegetables, and/or beans, stock or water, to make a quick soup.

Variations:

• Reduce onions to 3/4-1 cup then add 1/2 each of red, yellow and/or green bell peppers, cut in thin strips, after onions are tender. Stir briefly, sauté, then proceed with steps #3 and 4.

• Use 1-2 cups sliced onion and 2 cups thinly sliced button or crimini mushrooms or use 2 cups onions and 4 sliced shiitake mushrooms.

• Replace all or part of the onions with corn off the cob.

• Use 1-2 cups of onion and 1-2-cups finely cut carrot and/or rutabaga (cut in matchsticks or half moons). ❏

Alaria "Caviar" Condiment (Year Round)***

Soaking: 2-8 hours**
Cooking: 1-1 1/2 hours

Serves: 8-12 (or 4-5 meals for 2)
Serving size: 1-3 Tbsp. per person
Yield: 2- 2 1/2 cups

This condiment is delicious spooned over rice, millet, or pasta, especially with a few teaspoonfuls of roasted sunflower or pumpkin seeds, or roasted, chopped walnuts. Mild red pepper and hickory smoke flavoring add a bacon-like flavor. It has a slightly fishy, almost caviar-like taste and keeps for several weeks in the refrigerator. As a condiment it is best served by the spoonful rather than by the quarter– or half–cup!

2 cups tightly packed, dry, alaria sea weed

3 cups water (slightly more if boiling)

2-3 Tbsp. tamari (natural soy sauce) *or* shoyu

Optional, 2-4 Tbsp. brown rice vinegar *or* natural apple cider vinegar

Optional, 1/4-1/2 tsp. mild red pepper, powder*(ancho, Anaheim, or chipotle)*

Optional, 1 tsp. liquid smoke

1. Soak alaria in a small bowl in the above volume of water for 2-8 hours to soften. It is helpful to place a smaller bowl on top of the sea vegetable to keep it submerged in the liquid.

2. Pressure cook with the soak water for 1 hour.

3. After pressure cooking, remove lid, mince finely then and add tamari or shoyu. Add spice and/or liquid smoke as desired. Bring to a low boil, reduce heat and simmer away excess liquid.

4. Spoon into a pint sized glass jar or bowl.

Storage: Cover and refrigerate when cooled. This condiment will keep for several weeks, though you may go through it sooner!

Serving suggestions: Spoon a tablespoon or two over rice, millet or a two grain combination with a sprinkling of dry roasted, chopped nuts, umeboshi roasted pumpkin or sunflower seeds, a dab of ghee, or teaspoon of oil. Also serve with greens and a colorful root, round or ground vegetable soup, stew, or side dish.

More serving ideas:

- **Toast with Vegetarian Caviar:** A bit strange to the uninitiated, this one's for diehard seaweed fans! Spoon a small amount of Alaria condiment on toast or steamed bread, sprinkle with a dash of dry roasted, chopped nuts or spread bread with tahini first. Or top with steamed, poached, or pan fried tofu. If desired, top with steamed kale or collards for sandwich.

- Serve over soft oatmeal, rice, or millet porridge with 1/2-1 Tbsp. chopped, dry roasted walnuts, hazelnuts, or sunflower seeds. Add a sprinkle of fresh or dried chives, scallions, or parsley, and steamed, sautéed or parboiled greens.

- Serve over noodles that have first been topped with a dash of olive or toasted sesame oil or thinned sesame tahini. Sprinkle with dried or fresh, minced chives. Figure 2 Tbsp. alaria condiment and 1-2 tsp. oil, ghee, or butter, or sesame tahini per 2-3 cups cooked warm pasta. Serve with soup or stew and cooked greens or mixed vegetables.

Variations:

- **See Wild Nori Condiment**
- **See also Sea, Sage & Sunflower Spread.** ❐

Wild Nori Condiment (Any Season)

Prep: 15-20 minutes
Cooking: 1-1 1/2 hours

Yield: 2-1/2 cups
Serving size: 1- 3 Tbsp. per person

This delicious sea vegetable condiment lasts for several weeks in the refrigerator and makes a delicious mineral rich topping for rice, millet, whole grain pasta, or vegetables. Wild Nori tastes a bit like caviar when cooked into a thick paste. Laver is the name for the same sea vegetable found in Scotland, Ireland, and Wales. (Refer to the resource list in the back of the book for mail order sources for wild nori.)

Note: You can make this tasty condiment with or without spices.

2 1/2-3 cups loosely packed wild nori or laver (in dry form)—see variations below

3 cups water, or slightly more to cover sea weed

1-2 Tbsp. tamari or shoyu soy sauce

Optional, 1/2-1 tsp. cumin powder, or to taste

Optional, 1-2 Tbsp. mirin (sweet cooking rice wine)

1. Dry roast sea vegetables. See Basic Dry Roasted Sea Vegetable Procedure.

2. Grind to a powder in a suribachi then measure out 1/2-2/3 cup of sea vegetable powder or flakes. Cover with water and allow to soak for several minutes. Depending on whether you are using Atlantic or Pacific Coast nori, you may need to add more water. In our experience, the nori from Maine, (Atlantic Coast) swells and soaks up more water than the Pacific Variety (from California). Add tamari or shoyu. Add cumin and mirin if desired.

3. Bring to boil, cover, reduce heat to low and simmer for 30 minutes or until a thick paste is created. (We slip a heat deflector under the pot to prevent burning.) If too watery, simmer away excess liquid after removing lid. Taste and add more cumin if desired.

Serving suggestions: Use as a condiment for cooked whole grains or steamed vegetables, to marinate salads, or add a spoonful to leftover steamed broccoli, cauliflower, or beans to make an instant soup.

This condiment is especially good over rice, topped with a few teaspoons of roasted pumpkin, sunflower, sesame, or flax seeds. Or try it over Quinoa-Rice, Rice & Amaranth, Millet & Amaranth, Sweet Rice & Millet or some other two grain combination. Also serve with a side of greens and a colorful root or round vegetable dish.

Storage: Store in a jar in the refrigerator.

Variations:

- In place of cumin use ground mustard powder, chili powder, Italian herbs or 1 Tbsp. dried, rubbed sage.

- Omit cumin and add 1/4 tsp. red pepper powder (mild chipotle, anaheim, or ancho).

- Use a portion of this condiment as a dressing for tossed wild salad greens or parboiled vegetables. Toss vegetables with dressing to coat then allow to marinated for several hours.

- Replace 2 cups of dry nori with 1/2 cup roasted and ground Atlantic Coast Nori or 2/3-1 cup roasted, ground Pacific Coast Nori. Cook as above with seasonings.

- Add 1 tsp. liquid smoke in step #3 above, for a more bacon or sausage-like flavor. ❏

Sautéed Sunchokes with Dulse (Fall, Winter, Spring)***

Prep: 15-20 minutes
Cooking: 1/2 hour
Serves: 6-8 (or 3-4 + meals for 2)
Serving size: 1/2+ cup per person

Jerusalem artichokes *look* like a cross between a ginger root and a potato but they taste much sweeter, and entirely different! They bear no resemblance to the common green artichokes commonly found in grocery stores and fancy restaurants. You may find them labeled as "sunchokes" since they are a member of the sunflower family. They are wonderful in hearty winter or spring-time soups, stews, sautés, stove top casseroles, stir fry, and boiled salads too.

This dish has been particularly popular with cooking students and guests, even those who have never eaten or enjoyed sea vegetables! Once you try it, we think you'll like it. We like to serve it with steamed greens combined with root vegetables, brown rice, and a seed condiment. For company, we often make a red bean soup for contrast. Leftovers taste even better the second day and make a great quick soup or stew when combined with water or stock.

1 Tbsp. ghee *or* sesame or olive oil

1 large onion, cut in thin half moons or crescents

6-8 cups sunchokes, washed and scrubbed very well, then cubed or cut into 1" pieces

1/4 tsp. sea salt

3 cloves minced garlic

Optional 1 tsp. dried powdered cumin *or* sage

1 cup raw, dry dulse seaweed *or* 2/3 cup dry roasted dulse

1-3 tsp. tamari, shoyu (soy sauce) *or* umeboshi vinegar, or to taste

1/4-1/3 cup water to cover the bottom of skillet

1. Sort the dulse to remove any shells or stones. It is unnecessary to wash the dulse. Soak in water to just cover then chop finely or cut dulse with scissors while dry and omit soaking. Or, use 2/3 cup unsoaked, dry roasted dulse and crumble coarsely with your hands.

2. Warm the oil in a cast iron skillet or heavy stainless steel sauce pan or deep fry pan. Add onions and sea salt. Sauté over medium heat until wilted and translucent around the edges. Add garlic and cumin or sage. Stir and sauté for 3-4 minutes then add chopped jerusalem artichokes. Keep stirring, then add chopped, cut, or crumbled dulse and tamari, shoyu, or ume, and 1/3 cup water or enough to just cover the bottom of the skillet.

3. Bring to boil to create steam. Cover and simmer over low heat 20-30 minutes until tender and juicy.

4. Remove lid during last few minutes of cooking to cook away any excess water. Taste and add additional tamari or umeboshi vinegar if desired. Remove from heat and stir briefly.

Serving suggestions: Serve with cooked whole grains or pasta, steamed greens or pressed or parboiled salad, and a spoonful of sauerkraut or other vegetable pickles.

Storage: Refrigerate leftovers. Serve at room temperature or warm briefly by steaming in a bowl on a rack. Or, turn leftovers into a tasty soup or stew by combining with leftover soup, bean stew, water, stock and/or other bits of leftovers. (See Soups from Leftovers.)

Variations:

- Sprinkle individual servings with ground black pepper at the table if desired.

- For a rich gravy, dissolve 2-4 tsp. sesame tahini in 2 Tbsp. water. Stir this into the sauté during last few minutes of cooking. This is excellent over noodles, millet, or rice.

- **Carrots & Dulse:** Replace all or half of the sunchokes with rolling cut chunks of carrots.

- **Squash and Dulse:** Replace sunchokes with winter squash above. ❏

Sea Vegetables in Sesame Sauce
(Any Season)

Prep: 15-20 minutes
Soaking: 1-8 hours or overnight
Cooking: 40-45 minutes

Serves: 6-8 (or 3-4 meals for 2)
Serving size: about 1/2 cup per person

Reduce recipe by one-half as needed.

Even people who have never eaten sea weeds will like this dish. (Isn't anything better with peanut or sesame butter on it?) Really, just a dash of sesame, peanut or sunflower butter will mask the fishy taste that some newcomers to seaweed cuisine find so offensive. If you're already a fan of sea weed, make this dish for dinner at home or take to your next potluck. It's a great supplementary source of minerals and incredibly delicious. (This recipe was adapted from a recipe using arame—a Japanese sea vegetable—in Julia Ferre's *Basic Macrobiotic Cooking*.)

1 heaping cup dry sea palm or ocean ribbons (*yields ~2 cups after soaking*)

1 1/2-2 cups water to soak

1-2 tsp. unroasted sesame oil *or* ghee

1 large onion or leek cut in thin crescents or half moons

2-4 cloves garlic minced and/or 1-2 tsp. peeled, minced ginger root

Optional, 1 small, fresh chili pepper, minced finely
   or 1/8-1/4 tsp. chipotle, Anaheim *or* ancho red pepper powder (these are mild)

Optional, 1-2 tsp. dried powdered thyme, cumin or curry powder

2-3 pinches sea salt

2 carrots, halved lengthwise then cut in thin diagonals or matchsticks

1-3 tsp. tamari or shoyu, or slightly more as needed

1 cup water

2-4 Tbsp. sesame butter *or* sesame tahini (see variations below), dissolved in 2-6 Tbsp. water

Garnish:

Garlic chives or scallions, minced finely

1. Do not rinse sea vegetable, simply soak in water to just cover. Place a small bowl on top of the sea vegetable to keep it submerged in the water. Soak for 1-9 hours or overnight.

2. Remove sea vegetables from soak water and chop into 1/2 inch lengths. Reserve the soak water.

3. Add oil to a large cast iron skillet or heavy-duty stainless steel pot. Add onion, and a few pinches of sea salt. Sauté over medium heat until tender and translucent. Add garlic and red pepper if desired. Add herbs or spices, stir then add carrots. Add sea vegetable with enough soak water to just cover. Bring to boil, cover tightly, then reduce heat to low and simmer, covered, 30 minutes.

4. Dissolve seed or nut butter in remaining soak water. Add to vegetables and stir constantly. Turn flame to medium-low heat then simmer and stir to thicken. Remove from heat and garnish.

Serving suggestions: Serve as a condiment for brown rice, millet, or noodles, with soup and a steamed green or mixed vegetable side dish. Refrigerate leftovers and serve them as a condiment or combine them with other leftovers to make a quick soup.

Variations:

- Use peanut or sunflower butter in place of sesame butter above.

- In step #2, add 1/2 each of red, yellow, and green bell peppers, cut in thin 1/2-1 inch strips.

- Replace carrots with 2-3 cups cauliflower florets and 1 cup thinly sliced green beans or whole snow peas, added during the last 8-10 minutes of cooking. ❑

Herbed Pan Fried Sea Vegetable Chips (Any Season)

Prep: 20 minutes
Soaking: 6-12 hours or overnight
Cooking: 1 1/2 hours

Serves: 6-8 (or 3-4 meals for 2)
Serving size: 2 3-4 inch strips per person

You'll love these herb coated sea vegetable strips. They taste like a cross between potato chips and beef jerky! They make a tasty condiment on top of rice, millet, or vegetables.

For a colorful meal, serve these "chips" with a red or orange vegetable or bean soup (try azuki or kidney beans with leeks, squash, or parsnips), some brown rice cooked with millet, amaranth, or quinoa, a steamed or parboiled greens dish, and a roasted pumpkin or sunflower seed condiment. Leftover Sea Chips are also delicious crumbled over soups, salads, or morning cereal!

1 cup packed, dry, kelp or alaria sea vegetable

1 1/2 cups water to just cover sea vegetable

1 1/2 Tbsp. tamari or shoyu

1/2 cup arrowroot powder

1/8 tsp. sea salt

1 tsp. dried sage or cumin + 1 tsp. dried thyme
    + 1/2 tsp. dried marjoram

   or 1 Tbsp. garlic powder + 2-3 Tbsp. dried
   chives + 1 tsp. dried thyme

2 Tbsp. ghee or raw sesame oil *or* olive oil

1. Soak sea vegetable in water to just cover for 6-12 hours to soften. Put a jar on top to keep sea vegetable submerged in the soak water. (They can be cut with a scissor before soaking.)

2. Cut sea vegetable into 3-4 inch long strips, unless you have cut them before soaking.

3. Pressure cook 1 hour with soak water and tamari or shoyu.

4. Remove lid and simmer away excess liquid. (If boiling, bring to boil, cover, reduce heat to low, and simmer 1 1/2-2 hours, or until tender. When boiling, you will need to add more water to prevent burning.)

5. Mix herbs, sea salt and flour in a shallow bowl. Roll each strip in mixture to coat well. Pan fry in a lightly oiled skillet, cooking several at a time. When browned, flip over, cook the other side, and remove when done. Repeat process until all of kelp or alaria is cooked.

6. Place finished pieces on a baking sheet in the oven at 300° F to keep warm and to crisp them while cooking the rest of the batch. Oven baking for 10-15 minutes before serving makes the chips more crispy and tasty.

Serving suggestions: Serve 2-3 strips per person with grain, cooked greens or pressed or marinated salad, and condiments. Add a bean or veggie soup and/or a colorful root, round or ground vegetable side dish or corn on the cob.

Storage: Refrigerate leftovers and serve at room temperature or warmed briefly. ❏

Kale with Sea Palm, Shoyu & Mushrooms (Any Season)

Prep: 20 minutes
Soaking: 1/2 hour
Cooking: 40 minutes

Serves: 8 (or 4 meals for 2)
Serving size: 1/2-1 cup per person

** *Reduce recipe by one-half to serve 4 (or 2 meals for 2).*

This is a good dish to serve when introducing friends to sea vegetables. Serve this with a creamy squash, carrot, tomato, or beet soup, whole grain or noodles, and condiments. Leftovers are delicious rolled in pita or tortillas with scrambled tofu or cooked lentils. Leftover can also be packed for lunch with a cup of creamless cream of vegetable soup or bean soup, whole grain, a seed condiment, and pickles. The leftovers are also delicious served over morning cereal with a nut or seed condiment or a steamed egg plus scallions or chives.

1 1/3 cup dry sea palm sea vegetable, loosely packed
1 1/2-2 cups water to soak sea vegetable

Optional 2 tsp. ghee or sesame or olive oil
1 medium onion (preferably a sweet variety)
3-3 1/3 cups button or crimini mushrooms *or* 8-10 fresh or dried shiitake mushrooms
2 pinches sea salt
1-1 1/2 Tbsp. tamari soy sauce

Steamed or boiled vegetables:

1 medium-large bunch kale or collard greens, washed well
1/8-1/4 tsp. sea salt
Water to cover a pot by 1-2"

1. Soak sea vegetable in water to just cover for 2-8 hours with a plate or jar on top to keep it submerged in soak water. If using dried shiitake mushrooms, soak them with sea vegetable.

2. Oil-free sauté onion crescents in a wok or cast iron skillet with a few pinches of sea salt (to draw moisture out of the onions). Or sauté in oil with sea salt. Stir and brown onions. When soft and wilted, add mushrooms and another pinch of salt. Stir over medium heat until softer. Add 1-2 Tbsp. water as needed.

3. Remove sea vegetables from water, chop finely, then add to the skillet with onions, soak water and tamari. Bring to boil then reduce heat to low and simmer, covered, 1/2 hour or until liquid is absorbed. While sea vegetable cooks, prepare greens.

4. Bring 1-2 inches of lightly salted water to boil in a large pot. Layer greens in pot or stand them on their stems if using a tall pot. Cover and cook over medium-high heat for 6-10 minutes, until stems are very tender and vegetables are vibrant green. (Or, use Basic Procedure, Boiled Whole Greens).

5. Remove greens with a slotted spoon. Save cooking water for use as soup stock or in kuzu drinks. Chop stems finely then cut leaves into 1 inch squares or bite sized pieces.

6. In a serving bowl, toss greens with cooked mushroom and sea palm or ocean ribbons. Cover with a bamboo sushi mat then serve warm or at room temperature.

Storage: Refrigerate leftovers and take meal size portions out of the refrigerator at least 1/2-1 hour before serving to take the chill off. Use within 36 hours.

Variation:

• Replace kale or collards with 1 large head chopped and lightly steamed cauliflower or steam or parboil 8 cups of broccoli, including peeled and chopped stems, then toss with above ingredients.

• Replace sea palm with ocean ribbons. ❏

Macaroni Sea & Sunchoke Casserole (Fall & Winter)***

Prep: 20-30 minutes
Cooking: 1 hour + 15 minutes

Serves: 6-8 (or 3-4 meals for 2) if served with bread or rice
Serving size: 1 1/2-2 1/2 cups per person

The combination of sunchokes (Jerusalem artichokes) with dulse sea vegetable, and macaroni creates a flavor reminiscent of white meat fish or tuna noodle casserole while grated, dried mochi (available in most health food stores) provides a gooey, cheesy consistency. If sunchokes are unavailable, button or crimini mushrooms can be substituted with good results. A sprinkling of Flax or Sunflower Seed Condiment can also enhance this dish when added at the table.

Pasta:

12 oz. dry spelt or other whole grain pasta; spaghetti, rotini, fettuccini or elbows

2 quarts water for cooking pasta

1/4-1/2 tsp. sea salt

Dulse and sunchokes:

1 Tbsp. light or toasted sesame oil or olive oil

2-3 cups minced onion

2-3 cloves minced garlic

4 cups Jerusalem artichokes, washed well and cut into 1/2-1" pieces (see variation*)

2-2 1/2 cups loosely packed, dulse sea vegetable, sorted then scissor cut

1/2-3/4 tsp. sea salt

3/4 cup water

Herbs & mochi "cheese"

1 1/2 tsp. dried thyme

1/2-3/4 of a 12-ounce pkg. plain, mochi, thawed (1 1/2-2 cups when grated)

1-2 Tbsp. tamari or shoyu

Garnish: Black pepper and/or minced chives or scallions

+/- Flax or Sunflower Seed Condiment

1. Sort dulse well to remove any stones or shells! Cut with scissors or chop with a knife.

2. Cook, drain, and rinse pasta according to Basic Pasta Procedure, Set aside.

3. In a deep 3-4 quart pot or a wok, sauté onions in oil with a pinch of sea salt until translucent. Add garlic, sunchokes or mushrooms, and scissor cut dulse. Stir. Add salt and water, cover, bring to boil, reduce heat to low and simmer until tender (about 30 minutes).

4. Grate mochi with a cheese grater then toss with cooked pasta, dulse, sunchokes, herbs, and tamari. Transfer to a 3-4 quart casserole dish, cover, bake at 350° F for 40-45 minutes.

Serving suggestions: Serve warm with a side of greens; whole grain bread and/or rice; with or without a cup of soup or side of beans. (Try Spiced Red Bean Soup, Azuki Bean & Leek Soup, or puréed Cream of Carrot Soup.)

Storage: Refrigerate leftovers. Reheat entire casserole or meal size portions using covered-bowl-within-a-pot method.

Variations:

• Substitute oven roasted alaria or wild nori sea vegetable for dulse.

• Replace Jerusalem artichokes with button or crimini mushrooms, cut in thin slices. Cook as above. ❏

Chapter 7
Eat Your Beans, Tofu, Tempeh & Wheat Meat

Lean & Lively Bean Cuisine

Beans have been used by many cultures around the world, for centuries. They are nutritional powerhouses that can supply you with necessary nutrients. They can also help you to lose weight, lower your cholesterol, and improve your energy and endurance.

Beans won't leave you empty handed. In fact beans beat many animal products hands down! Besides being high in protein, beans are high in fiber (which fills you up and keeps things running through you smoothly), and low in fat.

A mere 3-8% of beans' calories come from fat, while a typical hamburger derives 65% of calories from fat. An average steak 82%, American cheese 73%, cream cheese 91%, and dark meat chicken 32%. Skinless chicken comes in at 18% fat, almost 5 times as much as beans!

So where's the protein? % of calories derived from protein	
T-bone steak	16%
Full fat milk	21%
Lamb chops	22%
Chickpea/garbanzo beans	23%
Blue cheese	23%
Cheddar cheese	25%
Red kidney beans	26%
Lima beans	27%
Low fat milk	28%
Lentils	29%
Swiss cheese	30%
Hamburger	34%
Dry soybeans	34%
Mung bean sprouts	43%
Soy bean curd (tofu)	43%

While beans can be found in the traditional diets of agrarian cultures from around the world, the science and art of bean cuisine has been perfected in Asia. The Far East has long been relying on a variety of beans—especially soy beans—for food and medicine.

Soybeans are one of the largest crops grown on U.S. farm land. Unfortunately, nearly 90% of them are fed to livestock and few indeed know how to properly prepare these foods for best digestion, nutrition, and a delicious taste. Did you know that most folks eat less than one teaspoonful of beans a day! What a shame. Not only are beans low in fat and high in protein and fiber. They are also an excellent source of complex carbohydrates and trace minerals and have been shown to help even out blood sugar levels, particularly for diabetics and people with hypoglycemia. They've also been shown to contain certain cancer protective compounds.

Although beans have a reputation in the West of being a poor man's substitute for meat, in the East beans and bean products are found on the plates of the rich as well as the poor.

Beans are economical

Besides being nourishing, beans are relatively inexpensive, costing just pennies per cup. Dried beans are very concentrated; all of their moisture has been extracted during drying and most have been reduced in size by one-third, so a little bit, once soaked and cooked, goes a long way.

Here's how we figure:

Dry beans:

weight	cups dry	cups cooked	cost	# of servings
1/4 lb.	2/3 cup	1 1/3-2 cups	$ .08- $ .20	3-6 (1-3 meals for 2)*
1 lb	2 1/2 cups	6 cups	$ .30- $ .90	12-18 people*

Servings per cooked bean dish:

Dry beans	Cooked yield in particular dishes	Serves
1 cup dry beans	2-2 1/2-cups cooked beans	6-8 (3-4 meals for 2)
1 cup dry beans	4-8 cups of bean soup or stew	4-8 (2-4 meals for 2)
1 cup dry beans	2-3+ cups cooked and refried beans	4-8 (several meals for 2)
1 cup dry beans	3-4 cups bean dip or paté	6-12 (6 with leftovers)

Notes:

* Exact number of servings will depend upon the preparation. For soup, stew, condiment, dips, and sauces we figure 1/2-2/3 cup dry beans serves 4. For refried beans, roughly 1 cup of dry beans serves 4.

**When cooking for two people, we typically soak 1/2-3/4 cup dry beans at a time. This will yield 4 servings (or 2 meals for 2) prepared as a soup, stew, or condiment.

What's a serving of beans?

- 1 cup (8-10 oz.) bean soup or stew
- 2-4 Tbsp. well-seasoned bean condiment (such as natto)
- 1/4-2/3 cup cooked beans, bean & vegetable side dish, or bean dip or paté
- 1-2 oz. tempeh *or* 2-4 oz. tofu (~1/4-1/2 cup cooked)
- 1/8-1/4 cup dry beans (before preparation)
- 1/2-1 cup soy yogurt or non-fortified soy milk (use less often than whole beans)

How much is enough?

We recommend 1-2 servings of beans, tofu, tempeh, or wheat meat 5-7x per week (Wheat meat may be counted in the bean group because it is so high in protein. Alternatively, it may be counted as *part of,* but not all of, your grain. It can also be combined with beans in the same dish, meal, or day, if used in small amounts.)

There are a variety of good reasons and delicious ways to eat beans. And there is an inviting array of beans to eat. All you need to make these foods part of nourishment for your life is a bit of knowledge and some simple and effective kitchen techniques.

Bean Cookery Basics

Flexible beans

Many beans can be used interchangeably, so don't be afraid to experiment. If a recipe calls for black turtle beans or kidney beans, you can safely substitute pinto or azuki beans. If a recipe calls for chickpeas, you can use great northern or white kidney beans. Since our recipes are just basic procedures, feel free to substitute whatever beans you have on hand (provided their cooking times are similar) to create your own unique recipes. Pay special attention to the soaking, cooking, seasoning, and serving tips which can help save you time, money, frustration, and digestive discomfort.

Beans & gas

Many folks think that beans and the copious production of gas are inevitably linked. However, there are ways to minimize the social and digestive discomfort.

Basic steps in bean cookery:

1) Sort, rinse and soak.

2) Drain, add fresh water and sea vegetable.

3) Pressure cook or simmer.

4) Season with sea salt and/or miso, tamari, or shoyu, plus herbs or spices.

Steps for avoiding gas:

1) Cook properly and fully.

2) Eat small volumes of beans with larger volumes of grains.

3) Avoid eating beans with fruits or fried foods.

4) Chew well.

We suggest that you cook only enough beans to last for two or three days and serve them in small amounts. Cooking a big pot of beans for the week can lead to eating more than you can digest and may create more gas than you can imagine.

Beans, like vegetables, lose most of their life force, aroma, and flavor when kept for an entire week. When frozen, most beans become gritty, watery, and far less tasty than when freshly cooked. The exceptions are well seasoned, fermented bean seasonings or condiments such as miso, tamari, shoyu, or tempeh or natto. Unlike most beans, natto keeps a few weeks in the refrigerator without spoiling. Miso, tamari, and shoyu last for years without spoiling. Both natto and tempeh hold up well in the freezer. Tofu can be frozen though the texture does change.

Sort & soak

Soaking and cooking beans in small volumes really doesn't take much time. Beans can be soaked all day or overnight and cooked while you are doing other things, even sleeping! First, sort beans to remove stones and other debris that often lurk within the bean bag or jar. (This can keep you from chipping a tooth or cracking a filling.) Wash off dirt and any gritty material.

Next soak. Soaking allows dried beans to absorb water and to soften. It also initiates the sprouting process Which makes more of the nutrients available. It is best to soak beans for a minimum of four to six hours and preferably eight to twelve. Western researchers have found that substances in the beans that inhibit digestion and assimilation can be inactivated by proper and lengthy soaking and by cooking in an alkaline solution (discussed below).

For convenience, sort, rinse, and soak beans before going to bed then drain and add fresh water and a strip of sea vegetable first thing in the morning. They can cook while you're eating breakfast or anytime later in the day. Alternately, you could soak them in the morning, then cook them in the evening. Beans can also be cooked all day or overnight in a crock pot or thermal cooker with or without soaking.

Proper cooking

Many people boil beans for hours in an attempt to render them soft. However, pressure cooking beans with a piece of kelp or kombu makes them far more digestible and it shortens their cooking time considerably. The sea vegetable contains substances which naturally enhance the flavor of and soften the fibers present in beans.

Although some beans—small red, azuki, black turtle, pinto, and kidney beans—may be soft after a lengthy soak and an hour of simmering, most others take several hours to soften by boiling. Chickpeas, black or yellow soybeans, whole dried green peas, and black eyed peas often take three to four hours to soften by boiling. If a pressure cooker is used, most small beans will be tender in twenty minutes and most large beans will be done in 30-40 minutes. Split peas, brown and red lentils don't need pressure cooking, though even they can be pressure cooked in a pinch,if a covered bowl-within-a-pot is used.

Due to their high fiber and starch content, beans should be thoroughly cooked before adding other ingredients such as vegetables, tempeh, wheat meat, vegetarian "sausage," herbs, spices, or salty seasonings. If lentils or split peas are used in soups, however, vegetables and spices may be added from the beginning because cooking time is generally less for these legumes.

Salting

Sun dried sea salt adds to the flavor and enjoyment of beans and bean products. But that's not all; Sea salt softens beans and adds substances which benefit digestion. From the Chinese medicine perspective, salt has a softening and downward energy. Cooking it into foods helps soften their tough fibers and makes food go down smoothly (rather than coming up in burps).

You may be familiar with the acid heartburn that can come from eating beans which are spiced but not salted. If salt (or miso or tamari) is omitted from a bean dish, you will likely come away from the meal with acid stomach, gas, bloating, or burping. While it is inadvisable to add salt to foods at the table, using some in cooking is of paramount importance to bring out flavor and facilitate proper digestion.

It is imperative to wait until beans are tender before salting and seasoning. One exception is when dry beans are soaked then cooked into a pot of brown rice or millet. In this case, the salt may be added directly to the pot before cooking and will not hinder softening if the mixture is pressure cooked.When preparing bean soups, stews, or sauces, you may add a small amount of salt to the softened beans and/or vegetables then season the pot more strongly with miso, tamari, or shoyu just before serving. Or, you may use sea salt as the only salty seasoning.

Add the spice

Herbs and spices, when used moderately, help to stoke the digestive fires, much as kindling added to a fire helps keep it burning. In most traditional cultures, herbs and spices are used to foster good digestion and assimilation. Onions, leeks, scallions and other pungent vegetables have also been used to warm beans and fuel digestion. However, it is important to use a light touch as some spices have a very hot energy and are easy to over use. Examples include garlic, ginger, chili, cayenne, black pepper, curry, and cardamom. These can overheat and dry out the body or cause profuse sweating and loss of vital energy when used inappropriately. Thus, it is generally best to to rely more often on herbs and spices with a more mild effect such as parsley, sage, rosemary, thyme, basil, oregano, dill, bay leaf, cumin, mustard, anise, cinnamon, onions, scallions, etc.

Though most herbs or spices are cooked into foods, some may be added at the table as garnishes. Minced fresh scallions, parsley, chives, garlic chives, arugula, and dill weed are good examples. For a more heating effect, dried chives, black pepper, the juice from grated ginger, or roasted garlic may be served with individual portions of cooked grains, beans, soups or stews. This allows each person to "season" his or her food to taste.

Skip the fruit and sweeteners

Many people unknowingly add ingredients to their beans which can severely hinder proper digestion. Fruits, sweeteners, and tomatoes have a cloying nature and can hinder digestion, creating stagnation and/or fermentation in the stomach. Consequently, you may want to limit the use of these foods for better digestion and health. (We suggest adding malt syrups to beans only infrequently, and sparingly.) Because avocados are very rich and consequently hard to digest (they are actually a fruit not a vegetable), if you eat them in the same meal with beans you may get indigestion and gas. Tomatoes can also be a problem if used often, in copious quantities, or by those with a weak digestive system.

Although it is common to use tomatoes (also a fruit) in bean dishes, this is often the cause of many of the digestive problems associated with eating beans. Tomatoes, and especially tomato sauce, have a very Cold energy which hinders digestion by dampening the digestive fire. Sun dried tomatoes are less Damp and Cold and thus can generally be used in bean dishes without undesirable effects, although even these are best used moderately and infrequently. (Refer to the vegetable chapter for more about tomatoes.) In place of tomatoes, try carrots, winter squash, and/or beets. They can add a sweet taste and vibrant red to orange color to bean dishes without producing gas, indigestion, or the sometimes harmful metabolic side-effects of tomatoes. Onions can also add a sweet flavor to bean dishes and will aid rather than hinder digestion.

Moderation

It's all too easy to "o.d." on beans because they are so tasty. However, turning them into soup or stew can greatly enhance digestion while making a little bit go a long way. As with other soups and stews, it is best to limit yourself to just one cup of bean soup in a meal. Taking seconds on bean soup can lead to digestive upset since soups contain a lot of fiber and water, and usually a fair amount of vegetables. Loading up on these can fill you up before you have eaten an ample and sustainable volume of grain. This can leave you very gassy soon after eating and very hungry a few hours later. When making bean side dishes it is helpful to remember to eat more grains than beans, using beans as a condiment.

Of bean products, tofu is particularly cooling and is best used moderately by vegetarians and vegans. Used too often or in too large a volume tofu can create a sluggish metabolism (by dampening the digestive and metabolic fires) and a very Cold condition. Moderation with tofu means that one would be best not to use it on a daily basis. Once or twice per week would be prudent, less for those who are already very Cold. (See the tofu section for more information.)

Chewing your beans

Foods like beans, whole grains, and fibrous vegetables are of a more complex nature than predigested, refined and overly processed food products. The fibrous walls of plant foods must be thoroughly broken down by cooking (the first step in the digestive process) and proper mastication (the second step of the digestive process) so that our digestive enzymes can do their work and we can get all of the nutrients locked inside the bean's cell wall. Unchewed beans are a likely cause of the digestive distress that so many people associate with beans. Setting aside 45-60 minutes for each meal, without the distraction of reading, writing, watching television, or working will allow ample time for you to chew well and to savor and enjoy every bite. Chewing makes a bigger difference than you might imagine. Try it!

Bean Cuisines Around the World

Throughout the world beans have played a major part in traditional diets. If you think meat or fish, chicken or turkey has to be the main dish, think again. Some of the most popular ethnic cuisines around the world use beans and grains as main dishes with animal products traditionally playing minor roles. If you want some inspiration in the bean department, think ethnic. In Japan small red beans are often cooked with rice or soup or sweetened and stuffed into pastries for dessert. In China, tofu has been used for centuries in soups, sauces, stir-fries and other dishes. Mediterranean and Indian cooks rely heavily on chickpeas and lentils to make dips, patés, soups, curries, croquettes, and even crispy pancakes! In Central and South America, beans are commonly used to make burritos, enchiladas, chili, dips, and casseroles. In Indonesia, soybean tempeh is used to make shish-kabobs, sauces, burgers, cutlets, and stews. Countless other examples of bean-grain based meals exist.

Common Methods of Preparing Beans & Bean Products

Everyday Bean Preparations:

Bean soups, stews, and chili**
Beans cooked with millet
Beans cooked with rice
Beans cooked with wheat meat or tempeh
(e.g., "meat" balls, burgers, or casserole)
Refried beans

Everyday Tofu Preparations:
(Quickest & Easiest Preparations)

Scrambled Tofu with sea vegetable
Tofu in quick/clear soup broth
Tofu in stir fry or sautées**
Soy milk in creamed vegetable soups & sauces

Occasional or Seasonal Use
Bean Preparations:

Refried or baked beans **
Bean dips and spreads
Bean sauces and condiments
Bean and vegetable casseroles**
Bean burgers and loaves**
Fillings for steamed buns, tamales, won tons
ravioli, calzone, tacos, burritos, enchiladas
Bean salads**

Occasional or Seasonal Use
Tofu Preparations:

Tofu dips and spreads
Tofu fillings for steamed buns, calzones, tacos
    pot pies, won tons, ravioli, tamales, etc.
Tofu salad dressings
Tofu burgers, loaves, and meat-less balls
Tofu & Egg Salad or Egg-less Tofu Salad
Tofu & Egg Omelets & Scrambles
Tofu shish kebobs
Tofu in dumplings, breads, and biscuits
Tofu in casseroles

- **Ecological, economical & health considerations:** We suggest soaking and cooking beans (as you need them). Canned beans are inferior in taste, far more expensive, and much less ecological (they require a lot more energy to can and ship) than dried beans. Though at first it might seem like a lot of work, bean cookery requires very little hands-on time or attention. They can be soaked and cooked with just 15 minutes of hands-on prep!

- **Time considerations:** Our regular use bean preparations are just that—what we use on a daily basis. They take very little time and are easy to prepare. Our occasional or seasonal use preparations take more time to prepare—more than you may have on a daily basis. For this reason, we save these more involved dishes for dinners with friends, holidays, weekends or when we have a little more time to play in the kitchen.

- **Seasonal considerations:** Some bean dishes—such as bean salads and dips, which are usually served cool or close to room temperature—are more appropriate for warm weather. Others—such as baked bean casseroles—are more appropriate in cold weather. Still other bean dishes are somewhere in between, making them suitable for year round use. Some of the year round preparations we use include stove top bean casseroles and skillet dishes; bean soups, stews, and chilis; bean filled tamales, won tons, or steamed buns; refried beans; burritos; bean "meatballs;" and bean sauces. Throughout most of the year, for best digestion, we generally serve beans in warm and moist or soupy preparations

Basic Procedure, Soaking & Cooking Beans (Year Round)***

Prep: 5 minutes
Soaking: 4-8 hours or overnight
Cooking: pressure cook 20-45 minutes *or* simmer 1-4 hours *or* all day—5-12 hours in a crock pot

Yield: 2-2 1/2 cups cooked beans
Serves: 4-8 as soup or stew
or 6-8 as a condiment *or* side dish

With a little pre-planning and prep (the night or morning before) you can have tasty, easily digested beans, in a "jiffy." Soaking is recommended, even for lentils, and will, in some cases, reduce cooking time. Pressure cooking is helpful for most large beans, aids digestion and cuts the total cooking time at least in half.

We recommend soaking beans and legumes for at least 4-8 hours. If you're short on time and you choose beans that have not been soaked ahead, use quick cooking varieties such as azukis, small red beans, lentils, or split peas. These can be boiled in a pot or pressure cooked in a covered bowl. Pour boiling water over the beans, cover, and allow to soak 1/2-1 hour before cooking. Soaking for the full time is advisable because it breaks down substances which can inhibit digestion and absorption.

For a firm bean suitable for use in bean salads or casseroles, cook with a little less water and reduce cooking time. Cold or chilled bean dishes are more difficult to digest than warm dishes so it is best to serve all bean dishes warm, or at least close to room temperature.

Basic Ratio:

1 cup dry beans
  (kidney, anasazi, small red, garbanzo, black turtle, whole dried peas, black eyed peas, azuki/aduki , navy, bolita, canelloni, etc.)

3 cups water to soak

1 1/2-3 cups fresh water to cook (less for pressure cooking, more for boiling)

3-4" piece kelp, kombu, or alaria sea vegetable

Optional, 1 bay leaf

1. Sort beans and remove any stones. Rinse then drain in a strainer. Transfer to a glass or stainless steel bowl or the pot you intend to cook them in.

2. Add three times more water than beans. Leave the pot or bowl uncovered or cover with a bamboo sushi mat. Soak for at least 4 hours and preferably 8-12 hours or overnight. (In a pinch, lentils or azuki beans may be cooked with little or no soaking.)

3. Pour off soak water and add fresh water to cover 1/2-1 inch over beans. Add a piece of kelp, kombu, or alaria sea vegetable. Add a bay leaf if desired. (This further enhances digestion.)

4. **To boil:** Bring to boil in a 2-4-quart pot over medium heat. Cover, reduce heat to low and simmer until tender, 1-1 1/2 hours for small beans or 1 1/2-4 hours for large or extra hearty beans such as chickpeas or yellow or black soybeans. (Soaking for 12 hours will reduce cooking time.) Add more water as needed to prevent beans from boiling dry.

To pressure cook: If cooking 2 or less cups of dry beans in a 3-6 quart pressure cooker, use the bowl-within-a-pot method. Bring to full pressure over medium heat (high heat can cause the bean skins to block the pressure valve). Allow it to hiss loudly for 3 minutes then reduce heat to medium-low and cook for indicated time: 20-30 minutes for small beans, 30-40 minutes for large. Remove from heat and allow pressure come down naturally (10-15 minutes), or run cold water over the pot to release the pressure and open lid sooner. (Reduce cooking time for firmer beans.)

To crock pot cook: Soak beans as above, drain, then add fresh water and kelp or kombu. Water should cover 1/2-inch over the beans. Turn on high, cover, and cook for 4-5 hours. Or cook 1 hour on high then 6-9 hours on low. Exact cooking time will vary with soaking times and beans used.

5. Use cooking liquid or strain off and reserve for use in soups, stews, sauces, or gravies. (Bean cooking juices, particularly from garbanzo beans or white or yellow soybeans, makes incredibly rich and tasty soups, sauces or gravies without oil.)

Basic Procedure, Covered-Bowl-Within-A-Pot Method for Beans***

Prep: 10 minutes
Soaking: 4-12 hours or overnight
Cooking: 25-30 minutes

Yield: 2-3 cups cooked beans
Serves: 6-8 as soup or stew
or 5-8 as condiment or side dish

We use this method to pressure cook a small volume (2 cups or less) of beans. Since the two of us don't eat buckets of beans, we usually cook just 1/2-3/4 cup dry beans at a time. Normally you must fill a pressure cooker at least half full for it to work properly but this method allows you to cook a small volume. An added benefit is that there is no danger of the beans burning (when using enough water in the pressure cooker) because the beans are not directly on the bottom of the pot. This method also prevents the bean skins from clogging the pressure valve, even if you use lentils, split peas, or soybeans, beans that are not normally safe to pressure cook on their own. This method can also be used to cook small volumes of barley or whole oats for a soup, sauce, or purée.

Note: Use a small stainless steel bowl which fits inside your pressure cooker with room to spare. There should be about 1/2 to 2 inches around all sides of the bowl. (You can also use something called an Ohsawa pot, a heat-proof ceramic dish with a lid, designed for use inside a pressure cooker. See Mail Order Resources.)

Equipment:

32 oz. stainless steel bowl

2 liter (4-6 quart) pressure cooker

Basic Ratio: 1 cup dry beans
(kidney, aduki/azuki, anasazi, black turtle, black soy, navy, or pinto beans, chickpeas, etc.)

3-4 cups water for soaking

4" piece of kelp or kombu sea vegetable

1 1/2-2 cups fresh water for cooking

1. Rinse and sort through beans to remove stones. Soak 4-8 hours or overnight.

2. Drain beans, place in a small stainless steel bowl. (If using dried chestnuts, do not pour off the soak water; chestnuts should always be cooked in their soak water.) Add sea vegetable and fresh water to cover 1/2-1 inch over the beans.

3. Fill a pressure cooker with 1/2-2/3 inch of water. Insert the bowl containing the beans. The water should surround one-third of the bowl's height. If the water comes up higher, remove the bowl and pour off some of the water. (If the water is too high, it can cause the bowl to tip over.) Cover the bowl with a heat proof saucer. (See notes below for cooking two things at once in a pressure cooker.)

4. Bring to pressure over medium-high heat then reduce heat to medium or medium-low. (With this method, you can cook beans at a higher temperature than when cooking them directly in a pot.) Cook 10-15 minutes for lentils or split peas; 15-30 minutes for dried chestnuts, or kidney, navy, black eyed pea, black turtle, small red, pinto, navy, azuki, or other small beans; 30-40 minutes for garbanzo, black or yellow soybeans, or other large or tough beans. (Reduce cooking time for beans that have soaked 12 or more hours and/or if a firm texture is desired for a bean salad.)

5. Turn off heat. Wait for pressure to come down naturally or run the pot under cold water to bring the pressure down more quickly. Use a pot holder to first remove the bowl's cover, then remove the bowl.

Storage: If not using beans right away, refrigerate in glass jars or ceramic, glass, or pottery bowl covered with a plate. Use within several days for optimal flavor and nutrition. ❑

Pressure Cooking Two Different Beans in the Same Pot

Prep: 5-10 minutes
Soaking: 4-12 hours or overnight
Cooking: 20-30 minutes

Yield: 2-3 cups cooked beans
Serves: 6-8 as soup or stew
or 4-8 as condiment or side dish

The bowl-within-a-pot method is particularly handy for single people or small families as it allows you to separately cook two different types of beans in the same pot. When using this technique, you save energy and time and increase the variety in your diet.

Bean #1 (To be cooked in a 16-ounce stainless-steel bowl or Ohsawa pot)

1/2 cup dry beans
(small red beans, azuki or aduki, kidney, navy, or other beans)
2 cups water for soaking

3-4" piece kelp or kombu sea vegetable
1-2 cups fresh water (to cover 1/2-1" over beans)

Bean #2 (To be cooked in the space between the bowl and the pot's sides)

1/2 cup dry beans
(chickpea/garbanzo beans, black turtle, pinto, white beans, or other)

2-3 cups water to soak

3-4" piece kelp or kombu
1 1/2-2 cups water for cooking (or as needed to cover 1"over beans)

1. Sort, wash, and drain beans in their separate batches. Soak and drain each as per Basic Procedure.

2. Assemble as indicated above, placing one type of bean in a small bowl, covered with a heat-proof saucer, inside the pressure cooker. Pour the other beans with their cooking liquid into the space between the first bowl and the sides of the pot. Add a bit more water to the surrounding area to prevent burning.

3. Seal the pot and pressure cook as described in the Bowl-Within-A-Pot Method above but use a medium-low heat. The pot should hiss gently as it cooks. If you turn the heat too low and the pot loses pressure, raise the heat and bring the pot to pressure again then lower it slightly. Cook as above, 20-40 minutes, depending upon the type of beans used and the type of dish you will use them in. (Cook beans al dente for bean salads.)

4. Remove pot from the stove when cooking time has elapsed. (Allow pressure to come down naturally or run cold water over the pot.) Open the pot remove the lid, carefully remove the bowl, then remove the beans remaining in the pot. (Use an oven mitt!)

5. Use these beans in any recipe you desire.

Storage: Store any beans you do not use immediately in wide mouth jars, covered when cooled, then refrigerate.

Basic (Vegetarian) Refried Beans (Year Round)***

Prep: 15-20 minutes
Cooking: 20-45 minutes
Serves: 4-6 (or 2-3 meals for 2)
Serving size: 1/2-2/3 cup per person

These refried beans are traditionally thick and pasty. You can either make them mild or spicy. We prefer to make them mild. For a bacon fat flavor, (minus the bacon), add some hickory smoke to this dish.

2-3 cups cooked beans, from 1 1/2 cups dry beans
  (use azuki/aduki, small red, pinto, anasazi, black turtle, or kidney beans)

1/8-1/4 tsp. sun dried sea salt

2-3 tsp. ghee or light sesame oil (or olive oil)

2-4 cloves garlic **or** 1 clove elephant garlic, minced finely

1/2-1 tsp. cumin, powdered

Optional, 1/8-1/4 tsp. powdered red pepper, or to taste
  (ancho, Anaheim, or chipotle)

Optional, 1 Tbsp. prepared mustard **or** 1-2 tsp. dried mustard

Optional, 1 tsp. hickory smoke seasoning (liquid)

1 Tbsp. dark miso or tamari **or** 1/2 tsp. sea salt

Additional water or bean cooking liquid as needed

Garnish: Scallions, parsley, or cilantro, minced finely or fresh or dried chives

1. Prepare and cook beans as per Basic Procedure, Beans page 315.

2. When tender, drain and reserve cooking liquid. Add 1/2 tsp. salt to beans. With a potato masher, mash beans with the strip of sea vegetable and enough cooking liquid to moisten. This may be done right in the pot.

3. Heat ghee or oil in a cast iron skillet or wok over medium-low heat. Immediately add mashed beans with spices. Stir with a wooden spoon. Beans will dry as you stir. Reduce heat to medium or low as needed. Add a bit more liquid as needed to keep the beans somewhat moist. Keep stirring and scrambling.

4. Add miso or tamari and continue to stir for 10 minutes. Scrape any crust from the bottom of the pan and mix it back into the beans.

5. Cover, reduce heat to low, and simmer (using a heat deflector). Simmer 10 minutes or up to 40 minutes. If beans will not be used right away, cook for the longer time but add more liquid as needed to keep them from drying out.

Serving suggestions: Serve over whole grain flour tortillas, pita, millet slices, polenta, or brown rice. Flat Breads, are also good with these beans (try chestnut, millet, corn, wheat, or spelt flat bread). If desired, sprinkle on a bit of black pepper at the table and/or a dollup or two of Tofu "Sour Cream." Round out the meal with a quick boiled, pressed, or marinated salad (or two of these). A puréed squash, carrot, beet, or summer corn soup also makes a nice addition as does corn on the cob in the summer and fall. You can also make burritos or tacos with these beans, served with the same side dishes.

Storage: Refrigerate leftovers. Use to fill won ton, steamed bun or ravioli dough. Turn leftovers into a quick soup with other leftovers such as cooked sweet vegetables, a sea vegetable side dish, dried minced vegetables, tofu or wheat meat, other leftover soups, and/or water. (See soups from leftovers.)

Rachel's Refried Beans (Year Round)***

Prep: 15 minutes
Cooking: 15-30 minutes

Serving size: 1/2-3/4 cup per person
Serves: 8 (or 4 with leftovers)

This is another basic bean recipe to add to your repertoire. It's a snap to make and incredibly versatile! We always make extra refried beans—the leftovers can be turned into quick soups, sauces, spreads, or fillings for steamed buns, sandwiches, or tamales the next day.

1 Tbsp. ghee or light sesame or olive oil
1 large onion, minced finely
1/8-1/4 tsp. sea salt
1/2 cup water
2-3 cloves garlic, minced finely
5-6 cups cooked beans (*from 2-3 cups dry beans; kidney, azuki, anasazi, or pinto beans*)
1/4 tsp. red pepper powder (*ancho, chipotle, or Anaheim*)
1 tsp. cumin powder
2 Tbsp. tamari soy sauce *or* 1-2 Tbsp. red miso or dark barley miso
2 cups bean cooking juices, water, or part vegetable soup stock
Optional, 1 Tbsp. prepared mustard

Garnish:

1/2-1 cup fresh, minced scallions, chives, parsley, cilantro *or* 1-3 Tbsp. dried chives
Optional, ground black pepper

1. Sauté onions and sea salt in oil or ghee, stirring until translucent. Add garlic, stir and add 1/2 cup of water. Simmer and stir over medium heat until onions become soft, about 5-10 minutes.

2. Add cooked beans, spices, and 2 cups of bean cooking liquid or water. Bring to a low boil, to prevent burning slip a heat deflector under the skillet or pot, cover, reduce heat to low, and simmer until beans become mushy, about 15-20 minutes.

3. Add miso or tamari then mash the beans in the pan using a potato masher or large slotted spoon. Simmer uncovered to cook away excess liquid. Taste, and adjust seasonings as needed. Garnish with minced scallions, chives, or parsley. Add ground black pepper at the table if desired.

Serving suggestions: Serve over polenta, millet slices, mochi waffles or with corn bread, tortillas, and/or rice; with pressed, marinated, boiled or tossed salad and condiments. Add a colorful root or round vegetable soup or corn on the cob and/or Tofu Sour Cream.

Storage: Refrigerate. Reheat using the covered-bowl-within-a-pot method or steam in a cup on a rack. Leftovers can be used as a sandwich spread or filling for steamed buns, won tons or tamales or made into a quick soup or sauce. (See Almost Instant Refried Bean Soup.) ❑

Basic Procedure, Bean-n-Oat Burgers (Any Season) ***

Prep: 20-30 minutes
Cooking: 30-90 minutes for beans + 1 hour for burgers

Yield: 6-8 burgers (or 3 meals for 2)
Serving size: 1 burger per person

The brown lentils and walnuts in this recipe provide a meaty taste without the meat. Oats replace the usual egg-binder in most burgers and add more fiber and whole grain goodness.

Lentils (*if using~2 1/2-3 cups soft, cooked lentils or other beans, see variations below*)

1 cup brown lentils, uncooked
2 1/2-3 cups water
4" piece kelp or kombu sea vegetable

Additional ingredients:

2 cups rolled oats
2 Tbsp. tamari or dark red or brown miso
1/4-1/3 cup walnuts, coarsely chopped

2 Tbsp. peanut or sunflower butter

2 Tbsp. dried onion granules or flakes

1-2 Tbsp. dried or fresh, minced parsley or chives

1 tsp. dried thyme

1 tsp. dried, rubbed sage *or* cumin, oregano, or thyme

1/4 tsp. dried, crushed rosemary

Optional, 1 tsp. garlic powder or granules

1/4 cup water or slightly more as needed to make a smooth mixture

Garnishes & relishes

Prepared Mustard (*natural yellow, dijon or stone ground*)

Grain Mayo (see index for recipe)

Sauerkraut, sliced dill pickle, onion pickles, or natural pickle relish

1. Sort, rinse, and drain lentils. Soak in above volume of water several hours or overnight, if possible. (Lentils can be cooked in their soak water or with fresh water.)

2. Bring lentils to boil, cover, reduce heat to low and simmer 30-40 minutes or until tender. Or, pressure cook 20 minutes using the Covered-Bowl-Within-A-Pot Method or cook 4-5 hours on high or 6-8 hours on low in a crock pot.

3. Mash lentils then add remaining ingredients. Form into a moist, pliable batter the consistency of soft cookie dough. Add a bit more liquid if too dry to hold together. Add slightly more oats if too wet to form into patties.

4. Divide into 6-8 portions using an ice cream scoop or metal 1/2 cup measuring cup. Form into balls then flatten into burgers about 1/3 inch thick. Make the edges round or square them off with the sides of your hands. Place on a well oiled cookie sheet.

5. Bake at 350-375° F for 30-40 minutes. Flip over half way through cooking time. Do not over-bake, just cook until firm. Remove from oven and transfer to a cooling rack or plate.

Serving suggestions: Serve on baked or steamed whole grain buns or wrap in flour tortillas. When using pita or tortillas you can tuck your veggies right in the pocket for easy transport. Skip the chips and serve corn on the cob, hot air pop corn , or baked parsnip fries. Add pressed or marinated salad or cooked greens with relishes and/or a cup of soup.

Storage: Refrigerate leftovers. Steam briefly on a plate atop a bamboo or metal steamer or serve at room temperature for pack lunches.

Variations

Garbanzo Burgers

3 cups cooked garbanzo beans (*from 1-1 1/2 cups dry beans*)

1/2 cup bean cooking liquid or water

2 cups rolled oats

2-3 Tbsp. light, yellow, or mellow miso (or red or brown miso)

1/3 cup sunflower seeds, preferably ground to a powder

2-3 Tbsp. sunflower or sesame butter or sesame tahini

3-4 Tbsp. nutritional yeast flakes or powder (not brewer's yeast)

2 Tbsp. dried onion granules or flakes

1-2 Tbsp. dried or fresh, minced parsley or chives

2 tsp. garlic powder or garlic granules

1 tsp. dried, powdered cumin

3/4-1 tsp. dried, rubbed sage, oregano, thyme (or a combination)

1 tsp. dried, crushed rosemary or oregano

Optional, 1/4 tsp. ground black pepper or red pepper powder

Optional, 1/8 tsp. celery seed

• **Other Bean Burgers:** Use black turtle, pinto, azuki/aduki, navy, anasazi, kidney or other beans in the variation above. (Use 3-4 cups of water to soak if starting with dry beans.) Use whatever spices or herbs you like—Italian, Mexican, Indian, Chinese, etc. Vary the seeds, nuts, nut butters or dried vegetables, as you like.

Basic Procedure, Smokey Baked Beans (Fall, Winter, Spring)

Prep: 15 minutes
Soaking: 6-8 hours or overnight
First cooking: 1/2-1 hours for beans
Second cooking: 1-2 hours

Serves: 8-9 (or 3-4 meals for 2)
Serving size: 1/3-2/3 cup per person

For a vegetarian version of baked beans and pork—with a meaty texture—add some wheat meat (seitan), Pressure Marinated Tempeh, tempeh "sausage" links, or our Tempeh "Bacon" (This lends a meaty texture and taste reminiscent of pork and beans.) For a smokey flavor and sweet taste without sugar, we often add dried, soaked, chestnuts to our beans.

Dried beans (or use 3-4 cups cooked beans)

1 1/2 cups dry beans, one *or* two varieties, *or* 1 cup dried beans + 1/2 cup dried chestnuts *(azuki, anasazi, small red beans, black turtle, kidney, or pinto beans)*

4 cups water

4" strip of kelp or kombu sea vegetable

3-4 cups water, less to pressure cook, more to boil, *(if using chestnuts, include the soak water when cooking)*

Other ingredients:

1 medium onion, cut into thin crescents

2-3 tsp. ghee or light sesame or olive oil

1/8-1/4 tsp. sea salt

2-3 cloves minced garlic

2 Tbsp. dark or red miso

1-1 1/2 cups of bean cooking liquid *and/or* water or soup stock, or more as needed

2 tsp. dried mustard *or* 2 Tbsp. prepared mustard *or* 1 Tbsp. peeled, finely grated fresh ginger

Optional, 1 cup minced or ground wheat meat (seitan), Pressure Marinated Tempeh "Bacon," or commercial vegetarian sausage links (low-fat type), sliced in rounds

Garnish:

Minced fresh scallions, chives, garlic chives, parsley, arugula, or dried chives

1. Sort, soak, and cook beans as per Basic Bean Procedure, page 315 If using chestnuts, soak these separately in water to cover. Combine chestnuts and chestnut soak water with drained beans and additional fresh water before cooking.

2. Sauté onion in ghee or oil over medium heat in a heavy dutch oven or oven-proof stainless steel casserole. Sauté until almost translucent. Add salt and garlic, stir, add 1/2 cup of water or stock. Sauté 3-4 minutes.

3. Add cooked beans or beans and chestnuts, chopped seaweed, cooking liquid or water, and ginger or mustard. Stir and add wheat meat or tempeh if desired. Cover casserole pot, bring to boil on top of the stove, then transfer to a preheated 350°F. oven. (If you have sautéed in a regular saucepan, bring mixture to boil in the saucepan then transfer to a heat-proof casserole dish.).

4 Bake for 1-2 hours. Stir once or twice. If much liquid remains in the pot after 1 to 1 1/2 hours, remove the lid and cook for another 15-20 minutes. If too dry, add a bit more liquid.

Serving suggestions: Garnish and serve with a broth or colorful vegetable soup; rice and/or tortillas, corn bread or steamed buns; and cooked greens or salad. (Leftover baked beans can be turned into a soup or sauce.)

Variations:

- Add 2 cups corn off the cob in step #3 above.

- Omit wheat meat or tempeh and add 1 tsp. liquid hickory smoke in step #2 above. ❏

Basic Procedure, Bean Salad (Spring, Summer, Early Fall)

Prep: 20-30 minutes
Marinating: 1-5 hours
Serves: 4-6 (or 2-3 meals for 2)
Serving size: 1/3-3/4 cup per person

This is a wonderful warm weather salad. Traditionally the lentil version is served with brown rice and/or pita bread and salad. This makes the perfect picnic, pack lunch, or potluck dish. Make it first thing in the morning then allow it to marinate all day, or make it in the evening before bed.

Beans:

2-2 1/2 cups firm, cooked drained beans
   (from 1 cup dry lentils, chickpeas, black turtle, kidney, navy, pinto or other beans)

1/2 cup chopped, fresh parsley or cilantro
   or 8 scallions, minced finely

Marinade:

1/4 tsp. sea salt

2 tsp. tamari or shoyu, *or* umeboshi or apriboshi vinegar

1 Tbsp. ghee *or* olive or light or toasted sesame
   oil or flax seed oil

1-3 cloves garlic, minced finely

1 1/2-3 tsp. brown rice vinegar *or* cider vinegar

Cooking liquid as needed

Optional, 1-2 Tbsp. fresh, minced herbs—1 or
   more varieties,
   or 1-2 tsp. dried, *(basil, oregano, thyme,
   dill, marjoram, or other)*

Other ingredients:

1-2 cups parboiled vegetables—2-4 colorful
   varieties—cut finely
   *(red or white onions, carrots, celery, red
   radish, red, yellow or green bell pepper, red
   radish, corn off the cob, green beans, etc.)*

Optional, 1 cup diced or shredded wheat meat
   or seitan

1. Save bean cooking liquid. Toss cooled and drained beans with pungent green garnish. Add parboiled, drained vegetables.

2. In a measuring cup, mix marinade ingredients with enough bean cooking liquid or water to produce 1/3-1/2 cup marinade. Toss with beans. Add wheat meat and/or minced raw or parboiled vegetables. Cover and refrigerate for 4-8 hours before serving.

Serving suggestions: Serve close to room temperature, with tortillas, pita, steamed buns, crackers, or rice, with cooked green or mixed vegetables or pressed or marinated salad, and a colorful vegetable soup.

Ideas:

- **Armenian Lentil Salad:** Use lentils and olive oil with oregano. Add carrots, onions, and/or celery.

- **Greek Lentil Salad:** Use lentils or chickpeas and olive oil. Add carrots. Omit parsley and scallions then add 1/4 cup freshly chopped olives, 1/2 cup raw or 1/2-1 cup parboiled yellow or red onion, 1-1 1/2 Tbsp. finely minced fresh or 1-1 1/2 tsp. dried oregano and 2-3 cloves minced garlic.

- **Mexican Bean Salad:** Use black turtle, anasazi, or kidney beans. Add fresh corn, carrot, and celery or bell pepper. Or, 6 sun dried tomato halves, minced, carrot or corn, and/or onions. Use tamari or umeboshi. Add 2 tsp. chili powder or 1/4 tsp. ancho, Anaheim or chipotle pepper powder, 1/2 tsp. dried cumin, and 1-2 cloves garlic. Optional, 3-4 Tbsp. chopped olives.

- **Italian Bean Salad:** Use white kidney, navy, or canelloni beans or chickpeas with olive oil, and umeboshi. Add 3-5 soaked, chopped, sun dried tomato halves, 1 Tbsp. fresh, minced basil or 1 tsp. dried, 1 1/2 tsp. fresh or 1/2 tsp. dried oregano and/or thyme, 3 cloves garlic, and 1/2 cup red onion or leek (parboiled) and 1/4 cup carrot and/or celery (also parboiled).

Chick-n-Pea Sourdough Dressing (Fall & Winter)

Prep: 30 minutes
Soaking (peas & beans): overnight
Cooking: 3-6 hours (to dry bread cubes)
+ 30 minutes (to sauté veggies & roast seeds)
+ 40 minutes (to bake entire casserole)

Yield: 3 loaf pans of stuffing
Serves: 15 with leftovers
Serving size: 1 scoop per person

***Reduce recipe by 1/2 if desired**

With this tasty dish, you won't miss the traditional heart-stopping stuffing! But don't limit it's use to Christmas and Thanksgiving. It also makes a great potluck or Sunday dinner dish. This richly seasoned holiday side dish will bring rave reviews and many recipe requests. Chickpeas and dried green peas give this dressing a poultry-like taste. By using a pressure cooker and the optional sea vegetable (which contains glutamic acid, a natural tenderizing agent) you can cut the legume cooking time in half. (Use precooked chickpeas in a pinch.)

16 cups cubed bread (yields 8 cups when dried)
(Try sourdough or yeasted bread: whole wheat, rye, spelt, barley, or other whole grain type)

Dried Beans (or use 3 cups cooked beans + 3 1/2 cups water)

3/4 cup dry chickpeas

1/4 cup whole dried green peas

3 cups water to soak

6" piece kelp or kombu sea vegetable

1/2 tsp. sea salt (added one pinch at a time at different stages)

2-3 cups fresh water to pressure cook
(**or** 3-3 1/2 cups water to boil)

3 1/2 cups additional water

1/2 tsp. sea salt

Vegetables:

1 Tbsp. ghee or light sesame oil

1 diced onion, minced

3 stalks celery, minced

6 cups button mushrooms, chopped finely

Herb mixture:

1-1 1/2 Tbsp. sea salt

2 Tbsp. dried, rubbed sage

1 Tbsp. dried thyme

1 Tbsp. dried oregano

1/2 tsp. cumin powder

1/2 tsp. black pepper

1 cup dry sunflower seeds

1. Cube bread. (This is a good way to use up stale bread, but fresh bread can also be used.) Place on cookie sheets in the oven then bake at 140°F for 4-6 hours or overnight, until crispy and dry. This can be done one or more days in advance. Store toasted cubes in a sealed glass jar.

2. Roast sunflower seeds in a dry cast iron skillet or wok over medium high heat until fragrant and golden, about 10 minutes. (See Basic Procedure, Roasted Seeds.)

3. Soak chickpeas with dried green peas and 3 cups water for 6-12 hours or overnight. Before cooking, throw off soak water and add fresh water to replace the amount you poured off then add sea vegetable.

   To pressure cook: Bring to pressure and cook 40-45 minutes.

   To simmer: Cover, bring to boil, reduce heat to low and simmer 2-3 hours, until soft. Add additional water as needed to keep beans covered.

4. Purée beans and peas in blender with cooking liquid, sea salt, and additional 3 1/2-4 cups water. Set aside. *Alternatively*, substitute 3 total cups cooked chickpeas and/or green peas for above dry peas, then add 3 1/2-4 cups of bean cooking liquid or water. Purée as above with sea salt.

5. Heat ghee or oil in large wok or cast iron skillet. Immediatley add and sauté onions with a pinch of sea salt for 1-2 minutes. Add celery and another pinch of salt then sauté one minute. Add mushrooms and a pinch of salt then sauté over medium heat until soft and translucent. (Adding the sea salt with each vegetable draws the vegetable juices out so that less oil is needed.) Stir and cover. Reduce heat to low and simmer 15 minutes or until vegetables shrink and smell rich.

6. Add herbs and 1-1 1/2 Tbsp. sea salt to vegetables and stir well to distribute. In a large mixing bowl combine sautéed vegetables, roasted seeds, bread cubes and puréed bean sauce. Stir to evenly distribute ingredients then spoon into 3 lightly oiled bread pans. Cover tightly with a lid or foil.

7. Bake at 350°F. for 30-40 minutes. Stuffing may be assembled a day in advance then baked or heated just before serving.

Note: Cooking stuffing in covered bread pans is essential; shallow oblong pans or casserole dishes will not produce the same results. They will cause the stuffing to dry out.

Serving suggestions: Serve with a puréed squash, carrot, or rutabaga soup, a low-fat gravy; steamed greens or pressed salad; and pan-fried, steamed, or grilled tempeh or wheat meat cutlets. Pickles and Millet "Mashed Potatoes" are optional.

Storage: Store leftovers in a covered bowl in the refrigerator. Reheat small portions using the covered-bowl-within-a-pot method. Use within two or three days.

Leftover tips: used

• Leftover stuffing can be heated and to fill already baked squash halves, ravioli, tamale dough, or simply warmed and served with gravy.

• **Stuffing in Your Pocket:** Fill pita pockets or flour tortillas with stuffing and minced or sliced leftover tempeh or wheat meat cutlets, steamed greens or pressed salad, and a dab of mustard or gravy. ❏

Natto

Natto, a traditional Japanese condiment made from fermented soybeans, is revered for its medicinal properties. It is easy to digest and can help boost iron absorption, particularly if eaten at the same meal with cooked leafy greens. Fermentation by friendly bacteria makes natto rich in biologically active vitamin B-12, particularly if it is home-made. (Under conditions which are too-sterile, the beneficial bacteria may not be as prolific). Like both yogurt and unpasteurized miso, natto is rich in other beneficial bacteria.

Though it is loved by many in Asia, natto it is an acquired taste for most Americans and Europeans. Its stringy appearance and strong smell, a bit like brie or aged roquefort cheese, initially puts some people off. On its own natto is rather bland, but it is fabulous mixed with a bit of tamari, shoyu, or umeboshi, with or without mustard or wasabi paste, and scallions or chives. Some love it, others don't.

A typical serving of natto is several tablespoons per person, used as a condiment, served over rice, noodles, inside nori-maki sushi, or added to warm soup just before serving.

Homemade natto is far superior to the frozen kind sold in many Asian markets. Although it is more commonly and traditionally made with yellow soybeans, natto can be made from any kind of beans. We have made it with black soybeans, chickpeas (garbanzo beans), and even peanuts.

Natto is particularly good in spring and summer months because it is fermented and slightly sour and this flavor, according to Oriental nutrition, is beneficial in the spring. Because natto is usually served at room temperature rather than warm, the warmer months would be the ideal time to consume it. We like to serve it a couple of times a month during theses seasons.

Basic Procedure, Natto (Any Season)

Prep: 20 minutes
Soaking: 8-12 hours or overnight
Incubation: 36-48 hours
Cooking: 30-60 minutes, depending on beans

Yield: 6-7 cups cooked
Serving size: 2-5 Tbsp. per person

** Reduce recipe by one half as needed.

Natto is made with a special starter or culture, which allows only a particular mold to grow. When made correctly, it will smell a bit like ammonia and the beans will be covered with a thick white mold after incubation!

3 cups dry black or yellow soybeans or whole raw peanuts or garbanzo beans

8-9 cups water

5" piece kelp or kombu sea vegetable

4-5 cup water, or enough to cover 1/2" over beans

One very tiny spoonful of Natto Starter (Use only the spoon which comes with the natto starter. See index for mail order companies.)

1. Sort beans, rinse, then soak overnight in above volume of water.

2. Pour off soak water. In a pressure cooker, combine beans, kelp or kombu, and fresh water to cover 1-2-inches over the beans. (When making a half batch, use the covered-bowl-within-a-pot method to pressure cook the beans after covering them with 1/2 inch of fresh water.)

3. Pressure cook 1-1 1/2 hours for yellow or black soy beans or 30 minutes for most other beans or peanuts. (Do not pressure cook lentils unless they are in a covered bowl.) Cook until soft.

4. Remove sea vegetable and set aside. (Chop and use in another dish or as a rice topping.) Drain liquid from beans and use it as a beverage (seasoned with a few drops of tamari or a pinch or two of sea salt per cup) or use it as soup stock.

5. Transfer beans or legumes to a large glass, ceramic, or pyrex bowl or casserole dish. Use a metal stem thermometer to monitor the temperature. When cooled to 120° F., use the spoon provided with the natto starter to measure out one tiny spoonful. (This *tiny* spoon is smaller than your pinky!) Stir thoroughly to distribute the starter.

6. Place beans in several cardboard Chinese take-out containers then close. (If unavailable, keep beans in a bowl then slip the bowl inside a brown paper bag.)

Keep in a warm place.
Pick one of the following:

a) a gas stove with the pilot light on

b) an electric stove with just the light on

c) an electric stove with a 100 watt bulb run in with a heavy-duty extension cord *or*

d) atop a small heating pad set to medium-low, with a blanket wrapped around the dish for insulation.

7. Allow beans to ferment for 36-48 hours. They are done when they have a strong ammonia-like smell and are covered with a thick white mold. They should have a sticky and stringy quality when stirred. They will smell strong. This is normal!

Storage: Stir then store in small bowls or wide mouth jars. Cover with a lid or small saucer and refrigerate. Natto keeps for several weeks in the refrigerator—plain or seasoned with salty or salty and pungent flavorings. (Alternatively, freeze portions of the natto in 1/2-1 cup amounts. It is best fresh but but freezing will not harm the beneficial enzymes in the natto or the flavor.)

Serving suggestions: Season 1/2-1 cup of natto with some salty seasoning prior to serving. You can vary the seasonings with different batches or meals. Seasoned natto tastes even better on the second day.

Variations:

- Use garbanzo beans (chickpeas) in the above natto recipe. Season with minced garlic or garlic powder and umeboshi, apriboshi, or light miso or tamari. A dash of herb seasoned olive oil or sesame tahini would also make a rich and tasty addition or try making Hummus dip with chickpea natto.

- Peanut Natto is great seasoned with tamari and scallions, served over Quinoa-Rice, Millet-Rice, Sweet Rice & Millet, or mochi, with a side of colorful root vegetables, and a pressed, marinated, or boiled salad.

- Use white kidney beans in place of soybeans then use the natto for a mock-cheese. Natto may be puréed in a suribachi for use in tacos, nachos, casseroles, or over pasta.

- Season your natto with your favorite ethnic spices and miso, tamari, shoyu, or sea salt. ❑

Seasoned Natto

Prep: 5 minutes or less
Serves: 8 (or 4 meals for 2)
Serving size: 2-5 Tbsp. per person

1 cup homemade natto

1/4-1/3 cup finely minced scallions with tops or chives

1 1/2 Tbsp. prepared mustard

1 Tbsp. + 2 tsp. tamari or shoyu

1. Mix all ingredients in a bowl or suribachi until well mixed and stringy.

2. Serve as above. ❑

Natto "Cream Cheese" Style Sandwich Spread

Prep: 15 minutes
Serves: 4-6 (or 2-3 meals for 2)
Serving size: 1/4-1/2 cup per person

This recipe comes from an old issue of *East West Journal*. The original recipe, created by Aveline Kushi, has been modified slightly. Homemade natto is far superior to store bought natto in this recipe. Different types of natto will produce dips with varying tastes and textures. You might want to try a different type of natto each time.

1/2 lb. firm or soft tofu

1/2 cup homemade chickpea, black soybean, or peanut natto

2 Tbsp. sesame tahini (or peanut butter if peanut natto is used)

1 tsp. apriboshi or umeboshi paste or 2 tsp. light miso*

1/2 cup minced sauerkraut
    or natural dill pickles

1. Steam or boil tofu for 10 minutes then drain.

2. Mash natto and tahini with ume, apriboshi or miso in a suribachi with a wooden pestle until sticky and gooey, or use a Foley food mill. Add tofu and continue to mash until smooth. (A food processor could be used, but a blender or standard mixing bowl will not work for this.)

3. When smooth, stir in sauerkraut or pickles. Garnish with chives, scallions, or parsley.

Serving suggestions: Serve as a spread on bagels, tortillas, sandwich bread, steamed buns, or brown rice cakes with a light vegetable soup or miso broth and a steamed or parboiled green vegetable side dish.

- **Aveline Kushi's version of Natto Cream Cheese Dip:** Use yellow soybean natto. This one sticks to the roof of your mouth, like real cream cheese. Use tamari or umeboshi paste to replace ume, apriboshi, or miso. She suggests serving this spread on sourdough whole grain bread with lettuce, dulse, and tomato.❑

Tempeh: The Soyfood with Culture

Tofu's Younger Brother

By now most Americans have heard the word "tofu" and have eaten it or at least seen it on supermarket shelves. Few Americans are familar with tempeh, but most of those who are regard it as a culinary treasure. The secret is texture. Tempeh is a soy product, but unlike tofu, tempeh is fermented and has a dense chewy texture. Its flavor is nutty or meaty and remarkably similar to that of meat or poultry when properly prepared. Tempeh can be used in any recipe that calls for meat or chicken, though it must first be sufficiently seasoned and pre-cooked by boiling or pressure-marinating in a salty solution for a rich flavor and best digestion.

How is Tempeh Made?

Tempeh is made in much the same way as yogurt or cheese. First, the soybeans are split and dehulled, then boiled for 45 minutes. The cooked beans are then cooled, dried, then innoculated with a friendly culture. The innoculated beans are then placed in a warm, 88 degree environment overnight. (This temperature closely resembles the climate of tropical Indonesia where tempeh has been the main protein source for centuries.) Returning in just over 20 hours one finds that a delightfully aromatic white frosting has bound the loose beans into a solid, firm cake. It is in this fermentation period that the real "magic" of tempeh is unleashed, transforming plain old soybeans into a gastronomic delight and a benefit to the body! The end result is a product that is even more nutritious than when the process began. It is also more digestible and its nutrients are more bio-availble.

> **Try Tempeh in:**
> - Stews
> - Chili
> - Baked bean dishes
> - Casseroles
> - Stir fry
> - Pot pies
> - Ravioli
> - Calzones
> - Won tons and pot stickers
> - Tamales and tacos
> - Stuffed Bell Peppers
> - Mock tuna salad spreads
> - Party dips and patés
> - Meat-less burgers (homemade or store bought)

Buying and Storing Tempeh

Once pre-cooked in a salty liquid or cooked into a dish, tempeh is best used within several days. Fresh or thawed tempeh should be used up within a week to ten days or it may be stored for longer periods of time (up to a year or more) in the freezer without significant loss of flavor or nutrients. You can thaw a whole package or cut a frozen block in half and thaw just what you need then wrap and freeze the rest in a sealed bag.

Making or purchasing fresh tempeh made by someone in your area is ideal. The taste is incredible if you eat it within days of being made. Store bought, processed tempeh burgers, mock "bacon," tempeh sausage links and other such products can be used, but they often have added fats as well as a long list of questionable ingredients. Thus, these should be used only occasionally. (Look for a product with the fewest and simplest ingredients.)

Tempeh Needs Special Care:

Aside from the seasoned and precooked, often deep fried, tempeh burgers sold in many health food stores, most of the tempeh found in the market is not thoroughly cooked: the soy beans have only been parboiled prior to innoculation. If the tempeh is white or beige in color, sold in an 8-ounce block, and the ingredient list says: soybeans and/or other beans, grains, or seeds, vinegar, and culture—you can bet that this is not a ready-to-eat product. (Some manufacturers steam their tempeh for 20 minutes prior to packaging, but in our experience this isn't enough.)

Soybeans are tough. They take far longer to cook and soften than most other beans and are notorious for being difficult to digest. In Asia, where the soy bean has been used as human food for centuries, extensive processing is standard procedure. Their indigestible parts are removed by mechanical processing, as in the making of tofu. Or, soybeans are cooked, then subjected to prolonged fermentation, usually in a salty (alkaline) solution as in the making of soy sauce, miso, and similar products. For centuries, the Chinese and Japanese have soaked, cooked and mashed soybeans, then made them into miso, tamari, or shoyu, products which are aged in an alkaline solution for a minimum of six months and often for three to five years. This aging process is quite literally a form of cooking under pressure, at a low temperature for a long period of time, with the aid of beneficial bacteria.

Soy beans are very nutritious. They are also very high in fiber and anti-nutritive substances (lectins, protease inhibitors, amaylase inhibitors, and trypsin inhibitors) which can interfere with proper digestion and mineral absorption. These are parts of the self-defense system of the soy bean, which tries to protect itself from digestion so that it can serve its function as the seed for the next generation of soy plants.

In Indonesia, tempeh is traditionally cooked briefly at a very high temperature (as in deep frying), or for a long time at a low temperature in an alkaline soy sauce solution (as in stews or other such dishes). These traditional practices make an otherwise problematic food more nutritious, digestible, tasty, enjoyable and medicinal.

Cooking: Less isn't always better

Many Americans think that the less cooking a food undergoes, the more nutritious it will be. However, this belief ignores the tough cell structure of vegetable foods, which need to be broken down by cooking or grinding. A raw foods diet can cause many health problems—including gas, diarrhea, and malnutrition—because the body is not able to extract the nutrients trapped in the cell structure of the vegetable and because the coarse fibers may push foods through the digestive system before we get a chance to extract the nutrients. Cooking is a form of predigestion; a crucial step, in fact.

Research in food chemistry has shown that lengthy soaking, and cooking in an alkaline solution (provided by seaweed, salt, and soy sauce) inactivates the harmful substances found in soybeans. If either of these steps is omitted, one is left with a high concentration of anti-nutritive substances. This preparation method is precisely the formula used to make miso, tamari, or shoyu in the Orient. It is also the procedure we recommend for cooking raw beans or for taking uncooked or lightly steamed, unseasoned tempeh and turning it into a highly digestible product.

We know of many people who have given up eating tempeh because they didn't care for the taste (they found it bitter) or because eating it produced more gas than they could bear. We've always enjoyed tempeh when it was properly seasoned and cooked. However, tempeh taken straight from the package and tossed into a stir fry or other briefly cooked dishes has always proven to be somewhat bitter, and a digestive disaster.

Boiling in a salty liquid tenderizes and drives the marinade into the tempeh. Prepared this way, tempeh is tastier and produces little or no gas. With this seasoned, well-cooked tempeh, we have won over many people who previously shied away from the so-called "ready to eat" tempeh.

Basic Procedure, Pressure-Marinated Tempeh (Year Round)***

Prep: 5 minutes
Cooking: 30-45 minutes
Serves: 4-6 (or 2-3 meals for 2)
Serving size: 1-2 oz. per person

8 oz. pkg. unseasoned tempeh *(soy, 3-grain, 5-grain, or other variety)*

2-2 1/2 Tbsp. tamari or shoyu

1 1/2 cups water (to pressure cook) or 2 cups water if boiling

4" piece kelp or kombu sea vegetable

1. **To pressure cook:** Place a whole or halved block of tempeh in the bottom of a pressure cooker. Add above ingredients. Place a small heat proof saucer directly on top of the tempeh to keep it immersed in the marinating liquid. Seal the pot and bring to pressure over medium-high heat. Reduce heat to medium and cook 30 minutes.

   To boil: Simmer all ingredients 1 hour in a saucepan with a tight fitting lid. Check periodically to be make sure that the tempeh doesn't boil dry and burn. You may need to add more water to keep the tempeh moist.

2. Remove lid and cook away remaining liquid, being careful not to burn the tempeh.

3. Remove tempeh from pot and save the kelp or kombu. (Use it in the dish you will be making or chop and spoon it over rice.)

Storage: Refrigerate tempeh and sea vegetable. Chop the sea vegetable strip; and add it to bean dishes, soups, or stews, or spoon it over whole grain. Use this seasoned tempeh within 3-5 days in any recipe that normally calls for meat, sausage, turkey, or chicken but reduce the salty seasonings for the dish since the tempeh will be fairly well seasoned.

Serving suggestions: See recipes in this chapter for using Pressure Marinated Tempeh.

Variation:

- Add 1/2-1 tsp. liquid hickory smoke flavoring to the marinade before cooking. ❑

Herbed Tempeh "Sausage" Cutlets (Fall, Winter, Spring)

Prep: 15-20 minutes
Cooking: 10-15 minutes
Yield: 4-8 cutlets
Serves: 4-8 (or 2-4 meals for 2)

These cutlets make a great condiment for rice or bread. They also make a tasty topping when crumbled over pizza or pasta, with or without a sauce. A little bit goes a long way.

1 Recipe Pressure Marinated Tempeh

Mixture for Dredging Tempeh *(you will have some leftover at the end):*

3/4-1 cup arrowroot powder *or* chickpea flour

2 tsp. dried powdered sage

1 1/2 tsp. thyme *or* half thyme, half marjoram

Optional, 1/4-1/2 tsp. cumin powder

Optional, 1/8-1/4 tsp. sea salt

1-2 Tbsp. ghee or raw sesame, olive or sunflower oil for skillet

1. Follow Basic Procedure, Pressure Marinated Tempeh above. Cut tempeh block in half, then in half again, then cut each piece into a thin slab (slicing through the center to make 4 thin squares) for burgers, otherwise cut into 16 thin, finger-long pieces, or triangles.

2. Mix herbs with arrowroot and sea salt. Dredge tempeh slabs in this mixture to coat thoroughly. (Reserve extra herbed flour coating; store this in a sealed jar for a later use.)

3. **To pan fry:** Put 1-2 tsp. ghee or oil in a cast iron skillet or fry pan. Pan fry several tempeh pieces at a time. Cover; cook several minutes on medium heat; then flip pieces once or twice until well-browned (almost charred) on both sides. Repeat with remaining tempeh.

   To steam: Omit oil. Place herb-coated tempeh on a heat-proof plate on top of a bamboo or metal steamer tray. Steam 30 minutes to create a shiny, smooth coating.

Storage: Transfer pan fried or steamed tempeh to a serving dish and cover with a bamboo mat until serving time.

Serving suggestions: Serve warm over rice or other whole grain, a side of cooked greens or mixed vegetables and/or pressed salad. Pickles and soup or root vegetables are optional. Cut tempeh into cubes and served over bowls of pasta topped with Beet Sauce Italiano or Parsnip White Sauce.

Note: The seasoned, cooked strips of seaweed can also be dredged in the herbed arrowroot or flour mixture and pan-fried until golden then chopped or simply spooned over rice.

Variations:

• Use wheat meat in place of tempeh above.

• **Tempeh Sausage Burgers:** Slice the block into 4 thin slabs, each roughly a square. Cook as above. Serve on baked or steamed buns with mustard and/or Grain Mayo or Tofu Mayonnaise with a few slices of Quick Pickled Onion Rings, sauerkraut, or quick pickled daikon. Add steamed greens or in the summer and early fall, try Mesclun greens or dark green lettuce with sprouts and tomato. Serves 4 ❏

Tempeh "Bacon"

Prep: 15 minutes
Cooking: 30-50 minutes
Serves: 8-10 as a condiment for soup or salad;
4-6 as a condiment for whole grain, pasta, or in stir fry;
or 4 as burgers

This dish was inspired by a recipe in *Vegetarian Times* Magazine. It can be made ahead of time and used to top soups, salads, pasta sauce, or whole grains. It's especially good tossed with steamed vegetables or added to stir fry, casseroles or stews. It's far lower in fat than real bacon and contains no cholesterol!

1/2-3/4 tsp. fennel seeds

1/2-3/4 tsp. cumin seeds

1/2-3/4 tsp. mustard seeds

4-5" strip kelp or kombu sea weed

8 oz. block of tempeh (*soy, 3-grain, 5-grain, or other), whole or cut in half*

2-3 Tbsp. tamari or shoyu

1/2-1 tsp. garlic powder

1 1/2 cups water to pressure cook *or* 2 cups water to simmer

1. Dry roast spice seeds in cast iron skillet or wok until they begin to pop. Stir constantly to prevent burning. Grind to a powder in suribachi or electric spice mill.

2. Put kelp or kombu in the bottom of a 1-quart sauce pan or pressure cooker. Top with tempeh. Mix powdered spice seeds, garlic, tamari, and water and pour over tempeh.

3. Bring to boil, cover, reduce heat to low and simmer for 45 minutes until all of the marinade is cooked into the tempeh. Or, pressure cook for 1/2 hour then remove lid and cook away liquid.

4. Cut tempeh into 8-thin slabs for use in sandwiches or on burger buns. Cut into 8-12 thin strips, crumble, or cut into cubes for a bacon-like topping or condiment. Optional, place tempeh on a baking sheet and broil until golden for "bacon. "

Serving suggestions: Use as "bacon" in baked beans, pasta salad, over cooked whole grain, tossed with boiled salad or steamed vegetables, or on top of soup. Or, toss tempeh cubes over pasta with Beet Sauce Italiano or serve with mounds of Kasha and Parsnip White Sauce. Serve any of these with a side of cooked leafy green or mixed vegetables, and sauerkraut, chopped dill pickles, or home made vegetable pickles.

Storage: Refrigerate leftovers in a covered glass or stainless steel container. Use within a week.

Variations:

• Dredge thin slices of Tempeh "Bacon" in arrowroot or rice, barley, or corn flour. Pan fry until golden brown in a lightly oiled skillet.

• Roll thin triangle shaped pieces of seasoned, cooked tempeh in arrowroot then steam on a metal steamer basket or on a plate atop a bamboo tray for 20-30 minutes. ❏

Vegetarian Chorizo (Any Season)

Prep: 15 minutes
Cooking: Depends on preparations
Yield: 1 1/2 cups filling
Fills: 18 small tamales *or* 12 steamed buns (raw dough)

**Figure 1-3 Tbsp. filling per steamed bun or tamale or 1-2 tsp. per won ton or ravioli

This version of chorizo, a spicy sausage preparation, is completely vegetarian and low in fat. Tempeh gives this version a rich and hearty flavor. It can be made a day in advance and is delicious inside ravioli, won ton, or steamed bundough. Increase the spices as you like.

1 recipe Pressure Marinated Tempeh (an 8 oz. tempeh block and a strip of sea vegetable)

4 cloves garlic, minced

1-2 whole, small, dried red pepper, minced finely *or* 1/2 tsp. mild red pepper powder (*Anaheim, chipotle, or ancho*)

1-2 Tbsp. chili powder

2-3 tsp. organic apple cider vinegar *or* 3-4 tsp. brown rice vinegar

1 tsp. powdered cumin

1 tsp. powdered sage

1/2 tsp. powdered thyme

1/2 tsp. crushed, roasted fennel seed

Optional, 1/4 tsp. ground black pepper

1 Tbsp. tamari, shoyu, or dark miso

1. Mash tempeh and the sea vegetable it was cooked with in a bowl or suribachi. Add remaining ingredients. Mix and mash well. Use as you would use sausage in any recipe; figure just 1-3 ounces per person.

Storage: If making chorizo in advance, cover and store in the refrigerator to allow flavors to develop. Use within 3-5 days. ❏

Chinaman's Purse (Filling for steamed buns)

Prep: 30 minutes
Cooking: 15 minutes + 10 to rest
Rising: 15-30 minutes (with Rapid-Rise Dough) *or* 1-1 1/2 hours with Standard or Slow-Rise Dough
Fills: 8-12 buns

Serves: 8 accompanied by rice or noodles
Serving size: 1 bun per person with rice or other grain; 2+ per person as the only grain in a meal

This dish is sure to be a hit. Its name comes from the purse-like appearance it creates when this filling is tucked into raw bread dough and the top is twisted shut to create a small pouch or pouches. These are a joy to eat and the same filling may also be used to fill tamales if you like.

Filling (for 8-12 buns):

1 recipe (8 oz. block) Pressure Marinated Tempeh, page 329

2-3 tsp. ghee or light sesame oil

1-2 tsp. peeled, finely minced ginger root

2 medium scallions, white and green part, finely chopped

2 small shiitake mushrooms, finely chopped (*fresh or soaked, dried variety*)

1/2 cup mung bean sprouts

scant 1/8 tsp. sea salt

1-1 1/2 recipe Basic Bread Dough (*whole wheat, barley, or spelt*).

1. Sauté vegetables in ghee or oil with sea salt for 2-3 minutes. Grate tempeh and add to vegetables. Mix well.

2. Divide filling into 8 portions for a single batch of dough or 12 portions for 1 1/2 recipe of dough. Arrange on a plate, cover loosely, and set aside.

3. Prepare Basic Bread Dough as per instructions. Divide dough into 8 portions for a single batch of dough or 12 portions for a recipe and a half of dough. Fill, rise, and cook as per Basic Steamed Buns Procedure.

Serving suggestions: Serve while warm with rice, boiled salad, glazed greens, or stir fry plus a light soup and pickles. If made ahead, resteam on plates (on bamboo trays) or wrapped in a cotton or linen towel. Serve at room temperature in pack lunches, with other leftovers.

Storage: Store in the refrigerator wrapped in a paper, wax, cellophane, or plastic bag. Use within two or three days.

Variations:

• Use this filling for tamales.

• Substitute 1 1/2 cups minced or ground wheat meat for tempeh and prepare as above. ❏

Stir-Fried Vegetables with Tempeh or Wheat Meat (Any Season)

Cooking: 8-10 minutes to stir fry
Prep: 15 minutes
Serves: 5-6 (or 2 1/2-3 meals for 2)
Serving size: 3/4-1+ cup per person

In this recipe you can use Pressure Marinated Tempeh or wheat meat (seitan). Quick cooking over a high heat seals in the flavors. Leftovers are delicious the second day served over rice, wrapped in flour tortillas or pita breads, tossed with noodles, or turned into a quick soup with stock or water and other leftovers.

6 oz. Pressure Marinated Tempeh
    or 3/4-1 cup wheat meat/seitan *(regular, original, hearty, or chicken-style)*
2-4 tsp. light or toasted sesame oil *or* olive oil
1 1/2 tsp. light sesame oil (or olive oil)
1 1/2 tsp. finely grated ginger root
Optional, 1-1 1/2 tsp. minced garlic
2 cups onion, cut in thin crescents or scallion whites and roots, cut in 1/2-1" pieces
4-5 cups asparagus, cut into thin diagonals (discard tough parts of stems) *or* 6-7 cups Chinese greens, broccoli, cauliflower or a combination of several different vegetables

Sauce:

1/4 tsp. sea salt
1-1 1/2 tsp. tamari or shoyu
1/4 cup water or soup stock

1. Thinly slice tempeh into 1 inch long 1/4-1/2 inch wide pieces or cut wheat meat into strips.

2. Mix sauce ingredients and set aside.

3. Stir fry ginger and/or garlic in a wok or cast iron skillet over medium-high heat. Immediately add onions, scallions or leeks and stir. Add tempeh or wheat meat and stir fry for about 2 or 3 minutes.

4. Add remaining vegetables one kind at a time, stirring for 1-2 minutes after each addition. Add sauce mixture, cover, and cook over high heat 4-6 minutes or until vegetables are just barely tender yet still crisp.

5. Transfer to a serving dish and cover with a bamboo sushi mat.

Serving suggestions: Serve as condiment for whole grain, polenta, or noodles, with a cup of vegetable, sea weed, or bean soup, and pickles or pressed or marinated salad.

Storage: Refrigerate leftovers. Serve them at room temperature or briefly reheat by steaming in a dish.

Variations:

• Replace asparagus with any seasonal vegetables *(broccoli, cauliflower; quartered brussel sprouts; kale; Chinese greens; or a combination of several colorful vegetables—rutabaga; daikon; carrot; yellow, red, or green bell pepper; jerusalem artichoke; pea pods; shiitake, crimini or button mushrooms; or several of these with greens).*

Note: All vegetables should be cut into paper thin strips, slivers, matchsticks, rounds, or halved florets, to facilitate speedy cooking. The longest cooking vegetables should be added to the skillet or wok first. ❏

Tuscan Tempeh Casserole (Stove Top) (Spring, Summer, Fall) ***

Prep: 15 minutes
Cooking: 25-30 minutes
Serves: 5-6 (or 2-3 meals for 2)
Serving size: 1/3-2/3 cup per person

This delightful dish is unlike most Western-style casseroles. While most casseroles are suited for winter weather because they are baked, this one needs no baking and cooks fairly quickly. Suitable for use in any season, it provides a colorful, nourishing, and rich tasting topping for rice, millet, polenta, or any mixed grain combination.

1 recipe Pressure Marinated Tempeh, *or* ~1-1 1/4 cup low-fat vegetarian "sausage" links, tempeh burgers, or chicken-style wheat meat, cut into dice or thin strips

1 Tbsp. ghee or light sesame or olive oil

2-4 cloves minced garlic *or* 1-2 cloves elephant garlic, minced finely

1 packed cup button or crimini mushrooms *or* 1-2 large shiitake, cut into thin slices

1/8 tsp. sea salt

1/2 medium onion, cut into thin crescents or half moons

4 sun dried tomato halves, cut finely

1-2 Tbsp. dried bell pepper flakes *or* 1/2 cup fresh, minced red, yellow and/or green bell pepper

1/2 cup water or pasta water

1-1 1/2 tsp. dried, crushed oregano or basil *or* 2 Tbsp. fresh minced oregano, thyme, or basil

1/4 cup fresh Italian, Chinese, or common parsley, minced finely

1. Cut tempeh into 1/2 inch cubes then cut each in half through the center to create thinner pieces. Set aside. If using sausage, cut into thin rounds. If using wheat meat, cut into thin lengths or dice.

2. In a wok or saucepan, sauté onions in ghee or oil for 2-4 minutes or until tender. Add garlic then mushrooms and salt. Stir. Add tempeh, wheat meat, or "sausage". Sauté several minutes then add sun dried tomato and dried bell pepper flakes or fresh bell pepper. Continue to stir, add water and dried herbs, cover, reduce heat to low, and simmer 30 minutes. (If using fresh herbs, add these during the last 10-15 minutes of cooking.)

3. Remove lid, stir, and simmer away excess liquid. Remove from heat, add parsley, and stir.

Serving suggestions: Serve as a condiment for rice, polenta, or a mixed grain combination. Tamari or Ume Seasoned Pumpkin Seeds or Walnut Condiment make an excellent topping. (See index for recipes). Other complementary dishes include creamless cream of vegetable soup and steamed or parboiled leafy green or mixed vegetables.

Storage: Refrigerate in a covered bowl. Reheat by briefly steaming in a cup on a rack or simply remove from the refrigerator 30-60 minutes before serving then serve at room temperature. Leftovers can also be turned into a soup or stew when combined with water, soup stock and/or leftover cooked root or round vegetables.

Variation:

- Reduce tempeh above to 4 oz. (1/2 recipe) or use 4 oz. tempeh burgers then add 1/2-2/3 cup chicken-style or light wheat meat or vegetarian sausage links. Prepare as above.

- **Tuscan Bean Casserole:** Reduce tempeh to 4-oz. or wheat meat to 1/2 cup then add about 1-1 1/2 cups cooked chickpeas (garbanzo beans). Prepare as above. ❏

Tempeh Taco Salad (Summer & Fall)

Prep: 30 minutes
Cooking: 15 minutes + 10-15 to sauté filling
Serves: 6-8 (or 4 with leftovers)
Serving size: 1/2 cup mixture per person

This colorful salad looks like the standard beefy version except that the honors go to tempeh or wheat meat. This recipe is on the mild side, so feel free to spice it up to suit your taste. For best results, assemble the tacos 15 minutes before serving so the shells don't get soggy.

Shells:

7-8 plain corn or wheat tortillas, baked inside bowls until crisp then cooled (see below)

Filling:

1 red, yellow or green bell pepper, seeds removed then minced

1/2 medium onion, minced

1 Tbsp. ghee **or** sesame or olive oil

2-3 cloves garlic, minced

Optional, 1/2-1 tsp. cumin powder

Optional, 2-3 tsp. chili powder **or** 1/8 tsp. ancho or chipotle pepper powder

1/2 cup minced olives or salt-pickled olives *(found in Oriental grocery stores)*

1 1/2 cups cooked black beans *(from 1/2-3/4 cup dry beans)*

1 Tbsp. ghee **or** sesame or olive oil

8 oz. block tempeh (any variety)

Garnish:

6-8 cups washed, dried, shredded red leaf or romaine lettuce

4-5 cups of alfalfa or clover sprouts

7-8 small cherry tomatoes

Optional, Tofu "Ricotta" or Tofu "Sour Cream,"

To make shells:

1. Make slits on four outer edges of each tortilla. Place each tortilla inside a small heat-proof soup bowl then form to sides of bowl.

2. Bake on cookie sheets at 350°F until lightly crisped.

3. Allow to cool then remove from bowls and set aside. (You can purchase premade taco shells instead and heat them briefly before serving, if desired. Figure two taco shells per person, in this case.)

To make filling:

1. Sauté onions, garlic and bell pepper in 1 Tbsp. ghee or oil until wilted, about 3-4 minutes, over medium heat. Add spice. When vegetables are tender, toss with cooked, drained beans and set aside.

2. Grate thawed tempeh with a cheese grater. Sauté until golden in 1-2 Tbsp. oil. Reduce heat to low and simmer, covered, until tender and lightly browned, (10-12 minutes).

3. Toss tempeh with beans and veggies. Add minced olives, toss again, then allow to cool.

To assemble taco salads:

1. Place 1 bowl-shaped taco shell on each plate. Fill with 1/2 cup shredded lettuce. Top with 1/2-3/4 cup bean-veggie-tempeh filling. Top each with a small handful of sprouts and/or a cherry tomato. Add a dollup of Tofu "Sour Cream", or tofu "Ricotta" if desired. (Or, fill premade taco shells.)

2. Serve one or two ice cream scoops full of rice (or rice cooked with sweet corn or quinoa) per person. Top each serving of grain with a tablespoon of Tamari or Umeboshi Seasoned, Roasted Pumpkin Seeds or grated cheese.

Variations:

- Use pinto, kidney, anasazi or azuki beans.

- Use 1 1/2 cups shredded or minced chicken-style, hearty, or original wheat meat or seitan in place of the tempeh.

- Omit taco shells/corn tortillas. Instead roll filling in soft whole wheat or spelt tortillas or chapatis. Figure 1-2 tortillas per person.

- **Burritos:** mix taco filling with an equal volume of cooked brown rice then fold burrito style in tortillas. Figure about 1/3-1/2 cup filling per burrito. ❏

Tofu Terrific

Tofu is a soft bean curd that resembles cheese and is made from the milk of soybeans. Though many associate tofu with Asian cookery, in the last ten years the natural foods movement has brought tofu into the limelight for vegetarians and non-vegetarians alike.

Tofu's rather mild taste, which some may at first find bland, is actually a plus. Tofu picks up the flavors of whatever you mix, mash, cook or season it with and thus lends itself to a wide range of applications. It makes a perfect all-purpose replacement for meat, chicken, eggs, milk, yogurt, or ricotta or cream cheese. Tofu can be used in soups and stews; pot pies; stir fries; as the base for dips, spreads, sauces, and dressings; in casseroles, omelets, scrambles, and egg salad-type spreads; as a filling for steamed buns, tamales, won tons, ravioli, and manicotti; or to replace or extend eggs.

Purchase and storage of tofu

Tofu typically comes in 12 to 16-ounce blocks. Check the pull date when buying it to make sure that it hasn't expired, or isn't about to. Though you need not use an entire block of tofu all in one meal or all in one dish, it is advisable to use the tofu within five to six days of purchase for best results.

Once opened, transfer the tofu to a wide mouth jar or bowl and cover with fresh water. Change the water daily to prevent premature spoilage. Discard tofu that is pink, slimy or smelly—it has gone terribly bad! Tofu can be frozen to prolong its shelf life and alter its texture. Once frozen it keeps for months. When thawed, it becomes sponge-like and porous and will have a meatier texture. Frozen, thawed tofu is not well suited for dips, or patés but it's excellent in chili, stew, stir fry, or casseroles.

Seasoning & cooking tofu

In Asian countries tofu's cooling effects are usually balanced by marinating and/or cooking with hot spicy seasonings such as ginger, garlic, or chili pepper which act to spark the digestive fire. Interestingly, in Buddhist monasteries, tofu has been used to reduce the libido of monks—as it is said to dampen the fire to the Gate of Vitality (the Kidneys) and one's passions. Even when cooked, tofu can put out the digestive fire when consumed in excess.

Tofu is most easily digested when cooked in well seasoned, savory dishes. Cooking and adding herbs or spices and a salty seasoning can eliminate most, if not all, of the digestive difficulties associated with tofu. Using it moderately, not more than a couple of times per week, and in small portions (2-4 oz. per person) helps.

Since tofu is already fairly high in fat (about 50%), it is wise to try to limit the amount of added fat that you mix or cook with it. Deep-fried tofu preparations are incredibly high in fat and can be hard to digest. Cold or sweetened tofu dishes are ever more burdensome to the digestive system.

Because tofu has such a cooling effect on the body, it should be cooked and served warm (in soups, stews, casseroles, etc.). The occasional room temperature preparation in warm or hot weather is not a problem, though. Tofu dips, spreads, and sauces should be taken out of the refrigerator 30-60 minutes before serving to bring them closer to room and body temperature. Frozen or cold, sweetened tofu offers double trouble since its cold temperature dampens the digestive fire and the added oils, nuts, fruit or sweeteners put a heavy burden on an already taxed digestive system. Avoid these altogether.

Despite what you may have heard or read, and regardless of what type of sweetener or oil is used, sweetened soy milk or tofu products such as custards, puddings, "cheese" cakes, smoothies, dessert toppings and sweetened beverages (especially if chilled) are a detriment to health. Common signs of trouble from eating tofu desserts may include gas, bloating, indigestion and/or diarrhea, headache, coldness in the extremities or interior of the body, allergies, excessive mucus, weight gain, painful menstrual cramps, or more serious disorders.

What Can You Do With Tofu?

The uses for tofu are endless. Slice, chip, dice, mash, blend, purée, frappé, or whip it. Marinate it, bake it, broil it, grill it, stir fry or sauté it, braise it, stew it, or simply season and serve it.

- Cube and toss into
  - soups and stews
  - stir fries
  - casseroles
- Scramble it
  - with land vegetables and herbs and/or sea vegetables
  - with veggies and wheat meat or eggs
- Freeze; drain; chop; add it to chili or stir fry
- Blend with seasonings to make
  - creamy, dreamy sauces and spreads
  - dips and dressings
- Purée for mock sour cream, mock cream cheese, or cheese-like dips
- Mash it with seasonings for dips, spreads, salads, or burgers, alone or combined with
  - hard boiled eggs
  - soy yogurt
- Purée and use as an egg or cheese replacer or extender in
  - quiches and casseroles
  - egg-salad
  - omelets and scrambles
  - corn bread, muffins & other baked goods
- Crumble over pizza
- Mash or blend with seasonings then stuff inside
  - pot pies
  - calzones
  - sandwiches
  - tacos, burritos and tamales
  - gyoza or won tons
  - ravioli, manicotti, or lasagna
- Marinate then
  - broil or bake

  - grill it on shish kebob skewers

- If you or some of your family members still use animal flesh foods, you can use tofu to wean away from these less healthful foods. Tofu can be uses as a "hamburger helper" or extender in

  - fish burgers or croquettes
  - meat loaves and meatballs
  - burgers and croquettes
  - casseroles and dips
  - chicken, turkey, or tuna salad

Types of tofu:

There are many varieties of tofu on the market—made differently, packaged differently, with different tastes and textures. Some have definite advantages over others.

Traditionally tofu was made firm by the use of nigari (the minerals left after drying sea salt). Tofu made with nigari is usually firmer, a bit tastier (we think), has a better texture, and is richer in minerals. Tofu made with calcium sulfate is also rich in bone building nutrients and is a good second choice. Recently, however, some companies have begun to make tofu with unnatural additions. Gluconalactone is one such addition used in the production of aseptically packaged tofu. This relatively tasteless tofu is a far cry from traditionally made tofu.

The best tofu is fresh, found in the refrigerator section of your local market, and made in your area. (Check the pull dates for the freshest tofu.) The best tofu is also stored in water packs or air-tight bags. You will find this tofu in soft, firm, and extra firm styles.

Soft tofu works well for creamy preparations (those you wish to purée or whip and use in place of milk; yogurt; cream, ricotta or cottage cheese; or to replace eggs in baking). Firmer tofu is better for dishes in which a firmer texture or consistency is desired (burgers, cutlets, shish kabobs, meat-less loaves, or stews).

It is fun to come up with healthier and fresher facsimilies of commercial tofu dips, dressings, and entrées. The prepared tofu dishes available at your local market or health food store are often expensive and less than fresh when compared to homemade tofu products, though you may want to try some of them to get new ideas and inspiration. However, especially avoid extremely high fat tofu products such as deep fried tofu burgers, fried tofu sausages, tofu luncheon meats, and tofu frozen dinners. Also, many premade, packaged tofu products contain a wide array of preservatives, flavorings, fillers, and other artificial or isolated substances and are overly processed and packaged. So do read labels! And be a conscious consumer.

Scrambled Tofu (Any Season) *** (for topping pasta, rice, bread, or tortilla roll-ups)

Prep: 15 minutes
Cooking: 10-15 minutes.

Yield: 3-5 cups
Serving size: 1/2-3/4 cup per person
Serves: 4-6 (or 2-3 meals for 2)

This is one of our favorites. We usually serve it over plain cooked pasta or Sesame Buttered Noodles although it is equally as delicious served over brown rice or rolled in chapatis or soft wheat tortillas. Be sure to make a double recipe if you want second day leftovers for breakfast, pack lunches, or supper.

2-3 tsp ghee or sesame oil or sunflower oil

1/2-1 cup minced onion

2 pinches sea salt

1/2-3/4 cup pasta water or water

1 pound (16 oz.) firm or soft tofu, crumbled

   or 8-10 oz. tofu and 3/4 cup shredded wheat meat/seitan

1-1 1/2 Tbsp. tamari, shoyu or miso or 2-4

Tbsp. salty wheat meat or tempeh broth

Optional, 1-3 cloves minced garlic

4-8 Tbsp. crumbled, dry roasted wild nori, kelp, alaria, or sea palm or two 4" strips leftover cooked kelp, chopped or mashed (from pressure-marinating tempeh)

Garnish:

Chopped parsley, scallions, or chives

1. Sauté onion in ghee or oil with sea salt until lightly browned. Add seaweed if desired. Add part of the pasta water and simmer until tender. Add 1-2 cloves minced garlic if desired.

2. Add tofu (or tofu with wheat meat or seitan) . Stir, add an additional 1/3-1/2 cup water or pasta water. Add tamari, shoyu, miso or wheat meat broth. Stir and simmer for 5-6 minutes then cook away excess liquid. Garnish, and serve.

Serving suggestions: Serve with whole grain, pasta, or bread (or two of these); steamed or quick-boiled green or mixed vegetables; and a colorful orange or yellow vegetable side dish or soup. Pickles also make a nice addition.

Storage: Refrigerate leftovers, if any. Serve at room temperature or briefly steam in a bowl.

Variation:

• Omit sea vegetable above; add 2 shiitake mushrooms or 6 button or crimini mushrooms cut in thin slices and 1 stalk minced celery in step #1 above. Also add 2 Tbsp. nutritional yeast flakes for a more cheesy taste, if desired. (Do not add baker's yeast or brewer's yeast! They are not the same.)

• Roll in Chapatis lined with romaine lettuce or Mesclun greens, scallions or chives, and sauerkraut. ❏

Mocheese
(for tamales, steamed buns, or pizza)

Prep: 15-20 minutes
Cooking: depends upon the dish
Fills: 18 tamales, 8 steamed buns, many won tons or gyoza *or* 1 medium pizza

This smooth and gooey filling has a taste and texture like that of cheese. It makes a fabulous filling for tamales, steamed buns, and won tons. (Be sure to make the filling before you make the dough for any of these items.) For a fabulous cheese-less pizza, spread Mocheese on a bare or red-sauced whole grain pizza crust then top with thinly sliced button, crimini or shiitake mushrooms, olives, and bell peppers (when in season). Add chives, basil, oregano, or a combination of several of these. Bake and...enjoy!

Mocheese:

1/3 lb. (5-6 oz.) soft tofu, mashed in a food mill

1/2 of a 12 oz. block mochi, *(plain, garlic sesame, or basil flavor)*, thawed, grated

5 Tbsp. millet miso or other sweet, yellow, mellow or light miso

2-4 Tbsp. corn or flax oil (or sesame tahini)*

Optional, 2 Tbsp. nutritional yeast flakes (for a more cheesy taste)

1 recipe Masa Dough
or 1 recipe All-Purpose Bread Dough

1. Combine filling ingredients. Mix well. Divide filling into 8-18 portion (depending upon the dish you will be making). Set aside on a plate.

2. Prepare bun, tamale, or won ton dough. Fill using Basic Steamed Bun Procedure, Tamale Procedure, or see Pizza Procedure. Figure 2 Tbsp. "Mocheese" filling per tamale or steamed bun or 2 tsp. per won ton wrapper.

3. Allow dough to rise (if using bread dough) then cook as per the dough recipe you use.

Serving suggestions: Serve Mocheese filled or topped grains warm, with a low-fat or oil-free green vegetable side dish, soup or a colorful root vegetable dish, and pickles. ❏

Mochi Pizza Pie (Any Season)***

Prep: 20 minutes
Cooking: 40-45 minutes
Yield: 10-inch pie dish
Serves: 2 as a main dish or 4-8 as a side dish with rice

Don came up with this perfect pie right after Grainaissance came out with their Pizza flavored mochi. It's a quick and easy one-dish meal that's sure to please. Mochi is an essential ingredient. Most health food stores stock it in the freezer or refrigerator case. (We keep our home freezer stocked with plain and flavored varieties.) Pizza flavored mochi gives the most authentic taste but garlic-sesame, basil, or plain mochi can be substituted with good results.

Crust:

3/4 cup corn flour *or* masa harina flour

2 Tbsp. finely ground sunflower seeds (or substitute pumpkin or flax seeds)*

1/4 tsp. sea salt

1/3-1/2 cup water, or more as needed to make a smooth mixture

Oil for pie plate

Filling:

6 oz. tofu (by weight; almost one-half of a 16 oz. block)

1 Tbsp. sweet, white, yellow, or mellow miso

Topping:

1/2 of a 12 oz. package Pizza flavored mochi *(Grainaissance or other brand)*, uncooked

1/4 cup water

Optional, 1/2 cup pitted black olives, chopped

Garnish: Minced parsley

1. Oil a 10 inch deep pie plate. Mix flour, salt, and ground seed meal. (We use a coffee-spice mill or Osterizer to powder the seeds.) Add enough water to make a smooth, pasty mixture. Press dough into the bottom of the pie plate and 1/2-inch up the sides of the pan.

2. Mash tofu with white miso and spread over the crust.

3. Grate uncooked mochi with a cheese grater. (Thaw it first.) Add water then sprinkle mochi over pie.

4. Cover with foil and bake in a 400° F oven for 30 minutes. Remove cover and bake 20 minutes until slightly bubbly and gooey.

5. Remove from oven and allow pie to sit for 15 minutes before slicing into 8 pieces and serving.

Serving suggestions: Garnish and serve with quick-boiled or steamed greens or mixed vegetables and pickles. Optional, a colorful squash, carrot & parsnip, beet, or corn soup or side dish.

Storage: Cover and refrigerate leftovers. Cover and reheat in a 300° F oven before serving.

Variation:

- Sprinkle 1/2 cup grated or minced sausage-style wheat meat or chopped vegetarian sausage over tofu mixture before topping with plain, basil, or garlic-sesame flavored mochi. Bake as above. Or, use pizza mochi with regular-, hearty-, or plain wheat meat.

- **No pizza mochi?** Add to grated plain mochi— 2-3 Tbsp. Pizza herb blend (found in most grocery stores). Or add 1-2 Tbsp. dried tomato powder or 4-6 minced sun dried tomato halves, 1-2 tsp. garlic powder + 1/2 tsp. each dried basil and oregano + 1/4 tsp. powdered thyme + 1-2 pinches ground red pepper powder. Dissolve 1 Tbsp. light miso or 1/2 tsp. sea salt in 1/4 cup water then add to mochi then omit the extra water. Proceed as above.

- Replace sunflower seed meal with pumpkin or flax seed meal or 1 1/2 Tbsp. sesame or sunflower butter. ❏

Spanokopita

Prep: 20-30 minutes
Cooking: 30 minutes (filling) + 20 minutes

Yield dough: 2 top + 2 bottom crusts,
Yield: 2 pies; 8 slices per pie (16 slices total)
Serves: 8-16 accompanied by rice
Serving size: 1-2 slices pie per person

Here's a simple version of a classic Greek pie. If fresh spinach is unavailable, use kale, collards, mustard greens, or a mixture of several fresh greens. Make a big batch if you are cooking for more than two people since leftovers are even better the next day and make the perfect pack lunch or picnic food. This no fuss, simple, and satisfying crust can be used for other pies including pumpkin, apple or fruit pies, savory main dish pies, pot pies, or turnovers. It is substantially lower in fat than conventional pie crusts and filo dough yet incredibly moist and satisfying.

Filling:

2 large bunches spinach*

1 lb. tofu, soft or silken variety

3 Tbsp. arrowroot

1 tsp. sea salt

4 Tbsp. brown rice miso *(light, yellow, mellow, or sweet)*

Pie Crust:

2 1/2 cups spelt flour, whole wheat pastry flour, or hard white wheat flour

1 cup + 2 Tbsp. water

2 Tbsp. corn oil **or** raw butter or ghee

2 tsp. sea salt

Flour to dust pie plates

To make filling:

1. Wash spinach, dry, chop fine. Mix with sea salt and squeeze to wilt. (Knead in a bowl, rubbing leaves together until watery and soft.)

2. Put tofu through a hand food mill or a food processor (do not add any liquid). Mix with remaining filling ingredients and set aside.

To make crust:

1. Liberally oil two 9-10 inch pie plates and dust with flour.

2. Bring water, salt and oil (or butter or ghee) to boil. Add to flour, stir, then knead briefly, in the bowl to form a soft dough.

3. Divide in half then divide each half into two balls, one slightly larger than the other. You should have four dough balls.

4. Roll one large ball into very thin to 11 inch diameter. Place on flour dusted pie plate. Repeat with the other large ball.

5. Roll one small ball into a thin 9-10 inch diameter then repeat with second small ball.

To fill:

1. Place 1/2 of spanokopita filling on one large crust. Cover loosely with smaller crust. Fold bottom-crust edge over upper-crust edge. Poke holes in the upper crust with the tines of a fork in 3-4 places. Brush the edges with water. Repeat for the other pie.

2. Preheat oven to 400° F.

3. Bake pies for 20-30 minutes, uncovered, basting edges with water after 10 minutes. When done, cover with a towel and let stand 10 minutes before slicing.

Serving suggestions: Serve with a colorful root vegetable soup or side dish and rice or pita breads. Add pickles or relish as desired.

Storage: Refrigerate leftovers. Serve at room temperature or steam in a covered dish.

Variations:

- Make 16 individual pot pies in muffin tins, each oiled and filled with dough, topped, sealed, poked with a fork, and baked 15-20 minutes as above.

- **All-Season Spanokopita:** For spinach, substitute kale, Chinese mustard greens, or Chinese broccoli, cut paper thin. Discard woody parts of stems and mince the rest finely. Prepared as above.

- Use this filling to stuff steamed bun dough, tamales, calzones, or to top pizza dough. ❏

For more tofu recipes:

- See spreads and sauces.
- See pasta section.

Don's Tofu Quiche with corn crust

Prep: 20 minutes
Yield: 1 9-inch pie

Cooking: 40 minutes
Serves: 6-8 accompanied by bread or rice

This resembles the spinach pies that are traditionally made with feta cheese. We use kale or collard greens in place of spinach in this recipe. These hearty greens are rich in calcium and iron and can be found throughout most of the year. These greens also have more texture than spinach and a wonderful taste. For a sweet taste, add fresh corn off the cob when it's in season.

Serve this with a puréed carrot, winter squash, or tomato soup or clear miso broth. Add a boiled, pressed or marinated salad or steamed greens, and whole grain bread or rice.

Crust:

1 cup corn meal

1/4 lb. tofu, crumbled or mashed in a suribachi or food processor

2 tsp. ghee or corn, sunflower, or sesame oil

1/8 tsp. sun dried sea salt

Soy milk to make dough pliable enough to pat into a 9" pie plate

Filling:

2-3 tsp. sunflower, olive, or light sesame oil

1 medium onion, chopped finely

3/4 lb. tofu puréed in a hand food mill or food processor

1-2 Tbsp. light or sweet miso

2 cups steamed kale, chopped finely, stems minced *or* use collard greens if kale is unavailable

Optional, 1 1/2 cups corn off the cob

1 cup grated, plain or garlic sesame mochi (sold dried, refrigerated, or frozen)

1 Tbsp. arrowroot powder

Few drops tamari soy sauce

1. Liberally oil a 9 to 10 inch pie plate.

2. Mix crust ingredients and gently form into a ball with your hands. Press crust mixture into the bottom and side of pie plate and set aside.

3. Sauté onion in a wok or cast iron skillet over medium heat, stirring until translucent.

4. In a mixing bowl, stir puréed tofu with chopped, cooked kale, sautéed onion, and corn. Add grated mochi, miso, a few drops of soy sauce, and arrowroot powder.

5. Stir well and spoon into the pan. Bake at 350°F uncovered for 40 minutes or until set and slightly golden on top. Cool 15-30 minutes then slice and serve.

Serving Suggestions: see notes above.

Storage: Refrigerate leftovers and serve warmed or close to room temperature.

Variations:

- **Millet Crust:** Replace cornmeal with ground millet meal. Or, mix 1-1 1/2 cups of cooked millet with tofu, oil, salt, and soy milk and then proceed as above.

- Add 6 soaked, chopped sun dried tomato halves to the above filling.

- Add 1-2 cloves minced garlic when sauteing onion. Then add 1/2-1 1/2 tsp. powdered cumin to pie filling. ❏

About Soy Milk:

The pros and cons of using soy milk

Soy milk has benefits and drawbacks

First the benefits. Turning soybeans into milk makes these otherwise hard-to-digest-beans more digestible by removing some of the fiber. Soy milk doesn't involve the taking of milk from other animals and does not support the inhumane practices of our modern dairy industry. Thus it is a very ecological and human "milk." Further, soy milk is less allergenic than cow's milk, making it appropriate for children who have been weaned from the breast and for adults who no longer need human breast milk, and surely do not need milk from the breast of cows or goats. Another of soy milk's virtues is that it can be substituted one for one in almost any recipe that calls for milk: cream soups; white sauces; casseroles; pancake and waffle batters; corn bread; biscuits; or in tea or grain coffee.

Now for the drawbacks. Soy milk contains substances which can inhibit proper digestion and mineral absorption, particularly if consumed "raw," (that is, if it is not cooked sufficiently, cooked into a dish, or heated briefly before serving). Soy milk comes from the soybean, the bean highest in fat and very high in protein. Thus soy milk is relatively high in fat and protein and can be hard to digest, particularly if eaten too frequently or in too large a volume.

Like tofu, soy milk has a very cooling and dampening effect and when taken to excess, or by those with a Cold condition and/or digestive weakness, it can create problems. (Soy milk is a Yin tonic according to Oriental dietary classification, which means that it adds to the substance or "yin" aspect of the body).

Consumed too frequently, in too large a volume, or iced, chilled, frozen, or sweetened, soy milk can create many of the same problems as animal milk: gas, bloating, indigestion, mucus accumulation, diarrhea, or excessive weight gain. By dampening the digestive fire, it can cause a Cold condition and the accumulation of Phlegm.

(From the western perspective, soybeans contain a thyroid inhibiting substance which, if not properly broken down by thorough cooking and seasoning, can slow down one's metabolism and impair one's ability to digest food and to keep warm.)

For these reasons, it is best to use soy milk moderately, particularly if you have weak digestion, allergies, cold limbs, or excess weight to lose. We suggest using it as an occasional food (perhaps just a couple of times a week, if that) mainly in cooked dishes.

If used as a beverage, soy milk should be seasoned with a pinch of sea salt or a dash of miso and warmed to offset its cold and dampening effects. A pinch of spice such as cinnamon, nutmeg, ginger or black pepper can also help. If you are on a very low-fat therapeutic diet, you may want to use soy milk even less frequently. For the very active—athletes, active children, laborers, or those needing to gain weight (or those with Yin deficiency), soy milk may be used slightly more often; however, it should be served warm or at least room temperature (brought to a boil, then cooled), unsweetened, and without the addition of fruit.

Replacing soy milk

You will also discover that soy milk can be replaced with grain, seed, or nut milks in many recipes. [See our Oat-Cream of Vegetable Soup.] Soy milk can also be made into yogurt, a process which adds more intrinsic "heat" to the soybeans, thereby aiding digestion, and adding beneficial bacteria. Soy milk can also be made into extraordinary sauces and salad dressings thickened with arrowroot, kuzu, or agar agar. We love using it in Stroganoff and "Cream" soups.

Soy milk and babies

Although soy milk is very nutritious, it is quite different from human milk in composition and should never be used as a replacement for human mother's milk.

Purchase of soy milk

Avoid vitamin or mineral fortified soy milks at all costs! They contain substance that are not normally present in soybeans. We can't imitate nature in all her wisdom and no chemically derived vitamins can ever replicate what is found in whole and unadulterated foods. There is research to support the premise that taking man-made or extracted nutrients in pill or supplement form upsets proper mineral metabolism and creates imbalances in the human body. It is better to get your calcium from daily servings of cooked, dark green leafy land vegetables and sea vegetables; weekly servings of tofu and/or tempeh; kidney beans and other legumes; occasional tahini based sauces, spreads, or dressings; corn tortillas, tamales and arepas; daily pumpkin, sunflower, sesame, and/or flax seed condiments; and whole grains such as millet, brown rice, amaranth, quinoa, teff, buckwheat, etc. Raw goat milk or yogurt is another option for those who choose to use dairy foods. Whole foods such as these supply ample amounts of iron, calcium, and other essential macro and micro nutrients. Whole foods supply all of the nutrients we need in a more ecological, economical, and balanced and natural manner than do supplements and fortified foods.

Fresh is best

When buying soy milk, look for a fresh locally made, unsweetened brand: plain or "original." (Save sweetened soy milks for special occasions.) Some brands contain kelp, kombu, or Caragheen sea vegetable which acts as a tenderizer for the soybeans and makes the milk more flavorful and digestible. Some brands contain oil, others don't. We recommend the oil-free varieties. You will have to read labels carefully. The addition of oil to soy milk is unnecessary, after all most soy milks derive 50% of their calories from fat naturally. The addition of oil just adds to soy milk's already high-fat content and can make the milk even more difficult to digest. Experiment to find the brand you like best.

Storage of soy milk

Refrigerate aseptic packages (cartons) of soy milk after opening and use within one week to ten days. If the milk sours, you can use it like buttermilk in pancakes, waffles, biscuits or breads. Soy milks that are sold in the refrigerator or freezer case should be kept under refrigeration and used within the same period of time.

Turning soy milk into buttermilk

To make soy milk taste like buttermilk, for use in cooking or baking, simply add one tablespoon of brown rice vinegar or apple cider vinegar per 7/8 cup of soy milk, then use in your favorite recipe.

Going Green With Wheat Meat

Where Does Wheat Meat Come From, Anyway?

Seitan (also called "wheat meat") has been used in China and Japan for centuries. It is usually made from whole wheat or wheat gluten flour, water, tamari or shoyu soy sauce, and herbs or spices. Some peoples vary the types of flour they use. For example, one company adds bean flour for a meatier taste while others vary the herbs, spices, or salty seasonings.

Wheat meat is becoming so popular in the U.S. and Canada that many companies now offer it in a variety of flavors—BBQ, hickory smoked, sausage-style, chicken-style, etc. Shapes range from easy to slice blocks that resemble beef brisket or roast to burger and sausage patties, links, luncheon meats, and chicken-like breasts and pull-apart pieces. We suggest buying those products with the simplest, fewest, and most natural ingredients.

Seitan and other wheat gluten products typically sell for $5-9 a pound. This may sound like a lot— it's more than one would pay for meat— but meat would cost a heck of lot more than it does if our government didn't subsidize the meat industry and if the true cost of water and grain were factored in to the cost of modern meat. Besides, a little bit of wheat meat goes a lot farther than meat, particularly if it is added to another dish, rather than served as the main-dish. There is absolutely no need to figure on an eight or sixteen ounce serving of wheat meat per person in a meal!

To be even more ecological and economical, you can make wheat meat or seitan yourself; it's not difficult. If you use vital wheat gluten, you can make a big batch with less than 30 minutes of hands on preparation. You can freeze some of your homemade wheat meat in meal-size portions. If you use whole wheat bread flour, the traditional way, it's a bit more time consuming to make, but still do-able.

Not just for the transition.

Wheat meat can be a bridge because it allows you to change your diet and still use many of your favorite recipes, without feeling as if you had to give up the familiar tastes and textures of the meat-based dishes you know and love (or loved). Wheat meat and seitan can be used to replace any type of meat or poultry in recipes, with little or no adjustment (although you will need to scale down the portion size and reduce the amount of fat and seasonings). If you love, or once loved, meat or poultry you may be pleasantly surprised to find that you don't even miss it when you use wheat meat. In fact, it has such a similar appearance, taste, and texture to the real thing that some vegetarians won't eat it!

But wheat meat isn't just for vegetarians or those in "transition." Wheat meat offers the protein, texture, appearance, and a similar taste to meat without the environmental side-effects of factory farmed meats and the modern American meat-habit. Wheat meat products also offer the culinary versatility of both meat and poultry. Wheat meat is virtually fat-free and totally cholesterol-free, making it an ideal food for regular use.

If you're already a vegetarian and don't want, need, or miss meat dishes, don't turn your nose up at wheat meat. It can still be of benefit to you. It is not just a meat "substitute." Think of it is a chameleon. Wheat meat has a texture to play with that opens up a world of culinary options otherwise unavailable. Although beans, tofu, and tempeh have, done a lot to open up a wider world of culinary possibilities, wheat meat can do what these foods have done and more.

Using Wheat Meat

Wheat meat is best served in moderate portion sizes of two or three ounces per person (or roughly 1/4-1/2 cup).

You can use it as is, by slicing, dicing, mincing, grinding, or chopping then adding it to your favorite soups, stews, salads, sauces, sandwiches, stir fries, stuffings, fillings, casseroles or other dishes, with little or no cooking.

Wheat meat can also be dressed up with sauces, marinades or seasonings and used to make French, Italian, Mexican, Spanish, Korean, Japanese, Chinese, English, Greek, German, or good-old American fare. For example, you can use it to make popular Mexican dishes like chili, fajitas, tacos, burritos, tamales, or enchiladas, to make French-style quiches, patés, stroganoffs, and stews.

Try it in Italian dishes like lasagna, calzones, ravioli, pizza, pasta dishes, and other creations. In Hungarian cooking, wheat meat is at home in stuffed cabbage leaves, goulash, and fried cabbage dishes.

You can create popular American dishes such as beefy stews, mock chicken and meat-like salads, ham and cheese look-alikes, French-dip and reuben sandwiches, gourmet burgers, meat loaves, beef-like jerky, and a wide array of appetizers and other familiar dishes with wheat meat.

Wheat meat also holds its own in Chinese-style preparations as well, so one can create sweet and sour mock pork, stir fries, filled buns, and dim sum appetizers. The possibilities are as endless as your imagination!

You can play with the style of preparation (and the amount of moisture the wheat meat is allowed to absorb) to create a wide array of different tastes and textures. Like a chameleon, wheat meat picks of the flavor of whatever you cook or serve it with, though some companies make it so flavorful that you really don't have to do much to it but heat it and eat it.

The brand of wheat meat that you choose makes a difference. Some companies make a very dense "meaty" textured product while others make a more soft and spongy one. Some brands are very salty while others are more lightly seasoned. You may want to experiment with a variety of cooking methods and condiments until you come up with the perfect preparations for your needs and tastes.

The Keeping of Wheat Meat

Some companies sell wheat meat in sealed jars on the dry goods shelf. Other companies sell it in vacuum sealed packs with some of the cooking brine, similar to the way tofu is generally packaged. It may also be sold in sealed plastic packs that resemble luncheon meats and tofu burgers. Still other companies sell wheat meat and wheat meat products in boxes or sealed bags in the freezer. Due to increasing demand, wheat meat may soon be sold in bulk just as tofu was once sold in co-ops in the late sixties and early seventies.

Most companies recommend keeping wheat meat for 7-10 days in the refrigerator, or frozen for longer periods of time. It can be frozen with or without the cooking broth, depending upon personal preference and the particular type of product you buy. Unlike meat and poultry, wheat meat is not harmed by thawing and refreezing, so you needn't worry about using it up in a short period of time. If you inadvertently thaw more than you need you can simply refreeze the unused portion without risk or fear of food poisoning or damaging he product.

WHEAT MEAT CAN BE USED IN MORE WAYS THAN YOU CAN IMAGINE

Chop, mince, shred, or grind it in a meat grinder then add it to:

- Vegetable stir fries
- Soups, stews, and chili
- Stove top or oven-baked casseroles
- Baked beans
- Sautés
- Spaghetti sauce
- Pasta, rice, or vegetable salads
- Shish kabobs
- Fillings for pot pies, tamales, and turnovers
- Fillings for won tons, gyoza, ravioli, or dim sum appetizers
- Stuffings for pumpkins, bell peppers, tomatoes, or cabbage leaves
- Goulash, stroganoffs, sauces, and gravies
- Meat or meat-less loaves, burgers, meatballs, and rissoles
- Tacos, burritos, and enchiladas
- Stove top casseroles
- Pizza

Slice it into cutlets and dredge it in flour or shake-and-bake coating mix then:

- Pan fry it for meat-less cutlets, strips, and chicken-like or meat-like appetizers or sandwich stuffers and sushi fillings
- "Oven fry" or pan fry for mock chicken nuggets, fried-"chicken," or steak-less fingers

Slice it like luncheon meat and use it to make:

- Veggie reubens
- Veggie club-sandwiches
- French dip sandwiches
- Ham-less and cheese sandwiches
- Pastrami look-alike
- Mock ham and cheese
- Any other sandwich favorite

Poach it in an herb and wine or sake based-marinade for gourmet sauces, stews, and side dishes

Basic Wheat Meat from Gluten Flour

Prep: less than 10 minutes
Cooking: 30 minutes at pressure *or* 1 hour if simmered

Yield: about 1 cup
Serves: 3-4 (or 1 1/2-2 meals for 2)

** *Double recipe as needed.*

Wheat meat is a snap to make when you start with gluten flour. It can be used in a myriad of ways—in stews, chili, stir fries, sandwiches, shish-kebabs, salads, casseroles, or anywhere you used to use meat, poultry, or fish. (But don't plan on 8-ounce steaks, we usually figure just 2-3 ounces per person, about 1/4-1/2 cup). You can make enough to last for a few days or a week at a time.

You'll find gluten flour in health food stores or by mail. You can also buy flavored wheat meat mixes. (See notes below.)

1/2 cup gluten flour or vital wheat gluten flour

1/2 tsp. garlic powder

1/8 tsp. red pepper powder *(we prefer mild varieties—chipotle, ancho, or Anaheim)*

Optional, 1-4 Tbsp. walnuts or sunflower seeds *(this produces a richer, meatier product)*

1 1/2-2 Tbsp. tamari or shoyu

1/2 cup water

1. Mix all dry ingredients in a bowl. In a separate bowl mix wet ingredients then stir into dry. (To use nuts or seeds, blend with liquids in a blender before adding to flour or powder sunflower seeds in a coffee-spice mill.) Mix very well using a large mixing spoon then your hands. Form into a ball.

   Note: If you plan to use the wheat meat in a recipe that calls for oil, nuts, seeds, or a nut or seed butter sauce, reduce or omit nuts and seeds from the wheat meat dough otherwise you will create a very high fat dish.

2. Oil a small stainless steel bowl (16 oz. size). Put the ball of dough in bowl. Cover bowl with a wet cheesecloth then secure with a rubberband or string.

3. Put bowl in a stainless steel pressure cooker, and surround bowl with water filled to 1/3 the height of the bowl. Bring to full pressure, reduce heat to medium and pressure cook 30 minutes. To boil, use the same bowl-within-a-pot method but bring to boil, reduce heat to medium-low and cook for 1 hour.

4. Remove gluten from bowl. Allow to cool before slicing. (**Note:** For sandwiches, slice paper thin.)

Serving suggestions: Add chopped wheat meat to your favorite recipe. Or, slice wheat meat made with nuts or seeds and serve over whole grain, pasta, or bread, with greens, a root, round or ground vegetable soup or side dish, and condiments. (Steam heat if desired.) Alternatively, wheat meat made without nuts or seeds can be heated by steaming, grilling, or pan frying. (Served as above.)

Storage: Refrigerate in a covered wide mouth jar or glass or stainless steel bowl

Variation:

- Purchase flavored wheat meat mixes such as **Knox Mountain Farms' Not-So Sausage, Wheatballs,** or **Chick 'n Wheat.** If you can't find them at your local co-op or health food store, call (603) 934-4757 to order or refer to our Mail Order Resources. ❏

Note: Wheat meat and seitan are different names for the same product.

Basic Procedure, Seitan Stroganoff (Fall & Winter) ***

Prep: 20-30 minutes
Cooking: 45-50 minutes
Serves: 6-8 (or 3 meals for 2)
Serving size: 1/2-1 cup per person

This recipe is meat-less, dairy-free, far lower in fat than conventional stroganoffs and incredibly versatile. Seitan (also called wheat meat) replaces meat in this classic dish. But even if you're not a vegetarian or a fan of wheat meat, you're in for a surprise! For a fancier meal, add a side of garlic bread or steamed buns and a light vegetable soup.

2-3 tsp. ghee *or* sesame oil or olive oil

2 medium onions, cut into thin crescents

1/8-1/4 tsp. sea salt

4 cups packed mushrooms, thinly sliced *(preferably button mushrooms + 1-2 shiitake or crimini mushrooms)*

Wheat meat and seasonings:

1-2 bay leaves

2 cups wheat meat or seitan, cut into thin strips or torn into thin, small bite-sized pieces *(original/hearty, chicken-style, or homemade)*

1/2-3/4 cup water or part wheat meat broth

1 1/2 tsp. dried herbs *or* 1 Tbsp. fresh herbs, minced finely *(thyme + basil or oregano; or marjoram, etc.)*

Optional, 1 Tbsp. mirin (sweet cooking rice wine) *or* 2-3 Tbsp. sake, mirin, wine, or sherry

Sauce:

3 Tbsp. arrowroot powder *or* kuzu root powder/starch

1-1/4-1 1/3 cups fresh, plain, unsweetened soy milk

1-2 Tbsp. light, yellow or mellow miso or tamari soy sauce *or* 2-5 Tbsp. wheat meat broth *(use lesser amount of miso or tamari if wheat meat is very salty and/or salty wheat meat broth is used above)*

Garnish: Fresh or dried chives, parsley, edible flowers and/or black pepper

1. In a heavy pot, (preferably a dutch oven or enamel lined cast-iron pot), sauté onion in ghee or oil over medium heat. Add sea salt and stir until browned. Add mushrooms, stir, cover, reduce heat to low, and cook for 20 minutes, until mushrooms become watery and wilted. (No additional water is needed; the mushrooms will release water as they cook down.)

2. Layer bay leaves, cut wheat meat and dried herbs over vegetables. (If using fresh herbs, add them after cooking.) Do not stir, simply add 1/2-cup liquid (3/4 cup if using very dense or dry wheat meat). Cover, bring to boil, reduce heat to low, and simmer 15 minutes or until tender and juicy.

3. In a blender, Osterizer (mini-blend container), or suribachi, purée sauce ingredients until smooth. Add this to the stew pot and stir to thicken, about 5 minutes. Turn off and remove from heat. If using fresh herbs, stir these in now.

Serving suggestions: Ladle over noodles, brown rice, millet, or polenta. Garnish as desired. Serve with a side of steamed green or mixed vegetables or a parboiled or tossed salad. For a fancier meal, also serve steamed buns or baked bread or sweet potatoes, and a light, creamy vegetable soup.

Storage: Refrigerate leftovers and reheat using the covered bowl-within-a-pot method. Or thin leftovers with water, stock, or soy milk to make a quick and tasty soup the second day.❏

Burdock Stroganoff (Fall & Winter)

Prep: 20 minutes
Cooking: 50 minutes
Serves: 6-8 (or 3-4 meals for 2)
Serving size: 1/3-1/2 cup per person

Burdock root adds an unusual twist and a hearty taste to this version of the popular Russian dish. While this dish is similar to our basic Seitan Stroganoff, it is much richer and so we serve it in much smaller amounts. It is really more of a sauce or gravy than a stew.

Vegetables and Wheat Meat:

1 1/2-2 tsp. ghee or untoasted sesame oil

1/2 large onion, minced finely

1/8-1/4 tsp. sea salt

2 cups well scrubbed (but not peeled) burdock root, cut into 1/4-1/2" rounds

2 cups (packed) mushrooms, cut finely

2-2 1/2 cups wheat meat/seitan, cut into cubes or long strips

Sauce:

1/2 cup sesame tahini (raw or roasted variety) *or* sesame butter

1/3-1/2 cup water, or slightly more as needed to blend

1 1/2 tsp. dark or red miso *(brown rice, buckwheat, soybean, or barley variety)**

Garnish:

Scallions, parsley, chives, or paprika

1. Sauté onions in ghee or oil, with sea salt, over medium heat. When tender and translucent, add chopped burdock root and continue to stir. Add mushrooms, stir, then cover and simmer for 10 minutes until wilted. Add wheat meat or seitan, cover, turn heat to low, simmer for 30-40 minutes.

2. Dissolve tahini or sesame butter and miso in water to make a paste. Pour this into the pot and stir to thicken. If too thick, adjust by adding water a tablespoon at a time, as needed, and stir to thicken.

Serving suggestions: Spoon over brown rice, millet, or noodles and add a side of quick-boiled greens or steamed greens tossed with sauerkraut or rice vinegar. Also serve a cup of carrot, squash, beet or tomato soup. This dish is also delicious over baked potatoes with a side of pressed or boiled salad and bread.

Storage: Store in a covered bowl in the refrigerator. Reheat using the covered-bowl-within-a-pot method. Or, turn leftovers into a hearty soup with additional water or stock and a bit more miso or tamari.

Variation:

• Use tamari or shoyu to replace miso above.❏

Hungarian Goulash (Fall, Winter, Spring) ***

Prep: 20 minutes
Cooking: 40-45 minutes
Serves: 6-8 (or 2 meals for a family of 3)

Numerous variations of Hungarian Goulash exist and each family has its favorite. Don, who is half-Hungarian, adapted his family favorite. We've replaced the meat with wheat meat while smooth and creamy tahini paste replaces the more traditional sour cream. When tomatoes are out of season, we use winter squash instead.

2 tsp. ghee or light sesame oil

2 medium-sized white onions, cut finely

1/4 tsp. sea salt

1 Tbsp. paprika

Sauce #1 (Fall, Winter, Spring & Early Summer):

2 1/2-3 cups winter squash, cut in 3/4" cubes

3/4 cup water or vegetable stock

1 cup natural sauerkraut, drained

2 cups chopped wheat meat or seitan (*chicken style, hearty/original, or plain variety*)

1/2-3/4 cup water or part vegetable stock (*more liquid for dry and dense wheat meat or seitan, less for soft, moist, and wet seitan*)

use for either method

Sauce #2 (Summer & Early Fall):

2 cups chopped tomatoes

1/2 cup tomato purée

Tahini Cream:

2 Tbsp. light or sweet miso

3-4 Tbsp. sesame tahini (raw or lightly roasted variety)

4-6 Tbsp. water

Garnish: chives, scallions and/or black pepper

1. Pick sauce #1 or sauce #2. Sauté onions in a 4-quart dutch oven pan or heavy pot over medium heat. Add a few pinches of sea salt to draw out additional moisture. Sauté until tender and translucent. Add paprika and squash or tomatoes and tomato purée. Stir briefly. Add water or stock if using squash. Cover, bring to boil, reduce heat to low, and simmer 20-25 minutes or until almost tender.

2. Layer sauerkraut and wheat meat over vegetables. Do not stir. Cover and return to a low boil then reduce heat to low and simmer 15-20 minutes until everything is tender and juicy. Most of the liquid should be absorbed.

3. In a suribachi, small bowl, or Osterizer mini-blend container, purée light miso, tahini, and water. Add additional water as needed to produce about 1/2 cup purée (or slightly more). Add this to the pot and stir to thicken, about 3-4 minutes, then turn off and remove from heat.

Serving suggestions: Serve over noodles or rice, with or without freshly baked whole grain peasant bread. (Try barley, rye, spelt, or kamut bread.) A small cup of vegetable soup or miso seasoned broth is also nice. Add a side of steamed greens, boiled salad, or mixed vegetables.

Storage: Refrigerate leftovers in a stainless steel bowl. Reheat using the covered-bowl-within-a-pot method. Transform into a soup with additional water or stock if desired. ❏

Variation:

- **Wheat Meat in Peanut Sauce:** Replace tahini with peanut butter. Replace paprika with 3 cloves minced garlic and/or 1-2 tsp. minced ginger root and 1/4 tsp. mild red pepper powder.

Basic Procedure, Pan-Fried Wheat Meat Cutlets (Any Season)

Prep: 15-30 minutes
Cooking: 15-30 minutes
Serves: 6-8 (or 3-4 meals for 2)
Serving size: 2-3 small cutlets per person

These cutlets look so much like meat that you might fool more than a few friends. These are juicy and tender on the inside with a slightly crispy herbed coating on the outside. They are meant to be a condiment, rather than a main dish, served with grain and relishes.

Note: You don't need a lot oil to pan fry. A little bit goes a long way if you use a moderate temperature and a little patience.

Herbed coating:

1 1/3 cup arrowroot **or** barley, chickpea, or corn flour

1/3-1/2 tsp. sea salt, ground finely

1 tsp. each of thyme, sage, and marjoram **or** basil, oregano, and either thyme or marjoram

Wheat Meat Cutlets

1 1/2-2 cups wheat meat/seitan *(about 12-16 cutlets, 3-4" across)*

3 Tbsp. salty seitan broth, soup stock, or water, as needed to moisten

1-3 Tbsp. ghee *or* sesame oil or olive oil for the skillet

1. Dry roast salt for several minutes in a wok until moisture has evaporated and crystals are opaque and dry. (Good quality, sun dried sea salt is wet and needs to be dry roasted in order to be ground.) If salt is coarse, grind in a suribachi. Mix with remaining coating ingredients.

2. Slice wheat meat into 1/3-inch thin cutlets or finger-like strips. Dip in stock or broth then dredge in the dry coating mixture until thoroughly coated. Transfer to a plate. Repeat with remaining cutlets. Reserve extra coating mix in a sealed glass jar for another time.

3. Heat 1 tsp. oil in a 10 to 12-inch cast iron skillet or heavy saucepan over medium heat. When oil is hot, add several cutlets. Cook 4-5 minutes on each side, pressing down with a spatula until they sizzle and become slightly charred. Cover the skillet for several minutes to steam.

4. Transfer cutlets to a plate. Cover with a lid or plate to keep warm then cook remaining cutlets with additional oil as needed. (You won't need much.)

5. Serve warm. If cooked in advance, reheat by steaming on an uncovered plate, on top of a bamboo steamer or metal steamer basket, or serve at room temperature for lunch.

Serving suggestions: Serve over whole grain brown rice, polenta, or bread with cooked greens or mixed veggies. Add a few minced pickles and/or mustard and/or Grain Mayo or Tofu Mayo. A puréed squash, rutabaga, parsnip, or corn soup also makes a nice addition. A bean, tofu, carrot or beet sauce can be used as a topping, though the cutlets are very delicious plain or with a dab of mustard and sauerkraut. Leftovers are great to have on hand and make terrific sandwich fillers.

Storage: Refrigerate leftovers. Serve at room temperature or briefly steam heat on a plate.

Leftover tips:

- Chop leftover cutlets and add to chili, baked beans, stir fry or spaghetti sauce.
- Slice leftovers and serve as an appetizer with sweet and sour sauce, mustard, Beet Sauce Italiano, or other savory or spicy sauce. ❏

Basic Procedure, Oven "Fried" Mock Chicken or "Steak" Fingers

Prep: 20-30 minutes
Cooking: 20-30 minutes
Serves: 8 (or 3-4 meals for 2)
Serving size: 2-3 pieces per person

This recipe provides that rich fried-chicken taste without all the traditional heart-stopping fat. These tasty cutlets are crispy on the outside and moist and tender on the inside. Try it with regular or chicken-style wheat meat. Plan for leftovers, you will want them the next day.

Wheat meat or tempeh:

3 cups (~16 pieces) chicken-style wheat meat, or thinly cut hearty/original wheat meat or seitan *or* 2, 8-ounce blocks Pressure Marinated Tempeh

Wet coating:

1/2 cup soft tofu puréed with ~1/3 cup soy milk or water *or* plain soy yogurt

3-4 tsp. tamari, shoyu, or light or dark miso

Breading:

1 1/2-2 cups finely crushed or powdered fat-free crackers or bread crumbs *(RyVita, RYTAK, Wasa, RyeKrisp, or other)*

1/2-2/3 tsp. dried, oregano, sage, or cumin powder

1/2 tsp. dried thyme or basil

Optional, 1/2 tsp. dried garlic granules

Sesame or olive oil to coat the baking pan

1. Preheat oven to 350° F. Oil a large cookie sheet (one with sides to catch the juices) or a cake pan. Or line sheet with parchment paper.

2. Cut wheat meat into 14-16 thin slabs or use pre-cut "chicken-style" wheat meat. If using tempeh, cut each block into 16 thin slices.

3. In a shallow bowl mix wet coating ingredients and set aside. In a separate bowl, mix breading ingredients. (Crackers may be crushed in a suribachi.)

4. One at a time, dip pieces of wheat meat or tempeh in wet coating mixture, turning to coat thoroughly, then roll in breading to coat liberally. Arrange pieces on oiled or parchment lined baking sheet or cake pans.

5. Bake uncovered in the middle to upper third of the oven, about 25-30 minutes or until lightly golden and crispy.

Serving suggestions: Serve with a cup of bean or vegetable soup; corn bread, rice, Millet-Squash Squares, Millet & Corn Slices, or Millet "Mashed Potatoes" with gravy. Add a pressed, marinated or boiled salad. Pickles are also nice. In the winter, you could serve baked sweet potato or winter squash on the side. In the summer serve corn on the cob.

Storage: Refrigerate leftovers in a covered bowl. Remove from the refrigerator 30-90 minutes before serving and eat at room temperature, or crisp in the oven or toaster oven, on a baking sheet, at 350° F for 10 minutes before serving.

Variations:

- Replace above herbs with 1 tsp. powdered sage + 1-1 1/2 tsp. paprika + 1/8 tsp. black pepper or mild red pepper powder.

- Use masa harina flour to replace cracker crumbs in the above recipe.

- **Oven-Fried Falafel Flavored Wheat Meat:** Omit cracker crumbs, herbs/spices, sea salt, miso, tamari, and shoyu. Substitute dry falafel mix for the breading above. ❏

Hungarian Stuffed Collard or Cabbage Leaves (Year Round)***

Prep: 20-30 minutes
Cooking: 2 1/4 hours *or* 4-6 hours in a thermal cooker

Yield: 4 stuffed leaves
Serves: 4 (or 2 meals for 2)
Serving size: 1 cup stew (includes 1 filled leaf) per person

This dish can be made throughout the year and assembled in about 30 minutes. We often make it once a week for several weeks in a row, in late summer, early fall, or throughout the winter. We never get tired of it because it can be endlessly varied with the addition of different herbs and spices. Winter squash is a favorite for the sauce, though tomatoes may be used occasionally in late summer and early fall, in season. We serve this as a stew, over individual bowls of rice or noodles or with a side of steamed buns or baked bread with a low fat spread. (Try rye, barley, soy, buckwheat, spelt, wheat, or chestnut bread.)

Sauce #1 (late summer and early fall)

1 Tbsp. ghee or olive oil

1-1 1/2 cups diced onion

2 cups chopped fresh tomatoes

1/2 cup fresh tomato purée

1/2-2/3 cup natural, organic sauerkraut

Sauce #2 (late fall, winter, and spring)

1 Tbsp. ghee or olive oil

1-1/2 cups diced onion

2 cups diced sweet winter squash (*kabocha, buttercup, hokaido, or butternut*)

1 1/4 cup water (1 cup if thermal cooking)

1/2-2/3 cup natural, organic sauerkraut

Filling:

2/3 cup gluten flour (or vital wheat gluten flour)

2 Tbsp. dried onion flakes (+/- 2 Tbs. dried parsley flakes)

1-2 tsp. garlic powder

2 tsp. dried, powdered herbs (thyme, oregano, basil, sage, cumin, or several of these)

1/8 tsp. mild red pepper pepper (ancho, Anaheim, or chipotle)

Optional, 3 Tbsp. nutritional yeast flakes (for a chicken-like flavor)

2-4 Tbsp. chopped walnuts **or** sunflower seeds

2/3 cups water

1 1/2-2 Tbsp. dark miso, tamari o shoyu (**or** 2-3 Tbsp light miso for a chicken like flavor).

Optional, 1/2 tsp. liquid smoke/hickory smoke flavoring

Wrapper: 4-6 large savoy cabbage or hard cabbage leaves or collard leaves

Garnish: Fresh, minced parsley, chives, scallions, and/or ground black pepper

1. If using cabbage, remove four outer leaves from head of cabbage. If using wrinkled cabbage, turn the head up-side-down, running warm water over and between the leaves while gently peeling or cutting them off the rest of the head. If using collard leaves, including the stems. Leave the center rib intact for both cabbage leaves and collards. Steam leaves until just tender, about 5 minutes, on a steamer basket or in a pot with 1/2-inch water. Remove leaves and cool in a dish on the counter.

2. In a 3 or 4-quart casserole dish or Dutch oven pot, sauté onions in oil until tender and translucent. Add chopped tomato or squash and a few pinches of salt. If using tomatoes, purée one diced tomato, without added liquid, in a blender or Osterizer mini-blend container. Add this (or the recommended volume of water if squash is used) to the pot along with sauerkraut. Bring to a low boil, cover,reduce heat to medium-low, and simmer 10-15 minutes.

3. In a mixing bowl, combine dry ingredients. Purée water and miso or tamari (+/- liquid smoke) in a blender. Add to the dry ingredients while mixing with a sturdy spoon. Form into a smooth ball. Divide into 4 balls of equal size and shape each into a small log.

4. Place one cabbage or collard leaf on the counter with the stem end (vertical) toward you. If leaves are torn or small, use two overlapping leaves. Place a "meat" ball log horizontally across the width of the leaf, on the end closest to you. Fold the bottom of the leaf around until just covered then fold in the left side of the leaf, then the right side, then tightly roll the ball away from you until completely wrapped. Set packet seam-side down on top of the sauce in the casserole dish. Repeat with the other "meat" balls.

5. Optional, cover cabbage balls with a small heat proof saucer or a plate which is smaller than the diameter of the pot. This keeps the leaves from opening up in the pot. Cover pot, bring almost to a boil, reduce heat to low, then cook, for about 2 hours. (Use a heat deflector under the pot if necessary, to prevent burning.) Or, cook for 4-8 hours in a thermal cooker.

Serving suggestions: Ladle 1 stuffed cabbage or collard leaf with a portion of the sauce into each serving bowl. Garnish as desired. Serve with several hefty slices whole grain bread—dinner rolls, steamed buns, or dinner pancakes. (Or, serve stew over individual bowls of rice or noodles.) Round out the meal with a small serving of pressed or marinated salad or quick-boiled greens.

Storage: Immediately portion leftover cabbage or collard leaves, with some of the sauce, into a heat-proof stainless steel bowl for easy reheating the next day. Cover with a small heat proof saucer and refrigerate when cooled. Reheat using the covered-bowl-within-a-pot method. ❑

Wheatloaf (Fall, Winter, Early Spring)

Prep: 20-30 minutes
Cooking: 1 hour or 8-10 hours in a crock pot

Yield: 1, standard loaf pan, 8-10 slices
Serves: 4-6 (or 2-3 meals for 2)
Serving size: 1-2 slices per person

Here's a healthier meatless version of mom's meatloaf. It's incredibly low in fat, cholesterol-free, and full of memories.

Binder & Seasonings:

2 Tbsp. tamari, shoyu, or dark miso *or* 3-4 Tbsp. light miso for a chicken-like loaf

1/2-2/3 cup mashed, soft tofu *or* 2/3 cup puréed, cooked chickpeas for a chicken-like loaf

1/2-2/3 cup warm water or mushroom soaking liquid

2 Tbsp. arrowroot powder *or* ground raw flax seeds

Other ingredients:

2-2 1/2 cups packed, shredded or ground wheat meat/seitan *(hearty, original, or chicken style)*

1 cup rolled oats *or* bulgar wheat or spelt bulbar

3 Tbsp. dried onion

2 Tbsp. dried bell pepper flakes

2 Tbsp. dried parsley *or* 4 Tbsp. fresh parsley, minced finely

2 tsp. dried garlic granules or powder

1 1/2-2 tsp. dried herbs or spices
(e.g., 1 tsp. sage + 1/2 thyme + 1/4 tsp. each marjoram or basil + oregano or poultry seasoning)

Optional, 1 Tbsp. prepared, unsweetened, preservative-free natural mustard *or* 2/3-1 tsp. dry mustard

Optional, 2 shiitake mushrooms, soaked in hot water to cover, then drained and minced

(save soak water to use in binder above)

Ghee or sesame or olive oil

Garnish: Fresh or dried, chives, prepared mustard, or other

Optional, low-fat or oil free vegetable sauce, gravy, or mustard, ***and/or*** pickles and relishes

1. If using shiitake mushrooms, soak in hot water to cover for about 30-60 minutes. Drain but save soak water to use in binder. Mince shiitake and set aside.

2. Grind flax seeds in a coffee spice mill or Osterizer. Combine binder and seasoning ingredients in a blender, Osterizer, or suribachi. Blend until smooth and creamy like yogurt. Add a bit more water (or mushroom soak liquid) if needed.

3. In a large mixing bowl combine all ingredients. Mash well. Mixture should resemble raw hamburger.

4. Lightly oil a 9 x 2-inch loaf pan. Dust with sesame seeds or bread crumbs if desired.

5. Press in mixture, flatten on top, cover, and bake at 350° F for 45 minutes. Uncover and bake 20 minutes until firm to the touch and lightly golden on top.

Serving suggestions: Slice and serve. We serve wheat loaf with brown rice, brown rice cooked with wild rice, or steamed buns. We also like to serve corn on the cob or baked or mashed winter squash, turnips, or sweet potato and/or a creamless cream of vegetable soup and pickles with this meal. At Thanksgiving serve with Mock Poultry Gravy or Parsnip White Sauce.

Storage: Refrigerate. Warm in the oven or heat using the covered-bowl-within-a-pot method.

Leftover tips:

• **Wheatloaf Sandwich:** Spread mustard and/or Grain Mayo on whole grain bread slices, buns, pita bread, or tortillas. Top with thinly sliced wheatloaf, natural sauerkraut, dill pickle or Quick Pickled Onion Rings and/or grated horseradish. Add greens or raw salad and tomato in hot weather or pressed or marinated salad and a light cream of vegetable soup.

Chapter 8
Creative Condiments

What are condiments

Condiments are special seasonings or seasoned foods that we add to foods at the table to spark the digestive fire or add missing flavors to various dishes. While some may be added by the cook in the kitchen, most are used at the table by the diner. Condiments can add to the eye appeal of a dish and can change the temperature or energy of a particular food or dish. In this way, diners, can selectively add condiments to individual portions of food in varying amounts to suit their needs, tastes, preferences, and desires. Condiments can also add variety to meals. They can be changed from meal to meal so that even if the same bread, rice or noodles are served two meals or days in a row, they will look and taste slightly different.

Since most of our food is slightly sweet (grains, beans, root, ground, and round vegetables), condiments round out our meals with other flavors. For health and enjoyment, it is important to include all flavors in our diets—sweet, sour, bitter, salty, and pungent but you needn't worry about getting all flavors in a single meal.

Condiments for health

Dry roasted, seasoned seed and nut condiments provide both salty and bitter flavors. Examples include Gomashio (sesame-salt), Flax Seed Condiment, Walnut-Salt, and Tamari Roasted Pumpkin Seeds. For freshness and flavor, these should be homemade rather than store bought. They can be used at the table, at a meal, sprinkled over whole grains, hot cereal, or pasta. They can also be used on vegetables from time to time. The bitter flavor stimulates digestion and is beneficial for everyday use. Dry roasted

and ground or crumbled sea vegetables also confer a slightly salty flavor and can be used as table condiments, alone or combined with roasted seeds or minced chives, scallions, or arugula.

Naturally pickled vegetables: sauerkraut; dill pickles; pickled onions, radishes, carrots, garlic or ginger; and naturally aged vinegars such as brown rice vinegar, apple cider vinegar, umeboshi and apriboshi vinegar or paste all provide a wonderful sour flavor. Some of these—like pickles and umeboshi or apriboshi vinegar and paste—have both salty and sour flavors. (Umeboshi and apriboshi vinegars are not true vinegars as true vinegars are not salty; rather, they are the brine left from salt pickling ume apricots or plums.) However, it is advisable to avoid using commercial vinegars which are often made with petroleum derivatives and high tech methods which reduce their nutritional value. Also avoid vinegars, pickles, or pickled foods containing sugar, artificial sweeteners, additives, preservatives, dyes, or MSG. Natural vegetable pickles are actually quite easy to make. (Most can be assembled in a mater of minutes and then left to ferment for three to six days or several weeks.) A limited variety of natural pickles can also be found in health food stores, co-ops, and reliable mail-order sources. Read labels carefully and bear in mind that most commercial pickles and vinegars are not naturally aged and therefore do not confer the medicinal benefits of their naturally aged counterparts.

Pungent or mildly spicy condiments for health include fresh green garnishes such as scallions, chives, parsley, cilantro, arugula, grated radish, and cabbage, onion or sunflower sprouts. Chives can be used fresh, in season, or dried; both forms are suitable for use at the table. These can be sprinkled over hot cereal, rice, noodles, soups, beans, or eggs. They spark the digestive fire and add interest to even the simplest dishes.

Black pepper, red pepper, grated horseradish, mustard, and dried ginger powder or the juice squeezed from freshly grated ginger also have a pungent to spicy flavor; however, these should be used with caution. Used in small amounts they can be good medicine for certain people, under certain conditions, and in certain contexts. Too much of these or other hot spices can aggravate certain conditions. When using dried herbs and spices, however, make sure that they have not been irradiated and use a light hand.

Prepared mustard (yellow, stone ground, or dijon) is another spicy, pungent and tasty condiment. It should be free of sweeteners, preservatives, additives, and artificial colorings. (Look for Eden, Westbrae, Edward & Sons or Co-Op brand in your local grocery or health food store.) Mustard may be used as a spread for bread to replace butter and other oily spreads. Though it sounds strange, it is actually quite tasty. If you want mayo with your mustard on burger buns, try our low fat, Grain Mayo or Tofu Mayo.

What to avoid

If your purpose is nourishment for life, you ought to avoid using certain things as table condiments—salt or sea salt, tamari, shoyu, soy sauce, umeboshi vinegar, salsa, ketchup, commercial mayonnaise or condiments that include sugar, other sweeteners, preservatives, or additives. Salt, tamari, shoyu, and soy sauce should be used to season foods in marinating, cooking, or in some cases when tossing steamed or parboiled vegetable before serving. Salt or soy sauce type products irritate the mucous membranes, add a harsh flavor, and easily lead to overuse when added at the table.

Oils and most salad dressings are heavy, rich, damp, hard to digest, and therefore oils are best used sparingly. In fact, most dressings should be used moderately . Too much oily and rich food burdens the digestive organs and can put out the digestive fire. This prevents the proper digestion and transformation of food into Qi (energy). We have provided several recipes for oil-free salad dressings, although a small amount of good quality, unrefined oil may be used on vegetables or grains at the table.

We recommend avoiding both salsa and ketchup/catsup. The main problem with salsa is that it has a Hot and Damp energy that can irritate the Stomach and Liver and dampen the digestive fire. Ketchup is the concentrated essence of the very Cold and Damp tomato (a fruit). It is a cooling condiment for hot energy foods like grilled hamburgers or charbroiled steaks. On a grain based diet it can easily create imbalance. If you want something that looks and tastes like ketchup or barbeque sauce, a more nutritious sauce or purée can be made from cooked beets combined with a much larger volume carrots or winter squash and onions.

Other condiments

Recipes for light and nourishing sauces are provided in this chapter though more can be found in other sections of this book. For example, almost any soup or stew can serve as a sauce for pasta while a bean dip, sauce, gravy, or a steamed egg can serve as a topping for polenta, pasta, bread, or rice.

Literally speaking, we may consider any side dish—whether it is made from land or sea vegetables, beans, tofu, tempeh, wheat meat, or eggs —in the category of condiments since they are all served alongside or used as topping for grains. However, this chapter will only focus on condiments which are served in far smaller portions than are side dishes.

Are condiments time consuming to make?

Most condiments needn't be made fresh for every meal and don't take a huge time investment. Seed condiments take fifteen to twenty minutes to make and can be made to last for a week to ten days at a time. Quick pickles can be made in under 20 minutes then left to ferment overnight or for three to five days (longer for Kim Chee or sauerkraut). Though some pickles are best used within a week or so, others—such as sauerkraut or Kim Chee—will last for months at a time. Sauces and gravies may take anywhere from fifteen to thirty minutes to make. These, however, are best made fresh and used within several meals or days.

Sprinkles & Spreads

Basic Procedure, Dry Roasting Seeds & Nuts (Year Round)***

Prep: 10 minutes
Cooking: 8-25 minutes, depending on kind/method
Yield: About 1 heaping cup
Serving size: about 1-3 tsp. per person at a meal

Seeds and nuts add a rich flavor and a crunchy texture to meals. They also add protein, calcium, zinc, iron, and other minerals to our diet. Because they are very high in fat (about 70-80% fat), they should be used as condiments in meals—eaten by the teaspoon or tablespoonful rather than by the fistful. Dry roasting brings out a rich flavor and makes them more tasty and digestible. In some cases, dry roasting and grinding seeds with sea salt actually *reduces* the amount of fat per teaspoon because dry roasting makes the seeds increase in size and volume. For example, 3/4 cup raw seeds will produces 1-1 1/4 cups of prepared seed condiment while 1 cup raw seeds produces 1 1/2 cups of seasoned, ground condiment.

When making seed or nut condiment we make a single batch of one or two kinds or a double batch of one, starting with 3/4 to 1 1/2 cups of seeds. This produces an amount that two people can use within one or two weeks. It is not a good idea to make seed condiments to last for more than two weeks as the flavor goes quickly.

Unsalted roasted seeds and nuts make great toppings for fat-free grain or fruit desserts; dinner grain (with a salty sea vegetable condiment); breakfast cereal (with umeboshi or apriboshi paste); or salads or cooked vegetables (combined with a salty and/or tangy marinade or oil-free dressing). Nuts can also be ground with miso to make delightful spreads and sauces.

Seed or nut condiments make a daily appearance on our table, as a replacement for the salt shaker and the butter dish. (Read on for recipes.)

Oven roasting (raw, shelled seeds or nuts):

Sunflower seeds
Pumpkin seeds (green variety)
Walnut or pecan halves
Almonds, hazelnuts, peanuts, or pine nuts
Other raw nuts from your region or bioregion

Stove top roasting (raw, shelled seeds or nuts):

Sunflower seeds
Pumpkin seeds (green variety)
Unhulled brown sesame seeds
Unhulled black sesame seeds
Whole flax seeds
Pine nuts or pignolias

1. Sort sesame seeds to remove any sand or stones. Rinse sesame, sunflower, or pumpkin seeds in a fine mesh strainer and drain briefly.

Note: Rinsing sesame seeds removes the natural tannins which impart a bitter taste and protect the seeds from pests. Do not rinse flax seeds. Nuts may be rinsed or not rinsed.

Also note: In most cases, it is best to roast just one or two cups of seeds or nuts at a time.

Oven Roasting Method:

2. Use this method for nuts or sunflower or pumpkin seeds. (Other seeds are a problem in the oven because they pop all over the place as they roast and make a mess.) Place one variety of seeds or nuts on a cookie sheet or in a cast iron skillet. (If roasting two different types, place them in separate pans.) Roast in a 300° F. oven for 15-30 minutes or until golden and aromatic. Check often, stir several times, and set a timer to prevent burning.

3. When done, you may refer to step #3 below to season. Leave seeds or nuts unseasoned if you wish to use them as a garnish for dessert or to add to another dish. Season with sea salt, tamari, shoyu, or ume for use as a condiment.

Stove Top Method:

1. Do not use this method to roast large nuts; they will not cook through to the core. Roast only one kind of seed or nut at a time. Toss seeds or small nuts into a dry wok or cast iron skillet. Dry roast over medium-low, this usually takes 6-10 minutes. Stir continuously in a circular motion with a wooden spoon. If heat is too high the seeds will burn on the outside yet remain raw on the inside. Nuts and seeds are done when lightly browned and aromatic. (Seeds burn easily so watch the heat.) Sesame, pumpkin, poppy, and flax seeds pop as they roast so reduce heat if they start popping out of the pan. If using an electric stove, you may need to briefly remove the skillet from the burner if the seeds start popping wildly.

2. When done, transfer to a bowl and either allow to cool or season right away with sea salt, tamari, shoyu, umeboshi, or apriboshi as Basic Seasoned Seed & Nut Condiments. Leave seeds or nuts unseasoned if they will be added to another dish. Season with a salty seasoning for use as a condiment.

Storage: Store in a sealed jar. Refrigerate seeds or nuts if unsalted to prevent rancidity.

Basic Procedure, Seasoned Seed & Nut Condiments, Ground (Year Round) ***

Prep: 10-15 minutes
Cooking: 8-10 minutes on top of the stove
  or 20-30 minutes in the oven

Yield: about 1 1/4-1 1/2 cups, depending on type
Serving size: 1-4 teaspoons per person, per meal

** If you are very active or cooking for more than two people, it pays to make a double batch each time.

We take something high in fat—nuts and seeds—and make them more balanced, digestible and nutritious by dry roasting, adding a salty seasoning, then grinding or chopping so that they can be made to go a long way. They should be used in small amounts—teaspoonfuls—lest they create digestive distress, weight gain, oily skin, or flatulence. However, they can be used daily, at every meal, if you like.

Some seasoned seeds and nuts taste meaty like bacon bits while others taste buttery. They add valuable vitamins, minerals, and essential fatty acids. They also help you to eat more grains. They are to be used at the table rather than in cooking and will enliven even the simplest of grains. They are particularly good sprinkled over hot cereal, noodles, brown rice, millet, polenta, bread, or baked vegetables. (Remember, they are very rich and are not meant to be used as a snack or by the handful. Because nuts are higher in fat than seeds and tend to be harder to digest we use them more often than seeds.

Tip: Always keep a jar or two of seed or nut condiment on the table. Be sure to make only enough to last for 1-2 weeks at a time. They lose their flavor and freshness after that.

Note: These condiments are best made while the seeds or nuts are still warm. Grinding by hand is best, in a suribachi so that the oil in the seeds will coat the sea salt evenly distributing it and making it easier to assimilate. (See previous page for more on seeds and nuts.)

Helpful hint: Measure seeds before roasting; measure nuts before or after roasting. Sesame, flax, and pumpkin seeds increase in size after roasting and this can alter your ratio.

Rule of Thumb: 3/4-1 cup raw seeds or nuts: 1 Tbsp. sun dried sea salt or 3/4-1 cup raw seeds or nuts: 3-4 Tbsp. tamari, shoyu, or umeboshi or apriboshi vinegar

16:1 = 1 cup raw seeds: 1 Tbsp. sea salt
32:1 = 2 cups raw seeds: 1 Tbsp. sea salt
  or 1 cup raw seeds: 1/2 Tbsp. sea salt

What is the right ratio for you? We suggest
16:1 to 32:1 for adults;
18:1-32:1 for children;
or make it salt-free if you like

Use 24:1 or 32:1 if you wish to use more than a few teaspoons of the condiment at a meal or are trying to lose weight or want to reduce your sodium intake.

Salted, Roasted, Ground Seed or Nut Condiments:***

1 cup raw shelled seeds *(pumpkin, sunflower, sesame, flax, or poppy seeds)*
   or 1 cup raw shelled nuts *(walnuts, almonds, pine nuts, peanuts, hazelnuts, etc.)*
1/2-1 Tbsp. sun dried sea salt

1. Dry roast and stir measured amount of sea salt over medium heat in a cast iron skillet or wok until it shimmers and turns opaque, about 3 minutes. True sun dried sea salt is slightly wet because it is free of anti-caking agents and bleaches. Roasting dries it so it can be easily ground.

2. Transfer to a medium or large sized (9-12-inch) suribachi (ceramic mortar with ridges) and grind to a coarse powder with a suricogi (wooden pestle), about 2 minutes.

3. Measure out seeds or nuts. Rinse sesame, sunflower, or pumpkin seeds. (See notes above for proportions. 16:1 or 24:1 is a good ratio for most people.) Dry roast as per Basic Procedure above.

4. Add dry roasted seeds or nuts to the suribachi and grind seeds or nuts with the sea salt using a suricogi (wooden pestle) in a circular motion, until about 80% powdered.

Tips for grinding: It is not necessary to push hard or make wide stirring motions, just make small circles and push gently in the center of the bowl. The spiral ridges do the crushing and will move the ground seeds up the sides of the suribachi. Leave the condiment a little chunky for added texture. Grinding usually takes about ten to fifteen minutes. *However,* due to their high fiber and lower fat content, flax seeds will take longer to grind than other seeds or nuts. So be patient. We grind flax seeds until about 90% of the seeds are powdered. If your seeds do not grind easily, they probably need to be roasted a bit longer. You can return them to the skillet and roast again.

5. Spoon condiment into a jar or jars. Allow to cool then cover with a lid. Do not wash the suribachi right away; instead, add two cups of water to the suribachi. Brush with a vegetable scrub brush to release seeds from the crevices, then pour off and save the liquid to cook breakfast cereal in or for making soup.

Favorite Salted (Ground) Seed Condiments:
- **Buttery Flax Seed Condiment**
- **Pumpkin Seed Condiment**
- **Sunflower Seed Condiment**
- **Sesame Seed Condiment (Gomashio)**

- **Two-Seed Sprinkle:** Sunflower & pumpkin seeds or pumpkin & flax seeds with sea salt.
- **Three Seed Sprinkle:** 1/3 sesame or flax seeds, 1/3 pumpkin seeds, and 1/3 sunflower seeds. Dry roast each type of seed separately then grind them all together with the salt.

Favorite Salted Nut Condiments:
- **Buttery Walnut Condiment:** Freshly roasted walnuts ground with sea salt.
- **Walnut & Sesame-Salt Condiment:** Half walnuts, half sesame seeds. Roast them separately but grind them together.
- **Bacon-Free Bits/Pine Nut Condiment:** Fresh roasted pine nuts ground with sea salt.

Variations:
- **Ground, Herbed Seed or Nut Condiments:** Add 1 Tbsp. dried, ground herbs *or* 1-2 tsp. spices to suribachi when grinding Salted, Roasted Seed or Nut Condiment. Try powdered sage, garlic, oregano, chili powder, or cumin.
- **Spicy Walnut-Salt Condiment:** Before grinding the roasted nuts with the sea salt, add dried herbs or spices. For a hot and spicy Mexican flavored condiment to rev up a cold body, use 2-3 tsp. garlic powder + 2-3 tsp. cumin powder + 2-3 tsp. onion powder +/- 1/8 tsp. red pepper powder or 2-3 tsp. chili powder per cup nuts.
- **Pesto Walnut Condiment:** Add 2-3 tsp. dried basil or Italian spice blend + 2-3 tsp. garlic powder + 1/2-1 Tbsp. sea salt + 1 cup roasted walnut halves. Or, use pine nuts or almonds to replace walnuts. ❑

Basic Procedure, Brine Seasoned Seed & Nut Condiments (Year Round)***

Prep: 10-15 minutes
Cooking: 10 minutes on top of the stove
   or 20-35 minutes in the oven
Yield: about 1-1 1/3 heaping cup
Serving size: 1-4 teaspoons per person, per meal

Brine Seasoned, Seed or Nut Condiments, whole

3/4-1 cup raw or dry roasted seeds or nuts

1-3 Tbsp. tamari, shoyu, or umeboshi or apriboshi vinegar *or* 1 Tbsp. sea salt dissolved in 3 Tbsp. warm water

1. Dry roast raw seeds or nuts as per Basic Procedure.

2. While warm seeds are still in the skillet add tamari, shoyu, ume or apriboshi vinegar (brine), or salt brine, a little at a time. Continue to stir over medium heat to evenly distribute and evaporate the liquid. Stir until nearly dry. Alternatively, toss oven roasted seeds or nuts with salty liquid and immediately return to oven or toaster oven. Bake at 250-300° F. until dry, about 10-12 minutes. (Herbs or spices may be added to the brine. See notes below).

3. Transfer to an uncovered wooden, glass, ceramic, or stainless steel bowl and allow to cool thoroughly. Use a fork or your fingers to break apart seeds that have stuck together. Leave seeds whole or grind them to a coarse powder in a suribachi. Chop nuts by hand or coarsely grind in a suribachi. Store in a glass jar with a lid.

Serving suggestions:

• Keep the jar on the table with a teaspoon nearby for serving. Keep a portion of this condiment in a tiny vial, in your purse or briefcase when traveling or eating meals away from home.

• Sprinkle 1-3 teaspoons of seed or nut condiment over individual servings of breakfast cereal, dinner grain, noodles, or bread; serve with pressed, marinated, or boiled salad, or steamed vegetables; add a side of soup or stew and/or a root vegetable or sea vegetable dish or condiment if desired. Use seed or nut condiments within 1-2 weeks for best flavor and nutrition.

Favorite Brine Seasoned Seed Condiments:

• **Tamari Roasted Sunflower Seed Condiment**

• **Umeboshi Roasted Pumpkin Seed Condiment**

Favorite Brine Seasoned Nut Condiments:

(**Note:** Chop or grind these condiments coarsely after seasoning.)

• **Umeboshi Roasted Walnut Condiment**

• **Tamari Roasted Almond Condiment**

• **Tamari or Umeboshi Seasoned Peanut Condiment**

• **Umeboshi Roasted Pine Nut Condiment**

Variations:

• **Herbed, Seasoned Seed or Nut Condiments:** Add 1 Tbsp. dried, ground herbs or 1-2 tsp. ground spices to the suribachi when grinding Salted, Roasted Seed or Nut Condiments or add the herbs or spices to the brine when making Brine Seasoned Seed or Nut Condiments. Try powdered sage, garlic, oregano, Italian spice blend, chili powder, or cumin.

Favorite Herbed Seed or Nut Condiments:

Note: The following seeds can be left whole or ground coarsely after seasoning. Nuts, however, should be chopped finely or ground coarsely.

• **Sage Seasoned Sunflower Seed Condiment:** made with salt brine or tamari.

• **Garlic Pumpkin or Sunflower Seed Condiment:** made with salt brine, tamari, shoyu, or umeboshi or apriboshi vinegar.

• **Chili Seasoned Pumpkin Seed Condiment:** made with salt brine or tamari. ❏

- **Hickory Smoked Pumpkin or Sunflower Seed Condiment:** Roast 3/4-1 cup raw seeds as per Basic Procedure then add 1 Tbsp. liquid Smoke/Hickory Smoke along with 3 Tbsp. tamari, shoyu, or umeboshi or apriboshi vinegar. If desired, also add 1/8-1/4 tsp. red pepper powder or 1 tsp. dried, rubbed sage, garlic powder, or cumin.

- **Hickory Smoked Walnut Condiment:** Roast as per Basic Procedure, For each 1 cup walnuts add 1 Tbsp. liquid Smoke/Hickory Smoke with 3 Tbsp. tamari, shoyu, or umeboshi vinegar. Optional, 1/4 tsp. mild red pepper powder (ancho, ahaheim, or chipotle) or 1-2 tsp. dried, rubbed sage.

- **Walnut, Umeboshi & Red Pepper Condiment:** Use umeboshi or apriboshi vinegar brine with 1/4 tsp. red pepper powder (chipotle or ancho are best). Optional, 1-3 tsp. garlic powder. Grind nuts after roasting, seasoning, and drying in the oven.

- **Spicy Peanut Condiment:** Add 1/4 tsp. red pepper powder or 2-3 tsp. curry powder to 1 1/2-1 cup dry roasted peanuts and 1 Tbsp. sea salt or 2-3 Tbsp. tamari. (If using tamari, you will have to dry the seasoned nuts in the oven before chopping or grinding.) ❏

Spreads

Herbed Tofu Cream Cheese (Spring, Summer, Fall)***

Prep: 15-20 minutes
Cooking: 10 minutes

Yield: 2-2 1/2 cups
Serves: 6-8 (4 meals for 2) *or* more as an appetizer
Serving size: 2 Tbsp. or 1/3-1/2 cup per person

This dip has a taste and texture reminiscent of sour cream-n-onion dip. It makes a delectable filling for sandwiches or tamales or steamed bun dough. You can use it to top bagels, sliced steamed buns, mochi puffs, crackers, pasta, steamed vegetables, or marinated beets.

16 oz. block (1 lb.) traditional or firm tofu

2 Tbsp. white, yellow, mellow or sweet miso

2-3 tsp. umeboshi or apriboshi paste *or* 1 Tbsp. umebosh or apriboshi vinegar

Optional, 1-2 Tbsp. raw or lightly roasted sesame tahini

2-3 Tbsp. water, or more as needed to mix

3 cloves minced garlic *or* 1-1 1/2 Tbsp. dried garlic powder

3 Tbsp. dried chives *or* 1/2 cup fresh chives or garlic chives, minced finely

1/4-1/3 cup minced scallions, parsley, or fresh dill, for garnish or mixed in

1. Steam tofu on a metal steamer basket or immerse in 2-3 inches of water and boil 10 minutes. (This makes the tofu more digestible and kills any bacteria if the tofu is less than fresh!). Drain tofu over a strainer or colander to remove excess water.

2. In a blender, Foley food mill, or food processor, mix tofu with remaining ingredients (except for garnish) and process until smooth. Don't add more water unless needed or spread will become runny. If using a blender, turn it on and off a few times and scrape sides with a spatula. If possible chill several hours before serving to allow the flavors to develop.

Serving suggestions: Serve at room temperature with bread, mochi "bread sticks," mochi waffles, or spooned over pasta; with a side of cooked greens or a pressed, marinated, boiled or seasonal raw salad. A vegetable soup or wheat meat stew would also be a nice addition for a hearty main meal.

Storage: Refrigerate leftovers and use within 2-5 days for best flavor and nutrition.

Variations:

- **Tofu French Onion Dip/Spread:** Dry roast 1/3-1/2 cup dried onion flakes in a cast iron skillet over medium heat, stirring constantly or in a 300° F. oven until lightly browned and aromatic. Prepare tofu spread as above but use parsley (not scallions or dill) with the garlic and chives. Stir onion flakes into tofu mixture at the end of step #2.

- If ume or apriboshi paste or umeboshi vinegar are unavailable, simply omit these.

- **Terrific Tofu Cream Cheese Sandwiches:** Start with sliced whole grain bread or pita pocket halves, tuck in assorted steamed vegetables or summer salad greens with cucumber or onion pickles and/or sprouts. Figure two sandwiches or four pita pocket halves or three or four flour tortillas per person for a portable lunch or quick supper. A light cream of vegetable soup makes a nice accompaniment.

- **Tofu Pesto Dip or Spread:** Add 1/2-1 cup fresh, minced basil to above recipe; use walnut or olive oil and add 3 cloves minced garlic (or use garlic oil) in place of tahini. Try Tofu Pesto Cream Cheese Sandwiches.)

- **Tofu Pesto Dressing:** Add more water to the above variation to make desired consistency.

- Experiment with different herbs. Stir 2-4 Tbsp. drained capers into puréed dip.

- **Terrific Tofu Mayo:** Steam 1 lb. of tofu as above then blend in 2 Tbsp. olive oil, 2 Tbsp. umeboshi vinegar or 1 tsp. sea salt, 1 tsp. dry mustard, 1/8-1/4 tsp. mild red pepper powder. If using salt, add 1-2 Tbsp. rice vinegar.

This makes a great coating for Pressure-Steamed beets or potatoes, steamed vegetables, boiled or pressed salad, or macaroni. ❑

Tofu "Sour Cream" or "Ricotta"

Prep: 15 minutes
Cooking: 10 minutes

Yield: about 2 heaping cups
Serving size: 2-4 Tbsp. per person

Use this to replace sour cream or ricotta cheese in pasta dishes or on tacos, burritos, enchiladas, or baked potatoes. You can also tuck it into pita sandwiches with steamed vegetables or salad or use it as the base for various dips and spreads. It's fabulous tucked inside steamed buckwheat buns (before the dough is steam cooked) or used to coat steamed cauliflower, carrots and green beans; broccoli; asparagus; or cooked beets.

1 lb. (16 oz.) soft or firm tofu

1-2 Tbsp. umeboshi vinegar **or** 2-3 tsp.ume paste

1-2 Tbsp. light miso

1/4 cup water, or as needed to blend

Optional garnish, scallions, chives, garlic chives, or minced red onion to garnish.

1. Steam tofu as per previous recipe. Drain over a strainer or colander to remove excess water.

2. In a blender, Foley food mill, or food processor, mix tofu with remaining ingredients (except for the garnish) and process until smooth like sour cream. Don't add more water unless needed or spread will be too runny. Turn blender on and off and scrape the sides with a spatula as needed to mix. Chill several hours before serving to develop flavors

Serving suggestions: Spoon over bread, steamed vegetables, puréed vegetable soups such as puréed carrot, beet, or corn, **or** chunky bean soups such as black bean, minestrone, Spiced Red or Black Bean Soup.

Storage: Refrigerate in a covered bowl or glass jar. Use within several days to one week.

Variations:

- Replace umeboshi or apriboshi with 1/2-1 tsp. sea salt then add 1 Tbsp. brown rice vinegar or apple cider vinegar. ❑

Tempeh "Mock Tuna" Spread

Prep: 20-30 minutes
Cooking: 30 minutes to roast sea vegetable
  + 30 minutes for tempeh

Yield: scant 2 cups
Serves: 5-6 (or 2-3 meals for 2)
  or 8-10 as an hor d'oeuvre

This tastes so much like tuna salad that our friend Tim Morris reported that his cat went absolutely wild when he made it. It's completely vegetarian, made from soy tempeh (a protein-rich cousin of tofu) and alaria (a mineral rich seaweed harvested off the coast of Maine or Canada). The sea vegetable adds a fishy taste and loads of minerals and sesame tahini makes it creamy without the mayo. You can serve this for lunch or supper as a side dish or party appetizer, or use it as a filling for steamed bun dough.

Sea vegetable (for the fishy taste):
6-8" piece alaria seaweed

Tempeh:

8 oz. pkg. unseasoned, tempeh*
(soy, 3-grain, 5-grain, wild rice, or other)
1 tsp. tamari or shoyu *or* 1/4 tsp. sea salt

Remaining ingredients:

2-3 Tbsp. sesame tahini (or sesame butter)
1-2 tsp. umeboshi or apriboshi paste, vinegar *or* juice from ume plum or apriboshi container *or* 2 tsp. brown rice vinegar or apple cider vinegar
1/2 Tbsp. dark miso (or tamari or shoyu)
1/2-1 tsp. dry mustard powder *or* 2 tsp. prepared mustard
2-3 Tbsp. chopped onion or minced scallions
1/8 tsp. celery seed
Optional, chives, parsley or scallions as garnish

1. Dry roast sea vegetable in the oven, on a baking tray or cast iron skillet at 200-225° F. for about 30 minutes or until crisp. This can be done several several hours or days ahead. (Alaria can also be roasted overnight in a gas oven with just the pilot light on.)

2. Place tempeh and sea vegetable in a small pot. Add tamari, shoyu or sea salt and water to just cover. Cover the pot with a lid, bring to boil, reduce heat to low and simmer 40-50 minutes or pressure cook 30 minutes. Remove lid and simmer away excess liquid.

3. Mash remaining ingredients in a suribachi or food processor. Crumble and add tempeh. Chop and add alaria. Mix. Add a few tablespoons of water if needed to mash. Refrigerate 1 hour or longer to allow flavors to mingle.

Serving suggestions: Serve at room temperature, on sliced steamed buns, pita pockets, loaf bread, or rice cakes. Top with lettuce, cucumber, sprouts and/or tomatoes in the summer or top with steamed or parboiled greens or mixed vegetables any time of year. Add a cup of cream-less cream of vegetable soup, pickles, and a side of brown rice for a more hearty meal.

Storage: Refrigerate leftovers in a jar or covered bowl. Use within 3-5 days.

Variations:

• Add a dash of natural pickle relish and minced parsley and reduce the ume vinegar or paste.

• Experiment with other herbs. Try 1 tsp. dried dill or 2 Tbsp. fresh, minced dill weed.

• **Tempeh-Potato Salad** or **Save the Tuna-Macaroni Salad:** Dilute dip with a small volume of water; toss over cooked, chopped potatoes or elbow, rotini, or macaroni noodles; add minced celery and onions or scallions. Refrigerate for several hours or overnight. Serve on a bed of Mesclun greens (a wild salad mix), escarole, endive, radiccio, or oak leaf lettuce. ❏

Hummus Tahini Dip (Spring, Summer, Fall)***

Prep: 15-20 minutes
Cooking: 0 if beans are cooked ahead

Yield: about 3 1/2 cups
Serves: 8-12, depending on serving size and side dishes; fills 16-18 tamales or buns **or** 10-12 sandwiches
Serving size: 1/2-2/3 cup per person as a side dish **or** 1/4 cup per person as an appetizer

*** Halve recipe to serve 4 (or 2 meals for 2.)*

Here's a reduced fat version of a popular Middle Eastern dip. Brown rice vinegar or apple cider vinegar stand in for the traditional lemon juice in this recipe. (Umeboshi or apriboshi also add an extra rich and zingy flavor.) This dip can be served as an appetizer or a side dish to be scooped up with pita breads, rice cakes, or crackers. It also makes a great rice topping, sandwich, taco, or burrito filler, or stuffing for steamed bun or tamale dough.

3 cup cooked chickpeas (garbanzo beans)

2-3 Tbsp. lightly roasted or raw sesame tahini

3-4 Tbsp. brown rice vinegar **or** 2-3 Tbsp. apple cider vinegar

2-4 cloves minced garlic

Optional, 1/2-1 tsp. powdered cumin

1/4-3/4 cup stock from cooking beans, and/or additional water as needed

Optional, 1-3 Tbsp. olive oil (extra virgin or virgin)

Salty seasoning, pick one:

2 Tbsp. white/yellow, or mellow miso
   or 2 Tbsp. umeboshi/apriboshi vinegar
   or 1 Tbsp. ume paste
   or 1 Tbsp. light miso + 1 Tbsp. umeboshi or apriboshi vinegar
   or 3/4 tsp. sea salt, or to taste

Garnishes:

1/2 cup freshly minced parsley, chives, garlic chives, cilantro, or scallions

Paprika, ground

1. Run all ingredients except garnishes through a hand food mill or food processor or mash in a suribachi. (It's nice left a bit chunky so you may wish to purée only two-thirds of the beans then stir the rest in after adjusting the liquids and seasoning.) Adjust consistency by adding bean cooking liquid a little at a time. Taste and adjust seasonings as needed.

2. Spoon all or part of the spread into serving bowls. Cool for one hour or more or refrigerate for several hours or overnight before serving. Sprinkle with paprika and a green garnish.

Serving suggestions: Serve with loaf bread, flat bread, pita, tortillas, steamed buns or crackers with or without brown rice. Add a side of colorful steamed or parboiled green, yellow, and red vegetables (kale, collards, broccoli, cauliflower, red or green bell pepper slices, celery, red radish, or carrot slices, leeks, etc.) or pressed salad and cream-less cream of vegetable soup. In the heat of summer, serve with fresh tomatoes, wild salad greens, and sprouts.)

Storage: Refrigerate leftovers in covered glass jars or bowls. Use within 3-6 days.

Variations:

• Reduce salty seasoning above then stir in natural pickle relish or minced dill pickles for an egg-salad-like dip.

• For fermented hummus, use Chickpea Natto in place of plain cooked chickpea in the above recipe. Prepare as above or you may wish to halve the amount of tahini and/or olive oil. ❏

Grain Mayo (Year Round)***

Prep: 10 minutes
Cooking: 3-4 minutes

Yield: 2/3-3/4 cup
Serves: 6-10 (or 3-5 meals for 2)
Serving size: 1-2 Tbsp. per person

Unlike most mayos this one is grain-based, with a hint of sesame tahini. It's creamy and rich tasting, but far lower in fat than most. It makes a tasty spread for whole grain buns with our Basic Bean Burger, Tempeh Bacon or Tempeh Sausage Cutlets, or with a commercial (low-fat) tempeh or wheat meat burger.

1/2 cup leftover oatmeal, rice porridge, or other soft grain

4 tsp. sesame tahini *or* 2 tsp. flax, corn or sesame oil

2-3 tsp. light or sweet miso *or* 1/8 tsp. sea salt

1/3-1/2 cup water, or more as needed to blend

1 Tbsp. brown rice vinegar *or* cider vinegar

1/4-1/2 tsp. yellow mustard powder *or* 2-3 tsp. prepared mustard

2 pinches red pepper powder (Ancho, Anaheim, Chipotle) *or* ground black pepper

2-3 tsp. arrowroot powder or 2 tsp. kuzu root powder

1. In blender or Osterizer (mini-blend container), purée all ingredients. Add a few extra tablespoons of water as needed to make a smooth and creamy consistency similar to a thick milk shake.

2. Transfer to a small saucepan. Heat to medium and stir to thicken. Turn off and transfer to a small heat proof dish. Allow to cool on the counter or in the refrigerator until thick.

Serving suggestions: Serve as a spread for burger or hot dog buns or sandwich bread.

Variation:

* If leftover rice or dinner grain is used, increase the water as needed to make it smooth and creamy. Proceed as above. It will thicken when heated. ❑

Sweet Miso & Squash "Butter" (Fall & Winter)

Prep: 15 minutes
Cooking: 1-1 1/2 hours or 8-9 hours ina crock pot

Yield: about 5-6 cups
Serves: 4-12 (or 2-3 meals for 2)
Serving size: 1/4-1/2 cup per person

** *Reduce recipe by one-half as needed.*

Double this recipe if you're cooking for a crowd and want leftovers. Second day servings become sweeter and can be transformed into instant soups, stews, sauces, toppings, or fillings. Light miso adds a rich and buttery taste. In a pinch, the squash can be steamed to save time though it will be far sweeter when baked.

1 Tbsp. ghee or sesame or corn oil

6-8 cups cubed winter squash (1 medium to 3/4 of a large squash) *(butternut, kabocha, sweet mama, buttercup, Hokkaido, delicatta or sweet dumpling)*

1/4 tsp. sea salt

1 Tbsp. white, yellow, mellow, sweet, chickpea or millet miso

1. Preheat oven to 350° F. Halve squash; scoop out and discard seeds and pulp. Peel skins for a deep orange "butter."

2. **To bake:** Add oil to a 3-4-quart heavy casserole dish, preferably enamel lined cast iron, a stainless steel Dutch oven pot, or a Corningware dish. Add squash and salt, cover, and bake 1-1 1/2 hours or until soft.

   To cook in a pot: Layer oil, squash and salt in a crock pot. Add 2 Tbsp. water, cover, and cook on high for 1 hour then reduce setting to low and cook 8-9 hours, all day or overnight, or cook in the crock pot on high for 4 hours. Or cook in a thermal cooker for 2-6 hours.

3. Mash with a potato masher or purée in a Foley food mill with miso. (If an enamel lined cast iron pot is used, remove the squash from the pot before mashing to avoid ruining the finish on the pot.) Be sure to use light, yellow or mellow miso paste which has a fruity sweet

taste and a buttery appearance. Dark miso will overpower and adversely affect the taste of this dish. Transfer to a serving bowl.

Serving suggestions: Serve with a light broth or bean soup; cooked whole grain (such as millet or rice) and/or bread; and steamed greens or pressed or marinated salad. You can also spread this squash purée over mochi waffles, pancakes, corn bread, millet loaf, bread, or biscuits, or serve it as a side dish like mashed potatoes.

Leftover tips:

• Turn leftover squash butter into toppings or fillings for burritos, tacos, sandwiches, pancakes or waffles, enchiladas, pot pies, pirogis, won tons, or pastries.

• **To make a soup or stew:** Thin leftover squash butter slightly with water or soup stock (to make soup, sauce, or stew) and combine with leftover chopped wheat meat, tempeh, beans, or vegetables. Warm, adjust with miso or tamari if needed, garnish and serve.

Variations:

• **Parsnip Butter:** Replace squash with washed, scrubbed, diced parsnips or parsnips combined with a smaller volume of onions. Cook as above. Purée in a blender or food processor.

• **Carrot & Parsnip Butter**

• **Sweet Potato or Yam Butter:** Replace squash with washed, scrubbed and peeled red garnet or jewel yams or white sweet potatoes. Cook as above. This is great on top of mochi waffles, pancakes, or biscuits. ❏

Millet "Butter" Spread***

Prep: 5-10 minutes
Cooking: 40 minutes

Yield: scant 2 cups
Serves: 10-14 (or 5-8 meals for 2)
Serving size: 1-3 Tbsp. per person

This golden, creamy spread makes a great alternative to butter. It keeps for a week in the refrigerator and is great on top any kind of bread, waffles, pancakes, or biscuits or over baked sweet potatoes. The flavors heighten after 12-24 hours.

1 1/2-2 Tbsp. corn oil (or flax oil)

1/2 cup millet, rinsed and drained

1/2 tsp. sea salt

2 cups water

2 Tbsp. arrowroot dissolved in 1/4 cup cold water

2 Tbsp. white, yellow, mellow, sweet white, or millet miso

1. In a 2-quart saucepan, combine millet, water, sea salt. Bring to boil, cover, reduce heat to low and simmer 35 minutes, without stirring! (Use a heat deflector on a gas stove, to prevent burning.)

2. Add oil and purée in a blender or food processor until smooth. Dissolve arrowroot in cold water; add to purée with miso; purée again then return to a sauce pan. Bring to a low boil then reduce heat to low and simmer and stir until thickened, about 3-5 minutes.

3. Pour into a small glass bowl, crock, or wide mouth jar and allow to cool and firm up.

Storage: Store in the refrigerator.

Serving suggestions: Remove from the refrigerator 20-30 minutes before serving. Use within about 1 week.

Variation:

• **Garlic-Millet Butter:** Add 2-5 cloves minced fresh garlic or 1 clove elephant garlic in step #1 for a milder taste or to step #2 for a stronger taste. Or add 2-6 cloves of roasted garlic when puréeing the "butter" in step #2 above. ❏

Sweet Miso Onion Butter
(Fall, Winter, Spring)***

Prep: 15-20 minutes
Cooking: 1-8 hours

Yield: 2-3 cups onion butter or 4 cups sauce
Serving size: 1/4-1/3 cup as diluted gravy *or*
2-3 Tbsp. per person as a spread for bread

Onions cooked for a long time over low heat, caramelize and turn golden-brown like apple butter. The sweet and savory flavors are delicious ladled over Millet & Squash Squares, or spread on biscuits, steamed slices of bread, fat-free Minute Made Mochi Waffles, or rice. .

1-2 tsp. light sesame or sunflower oil

10 cups packed, finely chopped white onions
(*Walla Walla Sweets or Vadalia's are best*)

1/8-1/4 tsp. sea salt

1-3 Tbsp. sweet, light, yellow, mellow, chick-pea, or millet miso

1/2 cup water to dilute miso

Optional, 1-2 cups water to make into a sauce

A cast iron skillet, heavy pot or wok with a tight fitting lid is best for this preparation.

1. Mince onions then sauté in oiled skillet or pot for several minutes over medium heat. Stir constantly until soft and translucent. Add sea salt to bring additional moisture out of onions. Keep stirring. Add a few tablespoons water if needed to moisten. Cover, reduce heat to low and simmer 1/2-1 hour or for 2-8 hours for a richer, sweeter taste. Additional water is usually unnecessary since onions have a high water content. Keep the heat low to prevent burning.

2. Dissolve miso in water to create a frosting-like consistency. (Use more miso if onion butter has cooked for just 1/2-1 hour, to increase the sweetness. Use less miso for long cooked onion butter.) Add to skillet, stir, cover and simmer on low heat for 5-10 minutes or up to 30 minutes, or until a thick paste is created.

3. Remove lid to cook away any excess liquid to create an apple sauce or apple butter consistency. To use as a gravy for millet loaf or other dishes; add additional water and simmer to thicken slightly.

Serving suggestions: Spoon over whole grain, pasta, bread, waffles, or pancakes. Serve with a side of cooked, pressed or marinated dark greens or mixed vegetables. Also add a cup of soup, stew, or an orange or yellow vegetable side dish.

Storage: Store in a glass jar in the refrigerator. It is best when fresh and, used within several days, though the miso will help preserve it for a week.

Tips:

- For a mildly sweet dessert, use onion butter to sweeten cookies (as a replacement for apple-sauce, apple butter, other liquid sweeteners).

- Use as a topping for pasta, with a seasoned nut or seed condiment or raw, chopped nuts.

- Use as a sauce for pizza, alone or with tempeh "sausage," wheat meat, or other vegetarian product. Add chopped olives or nuts, and/or basil, oregano, or thyme. Then bake as per basic pizza. See index for Pizza Bianca.

Variations:

- Vary the taste by using different types of light miso or by using different types of onions. ❏

Garbanzo Butter

Prep: 30 minutes
Cooking: 45 minutes to 2 hours (beans)+ 15-20 minutes
Setting: 1-2 hours

Serves: 8-12
Serving size: 1-3 Tbsp. per person

Unlike hummus, a popular chickpea dip or paté, this is meant to be used by the teaspoon or tablespoonful to replace butter on bread. It also makes a nice topping for rice, complemented with a sprinkle of chives or black pepper.

Beans:
(or start with 2-2 1/4 cups precooked beans)

1 cup dry chickpeas (garbanzo beans)

3 cups water to soak

1 1/2-2 cups fresh water for cooking (less for pressure cooking, more for boiling)

4" piece kelp or kombu sea vegetable

Seasonings:

3/4 tsp. sea salt

1 Tbsp. corn oil

1/2-1 tsp. sea salt

1/4 cup nutritional yeast flakes (not brewers yeast!)

2 Tbsp. arrowroot or kuzu dissolved in 1/4 cup cold water

1. Prepare dry beans as per Basic Procedure, Beans.

2. Add 3/4 tsp. sea salt to cooked beans and cooking liquid. Simmer 10-12 minutes then drain beans and reserve cooking liquid. Measure out 2-2 1/4 cups cooked beans and 1 cup of cooking liquid. Set extra beans aside for use in soup, stew, salad, or other dishes. Save extra cooking liquid for use as a soup stock or gravy (it works marvelously for this).

   If using precooked beans: Add 1 cup water and 1/2-3/4 tsp. sea salt to 2-2 1/4 cups of cooked beans. Simmer 5-10 minutes on low heat.

3. Blend beans, 1 cup bean cooking liquid, and seasonings in a blender, food processor, or Foley food mill with remaining ingredients including arrowroot or kuzu and water. Add a few tablespoons of liquid as needed to blend.

4. Return bean mixture to a saucepan. Stir to thicken, about 5-6 minutes. Transfer to an 8" round cake pan or shallow dish. Allow to firm up for 1-4 hours at room temperature (or in the refrigerator in warm or hot weather) before serving.

5. Cut into 1 inch squares to serve. The flavors will heighten after 12-24 hours.

Serving suggestions: Serve at room temperature as a topping for whole grain, baked or steamed bread, mochi waffles, or noodles; with a side of cooked greens or mixed vegetables; and a soup, stew or a colorful orange, red, or yellow root, round, or ground vegetable dish.

Storage: Refrigerate leftovers; use within 3-6 days.

Tips:

• For a tasty lunch-time sandwich, spread Garbanzo Butter on tortillas, pita bread, halved steamed buns, or loaf bread then top with steamed greens or mixed vegetables or with Mesclun greens and pickles in very hot weather. ❏

Sea-Sage & Sunflower Spread (Year Round)

Prep: 15-20 minutes
Oven roasting: 30 minutes
Cooking: pressure cook 1 hour or simmer 1 1/2-2 hours

Yield: 1 1/2-1 3/4 cup
Serves: 8 (or 4 meals for 2)
Serving size: 1-2 Tbsp. per person

This basic recipe can be made with kelp, kombu, wild nori, or alaria sea vegetable. It can be spooned over rice, millet or other grains; used as a spread on bread or biscuits; or tucked inside steamed bun dough. The taste is slightly fishy, like caviar. This condiment keeps for several weeks in the refrigerator, well seasoned with tamari or shoyu.

1 cup, tightly packed, dry roasted alaria, wild nori, or kelp sea vegetable

1 1/2 cups water (2-3 cups if boiling)

2-3 Tbsp. tamari or shoyu (natural soy sauce)

1 Tbsp. powdered sage, or a bit more as desired

2 Tbsp. sunflower butter

Water to thin as needed

1. Dry roast sea vegetables in a 225° F. oven, on a cookie sheet or cast iron skillet for 20-30 minutes or until crispy. Crumble coarsely.

2. **To pressure cook:** In a pressure cooker combine crumbled sea vegetable, water and tamari or shoyu. Pressure cook 1 hour. Add sage and simmer away excess liquid.

   To boil: Bring sea vegetable, water and tamari or shoyu to boil in a saucepan then simmer, covered, over low heat for 1 1 1/2-2 hours. Add sage during last 30 minutes. Add a bit more water as needed to keep sea vegetable moist and prevent burning.

3. When tender, if wild nori or dulse are used, mash in a suribachi with sunflower butter. Add a few tablespoons or more of water to thin to desired consistency. For other sea vegetables purée in the blender until smooth. This spread should make a thick paste and be slightly salty. Add a bit more sage if desired.

Storage: Store it in a glass jar in the refrigerator.

Serving suggestions: Serve just 1-3 Tbsp. per person per meal on bread or mochi waffles, with a side of greens or mixed vegetables and a cup of bean soup or a deep orange root or ground vegetable soup. This condiment keeps several weeks, though you may go through it sooner!

For a Native American meal, serve this spread with:

3-Sisters Soup, or Squash, Corn & Tomato Soup

Corn Flat Breads, Arepas, or a loaf bread (made with spelt or wheat and cornmeal) or serve over Posole-Rice.

Add a side of Boiled Salad or Quick-Boiled Vegetables (mustard and turnip greens with onions or leeks and sunchokes and garlic).

Cap off the meal with Rosehip & Apple Compote or Chestnut & Blueberry Custard. (See index for recipes.)

Leftover tips:

- Save as a filling for ravioli or won tons (1-2 tsp. each) or use 1 Tbsp. per steamed bun. ❏

Basic Procedure, Miso-Vegetable Condiments

Carrot Top Miso Condiment (Year Round)

Prep: 10 minutes
Cooking: 15-20 minutes
Yield: 1 cup
Serving size: about 1-3 teaspoon or to taste

Miso vegetable condiments are infrequent fare in our house, but tasty none the less. Carrots are usually sold without their mineral rich tops unless you shop at the local farmers' market or co-op. Their leaves are very high in plant-based (non-heme) iron and have a wonderful parsley-like taste when cooked. Carrot tops are very, very sandy and need a very thorough soaking (in cold water) and several good rinses. The tops are a bit bitter on their own but get much sweeter when cooked with the roots (carrots) or with miso or sea salt, as is done in this recipe. This preparation is salty like a pickle, and is meant to be served as a condiment rather than as a side dish. It keeps for a few weeks in a glass jar in the refrigerator. Spoon it over cooked whole grain rice, millet, polenta, or breakfast cereal, then top it off with 1-2 teaspoons of roasted, seasoned or unseasoned pumpkin or sunflower seeds.

Rule of thumb: *1 part miso per 6 parts chopped carrot tops (1/4 cup miso per 1 1/2 cups minced, tightly packed carrot tops).*

1 Tbsp. ghee or light sesame oil ***or*** olive oil

2 cups washed and finely minced carrot tops*
   (See variations below)

2 pinches sea salt

1/8-1/4 cup (1-4 Tbsp.) dark miso
   (barley, black soy bean, hatcho, buckwheat, 3-year brown rice, or red)

1/4 cup water

1. Soak carrot tops in a bowl of cold water and shake to remove sand. Repeat then rinse under running water (Carrot tops are very sandy and must be cleaned well or the dish will be inedible.) Mince carrot tops finely

2. Add ghee or oil to a cast iron skillet or wok. Sauté carrot tops for several minutes until soft. Add sea salt to draw out moisture then add a few tablespoons of water if needed to moisten. Cover and simmer on low heat for 5-6 minutes.

3. Dissolve miso in water and add this to skillet. Cover and simmer on low heat for an additional 8-10 minutes—until a thick paste is created. Remove lid and simmer away any excess liquid.

Storage: Store in a glass jar in the refrigerator and use as a condiment on top of whole grains, noodles, or morning porridge, or stirred into soup as a seasoning. Use within 1-2 weeks.

Variations:

- **Red Pepper Miso Condiment (Summer, Fall):** Use fresh Jalepeno, Anaheim, Habanero, or other red or green peppers in season. Use 1 Tbsp. oil to sauté 2 chopped, fresh red peppers; add 2 heaping Tbsp. dark barley, soy bean, or brown rice miso. This is great on millet, polenta, brown rice cooked with sweet corn, or morning cereal, topped with roasted pumpkin seeds.

- **Sweet Onion-Miso Condiment:** Use Walla Walla Sweet or Vadalia onions or other white onions in the above recipe, but use 4 cups of onions instead of 2 cups. Use light, mellow, yellow, or sweet miso in place of dark miso. (See also "Onion Butter".)

- Reduce miso by one-half for a less salty condiment if you want to serve it by the tablespoon rather than the teaspoonful if it tastes too salty to you. ❏

Leek Miso Condiment:
(Spring, Summer, Fall)

Prep: 10 minutes
Cooking: 10-12 minutes

Serves: 6 (or 3 meals for 2)
Serving size: 1-2 Tbsp. per person

This condiment can be used instead of butter or sea vegetable condiment to top cooked whole grain or noodles.

Suggested ratio: 1 Tbsp. miso per 2-3 cups cut, packed, raw vegetables

1-2 Tbsp. ghee **or** sesame or olive oil

4 medium to large leeks, washed and chopped finely (about 4 packed cups)

1/8 tsp. sea salt

1-2 Tbsp. barley, black soybean or brown rice miso

1. Cut leeks in half. Rinse under cold water, running your fingers through leaves to remove sand. Be very meticulous; leeks are very sandy inside. Cut leeks into thin rounds using entire vegetable, white and green part. Discard the outer leaf if rough; save the tiny hair like bits on the end for soup stock.

2. Sauté leeks in oil over medium heat. Stir constantly. Add salt to bring out moisture. Stir until soft and translucent, about 7-8 minutes. They should reduce in volume by one half.

3. Dissolve miso in a tablespoon or two of water, add to skillet and stir well to evenly distribute miso. Simmer on low for 2-3 minutes. Turn off and transfer to a small jar.

Serving suggestions: Serve over dinner grain or breakfast porridge with a dry roasted or umeboshi seasoned pumpkin or sunflower seeds.

Storage: Store condiment in the refrigerator and use within 1 week to ten days.

Variations:

• **Scallion Miso Condiment:** Use 4-6 cups chopped scallions in place of leeks. ❏

Sauces Salad Dressings
& Gravies

Mochi-zy Chickpea Sauce (Any Season)

Prep: 15-20 minutes
Cooking: 1 hour + 1 minutes

Serves: 4 (or 2 meals for 2)
Serving Size: 1/3-1/2 cup per person

For a rich tasting sauce without oil or cheese, chickpeas and mochi can't be beat. This sauce makes a great topping for polenta, millet slices, rice, or pasta. It can also be used as the base for a six-minute soup when combined with leftover cooked vegetables and stock or water.

1 1/4 cups cooked chickpeas/garbanzo beans (*from 1/2-2/3 cup dry beans*)

1/2 cup dried chives **or** 1-1 1/2 cup fresh, minced chives

~1 1/2 cups water

1/4 tsp. sea salt

1/2 packed cup grated mochi (plain, uncooked, thaw before grating)

Optional, 2 Tbsp. nutritional yeast flakes

1-2 Tbsp. sweet, white, yellow, mellow, chickpea, or millet miso

1. Combine chickpeas, chives, water, salt, and grated mochi in a 2-3 quart pot. Add nutritional yeast for a cheesier taste if desired. Bring to a low boil, simmer over medium heat and stir until thick (about 3-5 minutes).

2. Purée mixture in a blender or Foley food mill. Add miso and purée again. Serve immediately or return to the saucepan, cover, and heat on low with a heat deflector under the pot.

Serving suggestions: Serve warm over polenta, millet slices, rice, or noodles, a colorful vegetable soup, or a mixed vegetable side dish.

Storage: Refrigerate leftovers and reheat using the covered bowl-within-a-pot method.

Variations:

- **Sticky Black Bean Sauce:** Replace chickpeas with black turtle beans. Replace light miso with red or dark barley miso. Prepare as above. This is especially good over steamed masa balls, polenta or millet, or in enchiladas.

- **Herbed Mochi-zy Chickpea Sauce:** Replace plain mochi with garlic-sesame, basil-garlic, or pizza flavored mochi. Or, use plain mochi above but add 1 tsp. garlic powder + 1/2 tsp. each of dried basil, oregano and/or thyme. ❏

Tofu Tartar Sauce (Spring, Summer, Fall)

Prep: 15 minutes
Cooking: 5-7 minutes

Serves: 8-9 (or 4 meal for 2)
Serving size: 3-4 Tbsp. per person

*** Reduce recipe by 1/2 to serve 4-5 (or 2 meals for 2).**

For a smooth and creamy tartar sauce, a blender or food processor is a must. You can make the sauce ahead of time, up to 48 hours ahead if the tofu is fresh, then serve it a few days in a row. This makes a great topping for tempeh or wheat meat burgers, pan fried wheat meat cutlets, steamed broccoli and carrots, burritos, tamales, tacos, or baked potatoes.

1 lb. soft or silken tofu

2-3 Tbsp. white, yellow, sweet, or mellow miso

1/4 cup water or more as/if needed to create desired consistency

1 tsp. dried oregano or basil *or* 1 Tbsp. fresh, minced very finely

1. Steam tofu for 5-7 minutes. Drain well.

2. Purée all ingredients in blender to desired consistency (close to that of sour cream, yogurt or a thick dressing).

3. Chill slightly. Serve room temperature.

Serving suggestions: See notes above or try the following. ❏

Basic (Red Sauce) Beet Sauce Italiano (Any Season)***

Prep: 15-20 minutes
Cooking: 30-50 minutes
or 2-8 hours in a thermal cooker

Yield: 6-7 cups of sauce
Serves: 6-7 (or 3 meals for 2) over pasta or millet loaf
Serving size: 3/4-1 cup per person for pasta
or 1/2 cup per person over millet or meatless loaf

This mock-tomato sauce is great in the winter and spring when good-tasting fresh tomatoes are hard to find (and not in season) but good winter squash and beets are abundant. Thickness will vary with the density of your squash or carrots, so adjust it to your liking. This sauce is tasty over millet or wheat meat loaf, noodles served with wheatmeat balls, Tempeh Sausage, Tempeh Bacon, or smoked tofu (use bowls rather than a plates for pasta), or use in lasagna or pizza, enchiladas, sloppy joes, or casseroles. It also doubles as a "tomato-like" soup. Make enough to last a few days then mix it with other leftovers to make fast new soups or casseroles.

Basic ingredients:

3-4 whole garlic cloves

1 cup onion, chopped finely

4 cups carrot or buttercup, butternut or kabocha squash, or Hokkaido pumpkin, or carrot and squash, cut in 1/2-1" pieces

1/2-3/4 cup beet root, peeled and diced

Optional, 1 stalk celery, minced

Optional, 1/2 cup button or crimini mushrooms *or* 3 fresh or dried shiitake mushrooms, sliced finely

3 cups water or part vegetable stock

Additional water if needed after cooking

1/8-1/4 tsp. sea sea salt

Seasonings:

2-3 Tbsp. dark miso or tamari soy sauce *or* 1 Tbsp. half dark miso, shoyu, or tamari + 1-1 1/2 Tbsp. umeboshi vinegar

1 Tbsp. Italian herb blend (basil, oregano, thyme, marjoram, etc.)*

Optional, 1/4 tsp. mild red pepper powder

Optional, 1 Tbsp. apple cider vinegar

Optional, 1 Tbsp. dried parsley, dried chives *or* 3 Tbsp. fresh, minced parsley or chives

Optional thickener:

1 Tbsp. arrowroot or kuzu root powder

1/4-1/2 cup cold water

1. Combine basic ingredients in a heavy pot or pressure cooker. Cover, bring to a boil, reduce heat to low, and simmer 30-40 minutes until soft or pressure cook 20 minutes or cook 2-6 hours in a thermal cooker.

2. Purée in a food mill or blender. Add herbs or spices and seasonings and purée again. Return to pot.

3. Dissolve arrowroot or kuzu in cold water and add to sauce. (This keeps sauce from separating.) Bring to boil then reduce heat to low, stirring constantly to thicken. Simmer over low heat for 10 minutes. Add more water if too thick.

Serving suggestions: Serve over whole grain or pasta or in or over a bean, tofu, tempeh or wheat meat dish to replace tomato or cream sauce. Serve with a green or mixed vegetable side dish. Add soup and pickles if desired.

Variations:

- For a richer marinara sauce, add 1/2-1 Tbsp. olive oil to sauce in step #1 or sauté mushrooms then add to puréed sauce.

- Increase spices or change the spices to suit the dish you are making. For non-Italian dishes, replace herbs or spices above with 1 tsp. cumin powder, 1 tsp. thyme, 1/2 tsp. ground fennel, 1/4 tsp. black pepper and/or 1 Tbsp. prepared mustard or 1 tsp. dry mustard.

- Reduce water used and omit arrowroot then use as a soup and/or sauce for other dishes.

- Serve over Millet "Polenta," Millet with Lentils, Millet with Chickpeas, or Green-Pea Millet Slices. (See index for recipes.) ❏

Parsnip White Sauce Sauce (Fall, Winter, Early Spring)

Prep: 10-15 minutes
Cooking: 30-40 minutes

Yield: 5 cups
Serves: 6-8 (or 3-4 meals for 2)
Serving size: 1/2-3/4 cup per person

Parsnips and oats make a delightful velvety-smooth white sauce served over mounds of buckwheat, Millet & Lentil Slices or wheat meat loaf, bread, biscuits, or pasta. Make enough for the next day. You can use it as a hearty sauce or a soup when combined with leftovers.

2-3 tsp. ghee *or* light sesame oil or olive oil

1/2 large onion, minced

1/8tsp. sea salt

3 cups diced or thinly sliced parsnips

1/2 cup water (3/4 cup if boiling)

3/4 cup rolled oats

2 tsp. sea salt

3 cups water

1. Sauté onions in ghee or oil with salt until soft, stirring continuously. Add chopped parsnips and 1/2-cup water. Bring to pressure and cook 15 minutes. If boiling, chop parsnips more finely, cover, bring to boil, reduce heat to low, and simmer 30 minutes or until tender.

2. Add oats, (and remaining water and sea salt.) Cover and bring to boil, reduce heat to low and simmer, covered, for 30 minutes with a heat deflector under pot to prevent burning.

3. Purée in blender, food processor or Foley food mill. Taste. Sauce should be slightly thick. If too thick add a dash of water. It will thicken as it cools or when refrigerated.

Serving suggestions: Ladle over pasta or millet or polenta mounds. Add a side of salad or cooked leafy green vegetables and optional Tempeh Sausage, Tempeh Bacon, or Pan Fried Wheat Meat Cutlets and a colorful orange or yellow vegetable soup, and cucumber, radish, or onion pickles. ❏

Creamy Green-Garlic Sauce, for pasta (Spring, Summer, Early Fall)

Prep: 15-20 minutes
Cooking: about 20 minutes

Yield: 6-7 cups
Serves: 6-7 (or 3 meals for 2)

** Reduce recipe by one-half to serve 3-4 (or 2 meals for 2).

This is a great pesto alternative. It has a rich, creamy taste and texture. It is low if fat and oil-free, something few pasta sauces can boast. It is particularly nice over kamut or spelt pasta or brown rice udon noodles. You'll find endless ways to create imaginative meals!

3 medium white onions, cut into thin crescents

1 cup of pasta water (the secret to the sauce!)

1 pinch (1/8 tsp.) sea salt

8 cups broccoli tops and peeled, chopped stems

1 cup pasta water

1/2-1 1/4 cups firm tofu (*more tofu for a richer taste, less tofu for a leaner, greener sauce*)

4-6 small cloves of garlic, minced finely

1 Tbsp. light, yellow, or mellow miso (*tamari or dark miso may be substituted*)

+/- Additional miso, tamari, shoyu, to taste

2 tsp. umeboshi or apriboshi vinegar **or** 1-1 1/2 tsp. umeboshi or apriboshi paste

pasta water to thin as needed

1. Add sliced onion crescents to a wok or large 2-quart sauté or saucepan with 1 cup pasta water and sea salt. Bring to low boil and simmer until onions are glazed and water has evaporated, about 10 minutes. Stir periodically. Add chopped broccoli stems (do not use end of the stalk or the tough or woody stems) and florets to wok along with one more cup of pasta water. Cover and cook just until broccoli turns bright green and softens a bit.

2. In a blender combine tofu, garlic, and miso or tamari. Add umeboshi or apriboshi. Blend until smooth then add broccoli-onion mixture, blend again and add a dash of pasta water if needed to make a thick paste. Taste, add a few more drops of umeboshi or apriboshi vinegar, or miso or tamari if needed.

Serving suggestions: Serve warm sauce over pasta with a side of cooked carrots, beets, daikon, or a mixed root vegetable dish (See index for nishime vegetables.)

Storage: Refrigerate leftover sauce in a covered bowl or jar. Use as a bread spread or reheat using the covered bowl-within-a-pot method. (You can also dilute some of the sauce for use as a creamy soup.)

Leftover tips: Turn leftover sauce into creamy soup by thinning with water or vegetable soup stock. Simmer or heat in a covered bowl; season with tamari or miso and serve with grain and a colorful carrot, beet, or mixed vegetable side dish.

Variations:

- Add fresh basil, oregano, or thyme to the above recipe.

- **Cauliflower "Cream" Sauce (Summer, Fall):** Use cauliflower in place of broccoli and use light, yellow, or mellow miso and umeboshi or apriboshi to season. Add sautéed or steamed mushrooms before serving if desired.

- **Squash Cream Sauce (Fall, Winter):** Replace broccoli with cooked winter squash. Add to soft onions in step #2 with ~1/2 tsp. cinnamon, nutmeg or allspice, or basil, oregano and/or thyme. Season with light or yellow miso and omit the ume or apriboshi. Serve with a side of cooked greens. Add a sea vegetable side dish if desired. ❏

Pesto Presto (Spring, Summer & Fall)

Prep: 20 minutes
Yield: 1-1 1/2 cups
Serving size: 1-2 Tbsp. per person

This yummy pesto has no cheese and calls for less oil and nuts than most pestos.

2 Tbsp. olive oil

3/4 cup water, or more as needed

2-3 Tbsp. brown rice vinegar or apple cider vinegar

3-6 cloves minced garlic

1/4-1/2 tsp. sun dried sea salt **or** 1-2 tsp. umeboshi or apriboshi vinegar

2 cups fresh basil leaves or arugula, washed, dried and minced (stems removed)

1 cup crushed cracker crumbs *(Ryvita, Rye-Crisp, RyTak, or other fat-free crackers)*

1 Tbsp. white, yellow, mellow, sweet or light miso, or to taste (see variations*)

1/2-3/4 cup dry roasted or raw, coarsely chopped walnuts, almonds, or pine nuts

1. In a food processor, blender, or Foley food mill, combine everything but the nuts. Blend until smooth. Add slightly more stock or water if needed to make a smooth, sour cream-like texture.

2. Transfer to a small bowl or wide mouth jar and stir in the chopped nuts with a spatula.

Serving suggestions: Serve by the tablespoon over pasta, polenta, bread, or rice with a side of cooked greens or mixed vegetables. (You can also dilute a small volume of pesto then toss it over steamed or parboiled vegetables. or tuck a tablespoon of pesto inside steamed bun dough or tamale dough for a truly international treat.)

Storage: Refrigerate leftovers in a glass jar. Use within 1-3 weeks or freeze portions as desired. Serve at room temperature.

Variations:

- **For a more aged "cheese" flavor,** replace all or part of the miso with umeboshi or apriboshi paste or ume or apriboshi vinegar.

- **When fresh basil is scarce:** Replace fresh basil with fresh parsley (cleaned well to remove sand or grit) then add 2-3 tsp. dried basil or 2-3 Tbsp. fresh basil leaves, washed, dried, and minced.

- Thin a portion of the pesto with water and use as a salad dressing. ❏

Oil-Free Herbal Dressing (Any Season)

Prep: 10 minutes
Yield: 2 1/2 cups
Serving size: 2-3 Tbsp. per person

This delicious salad dressing has a creamy and tangy taste that complements cooked vegetable salads. It contains no added fat and can be whipped up in minutes.

1 Tbsp. arrowroot or kuzu powder + 2 cups water

3 Tbsp. umeboshi vinegar

1 Tbsp. brown rice vinegar **or** organic apple cider vinegar

1/2-1 Tbsp. tamari or shoyu

2 tsp. dried basil or oregano

1 Tbsp. dried chives

Optional, 2 cloves minced garlic

3/4-1 cup leftover cooked rice, millet or oatmeal

1. Dissolve arrowroot in cold water then bring to boil over medium heat. Reduce to medium-low and stir continuously until thickened, about 3-5 minutes.

2. Blend remaining ingredients to make a smooth liquid. Pour arrowroot mixture into blender and whip until smooth. If too thin add an additional 2-3 Tbsp. cooked grain and purée again. Adjust seasonings as needed. Dressing will thicken as it cools.

3. Pour into a gravy boat or glass jar and serve. Leftovers keep for 1 week in the refrigerator. ❏

Easy Oil-Free Mustard Vinaigrette (Any Season)***

Prep: 10 minutes
Yield: about 1 1/4 cups
Serving Size: 1-3 Tbsp. per person

We don't make dressings much, but when we do, this is a favorite. It has become our "house dressing." It's creamy and smooth without added fat and keeps well.

2-3 Tbsp. white, yellow, sweet, or millet or chickpea miso

1-2 Tbsp. prepared yellow, dijon or stone ground mustard (natural variety)

2-3 Tbsp. brown rice vinegar **or** 1 Tbsp. apple cider vinegar

1 clove minced garlic

1/4 tsp. dried thyme or oregano

1/2 tsp. dried basil

1/2 cup water or more as needed

1/2- 2/3 cup leftover cooked barley, rice, millet, oats, barley & millet or other

1. Whip all ingredients in the blender until smooth.

2. Taste and adjust seasonings adding more water if too thick or more grain if too thin.

Serving suggestions: Serve over raw or blanched vegetable salads.

Storage: Refrigerate in glass jars; use up within 2 weeks. ❏

Basic Procedure, Easy As 1-2-3 Dressing (Any Season)***

Prep: 5 minute or less
Yield: dressing for 3-4 cups cooked vegetables

This is not the kind of dressing that's served at the table. Instead, it is tossed over boiled salad or steamed vegetables in the kitchen, before serving. We mix up just enough of this quick sauce for a given batch of vegetables, varying the flavors a little each time.

Rule of Thumb: For every 3-4 cups steamed or parboiled vegetables combine the following:

2-4 tsp. oil **or** 1 Tbsp. nut or seed butter *(toasted sesame, light sesame, flax,* **or** *olive oil* **or** *sesame tahini,* **or** *sesame, sunflower or peanut butter)*

2 tsp. tamari, shoyu or umeboshi or apriboshi vinegar (or a combination of two of these) **or** 1 Tbsp. light, yellow, mellow, or sweet miso **+** water to blend

Optional, 2 tsp. brown rice vinegar, organic apple cider vinegar and/or prepared mustard or pickle juice.

1. Combine oil (or nut or seed butter and water) with 1 or 2 salty seasonings. Add vinegar or mustard if desired. Mix until smooth.

2. Toss over a bowl containing 3-4 cups of cooked, drained vegetables. Serve immediately or cover with a bamboo mat.

Variation:

- Omit oil then toss vegetables with 1-2 Tbsp. dry roasted seeds or chopped roasted nuts.

- **Oil-free dressing:** Omit oil, nuts/seeds above and use only salty and sour seasonings. (Ume vinegar + tamari/shoyu; tamari/shoyu + rice vinegar) Add flax oil at the table if desired.

- **Herbed/Spiced 1-2-3 Dressing:** Add 1-2 pinches or 1/2 tsp. of dried herbs or spices to basic dressing. (e.g.,powdered garlic, ginger, cumin, mild red pepper, dill weed, basil, oregano, or thyme.) ❏

Groovy Gravies

Tamari Thyme Gravy or Soy-n-Sage Gravy (Fall, Winter, Spring)

Prep: 15 minutes
Cooking: 10 minutes + 45 minutes

Serves: 8 (or 4 with leftovers)
Serving size: 1/2 cup per person **or** 1 cup per person as a soup replacer

Reduce recipe by 1/2 to serve 4 (or 2 meals for 2).

This tasty gravy is light and easy to digest, unlike most heavy and fatty recipes which rely on animal fat and/or cooking juices or an excessive amount of oil. Fresh or leftover gravy can be used in a myriad of ways—served over baked squash, warm biscuits, polenta, millet mash, or pasta, or used to dunk bread in.

1 cup spelt or barley flour **or** whole wheat pastry flour

1 Tbsp. ghee **or** light sesame oil

1/2-3/4 tsp. sea salt

1 Tbsp. dried thyme (or substitute rubbed sage)

6 cups water, part vegetable stock

2-3 Tbsp. tamari, shoyu, natural soy sauce or dark miso

1/2 cup water and/or soup stock

3 Tbsp. arrowroot powder or kuzu

Additional water or herbs as needed

1. Heat oil in a cast iron skillet. Add flour and roast in oil, over medium or medium-low heat until golden and aromatic, about 8-10 minutes. Watch it carefully so it doesn't burn. For a fat-free gravy, dry roast flour in an unoiled skillet or wok.

2. Combine water, stock, flour, salt, and seasonings in a blender. Purée until smooth. Or, let flour cool 20-30 minutes then mix with cold water or stock, a little at a time. Bring to boil over medium heat; whisk and stir constantly. Reduce heat then simmer on low, covered, for about 20-30 minutes. (Slip a heat deflector under the pot to prevent burning.)

3. Dissolve arrowroot or kuzu in cold water and add to gravy. Stir to thicken. Simmer 15 minutes. Taste and adjust seasonings as needed. If too thin, remove lid, simmer, and stir several minutes. If too thick add a bit more water, stir and simmer until heated through and thick. Transfer gravy to a serving bowl.

Serving suggestions: Try it over Millet-Lentil or Millet-Chickpea "Polenta" Slices, Millet "Mashed Potatoes," or mounds of buckwheat; with Tempeh "Sausage" or Tempeh "Bacon" or wheat meat cutlets. Add a side of greens or mixed vegetables; an orange or yellow vegetable side dish or soup and/or bread. Or, serve gravy in soup cups (3/4-1 cup per person) and dunk bread in then serve with greens and an orange/yellow vegetable, or with greens and tempeh or wheat meat.

Storage: Refrigerate leftovers and heat using covered-bowl-within-a-pot method.

Leftover tips: Gravy can also be combined with cooked beans, baked or puréed squash, or other leftovers to make quick soups, stews, sauces, or pot pie fillings. ❏

Mock Poultry Gravy
(Fall, Winter, Early Spring)

Prep: 8-10 minutes
Cooking: 40 minutes

Yield: about 5 cups gravy
Serves: 5-8 (or 3-4 meals for 2)
Serving size: 1/2-3/4 cup per person
or 3/4-1 cup per person as a soup replacer

** *Increase recipe as needed.*

This simple gravy has a rich poultry-like flavor without the fat or animal products found in most gravies and sauces. Arrowroot gives it a thick and smooth consistency and roasted barley flour adds a rich flavor. This gravy goes well with a variety of fall and winter dishes, before and after the holidays. Leftovers can be used in numerous ways. (See suggestions below.)

1 Tbsp. toasted or light sesame oil

3/4 cup barley flour

4 1/2 cups vegetable soup stock and/or water

1-1 1/4 tsp. sea salt

1-1 1/2 Tbsp. shoyu or tamari

1 1/2 Tbsp. arrowroot powder

1/4 cup cold water

1. Heat oil in a cast iron or stainless steel skillet over medium heat. Roast flour in oil, stirring constantly until golden brown and aromatic. Reduce heat to prevent burning. Flour should smell nutty after 6-8 minutes.

2. Remove roasted flour from skillet to prevent burning. Purée it with the 4 1/2 cups liquids in the blender. Or, let it cool in a bowl for 20-30 minutes then mix with the cool or cold stock, a little at a time. Bring to boil over medium heat, whisking or stirring constantly. Add tamari or shoyu and sea salt, and continue to stir. Add herbs if desired.

3. Dissolve arrowroot starch in cold water. Add to gravy and stir to thicken, about 8-10 minutes; cover; reduce heat; and simmer for 25-30 minutes on low, with a heat deflector under the pot. Stir often to prevent burning. If too thin, simmer several minutes with the lid off or dissolve additional arrowroot in a few tablespoons cold water, add, and simmer to thicken. If too thick, add a bit more water. Transfer to serving bowls.

Serving suggestions: Ladle over grain, tempeh, wheat meat, bean, or vegetable dishes. For the holidays, serve it over Easiest Ever Bread Cube Dressing, Chick-n-Peas Sourdough Dressing, Millet "Mashed Potatoes," or Tempeh Cutlets.

Storage: Refrigerate leftovers and heat using the covered-bowl-within-a-pot method.

Variation:

* If the dish you will be serving the gravy over does not contain herbs or spices, add 1 Tbsp. dried sage, thyme, marjoram, or "poultry" seasoning—in step #2 above. ❑

It's A Real Pickle

What's a Pickle for?

Pickles aren't just for burgers or sandwiches. They can be tossed with cooked vegetables or served as a complement for hot cereal, noodles, rice, and other grains. A wide variety exist beyond dill pickles and sauerkraut. In fact, almost any vegetable—from red radishes to zucchini can be pickled.

Why Do We Need Pickles?

Naturally pickled vegetables offer a wealth of beneficial microflora similar to the lactobacillus acidophilus bacteria found in good quality yogurt. Vegetable pickles add to the friendly bacteria in our gut which help to digest and assimilate grain and vegetable foods.

It is ideal to make your own pickles. It doesn't take alot of time and you needn't make large vats. Pickles can be made in any quantity and most can be made in half an hour or less. You can create an endless variety of pickles using the season's freshest produce. A rainbow of colors and a wide range of flavors are possible. Even if you've never made pickles, give it a try. You won't believe how easy it is.

Note: The amount of sea salt used in pickle recipes can be varied to make either mild or salty pickles, however less salty pickles will not keep as well. We suggest using the minimum amount of sea salt or seasoning listed in the following recipes as this will control the growth of undesirable bacteria.

How to Press Pickles:

1. Wash vegetables and cut into thin rounds, half or quarter moon slices or slivers. Place in a glass, pyrex, or stainless steel mixing bowl. Rub vegetables between your hands and crush with salt until wilted and tender or put in an appropriate bowl, crock, or jar then cover with a salty brine, as per recipe.

2. Pack vegetables into *one* of the following containers. Pour the liquid brine over the vegetables or the juice that came out in crushing over vegetables:

(a) a plastic pickle press (from an Asian grocery store), then screw lid on tightly

(b) a large glass or ceramic bowl or crock with a plate that fits inside the container without touching the sides then put a heavy weight or jar full of water on top of the plate to apply pressure. Put a clean cloth over the entire container to keep dust out

(c) a large jar then select a smaller jar which fits inside the rim of the first jar, fill the smaller jar with water and place it on top of the vegetables to apply weight.

3. The brine should rise up to cover the vegetables within 1-2 hours. Otherwise more salt, tamari, shoyu, or ume/apriboshi vinegar is needed or vegetables need to be crushed more thoroughly.

4. Apply enough weight to keep vegetables submerged as they pickle. Ferment or press at room temperature, away from direct sunlight or heat (on the counter in a corner). Allow to sit for 1-4 days, depending upon type of pickle. The longer they sit the more pickled and fermented they will get. We let most pickles sit for 3 or 4 days, though sauerkraut takes several weeks to ferment.

Storage: After 1-4 days, place pickles with brine in jars and refrigerate. (Onions and cabbage are best pickled 3 days; radishes or very sweet onions can be served after a day of pickling.) Use within several weeks to two months. Some types of pickles will last longer.

Notes:

- If mold occurs while pickling, either the brine didn't have enough sea salt, tamari, shoyu, or umeboshi or apriboshi vinegar or the vegetables weren't fresh or cleaned well.

- If mold develops while pickles are in the refrigerator, the vegetables were too old. Scrape off the mold and eat the pickles if they smell okay. You'll have to experiment.

- **For more pickles, see:** *Basic Macrobiotic Cooking*, by Julia Ferre or *The Book of Miso*, by William Shurtleff. ❏

Basic Procedure, Salt Pickled Vegetables (Year Round)***

Prep: 15-20 minutes
Marinate: 3 days

Yield: 1 quart (3-4 cups)
Serving size: 1-2 Tbsp. per person

These tasty pickles are easier to make than you would ever imagine. They only take about 20 minutes to assemble. You just need a good sharp vegetable knife, a suribachi with a wooden pestle, a large bowl for mixing, and either a pickle press, several wide mouth jars, or a crock and a small saucer or jar for pressing. They'll be ready to eat in 3-4 days.

Ratio: About 1-1 1/2 tsp. sea salt per 4 cups cut vegetables. Pickles made with less salt will be milder but will not last as long as pickles made with more salt.

8 packed cups vegetables, cut in thin shreds, quarter moons, half moons or crescents —1 or 2 varieties
(white, green, or purple cabbage, white, yellow, or red onions, cucumber, or other)

2-3 tsp. sea salt

Optional, 2 bay leaves

Optional, other herbs or spices

1. Wash cabbage or scrub carrots or other vegetables. If onions are used, halve them and remove outer peeling. Cut the vegetables finely. If using ginger root, peel with a potato peeler. If cabbage is used, grate or mince cores.

2. Place vegetables in a large mixing bowl. Crush salt into vegetables using your hands to rub the vegetables against each other until they start to wilt and release water. When using purple cabbage or red onions, use a large suribachi and suricogi (wooden pestle) to crush the vegetables so your hands do not turn purple. When vegetables have wilted, add bay leaves or other herbs if desired.

3. Transfer vegetables and brine to a plastic pickle press, ceramic crock, wide mouth jars, or a glass mixing bowl. (Place bay leaves on the bottom, if used). Press vegetables down and wipe any pieces off the sides of the jar, press, or crock. Use an uncut cabbage leaf to cover the vegetables then cover with a saucer and a weight, a smaller jar full of water, or a pickle press lid. Within 1-2 hours water level should rise above the vegetables. If not, add a bit more sea salt and rub it thoroughly into the vegetables until more water is released or place a heavier weight on top.

4. Let the vegetables pickle at room temperature for 3-5 days then transfer pickles and brine to smaller glass jars and refrigerate.

Storage: Always store pickles covered with their brine. Mosr pickles will keep for several weeks or up to three months.

Serving suggestions: Serve 1-2 Tbsp. per person at meals where pressed or marinated salad is not served. Add pickles to salad or sandwiches; toss them with steamed greens or mixed vegetables, or cooked sea vegetables; or serve them atop hot cereal, rice, bread or noodles.

Favorites:

- **Onion Pickles:** These are sweet and a favorite on top of morning cereal, rice, or buns.
- **3-Day Red Cabbage Pickles** with dill or caraway (Fall, Winter)
- **3-Day Green Cabbage Pickles** with dill, caraway, or garlic (Fall, Winter)
- **3-Day Carrot Pickles** with fennel or caraway (Fall, Winter, Spring)
- **3-Day Red Radish Pickles** (Summer, Fall)
- **Cucumber Pickles** with dill and garlic (Summer, Fall)

Variations:

- **Herbed Pickles:** Add 1 Tbsp. crushed caraway, cumin, fennel or mustard seed or 1/4 tsp. red pepper powder, or several cloves of fresh minced garlic in step #2 above.
- **Mix two vegetables:** onions or leeks + cabbage; cabbage + grated carrot. ❏

Basic Procedure, Quick Tamari, Shoyu or Umeboshi Pickles (Year Round) ***

Prep: 10 minutes
Marinate: 2-3 days
Yield: about 1/2-1 cup pickles
Serving size: 3-4 slices or about 1- 2 Tbsp. per person

These pickles are not difficult to make nor do they take a lot of time. They can be assembled in 10 minutes, placed in a bowl or pickle press, and allowed to sit for 24 hours or up to 3 days at room temperature. They are tastiest after three days. They require no additional attention and last for weeks in the refrigerator. They can be served as a condiment for whole grain; chopped and tossed with steamed greens; added to pasta salads; spooned on top of bread with a spread; tucked into a sandwich or tortilla roll up; or added to salads.

1 1/2 cups packed, finely cut, fresh vegetables—one variety
   (e.g., white or red onions, cut in thin crescents or half moons; daikon radish or red radish cut in paper thin rounds +/- minced tops; finely cut red or green cabbage; **or** kirby cucumbers, cauliflower, or other vegetables cut in 1/4-1/2-inch slices)

1/4 cup umeboshi or apriboshi vinegar **or** 1/4 cup tamari or shoyu, **or** a combination of two of these

2-4 Tbsp. pure water

1. Wash and scrub vegetables with a natural bristle brush. If onions are used, remove outer peeling but skip the washing. Finely cut vegetables into rounds, half-moons, quarter-moons, or other slices and place in a plastic pickle press with a screw on lid, a ceramic crock with a smaller saucer which fits inside the crock or a small bowl or a wide mouth quart jar with a smaller bowl or jar full of water used to press down on the vegetables, keeping them under the brine.

2. Mix umeboshi, apriboshi, tamari, or shoyu with water. Pour over vegetables. Press vegetables in a pickle press, bowl, crock, or wide-mouth jar with a weight on top. The liquid should initially come up to one-half the height of the vegetables. It need not cover them completely; the pressing will draw additional liquid from the vegetables and this will rise up over them within 1-2 hours.

3. Leave the vegetables for 24 hours or up to 3 days to pickle on the counter. In hot weather, refrigerate after 1-2 days.

Storage: Refrigerate pickles in their brine in glass jars or covered crocks. Use within 1-2 months.

Favorites:

- **Umeboshi or Apriboshi Onion Pickles (Year Round):** If desired, add 2 tsp. dried or 2 Tbsp. fresh, minced dill weed.

- **Pickled Pink Radish (Summer, Fall):** Daikon or small red radish slices pickled in umeboshi or apriboshi.

- **Umeboshi/Apriboshi Pickled Cauliflower or Cucumber (Summer & Fall):** Tiny pickling cucumbers cut in paper thin rounds or half-moons.

- **Tamari Pickled Radish or Turnip (Summer, Fall, Winter):** Small white radish or daikon radish slices.

- **Umeboshi Pickled Cabbage (Fall, Winter, Early Spring):** Use hard purple or green cabbage cut in fine shreds. Add a dash of dill weed if desired.

Variation:

- **Vinegar pickles:** Replace ume, apriboshi, tamari, or shoyu with 1 tsp. sea salt. Replace the water with brown rice vinegar. Prepare as above.

Favorites:

- Onions with sea salt and rice vinegar.

- Red radish slices with sea salt and rice vinegar.

- Cucumbers pickled with sea salt, brown rice vinegar, garlic, and dill weed. ❏

Basic Procedure, Don's Dills (Summer & Fall)

Prep: 15-20 minutes
Pickling: 3-4 days
Yield: 1 pint (2 cups) of pickles
Serving size: 2-4 thin slices per person

These have no added vinegar, sweeteners or preservatives and are much tastier than most store bought dills. However, they won't keep as long as store bought varieties. We make several jarfuls in the early fall so we will have them around after the fresh, locally grown cucumbers are gone.

4 cups packed, thinly sliced pickling cucumbers

3-4 cloves garlic cut in thin slivers **and/or** 1/4 cup chopped onion or scallion

3 sprigs fresh dill weed

1 1/2-2 tsp. sea salt

1. Wash cucumbers and cut into thin rounds. Chop and add garlic and/or onion. Add salt.

2. In a bowl, crush the salt into the vegetables, rubbing until they start to wilt and release water. Place vegetables and brine in a plastic pickle press, a ceramic crock, or glass bowl as per Basic Pickle Procedure. (The larger volume of salt will make them last longer.)

3. Within several hours the water level should rise above the vegetables. If this does not happen you will need to add a bit more sea salt and rub it thoroughly into the vegetables until more water is released. Let pickles sit for 3-4 days at room temperature.

Storage: Store pickles with their brine in covered 8-, 16, or 32-ounce glass jars, in the refrigerator. Use within 1-3 months for best results.

Variations:

- Add 2 Tbsp. fresh or 2 tsp. dried tarragon.

- Add 1 cup finely cut white onion and 1-1 1/2 tsp. sea salt to the above recipe.

- Add 6-8 black peppercorns. ❑

Mustard & Miso Pickled Sprouts (Winter & spring)

Prep: 10 minutes
Serves: 8-10 small **or** 4-5 medium servings

Marinate: 30 minutes **or** 1-3 hours
Serving size: 1-3 Tbsp. per person

Mustard and miso turn run of the mill sprouts into a flavorful pickle-type condiment. Leftovers keep for 1-3 days and can be added to salads, sandwiches, or burritos, or used to top bread or rice. These are mildly pungent and add a nice contrast to almost any meal.

4 packed cups alfalfa, clover, or mixed sprouts

3 Tbsp. prepared mustard (dijon, or stone ground natural variety)

2 Tbsp. light, yellow, mellow, sweet, or millet miso

3 Tbsp. water

1. Mix water, miso and mustard until smooth.

2. Place sprouts in a bowl. Pour puréed sauce over sprouts and mix. Allow to marinate for 1-3 hours before serving.

Storage: Store in the refrigerator in glass jar or covered bowl. Use within two days.

Serving suggestions: Serve at room temperature, 2-3 Tbsp. per person. ❑

Quick Pickled Onion Rings (Any Season)***

Prep: 10 minutes
Marinate: 4-8 hours or overnight

Yield: about 1 cup
Serves: 8-10 (or 2-4 with leftovers)

These sweet and delicious pickles take just 10 minutes to assemble and need just 4-6 hours to sit. Thin slices are perfect on top off sandwiches or veggie burgers. They are especially good on Basic Bean Burgers, wheat meat burgers, Tempeh Gyros, Squash-Wiches, "Yam"-Wiches, or sandwiches made from tofu or bean dips. Make a larger batch if you want leftovers to last several days. These will get sweeter as they sit.

2 cups onions, Walla Walla Sweets, Vadalia, or other, cut in thin slices
1 Tbsp. brown rice vinegar
1/4-1/3 tsp. sea salt (more if they will not be used up within a couple of days)

1. Peel onions, then cut into thin rings.
2. Mix all ingredients well, rubbing onions in a bowl until they start to get a little watery.
3. Press 4-8 hours with a plate and weight on top. (See Pressing Technique, page 379.)

Storage: Store in a jar with the brine, in the refrigerator. Use within 1-2 weeks for best results.

Serving suggestions: Serve several slices per person in sandwiches or with bread or rice. (Try them with our Tempeh Gyros or Basic Bean Burgers, or toss with steamed broccoli or kale, plus cauliflower and carrots or red radish then add a dollup of Tofu Sour Cream or Tofu Tartar Sauce.) They are also tasty, minced and served over hot cereal with roasted seeds or a steamed egg and a side of cooked leafy greens. Or serve over hot cereal or millet, rice, or polenta with parboiled or steamed vegetables that have been tossed with tahini, sunflower, or sesame butter that has been thinned with water. ❏

Basic Beet Root Relish (Year Round)

Prep: 5-10 minutes
Cooking: none

Yield: 2/3 cups
Serving size: 1-3 Tbsp. per person

This refreshingly sweet salad can enliven even the simplest meal. Leftovers will keep for several days.

1 small to medium beet, about 2/3-3/4 cup packed
Fresh horseradish (1-1 1/2 tsp. finely grated)
1/2-1 tsp. tamari, shoyu, or umeboshi or apriboshi vinegar +/- 1 tsp. rice vinegar

1. Wash but do not peel the vegetables. Use a vegetable scrub brush to clean them.
2. Use the smallest hole on an all-purpose grater (the size used for Parmesian cheese). Grate the beet into a small dish. Grate and add about 1 tsp. horseradish. Mixture should be juicy.
3. Add tamari, shoyu or ume or vinegar and/or rice. Stir.

Serving suggestions: Serve as a relish with whole grain, pasta, or bread, with cooked greens, soup, stew, tempeh, or beans and seed and/or sea vegetable condiments. It's also delicious on bread (alone or with a tofu, tempeh, or tahini spread).

Storage: Refrigerate leftovers in a covered jar or bowl. Remove from refrigerator 1/2 hour before serving. Use within 24 hours.

Variations:

- **Carrot & Beet Root Relish:** Use one large carrot and one small beet in above recipe. Omit horseradish.

- **Carrot & Daikon Relish:** Use half carrot and half daikon radish. Omit horseradish. ❏

- Replace salty seasonings with cider or rice vinegar.

Quick & Easy Kim-Chee Pickles (Fall, Winter, Spring)

Prep: 15 minutes
Pressing: 1-3 hours
Marinate: 3-5 days or more

Yield: about 3-4 cups pickles
Serving size: 2-4 Tbsp. per person

These pickles spark the digestive fire and stimulate circulation. Unlike some of the more traditional versions which literally set your mouth on fire, this version of Kim-chi is *very* mild. For a spicier version, increase the garlic and ginger and/or add cayenne or fresh chili pepper.

These pickles last for months and improve with age, though you can dig into them in as few as 4-5 days. While you can make them any time of year, we especially enjoy making them when chinese cabbage is abundant. This recipe is adapted from one in *Cooking with Japanese Foods* by Jan Belleme.

1 small head nappa or Chinese cabbage, cut in
   1/2 to 1" squares

1 carrot, cut in thin slivers or match sticks

1 leek washed and finely cut, 1 medium onion,
   thin crescents **or** 5 minced scallions,

1 Tbsp. sea salt

1-2 Tbsp. minced garlic

2-3 tsp. peeled and minced fresh ginger root

Optional, 1 fresh anaheim or ancho chili pepper, minced finely **or** 1/4 tsp. mild red pepper powder (*chipotle, Anaheim, or ancho*)

1. In a large suribachi crush sea salt into vegetables with a wooden pestle until watery and translucent around the edges. This can also be done by hand in a mixing bowl, crushing and kneading as with pressed or marinated salads.

2. Stir in minced garlic, ginger, and chili or red pepper powder. Press as per Basic Procedure for Pressed Salad. A plastic pickle press with a screw on lid works best, but you can improvise with a bowl or crock topped with a plate and gallon jug of water for weight. Allow to press at room temperature 1-3 hours until brine rises above and covers vegetables.

3. When brine rises above vegetables, pack into one or more wide mouth glass jars along with the brine liquid. Screw lids on jars and store in a fairly cool dry place away from direct sunlight (corner of the kitchen counter, a pantry or other such place). Let sit out for 3-5 days then transfer jars to the refrigerator.

Storage: Kim chee is ready to serve after 5 days but will improve with age the longer it sits in the refrigerator. The flavor will change after several weeks and even more after several months. The salt acts as a preservative and kim chee will last for well over a year in the refrigerator.

Serving suggestions: Serve 1-3 Tbsp. per person at a meal, as desired. They're great on bread with diluted sesame butter and steamed greens, in tempeh or wheat meat sandwiches, or with veggie burgers. You can also serve a spoonful or two of pickles alongside brown rice (or a mixed grain) with a seed condiment; stir fried, sautéed or parboiled vegetables; and soup or a bean, tofu, tempeh, or wheat meat side dish.

Variations:

- For hot kim chee add 1-2 tsp. mild red pepper or, cayenne or increase the fresh red pepper before pressing the vegetables. Be careful, it's easy to go overboard with the pepper. Try it mild the first time.

- Use different types of cabbage, grated daikon radish, scallions, celery, etc.

- Small jars of kim chee make excellent Christmas gifts! ❏

Umeboshi or Apriboshi Paste
(Year Round) ***

Prep: 10-15 minutes
Serving size: 1/2 tsp. per person
or as needed in a recipe

This salty, slightly sour and tangy paste is made by mashing umeboshi or apriboshi plums with a bit of water. As a seasoning, it adds a rich, aged flavor to tofu, bean, or egg-based patés, dips, spreads, sauces, and salad dressings. It also adds a wonderful, rich, almost buttery taste when smoothed sparingly over breakfast cereal and then topped with a steamed, poached, or 1,000-year egg or chopped roasted nuts or seeds, with chives, scallions, or parsley. It can also be spread very thinly over steam-warmed bread or corn on the cob instead of butter.

This pickled plum/apricot paste needs no refrigeration and, like the salty-brine pickled plums or apricots it comes from, it will last almost indefinitely. The pits can be used to make ume tea or juice for seasoning various dishes.

About 6-8 umeboshi or apriboshi pickled
    plums/apricots
3-4 Tbsp. water, or as needed

1. Remove pits from the plums or apricots and set aside (they can still be used).

2. In a suribachi, mash the plums or apricots with the water to make a smooth paste. Add additional water, a few teaspoons at a time, as needed. The consistency should be like jam or chutney.

Hint: Move the wooden pestle in small circles around the bottom of the suribachi, rather than using a pounding or up and down motion.

Storage: With a spatula, scrape the pickled paste into a small, wide-mouth jar. Cover and store in a cool dry place such as a cabinet or on the table. Always use a clean spoon to dip into the jar so as not to introduce new bacteria and cause mold to grow.

Serving suggestions: Use sparingly in cooking or making sauces, dressings, dips, and spreads, or use at the table (over hot cereal or on bread). A little bit goes a long way. Be very careful not to use too much or you will over-salt and overpower your foods. If used to season other dishes such as dressings or sauces (in place of salt or tamari), add just a little bit at a time. As a table condiment, about 1/4-3/4 tsp. per person in a meal is usually enough.

Using the pits:

1. In a small saucepan, combine a handful of umeboshi or apriboshi pits with several cups of water. Cover and bring to boil; reduce heat to low and simmer for 20 minutes.

2. Strain off the pits and discard (preferably to a compost bin). Save liquid and use it for the following:

#1: Cook the ume tea in with morning cereal to replace a portion of the water and all of the salt (try 1/2 cup of this ume or apribosh juice in place of 1/2 cup water in a batch of hot cereal to serve two).

Cook as per basic cereal recipe. This cereal will taste very rich and buttery! We like to stir in roasted dulse, then top with scallions or chives and a Seasoned Seed Condiment.

#2: Use this liquid as part of the stock in soup or stew and reduce the amount of added sea salt, miso or tamari in a given recipe.

#3: Use the ume or apriboshi pit liquid as a cooling summer drink, served warm or at room temperature. ❏

Condiments p. 386

Chapter 9
Nourishment For Breakfast

For what is breakfast, but a breaking fast?
— Henry David Thoreau

Breaking the Fast

The fast pace and odd hours of modern life seem to have made "breaking fast" a thing of the past. Many Americans face long morning commutes to stressful jobs. Usually they feel that they barely have time to get ready for work in the morning, let alone eat. They skip breakfast for lack of time or if they do eat, they often scarf down a danish and cup of coffee or a glass of juice on the run.

Of course, in order to be able to *break* fast, you first have to fast, and usually those who aren't hungry in the morning are those who haven't fasted (i.e, they've eaten late at night). With the odd hours of modern schedules, which are arranged around the needs of industry and commerce, not of human health, late-night eating is not uncommon.

Research confirms that breakfast has become an "old-fashioned" thing. One in four American adults never eats breakfast and 9% of Americans eat breakfast only occasionally. Young adults are the most frequent breakfast skippers, and perhaps one-third to one-half of teens skip the morning meal. In contrast, Americans over fifty-five are among the most likely to eat breakfast: at least 70% of men and women over the age of 55 report that they eat breakfast everyday.

Fifty years ago, people in the over fifty-five crowd were being advised by their mothers and grandmothers to eat a hearty breakfast to get the day off to a good start. It was, as they said, "just common sense" that a healthy and energetic person was "early to bed and early to rise," and needed plenty of warm fuel to rekindle the inner Fire. The sages of traditional Oriental medicine discovered that this common sense—it is common in all traditional cultures— reflects knowledge of the actual biorhythms of human nature.

According to traditional Oriental medicine and the medical knowledge of many other traditional cultures, the stomach is most receptive to food between the hours of 7:00 and 9:00 a.m., and the body is most efficient at transforming food into human matter and energy between the hours of 9:00 and 11:00 a.m. This is natural. Before we become active, it is important to gather some energy. This means that the morning meal ought to be one of the largest of the day.

Western science has confirmed this ancient view of Oriental medicine (and grandmothers everywhere!). Researchers have found that those who take the majority of their food before noon have less tendency to gain weight, when compared with those who eat late in the day. This means that food consumed before noon becomes energy, rather than excess matter (stored fat). Researchers have also found that those who eat breakfast consistently out-perform breakfast skippers in both mental and physical activities.

What happens when you skip breakfast?

Skipping breakfast often leads to low-energy levels, an uncontrollable appetite later in the day, and snacking, binging, or late-night eating which interferes with proper digestion and a good night's rest. Overeating and late-night eating also tend to create a host of health problems, including unwanted weight gain, morning sluggishness, fatigue or depression, a feeling of heaviness, mucus in the throat or nasal passages, and a weak appetite first thing in the morning.

The breakfast skipper is often a victim of a self-perpetuating downward spiral. Since those who skip breakfast tend to eat large meals at the end of the day, when food is poorly digested, they usually have little or no appetite in the morning. This is only natural—after all, if dinner from the night before is still sitting there in your intestines undigested. Then it is unlikely that you will feel hungry, And so the cycle starts again. To remedy this situation, start by eating something for breakfast and lunch one day, then eat little or nothing for dinner. The next morning, you will probably have a strong appetite for breakfast! Then you can begin to eat as nature intended: breakfast like a king, lunch like a prince, and dinner like a pauper. Since you won't be going to bed full, you will probably find that it is also easier to get up in the morning (after a good night's rest). Changing your body rhythms and eating in harmony with daily energetics will help make you more alert and energetic in the morning. It can improve your digestion and health problems related to poor digestion and can help you to shed excess weight if need be.

If you've typically been a breakfast skipper or morning skimper, try making breakfasts ahead, planning and preparing the night before so you don't have to fuss first thing in the morning. This can make a world of difference when you are making the switch from being a late-night eater to a morning-bird. Once you get the hang of it, you'll be able to whip up new and exciting breakfasts with just a few minutes of hands-on prep time. And you'll be far more alert, energetic, and productive as a result.

The Tao of Breakfast

Breakfast comes after we arise from a death-like slumber. In the morning we are reborn; we recapitulate the developmental stages of our infancy, moving from lying to crawling (out of bed) to standing to walking. In the early morning, our digestive system is as sensitive as that of an infant. Thus, for our main food in the morning, the textures and nutritional values of mother's milk or infant food are most appropriate. Whole grains have a protein to carbohydrate ratio and a sweet flavor that virtually duplicates human mother's milk. This suggests that soft grain porridge would be a particularly suitable staple food around which to build a nourishing breakfast.

As we noted above, traditional Oriental medicine has determined that the Stomach is the organ most active between 7:00 and 9:00 a.m.—the time when we commonly consume breakfast. The

---

What's Good about Breakfast

Eating breakfast improves concentration and learning ability: A 1987 study conducted by the Boston University School of Medicine, Tufts School of Nutrition, and Boston City Hospital confirmed the ancient knowledge that breakfast improves mental functioning. In this study, elementary school children (third through sixth graders) who ate breakfast scored higher on tests and were less likely to be tardy than those who skipped their morning meal. Breakfast skippers displayed more trouble with problem solving and concentration than breakfast eaters.

Eating breakfast helps prevent obesity: A study of 1,797 preteens, conducted by Cornell University nutritionist Wendy Wolf, showed that children who skipped breakfast were more likely to be obese than breakfast eaters. Breakfast skippers were more likely to resort to eating more high-fat and high-calorie snacks and sweets later in the day. Obesity in childhood is associated with an increased risk of developing heart disease, diabetes, and respiratory disease later in life. As much as 40% of obese children and 80% of obese teenagers become obese adults.

Stomach likes warm and moist foods, and dislikes dry and cold foods. Thus, to harmonize with the morning energy, it may be best to take the advice of your grandmother and have warm porridge (or steam-heated leftover rice) rather than dry toast or cold-and-dry cereal for breakfast.

Most Americans are accustomed to having fruit and sugars at breakfast. However, fruits generally are very heavy, cooling and sedating, according to Oriental herbalists. This energy is just the opposite of the light and uprising tendency of morning-Qi (energy) and thus these are not particularly appropriate or nourishing foods for the first meal of the day. The sugar in fruit and sweeteners or jams can easily overwhelm the Spleen (similar to the stomach and spleen of western anatomy), leading to the accumulation of Dampness. Since Dampness is viscous and heavy, the use of sweet foods at breakfast can create heavy feelings in the limbs and a fuzzy feeling in the head. The cold and damp nature of sweets or fruit may be temporarily stimulating but can, in fact, put a damper on the digestive "fire" of the Spleen entirely, leaving it unable to transform more nourishing foods into Qi (vital energy). This may lead to the all-too-common experience of mid-morning, low energy "blues," and cravings for stimulants such as coffee or more sweets.

Morning time also corresponds to Spring time. Both spring-time and morning are characterized by a yang-uprising energy. To harmonize with morning-Qi, breakfast can include more yang, ascending, warm energy foods with a mildly pungent taste. These may be leftover or freshly prepared by steaming, stir-frying, quick-boiling, or fermenting, techniques which have an en-livening energy. Steamed, sautéed, or quick-boiled leafy greens and pungent onion family vegetables fit this bill, as do naturally pickled (not vinegar or sugar preserved) vegetables—especially pickled pungent greens, radishes, or onions. Fresh or dried chives, scallions, or parsley can be just the thing to spark the digestive fires as well. Things that sprout or grow upward help us to rise to the challenge of a new day.

No one would think of feeding an infant bacon, sausage, steak or other such foods. According to traditional Oriental medicine, these sorts of foods are very difficult to digest. If flesh foods are taken in quantity at this time, when we are attempting to re-awaken, the result may be that, before we know it, we are digesting ourselves back to sleep! Hence, Oriental medicine would suggest avoidance or very limited use of animal foods at breakfast. Used sparingly as topping for grain—a few teaspoons of a seasoned, roasted nut or seed condiment, or a steamed or lightly poached egg would be most appropriate to enhance the meal without smothering the digestive fire. Or one might occasionally enjoy a bit of soy yogurt as toppings for hot cereal, rice, vegetables, or a low fat tofu, grain, or vegetable-based spread on bread.

Life began in the salty sea. Sea vegetables are perhaps the oldest uprising forms of life on the earth, stretching themselves from the dark depths of the ocean toward the warm light. Since morning is the time we begin life anew, a small

volume of salty condiments or sea vegetables are also appropriate food for breaking the fast and enlivening our grain foods.

Breakfast the Orient-al Way

A Nourishment For Life breakfast may be quite a bit different from what you're accustomed to. Such a meal will revolve around large volumes of whole and minimally refined—and softly cooked as porridge or dinner grain— grains as the foundation, with land and/or sea vegetables as side dishes, and seeds, nuts, or occasionally free-range eggs used as condiments. And such a breakfast will be more savory than sweet. However, many grains and vegetables have a subtle sweet taste that will grow on you the longer you eat them and the more thoroughly you chew them.

You might not like some of the foods in the beginning, and you might not think you can eat so much grain or so many vegetables and little or no animal food. But if you persevere, for the sake of improved personal and planetary health, with-in a few weeks you may be surprised to find that you enjoy and even crave savory grains (and perhaps vegetables too) first thing in the morn-ing! We have watched numerous friends and cooking students go through this process, replac-ing long held habits, tastes, and preferences with healthier, more economical and ecological habits. Give it a try, go with the grain!

Vegetables for breakfast?

Many Americans seem to think that they could "never" eat savory food and vegetables for break-fast. At first, it seems just too weird and foreign. And yet a savory breakfast containing vegetables is not unknown to the American palate. Most people have had savory breakfast foods such as hash browns and vegetable omelets filled with mushrooms, onions, and even broccoli, or a glass of tomato juice, or ketchup on scrambled eggs served with home fries.

When we look at breakfasts around the world, savory breakfasts containing vegetables are far more common than the dessert-style breakfasts had by most Americans. In fact, the American sweet breakfast, in the world context, is the most weird and unusual. In the British Isles, oat porridge with dulse sea vegetable was once traditional fare. In Asia—India, Tibet, China, Japan, and Korea—people eat cooked vegetables and/or pickles with their cereal. In her book, *How To Cook And Eat In Chinese*, Buwei Yang Chao comments that in China "It is true that we sometimes eat congee or thin boiled rice at breakfast, but to put milk and sugar in it—weak! No, sweet things have their places." In China most folks sit down to a savory porridge called congee, which is typically topped with a pickled egg, chopped meat, fish, or chicken, and cooked vegetables, spices, pickles, and scallions.

Though vegetables for breakfast may sound strange to the uninitiated, this practice isn't so uncommon and it is definitely a habit worth cultivating. Vegetables are far more nutritious than fruits. Adding more vegetables to your diet can go a long way toward bettering your health. Vegetables are very beneficial breakfast foods and the perfect complement to a piping hot bowl of porridge, freshly cooked rice, or a steam-warmed bowl of millet, rice, polenta, or noodles.

No fruit?

Of course habit has us equate hot or cold cereal with bananas, raisins, berries, sugar, honey, and milk—however, other toppings and condiment options do exist. Most people from traditional cultures around the world—where fruit production was never a priority —have enjoyed barley, millet, oat, rice gruel, or other porridges for centuries, and without fruit, syrup, or even milk. Fruit is not an essential part of breakfast, or of a a healthy diet. Cooked, pressed, or marinated dark green leafy vegetables, dark orange colored root and round vegetables, beans, whole grains and sea vegetables can more than meet your needs for vitamin C, potassium, iron, calcium, protein, and other essentials.

What else can I eat that's sweet?

Whole cereal grains and vegetables can give you a subtle sweet taste that nourishes without depleting. Many grains have a subtle sweet taste. Examples include: sweet brown or Thai black sweet rice, whole oats, millet, cornmeal, polenta, and/or fresh-frozen steam-peeled or dried chestnuts, any of which can be combined or added to other cereal grains for your morning meal. And if a sweeter taste is what you desire first thing in the morning, don't forget to soak your grains overnight; this initiates the sprouting process and brings out a much sweeter taste. Proper and lengthy cooking as well as the addition of sun dried sea salt—cooked into the cereal pot—will create a more flavorful and sweet cereal as well. (Thorough chewing also teases out the mildly sweet taste of whole grains.)

For a stronger sweet taste, sweet winter squashes, sweet potatoes, or fresh or dried sweet corn may be cooked into your cereal or served as a topping. Or, if you opt for dinner grain consistency rice or millet, you could add a cup of soup made from parsnips, carrots, squash, onions, or a combination of several sweet root and round vegetables. This is no more odd than having hash brown potatoes for breakfast. However, be forewarned that taken to excess even these super sweet vegetables can lead to flatulence and acid regurgitation, so it is advisable to keep grain as the main dish in any meal with everything else served as a side dish or condiment!

Free-range, farm fresh duck and chicken eggs also have a remarkably sweet taste that is not found in commercial, factory farmed eggs. So if you choose to include these foods in your diet, scout around to find a source of good quality eggs. These may be steamed in an oiled custard cup, poached, stir fried with vegetables, or scrambled with tofu and herbs and used occasionally to top hot cereal, rice, millet, or noodles, and veggies. Raw goat milk or yogurt also possess a mildly sweet and rich taste and can be used at breakfast by those who choose.

How about those nuts?

It's all too easy to overdo it with nuts and seeds. Though they may be tasty, they are very high in fat and hard to digest. For this reason, they are best used very sparingly. By dry roasting nuts and seeds, seasoning them with something salty—mineral rich sea salt, tamari, or umeboshi vinegar—then grinding them to a coarse powder, you can make a little bit go a long way. Used as a table condiment for grains, they will also be easier to digest than when eaten by the fistful.

Such nut and seed condiments can be used daily, at every meal if you like, as long as they are used in small amounts, two to four teaspoons per person at a given meal. Exact amount used will vary with the volume of grain you eat and the way the nuts or seeds are prepared. Or, coat steamed vegetables with diluted nut butter to serve over grain. Or, sesame butter to coat noodles. Or, cook a small amount of nuts or seeds right into the cereal pot. Another option is to top cereal with a couple of teaspoons of raw sesame or flax seed oil or nut oil.

Certain conditions create a craving for nuts, seeds, and large amounts of vegetable oil. Among followers of vegetarian, vegan, or ultra low-fat or fat-free diets if these diets contain (1) an excess of Empty, clearing, or cooling foods such as iced or cold foods, juices, raw foods, (2) an excess of fruits or vegetables, a lack of sufficient warming foods or of tonic foods (like rice and other grains), or (3) a deficiency of sea salt which nourishes the Essence and is needed for proper digestion and assimilation.

The proper use of a sufficient amount of good quality sea salt (or miso, tamari, or umeboshi) cooked into all of one's grains, beans, and soups can eliminate many sweet or oil cravings while enhancing the flavor and digestibility of foods. Good quality salty seasonings add vital minerals and bring out a rich and buttery taste even when little or no fat is added to a dish. Proper chewing is also crucial for the elimination of cravings for fats (and sweets). Further, cravings for nuts, seeds, and nut butters often cease when small quantities of seeds or seed condiments are used daily with grains and two to six teaspoons of cold pressed vegetable oil (or ghee) per day.

The Basics of Breakfast

Hot cereal or whole grain: A nourishing breakfast revolves around a warm bowl of porridge (soft cereal) or cooked whole grain (dinner grain consistency) comprised of a single grain such as millet, buckwheat, rolled oats, or brown rice, or a combination of two grains. Regardless of the kind of grain you choose, grains should provide 50-70% of the volume you eat at breakfast. With the basic formulas we offer here, you can create an endless variety of porridge possibilities.

Quick & easy porridge

Making breakfast really takes very little time.

Whole grain porridge can be cooked overnight on top of the stove on a very low heat with a heat deflector under the pot. If you're really pressed for time and find yourself harried or incoherent first thing in the morning, invest in a crock pot or thermal cooker. With it, you can cook whole grain hot cereals overnight then wake up to a soothing breakfast. You can also make extra cereal for use two mornings in a row (steam warming leftovers on the second morning) or make a simple porridge from leftover cooked dinner grain first thing in the morning. Warmed leftover rice, noodles, steamed buns or other steamed breads also make a satisfying breakfast. In the heat of summer, try Vegetable Muesli (our own unique concoction) or Cold-Cooked, Counter-Top Oats. These are more cooling preparations which require no cooking. However, warm grain is the ideal breakfast food for daily use.

Soft porridge is gentle on the system first thing in the morning. It is soothing to the digestive organs, waking them up slowly and gently. Porridge is also delicious, nutritious, incredibly inexpensive, and easy to prepare. If you play around with different grains and grain combinations, and try different savory toppings, condiments, and vegetable side dishes, you may be surprised to find that there's never a dull meal, even if it's an oat-meal!

Old Grains Make New Meals

Turning leftovers into breakfast cereal is ecological, economical, and makes for tasty cereals. Such a system allows you to practice a "waste nothing" way of cooking while adding incredible variety to your diet. Leftover whole grain, bread, and cooked vegetables can all be used to create tasty and nutritious breakfasts. Oftentimes, we cook leftover noodles, rice, or dried out bread in with our morning porridge. Sometimes we even add leftover baked squash, sweet potato, or corn cut off the cob to our morning cereal for a delectably sweet morning meal.

Dinner grain will do

If you are following the two-meal-a-day-plan (or 2-meals plus a light snack), it is best to serve thick dense dinner grain or thick porridge for breakfast. This will give you the staying power to go until one o'clock for your lunch meal. Grain that is very watery is less calorie dense and less likely to carry you for four or five hours. (If you opt for dinner grain, be sure to serve it warm with a cup of soup or stew or a yellow/orange vegetable side dish, plus a greens dish and condiments.) In this case, you might cook a fresh pot of rice first thing in the morning so you will have it for breakfast and lunch, or for all three meals (plus leftovers for a meal the next day).

Rich condiments: Breakfast cereal or dinner grain may be topped with one of the following: (a) 1/2-2 Tbsp. roasted, seasoned seed or nut condiment; (b) 1-3 tsp. nut or seed butter (thinned with water); or (c) 1/2-1 cup soy, seed, or nut yogurt or goat milk or yogurt. or (d) 1-2 tsp. nut or seed oil or ghee or raw butter.

Nut or seed butter may also be used as a light dressing for leafy green or mixed vegetables which may then be served over and eaten with hot cereal, rice, bread, or noodles. Or, skip the seeds and nuts and try topping your cereal with 1 steamed or poached egg, 1 diced red cooked egg, or 1/2 to 1 Chinese-style 1,000-year egg (a preserved egg which needs no refrigeration or cooking and resembles a hard boiled egg when extracted from the shell (use rarely).

A half teaspoon of umeboshi or apriboshi paste spread on cereal (with chives or scallions) adds a rich taste, even without the addition of roasted nuts, seeds, nut or dairy butter, or an egg. It might sound strange, but salty pickles, pickled plum paste or powdered miso taste incredibly rich and delicious on porridge with roasted sea vegetables. If you choose to add nuts or seeds here, cook them in with the grain or sprinkle roasted, unsalted seeds or chopped nuts over your umeboshi/apriboshi topped grain.

In warmer weather, soy yogurt can be a refreshing topping for your cereal or soy yogurt or soy, almond, sunflower or rice milk may be used to soak rolled grains for Vegetable Muesli.

Occasionally, you might want to cook a small volume of nuts or seeds into your cereal and skip the rich toppings. When weight loss is desired, it is advisable to skip the eggs and to stick with seed condiments or seed oils on your cereal. Animal products should be used sparingly by anyone wishing to achieve or maintain vibrant health. One should always seed good quality products from free-ranging animals.

Fresh leafy greens: You can benefit greatly by serving your cereal with a small cup of leafy green or mixed vegetables. Morning greens may consist of lightly steamed, stir fried, quick-boiled, parboiled, or sautéed vegetables or a pressed or marinated salad. Though you may prepare vegetables fresh for breakfast, leftovers from the previous day are a tasty and convenient time saver. (If vegetables for breakfast seem too foreign at first, you may wish to leave out the greens or replace them with leftover cooked sweet corn, winter squash, or sweet potato, then work your way toward incorporating greens into your morning meal. Please give it a try; you won't believe how good these foods taste at breakfast—and how good they can make you feel —until you try them.)

Steamed or parboiled vegetables can be plain or lightly coated with tamari, shoyu, or umeboshi, with a hint of oil or diluted seed butter, and served on the side in small custard cups or dishes or spooned over porridge with sea vegetable and seed condiments. Or, any of these salty seasonings (or sea salt or pickle juice) may also be added to the vegetables in the cooking

For this reason, remove leftovers from the refrigerator 20-60 minutes before serving to allow them to come to room and body temperature before a meal.

Other vegetables: If you are on a two-meal-a-day plan (two main meals—breakfast and lunch, with a fast until the next morning or a light dessert or snack taken in the late afternoon or early evening), you will want to add a second vegetable side dish at breakfast: a smooth and creamy soup, a hearty stew, a vegetable mash or purée, a sauté, or stewed, baked, nishime or kinpira-style root vegetables. Sweet root, round, or ground vegetables are ideal. Examples include carrots, parsnips, rutabaga, winter squash, sweet potatoes or yams, onions, sunchokes, sweet corn (in season), or a combination of several of these. These provide added nourishment, a sweet flavor, a grounding energy, and a complement to grains and greens. These can be freshly prepared first thing in the morning, leftover from the previous day, or cooked all night in a crock pot or insulated thermal cooker. Although this may sound strange, many of these sweet vegetables have a taste that is similar to fruit. These vegetables can be spooned, mashed, or spread on top of porridge or bread, served alongside your dinner grain or soft cereal and greens, or you might even cook one of them right into your cereal. (Like other foods, leftover cooked vegetables should be served warm or allowed to come to room temperature for 20-60 minutes before serving.

Pungent green garnish: A few teaspoons or tablespoons of a raw, fresh, and pungent garnish (or a few teaspoons of a dried pungent garnish) can enhance your appetite and your cereal. Examples include: fresh or dried chives, garlic chives, scallions, dill, parsley, grated horseradish, or sprouts. For convenience, you can mince up enough to last for a few days, then store them in small wide-mouth jars in the refrigerator for easy access. Dried chives travel well and also come in handy in the off-seasons when other fresh garnishes may not be locally available.

Sea vegetables: A bit of oven roasted sea vegetables (dulse, kelp, ocean ribbons, wild nori, etc.) or sea vegetable flakes (sea cress, dulse, etc.) makes another good addition to your cereal bowl. Sea vegetables are chock full of minerals. They are also potent anti-cancer foods and detoxifiers. (Refer to the sea vegetable chapter for

more on these super-foods from the sea.) Just crumble a handful into the bottom of your cereal bowl before adding hot cereal, then stir in cereal and top with other condiments. Or, shake some sea vegetable flakes or crumble roasted chip-like pieces on top of your porridge or dinner grain, along with a salty seed or nut condiment. Alternatively, soak and cook a four to six-inch piece of kelp, kombu, or alaria sea vegetable into the cereal or grain pot. If serving dinner grain for breakfast, you might want to top your grain with a tablespoon or two of sea vegetable condiment (Nori or Alaria Condiment, etc.) or cook some sea vegetables in with your greens or root vegetables.

Sea vegetables, like land vegetables, come in a wide variety of tastes, textures, flavors, and colors. However, you need not use them in large volumes—they are very concentrated—a little bit can go a long way. A few teaspoons or tablespoons of flakes or a handful of oven-roasted sea vegetable will provide ample benefit. (Refer to the sea vegetable chapter for more information.)

Savory and sweet pickles: Good quality pickles, when used in small amounts can aid digestion and add a rich taste to meals. These can be homemade or purchased from a health food store or quality mail-order source (see the index for Mail Order Resources). They are not a necessary ingredient at breakfast, though some find them to be refreshing first thing in the morning, tossed with boiled salad or steamed greens or simply eaten with grain. (Pressed or marinated salad, served with or instead of cooked greens, can also add a fresh energy to the morning meal.) Onions or red radish pickles in sea salt or umeboshi vinegar are particularly nice at breakfast.

An occasional one-half to one teaspoon of tart and tangy, pickled plum or apricot paste (called umeboshi or apriboshi) makes a tasty cereal condiment. It is very salty and sour so you don't need much, but it does bring out a really rich taste in the cereal. It is especially decadent spread over oat-based cereal or rice that has been cooked with nuts or seeds or topped with a poached egg or teaspoon or two of nut or seed oil (flax, sesame, or walnut) or raw butter or ghee.

Make time for breakfast

Think you don't have time to make a nourishing breakfast? This chapter will show you how to make nourishing meals efficiently, affordably, and ecologically. Using our methods, anyone can assemble a nourishing breakfast with just 10-25 minutes of hands-on preparation, especially if you have planned ahead and have leftovers around. While your breakfast cooks, you can take a shower, exercise, or prepare other things for the day—you can wash and soak whole grains and/or beans, assemble a soup or stew for lunch or supper, make a quick dessert for later, whip up a pressed salad, or pack a lunch or two.

Breakfast should be a very substantial meal, not a quick bite taken on the run. Skipping off without a full meal under your belt would be like starting on a long journey with your car's tank empty or only half full. You couldn't get very far on an empty tank, nor will you get far on an empty stomach. A nourishing breakfast should make up one-third to one-half of your daily caloric needs. For this you will need to allow ample sitting and chewing time.

If you want to make the most of your morning time, make breakfast—rather than dinner—a family-affair, then plan for a large early afternoon lunch (at one or two o'clock) and skip dinner or make it a light bite (or snack). Schedule it so that a good hour is allotted for sharing, eating, and communing over this most important morning meal. In this way, you will have quality time with loved ones before you have been tired out by a long day of activity and stress. You won't have to rush around the kitchen trying to pull together a big evening meal at the end of the day.

We recommend taking at least 45 minutes to a full hour to eat your breakfast, sitting down, in peace and without distraction. Your food will taste better, be more satisfying, and be more efficiently used by your body if you cultivate the art of eating consciously and chewing thoroughly. Chewing your food until it is totally liquefied (50-100 times per mouthful is ideal) will facilitate good digestion and absorption. Of course this takes practice and discipline since few of us are accustomed to putting so much into chewing, but you get out what you put in. And in case you didn't already know it. Digestion starts in the mouth (not in your stomach)! It may seem strange to chew so much but you will feel more satisfied and be better nourished as a result. If you are going to eat a lot at breakfast—and you should—you will need to allot sufficient time to take it all in. Try it, you may be amazed at the beneficial results! The journey toward sustainable eating starts with a single meal or mouthful just as the journey of a thousand miles starts with a single foot step. Taking time to make and eat a nourishing breakfast is the first step toward vibrant health for you, your family, your community, and the planet.

Things to do while your cereal cooks

While sea vegetables are roasting and cereal or dinner grain are cooking or being rewarmed, and/or breakfast veggies are cooking, you could:

1. Cook a pot of soaked rice or millet for lunch and/or supper.

2. Cook a pot of soaked beans.

3. Assemble and simmer a simple vegetable soup or stew for lunch, supper, or both.

4. Assemble a soup or stew, refrigerate it, then simmer it just before lunch or supper.

5. Make a pressed or marinated salad to last several days or the week.

6. Sauté, stir fry, or quick-boil vegetables to last for two or three meals.

7. Wash and soak grain to last for several meals.

8. Soak beans for supper or the next day's soup, stew, or side dish.

9. Assemble a soup from assorted leftovers (to be heated for breakfast or lunch, or for later use).

10. Pack a lunch: Heat water for the thermos. Heat soup, stew, or gravy to put inside. Pack salad or greens; pickles; condiments; and bread or leftover noodles, rice, or polenta. Heat tea or grain coffee for the thermos.

11. Assemble and cook a simple fruit dessert or whip up an almost instant amasake pudding for an after lunch or after dinner treat. Or, if making homemade amasake, soak the grain (to cook later) or cook the grain then leave it to ferment all day.

Things to Cook into Breakfast Cereal for Added Variety

Soaking uncooked grains overnight, then cooking them in the soak water with the addition of sun dried sea salt makes them more digestible. Grains become creamier and richer tasting when soaked (omit soaking for Crock Pot/Overnight Cooking methods); in a pinch, rolled grains can be cooked without soaking. If you cook seaweed, nuts, or seeds in with your grain, avoid adding more of these at the table.

Liquids:
(Add to grain when soaking)
Leftover pasta cooking water or corn silk tea
Leftover pickle juice or brine + water
    (especially from umeboshi pickled vegetables)
Suribachi scrapings + water
    (from making roasted seed condiments)

Whole Grains:
(Soak for best results)
Black or brown sweet rice
Pearled or pot barley
Job's tears (Chinese hato mugi or pearl barley)
Millet
Wild rice or wehani rice
Sprouted wheat or rye berries
Whole oat groats
Short or medium grain brown rice
Kasha (roasted buckwheat groats)
Unroasted, white buckwheat groats
Quinoa
Amaranth
Ivory or brown teff
Cooked posole (whole dried corn)

Seeds/Nuts: *(Use infrequently and soak with grain)*
Dried or fresh-frozen, peeled chestnuts
Chopped almonds, walnuts, or hazelnuts
Dried lotus seeds
Raw or roasted sunflower or flax seeds
Roasted, ground sesame seeds
Raw or roasted peanuts or pine nuts
Poppy seeds

Leftovers:
(Add just before cooking)
Cooked plain pasta
Cooked rice, millet, barley or other grain
Cubed polenta or millet loaf
Cubed dry stale bread, tortillas or buns
Shredded tortillas
Corn off the cob
Cooked squash or sweet potato
Plain or lightly buttered popcorn
Rye crisp crackers or stale fat free crackers, broken up

Land Vegetables:
(Add just before cooking)
Dried sweet corn (needs pre-cooking)
Fresh sweet corn, uncooked
Cubed winter squash, uncooked
Cubed sweet potato, uncooked
Diced cauliflower, uncooked

Cracked or Rolled Grains:
(Soaking is best but optional)
Cracked wheat
Bulgar wheat
Rolled wheat or spelt flakes
Rolled triticale/flakes
Kamut flakes
Rolled oats/oatmeal
Steel cut oats
Rolled rye flakes
Rolled or pressed barley flakes
Rolled millet
Other grain flakes
Couscous (whole wheat variety)
Corn meal or polenta

Other *(Use in small volume):*
(Soak and cook with the grain)
Kelp or kombu sea vegetable strip
Dulse sea vegetable
Wild nori sea vegetable
Dried or fresh shiitake mushroom
Dried or fresh, cubed lotus root

Rules of Thumb Breakfast Planning & Preparation:

WHAT'S A SERVING?
For each person, pick one of the following:

	Examples:
1/2-1 c. dry whole grain	Millet, brown rice, buckwheat, or other
1-1 1/2 c. dry rolled, cracked or flaked grain	Rolled oats, barley flakes, or rolled spelt
1-2 1/2 c. leftover cooked dinner grain	Leftover rice, millet-rice, rice & rye berries, or other
1-2 c. cooked dinner grain + 1/4 c. soft shelled grain	Leftover rice + dry millet, amaranth, or kasha
1-1 1/2 c. cooked dinner grain + 1/2 c. rolled/cracked grain	Leftover millet + rolled oats or barley flakes
2-3 c. cooked soft porridge	Soft rice, millet, polenta, buckwheat or other
1 1/2-3+ c. cooked dinner grain	Rice, millet, kasha, mixed grains, or other grain

WATER TO GRAIN RATIO:

For this much grain:	Add this much water to soak/cook:
1 cup rolled, flaked or cracked grain	1 1/2-2 cups water
1 cup whole, uncracked grain	2 1/2-4 1/2 cups water (less for very thick cereal)
1 cup of leftover dinner grain	1-1 1/2 cups water

- **Note:** If too thick after cooking, stir in an extra 1/2-1 cup water to create desired consistency.

- You may use pasta water, corn silk or corn cob tea, or egg shell stock in place of water.

RATIO OF SEA SALT TO GRAIN:

For this much grain:	Add this much sun dried sea salt:
1 cup whole or cracked grain	1/8 tsp. sun dried sea salt or sea minerals

COOKING TIMES:

Rolled or Cracked Grain:	Pressure Cook	Simmer	Overnight
Rolled oats, barley flakes or other	Don't pressure cook	30-60 minutes	8-12 hours
Kasha or other cracked grain	Don't pressure cook	30-60 minutes	8-12 hours
Soft shelled grains:			
Millet	30-45 minutes	30-60 minutes	8-12 hours
Millet + amaranth or teff	30-45 minutes	30-60 minutes	8-12 hours
Millet or bulgur + quinoa	30-45 minutes	30-60 minutes	8-12 hours
Hard shelled grains:			
Black or brown sweet rice	1-2 hours	1-2 hours	8-12 hours
Pearl or pot barley	1 1/2-2 hours	Best overnight	8-12 hours
Whole oat groats	Don't pressure cook	Best overnight	8-12 hours
Mixed hard shelled grains	1-2 hours	1-2 hours	8-12 hours
Hard + soft shelled grain:			
Brown rice + amaranth or teff	1-2 hours	1-2 hours	8-12 hours
Brown/sweet rice + millet	1-2 hours	1-2 hours	8-12 hours

- When combining hard shelled, soft shelled, rolled, or cracked grains, cook for the time required for the longest cooking grain (for example, amaranth + sweet brown rice = cook as for rice.)

Cooking Tips for Breakfast Cereal

Sea minerals and sea salt in cooking:

Cooking sun dried sea salt with grains makes them more flavorful and aids digestion. True sun dried sea salt, often sold as sea minerals, contains over 83 different minerals which are essential for healthy metabolism and the production of digestive enzymes (including hydrocholoric acid). Refined sea salt and other table salts, on the other hand, have been stripped of these vital minerals; they are almost pure sodium chloride (usually 99.9%), and most have anti-caking agents, bleaches, dextrose and other additives.

Importance of rinsing whole grains:

All *whole* grains—except amaranth, teff, and buckwheat/kasha—need to be rinsed and scrubbed in a bowl, then drained in a fine strainer before soaking and/or cooking. This process removes the dust, dirt, and coarse bran bits from the outer hull. Do not rinse or drain grain after soaking. Instead, simply add the sea salt and cook the grain in its soak liquid. Rolled and cracked grains should not be rinsed.

Why we soak our grains:

Soaking both whole and rolled grains prior to cooking (4-10 hours or overnight) makes them more tender and digestible. It can increase the amount of available nutrients by up to 50% because soaking initiates the sprouting process and breaks down substances found in the grains which may interfere with proper digestion and assimilation. Soaked grain will still need the same amount of cooking: however, it will be smoother, creamier and more nutritious than unsoaked grain. If you forget to pre-soak your grain, just select a cereal recipe that uses cornmeal, polenta, bulgur, buckwheat/kasha, whole wheat couscous, or rolled oats. If you're in a hurry grains may be cooked without prior soaking, though even these are better soaked. If you don't soak every time, it's not a problem.

No-stir, no-stick cereal cooking technique:

We like to keep things simple. Thus, we never stir our cereal while it's cooking, even if we've added leftover rice or vegetables to the pot or used two different grains. There is no need to stir unless you are making a cereal from flour alone. In fact, stirring cereal before it is done is not only unnecessary, but it can cause the grain to stick to the bottom of the pot. Stirring during cooking separates the starch from the grain and prevents steam from rising up and cooking the grain evenly and usually leads to burned pots and gummy grain. If you don't stir your cereal until after it's done, you will be free to do other things while your cereal cooks. When done, remove cereal from the heat and leave it covered for about ten minutes to allow the steam to condense and lift any stuck grains from the bottom. Then uncover, stir and enjoy. It is simple and you won't have to clean a burned pot.

Tips for the Morning Rush

Cook cereal ahead

You can cook hot cereal to last for two mornings, then resteam leftovers using the uncovered-bowl-within-a pot method or the bowl-on-a-rack method. The same goes for dinner grains such as plain rice, millet, or a two-grain combination. (We always cook these to last for two or three meals at a time.) These reheating methods prevent the cereal or dinner grain from burning and keep the flavors intact and leave you free to do other things while your cereal is heating.

The overnight crock pot or stove top methods of simmering cereal are other options. These methods allow you to cook cereal while you sleep, making your morning go a little more smoothly. In the heat of summer, our cooling Vegetable Muesli, Counter Top Oats or Cold Cooked Oats are also handy options. However, even in the heat of the summer, we still enjoy the nourishing qualities of cooked cereals nine mornings out of ten—we simply let our hot rice or cereal cool off a bit before serving.

Make extra side dishes the night before

Cook extra vegetables or have extra pressed or marinated salads and even soups on hand so that you will have enough for breakfast and/or lunch.

Basic Porridge
Making Procedures

Cereals from Scratch

The following cereals serve two (or 2 mornings for 1 person); to serve three, increase any recipe by one-half; to serve four (or 2 morning for 2 people), simply double any of the following recipes. **Note:** *If you are very active or eating only two meals per day, you'll probably need the larger amount of grain listed and a very thick cereal. We figure 1 1/2-2 cups rolled grain or 3/4-1 cup whole grain per person in this case.*

Basic Procedure,
Simmered Rolled or Mixed Grain
Porridge (Year Round)***

Prep: 5-10 minutes
Cooking: 30-35 minutes
Soaking: Preferably overnight

Serving size: 1 1/2-2 1/2 cups per person
Serves: 2 (or 2 meals for 1)

This is a quick, nourishing breakfast. It is equally tasty made from either a single grain or a combination of grains. You can mix and match. The possibilities, as you will soon see, are endless.

Pick one of the following recipes:

Rolled Grains Only:
2-3 cups rolled grains
(rolled oats, spelt, barley or kamut, flakes, etc.)
3 1/2 -5 cups water, pasta water, or corn tea
~1/4-1/2 tsp. sea salt
Additional water as needed after cooking

Rolled & Soft Shelled Grains:
1 1/2-2 cup rolled grain
1/2 cup soft shelled grain
(millet, amaranth, teff, quinoa, buckwheat, etc.)

3 1/2-4 cups water, pasta water or shell stock
~1/4 tsp. sea salt
Additional water as needed after cooking

1. Don't rinse rolled grains, cracked grains, amaranth, or teff. Rinse, scrub and drain millet or quinoa. Soak grains in the appropriate volume of water, at room temperature overnight. (Cover and soak the grain pot in the refrigerator in hot weather.) If you forget to soak, you can still make the cereal, it just won't be as creamy.

   Note: Don't throw off the soak water; cook the grain in this liquid. (You can also add roasted flour to this recipe. Refer to variations below for specifics. If roasted flour is used, add it to the pot just before cooking.)

2. Add sea salt just before cooking. Cover the pot and bring to a boil.

   If using a gas stove: Slip a heat deflector under pot before turning the heat to low. Simmer, covered, for 30-45 minutes, without stirring.

   If using an electric stove: Preheat the deflector on a separate burner on medium heat, then transfer the boiling pot to the deflector and reduce heat to a low setting. (Stoves vary greatly; you'll have to experiment to get the right setting.) Cook 30-45 minutes.

3. Turn off the heat. Let the pot sit undisturbed on top of the stove for 10 minutes (or longer if you're not yet ready to eat). The steam will lift any stuck cereal off the bottom of the pot. Stir vigorously, adding water a little at a time if cereal is too thick. If too thin, simmer and stir for several minutes, with the lid off, until it reaches the desired consistency.

Serving suggestions: Ladle into serving bowls, top with savory condiments and serve with side dishes.

Storage: Store leftovers in a bowl at room temperature, covered with a bamboo sushi mat. Re-heat by steaming in a bowl. Leftovers are handy to have for breakfast the next day ,reheated by themselves or combined with other leftover grains. (For other leftover ideas, see Uses for Leftover Grains.) ❏

Variations:

For the following variations, use the basic procedure and proportions of liquid and sea salt as in Simmered Rolled or Mixed Grain Porridge above. All cereals are suitable for year round use unless otherwise noted. Each recipe yields two servings.

Favorite Rolled Grain Cereals:***

- **Barley & Oatmeal:** 1-1 1/2 cups rolled barley + 1-1 1/2 cups rolled oats.

- **Three Rolled Grains:** 2/3-1 cup each—rolled spelt, rolled barley, and rolled oats.

- **Fresh Corn & Oatmeal (Late Summer & Fall):** When in season, add 1 cup corn off the cob before cooking your soaked oats.

- **Dried Sweet Corn & Oatmeal (Winter, Spring):** Add 1/4 cup of dried (dehydrated) sweet corn prior to soaking. (Dry summer sweet corn yourself or mail order it.)

- **Cornmeal & Oatmeal:** 1-1 1/2-2 cups rolled oats + 1 cup cornmeal. Or, 3 cups rolled oats + 1/2 cup cornmeal.

- **Bulgur & Oatmeal:** 1 cup bulgur wheat + 1-2 cups rolled oats.

Rolled & Soft Shelled Grain Cereals:***

- **Buttery Millet & Oatmeal:** 1-2 cups rolled oats + 1/2 cup rinsed millet.

- **Creamy Kasha & Oatmeal:** 1-2 cups rolled oats + 1/2 cup roasted buckwheat/kasha.

- **White Buckwheat & Oatmeal:** 1-1/2 cups rolled oats + 1/2 cup white buckwheat.

- **Earthy Ethiopian Teff-n-Oats:** 1-2 cups rolled oats + 1/2 cup ivory or brown teff.

- **Buttery Amaranth & Oatmeal (Fall & Winter):** 1 1/2 -2 cups rolled oats + 1/2 cup amaranth.

- **Polenta & Oatmeal:** 1-1 1/4 cups rolled oats + 1/2-3/4 cup dry polenta or cornmeal.

Other Rolled Grain Favorites:***

- **Roasty-Toasty Oats:** Use 1 1/2-2 cups rolled oats (or part rolled barley) + 1/2 cup dry roasted flour (whole red wheat, white wheat, spelt or barley flour, cornmeal, kamut or other).

Dry roasted flour adds a rich, nutty taste to cereal. We usually use the flour left over from flouring (rather than oiling) baking sheets for homemade pizza, bread sticks, or dinner rolls. This flour is much too good to throw out and adds the most marvelous flavor to oatmeal.

This cereal is especially tasty with crumbled, roasted sea vegetables stirred in and a roasted, seasoned seed or nut condiment sprinkled on top along with a dash of fresh or dried chives or scallions, and a side of cooked leafy greens or mixed vegetables.

- **Morning Mochi & Oatmeal (Fall & Winter):** 1-2 cups rolled oats + ~2 cups of thawed, uncooked, plain mochi, cut into 1/2-1-inch cubes.

Mochi is a traditional Japanese product made from sweet rice which has been cooked, pounded and dried. It can be found in the refrigerator or freezer section of most health food stores. Thawed, cut and added to hot cereal just before cooking, it adds a sticky texture and rich taste. ❏

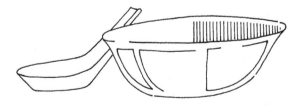

Breakfast Cereal Bowl
(You'll need a 24 oz. bowl for each person for a substantial enough breakfast)

Basic Procedure,
Simmered Soft Shelled Grain Porridge (Year Round)***

Prep: 10 minutes
Soaking: preferably overnight
Cooking: 30 minutes to simmer
Serves: 2 (or 2 meals for 1)
Serving size: 1 1/2-2 1/2 cups per person

We usually use millet, white buckwheat, or roasted buckwheat/kasha as the base. Tiny seed grains such as teff, amaranth, and quinoa tend to be harder to digest (due in part to their higher fat content and their sticky and gelatinous texture). It is better not to cook them solo; we combine them with a much larger volume of a mild flavored, low-fat, economical grain such as millet, buckwheat, oats, or short grain brown rice.

Basic Ingredients:

1-1 1/2 cups soft shelled grain
   (e.g., millet, kasha (roasted buckwheat), white buckwheat, a combination of two of these, or one of these grains mixed with a seed grain such as teff, quinoa or amaranth)
3-4 1/2 cups water or pasta water
1/8-1/4 tsp. sea salt
Additional water as needed after cooking

1. Place whole grains (except for buckwheat, kasha, teff or amaranth) in a bowl or cooking pot. Add water; scrub with your hands in a back and forth motion, then pour through a fine mesh strainer to rinse. Repeat several times until the water is mostly clear. Rinse quinoa in a fine mesh strainer. Add teff or amaranth to the pot after washing millet. Do not rinse kasha or buckwheat.

2. In a 2-4 quart cooking pot, soak grains in appropriate volume of water on the counter covered with a bamboo mat. (In hot weather, cover and soak in the refrigerator.) Don't throw off soak water, you will cook the grain in it.

3. Add sea salt just before cooking. Cover pot and bring to boil.

   If using a gas stove: Slip a heat deflector under the pot before turning to low. Simmer, covered, on low 30-35 minutes without stirring.

If using an electric stove: Preheat the deflector on a separate burner over medium heat, then transfer the boiling pot to the deflector and reduce heat to a low setting. (Because stove temperatures vary, you may have to experiment to get the right setting.) Do not stir.

4. Turn off heat and allow cereal to sit undisturbed on top of the stove for 10 minutes (or longer if you're not ready to eat yet). Letting it sit allows the steam to lift any stuck cereal off the bottom of the pot. When ready, stir vigorously with a rice paddle. Add a small amount of water, a little at a time, if cereal is too thick. If too thin, stir and simmer with the lid off for several minutes to thicken.❏

Variations:

For the following variations, use the basic procedure and proportions of liquid and sea salt as above. Or, cook overnight in a crockpot on low.) All are suitable for year round use unless otherwise noted. Each recipe yields cereal for two.

Favorite Soft Shelled Cereals with Millet ***

- **Morning Millet & Kelp:** 1-1 1/2 cups millet + a 4" piece kelp or kombu.

- **Millet & Polenta Porridge:** Millet and polenta.

- **Millet & Sweet Corn Cereal:** Add 1 ear fresh, in season sweet corn. Cut off the cob (~1 cup) before cooking. For added flavor, cook the fresh, bare corn cobs in with the cereal, then remove cobs before stirring and serving.

- **Morning Millet & Squash Porridge:** Add 1-1 1/2 cups diced winter squash or sweet potato before cooking. (We leave the skin on squash; peel sweet potato if you like.)

- **Millet & Amaranth Porridge:** Use 3/4-1 cup millet + 1/4 cup amaranth.

- **Morning Millet & Mochi Cereal (Fall & Winter):** 1/2-3/4 cup millet + 2 cups cubed, thawed, uncut, uncooked, plain mochi added before cooking. ❏

Easy Overnight Porridge (Stove-top or Crock Pot; Any Season)***

This method is mainly used in the Fall, Winter, and Spring. Using a crock pot, however, will not create extra heat in the kitchen and is thus convenient any time of year. Do not worry, the low temperature will not over-cook your cereal.

Prep: 5-10 minutes
Soaking: unnecessary
Cooking: 8 hours or overnight

Serving size: 1 1/2-2 1/2 cups per person
Serves: 2 (or 2 mornings for 1)

If your mornings are rushed or making time for breakfast is new to you, you can begin cooking your cereal *before* going to bed. Porridge can cook all night, unattended, on top of the stove or in a slow cooker. When you wake up, you will have a creamy, smooth, piping hot porridge that's ready to eat. This method is especially well suited for brown rice or whole oats, though millet is equally lovely cooked this way. Try a single grain or a two grain combination.

Basic Ingredients:

1-1 1/2 cups whole grain
   (*Short or medium grain brown rice, sweet brown rice, whole oats, pearl barley, kasha, millet, two of these or any one of these combined with a smaller volume of amaranth, teff, quinoa or polenta*)

3-5 cups water, corn cob or corn silk tea, or pasta water (less in a crock pot; more for stove top)

1/8-tsp. + a pinch sun dried sea salt

Optional, 4-6" piece kelp or kombu

Additional water as needed after cooking

1. Rinse and scrub any whole grains (except buckwheat, amaranth, or teff) and pour through a fine mesh strainer to drain. Repeat 2-3 times until rinse water is relatively clear.

2. Combine grain, cooking water, and salt in a heavy 2-4 quart pot with a tight fitting lid or a crock pot. If desired, add sea vegetable for extra flavor and tenderization.

3. **Stove Top Method (Fall, Winter, Spring):** Cover, bring to boil over medium-low heat, without stirring. Once cereal is boiling, slip two heat deflectors underneath, reduce heat to the lowest setting and simmer, covered, all night. If an electric stove is used, pre-heat the heat deflectors over medium-high heat on one burner while the pot comes to boil on another. Then transfer the pot to the pre-heated burner with the deflectors before reducing heat.

   Crock Pot Method (Any Season): Cover. Set on low and cook all night. Or cook for one hour on high, then turn to low.

For either method:

4. In the morning, before serving, stir vigorously. Add warm water a little at a time if cereal is too thick. Ladle into serving bowls and top with condiments.

Storage: Store leftovers in a glass or stainless steel bowl covered with a bamboo sushi mat. Reheat using the uncovered-bowl-within-a pot method or by steaming in a bowl on a rack, or combine leftovers with a soft shelled grain and cook 30 minutes. ❏

Porridge Under Pressure***

Prep: 5 minutes
Soaking: 6-12 hours or overnight
Cooking: 1/2-1 1/2 hours

Serves: 2 (or 2 mornings for 1)
Serving size: 1 1/2-2 1/2 cups per person

This method is used for hard shelled grains to render them soft and creamy. It is particularly good for barley, brown rice, sweet brown rice, Thai black sweet rice, or any of these combined with soft shelled grains like millet, amaranth, teff or quinoa. We also use this technique for millet combined with another soft shelled grain.

Caution: Do not use this method with rolled, flaked or cracked grains; they can block the pressure valve. Even when using amaranth, teff, or polenta, it is wise to combine them with a much larger volume of brown rice, sweet brown rice or millet to avoid blocking the pressure valves and to make a tastier and more digestible cereal.

1-1 1/2 cups hard or soft shelled grain, or a combination of two grains
(Short or medium grain brown rice, sweet brown rice, millet, etc.; two of these together; or any of these with amaranth, teff, quinoa, or polenta)

3-4 cups water, pasta water, or corn silk tea or corn cob tea

Optional, 4-6" piece kelp or kombu

Optional, 1/2-1 cup cubed winter squash, sweet potato, yam, corn off the cob
and/or 2-4 Tbsp. raw seeds or chopped nuts

1/8 tsp. + 1 pinch sea salt

1. Wash and scrub whole grain in a bowl or pot and pour through a fine strainer to drain. (Be sure to scrub thoroughly to soften the bran layer.) Repeat several times until rinse water is mostly clear.

2. In a pressure cooker, combine the grain and cooking liquid. Add a small piece of kelp or kombu sea vegetable if desired (it makes the cereal more creamy). If using nuts or seeds, add them now. Cover with a bamboo sushi mat and soak overnight on top of the counter. (Cover and refrigerate the pot in hot weather.)

3. Just before cooking, add sea salt. Add vegetables, if using.

   If pressure cooking: Seal the pot and bring it up to pressure over medium heat. Let it hiss for a few minutes; then reduce heat to low or medium-low and cook for the recommended time below.

   If boiling: Bring to a boil and slip a heat deflector under the pot before reducing heat to low.

   If using an electric stove: Bring cereal to a boil. Preheat heat deflector on a separate burner; meanwhile, over medium heat, transfer the boiling pot to the deflector before reducing the heat to low. (Stove temperatures vary so you will have to experiment to get the right setting.)

   For soft shelled grains: Millet; millet + quinoa, teff, amaranth, or polenta, cook 1/2 hour.

   For hard shelled grains: sweet or regular brown rice; barley; brown rice + cornmeal, or polenta or amaranth; brown rice + sweet corn, nuts, seeds, or chestnuts, cook 1-1 1/2 hours.

4. Remove pot from burner and allow it to sit for 10-15 minutes (this allows pressure to come down naturally and/or cereal to loosen from the bottom of the pot). Remove lid and stir vigorously. Add a bit more water if cereal is too thick. If too thin, stir briefly, uncovered, over medium heat.

Serving suggestions: Ladle out servings and top with the condiments and side dishes.

Storage: Store leftovers in a glass or stainless steel bowl covered with a bamboo sushi mat. Reheat using the uncovered-bowl-within-a pot method or by steaming in a bowl-on-a-rack, or combine leftovers with a soft shelled grain and cook 30 minutes. ❏

Favorite Brown Rice Cereals:

Note: Use short or medium grain brown rice when rice is called for. Also note: Simmer, pressure cook, or cook overnight. Refer to previous pages for procedure.

- **Rice & Buckwheat Porridge:** Use half of each.

- **Rice & Teff Porridge:** Use 3 parts brown rice to 1 part brown or ivory teff.

- **Rice & Hato Mugi Porridge:** Use 3 parts brown rice to 1 part hato mugi barley.

- **Brown Rice & Sweet Rice Porridge:** Use half of each.

- **Sweet Rice & Millet Porridge:** Use half of each.

- **Rice & Millet Porridge:** Use half of each.

- **Rice & Sweet Corn Cereal (Summer & Fall):** Add 1/3 cup dried sweet corn to 1-1 1/2 cups short or medium grain brown rice or rice with millet.

- **Sweet Rice & Squash Cereal (Fall, Winter, Early Spring):** Add 1 cup diced winter squash to rice or rice with sweet rice or millet.

- **Posole & Rice Porridge:** Use all rice or half rice, half millet. Add 1/4-1/3 cup cooked dried corn (posole) when soaking cereal.

- **Creamy Barley Congee (Year Round):** 1-1 1/4 cup pearled barley + 4" piece kelp or kombu sea vegetable (to tenderize). Optional, 1-2 small shiitake mushrooms.

Note: When cooked overnight with kelp or kombu sea vegetable, whole barley becomes soft and creamy. Without kelp or kombu, whole barley usually remains chunky, chewy, and very difficult to digest. Use the slightly polished "pearled" barley found in supermarkets and health food stores rather than the harder and more difficult to digest pot barley.

Whole Oat Porridge
(Late Fall through Winter)

•• **Cook as per Easy Overnight Porridge.** Though familiar with quick cooking rolled or instant oats, most Americans are unaccustomed to cooking with whole oats, or oat "groats" as they are often called. However, whole oat groats, when properly cooked, have a far richer, creamier, and sweeter taste than rolled varieties—and without added milk, cream, or butter! They are available in most health food stores, co-ops and some specialty bulk foods stores. Try the groats alone or in combination with other whole grains. Do not pressure cook them unless you use the covered-bowl-within-a-pot method, as they can block pressure cooker valves. Or, use an overnight cooking method instead; this is simple, works best, and produces the most creamy cereal.

Favorite Whole Oat Porridges
(Fall & Winter)

- **Oat Groat Porridge:** 1-1 1/4 cups whole oat groats.

- **Whole Oat & Millet Porridge:** Use half millet, half whole oats.

- **Whole Oat & Rice Porridge:** Use half short or medium grain brown rice, half whole oats.

- **Whole Oat & Buckwheat Porridge:** Use half kasha or white buckwheat, half whole oats.

- **Whole Oat & Sweet Rice Porridge:** Use sweet brown or black rice, half whole oats.

- **Whole Oat & Lotus Seed Porridge:** Add 1/4 cup lotus seeds before cooking overnight or when soaking whole oats.

- **Whole Oat & Chestnut Porridge:** Add 1/4 cup dried or fresh-frozen, steam-peeled chestnuts to oats before cooking overnight.

•Nutty Congee
(Mostly Fall, Winter & Spring)

Congee is a soft whole grain porridge served throughout Asia. In Asia, it is cooked much thinner than our usual thick porridge, in which case it must be served with a more substantial grain dish such as steamed buns or flat breads if one is to survive until the next meal! Congee can be made from almost any whole grain. A small volume of nuts can be added from time to time, for a richer taste. Different grain combinations and different nuts or seeds will produce different tastes and medicinal effects.

Favorite Nutty Congee Combinations:

(Pressure cook 1 hour or cook overnight if brown rice or sweet brown or black rice are used.)

- **Basic Nutty Congee:** 1-1 1/2 cups whole grain (one or two grains) + 2-6 Tbsp. raw peanuts, pine nuts, chopped walnuts or hazelnuts or sunflower or flax seeds or 1/4 cup dried or fresh-frozen steam-peeled, chestnuts.

- **Brown Rice Congee with nuts or seeds:** Use short or medium grain brown rice.

- **Short Grain Brown Rice Congee with nuts or seeds:**

- **Sweet Rice & Millet Congee + nuts or seeds:**

- **Millet Congee with nuts or seeds:** Pressure cook 30 minutes or cook overnight.

- **Chestnut Congee:** Dried or fresh-frozen chestnuts + one of the above grain combinations.

- **Walnutty Congee:** One of the above grain combinations + chopped walnuts.

- **Lotus Seed Congee:** One of the above grain combinations + lotus seeds.

- **Peanutty Congee:** One of the above grain combinations + peanuts.

- **Pine Nut Congee:** One of the above grain combinations with raw pine nuts.

- **Sunflower Seed Congee:** Add sunflower seeds to one of the above grain combinations.

Basic Procedure, Counter Top Oats; Cold-Cooked Oats (Warm weather)*** & Overnight Thermos Cereal (Year round for travel & busy times)•••

Prep: 10 minutes
Cooking: overnight (on the counter!)
Serves: 1
Serving size: 1 1/2-2 cups per person

•• **Double this recipe to serve 2.**

Unlike most cereals, this one is cooked right on the counter, in a covered bowl or inside a wide-mouth thermos. In the morning stir and serve this cooling and refreshing cereal at room temperature, topped with savory condiments and vegetable side dishes.

Note: The thermos method is especially handy when camping, backpacking, or traveling. You can even make it in a hotel room if you have a small hot pot to heat the water.

Per person, figure:

1-1/2 cup flaked/rolled grain (e.g., rolled oats), or cracked or powdered grain

1 3/4-2 cups boiling water

1/8 tsp. + 1 pinch sun dried sea salt

1/4-1/3 cup additional boiling or lukewarm water in the morning if cereal is too thick

1. **Thermos method:** Place rolled or cracked grain in a large wide-mouth thermos.

   Counter-top method: Place rolled grain in a 24-32-ounce heat proof pyrex or stainless steel bowl.

For either method:

2. Boil water with sea salt. Stir briefly to dissolve the sea salt then immediately pour over grain. Stir briefly and cover with a glass, stoneware, or china plate, saucer, or thermos lid. Allow cereal to sit overnight on a counter or tabletop.

3. In the morning, stir vigorously with a wooden spoon to create a sticky consistency. If desired, add an additional 1/4-1/2 cup water and stir again. Ladle into a large serving bowl. ❏

Basic Procedure, Vegetable-Muesli (Summer, Early Fall) • • •

Prep: 10-15 minutes
Soaking: overnight
Cooking: none

Serves: 2
Serving size: 1 1/2- 2 cups per person

*** Reduce recipe by 1/2 to serve just 1 person.**

Muesli, a popular Swiss cereal, is made from rolled grains which are soaked overnight in water, milk, or yogurt. This soothing cereal is particularly good for clearing excess Heat and stimulating the appetite during the hottest days of summer. (It's handy for travel or camping too!) Though quite tasty, this concoction is far too cooling for daily use or for cool to cold weather when we need to be cautious of foods and preparations which can harm the digestive fire.

Unlike most mueslis—which are loaded with fruit, nuts, seeds, sweeteners, and other hard to digest ingredients—ours relies on the subtle sweet taste of carrots and sweet corn. In very hot weather, we may infrequently add a small amount of grated apple or pear or leftover fruit compote, though it's best to leave the fruit out of your cereal except for very infrequent use. Its Damp and cloying nature can, when eaten in the midst of a meal or to excess, overwhelm the digestive organs and prevent proper digestion and assimilation (the transformation of food and Fluids into Qi or vital energy).

2-3 cups rolled oats (or part rolled kamut, spelt, or barley flakes)

2-3 cups rice, almond- or sunflower- milk, or plain unsweetened soy milk or yogurt,
or goat milk or goat yogurt
or half water and half milk or yogurt

1/4 tsp. sun dried sea salt ❏

Morning mix-ins (divide between 2 people):

Sweet corn shaved from 1 corn cob (~ 1 cup) *and/or* 1 fresh apple or pear, grated finely

1-2 carrots (grated very finely on the second to smallest holes of your grater)

1 packed cup red leaf, romaine, or Mesclun mix, minced finely, leaves and stems
or 1 1/2 cup pressed or marinated salad or leftover steamed, boiled or sautéed greens *(served on the side)*

Optional toppings:

+/-1-3 Tbsp. minced parsley, chives, scallions, or edible flowers

Optional 2-3 Tbsp. raw or dry roasted sunflower, sesame, or pumpkin seeds or chopped nuts

Optional 1/2-1 tsp. umeboshi or apriboshi pickled plum paste *or* 2 Tbsp. pickles

Optional 1/3 cup oven roasted dulse, crumbled *or* 2-6 tsp. dulse or other sea veggie flakes

1. In a 2-quart glass, pyrex, or pottery mixing bowl, combine rolled oats (or other rolled grain) with salt, and milk or yogurt or diluted yogurt and water. Stir well, cover with a dinner plate and refrigerate overnight. (Store in a cooler, ice chest, or cool place when traveling.)

2. In the morning, stir well and add 1/2-1 cup warm water if too thick. Grate apple or pear or cut corn off the cob. Grate carrot very finely to make it juicy. Divide these between two large (32 oz.) cereal bowls. Add minced salad greens to serving bowls or serve leftover cooked, pressed, or marinated vegetables over or alongside the cereal (in small custard cups).

3. Spoon cereal over individual bowls of raw vegetables, or vegetables combined with grated fruit. Sprinkle with scallions, parsley, chives, or fresh dill if desired. Stick crumbled pieces of dulse into cereal if desired or sprinkle on sea vegetable flakes at the table. Serve. Stir as you like, and enjoy! If desired, sprinkle on a seasoned seed or nut condiment or plain, dry roasted seeds or chopped nuts at the table for a buttery and rich taste. If serving pressed or marinated salad or cooked greens, serve on the side or spoon on top of cereal. ❏

Cereals from Leftovers

Basic Procedure, Leftover Dinner Grain Porridge (Year Round) ***

Prep: 5 minutes
Soaking: see notes below
Cooking: simmer 30 minutes or pressure cook 15 minutes

Serves: 2
Serving Size: ~ 2-2 1/2 cups per person

Don't discard last night's rice or millet, the rice you cooked two days ago, or any other leftover grain; it's perfect for breakfast. Simmered or pressure cooked with additional water, it will become soft and creamy. Plan for leftovers whenever you cook grains so you can pull together interesting, varied, and quick morning meals. Leftover dinner grain can be cooked alone or combined with rolled or whole grains to make new morning meals.

1. Place leftover grain in a saucepan with a measured amount of liquid. Do not stir or break up the grain or it will gum up, stick, and burn! Just cover it and bring it to boil over medium heat. (Use a large enough pot—a 2-4 quart pot to serve 2—and it will not boil over.)

2. **With a gas stove:** Slip a heat deflector under the pot, then reduce heat to low or medium-low and simmer, covered, for 20-30 minutes without stirring, or pressure cook 15 minutes.

   With an electric stove: Bring to boil as above. Heat a flame deflector on a separate burner then transfer the boiling pot to the deflector. Reduce heat to low or medium-low and simmer 20 minutes or pressure cook 15 minutes. Do not stir cereal as it comes to boil or cooks!

3. When cooking time has elapsed, turn off heat and allow cereal to sit undisturbed for 10 minutes. Stir vigorously with a wooden spoon or use a potato masher if a creamier texture is desired. If too thick, add warm water, a little at a time, and stir to create desired consistency.

Serving suggestions: Ladle into serving bowls and top with condiments and side dishes.

Leftover tips: Reheat leftovers at any other meal using the uncovered-bowl-within-a-pot method or by steaming-in-a-bowl-on-a-rack or use to make a creamy soup, sauce, salad dressing, or gravy.

Basic Ratio:

3-4 cups leftover dinner grain, brown rice or other (see ideas below••)

~2 1/2-4 cups water or pasta water

Additional water as needed after cooking

Examples of some dinner grains one might use:

- Leftover brown rice that was cooked with nuts, seeds, azuki beans, or chestnuts.

- Leftover brown rice that was cooked with millet, barley, amaranth, or teff.

- Leftover brown rice that was cooked with sweet rice, squash, green peas, or corn.

- Leftover millet that was cooked with amaranth, teff, barley, or sweet corn.

Variation:

- Add 1/2-1 cup diced leftover cooked winter squash or sweet potato to the cereal pot before cooking. Place it on top of the leftover rice but do not stir it in until after cooking. Or, add 1 cup of corn off the cob in the same fashion. ❑

Basic Procedure, Cereal from Leftover & New Grain (All Seasons) ***

Prep: 5 minutes
Serves: 2
Soaking: see notes below

Serving Size: ~ 1 1/2-2 1/2 cups per person
Cooking: simmer 30 minutes or pressure cook 15

Here's a great way to extend leftovers and add variety to your diet. Every few days you can make breakfast cereal by combining leftover dinner with a new (uncooked) rolled, cracked, or soft shelled grain. Cooked together, the resulting porridge is incredibly rich, creamy, tasty, smooth, and easy to digest. Even leftover millet, polenta, noodles, or dried out bread or tortillas can be added to the pot. You won't believe how good it is until you try it.

1. Combine rolled, flaked, cracked, or rinsed whole grain in a cooking pot with the recommended amount of liquid. Soak, uncovered, at room temperature, overnight if possible. (Cover and soak in the refrigerator in hot weather.)

2. In the morning spoon leftover cooked dinner grain, noodles, polenta, millet, or cubed bread on top of the soaked or unsoaked grain. Add sea salt. Do not break up the grain or stir it; simply cover the pot and bring it to boil over medium heat. (Use a large enough pot so the cereal won't boil over. We use a 2-4 quart pot.)

   If using a gas stove: Slip a heat deflector under the pot, reduce heat to low or medium-low and simmer, covered, without stirring, for 25-35 minutes.

   If using an electric stove: Preheat the heat deflector on one burner while the pot comes to a full boil on another burner. Transfer the boiling pot to the hot deflector, reduce the heat to low (or #3 setting) and cook as above without stirring. (Stirring the cereal as it cooks or before it is done will make it stick and burn!)

3. Turn off heat. If possible, let the cereal sit for at least 10 minutes (or up to 40 minutes if you are not ready to eat yet). This will loosen any stuck cereal from the bottom of the pot.) Stir vigorously with a rice paddle or a potato masher if a smoother texture is desired. If too thick, stir in a small amount of warm water.

Serving suggestions: Ladle into serving bowls; top with savory condiments and side dishes.

Leftover tips: Reheat leftovers at another meal, as per uncovered-bowl-within-a-pot method or by steaming in a bowl on a rack. Or use leftovers to thicken a soup, sauce, or pudding.

Variation:

- **Overnight Cereal From Leftovers:** Place uncooked rolled or soft shelled grain in a 2-3 quart saucepan (to serve 2). Add water or pasta water, salt, and leftover dinner grain. Cover pot, turn to low heat and bring to very low boil. Slip two heat deflectors the under pot, reduce heat to low, and cook all night. In the morning, stir well adding a bit more water if needed. Or, layer ingredients in a crock pot with uncooked grain on the bottom. Cook all night on low.

Basic Ratio:

1 1/2-2 1/2 cups leftover cooked grain
  (e.g., short or medium grain brown rice, sweet brown rice, millet, buckwheat, or a mixed grain combination)

1 cup (uncooked) rolled, flaked or cracked grain *or* 1/2 cup uncooked millet or buckwheat
  (e.g., rolled oats, kamut or spelt flakes, polenta, bulgar, or see soft shelled grains above)

1/8 tsp. sea salt

4-4 1/2 cups water, or pasta cooking water or corn silk tea or corn cob tea

Additional water if needed before serving

Note: If millet is added to your leftover grain, you can pressure cook rather than boil the cereal if desired. Pressure cook 15-20 minutes. ❏

Favorite Cereals from Leftovers (Any Season)***

- **Cream of Buckwheat & Last Night's Rice:** 1/2 cup (dry) kasha (roasted buckwheat) + 1 1/2-3 cups leftover cooked rice or a mixed whole grain combination.

- **Cream of Millet & Last Night's Rice:** 1/2 cup (dry) millet + 1 1/2-3 cups leftover cooked rice, cubed millet loaf, polenta, or mixed whole grain combination.

- **Noodle & Oatmeal:** 1 cup rolled oats (or other) + 2-3 cups leftover cooked noodles.

- **Polenta & Oatmeal: (Any Season)*** 1 1/2 cups rolled oats (or rolled spelt or barley flakes) + 2 cups cubed whole grain bread, millet loaf, or polenta.

- **Cornbread Porridge with Last Night's Rice:** 1 1/2-2 cups leftover dinner grain + 2 cups (leftover) cubed millet loaf, polenta, or corn bread.

Sunday's cornbread may be dry by Thursday, but it won't taste dry cooked into your morning cereal. In fact, it'll add a vibrant color and a sweet taste to any morning meal. Last night's polenta isn't bad cooked into cereal either; in fact, it's another morning favorite in our house.

- **Bread Cube Porridge:** 1 cup rolled oats + 2-2 1/2 packed cups cubed bread or 1-1 1/2 cups rolled oats + 1-2 packed cups cubed bread.

Don't throw out that dried old hunk, slice, or roll of bread. If it's too hard to cut, simply wrap it in a cotton-linen kitchen towel and steam it briefly to soften, then you can cut it. It'll be superb, slightly sweet, creamy, and very satisfying cooked in with oatmeal. You can use steamed buns, tortillas, pita, dinner rolls, French bread or other bread—even dried out bagels will work. Use any kind of bread from basic spelt or wheat to buckwheat, amaranth, soy, barley or the more exotic breads such as the chestnut bread listed in the bread chapter.

- **Noodle & Bread Cube Porridge with last night's rice:** 1-1/2 cups leftover rice (or rice that was cooked with a second grain, nut, bean or vegetable) + 1-1 1/4 cup leftover pasta + 1-2 cups cubed bread, stale or fresh (any variety made from whole grains).

You've heard of bread pudding and noodle pudding, but how about noodle and bread porridge? Leave no grains unused if at all possible (unless they've gone sour), that's our motto. The result: delectable cereals with contrasting tastes, textures and flavors. Whether you pick buckwheat, corn, spelt, or wheat noodles, or rye, wheat, corn, barley, or spelt bread, you'll enjoy this cereal.

- **Blue Chip or Cracker Special:** 1 cup rolled oats or 1/2 cup dry millet + 3 cups broken crackers or chips, or shredded or cut corn tortillas.

Corn chips shouldn't be a staple food: they're far too high in fat and hard to digest. Even the fat-free ones can burden your digestive system because of their crunchy, hard and dry texture. But, if you've got some left from a party or potluck, by all means use them in your morning porridge. Even tortillas that have become too dry to serve for supper will soften up nicely when cooked into leftover rice or with uncooked rolled oats. You can use these in place of the bread or leftover pasta above.

- **Leftover Squash, Sweet Potato, or Corn & Oatmeal:** 2-2 1/2 cups rolled oats + 1 cup leftover cooked, diced squash or sweet potato, or corn cut off the cob.

Note: A small volume, perhaps 1/3-1/2 cup of juice leftover from pickling vegetables in umeboshi or apriboshi vinegar, or from simmering the pits from these pickled plums or apricots, may be cooked in with each pot of cereal in place of sea minerals or sea salt, for a rich and buttery taste. ❑

How to make over 30 different cereals from millet:

We never tire of millet; in fact, we use millet almost as much as rice in our house. You could use millet every morning for over a month and come up with a different cereal each and every day! Here's how: (The same range of possibilities apply to buckwheat, oats, or brown rice).

- Millet & Amaranth Cereal
- Millet & Rolled Barley Porridge
- Millet & Cauliflower Cereal
- Millet & Cornmeal Porridge
- Millet & Lotus Seed Cereal
- Millet & Ivory Teff Cereal
- Millet & Brown Teff Porridge
- Millet & Orzo Mush
- Millet with Wild Rice Porridge
- Millet, Lotus Seeds & Squash Porridge
- Millet & Sweet Rice Cereal
- Millet & Black Sweet Rice Porridge
- Millet & Walnut Porridge (or filberts)
- Millet & poppy seeds
- Millet & sweet potato
- Millet & winter squash
- Millet & winter squash or sweet potato & peanut butter
- Millet Mush with Leftover Squash & Walnuts
- Millet & Bulgur Mush
- Millet & Hato Mugi Mush (Job's Tears/Chinese Pearl Barley)
- Millet & (Leftover) Millet Loaf Cereal
- Millet & Dried or Fresh Corn Cereal
- Millet & Chestnut Porridge
- Millet & Oat Groat Porridge
- Millet & Rice Porridge
- Millet & Cracked Rye Cereal

- Millet & Leftover Rice Porridge
- Millet & Leftover Noodle Porridge (+/-rolled oats)
- Millet & Leftover Polenta Porridge
- Millet & Leftover Rice w/seeds or nuts
- Millet & suribachi scrapings (from making seed or nut condiment)
- Millet & Pasta Water Porridge
- Millet Mush with leftover barley-rice
- Millet Mush with leftover rice & amaranth
- Millet Mush with leftover rice & polenta
- Millet Mush with any leftover dinner grain
- Millet & (Rolled) Spelt or kamut
- Millet & (Leftover) Bread Cube Mush
- Millet & rolled oats + cubed bread
- Millet Mush with Rye Crackers
- Millet & Popcorn Porridge

How to make over 30 different oatmeals

If you buy rolled oats in 50 pound bags as we have on several occasions, you get very creative. Here's an example of just some of the many different ways to have your oats and plenty of variety too!

These cereals rely on rolled oats (also called oatmeal): • •(see notes below)

- Millet & Oatmeal
- Roasted Buckwheat (kasha) & Oatmeal
- White Buckwheat & Oatmeal
- Barley & Oat (flake) Porridge
- Oats & Amaranth
- White Teff & Oatmeal
- Brown Teff & Oatmeal
- Quinoa & Oatmeal
- Polenta & Oatmeal
- Kamut & Oatmeal
- Barley, Spelt & Oatmeal
- Oats with dried chestnuts (precook chestnuts first)
- Oatmeal with winter squash
- Oatmeal with chopped nuts & squash
- Flax & Oatmeal
- Oatmeal with sunflower seeds
- Oatmeal & walnuts
- Oatmeal & poppy seeds
- Oatmeal with sweet potato
- Oats with fresh sweet corn
- Oats with leftover cooked rice
- Oats with leftover cooked noodles
- Oats with leftover cubed millet or millet loaf
- Oats with leftover cubed bread
- Oats with roasted flour (left from baking bread and flouring the baking trays)
- Oats with cubed polenta
- Oats with leftover seeded rice
- Oats with suribachi scrapings (from making seed condiment)
- Oats with leftover pasta water
- Oats with leftover barley-rice
- Oats with leftover rice & amaranth
- Oats with leftover bean-rice or chestnut-rice
- Oats with leftover rice & polenta
- Oats with leftover crumbled crackers
- Oats with leftover popcorn
- Oats with leftover cubed cornbread
- Oats with leftover rice and pasta

• • **Note:** Additional variety can be had by using whole oats in the winter, combined with other whole grains (brown rice, sweet brown rice, barley, millet, wild rice, chestnuts, etc,) or with nuts or seeds (pumpkin, sunflower, sesame, flax, walnuts, almonds, hazelnuts, chestnuts, lotus seeds, etc.), or sweet vegetables (winter squash, sweet potato, etc.), or by combining two grains with one sweet vegetable or a seed or nut. ❑

Home-Made Breakfasts in Hotels, Motels, and Camp Grounds:

- **Grains:** If you travel frequently and stay in hotels or motels, keep a supply of dry whole grain millet and rolled or cracked grains (e.g., oat, barley, spelt flakes or wholewheat cous cous) in your travel bag. Replenish your stash at grocery or health food stores. These will be more economical than restaurant meals.

- **Quick & Easy Cereal:** You can cook cereal for one or two people in a 2-4 quart crock pot. These can be plugged in anywhere. Alternatively, pack a wide-mouth 24-32 ounce thermos (1 per person) and a hot pot. The grain can "cook" on the counter in the sealed thermos or in a large glass or stainless steel bowl covered with a plate after pouring boiling water over it! (See index for Cold-Cooked Oats, Counter-Top Oats or Thermos Cereal.)

- **Equipment To Pack:** For each person, pack a mug for tea or grain coffee, large cereal bowl (wood or stainless steel), teaspoons, butter knife, and chopsticks. Take a stainless steel lunch box if you have one—for leftovers from restaurant meals. A one-person, hand-held cooler is good for single travelers, or take a larger cooler for car, train, plane or boat trips.

- **Emergency Bread Rations:** Pack home made or store bought whole grain breads (cornbread, rice bread, Essene sprouted bread, steamed buns, pita, chapatis, bagels, loaf bread, etc). Serve these with your cereal in— a pinch—instead of cereal. If you have enough space and ice in the cooler, take mochi and a non-stick electric waffle iron. You can make instant waffles with these in a motel room!

- **Handy Travel Toppings & Condiments:** Take a few vials of ready to use cereal toppings— dry roasted, one or two ground seed or nut condiments (e.g., Sesame-Salt or Walnut Condiment), dried chives or fresh scallions, sea veggie flakes, ume paste or mashed apriboshi pickled plums, white miso, and preserved 1,000 year eggs if you like. These need no refrigeration and can be taken almost anywhere (including restaurants) with ease. Stash these in a briefcase, back pack, or travel bag. If you have a cooler, you can pack cold pressed sesame, flax, walnut, or pumpkin seed oil to use as a cereal topping in place of seed or nut condiments. You can also take some homemade goat or soy yogurt on the road if you have a cooler.

- **Have Veggies Will Travel:** Fresh sprouts or leftover steamed or stir fried vegetables from restaurant meals are handy to serve with morning grain. Scallions or fresh or dried chives can be found in almost any grocery store when traveling by car. Pressed or marinated salads—made at home, to last for up to a week—can be toted in a hand-held or car size cooler to serve at any meal, even breakfast. Change the ice in the cooler daily if possible.

- **Take Your Tea:** Many restaurants carry herb teas, though you may want to keep a stash in your car, briefcase, purse, or travel bag; you'll save money taking your own and you will be able to drink it anytime. Take instant grain coffee, your favorite tea bags, and maybe a mug, too! A cup of herb tea or instant grain coffee will be a snap to make with a hot pot or electric element to heat up the water.

- **Dining Out For Breakfast:** Most restaurants serve hot cereal, and it's not always instant! *Order:* an extra large bowl of oatmeal or other hot cereal (i.e., a 2-cup portion) and a small bowl of steamed or stir fried leafy green or mixed vegetables. (They may think it strange but will oblige since most restaurants have broccoli, cabbage, Brussel sprouts, cauliflower, carrots, onions, etc. Some have kale garnishing the salad bar; ask for it steamed or sautéed with onions! Ask for raw, chopped parsley or chives for a garnish. You can order whole grain or sourdough bread, bagels or English muffins. Some restaurants are very progressive and carry decent whole grain bread. Order it unbuttered; skip the muffins (they're just cake in a cup and usually loaded with fat and sugar), pastries, donuts, and sweet rolls. Waffles and pancakes are okay if you top them with vegetables and/or a steamed/poached egg or homemade condiments. Pack ume or apriboshi paste, sea vegetable flakes, a small jar of roasted, seasoned seed condiment, and dried chives, if you like. These make handy additions to any restaurant meal.

Breakfast p. 412

Chapter 10
Getting Your Just Desserts

Getting Oriented to Just Desserts

Probably your first response to the title of this chapter is "Oh good! A chapter that is only desserts!" And you are right, this chapter is only desserts, but it is also about just desserts—that is, desserts that are appropriate and suitable for those who wish to live a long, healthy and honorable life. In order to get an oriental view of desserts—a view that can guide us to their appropriate use—we need to take a look at sweet foods from a variety of perspectives.

Fruit

Fruits are cooling and damp, very sweet and often sour as well. They generally are not very nourishing. On the contrary, one of the major actions of fruits—due to their richness in the soluble fiber pectin—is to cause the bowels to move. They are laxative and make us lax, or relax, sometimes too much! Accordingly, fruits are considered to be relatively Empty foods that drain rather than supplement the energies of the body. This is especially true of watery and soft tropical fruits such as bananas, oranges, pineapples, figs, and so on. In the modern American diet, these are often found counter-balancing the extremely filling effects of three egg omelets, steak, ham, etc. More hardy fruits from temperate regions—apples, pears, apricots, peaches, and so on—have a more moderate effect, than tropical fruits and are therefore more desirable in the context of a more vegetarian way of eating. However, even these are "emptying" and should be used sparingly by vegetarians or vegans.

Since fruit is very Cooling and quite Damp in nature, it can burden the Spleen, which likes warm and dry food. It is generally best to cook fruits, even in the warm seasons. That's probably why your grandmother made fresh berries into cobblers and pies. The addition of cinnamon to fruit desserts is another common practice in many culinary traditions. Cinnamon is warming and drying and thus counteracts the Cooling, Dampening effects of fruit. If you want raw fruit, the summer and fall—when the weather is usually warmer and dryer—are probably the best times for this.

Fruits generally are more moistening and cooling than other foods in their immediate effects, though copious consumption of them can create pathological Heat in the Stomach and Liver. Excessively sweet foods also damage the Kidneys, adversely affecting the teeth, bones and brain. Even western researchers have found higher rates of tooth decay among individuals who consume an excess of fruit or juice. This effect is due to their excessively sweet and sour flavors, and again the adverse effects are generally greater with tropical origin fruits which are generally more sweet and/or sour than temperate origin fruits.

Dried fruits and cooked fruits are generally more desirable than raw fruits. Drying reduces the Mucus-Damp generating quality of fruit, and cooking reduces the Cooling nature. Cooked, dried fruit is the most desirable for regular use in the context of a vegetarian way of eating such as Nourishment For Life. However, an excessive consumption of fruit can cause fatigue, vaginal discharges, coldness in the abdomen and/or the extremities, digestive weakness, and infections. If these problems are frequent, little or no fruit should be eaten. In fact, there are vegetables that can perform the same nutritional functions and offer a sweet taste without the more extreme effects of fruit. In China, fruit is very rarely used as either medicine or dessert, while vegetables are eaten at every meal.

Traditional Views of Fruits:

In traditional agricultural societies such as China, fruits were rarely cultivated with much enthusiasm. Fruits take large amounts of labor and irrigation, yet in comparison to grains and vegetables they produce a relatively small yield of extremely perishable food. This is also true of crops grown for sugar, such as sugar cane and sugar beets. For the most part, traditional agriculture was an attempt to get the most nourishing food possible with the least amount of trouble. For this reason, honey bees were not domestic animals until recent times, near the industrial revolution.

Sweet foods and fruits became major articles of diet only recently. The introduction of large volumes of sugar and fruit into the human diet came as a direct result of the imperialistic colonization and enslavement of the natives of Africa and South America. Large fruit and sugar cane or sugar beet plantations were created by the brute force of the wealthy and worked by enslaved and undernourished people who were/are paid low wages and made to work under inhumane conditions. Traditional agricultural people never put much energy into fruit growing except when forced or coerced to do so by rich people with excessive appetites. The traditional cuisines of the high civilizations of the tropical zones have revolved around starchy root vegetables and grains—such as rice, corn sweet potato and manioc—not fruit.

Among traditional agricultural peoples fruit was understood in a very common sense way and certain idioms grew out of this understanding. Since fruits and sweets spoil and decay rather readily, or attract large numbers of insects and other vermin, traditional wisdom held that those who eat a lot of it become spoiled and set themselves up for rampant decay or infestation by worms or bugs.

Traditional views of fruit appear in such idioms as "He's a fruit" and "She is as nutty as a fruit cake." These phrases, which convey the traditional view that fruit makes people "fruity," crazy, unstable, sexually impotent or spacey. In the Orient it is a said that ,"If there is a fruit tree in the back yard, the woman of the house will have no children." This conveys the Oriental medicine view that fruit has a "Cold" energy and that frequent consumption can injure the Yang energies, (the digestive and kidney fire), often leading to impotence, frigidity, infertility, or miscarriage.

Sweetener Dearest?

In general, the sweet taste is considered in Oriental medicine to be a tonic for the Spleen and Qi. However, this mainly applies to the substantial sweet-bland taste of grains and meats. The extremely sweet taste of fruits and most sweeteners is another story. This taste is more volatile and can harm the Spleen and weaken the muscles of the four limbs. Since this super-sweet taste represents the Earth element, and an excess of the Earth element harms the Water element, excessively sweet things also have a deleterious effect upon the Kidneys, bones, and teeth, all of which represent the Water element.

Refined sugar is probably the most commonly consumed sweet food. On the average, Americans consume their weight in sugar every year. What does this do for, or to, us? According to Oriental medicine, consumption of sugar generates Yang, firey energy in the body. It also produces fluids. Used as a medicine, temporary use of sugar can boost energy production and lubricate a dry throat. However, these ends can also be achieved by the use of honey, licorice root or other herbs, so sugar is not indispensible by any means.

Over consumption of sugar—we will discuss what that means later—overwhelms the Spleen leading to the production of Excess Damp and Heat. The Damp often lodges in the Lungs or Heart and vessels as Phlegm. Since the Lungs control the defensive Qi of the body, over consumption of sweet foods is at the root of degeneration of the immune system, such as is seen in the progression of AIDs and rheumatoid arthritis. Phlegm in the Heart can produce mental confusion, mental illness, or hyperactive personality, while Phlegm in the vessels can create Heart attack, stroke or atherosclerosis. Damp and Heat can also inflame the Liver, producing high blood pressure, emotional instability and/or propensity to anger. According to Tibetan medicine, sugar is quite dangerous. Tibetan doctors maintain that sugar increases the potency of the pathogens that create cancer. The actions of honey, maple syrup, high fructose corn sweetener, fruit juice, and fruit sugar are basically the same as that of refined sugar.

Concentrated sweeteners derived from the fermentation of grains—such as barley malt and rice syrup—have somewhat gentler effects. Unlike fruits, honey and refined sugars, malt syrups do not contain fructose. The sugars in them are merely the breakdown products of starch, and are similar to what our own digestive system produces in the digestion of grains. Indeed, these malts are really just predigested and strained grains. However, since they are not whole foods, they are easily over consumed, with much the same results as are found in the over consumption of fruits or refined sweeteners and so should be used aparingly.

Amasake is a fermented, predigested grain product that is richer in fiber and nutrients than any of the refined sweeteners. It is the most gentle of sweeteners, and the most nutritious. It tonifies the Middle Burner, tones and vitalizes the Blood, and supports the yang. It is the preferred sweetener since it has the least propensity to have adverse effects, and, due to its unrefined nature. It is also difficult to over consume. Amasake is an especially friendly food for women, as it will keep the Blood strong and moving, preventing and remedying a variety of menstrual disorders if consumed on a regular, yet moderate, basis.

Is Sugar a Food?

It is really important to understand the difference between sugar and food. Foods are not "pure" substances. When you eat a piece of chicken you are ingesting proteins, fats, and a wide variety of other nutrients. If you eat a piece of deep sea fatty fish, you get protein, fat, vitamins A & D, calcium, essential fatty acids, as well as other known and unknown nutrients. When you eat a cup of kale, collards or broccoli you get calcium, iron, beta-carotene, potassium, vitamin C, fiber and other essentials. From whole grain brown rice you get more than just carbohydrates—additionally you get protein, trace amounts of fat, B-vitamins, fiber, and many

other nutrients. We simply cannot reduce foods to a single nutrient. In contrast, refined sugar is a purified, single substance. It is 100% "pure" sucrose. This makes it more akin to drugs than to food. In fact, the process of producing sugar is not unlike the process by which cocaine is produced. White sugar even looks like cocaine. From this perspective, it would not be surprising to find that people easily become addicted to sugar, and that sugar has many adverse effects. Some people die or will kill for their sugar.

Just Desserts—A Social Justice Issue

Many of the dessert foods that Americans take for granted are available only because of the unjust cultural and economic imperialism of capitalist "development" of the "third" world. Third World peoples have had their land taken away and/or diverted from the production of more nutritious staple foods for the production of cash crops—sugar, cocoa, bananas, coffee, citrus, etc. and others—for the wealthy. As a result of having their land used for the production of export cash crops, these people must import food for their own consumption and almost invariably at a higher price than if they were to grow it themselves. Further, many of these enslaved people cannot afford the quality food they need to support their health and that of their families. Many of them also suffer from exposure to harmful pesticides, herbicides, and other toxic chemicals which are routinely used in their line of work. Consumers of these products may also suffer from ingesting the same poisons. In the end the health of these Third World peoples suffers, as does the health of the wealthy for whom these foods are grown.

People who grow, harvest, process and package our sweet luxury crops (even in America) are paid little for their time and often work in terribly unsafe conditions. They stand to lose more than they gain. Many of them also suffer from injuries suffered on the job due to inhumane work environments. Failing health due to a massive increase in sugar and processed food consumption further undermines the health of many farm and factory workers involved in the production of sugar, coffee, tobacco and tropical fruit products.

On an environmental level, many indigenous crops are lost as sugar, coffee and tropical fruit plantations crowd out more nutritious native plant foods. Further, the production of beet and cane sugar, coffee, chocolate, and tropical nuts and fruits requires large amounts of land, water, and energy to grow, harvest, process, package and ship. These luxury crops eat up valuable farm land, energy, and precious resources that could be put to better use.

Intensive mono-cropping of sugar, coffee beans, and chocolate, (as well as most other tropical origin products used for export), deplete our soils, often rendering them desolate, barren, and subject to soil erosion and run-off within a short period of time. Can anything containing any of these foods be called a just dessert?

Do Fruits Make You Ripe For Disease?

There's a growing body of scientific research that confirms the drug-like and detrimental effects of sugar on the human body. (Sugar consumption weakens and immobilizes the immune system, elevates triglyceride levels, can exacerbate hypertension, makes the blood overly acidic, draw minerals out of bones, can create anemia, and is linked to cancer, hypertension, heart disease and allergies!)

Dr. John Yudkin, in his groundbreaking book, *Sweet & Dangerous: The new facts about the sugar you eat as a cause of heart disease, diabetes, and other killers,* clearly states the truth about sugar: "There is no physiological requirement for sugar; all human nutritional needs can be met in full without having to take a single spoon of white or brown sugar or raw sugar, on its own or in any food or drink. Secondly, if only a fraction of what is already known about the effects of sugar were to be fully revealed in relation to any other material used as a food additive, that material would be promptly banned." His book details the links between consumption of sugar and occurrence of heart disease, gall bladder disease, cancer, and many other illnesses. Researchers have found repeatedly that sugar consumption reduces the capacity of the immune system, upsets delicate mineral and acid base balances in the body, induces osteoporosis, and causes enlargement of the liver and kidneys. All of this is merely a prelude to total confirmation of the traditional Tibetan and Oriental view of sugar as a substance that does little more than contribute to the degeneration of humankind.

In Keeping with Your Region and the Season

To harmonize with the seasons and your bioregion, select only fresh in season or dried fruits from your area (your state, a neighboring state, your region or your bio-region). It is also advisable to use preparations that harmonize with the season.

In hot weather make desserts that require little or no cooking. Examples include simmered fruits, light gels, aspics, steamed puddings, steamed or no-bake cookies, or fresh fruit or fruit salad.

In the winter, stewed fruits, baked apples, bread pudding and bake pies or cookies are delightfully appropriate.

Preparations suitable for any season include: amasake (made from almost any grain) served warm or at room temperature; simmered, steamed, stewed or poached fruit puddings, sauces, and compotes; chestnut or chestnut and fruit or grain-based puddings or sauces and other steamed desserts.

Energy & Time Efficient Desserts

In terms of energy use, it makes more sense to use quick and light stove top preparations more often than baking or other energy intensive methods. Many of the desserts you normally bake can be steamed, poached, or pressure cooked on top of the stove in a fraction of the time using much less energy. For example, rice puddings, bread puddings, pastries, turnovers, and some cakes can be efficiently steamed rather than baked, or cooked in a crock pot. We've even steamed a number of cookies. Most fruit desserts can be poached, stewed, steamed, pressure cooked, or cooked in a crock pot as well. As for your energy, you'll soon find that most of the desserts featured in this chapter take a minimum of preparation time and need very little attention as they cook. This is in stark contrast to most dessert recipes.

You will discover that simple homemade desserts cost much less than store bought cookies, cakes, brownies and other desserts which contain a long list of undesirable ingredients including concentrated and refined sweeteners and/or preservatives. Just because your cookies come from the health food store doesn't mean they're good for you. (These are often highly sweetened, full of oil, or rancid by the time you get them.) Even homemade amasake which may look very involved to make is actually quite easy, needs less than 30 minutes of hands on work, costs far less than store bought varieties and like other home-made desserts, usually tastes even better than store bought varieties.

Making Low-Fat Desserts

The desserts contained in this chapter are either very low in fat or fat-free. This is in dramatic contrast to most premade, commercial desserts which contain as much or more fat in a single serving than you need in an entire day! Our desserts use nuts, seeds, and oils in minute amounts—a few teaspoons of nuts or seeds or a single teaspoon of oil per person. (You really don't need much to produce a rich flavor.)

Downsizing Your Desserts

In terms of portion size, a scaled down version of your favorite desserts may be in order. A big slice of cake after a grain based meal is likely to leave you feeling loggy and lethargic. A small cup of fruit sauce or pudding is satisfying and far more digestible. Monster cookies and enormous Belgian waffle sundaes may be common fare in treacherously unhealthy diets that have a scarcity of whole grains and veggies, but on a nutritious grain centered diet, lighter and smaller desserts are much more appropriate. (We recommend using cookies, bars, and cakes very infrequently.)

For the most part, heavy or baked desserts will become less than appealing and won't sit well, once you shift to a grain-based, vegetable-rich diet. Notice the surprising lack of dessert selections in most Asian restaurants—a single fortune cookie or a piece of fruit. In Japanese cuisine light fruit gels called "kanten" or amasake puddings are the norm. Though steamed cookies, steamed filled pastries and other sweet desserts are sometimes eaten in Asian countries, these desserts are usually smaller and far less sweet than most American and European desserts.

Why So Many Dessert Recipes in a Book Which Discourages Desserts?

Most folks like desserts and we are no exception. Although we don't make desserts daily fare, we do make them now and then and we figure that you will likely do the same. We have endeavored to make the highest quality desserts for ourselves, our students and guests, and for you and yours.

Some of the desserts included in this chapter were designed for special occasions, Christmas, Thanksgiving, Halloween, birthdays, etc., while others were designed for potlucks, parties, or festive meals with friends. Some we have made many times over the course of several years; others we have made only once or twice but because we found them so popular, we wanted to include them in this book. Some are suitable for particular seasons, while others may be used any time of year. It is our hope that you will enjoy these tasty treats in the spirit of justice and moderation.

Causes and Cures for Sweet Cravings

You needn't be a slave to sugar, or to cravings for it. You need only be armed with the facts, alerted to some of the causes, and given some preventive strategies. After that, it is up to you to decide whether you want to have your life controlled by sweets. From the perspective of Oriental medicine, it is neither necessary nor advisable to eat concentrated sweets on a daily basis. Sweets cravings come from Qi or Yang deficiency, emotional factors and/or are a symptom or result of our modern way of life. However, there *are* solutions.

Emotional exhaustion and stress play a part in sweets cravings. It is not uncommon for such cravings to arise when one is lonely or emotionally exhausted. In this case, sweets may provide a momentary feeling of comfort, reward, relief or excitement. However, sweets are not a solution to these problems and will only make matters worse in the long run. Better solutions include meditation and breathing as well as regular aerobic exercise. These vitalize the body, promote a sense of calm and will help to release stress in a more healthy way. Being part of a supportive community, having significant relationships, and developing a life purpose are also important solutions to sweets cravings caused by loneliness.

Eating a restricted diet can also cause sweets cravings. Restricting the amount of food one eats, a common practice in the West—often done in an attempt to lose weight or to avoid becoming fat—can easily lead to a lack of energy and the desire to eat sweets. Further compounding this problem is the fact that many Americans in general, and dieters in particular, restrict the amount of grain they eat—out of a mistaken belief that grains are fattening. In actuality, grains provide the body with the long lasting and nourishing energy it needs to function best.

Although sugar and fructose provide a quick rush of energy, this energy is short-lasting because the fuel is without substance; it is energy with little that matters. Grains, on the other hand, contain energy (of the long-lasting kind) with substance; hence the fuel in grains is energy *that matters.* Both the solution to and the prevention of sweet cravings lies in eating an appropriate volume of foods, particularly grain foods, rather than restricting yourself to bird-sized portions or salad meals.

When people crave sweets, they hardly ever crave just fruits. How often have you heard someone say that they binged on half a dozen apples or an entire watermelon because they just couldn't stop or were so hungry? It seems that when people crave sweets, they typically go for foods which are concentrated, sweet and fatty, and often thick and heavy as well. Examples include: cookies, cake, donuts, ice cream, trail mix, chocolates, etc. In some cases these dense and heavy foods are the most "substantial" items a person may eat. This may be the case with many breakfast or lunch skippers and/or dieters who try to subsist on salads, yogurt and just a few crackers or a couple of slices of bread in a day. Who wouldn't want something dense and heavy to supplement such a diet?

A Cold condition can also be a cause of sweets cravings. This is particularly common among those vegetarians who eat large amounts of salad and tropical fruits while skimping on well cooked grains, legumes and hardy and/or cooked vegetables. It especially strikes raw foods vegetarian men. Sugar is like a spark. It fires people up and provides a temporary rush of energy. Thus, sugar (like coffee and alcohol) is often used by people who are Cold and deficient and in need of more warming foods. A better solution to the problem of sweets cravings due to coldness is to eat more grains and legumes; more sea salt, miso, and tamari; to use a small amount of oil and seeds daily; to use some warming herbs; and to avoid raw vegetables and juices and while limiting the consumption of fruit.

A fourth cause of sweets cravings is irregular or skipped meals. This leads to irregular energy levels, poor concentration, irritability, fatigue, confusion, depression and other symptoms that come from sudden drops in energy when the mind and body run out of "gas" This is typically called, "hypo-glycemia"—literally low blood sugar. Extreme hunger and sudden drops in energy are "normal" reactions to a lack of sufficient fuel. Though this hunger is often interpreted as a craving for sweets, it may simply be a strong desire for food, one which could just as easily be met by grains and starchy vegetable but which we may simply be accustomed to satisfying with empty sweet foods like cookies, pastries, soda pop, candy, chocolates, fruit juice, milk shakes, ice cream and other highly sweetened substances. The solution to sweets cravings due to irregular or missed meals lies in eating three grain-based meals each day at regular intervals (or perhaps two large meals and one snack.) Regular meals provide fuel for the body on an ongoing basis. Skipping meals deprives the body of the fuel it needs to run.

A fifth cause of sweets cravings can be an excessive consumption of protein. This usually comes from animal foods—meat, chicken, fish, eggs, cheese, milk, etc.—in the modern American diet. Too much protein upsets our body chemistry and can set up a craving for more carbohydrates to make balance. Since carbohydrate is the body's main source of fuel, it is only natural that we would seek this fuel. People often meet this "need" for carbohydrate with refined sugars or simple carbohydrates in the form of cookies, cakes, pastries, candy, sugary drinks, alcohol, or large amounts of fruits or fruit sweetened items. Needless to say, this is the not the ideal way to fuel the body. The solution here lies in basing one's diet on whole grains supplemented with moderate amounts of hardy vegetables, beans and legumes.

A final cause of sweets cravings is, for lack of a better word, brainwashing. We are constantly exposed to sweet foods and advertisements for sweet foods. The solution to this is to simply avoid the advertising and to just say "no!" (Get rid of your television set and many of your cravings may go with it!) Even if you are exposed you don't need to buy it. If you don't bring it home, you're less likely to eat it. Whatever you do with your cravings, don't indulge them, they'll only get stronger.

Cravings are like a stray cat

You feed them, they just keep coming back. If you feed them long enough, others will come, and they'll hang around too. (Surprised?) If you don't feed them, chances are they won't come back, or if they do, they won't hang around for very long. It's as simple as that. Feed them and they'll be with you forever and then before you know it more stray cats are hanging around, begging to be fed. Stop feeding them and they will go away—somewhere where someone else will feed them.

If you think that "if only I can get this food, then I'll be happy," you're in for a shock and a let down. It's all an illusion. When was the last time you had that food and were really happy, really satisfied, really content? Maybe you had it and then said, "I'll just eat one more piece and then I'll be happy. " Then one more, and one more and before you knew it you felt sick. You ate too much and then you didn't feel happy. Or you had that food then you had to have something else, and then something else, to be happy. It doesn't work: "When I get this, then I'll be happy", thinking just leads us down a blind alley, again and again. In fact, you may find that you become less and less happy the more you feed your cravings. Now you have to keep feeding the stray cat (the craving). It thinks you want it around. You fed it yesterday, and today it's hungry. Again it wines, it cries, it begs to be fed. It keeps pawing at the door. It even wakes you up at night. You have to stop. You have to let it go, let it go away. It will. Really. If you stop feeding it.

For the most part, cravings exist in our minds. You remember that last meal at the Thai restaurant? If you think about it enough, you'll probably start craving it. If you watch television with all its advertisements for food or you cruise the malls, don't be surprised if you are stimulated to eat. Similarly, if you insist on spending a great deal of time drooling over picture books of food or hanging out in coffee shops, delis, ice cream parlors or convenience stores, don't be surprised if you want to eat all the foods they offer. If you look at, smell, touch, think, dream and talk about food all of the time, you're bound to want to eat more—and to eat foods that aren't what you really need. Go to the movies and the smell of movie pop corn is bound to set your mouth watering. Stare in the bakery window and you'll be wanting pastries for sure.

To get out of the quick fix-rut you'll have to learn to plan ahead. As a wise old Chinese proverb so eloquently says, "Don't wait until you're thirsty to dig a well." This could just as easily be translated into "Don't wait until you're hungry to start cooking." You know you are going to get hungry later or tomorrow, so plan, shop and cook ahead so you've always got something on hand for the next meal (in anticipation of it). You know you'll be hungry at some point after breakfast, so make lunch ahead and pack it with you if you're going somewhere. You know you'll probably be hungry at dinner time—so have food on hand, ready to cook or cooked ahead. This will go a long way toward keeping you on track and eating well. Once you get the hang of planning ahead it won't take long to get good meals on the table or for you to feel the benefits. You'll be surprised. We guarantee it, if you study and practice our secrets for meal planning and preparation.

Cravings are an outgrowth of a fast and frenzied way of living and eating where one barely has time to eat, much less cook. Rush here, rush there. Stay out late, rush off to work. No time to eat. Work late, eat late, go out, then go to bed, (often on a full stomach). Get up and do it again. That's the pattern. One can get prepared food at any time—day or night—almost anywhere—so who needs to plan ahead? And with chasing after the dollar bill or working for a vacation who's got time to cook? The dizzying array of foods from which one can choose boggles the mind. (Is it any wonder food is on our minds so much? It's everywhere!)

Surely our ancestors did not have so many options in the food department, nor did they have the problems that come with the overwhelming abundance of foods in the refrigerator, in the freezer, or on the shelf—in a can, box or envelope. Our ancestors probably didn't have cravings either. They ate what they ate and then they were done with it. They probably didn't spend every waking moment agonizing over what to eat and what not to eat either. They probably didn't get up at two in the morning for a snack or a drive to the local eatery for a fix. They simply ate what was locally, seasonally and regionally available, fresh picked, fresh killed, pickled, or dried. They didn't have the luxury of fantasizing over their last or next meal. Really, they were much more free than we who have more choices than we know what to do with. We who live in wealthy nations are often trapped by our endless fascination with and obsession with food. The criteria is usually not "is it fresh?" More often it's "is it the right color, flavor, texture or aroma "and" will it satisfy our sensory desire for more stimulation?"

Americans are spoiled rotten (and not surprisingly, so are our teeth). Only people who live in luxury can have cravings. Here so many people are craving ice cream or coffee or chocolate chip cookies. We're used to getting whatever we want—however, it's not that way in many parts of the world where people are just concerned with getting a good meal and enough food on the table. They're not agonizing over whether to have chocolate or vanilla; they're just eating.

In Soviet Georgia, for example, it is a common practice for people to give up favorite foods for several weeks at a time, and throughout the year. They do this to overcome their weaknesses and to develop their character. It is not bad to have a fondness for something, or even a strong fondness, but indulging in it continuously is a way of rewarding your weaknesses. What you reward will persist. That doesn't mean that you never have these things you are so very fond of, but if you're so fond of something that you can't control yourself, can't think straight, can't stop, or think you have to have it or you'll be miserable, then you have a problem. If you can't say "no" to it—then it is controlling you. If you go without it until you don't want it, until you can eat just a little and stop, then you will be free. You will no longer be enslaved to a master: chocolate, ice cream, (or Rice Dream), cookies, cake, chips, or whatever it is that has you.

Recommendations for use sweet and fruits

Fruits should generally be chosen from local sources and used only when in season or dried. Fruits or natural desserts generally should not be used more than two to four times per week. It would be wiser and healthier to use them less often, perhaps once or twice per week (particularly for fruits and other concentrated sweeteners). They are certainly not essential parts of a health promoting diet. In fact, they are often at the root of many a health depleting diet.

The dessert recipes in this book use only fruits, juices, chestnuts, amasake or occasionally, malt sweeteners. In some cases, dessert may consist of even more natural preparations such as baked or nishime cooked winter squash or sweet potatoes, some corn on the cob; boiled, pressure cooked or roasted chestnuts; mochi; a rice cake with miso-tahini; or a bowl of popcorn. For reasons that have been given, these provide ample sweetness without the deleterious personal, social and ecological effects that are associated with the use of out of season or highly refined fruits and sweeteners. Remember, no one needs to eat sweets; we only do it for pleasure or sometimes for "medicinal" ends. If it gets to the point where you can't say no, it is no longer a pleasure, it is then a full blown addiction!

Vitamin C Beyond Citrus & Potassium Beyond the Banana

Fruits, sweets, and juices are relatively non-nutritious when compared to whole grains and vegetables. A comparison of oranges to broccoli shows that for an equal size serving, boiled broccoli has about the same amount of vitamin C as the orange but nearly 10 times the vitamin A and iron, 3 times the calcium, and twice as much of the B vitamin folacin. The leafy green kale contains twice the vitamin C, 4 times the calcium, 7 times the iron, and a whopping 45 times the vitamin A of an equal size serving of orange.

Bananas are often referred to as good sources of potassium, but lentils, sweet potatoes, yams, white potatoes and winter squash all have as much or more of this nutrient in an equal size serving. Compared to the banana, lentils have 17 times more protein, potatoes have 4 times more iron, and winter squash has 35 times more vitamin A. Surprise!

Making Low-Fat, Low-Impact Desserts

Don't let dessert sideline your health commitments. During the holidays or any time of the year, high-fat and/or cholesterol and sugar-laden desserts are the norm. The innocent looking cookies, cakes and pies at family get togethers, parties, potlucks, even co-ops and natural foods restaurants aren't just high in fat, most contain butter, lard, suet, or a great deal of oil, nuts, and/or seeds, and often milk, cream, eggs, or a combination of several of these ingredients.

Many well intentioned people don't realize just how much fat is in a tablespoon, quarter-cup, or cupful of oil, nuts, or seeds. A handful of nuts or a quarter cup of oil packs more calories than two or three cupfuls of breakfast porridge such as oatmeal. Even if the fruit cake, cookies, cakes, and pies you normally eat don't contain animal products (eggs, butter, cream, milk, etc.) most recipes contain two to ten times as much fat as you need in an entire meal or a day—in a single serving! Innocuous ingredients like vegetable oil, margarine, nuts, seeds and their butters, are all high in fat. So even if you skip the animal products and opt for vegan dessert-making, you could still end up with a recipe that's just as high in fat as the fare you arr trying to avoid.

Cut the fat

So what can you do? For low-fat baked goods, the butter, oil or shortening in a recipe may be replaced with apple sauce; puréed cooked fresh or dried fruit (raisin or prune purée work well), puréed, cooked fresh-frozen or dried chestnuts; mashed squash or sweet potato; puréed corn off the cob; or in some cases soy milk or amasake. These substitutes provide the necessary moisture for proper taste and texture, with fewer calories and virtually no added fat.

In most recipes for cookies, muffins, or brownie bars, total fat per recipe can be reduced to a maximum of 1-2 tablespoons vegetable oil (corn or light sesame for best results), or a similar volume of nut or seed butter if one of the above ingredients are used to create a moist batter. Sweet fat replacements should only be used in desserts. For savory baked goods, use vegetable purées, soy milk, chestnut, or tofu purées to replace the fat.

It is a good idea to keep the use of nuts, seeds, or nut seed butters to not more than 1/2-1 tablespoons per estimated/realistic portion size. For example, if a cookie recipe makes 12 large cookies or 24 small cookies, you can assume that most people will eat two large or three small cookies. That would mean that the entire recipe would serve about six people. So, it would be

Recommended Desserts

**Regular
Use Desserts:**

Amasake puddings
Chestnut desserts
Sweet vegetable desserts
Grain-based puddings
Simmered or stewed fruit desserts
Steamed or poached fruit desserts
Pressure cooked fruit desserts

**Seasonal, Party, or
Occasional Use Desserts:**

Bread puddings
Baked fruit desserts
Raw fresh fruits & fresh fruit salads
Fresh gels and aspics
Cookies, cakes and bars
Pies and pastries

Recommended Sweeteners

Sweeteners for Regular Use:

Chestnuts, chestnut purée and chestnut flour
Amasake pudding or nectar (beverage)
Mashed, baked or simmered winter squash
Mashed, cooked sweet potato or yam

Apple juice

Apple sauce or other fruit sauce
Raisins, or raisin or prune purée
Other fresh or dried fruit purée
puréed sweet corn, off the cob

Infrequent Use Sweeteners:

Brown rice syrup or powder
Barley malt syrup or powder

Celebration Use Sweeteners:

Maple syrup
Sorghum
Honey

Note: It is advisable to keep fat to a minimum in desserts, not more than 1 tsp. of oil or butter per person or 3 tsp. of nuts, seeds or nut butters (or not more than 1-2 Tbsp. fat per 3-4 cups flour in a recipe). All or most of the fat in cookies, cakes, puddings, and many other desserts can be replaced with apple sauce, apple juice, amasake pudding or beverage, raisin purée, chestnut purée, mashed squash or sweet potato, or a cooked fruit compote. Milk, cream, and eggs can also be replaced with little or no loss of taste or texture.

best to limit the nuts to 1/3 of a cup or 6 table-spoons of chopped nuts and to replace all of the oil or shortening. If oil is used in a cookie recipe, it is best to leave out the nuts or seeds or limit their use to 1-2 teaspoons per person serving. In most cookies, brownies and bars, you can safely replace the oil, butter or margarine with apple sauce,or amasake then add in a small amount of seeds, nuts or nut or seed butter.

To Eliminate milk, buttermilk & cream

Milk and cream may be replaced with Almond Beverage, Rice Dream Beverage, commercial amasake shake or nectar, sunflower or almond milk, Amasake Light, homemade amasake pudding or liquid, apple juice, soy milk (for savory baked goods), or puréed cooked oatmeal, rice, millet, squash, or stewed fruit, made the thickness of the items they are meant to replace! For desserts, you can use sweet versions of the products mentioned to replace the milk and/or cream and the sweetener as well. For savory baked goods, however, it is best to use unsweetened grain, soy-, or nut-, or seed-milks. (When using sweet concoctions to replace the milk or cream, often times will also be able to greatly reduce the amount of sweetener called for in a recipe.)

Omitting the Eggs

Replace eggs with a low fat alternative

For each egg use one of the following:

- 1/4 cup commercial, liquid egg-replacer (the least desirable option)

- 1 1/2 Tbsp. ground flax seeds mixed with 3 Tbsp. boiling water to make 1/3 cupful, allowed to sit 15 minutes, then whipped in a blender if possible

- 1 Tbsp. arrowroot flour or soy flour dissolved in 3 Tbsp. cold water, stock, juice, amasake nectar, or grain milk*

- 1/4 cup puréed tofu*

- Dissolve in 1/3 cup cool or cold amasake beverage or shake 1 Tbsp. arrowroot flour or kuzu +/- 1/2 tsp. non-aluminum baking powder*

- 1/4 cup water, juice, soy-, nut-, seed-, or grain-milk, or amasake nectar*

Notes:

- Avoid using sweet liquids in non-dessert preparations. Instead, use water, soup stock, or plain soy milk with an egg-replacing dry ingredient in savory and main dish preparations.

- Avoid using soy milk, tofu or soup stock in dessert items. Instead, use water or a sweet liquid.

You may replace up to one-fourth of the whole wheat bread or pastry flour in a recipe with oat, amaranth, barley or chestnut flour for a more moist, tender, and rich tasting baked good. Spelt flour can replace white flour, bleached or unbleached flour, or pastry wheat flour and will also help to produce a moist texture with added nutrition. Barley flour can often be used exclusively in cookies or it may be combined with oatmeal or pastry flour for pie crusts, pastries, muffins, or sweet dessert breads.

Reducing the sweeteners

Concentrated sweeteners may be replaced with puréed raisins or other dried and/or fresh fruits, applesauce, or commercial or homemade amasake beverage or pudding. (**Note:** Amasake Light, a new product, does not work as well as a sweetener as its thicker cousin, Amasake Shake.)

To replace 1 cup sweetener in your favorite recipe, take 1 cup of raisins (or prunes), simmer in 1 cup water or apple juice for 10 minutes, then purée. Or, use an equivalent amount of amasake. If you do use rice syrup, barley malt, maple syrup or other concentrated sweeteners, you can often reduce the amount called for in a recipe with good results, particularly if apple juice, amasake or chestnut purée have been used to replace the milk or if apple sauce, chestnut purée, prune purée, mashed squash, or other such ingredients have been used to replace the oil and/or eggs.

Occasionally, you may wish to use a bit more oil, nuts, or seeds in your desserts, just serve these dishes in small portions. If you get experimental, you might try to adapt your favorite recipes for banana, zucchini, or pumpkin bread or brownies. (*Hint:* Mashed banana can be replaced with cooked and mashed varieties of winter squash, sweet potato, yam, or parsnip.)

Does Artificial Sugar Equal Danger?

For the past 10 years the non-nutritive sweetener aspartame has been sold under the trade name Equal and used in other products under the name NutraSweet. It has been touted as a "safe and natural ingredient" because it is made from the chemical bonding of two amino acids, aspartic acid and phenylalanine. However, there is brewing controversy about aspartame's safety for human health. Would it be surprising if such an adulterated, man-made product caused health problems? Dr. H. J. Roberts has come forward with *Sweet'ner Dearest,* a book describing the medical complaints associated with the use of aspartame (trade name NutraSweet). The book details case histories of people afflicted with headaches, mood swings, and other symptoms associated with its use. (There are even studies linking the use of this sweetener with kidney and liver damage.) Roberts says 54% of American adults consume the sweetener which is now used in 4,200 products. Many of these people are unknowingly consuming the sweetener and exposing themselves to unnecessary risk.

Are you consuming aspartame? If so, you should know the risks and dangers. For more information, send a SASE to Aspartame Consumer Safety Network, P. O. Box 780634, Dallas, Texas 75378. They'll send you a brief article by Dr. Lendon Smith concerning aspartame. For a $15 contribution to this non-profit group you will also receive the 180 page book, *The Deadly Deception.* For more information on aspartame and other questionable food items read, *Safe Food: Eating Wisely in a Risky World,* by Michael Jacobson, PhD. (Living Planet Press.)

Sugar and immunity

Fructose, honey, sucrose and orange juice have all been shown to depress the immune system. (Loma Linda University study.).Fructose also elevates the level of triglycerides (which are shown to cause gout attacks and raise the risk of heart attack), to reduce the level of ATP (the livers main energy source), to promote tooth decay, to inhibit protein and RNA synthesis, to interfere with normal detoxification of ammonia (a by product of protein digestion). Thus, fruits and sweeteners should not form a large part of health supportive diet.

A Guide to Sweeteners

Sugars are made up of simple and complex carbohydrates. Examples of simple sugars include: sucrose and fructose. Examples of sweeteners with a high percentage of complex carbohydrates include barley and rice malt syrups. When sugars are taken out of their whole foods context they can overload the blood stream and interfere with proper blood sugar regulation and mineral absorption and metabolism.

Sweeteners containing more complex carbohydrates (particularly grain-based sweeteners which contain more maltose) have a more gentle, slow, and balanced effect on metabolism. However, all sweeteners, even the most wholesome and minimally processed, can still upset our systems when eaten too frequently or in large amounts. For this reason, we recommend eating desserts—including fresh and dried fruits, juices, and desserts made from them, as well as all concentrated sweeteners or products containing them—not more than two or four-times per week (amasake can be consumed three to five times per week if used instead of fruit or other sweeteners). It is unnecessary to eat desserts or even fruits on a daily basis—more nutritious and naturally sweet vegetables and well cooked, well-chewed whole grains, beans, and chestnuts provide ample sweetness and more nourishment.

Note: To avoid introducing new bacteria or inviting mold, always use a clean spoon to dip into a jar of liquid sweetener then wipe the sides of the jar with a clean sponge before sealing.

- **Amasake:** This fermented sweetener, made from an Asian variety of sweet rice is the least refined of the natural sweeteners and can be easily made at home. **(Note:** amasake can be made from grains other than sweet brown rice.) Left unstrained it contains all of the goodness and fiber of whole grains. Strained varieties are lower in fiber but still nutritious. Amasake (commercially sold as amasake) can be used to replace dairy products, butter, oil, and both dry and liquid sweeteners in baked desserts, puddings, custards, frostings, pie fillings, pastry dough, etc. (See side-bar.) Homemade amasake can be made the consistency of thick pudding, thin cream or milk;

commercial varieties typically have a thinner milk-like consistency. The flavor varies from brand to brand, with how much koji you use in home batches, or with they type of grain used. Aseptic cartons of commercial amasake can be kept for a year unopened, or as long as the package date suggests. Bottled amasake sold in the refrigerator case and opened aseptic cartons should be used within about a week or frozen for up to a year.

- **Barley malt syrup:** This sticky syrup is created through a natural enzymatic reaction which reduces the carbohydrates in whole, sprouted barley to simpler sugars (mostly maltose). Barley malt syrup contains some complex sugars and therefore is metabolized more slowly. It is thick like molasses and has a dark color and distinctly malty taste. It can be used in almost any baked good, though its taste may be a bit too strong or malty for delicate pastries, cakes and some cookies. (It's great in gingerbread, sweet potato pie, or molasses cookie or cake recipes.) Store in a sealed jar in a cool dry place or in the refrigerator. Barley malt also comes in a powder form; use this sparingly, in some recipes it can taste bitter or overpowering.

- **Brown rice syrup:** This naturally fermented sweetener is rich in complex sugars. It is made from whole grain rice and sprouted barley. It contains some protein, B- vitamins, and many minerals which are naturally present in whole grain rice. The taste is light and delicate with a slightly malty undertone. Liquid rice malt syrup looks more like honey than barley malt and can be used to replace equal portions of other liquid sweeteners. You can also use it in place of dry sweeteners if you adjust the recipe (see side-bar). Store in a sealed jar in a cool dry place. If any any surface mold develops, simply scrape it off. Brown rice sweetener also comes in a powder form which can be used to replace an equal volume of sugar.

- **Honey:** This sweetener is primarily comprised of simple sugars. The flavor, composition, and color of honey is as varied as the blossoms that feed the bees. The degree of filtering also varies widely. Raw honey has been lightly heated and filtered but still retains some enzymes and trace vitamins and minerals; however, these may be destroyed by the high heat common in baking. Store honey in a sealed jar in a cool dry place. If mold develops on the top, simply scrape it off. Since it is sweeter than sugar or rice malt, you will probably need to use less of it.

- **Maple syrup:** This sweetener is made from the boiled sap of the sugar maple tree. It takes *40 gallons of sap* to make *one gallon* of this popular sweetener. (Read labels— some grocery store brands contain maple syrup diluted with corn syrup or other sweeteners and artificial coloring and flavoring agents.) This is sweeter than rice syrup or barley malt. Some find it to be less sweet than honey, though others find it to be just as sweet. It comes in grades A, B, and C which are mostly related to the temperature and time used in processing. Higher grades, such as grade A, are usually lighter in color and flavor and a bit costlier. Grade B is darker in color and stronger in flavor. Maple syrup can replace liquid or dry sweeteners in your favorite recipe. When used to replace dry sweeteners, the amount of other liquids may need to be reduced, or the amount of flour may need to be slightly increased.

Sweetener Substitutions:

In most cases the amount of sweetener in a recipe can be reduced, often by one-half or more. (For more on replacing fat see "Adapting Your Favorite Recipe" in the bread chapter.)

Rule of thumb: Replace 1 cup of white, brown, or turbinado sugar in a recipe with one of the following:

1 cup amasake pudding or nectar
1 cup apple sauce
1 cup stewed fruit
1/2-1 cup raisin purée
2/3 cup honey
1 cup barley malt or rice syrup
1 cup prune purée
1 cup squash or sweet potato
(puréed in juice or water)
1-1 1/4 cup Fruit Source, granulated or liquid

1-2 cups apple juice or sweetened nut milk
(adjust the recipe to allow for extra liquid)
1/2-2/3 cup maple syrup
1/2-3/4 cup fruit juice concentrate
(or other dried fruit puréed in an equal
volume of water)
1 cup chestnut purée
1/2-1 cup rice malt powder
1 cup corn off the cob (puréed in apple juice
1 cup barley malt or rice syrup

Tips:

- When using a concentrated liquid sweetener to replace dry sugar in a recipe, it is advisable to reduce the liquid by 1/4-1/3 cup. If no liquids were called for in a recipe, add 3-6 Tablespoons of flour or arrowroot for each 3/4 cup of concentrated liquid sweetener.

- To measure thick, viscous unpourable syrup (such as barley malt or slightly old rice malt), place the opened jar in a pan of warm water for several minutes to liquefy. For easy cleanup, oil your measuring cup and other utensils before measuring thick syrups.

- Some syrups may liquefy batters and doughs (due to the natural starch splitting enzymes they contain). This is more likely when eggs are not used in a recipe. To counter this, you may wish to boil the malt syrup for 2-3 minutes (or steam it in an oiled cup) then cool it before adding it to a recipe.

Sweetener Comparisons by Composition:

Sweetener	% sweetness relative to white sugar	Type of carbohydrates
Amasake	70%	50% maltose, glucose, complex
Barley Malt	60%	65% maltose, 5% glucose, complex
Brown Rice Syrup	70%	50% maltose, 37% complex
Brown Sugar, packed	100%	96% sucrose
Date Sugar	75%	65% fructose, fiber
Fructose (granulated)	170%	100% fructose
Fruit Source	80%	20% sucrose, 20% fructose, 33% complex
Fruit Concentrate		
(Mystic Lake Syrup)	75%	21% fructose, 20% sucrose
Honey	130%	50% glucose, 50% sucrose
Maple syrup	60%	65% sucrose
Molasses, Blackstrap	50%	70% sucrose
Molasses, Sweet	70%	70% sucrose
Sorghum	60%	70% sucrose
Sucanat (dried cane juice)		96% sucrose
White Sugar	100%	99.9% sucrose

(This chart was provided by Goldie Caughlin of Puget Consumer Co-op in Seattle, Washington)

Amasake

What is amasake and what's it made from?

The Japanese word "amasake" literally means sweet (ame) fermented grain (sake). This thick pudding or beverage is made by inoculating cooked grains with the spores of aspergillus oryzae mold (found dry on koji), then leaving the grain to ferment in a warm place for 6-10 hours. During this time, the mold spores convert the starch in the grain to a disaccharide maltose, the same process that is accomplished in your mouth by your salivary enzymes when you chew grains well (until they are liquefied and taste sweet).

Is it good for you?

Amasake is, in a sense, predigested grain. And since it is virtually free of simple sugars, it is probably a more healthful dessert than fruits or other sweeteners, all of which contain significant quantities of fructose and sucrose. Fructose and sucrose have been shown to have a negative impact on health, particularly on our blood sugar and mineral metabolism. Amasake made from whole grains, however, provides all of the goodness and nutrition of whole cereal grains and a very sweet taste without a trace of fructose or sucrose. What other dessert or sweetener can offer so much in one package? Of course, the ideal way to get your amasake every day is to chew your grains well.

Amasake is valued for more than just it's sweet taste. In Japan, nursing mothers, hard working farmers and sumo wrestlers use amasake to provide strength and resistance to fatigue. If it is made from whole, unrefined or minimally refined grains it is far more nutritious than most other sweets and desserts. Unlike sugar, amasake is certainly not a source of "empty" calories.

Amasake makes the perfect dessert or after workout snack. It can also satisfy the sweet tooth after a meal without overburdening your digestive system the way many heavy or rich desserts can.

Making amasake

Koji spores are added to cooked whole grain and allowed to ferment for six to ten hours. This mixture is puréed then cooked briefly to stop the fermentation. Or, if it is very liquidy, amasake can be cooked down on top of the stove, on a very low heat, for one or several hours to reduce it to a thicker pudding. This thick, rich and sweet pudding is tastier than most of the liquid amasake found in health food stores and is suitable for use as a dessert on its own or combined with dried or fresh fruits, spices, nuts, seeds, or other ingredients. Whether you make it thin or thick, homemade amasake can be used in a myriad of ways.

Using amasake

Amasake can be used as a replacement for dairy products, sweeteners, and/or oil or butter in many baked goods, including pastry doughs and fillings, cookies, cakes, brownies, frostings and glazes. We often use homemade or commercial liquid amasake in pie crust or pastry dough to replace both the water and the fats. (See substitution lists for more ideas and tips.) Homemade amasake can also be diluted for use as a dessert beverage, though in our house we prefer to serve it as a thick pudding or to use it as an ingredient in other dessert preparations.

Amasake, beyond rice!

Though commercial varieties of amasake are usually made from sweet brown rice, amasake can be made from a wide variety of grains. We have enjoyed amasake made from millet, buckwheat, barley, roasted barley, sweet brown rice, Thai black sweet rice, or various combinations of two grains or one or two grains combined with fruits or nuts. In fact, at our wedding celebration, we opted for a luscious, creamy marshmallow-like amasake pudding (made from sweet brown rice or millet) in lieu of a traditional wedding cake. We found this dessert to be lighter and far more enjoyable than a rich, baked cake after a buffet laden with numerous whole grain, bean, and vegetable dishes. We have also served amasake birthday puddings in both summer (often simmered with or ladled over the season's freshest fruit) and winter (alone or with dried chestnuts or fruit, spices and/or nuts).

Commercial amasake comes in a rainbow of flavors—original (plain), almond, vanilla-pecan, mocha-java, sesame, etc. Grainaissance is the major supplier of amasake drinks, concentrates, and puddings on the West Coast and in the Midwest, though many smaller companies also exist. They make a great product.

Storing amasake

Once made, amasake is best used up within several days to one week (or two weeks at the (outside) since flavor is lost in prolonged storage. It is inadvisable to freeze homemade amasake since the flavor and the texture are altered greatly in the freezing process, resulting in a gritty or "grainy" textured and watery product. Baked goods such as cookies, cakes, brownies, or pastries made with amasake hold up to freezing far better than the actual liquid or pudding.

You can prolong the life of amasake without freezing it by putting warm, freshly made amasake in sterile canning jars (ball jars) then sealing the jars while the amasake is still hot or warm. Refrigerate the jars then use them within one to two weeks of opening. We suggest using pint or quart jars. We do not have extensive experience with this but we have kept amasake for a couple of weeks this way, with no loss of flavor.

Commercial amasake will last longer than homemade, particularly when purchased in aseptic packs (not the most ecological, but handy at times). Amasake is usually found refrigerated in the dairy case of health food stores. Sometimes it is sold frozen. Aseptic cartons can usually be found on the soy milk aisle. Frozen amasake should generally be used within three to ten days of thawing. Amasake, if purchased from the refrigerator case, should be used within about one to two weeks. Aseptic packs should be opened by the date on the package then used within seven to ten days.

Making a manageable batch

When cooking for two, it is best to make amasake in smaller batches starting with one or two cups of dry whole grain. One cup of dry whole grain will make enough amasake to serve three to six people as a pudding. Two cups of dry grain will make enough to serve six to ten people.

You can increase the yield of your homemade amasake in one of several ways:

- by combining it with fruits, chestnuts, seeds, or nuts;
- by combining it with flour, bread, bread cubes, or other grains for puddings or baked goods;
- by using it as a topping for fruit or sweet vegetable desserts, or
- by making it more concentrated and sweeter (with more koji) then diluting it with water for use as a sweet drink or sweetener

You can also make a larger batch of amasake, with more grain, to serve more people.

Amasake, a dessert for all seasons and all reasons

Amasake is light yet concentrated, making it suitable for use in any season and for any occasion. We have certain favorites in each season and some that we favor just about any time of the year, though you will no doubt find your own as you experiment with the amasake making process. We often serve amasake puddings or special desserts made from them for birthdays, anniversaries, holidays, or weeknight treats.

Although at first it might seem like a terribly time consuming project, making your own amasake is really quite simple. In making amasake you won't have to spend a great deal of time tending the pot. You only have to assemble the mixture then intervene at brief intervals to perform simple steps. (Total hands-on time is typically 30-60 minutes for either a small or large batch.)

Koji: The key to making amasake

Koji (the inoculated spores that will break the grain down into maltose) is essential for making amasake. Inexpensive and high quality organic brown rice koji is available by mail from South River Miso Company, listed in this book under Mail Order Resources. (Bulk discounts are available if you buy several pounds.) A little bit of koji will go a long way and it will last for a long time if stored in a cool dry place.

Note: 1 pound of koji can make enough pudding to serve 30-40 people, though you needn't make up a batch so large and use up all your koji at once. Smaller batches made more often are more practical, nutritious, delicious, and easy to prepare than are giant batches.

White rice koji is also available in many Oriental markets in the refrigerator section in 32- oz. plastic tubs. (In the Pacific Northwest, Cold Mountain Koji is available in some Asian markets. Other brands can be found in other parts of the country if you know what to ask for.) Be sure not to ask for amasake. Ask for koji as this is what you will need to make your own plain type amasake. The difference between brown and white rice koji is simple: brown rice koji is made from brown rice and contains all of the nutrients found in brown rice; white rice koji is made from white rice. Either variety of koji will transform whole grains into a delicious and nutritious pudding, beverage, or concentrated sweetener.

Koji keeps almost indefinitely in a cool dry place (in sealed jars). We've kept it for up to three years and found that it's strength was not diminished. Imported koji (found in the macrobiotic section at many co-ops and health food stores) is overpriced and not as active or "live" as either the white rice koji from Asian markets or the brown rice koji mentioned before.

Amasake Favorites For All Seasons:

- **Winter:** Buckwheat; buckwheat + sweet rice; sweet rice + rice; sweet rice + millet or any of these combinations + dried chestnuts or dried fruit

- **Spring:** Barley + sweet rice; roasted barley + sweet rice; millet; sweet rice + polenta or sweet rice + millet

- **Summer:** Sweet rice + polenta; cornmeal or millet + sweet corn; millet; millet + sweet rice; any of these flavors + fruit; or roasted barley + sweet rice

- **Fall:** Millet; sweet rice + millet (+/- chestnuts); sweet rice + dried corn; roasted barley + sweet rice or cornmeal + sweet rice

- **Year Round Favorites (see index for recipes):** Roasted barley + sweet rice; millet + sweet rice; black sweet rice + millet or plain brown rice; millet + fruit; millet + rice

Note: Some varieties of amasake (plain buckwheat, plain millet, or oat amasake) may need to be thickened with arrowroot or kudzu powder (a starchy powder from the root of a common weed in the Southern United States and in many parts of Asia), agar agar, or vegetarian gelatin powder/flakes. The above combinations can be enhanced with a little thickener if you want to make them smoother or if you find them to be too sweet and need to dilute them with extra water then thicken them back to a pudding state. Experiment with your favorite grains. You may find a favorite we've not tried.

The Many Uses of Amasake:

Homemade amasake is usually very thick and makes a pudding on its own, with no thickening. It can also be used in pastry, bar, and cookie doughs without alteration. Commercial amasake is generally sold as a beverage (refrigerated, frozen, or in aseptic packages) and must be thickened to produce a pudding or cream-like dessert topping.

Use amasake as a dessert or pudding:

- on its own
- combined with spices
- combined with chopped nuts and/or spices
- combined with cooked parsnips, winter-squash, or sweet potato
- mixed with instant grain "coffe," +/- almond or vanilla extract, +/- roasted, chopped nuts
- combined with fresh or dried fruit and cooked briefly
- mix the concentrate with chestnut flour and arrowroot or kuzu for pudding

Use amasake to make jello, aspic, or parfaits (with agar agar and/or kudzu or arrowroot)

- with grain coffee and raisins
- with flavored extracts
- with fresh or dried fruit
- with fruit juice and fresh or dried fruit

Use amasake as a topping for:

- fresh seasonal raw fruits or fruit salad
- stewed, baked, simmered, or steamed fruit
- pumpkin, sweet potato or fruit pies (to replace whipped cream)
- cakes, bars, brownies, and fruit cakes (thickened with arrowroot or kuzu first)

Use amasake as a sweetener:

- on cookies, cakes, brownies, and bars
- in custards
- in pie and pastry fillings
- in pastry dough

Use amasake to replace:

- maple or corn syrup, rice malt, or barley malt in baked goods
- oil, margarine or butter in baked goods (usually best used with apple sauce)
- water in dessert pie crusts or pastry crust for a sweet and flaky crust
- cake frosting, thickened with arrowroot or kudzu and spices as desired
- smoothies blended with fresh berries or other fruits and water if needed
- yogurt or sour cream in cookies, cakes, brownies, and bars
- yogurt, milk, and sweeteners in steamed dessert buns
- yogurt, milk, and sweeteners in sweet quickbreads or pastries
- milk and/or cream in bread-, rice-, or noodle puddings
- milk, cream, or yogurt in puddings, custards, and flans
- malteds, hot cocoa, or milk shakes. When heated briefly, may be diluted with water ❏

Perfect places to ferment your grain

- A gas oven with just the pilot light on or set temperature at 120° F.
- An electric oven with the light on or preheat oven to 140° F. (put the grain in and turn it off, then turn it on again for 15 minutes every few hours, leaving the grain inside
- Near a warm radiator
- On top of a small electric heating pad on medium-high with a blanket wrapped around the pot for insulation
- An electric oven with a 100 watt bulb run into the oven with a heavy duty extension cord (light on, oven heat off, door closed)
- An electric oven, set to "warm"

Rules of Thumb for Amasake Pudding:

- For every 1 cup of dry grain, figure 1 1/2-2 cups wate (more if boiling, less if pressure cooking)
- Figure 1/4 -1/3 cup of dry whole grain per person before cooking (to yield 2/3-3/4 cup pudding)
- Use 1/4 cup of koji per 1-1 1/2 cups dry (uncooked) whole grain
- For 2 cups dry whole grain: 1/2 cup koji to make pudding for 6-8 (1/2-3/4 cup each)

Rule of Thumb for Amasake Concentrate or Beverage:

****Note**: This makes a sweet amasake beverage, like the kind sold in health foods stores.
- For every 1 cup of *dry grain*, figure 4 cups water
- Figure 1/4 -1/3 cup of *dry whole grain* per person before cooking (yields 1 cup beverage)
- Use 1/2-3/4 cup of koji per 1 cup dry (uncooked) whole grain
- For 2 cups dry whole grain, figure 1-1 1/2 cups koji for a beverage to serve 6-8 (1 cup per serving);

    or a concentrate to make 8 cups of pudding (to be thickened with flour, arrowroot or kuzu);

    or for a sweetener to use in other desserts

To make amasake pudding which requires no added thickener, try these combinations:

Favorite Combinations	Flavor
equal parts sweet brown rice + millet	Marshmallow cream—very rich!
equal parts Thai black sweet rice + millet or brown rice	Black cherries—very fruity!
equal parts sweet brown rice + barley	Vanilla pudding—very smooth!
equal parts sweet brown rice + roasted pearl or pot barley	Mocha—tastes like chocolate mousse!
equal parts sweet brown rice + whole oat groats	Milky, runny and slightly sticky
equal parts sweet brown rice + roasted buckwheat	Bread pudding (if made with raisins)
equal parts sweet brown rice + cracked dry corn	Sweet, corny, and light
Sweet brown rice + brown rice or millet + chestnuts	Fruity, sweet, rich, and creamy
Millet + dried peaches, cherries, or apricots	Fruity, creamy

Basic Procedure, Making Amasake (Year Round)***

Prep: 30-40 minutes total
Soaking: 4-8 hours or overnight
First cooking: 30-60 minutes, depending on grain
Cooling: 30-45 minutes
Incubation: 6-9 hours, in a warm place
Puréeing: 10 minutes
Final Cooking: 1/2-1 1/2 hours

Serving size: 2/3-3/4 cup thick pudding
(made from 1/4-1/3 cup dry whole grain)
or 3/4-1 cup thinned beverage
Serves: see chart below

Amasake only requires about 20-30 minutes of hands-on time. When cooking for two, make a small batch from two cups of dry whole grain. This yields 6-8 servings of pudding, an amount two can use within a week or two. It is inadvisable to freeze homemade amasake as this alters its taste and devitalizes it. (If you inadvertently make too much, you could keep it in the refrigerator for up to two weeks or freeze the extra to be used later in baking.)

Amasake Ratio & Rules of Thumb:

Serves: 6-8 (or 3x for 2)	**Serves: 9-12**	**Serves: 12-16**
2 cups whole grain	3 cups whole grain	4 cups whole grain
4 cups water	6 cups water*	7-8 cups water*
1/2-3/4 cup koji	3/4-1 1/4 cup koji	1-1 1/2 cups koji
1/4-1/2 tsp. sea salt	1/2 tsp. sea salt	1/2-3/4 tsp. sea salt

Optional, kuzu or arrowroot for thickening

* ***Note:*** *For a liquid amasake concentrate, use a ratio of 1 cup dry whole grain to 4 cups water. After cooking and cooling, add 1/2-1 cup koji, depending on desired sweetness. This will produce 1 quart (4 cups) of liquid amasake concentrate. This may be used to replace commercial amasake liquid in recipes; to replace other liquid sweeteners, or it may be diluted then thickened to make pudding.*

1. Wash, drain and soak as per Basic Procedure, Brown Rice or Millet. Soak 4-12 hours or overnight.

2. Do not add salt to grain. Pressure whole grain or a grain combination which includes brown rice, sweet rice, or barley for 45-60 minutes or simmer 1 hour as Basic Procedure Rice.

   (If millet is used alone, pressure cook or simmer 30 minutes.)

3. When grain is done, stir thoroughly top to bottom then transfer to a glass, pyrex, or ceramic bowl. Insert a metal stem thermometer into the center of the grain. Leave grain uncovered and cool to 110-130° F.. stirring periodically to cool. **Note:** Too hot a temperature will render the koji spores inactive. (It should be cool enough to stick your finger in for 20 seconds without getting burned.)

4. Stir koji into warm grain, using a wooden spoon or rice paddle. The grain will be very thick but will thin out as it ferments. Cover the bowl or casserole dish with a glass plate or lid. Keep in a warm place for 6-8 hours or overnight. Temperature should remain at 120-140° F during incubation but no hotter or the koji spores will die. Stir with a wooden spoon several times during fermentation and check the temperature with a thermometer. Grain should start to smell sweet and become watery as it ferments. Taste after about 5 hours, if it's not very sweet, let it ferment for another 2-3 hours.

5. Purée fermented grain in a blender, food processor, or hand food mill. If you use a hand food mill, stir the bran-y part back into the smooth grain purée.

6. Final cooking, on medium or low heat, is necessary to stop the fermentation to prevent souring. This cooking also makes the amasake sweeter and thicker. Pour puréed grain into a saucepan. Add salt as per the basic recipe. Bring to a boil, reduce heat to low and simmer covered or uncovered 15-20 minutes. If pudding is very runny, cook on low for 45-60 minutes. (If using a gas stove, slip a heat deflector under the pot to prevent burning.) Stir periodically to avoid burning. Mix any thick caramelized browned lumps back into the pudding.

Notes: *If pudding is not sweet enough or thick enough, cook it down on low for 2-3 hours with a heat deflector underneath or cook for several hours on low in a crock pot. It will thicken and caramelize on the bottom. Stir several times as it cooks, being careful not to burn it.*

If your amasake is too sweet: Dilute some or all of it with an extra cup or two of water. Dissolve arrowroot powder (1 Tbsp. per cup runny amasake) in a dash of cold water then stir this into the amasake. Simmer on low for several minutes to thicken. Or, thin amasake with water and serve as a beverage, warmed slightly or served close to room temperature.

7. Cool uncovered, at room temperature; in a covered pot on a cold porch; or in the refrigerator.

Storage: Leave serving size cups on the counter if they will be served within 2-24 hours. Amasake will keep unrefrigerated for 48 hours in uncovered bowls or cups in a cool box or on the counter in cold weather, away from heat or direct sunlight. Store remaining pudding in a plate covered glass bowl or jars in the refrigerator. (Amasake thickens and sweetens considerably as it cools.) Use within several days to two weeks.

Serving suggestions: Portion into small dessert cups, 2/3-3/4 cup pudding per person. Serve close to room temperature or warmed briefly. (See also "Uses for Amasake".) ❑

Notes:

- Take meal size portions from the refrigerator 1/2-1 hour before serving to allow them to come up to room temperature. This facilitates good digestion and improves the flavor. (Ice cold foods chill the Stomach and the whole body and injure the Spleen and digestive fire.)

- **To warm amasake:** Portion into small custard cups and steam on a metal rack, bamboo steamer tray, vegetable steamer basket, or trivet for several minutes over boiling water.

- **Spiced Amasake:** For each 2/3-3/4 cup serving, add 2-3 pinches (1/8 tsp.) dried powdered ginger, cinnamon, nutmeg, or allspice or 1/2-1 tsp. juice from finely grated and squeezed ginger root. Spices may be stirred into room temperature pudding or before rewarming. You may combine spices with chopped, roasted nuts. Figure 1/2-1 Tbsp. nuts per person/per serving.

- **Nutty Amasake:** Sprinkle on or mix in 1/2-1 Tbsp. dry roasted, chopped walnuts, almonds, hazelnuts, or peanuts, or stir in 1 tsp. nut butter per 1/2-3/4 cup portion, before serving.

- **Mocha Amasake:** Stir in 1 tsp. instant grain coffee per serving of amasake pudding. Stir while warm or when reheating. (Try Kafree Roma, Yannoh, Pero, Inka, or other brand). This variation is delicious with roasted chopped walnuts or mixed with hazelnut butter. (*It really tastes like chocolate!*)

- **Amasake Beverage:** Follow the basic procedure for amasake making but use 4 cups water per cup of dry grain and use 1/2-1 cup koji per cup of uncooked grain. After fermentation, cook as above but for just 15-40 minutes to stop the fermentation. Use this in any recipe calling for commercial amasake beverage.

Favorite Amasake Combinations:

Basic Millet & Sweet Rice Amasake Pudding (Year Round)***

This tastes a bit like marshmallow cream. It is one of our favorites. It makes an excellent wedding pudding. (You'll avoid the hassle of making a cake and the indigestion from eating a big cake on top of a big meal if you opt for this lighter and easier to digest dessert.) Amasake is very concentrated, so when used as a drink or pudding it is best served in small amounts.

Prep: 30 minutes
Soaking: 6-8 hours or overnight
First cooking: 45-50 minutes + final cooking
Incubation: 6-9 hours or as needed
Final cooking: 1/2-1 hour

Yield: 9-10 cups
Serves: 8-12
Serving size: 2/3-3/4 cup per person

** *Reduce or double recipe as needed.*

1 1/2 cups brown sweet rice

1 1/2 cups millet

6 cups water

3/4 cup koji

1/4-1/2 tsp. sun dried sea salt (added after fermentation)

1. Follow Basic Amasake Making Procedure.

2. Serve plain or mixed with a small amount of spice and/or nuts or grain coffee powder. ❏

Luscious Purple Pudding: Black Sweet Rice Amasake (Year Round) ***

Prep: 30 minutes
Soaking: 6-8 hours or overnight
First cooking: 45-60 minutes
Incubation: 6-9 hours or as needed
Final cooking: 1/2-1 hour

Yield: 8-10 cups
Serves: 10-12
Serving size: 2/3-3/4 cup per person

This pudding is incredibly sweet. It tastes and looks remarkably like blackberry or raspberry fruit pie filling even though it is fruit-free! The secret is Thai black sweet rice, available by mail from Gold Mine Natural Foods (see mail order resources) or in many Oriental markets. A little bit of black sweet rice goes a long way in this rich tasting pudding; some even find it to be too sweet! To cut the sweetness, dilute it slightly with water then thicken it with a bit of arrowroot or kuzu.

1 1/2 cups black sweet rice

1 1/2 cups short or medium grain brown rice

6 cups water

3/4 cup koji

1/4-1/2 tsp. sun dried sea salt (added after fermentation)

1. Prepare as per Basic Amasake Making Procedure above.

2. Serve as pudding, as a dessert topping, or use to sweeten cookies, cakes, muffins, or pastry.

• **Plain Rice amasake:** Use all short, medium, or long grain brown rice. Or, use half sweet brown rice and half short or medium grain brown rice. ❏

Roasted Barley Amasake Pudding (Fall, Winter, Spring)***

Prep: 30-40 minutes total
Dry roasting: 20 minutes
Making barley tea: 10-20 minutes
Soaking: 8-12 hours or overnight
First cooking: 50-60 minutes
Incubation: 6-9 hours or as needed
Final cooking: 1/2-1+ hour

Serves: ~6-10
Serving size: 1/2-3/4 cup per person

This one really tastes like chocolate mousse. Roasted barley amasake has a rich, sweet, roasted taste like bitter-sweet chocolate, but without any added fat or caffeine. This thick pudding makes incredible low-fat brownies (see index), cake frosting, or cookies, though we usually serve it as is. This super sweet pudding will knock your socks off, so watch out!

1 cup pot or pearled barley (uncooked)

1 cup sweet brown or white rice (uncooked)

2 cups water

2 cups very dark barley coffee (cooked and strained)**

1/2 cup koji

1/2 tsp. sun dried sea salt (added after fermentation)

1. Dry roast barley in skillet or wok over medium flame, stirring constantly, until dark—almost black in color—and aromatic (about 15 to 30 minutes for a double batch). Allow to cool.

2. Rinse and drain sweet rice using a fine mesh strainer. In a pressure cooker, combine roasted barley, drained sweet rice, water, and barley "coffee". Soak 8-12 hours or overnight. Do not throw off the soak water; you will cook the grain in this liquid.

3. Pressure cook 1 hour as per Basic Procedure, Brown Rice (but without salt). Use a heat deflector under the pot to prevent burning the bottom.

4. Proceed as per Basic Amasake Procedure.

Storage: Store in a glass jar in the refrigerator.

Serving suggestions: Serve as a pudding or use as a base or sweetener for other desserts. ❏

Note: Since this pudding is sometimes too sweet, you may wish to either use it as a sweetener in making other desserts or dilute it with water then add a bit of arrowroot or kuzu dissolved in cold water, then thicken it by stirring it over a medium-low heat.

**Dark Barley Coffee: Put 4 cups water into a saucepan or a stainless steel percolator and add 1/4-1/3 cup roasted barley or barley coffee grinds, preferably in a tea ball (from an Asian market, health food store, or mail order company). Cover, bring to boil, reduce heat to low, and simmer 20 minutes or until dark and thick. Pour through a strainer and use the amount called for in the recipe or use Chicory or Barley & Chicory Coffee, Beverage chapter.)

Uses:

• **Roasted Barley Amasake Brownies**

• **Roasted Barley Amasake Frosting:** This pudding would make a good frosting for cake with or without a dash of vanilla extract, almond extract and/or roasted chopped walnuts.

• Combine some of the leftover pudding with chestnut purée for a chestnut-mocha pudding.

• **Minty Mocha Amasake Pudding:** Combine a small portion of thick roasted barley amasake with a few drops of peppermint extract. ❏

Chestnut Amasake Cream
(Fall-Winter)

Prep: 20-30 minutes total
Soaking: 6-8 hours or overnight
First cooking: 1 hour
Incubation: 6-9 hours or as needed
Final cooking: 1/2-1+ hour

Yield: 9 cups thick pudding
Serves: 12 as a pudding or 24 as a dessert topping
Serving size: 1/2-3/4 cup as a pudding
  or 1/4-1/3 cup as a dessert topping

** *Reduce recipe by 1/2 or more as needed.*

This is an incredible pudding. It can also be used as a whipped-cream alternative and non-dairy topping for holiday pumpkin/sweet potato pudding or pies, cakes, or baked apples. You can also use this to make cookies, pastry dough, or other desserts. Chestnuts can be mail ordered (dried or steam-peeled and fresh frozen), or purchased in a health food store, food co-op, Italian market, or specialty foods store. Buying chestnuts in the shell is not recommended as they take a great deal of time and effort to roast, clean, and prepare.

1 1/2 cups sweet brown rice

1 1/2 cups millet

1 cup dried chestnuts or fresh-frozen steam-peeled chestnuts

6 cups water

1/2-3/4 cup koji

1/4-1/2 tsp. sun dried sea salt (added after grain has fermented)

1. Rinse grains and drain. Combine in a 4-6-quart pressure cooker. Add the water and dried chestnuts. (**Note**: these are not water chestnuts but a different variety altogether.) If using fresh-frozen steam-peeled chestnuts, add them to the grain just before cooking. Soak grain and chestnuts for 6-12 hours.

2. Do not throw off soak water. Pressure cook 1 hour or bring to boil and simmer, covered for 1-1 1/2 hours. Incubate, purée, and cook down with sea salt as per Basic Amasake Procedure.

Serving suggestions: As pie topping, serve 1/4-1/3 cup per person; as a pudding, 1/2-3/4 cup per person. Or, use in baking cookies, pumpkin pies, bars, or quick breads to replace sweeteners and most of the oil. Or, use to replace soy milk or milk in sweet desserts. (~3/4 cup per person as a dessert/drink). ❏

Variations:

- **Millet & Polenta Amasake:** Follow above procedure, but use half millet, half polenta or coarse cornmeal and omit chestnuts (Use 2 cups water per cup dry millet, polenta, or cornmeal. Pressure cook or simmer 30 minutes as per Basic Procedure.)

- **Sweet Rice & Cornmeal Amasake:** In the basic amasake recipe, use half sweet rice and half cornmeal. Soak and pressure cook or simmer the two grains for 45-60 minutes before incubating as per Basic Amasake Procedure.❏

Basic Procedure, Fruity Amasake
Pudding (Fall, Winter, Spring)

Prep: 30 minutes total
Soaking: 6-8 hours or overnight
Cooking: 30 minutes
Incubation: 6-9 hours or as needed
Final cooking: 1/2-1+ hour

Yield: 10-12 cups pudding
Serves: 10-12
Serving size: 2/3-3/4 cup per person

Amasake pudding can be enhanced with dried fruit for a sweeter or more interesting taste and texture. Prepare a basic amasake pudding, add the dried fruit, then follow the procedure below.

3 cups soft shelled grain (millet, kasha, or polenta/coarse cornmeal, etc.)

5-6 cups water

3/4 cup koji ***

1/2 tsp. sun dried sea salt (added after fermentation)

1/2 cup dried fruit

1 cup water (to soak dried fruit)

2-3 Tbsp. arrowroot or kuzu, dissolved in 3-4 Tbsp. cold water

1. Rinse grain, soak, cook, incubate then purée as per Basic Procedure, Amasake. You may omit the soaking stage for kasha, polenta, or cornmeal.

2. In a bowl or saucepan, soak dried fruit in the recommended volume of water for 1 hour or overnight. Remove dried fruit from water, mince finely, then return to soak water in a saucepan. Bring to boil, cover, reduce heat to low and simmer 5 minutes.

3. To amasake add arrowroot or kuzu dissolved in suggested volume of cold water. Simmer and stir to thicken (~3-5 minutes). Next, add fruit and simmer on low heat to evenly distribute and thicken (~5-10 minutes). Remove from heat.

4. Mixture will thicken as it cools. Allow to cool at room temperature, uncovered or in a bowl or wide-mouth jar in the refrigerator.

Storage: Store in a covered glass jar or bowl in the refrigerator. Keeps for up to two weeks.

Serving suggestions: Serve as a pudding or use leftovers as per tips below.

Other tips & uses:

- Use to replace sweeteners and some of the oil in cookies, brownies, and quick breads.

- If too sweet for a dessert pudding, dilute some kuzu or arrowroot in cold water, add to pudding and stir over medium heat to thicken.

- This also makes a good cake frosting when puréed, with or without a dash of vanilla extract, almond extract and/ or roasted chopped walnuts or hazelnuts. ❏

Examples:

Millet & Dried Peach Amasake (Spring, Fall)

Prep: 30 minutes total
Soaking: 6-8 hours or overnight
Cooking: 30 minutes
Incubation: 6-9 hours or as needed
Final cooking: 1/2-1+ hour

Yield: 10-12 cups pudding
Serves: 10-12
Serving size: 2/3-3/4 cup per person

Homemade millet amasake is unlike commercial rice-based drinks. It is thick, creamy and makes a delectable pudding or sweetener for baked goods. You may experiment with different types of dried fruits.

3 cups millet

6 cups water

3/4 cup koji ***

1/2 tsp. sun dried sea salt (added after fermentation)

1/2 cup dried peaches (or other dried fruit)

1 cup water (to soak peaches)

2 Tbsp. arrowroot or kuzu dissolved in 4 Tbsp. cold water.

1. Prepare grain as per Basic Procedure, Amasake Pudding.

2. Soak the dried fruit for 3-8 hours. Chop finely, then simmer in the soak liquid for 30 minutes. Add fruit to amasake as per Basic Procedure, Fruity Amasake, above, then stir to thicken. Cool and store as per suggestions above.

Variations:

- Use dried cherries, blueberries, apricots, nectarines, prunes, or strawberries. If using brown rice, sweet brown rice or other hard shelled grain, or a mixed grain combination, to make the basic amasake, pressure cook grain for 45-50 minutes or simmer for 1 hour before incubating. If using cracked or rolled grains by themselves, simmer 25-30 minutes before incubating. ❏

Buckwheat-Raisin Amasake Pudding (Fall, Winter)

Prep: 30 minutes total
Soaking: optional 3-6 hours
First cooking: 30 minutes
Incubation: 6-9 hours or as needed
Final cooking: 1/2-2 hours

Yield: 10 cups
Serves: 10-12
Serving size: 2/3-3/4 cup per person

Buckwheat amasake tastes like thick, smooth, dark, rich chocolate mousse or bread pudding.

3 cups roasted buckwheat groats (kasha)

5 cups water

3/4 cup koji

1/2 tsp. sun dried sea salt

1/2-3/4 cup raisins

1/2-3/4 cup water (to soak raisins)

1 Tbsp. arrowroot or kuzu dissolved in 1 Tbsp. cold water

1. Do not rinse the kasha (roasted buckwheat). Soak for 2-8 hours or skip the soaking.

2. Bring to boil, cover, then slip a heat deflector under the pot and simmer on low, 20-30 minutes, with no salt added. Do not stir during cooking.

3. To incubate, follow Basic Procedure Amasake, page 432. To add fruit, follow the Basic Procedure for Fruity Amasake, (steps #2-#3). Let cool all day or overnight.

Serving suggestions:

- Serve as a pudding.

- Use to replace sweeteners and/or some of the oil in spice cookies, brownies, muffins, or ginger bread cookies and cakes. (Replace some of the oil with apple sauce and add additional raisins or a dash of barley malt if desired.)

Storage: Refrigerate in a covered glass bowl or jars. Use within 3-7 days. ❏

Almost Instant Amasake Pudding (Any Season)***

Prep: 5-10 minutes
Cooking: 5-10 minutes

Serves: 2-3
Serving size: 2/3-1 cup per person

This is a quick and easy recipe for a luscious, creamy, naturally sweet pudding. It is ideal for the times when you want amasake but lack the time to make it from scratch. It can be made in under ten minutes and is low-in fat. Commercial amasake comes in a rainbow of flavors. For this recipe you can use either the aseptic packs or the kind sold in small bottles in the refrigerator or freezer case of your local health food store. Or, substitute homemade amasake concentrate/beverage.

16 oz. (2 cups) commercial Amasake (*Vanilla Pecan, Almond, Sesame, or Original Amasake shake or beverage: Grainaissance or other locally made brands, made from whole grain brown rice*) **or** homemade amasake concentrate or beverage

3 Tbsp. arrowroot or kuzu root powder

1 pinch sea salt

Optional, 1/8 tsp. ground cinnamon, ginger, or pumpkin pie spice

1. Blend cold or room temperature amasake and arrowroot or kuzu starch in a blender. Add spice if desired. Pour into a 1 or 2-quart pot. Heat over a medium flame, stirring constantly until it thickens and boils, reduce heat and simmer 3-4 minutes.

2. Pour into two or three serving dishes and allow to cool for 1/2-6 hours at room temperature before serving or refrigerate until firm if you are in a hurry.

Serving suggestions: Once it has cooled and firmed up it is ready to eat. (If refrigerated, remove and allow to come to room temperature for 30-90 minutes before serving.)

If you have used a fat- and nut-free amasake (original flavor), sprinkle 1-3 tsp. chopped roasted almonds, walnuts, or hazelnuts over each cup before serving if desired.

Variations:

• Almost Instant Mocha Amasake Pudding (Any Season)***

Use Mocha-Java flavored amasake or dissolve 2 Tbsp. instant grain coffee powder (Kafree Roma, Pero, Inka, Caffix, or other) in the cold/cool almond, sesame, or original flavored amasake in step #1 above.

• Vanilla, Butterscotch, or Almond Amasake Pudding (Any Season)

Use original flavored commercial amasake and add 1/2 tsp. natural vanilla, almond, or butterscotch extract. (Skip the grain coffee powder.)

• Almost Instant Chestnut-Amasake Pudding (Any Season)***

Combine 2 cups of room temperature or cold commercial amasake beverage (any flavor) or homemade amasake concentrate with 1/2 cup chestnut flour, 1 Tbsp. arrowroot or kuzu root powder, and 1/8 tsp. sea salt. Purée in a blender. Optional: Add 1 Tbsp. tahini or hazelnut butter.

To simmer: Bring to boil in a saucepan then simmer and stir until thick. Cook 8-10 minutes on low.

To cook without stirring: (This produces a denser, fluffier pudding.) Pour into a 16-32 - oz. stainless steel bowl. Cover with a heat-proof saucer. Cook using the covered bowl-within-a-pot method, (see Table of Contents for cooking & reheating techniques) for 40-45 minutes. Stir. Spoon into 2-3 dessert cups. If using amasake which doesn't contain any nuts or seeds, sprinkle each serving with 2 tsp. chopped roasted nuts. ❑

More Puddings

Basic Procedure, Steamed Grain Pudding (Year Round)***

Prep: 15 minutes
Cooking: 1 hour

Serves: 8 (or 4 with leftovers)
Serving size: 2/3-3/4 cup per person

Reduce recipe by 1/2 to serve 4 (or 2x for 2)

It's a snap to make this pudding. You won't have to stir it while it cooks nor will you have to worry about it burning on the bottom. Steaming makes clean up a snap and creates a light and creamy texture. Suitable any time of the year.

1-1 1/4 cups raisins or currants

1 cup apple juice or apple cider

4 cups water

1 1/4 cups rolled or cracked grain *(oatmeal, barley flakes, wheat flakes, corn meal, etc.)*

1/4 cup sunflower seeds or chopped walnuts, hazelnuts, or almonds

1/2 tsp. sea salt

1 tsp. cinnamon (or other sweet spice)

Optional, 1/2 tsp. almond or vanilla extract

1. Mix all ingredients in a heat-proof glass (pyrex) or small stainless steel mixing bowl. Cover bowl with a heat-proof saucer or dinner plate and set on top of a metal disk, trivet, or rack on the bottom of a large pot. If using a stainless steel bowl, put the covered bowl directly in the bottom of the pot.

2. Add enough water to the pot to surround bowl up to 1/3 of its height. Cover the pot and bring to boil, reduce heat to medium and cook 1 hour.

3. After cooking time has elapsed, stir vigorously with a fork or wooden spoon to dissolve any lumps. Ladle into individual dessert cups or spoon into a square cake pan. Allow to cool to room temperature before serving. (If desired cut into small squares or serve from an ice cream scoop for a more attractive presentation.)

Serving suggestions: Serve close to room temperature or briefly steam heat on a rack.

Storage: Refrigerate leftovers that will not be eaten within 24 hours, otherwise, cover with a bamboo mat and store on the counter or in a cold box.

Variation:

- **To simmer, rather than steam:** Combine all ingredients in a saucepan. Whisk gently and bring to boil over a low heat, stirring constantly. Cover, reduce heat to low and simmer 45 minutes with a heat deflector under the pot to prevent burning. *On an an electric stove,* preheat deflector on a separate burner then put the boiling pot on the deflector before reducing heat. Cook as above.

Favorites: (Use sea salt in all recipes)

- **Steamed Barley-Raisin Pudding (Spring):** Rolled barley, sunflower seeds, raisins, and cinnamon.

- **Steamed Sunflower Oat Pudding (Fall and Winter):** Use rolled oats, sunflower seeds or chopped walnuts, and cinnamon.

- **Steamed Corn Pudding (Spring through Fall):** Use cornmeal, raisins, dried cherries or blueberries, and sunflower seeds, almonds, or hazelnuts. Increase liquid to 5 cups.

- **Steamed Wheat Pudding:** Use white wheat or whole wheat pastry flour with raisins; add hazelnuts, walnuts, or sunflower seeds; also add dried ginger powder or nutmeg.

- **Barley-Rice Pudding (Spring, Summer, Fall):** Use barley flour with brown rice or sweet rice flour. Use raisins and walnuts or replace nuts or seeds with 3 Tbsp. sesame tahini.

- Replace all or part of the cinnamon with ginger, allspice, nutmeg, or pumpkin pie spice. ❏

Basic Bread Pudding
(Late Fall, Winter)

Prep: 20 minutes
Soaking (before cooking): 1-3 hours

Cooking: 1 hour
Serves: 8-10
Serving size: 2/3-3/4 cup per person

****Note: If reducing recipe, save energy and cook by steaming unless your oven will be used to cook other foods.**

This simple bread pudding has gotten rave reviews. Whole grain sourdough or yeasted bread make without added oil or sweeteners produces the best results. Miso adds a brandy-like flavor and helps to balance the sweetness while aiding in digestion. Experiment with different spices as you wish. The flavor improves with age and second day leftovers are even better.

5 1/2 cups cubed fresh or stale sourdough rye, wheat, barley, or other bread*

1/2 cup raisins

1 heaping Tbsp. caraway seeds or powder (or substitute anise seeds or anise powder)

5 cups apples cored and diced, skins left on *(Granny Smith, Johnathon, Jona Gold, Pipin, Braeburn, Cortland, or other local apples)*

1 1/2-2 level Tbsp. sunflower or hazelnut butter, **or** sesame tahini

1 cup water

2 Tbsp. light, yellow, mellow, sweet, or red miso

2 cups commercial amasake beverage (original or almond flavor) **or** homemade amasake concentrate **or** Vanilla Rice Dream Beverage.

1/2-2/3 cup fruit juice sweetened apple butter, fruit sweetened jam, **or** additional amasake or rice milk beverage

1. In a large mixing bowl, combine first 4 ingredients.

2. In a suribachi or mortar and pestle mix and mash remaining ingredients then pour over apples and bread and stir to coat.

3. Oil a 2-quart casserole dish or two 9-inch pie plates or cake pans. Spoon mixture into pans. Cover with a glass or stainless steel lid. Allow mixture to sit for 2-4 hours before baking so the bread can soak up the flavors.

4. Bake covered pans or casserole dishes at 350° F. for 1 hour or until slightly firm and pudding starts to pulls away from the sides of the pan. Remove from oven and spoon into individual dessert cups. (An ice cream scooper works well for this and makes it look lovely.)

Serving suggestions: Allow to cool slightly then serve. Dessert can be made a day in advance to allow flavors to mingle even more.

Storage: Refrigerate. Serve room temperature or lightly reheat by steaming in cups on a tray.

Variations:

• In place of caraway, use 1 tsp. cinnamon + 1/2 tsp. nutmeg +/- 1/8 tsp. ginger powder.

• **Corn Bread Pudding:** Use leftover corn bread or corn buns in the above recipe.

• **Chestnut Bread Pudding:** Use leftover chestnut loaf bread, buns, or other bread.

• **Barley Bread Pudding:** Use bread made with part barley flour and part wheat flour.

• **Steamed Bread Pudding:** Spoon uncooked dessert into a stainless steel bowl or a heat-proof pyrex bowl. Allow some room for expansion during cooking. Cover with a heat-proof saucer. Steam 1 hour using the covered bowl-within-a-pot method (see reheating tips & techniques in Chapter 2).

• **Quickest Steamed Bread Pudding:** Combine 5 1/2 cups cubed bread + 5 cups amasake beverage or homemade amasake thinned to a milky texture + 1/2 cup raisins + 1/4 tsp. sea salt + 1 tsp. cinnamon. Cover with a plate and steam for 1 hour in a bowl on a rack, tray, or trivet (covered bowl-within-a-pot method). ❑

Creamy Dreamy Chestnut Custard (Any Season)***

Prep: 30 minutes
Cooking: 40-45 minutes

Serves: 6
Serving size: 2/3-3/4 cup per person

***Reduce recipe by 1/3 to serve 4 (or 2x for 2)*

This pudding is delectably smooth, creamy, sweet, and easy to digest. Leftovers are just as tasty the second day so make an extra portion or two! This, as well as Almost Instant Amasake Pudding or regular amasake pudding, and Rosehip & Apple Compote, have become our house desserts. We never tire of them nor do our guests. Chestnut flour is not as widely available in American stores as it is in Italy so you may have to order it by mail. (See Resources.)

1/2 cup packed raisins (or see fresh fruit variations below)
4 cups apple juice

1 1/2 cups water
1/4 tsp. sea salt
2 Tbsp. sesame tahini (or light sesame butter)
1 cup chestnut flour
2 Tbsp. arrowroot or kuzu root dissolved in 1/4 cup cool or cold water

1. Place raisins and apple juice in a pot. Bring to boil, cover, reduce heat to low, and simmer 10 minutes. (Skip this step if using fresh fruit.)

2. Puree the next four ingredients in a blender. Stir into the simmering juice mixture. Cover, reduce heat to low, and simmer 20 minutes.

3. Blend water and arrowroot or kuzu. Add to pudding and stir until it starts to thicken, cover pot then slip a heat deflector underneath and simmer on low 15-20 minutes until thick. It will thicken even more as it cools.

4. Spoon into serving cups. Allow to cool at room temperature then serve. Store at room temperature for up to 24 hours or refrigerate then remove portions 1/2-2 hours before serving.

Variations:

- **Mocha Chestnut Pudding:** Add 2 Tbsp. instant grain coffee (Kaffree Roma, Pero, Postum, Yannoh, or other brand) to the pot in step #1 above.

- **Chestnut & Dried Cherry or Blueberry Pudding:** Substitute dried cherries or dried blueberries for raisins. Select those free of additives, preservatives and sugar.

- **Fresh Cherry, Peach, Blueberry, or Apricot & Chestnut Pudding:** Omit raisins and the 1 1/2 cups water above. Skip step #1. Instead, blend juice, chestnut flour, salt, arrowroot and tahini or sesame butter in step #2. Bring to boil, stir, cover, reduce heat to low and simmer for 15 minutes. Add 2 cups fresh pitted cherries, berries, or chopped apricots, peaches, or nectarines then simmer, covered, on low heat, for 15 minutes or until very thick. It is helpful to slip a heat deflector under the pot once it comes to boil.

- Use hazelnut butter instead of tahini.

- See **Almost Instant Chestnut Amasake Pudding.** ❏

Chestnut or Maple Chestnut Pudding (Fall, Winter, Spring)***

Prep: 20-25 minutes
Soaking: 4-8 hours or overnight
Cooking: 1 hour if pressure cooking; 2 hours if simmering

Serves: 6
Serving size: 2/3-3/4 cup each

Dried chestnuts make a wonderfully sweet pudding that doubles as a sweetener for cookies, pumpkin pie, quick breads, brownies, or a pastry filling. Maple syrup is high in sugars and very labor intensive so we use it very infrequently. (It takes 40 gallons of maple sap to make 1 gallon of maple syrup!) For a sweet taste without maple syrup, replace the maple syrup with barley malt.

2 cups dried chestnuts or fresh-frozen steam-
    peeled chestnuts

3 1/2 cups water (5 cups water, if boiling)

1/2 tsp. sun dried sea salt

Additional water to thin to desired
    consistency, if needed

1/4 cup maple syrup **or** 1/2 cup barley malt
    syrup

Optional, 1 tsp. almond extract
    or maple extract (if maple syrup is omitted)

2 Tbsp. arrowroot powder or kuzu root dis-
    solved in 1/4-1/3 cup cold water

1. Soak chestnuts 6-8 hours or overnight in water. Do not throw out the soak water.

2. Pressure cook chestnuts in their soak liquid for 45 minutes or bring to boil and simmer covered, on low, in a pot with a heavy lid, for 1 1/2 hours or until tender.

3. Purée chestnuts in a Foley food mill, food processor or blender with cooking liquid. This should yield 3 2/3-4 cups purée. If not, add additional water. Add sea salt and maple syrup. If too thick, add water to thin. If using barley malt syrup, bring malt to boil and simmer and stir 2-3 minutes. Turn off and add to chestnuts.

4. Dissolve arrowroot or kuzu in cold water and add to purée. Simmer pudding over medium or medium-low heat and stir to thicken, about 5-10 minutes or cook in a covered bowl-within-a-pot for 20 minutes to avoid stirring.

5. Ladle into dessert cups. Allow to set up at room temperature It will thicken as it cools and will become even sweeter the second day.

Storage: Refrigerate leftovers if they will not be used within 24 hours.

Leftover tips:

- Mix leftover pudding with mashed, baked squash or sweet potato to serve as a pudding or pie, pastry, or turnover filling.

- Use to replace liquid sweeteners or yogurt in carob or grain-coffee based brownies or in cookie or cake batter. (You can use apple sauce to replace most oil in baked goods.)

Variation:

- Add 2 Tbsp. hazelnut butter in step #3. ❏

Parsnip Amasake Pudding
(Fall & Winter; Great for Halloween)

***Amasake must be made ahead or
purchased for this recipe**

Prep: 20-30 minutes
Cooking: 50 minutes

Serves: 6-8
Serving size: 3/4-1 cup per person

Parsnips are sweet, if you get a good batch. Combined with amasake they make a luscious, creamy pudding that's perfect to top off a festive meal. Start with thick homemade amasake (made from brown rice or brown rice with sweet rice or millet) or simply pick up some commercial amasake nectar or shake at the health food store. Leftovers are even sweeter on the second or third day and can even be used to make cookies, quick breads, or muffins (to replace the sweetener and most of the oil).

1 tsp. light sesame, sunflower or walnut oil to
   coat the bottom of a pot

3 cups parsnips, washed and minced

3 pinches sea salt

1/3 cup water (if pressure cooking) **or**
   1/3-1/2 cup (if simmering)

1/3 cup raisins

1/2 cup water

1/8 tsp. sea salt

4 cups commercial amasake shake, *(original or
   vanilla pecan flavor)*
   or 4 cups amasake concentrate
   or 4 cups thick amasake pudding

About 3 Tbsp. arrowroot powder or kuzu (1 1/2
   Tbsp. if using thick Amasake pudding.)

1/2-2/3 tsp. cinnamon or nutmeg, ground

1. Place oil in the bottom of a pressure cooker or large pot. Add minced parsnips and a pinch of sea salt. Sauté over medium heat, stirring constantly until soft and aromatic, 3-5 minutes.

2. Add 1/3-1/2 cup water. Pressure cook 15 minutes or cover, bring to boil, reduce heat to low, and simmer covered 30 minutes.

3. Meanwhile mix raisins and sea salt in a pot with 1/2 cup water. Bring to a boil, cover, reduce heat to low, and simmer 10 minutes. Add cinnamon or nutmeg.

4. Purée cooked parsnips, raisins, raisin cooking liquid, amasake, and arrowroot in a blender or foley food mill until smooth. Pour into a saucepan. Bring to a boil, then reduce heat to low and simmer 5-6 minutes until mixture starts to thicken, stirring constantly.

5. If mixture is too thin and/or too sweet, dilute an extra tablespoon of arrowroot in 1/2 cup cold water. Add this to the pot and stir to thicken. Ladle into individual dessert cups. Allow to cool at room temperature for 1-3 hours before serving.

Storage: Store leftovers in a glass jar in the refrigerator.

Serving suggestions: Serve pudding at room temperature. Garnish with a sprinkle of nutmeg if desired.

Variations:

- **Pumpkin Amasake Pudding:**
Replace parsnips above with cubed kabocha, buttercup, butternut, or hokaido pumpkin.

- **Sweet Potato Amasake Pudding:**
Use peeled red garnet or jewel "yams" or white sweet potatoes. (Thought these are labeled "yams," they are actually sweet potatoes! True yams are white and starchy, not yellow or orange. True yams are not sweet, nor are they grown in the U. S.) ❑

Super Simple Squash Custard or Pumpkin Pudding (Fall & Winter)***

Prep: 20 minutes
Cooking: 45-60 minutes
Cooling: 2-4 hours or overnight

Yield: 2 9" pie plates, 1 oblong pan, *or* 12 custard cups
Serves: 12-14

*** Reduce recipe by one-half to serve 6 (or 3x for 2).*

This is a pumpkin pie without the crust. Unlike most pies or custards, this one is low in fat, eggless and so easy that even the busiest cook can make it. You won't need to add any sweetener if you pick a sweet squash such as kabocha, hokaido, buttercup, sweet mama, butternut, or sweet dumpling. We don't use the starchier, less sweet sugar pie pumpkins, acorns, or canned pumpkins which cry out for a lot of fat and sweeteners. Serve this pudding solo, or for the holidays top with amasake pudding or chestnut "cream" or Vanilla Amasake Pudding.

2 cups apple juice or cider, preferably fresh

8-9 cups cubed winter squash (*buttercup, kabocha, hokaido, sweet dumpling, or sweet mama*), cubed *or* peeled and cubed butternut squash

2 Tbsp. corn oil *or* 3-4 Tbsp. hazelnut butter

1/4 tsp. sea salt

2 tsp. pumpkin pie spice

3 Tbsp. arrowroot *or* 2-2 1/2 Tbsp. kuzu root

1/4-1/2 cup cold water or apple juice

Optional topping:

Amasake Pudding, Maple Chestnut Cream Topping, *or* Chestnut Amasake

1. Wash squash, halve, then remove and discard the seeds from the portion you plan to use immediately. Cut squash into 1-inch cubes and place in a measuring cup, measuring out the volume needed. The skin may be left on the squash (if you are using any of the recommended squashes) and puréed with the flesh at the end of cooking. For a more delicate pudding, peel the squash before slicing.

2. In a 4-quart pot combine the first five ingredients. Cover and bring to boil over medium heat, reduce heat to low, and simmer 40 minutes or until soft. You may wish to use a heat deflector.

3. Purée squash mixture in a hand food mill or food processor. Return it to the pot. Dissolve arrowroot in a small portion of cold water or juice and add to the pot. Turn heat to low or medium-low and stir to thicken for several minutes. If too thick, add an extra 1/4-1/2 cup juice.

4. When custard starts to thicken, remove from heat, stir again, then ladle or pour into two round or square cake pans, pie plates, ceramic dishes, or 10-12 individual custard cups.

5. Allow to firm up several hours at room temperature or in the refrigerator before serving.

Serving suggestions: Remove dessert from the refrigerator 1/2-1 hour before serving to allow it to come to room temperature. Serve as is or topped with thick amasake pudding, chestnut purée, Maple Chestnut Cream, Nutty-Honey Sauce, or a sprinkle of chopped, dry roasted walnuts or hazelnuts. Use within three days for best flavor.

Storage: Refrigerate leftovers that will not be eaten within 24 hours.

Variation:

• Use thin homemade amasake concentrate or commercial amasake nectar to dilute arrowroot. ❏

Easiest Ever Fruit Desserts

Compotes, Sauces, Stewed Fruits & More

Rosehip & Apple Compote (Fall, Winter, Spring)***

Prep: 10-15 minutes (depending on size of apples)
Cooking: 15-20 minutes *or* 3-4 hours in a crock pot on low

Serves: 6-8
Serving size: about 2/3-3/4 cup per person

Reduce recipe by 1/2 to serve 3-4 (or 2 meals worth of dessert for two)

Apple compotes are a snap to make and always a hit with cooking students and guests. This is one of our three most favorite desserts (Creamy Dreamy Chestnut Custard and amasake are the others). If you're short on time assemble the compote just before sitting down to supper, leave it to simmer while you eat, then let it cool while you wash dishes. We usually make a smaller batch to serve four or two meals worth of dessert for the two of us (using the guidelines below) and we serve it solo or with a plain toasted nut topping.

Rule of thumb: Per person, figure 1 medium or 2/3 of a large apple + 2-3 tsp. raisins + 1-2 Tbsp. dried, seeded, rose hips (found in health food stores) + a pinch of salt + 1-2 Tbsp. water.

5 large or 6 medium Granny Smith, Macintosh, Braeburn, Jona Gold or Jonathon apples, or other tart apples from your state or region

1/2 cup dried, seeded, rosehips (little red flakes), sorted to remove any bits of the kernel

4-5 Tbsp. organic raisins (use slightly less if sweeter apples are used)

1/4 tsp. sun dried sea salt

~1/4-1/2 cup water, as needed to just cover the bottom of the pot

Optional Toppings

Nutty Topping #1

4-8 Tbsp. dry roasted, chopped walnuts, hazelnuts, or almonds

Nutty-Honey Sauce #2 (Best used only occasionally)

2 heaping Tbsp. sunflower or peanut butter
2 Tbsp. rice malt syrup or honey
3-4 Tbsp. water

1. Wash but do not peel apples. Halve and remove cores and seeds. Grate 3 apples and dice the rest. (In a hurry? Just dice all the apples rather than grating some of them.)

2. Layer ingredients in a 3-4-quart pot with a heavy lid, first dried, seeded rosehips, then raisins, then grated apples, then chopped apples, salt, and water. Cover, bring to boil, reduce heat to low, and simmer 15 minutes if part of the apples are grated, 30 minutes if ungrated. Or, pressure cook 15-20 minutes directly in a pressure cooker or a covered-bowl-within-a-pot. Do not stir during cooking.

3. Stir well and spoon into individual dessert cups. Allow to cool at room temperature for 1-5 hours. Or, refrigerate then remove portions from the refrigerator 30-60 minutes prior to serving to take the chill off.

4. *For topping:* Sprinkle 2-3 tsp. chopped, dry roasted nuts over each fruit cup or for sauce, combine and stir nut or seed butter with sweetener and water in a bowl or suribachi to form a smooth paste. Spoon over portions of fruit, about 1 Tbsp. sauce for each.

Storage: Refrigerate leftovers.

Variation:
Rosehip-Apple & Dried Peach Compote: Add 1/4 cup diced, dried peaches. ❏

Basic Procedure, Apple Sauce or Compote (Fall, Winter, Spring)***

Prep: 10-15 minutes
Cooking: 15 minutes if pressure cooking,
or 30-60 minutes if simmering

Serving size: 2/3-1 cup per person
Serves: 6-8 (or 3-4 meals for 2)

This is one of the easiest desserts to make and one of the most delicious. Apples are a treat any time of year, but particularly in winter months when many other varieties of fruit are not freshly and locally available. Raisins provide all the sweetness you need.

6-8 medium-sized apples—*(Empire, Granny Smith, Gravenstein, Cortland, Pipin, Macintosh, Jonathon, Jona Gold, or other tart or sweet apples, or a mixture of 2-3 varieties)*

1/3-1/2 cup raisins or slightly more minced prunes

1/4 tsp. sea salt

~2/3 cup water, enough to just cover the bottom of the pot

1 Tbsp. anise, fennel, or caraway seeds, whole or ground
or 1/2-2/3 tsp. powdered cinnamon

Optional, 1 Tbsp. arrowroot *or* kuzu *or* whole wheat pastry, spelt, or barley flour dissolved in 3 Tbsp. cold water

Optional, garnish, 1-3 tsp. chopped, dry roasted walnuts, almonds, or hazelnuts per serving

1. Wash and halve apples. Leave skin on. Remove seeds and core with a small spoon. Cut into 1/2-1 inch dice or cubes.

2. **To pressure cook**: combine apples, raisins or prunes, salt, liquid, and spices. Bring to pressure, reduce heat to low, and cook 15-20 minutes. Let pressure to come down naturally.

   To boil: Combine ingredients as above, but add water to just cover the bottom of the pot. Cover, bring to boil, reduce heat to low and simmer 40-60 minutes.

3. Remove lid. Mash fruit with a potato masher. If fruit sauce is too watery (or if you plan to use it in turnovers or a pie crust), dissolve arrowroot or flour in 2-3 Tbsp. cold water, add this to pot, and simmer and stir for 3-5 minutes over medium heat to thicken.

Serving suggestions: Serve warm or at room temperature. If desired, top with roasted, chopped nuts (1-3 tsp. per serving).

Storage: Refrigerate leftovers; take them out of the refrigerator 30-90 minutes before serving or briefly steam heat in custard cups on a bamboo tray or metal steamer basket before serving.

Variations:

- Try pears or a mixture of apples and pears.
- Increase raisins to 2/3 cup and/or replace water with apple juice for a concentrated sweetener for use in baking.
- Serve as is or purée and use in baking to replace oil, margarine, shortening, butter or sweeteners.
- **Fruit Filled Turnovers:** Use the above fruit compote as a filling for Dessert Won Tons then bake or steam as per Won Ton Procedure. (Use juice in the dough if desired.)

Favorites:

- **Caraway Apple Compote**
- **Anise Apple Compote**
- **Cinnamon Apple Compote**
- **Gingery Apple Compote:** Omit spices suggested above Instead, add 1 tsp. juice from freshly grated and squeezed ginger root after cooking the sauce.
- **Anise Pear Compote**
- Any of the above combinations with pears or apples and pears combined. ❏

Cranberry-Apple Sauce or Compote (Fall, Early Winter)***

Prep: 10-15 minutes
Cooking: 30-35 minutes (or 15 minutes at pressure)

Serves: 8
Serving size: 2/3-3/4 cup per person

***Reduce recipe by one half to serve 4
(or 2 x for 2).*

This festive fall dessert can be assembled in minutes and is sure to hit the spot after a hearty fall or winter meal. Granny smith apples are a favorite in our house. Their high pectin content acts as a natural thickener. If using another type of apple you may need to thicken the sauce with arrowroot or kuzu.

1/2-3/4 cup raisins *(the smaller amount when using sweet apples, the greater amount when using very tart apples)*

2 cups fresh cranberries, rinsed, and drained (see variations below)*

4 large or 5 medium Granny Smith, Jona Gold, Jonathon, Macintosh, Braeburn, apples

or other tart semi-sweet apples, washed, cored and chopped, skins left on

1/4 tsp. sea salt

Water to just cover the bottom of a pot by 1/4-1/2" (about 1/3-1/2 cup)

Optional, 1 Tbsp. arrowroot powder or kuzu dissolved in 1/4 cup cold water

Optional, 5 Tbsp. chopped, dry roasted walnuts or hazelnuts for garnish

1. In a large saucepan layer all ingredients except those that are optional. Cover, bring to boil, reduce heat to low, simmer 30-35 minutes, without stirring. Use a heat deflector if desired. Or, pressure cook fruit mixture for 15 minutes until tender.

2. Mash with a potato masher or stir with a wooden spoon. For a thicker consistency, dissolve arrowroot or kuzu in cold water, add to pot, then simmer and stir to thicken.

Serving suggestions: Ladle into individual dessert cups and allow to cool and set up before serving. If desired, garnish each with 1-3 tsp. chopped roasted nuts. Serve at room temperature.

Storage: Refrigerate leftovers and serve at room temperature or steam briefly in custard cups on top of a steamer tray or basket.

Variations:

- **Cranberry Apple Turnovers, Tamales, or Won Tons (Any Season):** Use the above fruit compote as a filling for any of these doughs. See index for wrappers.

- **Blueberry, Cherry, Peach, or Apricot-n-Apple Sauce (Year Round)***: Replace cranberries above with fresh berries, pitted cherries, peaches, or apricots. Omit or use half the amount of raisins if sweet rather than sour fruits are used.

- **Mixed Fruit Sauce or Compote (Year Round):** Combine 6 medium apples with 1/4 cup raisins and 1/4-1/2 cup unsulphured, dried, sugar-free blueberries, cherries, cranberries, prunes, apricots, or peaches. Add 1/4 tsp. sea salt and 1 cup water. Cook as above. Add arrowroot or kuzu mixture at the end, if desired. (See also Rosehip & Apple Compote.)

- **Cranberry Apple Crisp (Fall):** Use above fruit mixture but replace the water with apple juice. Bring mixture to a boil then add the arrowroot mixture and simmer for just 10 minutes to soften. Combine fruit with our low-fat crisp topping, layering in a 12 x 9 x 2 pan; bake as per Basic Fruit Crisp. ❑

Favorites:

- **Peachy Apple Sauce/Compote**
- **Prune & Apple Sauce/Compote**
- **Blueberry Apple Sauce/Compote**
- **Pear, Apple & Prune Sauce/Compote**
- **Pear, Apple, Apricot & Prune Sauce/Compote**

Basic Nutty-Apple Mousse
(Fall & Spring)***

Prep: 10 minutes
Cooking: Pressure cook 20 minutes
or simmer 35 minutes
Serves: 6-7

This delightful mousse takes just a few minutes to prepare and can be made up to a day in advance. You won't believe how easy it is to make and how good it tastes! Traditional mousses were never this easy. This one has a sinfully sweet, rich, and creamy taste yet it's low in fat and dairy-free. It is particularly enjoyable in the late fall or spring.

9-10 cups (about 5 large sized) Granny Smith apples, chopped finely, skins left on

3/4 cup raisins

1/2 tsp. sea salt

1/4 cup nut or seed butter *(e. g. , sunflower, sesame, peanut, or hazelnut butter)*

1/2 cup water (or apple juice for a richer and sweeter flavor)

1/2 cup cold water + 1 heaping Tbsp. arrowroot or kuzu

1. Pressure cook first 5 ingredients for 20 minutes. Or, bring to boil in a pot covered with a heavy lid, reduce heat to low, and simmer, 35-40 minutes.

2. Purée in a blender or food mill.

3. Return purée to pot. Dissolve arrowroot or kuzu in cold water and mix with fruit. Simmer over medium heat. Reduce heat and stir to thicken, 3-5 minutes.

4. Ladle into individual dessert cups. Allow to firm up at room temperature, 1-3 hours, or chill for faster results.

Storage: Refrigerate mousse and remove 30-40 minutes before serving to take the chill off.

Variations:

• Use Jona Gold, Empire, Cortland, or other tart, semi-sweet apples in the above recipe.

• Replace raisins with prunes or replace apples with pears.

• Try nectarines or peaches the above recipe but cook for less time. ❏

Favorites:

• **Sunflower Apple Mousse**

• **Peanutty-Apple Mousse**

• **Hazelnut & Apple Mousse**

Raisin Glazed Pears
(Summer, Fall, Winter)***

Prep: 10-15 minutes
Cooking: 30-40 minutes

Serves: 4-5
Serving size: 3/4-1 cup per person

Here's another quick and easy dessert that is sweet and satisfying. It often tastes better on the second day and leftovers can be used in endless ways! Pears are cool and sweet— just the thing to quench a summer thirst, lubricate a hot and dry throat, or clear a cough.

4 medium sized pears (*Bosc, Anjou, or other*), washed and chopped in 1/2-1" pieces, skins left on

1/2 cup raisins

1/8 tsp. sea salt

1/2 cup water

1 1/2 tsp. arrowroot or kuzu in 3-4 Tbsp. cold water

1. In a sauce pan combine first four ingredients. Bring to boil over medium heat, cover, reduce heat to low, and simmer 30-35 minutes or until very tender.

2. Dissolve arrowroot or kuzu in cold water and add to pot. Stir to thicken, several minutes— until clear.

3. Ladle into 4 or 5 dessert cups and let cool. Serve room temperature.

Variation:

• Add 1/2 tsp. cinnamon before cooking.

• **Raisin Glazed Peaches or Nectarines:** Use fresh peaches or nectarines instead of pears. ❏

Stewed Anise Pears (Fall, Winter)***

Prep: 10 minutes
Cooking: simmer 40-50 minutes
or pressure cook 15-20

Serves: 6-8 (or 4 with leftovers)

This simple dessert can be made in any quantity. It's a breeze to make and always a hit in cooking classes. (Anise counters the pear's overly cooling nature and aids digestion.)

Rule of thumb: Per person, 1 pear + 2 tsp. raisins + a pinch of anise + pinch of sea salt.

7 Bosc, Comice, Anjou or other pears, washed and cubed (skins left on)

1/4-1/3 cups raisins or minced prunes

1/4 tsp. sea salt

1 Tbsp. whole anise seeds

Water to just barely cover the bottom of the pot (~1/3-inch)

Optional, 1 Tbsp. arrowroot or kuzu powder dissolved in 3-4 Tbsp. cold water

1. Combine first 5 ingredients. Cover, bring to boil, reduce heat to low and simmer 40-50 minutes until tender, or pressure cook 15-20 minutes.

2. Leave chunky or mash with a potato masher. If mixture is too watery, dissolve arrowroot or kuzu in cold water, add to pot and simmer until thick. This method works well if you have inadvertently added too much liquid in cooking.

Serving suggestions: Serve warm or room temperature.

Variations:

• Use half apples and half pears.

• Use dried apricots or prunes to replace raisins. ❏

Fancy Fruit & Chestnut Desserts

Basic Procedure, Baked, Stuffed Apples (Fall & Winter) ***

Prep: 20-30 minutes
Cooking: 1 hour or 8 hours in a crock pot

Serving size: 1 medium or 1/2 large apple per person
Serves: 6-12

Here's a knock-out dessert that can be made to serve two or two dozen. It is reminiscent of the old fashioned butter, cinnamon, and brown sugar filled apples I remember eating as a child, but is lower in fat and contains no dairy or refined sugar. Granny Smith apples are a favorite but you can use almost any firm, crisp baking apples—just don't use red delicious, they tend to be very mealy!

To maximize energy and oven use, bake other things such as sweet potatoes, corn bread, loaf bread, lasagna, or a casserole at the same time.

***Note:** Make this 1 1/2 hours before serving, so that it can cool slightly. If you have leftovers, remove from the refrigerator 1/2-1 hour before serving to take the chill off.*

Rule of thumb: (Per person) 1 medium apple + 1 Tbsp. raisins + 1-1 1/2 tsp. nut or seed butter + 1 pinch cinnamon + 1/3 tsp. light or dark miso paste + 1/2 tsp. arrowroot + 1-2 tsp. water

Apples:

6 medium sized Granny Smith, Gravenstein, Macintosh, Jona Gold, or Braeburn apples

Sunny-Honey or Nutty-Butter & Raisin Filling:

2 Tbsp. sunflower or sesame butter **or** hazelnut, or peanut butter

2 teaspoons white, yellow, mellow, sweet white, millet or red miso paste

1/4 tsp. cinnamon

6 Tbsp. raisins, minced finely

1 Tbsp. arrowroot powder

1-3 Tbsp. water as needed

1. Preheat oven to 350°-375° F. Wash apples. Remove cores, leaving a hollow well in the center. Leave skins on. Trim edible bits from score and mix with the filling.

2. In a suribachi or mortar and pestle, mix filling ingredients and 1-2 Tbsp. water as needed to make a thick paste. Divide filling between the apples and stuff into the hollows. The filling may peek over the top of each apple.

3. Put apples in a 9-10 inch cake pan, casserole dish, pie plate, or baking dish with sides. They should be touching so they don't tip.

4. Bake covered or uncovered in the middle of the oven for 1-1 1/4 hours or until apples bubble, skins have softened, and a knife or toothpick can be easily inserted. (Don't let them over bake or the apples will collapse and melt into a sauce.)

Variations:

• **Crock Pot Baked Apples:** Arrange 2-6 stuffed apples in a crock pot/slow cooker. They can be stacked. Add 1/4-1/3 cup water, depending on number of apples. Cover and cook on low for 8 hours.

• Dilute the above filling with water or juice and use it to stuff sweet steamed buns, steamed or baked Dessert Won Tons, or tiny turnover pastries. Figure 2 Tbsp. filling per uncooked steamed bun or 1 tsp. per dessert won ton. (See Bread Chapter for Steamed Dessert Buns or see Pasta cahpter.)❏

Steamed Chestnut-Apple Compote (Fall, Winter, Spring)

Prep: 15-20 minutes
Soaking: 4-8 hours for dried chestnuts
Cooking: 1 1/2-1 1/3/4 hours

Serves: 6-8
Serving size: 2/3-3/4 cup per person

Combined with apples and raisins, chestnuts make a delectably sweet and satisfying dessert. They're low in fat and full of flavor. Steaming makes for a light spring-time pudding, though this is an enjoyable dessert any time of year. A large glass or stainless steel bowl is necessary for steaming. If a pyrex or other breakable bowl is used, slip a small metal rack, disk or plate between the pot and the bowl to prevent breakage. (Chestnut flour can be mail ordered, see Mail Order Resources.) This is the perfect dessert to cap off an Italian meal.

1/2 cup dried chestnuts **or** 1 cup steam peeled, fresh-frozen chestnuts

1 cup water

7 cups apples, chopped (*preferably Granny Smith, Jona Gold, Jonathon, or Cortland variety*)

1/2 cup raisins

1/2 cup chestnut flour

1/2 tsp. sea salt

1 tsp. cinnamon

1. In a pot, soak raisins and dried chestnuts overnight in the water. If using fresh or fresh-frozen steam-peeled chestnuts, add them to the soaked raisins just before cooking.

2. Do not drain off the chestnut-raisin soak liquid. Cover, bring to boil, reduce heat to low and simmer 45 minutes. Or, pressure cook 20 minutes. Remove the lid and cook away any excess water.

3. Combine apples and chestnut-raisin mixture with salt, flour, and cinnamon. Place in a 3-quart stainless steel or heat-proof glass mixing bowl. Toss thoroughly.

4. Put the stainless steel bowl directly in the bottom of a large sauce pan filled with 2 inches of water. There should be at least 1/2 inch between sides of bowl and sides of pot to allow steam to rise above the bowl. If using a glass/pyrex bowl, first place a metal rack or round disk under bowl to elevate it slightly above the bottom of the pot. Cover the bowl with a heat-proof dinner plate or saucer. Cover the pot, bring to boil, and steam on medium high for 1 hour. Check water level during cooking. Add more hot water to the the pot, to surround the bowl, as needed.

Serving suggestions: Ladle into individual dessert cups and serve room temperature or slightly warm. ❏

Raisin Glazed Chestnuts (Fall, Winter & Spring Favorite)***

Prep: 20 minutes total
Soaking: 4-8 hours for dried chestnuts
Cooking: 45 minutes
Cooling: 1-3 hours before serving

Serves: 8
Serving: size: 1/2-2/3 cup per person

***Reduce recipe by one-half to serve 4
(or two times for two people)*

Plump and juicy glazed raisins surround sweet succulent chunks of chestnuts for a melt-in-your mouth taste that will satisfy even the most ardent sweet tooth! Slightly softer than a jello and firmer than a pudding, this elegant dessert makes a grand finale to any meal, without a lot of hassle. A little bit goes a long way so plan on just 1/2-2/3 cup of this dessert per person.

Chestnuts:

2 cups dried chestnuts *or* 3 cups fresh-frozen
    steam-peeled chestnuts

1 cup water (1 1/2-1 2/3 if boiling)

1 cup apple cider or apple juice

Raisin sauce:

1 cup apple cider or apple juice

1 cup water

1/2 cup raisins

reserved chestnut cooking liquid

1/4 tsp. sea salt

1/4 tsp. cinnamon

Glaze:

1/2 cup cold water

2 Tbsp. arrowroot or kuzu root powder

1. Soak chestnuts in the liquids overnight at room temperature or in the refrigerator. Pressure cook, in the soak liquid, for 45 minutes. (Pressure cook using the bowl-within-a-pot method) or bring to a boil, reduce heat to low, and simmer 1-1 1/2 hours until tender.

2. Drain and reserve liquid.

3. *Sauce:* Combine raisins, apple cider, water, chestnut cooking liquid, sea salt, and cinnamon. Bring to boil, reduce heat to low and simmer 10 minutes.

4. *Glaze:* Mix arrowroot or kuzu in cold water. Dissolve into raisin sauce. Stir and simmer until clear and thick.

5. Add chestnuts, stir, then spoon into serving cups. Allow to cool at room temperature. ❑

Fruit Crisps & Pies

Apple Pie with Magic Millet Crust (Fall & Winter)

Prep: 30 minutes
Cooking: 1 hour
Yield: 1 9-10" pie
Serves: 6-8

This marvelous apple pie makes it's own crust. There's no messy pie crust to roll out, no dough to knead, and the cleanup is a snap. The secret is millet which settles in the bottom of the dish to make a firm yet moist and slice-able wheat-, flour-, and oil-free crust. It is by far one of the easiest pies you will ever make. I was not always a millet lover, but was quickly converted with this heavenly dessert which my husband made during the first few weeks of our moving in together. It has remained a favorite in the years since then.

Note: A crust will not be formed if this dessert is baked in a casserole dish or oblong pan with sides. A pie plate is essential for forming a crust.

7 medium Granny Smith apples (or substitute
    Braeburn, Cortland, or other tart apples)

1/2 cup raisins

1/4-1/3 cup walnuts, chopped finely or ground
    in a suribachi or mortar and pestle

1/8 tsp. sea salt

1/2-1 tsp. cinnamon

1 Tbsp. arrowroot

2/3 cup millet (uncooked)

1/2 cup apple juice or fresh apple cider

1. Preheat oven to 375° F.

2. Grate apples and toss in a bowl with raisins, walnuts, salt, and cinnamon. Mix well.

3. Divide mixture in half and place in two separate bowls. Add arrowroot to one bowl, millet to the other. Pour boiling apple juice over the apple and millet mixture.

4. Put millet and apple mixture on the bottom of a deep 9 inch pie plate. Push mixture up the sides and bottom of pan to form a crust.

5. Pour arrowroot and apple mixture over millet mixture. Cover the pie plate with a lid or foil and bake in a 375° F oven for 1 hour.

6. Remove from oven. Use a large spoon to smooth the top. Let cool thoroughly before slicing. Cut into 6-8 slices. ❑

Pumpkin or Sweet Potato Pie (Fall & Winter)***

Prep: 20 minutes
Cooking: (filling): 1 1/4 - 1 1/2 hours
Cooling: 2-4 hours or overnight

Yield: one 10 inch pie plate or casserole dish
Serves: 8 (or 4 with leftovers)

Pumpkin pie is a favorite throughout fall and winter. Squashes such as kabocha, buttercup, sweet mama, and honey delight squash or hokaido pumpkin need very little sweetening. They taste richer than canned or fresh sugar pie pumpkin. If desired, top with Chestnut Amasake Cream, Maple Chestnut Pudding, thick amasake or quark.

Rule of thumb: *3 cups filling per 9" shallow pie plate; 4 cups filling per 10" deep dish pie.*

Filling*:*

1 medium to large kabocha, hokaido, sweet
    mama, or buttercup squash (3 pounds)
1 cup apple juice or water
1 tsp. sea salt
2 tsp. pumpkin pie spice
    (**or** *1 tsp. cinnamon + 1/2 tsp. nutmeg + 1/4*
    tsp. ginger powder + 1/4 tsp. cloves,
    powdered)

1/2-1 tsp. vanilla extract
1/2 cup maple syrup, rice syrup, or commercial
    amasake shake or nectar **or** homemade
    amasake concentrate

Crust:
1/2 recipe Spanokopita Pie Crust

Binder:
2 Tbsp. arrowroot **or** 1 1/2 Tbsp. kuzu root
    starch
2 1/4 tsp. agar agar
1/4 cup apple juice, amasake nectar or concen-
    trate, **or** Rice Dream Beverage
Optional, 2 Tbsp. sesame tahini or peanut or
    hazelnut butter

1. Wash pumpkin or squash. Remove skins. Discard seeds and pulp. Cut into 1-1 1/2 inch cubes. Combine squash with 1 cup water or juice and salt. Pressure cook 20 minutes, or cook on low, in a pot with a heavy lid, for 40-45 minutes or until very soft. Alternately, bake squash halves as per Basic Procedure, or cook with 1/3 cup liquid for 6-8 hours on low in a crock pot.

2. Purée squash in a blender, food processor, or foley food mill, with cooking liquids, spices, vanilla, and sweetener. Add nut butter if desired. (If using baked squash, add the liquid and salt when puréeing. Add slightly more liquid as needed to make a smooth purée.

3. Oil pie plate. Roll dough on a pastry cloth or place ball of dough in the center of the pie plate and press it across the bottom and up the sides. Crimp edges. Bake 15 minutes at 350° F.

4. Dissolve binder ingredients in chilled or room temperature liquid. Bring to boil, simmer, and stir over low heat for 2-3 minutes to thicken. Add to squash mixture and stir.

5. Spoon purée into prebaked crust, bake at 350° F.-375° F. for 30-35 minutes or until firm and golden. Cool at room temperature for several hours or chill overnight before slicing and serving.

Variations:

- **Sweet Potato Pie:** Bake 3 pounds red garnet or jewel or white sweet potatoes. Peel. Proceed as if using baked squash in Step # 2.

- If using baked, crock pot, or nishime squash or sweet potato, juice or water may be replaced with amasake or almond milk. ❏

Basic Procedure, Fruit Crisp (Year Round)

Prep: 20 minutes
Cooking: 1 hour + 10 minutes
Serves: 8-10
Serving size: 3/4-1 cup per person

Unlike most fruit crisps, this one contains no refined sugar, honey, or syrups. It's also oil-free and very low in fat. We use this basic recipe throughout the year with everything from apples to peaches and blueberries. We often mix apples with a second, in season fruit.

Apple Syrup (glaze for fruit):

1 cup apple juice
2 Tbsp. arrowroot or kuzu root starch
1/8 tsp. sea salt

Fruit:

8-10 cups apples, one variety or a combination of two (6 large or 8 medium-sized) *(Granny Smith, Braeburn, Johnathon, other tart apples or sweet -sour baking apples)*

Crisp topping:

1-1/2 cups rolled oats
1/3 cup whole wheat pastry flour, hard white wheat flour, or spelt flour
1/2-3/4 cup nuts or seeds *or* seeds and nuts
    (chopped walnuts, almonds hazlenuts, or sunflower or poppy seeds)
1 1/2 tsp. cinnamon

Raisin Purée (all-purpose sweetener):

1 cup water, apple cider, or apple juice
3/4 cup packed raisins
1/4 tsp. sea salt

1. Dissolve arrowroot or kuzu and salt in cool or cold juice. Simmer over low heat, stir to thicken, then turn off and set aside.

2. Wash and halve apples. Leave skins on, remove cores, chop apples into thin rounds, half-rounds, or slices. Toss into a mixing bowl. Add thickened juice, stir, and set aside.

3. Simmer raisins, water or juice, and salt for 10 minutes. Meanwhile, combine dry topping ingredients in a separate bowl.

4. Purée raisin mixture in a blender or food processor to make a paste. Add water as needed to make 1 cup purée. Add to dry topping. Stir to make a cookie-like dough.

5. Arrange half of the apple mixture in a 12 or 14 x 9 x 2 inch oblong baking pan or two 9 inch square pans or pie plates. Top with half the crisp topping. Add remaining apples, then top with remaining crisp mixture.

6. Cover, and bake at 350° F. for 20-25 minutes. Remove cover and bake 20-25 minutes to crisp. When making dessert bake covered for 20 minutes, then allow to cool at room temperature for several hours or refrigerate. Before serving, bake the crisp uncovered for 20-25 minutes.)

Serving suggestions: Serve warm or close to room temperature. Cover and refrigerate leftovers that will not be eaten within 24 hours. Allow leftovers to come to room temperature. If desired top with quark (yogurt cheese).

Variations:

- **Blueberry & Peach Crisp:** Omit apples. Combine 4 large peaches with 1 quart (4 cups) washed and drained fresh blueberries. Replace poppy seeds with walnuts, sunflower seeds, or half of each. Proceed as above.

- **Use other fruits:** blueberries and apples, cranberries and apples, peaches and apples, cherries and apples, or marionberries or logan berries with apples.

- Replace raisin purée with 1/2 -3/4 cup rice malt syrup or fruit syrup . Mix with crisp topping ingredients.

- Replace apple juice syrup with 1/2 cup rice malt, honey, or fruit syrup.❏

Summer & Early Fall Desserts

Fruit Salads & Gels

Bing Cherry Gel (Summer, Early Fall)

Prep: 15 minutes to pit fruit
Cooking: 10 minutes
Cooling: 2-3 hours to set

Serves: 8 (or 4 with leftovers)
Serving size: 2/3 cup per person

**** *Reduce recipe by one half to serve 4
(or 2x for 2)***

This dessert is easy to make and so delicious. Make when cherries are fresh and abundant.

1 quart (4 cups) fresh bing cherries, (or other varieties), washed, pits and stems removed

2 cups apple juice (reserve 1/4 cup)

1/8 tsp. sea salt

1 1/2 Tbsp.s agar agar flakes *or* 1 1/2 tsp. agar agar powder

1 1/2 Tbsp. kuzu root powder *or* 2 Tbsp. arrowroot powder

1. Place juice in large pot, reserving 1/4 cup for dissolving arrowroot or kuzu. Add agar agar, cherries and sea salt. Bring to boil, cover, reduce heat to low and simmer for 6-8 minutes.

2. Dissolve kuzu or arrowroot in 1/4 cup of juice, then add to the simmering liquid. Stir briefly to thicken, then turn off heat. Ladle into 8 individual custard cups or small bowls. Allow to cool and firm up at room temperature (2-3 hours) or in the refrigerator.

Serving suggestions: Serve close to room temperature.

Storage: Refrigerate leftovers.

Variations:

• Replace cherries with other seasonal fruits.

❏

Very Berry Gel (Summer, Early Fall)

Prep: 5 minutes
Cooking: 10 minutes
Cooling: 2-3 hours to set

Serves: 6
Serving size: 2/3 cup per person

1 3/4 cups apple juice or apple-berry juice

1/8 tsp. sea salt

1 Tbsp. agar agar flakes *or* 1 tsp. agar agar powder or unflavored vegetarian gelatin

1 1/2 pint fresh berries, 1-2 varieties *(blackberries, blueberries, loganberries, raspberries, cherries, strawberries, or marionberries)*

1/4 cup apple or apple-berry juice

2 Tbsp. arrowroot powder *or* 1 1/2 Tbsp. kudzu root powder

1. In a 3-quart saucepan, combine 1 3/4 cup juice with agar agar or vegetarian gelatin and sea salt. Bring to boil, cover, reduce heat to low and simmer 6-7 minutes until agar or gelatin dissolves.

2. Meanwhile, rinse and drain berries. Dissolve arrowroot or kuzu root starch into 1/4 cup juice. Add this to the pot and stir. Add berries, stir, and turn off heat.

3. Ladle into small cups and allow to cool at room temperature for 2-3 hours, or chill in the refrigerator, until firm.

Serving suggestions: Garnish each serving with a fresh mint leaf, if desired. Serve close to room temperature.

Storage: Refrigerate leftovers that will not be served within 6 hours. ❏

Very Berry-Amasake Jello
(Summer, Early Fall)***

Prep: 15 minutes
Cooking: 12-15 minutes
Setting: 2-4 hours

Serves: 6 (or 3 days of dessert for 2)
Serving size: 2/3-1 cup per person

2 cups apple juice or blueberry-apple juice or amasake beverage or concentrate

1 1/2-2 tsp. agar agar powder *or* 1 1/2-2 Tbsp. agar agar flakes or equivalent of vegetarian gelatin

1/8 tsp. sea salt

1 1/2 pints (3 cups) fresh blueberries *or* 3 cups pitted, fresh cherries

2 tsp. arrowroot or kuzu root powder

1/2 cup commercial amasake nectar or shake (original, vanilla-pecan, or almond) *or* homemade amasake concentrate or beverage *or* vanilla Rice Dream Beverage

1. In a 3-4 quart pot, combine first four ingredients. Cover, bring to boil, reduce heat to low, then simmer for 8-10 minutes.

2. Meanwhile, dissolve arrowroot or kuzu in 1/2 cup of cool or cold amasake or Rice Dream Beverage. Stir this into the pot. Simmer and stir to thicken, 4-5 minutes or until it becomes clear, and turn off heat.

3. Ladle into 6-8 dessert cups and allow it to firm up at room temperature, 2-4 hours.

Serving suggestion: Serve at room temperature. Sprinkle each serving with 1-3 tsp. chopped roasted almonds, walnuts, or hazelnuts, if desired.

Storage: Refrigerate leftovers.

Variation:

• **Basic Amasake Fruit Jello:** Use other fresh seasonal fruit in place of berries or cherries (chopped peaches, pears, nectarines, or raspberries.) If using a tart type of fruit add 1 Tbsp. honey or rice malt syrup in step #2 above. ❏

Cherry Amasake Creme
(Summer/Early Fall)***

Prep: 20 minutes (to pit cherries)
Cooking: 12-15 minutes

Serves: 4-5
Serving size: 1/2-3/4 cup per person

This recipe combines smooth, sweet, and creamy homemade amasake pudding with fresh seasonal fruit to create an ambrosial concoction. No added fat, no sugar, and no regrets! Try this with fresh blueberries, peaches, or other seasonal fruits. This is a warm weather favorite.

1 pound fresh cherries

1/4-1/3 cup water

1/8 tsp. sun dried sea salt

1 1/2 tsp. arrowroot or kuzu dissolved in 1-2 Tbsp. cold water

2 cups amasake pudding (thick homemade variety)

1. Pit cherries. Combine with water and sea salt in a pot. Cover, bring to boil, reduce heat to low and simmer 10 minutes. Allow to cool 10 minutes.

2. Mix arrowroot or kuzu into cherries. Stir to thicken over medium heat. Mix in amasake, stir well, spoon into individual dessert cups.

3. Allow to cool at room temperature before serving.

Storage: Refrigerate any leftovers in a glass jar or custard cups.

Variations:

• **Use other seasonal fruit:** Fresh blueberries, chopped ripe nectarines, apricots or peaches, etc. ❏

Apple-Peach & Raisin Jello (Summer, Early Fall)

Prep: 10 minutes
Cooking: 5-15 minutes
Cooling: 2-3 hours
Serves: 5
Serving size: 3/4-1 cup per person

Double this recipe if you're expecting company. It's sure to be a hit. It is easy on both the cook and your digestive system. Other varieties of seasonal fruit such as melon, berries, nectarines, or cherries may be substituted for the peaches, depending upon availability.

3 large, fresh peaches
1/8 tsp. sun dried sea salt
2 cups apple juice
1/4 cup raisins
2 1/4 tsp. agar agar flakes or other unflavored vegetarian gelatin
1/8 tsp. sea salt

1/2 cup apple juice (cold or room temperature)
2 1/4 tsp. arrowroot or kuzu

1. Dice peaches and mix with sea salt. Divide fruit between 5 dessert cups.

2. Combine 2 cups of juice with raisins, agar agar or gelatin, and remaining salt in a pot. Bring to boil, cover, reduce heat to low, and simmer 6-10 minutes with agar.

3 Dissolve arrowroot or kuzu in remaining juice and stir into pot. Bring to a low boil, then turn off the heat. Pour juice mixture over fruit cups.

4. Allow to cool at room temperature for 2-6 hours before serving or speed up the process by refrigerating.

Serving suggestions: Serve at room temperature. If refrigerated, remove 1/2-1 hour before serving to avoid spoiling digestion.

Variations:

• Replace peaches with nectarines, pears, or 3 cups of fresh berries. ❏

Strawberries-n-Amasake Cream (Summer/Early Fall)***

Prep: 15 minutes
Serves: 6-8 (or 4 with leftovers)
Serving size: 3/4-1 cup per person

1 quart fresh strawberries
1/8 tsp. sea salt

2 cups thick homemade amasake pudding *(plain, millet-sweet rice, millet, or barley & rice amasake)*

1. Wash berries. Cut into thin slices. Gently mix with sea salt and allow to stand 1/2 hour.

2. Spoon berries into individual serving cups (about 1/3-1/2 cup per person), then cover each fruit cup with 1/4-1/3 cup of amasake pudding. Serve.

Variation:

* **Peaches-n-Cream:** Substitute freshly sliced peaches for strawberries.

* **Blueberries-n-Cream:** Replace strawberries with fresh blueberries. ❏

Layered Amasake Fruit Parfait (Summer Favorite)***

Prep: 20 minutes
Cooking: 1-1 1/2 hours

Serves: 8-10 as a 2-layer dessert
or 8 as a 3-layer dessert

***Halve or increase entire recipe or single layers as needed.**

This creamy layered parfait derives it's sweetness from cooked fresh fruit and amasake. It contains no added oil, dairy products, or sugar. You can make your own amasake pudding or purchase the commercial variety in most health food stores. (Buy original, plain, vanilla pecan, or almond flavor.) Make this a 2-layered dessert with cooked fruit on the bottom and vanilla amasake topping or make a blueberry bottom with a vanilla topping. Or, for a real treat, make a deluxe 3-layer parfait!

Apple & Pear (bottom layer: 8 servings @1/3 cup each or 3 single desserts)

2 cups chopped Empires, Jona Gold, Macintosh, Braeburn, or Ida Red apple, or combination, skin left on

2 cups very ripe pears, diced

1/8 tsp. sea salt

3 Tbsp. water or apple juice if simmering (see below)

1. Pick a cooking method.

   To pressure cook: Combine fruit and sea salt in a pressure cooker. Seal pot and bring up to full pressure. Reduce heat to low and cook for 20 minutes. There is no need to add water or juice if pressure cooking.

   To boil: Add a few tablespoons of water or apple juice to the fruit and sea salt. Bring to boil in a pot with a tight fitting lid. Cover, reduce heat to low, and simmer 1/2 hour or until fruit is very soft and smells sweet.

2. Spoon into 8 parfait glasses or dessert cups or into a 2 quart glass mixing bowl or pyrex pan, or spoon into 4 cups for a two-layer dessert. You will then top this fruit with a layer of Vanilla Amasake Flan.

Vanilla Amasake Flan (middle layer: 8 servings @ 2/3 cup each or 3 single desserts)

6 cups commercial original or plain amasake or homemade amasake concentrate (liquid)

or 4 1/2 cups thick homemade amasake pudding diluted with 1-1 1/2 cups water

2 1/2 tsp. agar agar powder

or 2 1/2 Tbsp. agar agar flakes

or 1 agar agar bar torn into pieces

or 2 1/2 tsp. unflavored vegetarian gelatin

2 Tbsp. arrowroot or kuzu root powder

2 pinches sea salt

1. Reserve 1/4 cup of the amasake. Combine the remaining amasake and agar agar (or gelatin) in a 3-quart sauce pan. Bring to boil, cover, reduce heat to low, and simmer 8-10 minutes to dissolve agar agar or gelatin flakes.

2. Dissolve arrowroot or kuzu in 1/4 cup reserved amasake or cold water. Add to pot and stir 2-3 minutes until clear. Mixture should start to thicken and will firm up like jello as it cools.

3. Allow mixture to sit in the pot for another 10 minutes, then ladle over the first fruit layer or spoon into 3 individual serving cups to serve as a dessert on its own.

4. Allow mixture to set up at room temperature, about 2 hours, or 1 hour in the refrigerator. If desired, make a third layer with blueberry or cherry amasake.

Serving suggestions: Serve close to room temperature and refrigerate leftover pudding. Use up within several days.

Variations:

- For a fluffy white cream topping, allow vanilla amasake mixture to set up in a separate bowl, then purée in a blender or food processor and spoon over fruit cups. This makes a great non-dairy whip topping for pies too.

Blueberry Amasake (top layer: makes 8-9 @1/3 cup servings or 3 single desserts)

1 1/2 cups fresh blueberries (see variations below)*

2 pinches sea salt

3 cups thick homemade amasake pudding

(made from rice, millet, millet & sweet rice, or other grains)

1. Gently rub sea salt into fresh berries and place in a 2-quart sauce pan. (The sea salt will draw moisture out of the berries.) Cover berries with thick homemade amasake pudding. Cover pot, bring to boil over medium heat, then immediately turn to low. Simmer 8-10 minutes. Stir after cooking time has elapsed.

2. Ladle into 3-5 serving cups to serve alone or as the final layer or spoon blueberry amasake into dessert cups and top with the vanilla amasake jello and allow to firm up.

Variations:

- **Just Blueberry Amasake Pudding or Vanilla Amasake Flan:** Serve just one of these puddings for dessert—just blueberry amasake or stewed fruit with Vanilla Amasake Flan on top. To do this, increase above recipes as needed. Figure 2/3-1 cup of dessert per person.

- **Fresh Strawberry or Cherry Amasake Pudding:** Use fresh strawberries or pitted cherries to replace blueberries above. Increase recipe as needed to serve desired number of people.

- **To use commercial amasake nectar/beverage:** Dissolve 1 Tbsp. agar agar flakes and 1 Tbsp. arrowroot or kuzu into cold or room temperature commercial amasake nectar, then prepare as above. ❏

Uncooked Fresh Fruit "Puddings" & Salads (Summer, Early Fall)***

Uncooked, fruits make delectable fruit salads and raw puddings, just the thing to cap off a soothing summer meal on a scorching hot day. To avoid putting out your digestive fire it is best to keep portions satisfyingly small. Sea salt draws out the fruit's naturally sweet taste and raisins add additional sweetness . We often add a dash of chopped dry roasted nuts or seeds to the mixture for a delicate crunch.

Though fresh fruit can be a welcome treat in warm weather, it is best avoided in the winter or in cold weather. If your digestion is weak, skip the raw fruits. Instead try an amasake or chestnut dessert or one of our fruit compotes. (These desserts are even better the second day, so you might want to make them the night before then serve them at room temperature the next day. Try fresh peaches, apricots, nectarines, blueberries, cherries, or mixed summer fruits.)

Rule of thumb: *Per person, figure 1 medium to large or 2 small pieces of very ripe fruit + 1-1 1/2 Tbsp. raisins or other dried fruit. Add 1/8 tsp. sea salt per 5-6 servings (mixed in with the fruit).*

Basic Procedure, Fruit & Nut Salad (Late Summer/Early Fall)

Peach & Walnut Fruit Salad

Prep: 15 minutes
Serves: 5-6
Serving size: 3/4-1 cup per person

This dessert has a sweet, nutty taste and crunchy texture. It's sure to become a summertime favorite!

6 large peaches, diced
1/3-1/2 cup raisins
1/8 tsp. sea salt
1/4 cup chopped, roasted walnuts

1. Dry roast nuts on a dry cast iron skillet or cookie sheet in a 250° F oven for 10-15 minutes or until aromatic. Watch them closely so they don't burn.

2. Toss fruit and salt into a mixing bowl and mix with a spoon until soft, leaving noticeable chunks, or mix until smooth like pudding. Chop nuts finely and mix into fruit.

3. Refrigerate several hours or overnight or spoon into individual serving cups and allow to set at room temperature for 1-3 hours before serving.

Variations:

- **Nectarine Salad:** Substitute 7 nectarines for peaches above.

- **Sunny Nectarine-n-Raisin Salad:** Use nectarines for peaches above and replace walnuts with unsalted, dry roasted sunflower seeds.

- **Blueberry-Raisin Salad:** Use 4 1/2-5 cups blueberries + 1/2 cup raisins + 1/8 tsp. sea salt + 2 Tbsp. roasted sunflower seeds or chopped, dry roasted hazelnuts or walnuts.

- **Uncooked Apricot Pudding:** Use apricots in place of peaches but use more of them. Figure about 2-3 apricots per person. (This turns into a pudding if you mix it very well.)

- **Blueberry & Dried Peach Salad:** Use 5 cups fresh blueberries, washed and drained + 6 Tbsp. minced, unsulphured, dried peaches or apricots + 1/2 cup apple juice or water + 1/4 tsp. sea salt. Optional, 1/4 cup roasted sunflower seeds, walnuts, or hazelnuts.

- Mince dried fruit and simmer with sea salt and juice or water for 10 minutes. Cool, toss with berries and stir. Cover and refrigerate. Ladle 3/4-1 cupful of fruit salad into each dessert cup. Sprinkle or toss with seeds or chopped nuts and/or amasake pudding. ❏

Fancy Treats
Cookies, Brownies, Bars, & Cakes

The following desserts are a little more involved to make and typically contain more ingredients than the previous desserts. Some are much richer, and most are harder to digest than simple fruit or amasake based desserts. Thus, we recommended making them infrequently.

Nutty No-Bake Peanut Butter Cookies (Year Round)***

Prep: 20 minutes
Cooking: none
Resting: 1-2 hours or overnight before serving

Yield: 16-24 cookies/balls
Serves: 8-12
Serving size: 2-3 per person

This is a great dessert to make with young kids. It is especially handy for potlucks, parties, informal dinner parties, or a quick mid-week dessert for the cookie monsters. These are very rich so it is best to figure not more than three cookies per person. Just savor every bite! (When cooking for two, make a half batch to avoid eating too many or having them too many days in a row.)

1/3 cup raisins
1/3 cup + 1 Tbsp. honey or rice malt syrup
1/3 cup natural peanut butter
2/3 cup packed, very finely grated carrot
1/8-1/4 tsp. vanilla or almond extract
1/4-1/2 tsp. sea salt

Optional, 1 Tbsp. dry roasted sesame or sunflower seeds

1/4-1/2 tsp. sea salt (if using unsalted nut or
seed butter)

1 3/4-2 cups rolled oats

1. Chop raisins finely so that they can be evenly
distributed throughout the dough.

2. Grate carrots on the second to the smallest setting on your grater so they'll be juicy and
spread evenly throughout the mix. (This is the
hole normally reserved for parmesan cheese.)

3. In a mixing bowl combine everything but the
oats. Mix with a fork or spoon. Add the oats
then mix again. Cover the bowl with a plate
and allow the mixture sit on the counter for
1/2-1 hour to allow the oats to soak up moisture, soften, and become more digestible.

4. Oil your hands lightly to keep the dough from
sticking, then form dough into tablespoon-
sized balls and roll tightly in your hands. You
should end up with 16-24 balls. Place on a
plate and let sit for 1/2-1 hour.

Serving suggestions: 2-3 balls per person.

Storage: Store leftovers in wax paper bags, a
cookie tin, or in a bowl in a cool dry place.
Refrigeration is optional if cookies will be
eaten within 2-3 days.

Variations:

• Use sunflower, almond, hazelnut, or sesame
butter in place of peanut butter above. ❏

Buckwheat, Sesame & Chestnut Gems (Fall, Winter, Early Spring)

Prep: 20-30 minutes
Cooking: 12 minutes

Yield: 3 dozen 2 inch cookies
Serves: 12-18 (or 6 with leftovers)
Serving size: 2-3 per person

These delightful cookies have a rich and robust
taste without all the fat. Chestnut flour and
raisins add moistness and a sweet fruity taste,
sesame seeds add crunch, and buckwheat flour
gives body, texture, and added moistness.

Buckwheat flour can be found in most grocery
and health food stores and is a favorite in cookies, cakes, breads and tortillas. These cookies are
simple to make, have only six ingredients and
are simply delicious to eat! (Adapted from a
recipe for buckwheat cookies by macrobiotic
chef extraordinaire, Michael Abeshera.)

1 cup raisins

2 cups water or apple juice

1/4 tsp. sea salt

3/4 cup sesame seeds, unhulled brown variety

1 1/2 cups buckwheat flour

1 1/2 cups chestnut flour

1. Preheat oven to 350° F. In a small sauce pan,
bring to boil raisins, salt, and water or juice.
Cover and simmer 10 minutes, over medium-
low heat.

2. Meanwhile, dry roast sesame seeds in a cast
iron skillet or wok, stirring constantly until
aromatic, lightly browned, and a bit puffy.
(See Basic Procedure Dry Roasted Seeds &
Nuts.)

3. Add 1/2 cup roasted seeds to raisin mixture.
Reserve the remaining sesame seeds for dust-
ing the pans. Set mixture aside, and allow to
cool.

4. Dust 2 stainless steel cookie sheets with
sesame seeds. This will keep the cookies from
sticking to the pans.

5. Mix flours. Add raisin-sesame seed mixture
and stir to create a smooth dough. With a
tablespoon, form into balls and place on cookie sheets, 1 inch apart. Flatten to silver dollar
size. Bake for 10-12 minutes, or until browned
on the bottom. Do not over-bake or cookies
will become dry. (They'll firm up as they
cool). Remove with a metal spatula or pancake turner and place on wire racks to cool.

Storage: Store in wax paper bags or in a glass jar
or bowl, loosely covered. Use up within 2-5
days. (Save sesame seeds from cookie sheet,
and add them to morning cereal before or after
cooking.) Baked cookies can also be frozen in
small batches in zip-lock freezer bags. ❏

Mock Chocolate, Roasted Barley Amasake Brownies
(Fall, Winter, Spring)***

Prep: 20 minutes
Soaking (beans): 6 -12 hours

Cooking: 60-90 minutes for cooking beans
60 minutes for baking brownies
Serves: 12

These brownies look chocolatey but contain no cocoa or carob. The dark color, rich, roasty taste, and slightly bitter flavor reminiscent of chocolate comes from black turtle beans, roasted barley, and kelp or kombu sea vegetable. The batter is dairy-free, wheat-free, and far lower in fat than most brownie batters. Raisins and amasake lend a complex sweetness. Roasted barley amasake is the key to this recipe. It is not available in health food stores and nothing in the stores can compare to this dark, thick, and rich brew that holds its own as a pudding for dessert. Roasted barley amasake is the key to this recipe. You may substitute mocha amasake pudding if you can find it, but it won't be quite the same.

1 cup black turtle beans
2 1/2 cups water

4" piece kombu seaweed
Fresh water for cooking (to replace the soak water you pour off)

1/4 tsp. sea salt
1 1/2 cup raisins
2 Tbsp. roasted sesame tahini **or** sesame butter
Optional, 2 Tbsp. corn or sunflower oil
1/3 cup chopped walnuts
1 cup brown rice flour **or** sweet brown rice flour
1 cup Roasted Barley Amasake Pudding

1. Rinse beans, then soak in water all day or overnight.

2. Drain beans and add fresh water and kelp or kombu. Pressure cook 30-45 minutes or simmer 1-1 1/2 hours or until tender, adding a bit more water if needed to keep the beans from boiling dry. Or cook beans in a crock pot. If pressure cooking, bring pressure down before proceeding with the next step.

3. Add salt, raisins, and about 1/2 cup additional water to tender beans. Pressure cook for just 10-15 minutes or simmer for 20 minutes, covered, on low heat. Purée in a foley food mill or food processor. Mix in remaining ingredients.

4. Turn into a 9 x 13 inch glass pan (no oil needed). Bake for one hour at 375°F.

5. Cool thoroughly, 3-12 hours, before slicing.

Storage: Refrigerate leftovers in a covered container or freeze in small portions in zip lock freezer bags. Frozen brownies should be thawed on the counter or in the refrigerator in their container. Or, they may be briefly steam heated on a plate, on top of a metal steamer tray or bamboo steamer basket to warm and freshen before serving.

Variations:

- For an even sweeter taste, use apple juice in place of water to cook beans.

- Use peanut or sunflower butter in place of roasted sesame tahini or sesame butter.

- Use azuki/aduki beans in place of black turtle beans.

- In place of roasted barley amasake pudding, use thick chestnut purée or add 3-4 Tbsp. instant roasted grain "coffee" powder to millet, sweet-rice or sweet-rice-and-millet-based homemade amasake pudding. Or use commercial mocha flavored amasake pudding (not the beverage.) ❏

Steam-Baked Chestnut-Apple Cake/Chestnut Un-Cheese Cake (Any Season)

Prep: 20 minutes
Rising: 15-30 minutes
Cooking: 50 minutes
Cooling (before serving): 2-3 hours

Yield: 1 10-inch cake
Serves: 10-12

Don't let the simplicity of the ingredients fool you. Chestnut flour lends a smooth, rich texture to this cake. Steam baking (cooking in a covered casserole dish) makes for a moist cake with a minimum of oil. The inside stays moist while the outside develops a thin skin. It slices like cheesecake and has a similar appearance and texture. A covered round or square casserole dish with a lid seals in moisture and flavor and is essential for making this cake. This cake is very good on its own though you could to top it off with a cooked fruit sauce. This dessert is a real treat for and potlucks, special occasions. (We don't use baking soda with any frequency, but we came up with this recipe several years ago and it was so popular that we decided not to alter it.)

Dry ingredients:

2 cups chestnut flour

2 cup spelt flour **or** whole wheat pastry flour (**or** replace 1 cup spelt flour or pastry flour with 1 cup white spelt flour or unbleached wheat flour)

1/4 tsp. sea salt

1 Tbsp. baking powder

Liquids:

1 cup apple juice

2 cups thick apple sauce*

2 Tbsp. corn oil or light sesame oil

1 tsp. pure almond extract

1. Preheat oven to 350° F. Oil a 4-quart enamel lined cast iron pot (Le Crueset type) or a stainless steel dutch oven pot (9 or 12-inches in diameter) with a heavy lid. Dust with flour.

2. Mix wet ingredients and set aside. Sift dry ingredients, then slowly stir into wet. Pour mixture into oiled and floured baking pot or pan. Put a lid on the pot and bake for 50 minutes or until it tests done and a toothpick comes out clean.

3. Uncover and let cool at least 2 hours before serving or removing from the pan. Cake will appear to "fall" as it cools, but this is expected. The cake will firm up as it cools, so don't serve it right away.

4. Before serving, run a knife or firm spatula around the edges of the pan. Slice into 10-12 pie-shaped pieces and lift from the pan. Slices should look a bit like cheesecake.

Serving suggestions: Serve plain or with a light, naturally sweetened topping made from apple-strawberry or apple-cherry juice thickened with arrowroot or kuzu. Or, top with quark

Storage: Cover loosely. Store at room temperature for 48 hours or cover and refrigerate.

* **Homemade apple sauce:** Pressure cook 15 minutes or simmer on low 1 hour: 4 diced apples, 1/8 tsp. sea salt, 1/4 cup apple juice. Mash well, stir in 1 Tbsp. flour, then simmer away any excess liquid. Measure out 2 cups for recipe. Reserve the rest for other uses.

Variation:

• For a lighter chestnut cake, omit baking powder. Add 2 1/2 tsp. Active Dry Yeast to flour mixture. Prepare as above but heat juice to 110°-120° F (no hotter) before combining with other liquids. Mix wet ingredients with dry. Allow to rise in a warm place, in a covered bowl, for 1 hour or until doubled. Stir, pour into oiled casserole pot. Let rise until doubled, 30-60 minutes. Bake as above. ❏

Low-Fat Holiday Fruit-Nut Bread
(Fall & Winter)

Prep: 20 minutes
Rising: about 15-30 minutes if using yeast
Cooking: 1 hour
Cooling: at least 4 hours

Yield: 2 small loaves, 16 slices per loaf
Serves: 16-32
Serving size: 1-2 slices per person

This wheat, dairy, egg, and cholesterol-free loaf is perfect for holiday gatherings. It makes a great gift, too. Spelt and barley flour create a moist loaf that can be served plain. It's fairly rich so small servings are advisable. (Yeast is preferable to baking soda or baking powder in this and all other baked goods. Yeast assists digestion while baking soda and baking powder may, in fact, hinder good digestion and destroy some of the nutrients in the flour.)

Wet ingredients:

1 cup raisins

1 cup apple cider or apple juice, heated

2 cups amasake nectar or shake (almond or original) or vanilla rice milk beverage

1/2 cup apple sauce

1/2 cup apple cider or apple juice

Dry ingredients:

1 cup dried unsweetened apricots, coarsely chopped

1 cup raw walnuts or hazelnuts, chopped coarsely

3 cups spelt flour *or* hard white wheat flour

2 cups barley flour

1/2 tsp. sea salt

1 Tbsp. non-aluminum baking powder

Optional, 1 tsp. cinnamon or allspice

Optional, 1/4-1/2 tsp. dried, powdered nutmeg or ginger

2 9x5-inch bread pans

Oil to grease pans

Barley, wheat, or spelt flour to dust pans

1. Preheat oven to 350° F.

2. In a blender purée 1 cup raisins in 1 cup hot apple cider or juice. Combine and purée remaining wet ingredients, then set aside.

3. In a large mixing bowl, combine dry ingredients. Add to liquid ingredients and stir until thoroughly mixed. Do not over mix or batter will become rubbery.

4. Spoon into 2 well oiled and lightly floured bread pans (8 1/2" x 4 1/2"). Bake 1 hour, or until bread starts to pull away from the sides of the pans and a toothpick inserted in the center comes out clean.

5. Remove from oven and cool at least 4 hours before removing from pans or slicing. Bread will be soggy and doughy unless cooled sufficiently before slicing. You might even want to make it a day or two in advance.

Storage: Once cooled, store in the refrigerator, in plastic or cellophane bags. Slice to serve. If you want warm bread, wrap several slices in a clean cotton towel, put this on a plate, on top of a bamboo steamer tray, and steam for several minutes over boiling water. Use within 1-2 weeks.

Variation:

• Use dried (unsweetened) cherries, blueberries, or peaches to replace dried apricots above.

• Omit baking powder. Add 2 1/2 tsp. Rapid-Rise Yeast to the flour mixture. Heat the juice to 125° F (no hotter) in step #2. Be sure to use a thermometer. Proceed as above but let batter rise until almost doubled in bulk (about 15-30 minutes) before baking. Do not allow it to over-rise. ❏

Desserts p. 464

Chapter 11

Quenching That Thirst For Life

The 8-Glasses-A-Day Myth

Contrary to popular thought, it is neither necessary nor desirable to drink large volumes of fluid every day, provided that your diet is composed primarily of cooked grains and vegetables. Excess of anything is harmful, and over consumption of fluids is no exception. From the perspective of Oriental medicine, drinking too much fluid stresses the Spleen, Lungs, Kidneys, and digestive organs, all of which must labor to process and excrete the excess.

The popular notion that we need to drink eight glasses of fluid per day has arisen to compensate for the lack of soups, whole grains, porridge, and vegetables in the Western diet. Meat, bread, crackers, and sugar-rich products are relatively dry foods that can cause an excessive thirst, particularly if such foods are the staples of one's diet. Perhaps the primary cause of strong thirst in most modern diets is the consumption of sugar-rich foods. Sugar-rich blood needs plenty of water for dilution. Diabetes is the extreme of sugar-rich blood, and it is sometimes referred to as the "wasting and thirsting" disease. When blood sugar levels are high, one becomes very thirsty and, in order to rid the body of excess sugar, urination is profuse.

Like water to sugar

Water is attracted to and collects wherever there is a high concentration of sugar; this is why fruits and sugar cane are sweet and juicy, and naturally sweet products such as honey and maple syrup (tree sap) are liquids. Thus, when we eat fruits, sugar, honey or other concentrated sources of sugar or drink fruit juices, we will have great thirst. Indeed, fruit juices and other sweet beverages create rather than quench thirst.

According to Oriental medicine, chronic consumption of sweet foods—including fruits and juices—creates pathological heat. Excess sugar in the blood raises the metabolic rate. This generates heat. Also, the metabolism of sugar generates Phlegm, in the form of fat. This fat-phlegm congests the fine channels of the body. When the channels and organs are congested, the life force cannot circulate freely; this also generates heat. All of this heat generates thirst. In essence, the thirst is for fluids to flush the excess sugar out of the organs and blood.

From the perspective of Oriental medicine, the Spleen, Kidneys, Liver and Lungs are most harmed by sugar. Thus, in the medicine of the Orient, consumption of sugar is recognized as a major cause of digestive disorders, diabetes, kidney disease, osteoporosis, premature loss of hair, obesity, chronic infection, weakened immunity, and lung problems such as respiratory allergies and asthma.

Salt and thirst

Some people think that salty foods cause thirst. However, vegetable foods properly prepared with salty seasonings rarely are themselves the cause of great thirst. This may seem surprising, yet our experience and centuries of experience in Asia show this to be true.

In the traditional cuisines of Japan and China, where the consumption of salt—via salted foods, miso soups, tamari, and pickles—is fairly high, water is rarely served and tea is commonly served in very small cups. A moderately salt-rich diet, one that is also low in simple sugars, does not exacerbate thirst. According to Oriental medicine, salt has a cooling and moistening quality that relieves thirst. Hence, in order to alleviate excessive thirst, some athletes have used salt tablets, along with liquids, in summer training. Although some people find that salty movie popcorn or pretzels make them thirsty, these foods are not just salty. They are also very, very dry, and dry foods typically attract wet foods. You may notice that lightly salted or even unsalted crackers, chips, or popcorn create the same desire for liquids. It is important not to confuse dryness with saltiness! (The quality of the salt and how it is used also needs to be factored in.)

Drinking in America

When Americans do drink, they rarely choose pure water or mild and nutritious herb teas. The most popular beverages are soda pop, coffee, fructose sugared or fruit sweetened drinks, and black tea. Soda pop, whether "diet" or regular, creates Damp and Heat, damages the Spleen and Kidneys, exhausts the Yang, dehydrates the body and increases thirst. These pathologies may be experienced as phlegm, congestion or edema, ulcers, acid heartburn, and/or fatigue. Soda and sugary beverages also interfere with proper mineral metabolism, particularly that of iron and calcium. Sweetened fruit drinks and pure fruit juice have similar effects.

In Oriental medicine, coffee, both regular and decaf, are said to consume the Kidney Essence and transforms it into qi. Coffee also upsets the body's proper mineral balance and is linked to osteoporosis. (This connection is now being recognized by many doctors in the west.) Coffee's net effect is to produce temporary energy at the expense of literally burning out the Kidney substance and exhausting the Yang (the fire of life and vitality). Drinking coffee is like buying on credit and spending beyond your means. At some point you discover that you have emptied your reserves (drained your bank account) and have little or nothing left to live on (or to pay your debt). Black tea has a similar effect. In short, none of these beverages are nourishment for life. On the contrary, they are very addictive and destructive at the same time, depleting the body and consuming the very foundation of one's life.

Cold vs. Hot: Icy Follies

Americans have been sold the idea that ice cold drinks are satisfying and refreshing. Yet drinking chilled beverages damages the body. The human body is roughly 100° F. Whenever we put incold fluids or eat cold food, all of the organs must labor to heat that substance to 100° F before it can be absorbed. This drains the Yang (the body's fire and reserves), weakens the body, and creates cold stagnation. Fatigue, poor digestion, depressed spirit, menstrual cramps, and many other problems are caused and/or perpetuated by the consumption of cold things. Therefore, all fluids should be taken warm, or at least close to room temperature. This is true even in warm weather. Consumption of ice cold fluids causes the body to temporarily overheat in an attempt to bring the fluid to body temperature. In hot weather, it is better to drink warm fluids made from herbs that cause mild sweating which will release, rather than smother, the excessive heat.

When should I drink?

It is generally unwise to drink fluids, other than soup or stew, with meals. Miso soup is the ideal beverage to take with meals as it facilitates digestion. (Note, we consider any soup, stew, or gravy seasoned with miso to be a miso soup, whether corn, winter squash, pinto bean or split pea soup or a hearty gravy.) Soup should be used throughout the first part of meal, eaten gradually, in combination with other foods rather than as a first course. For example, one should take a bite of soup or stew followed by a bite of grain or grain topped with a condiment, then a bite of soup, then a bite of grain, and so forth, until one's cup of soup is gone. Or, you may eat a bite of both simultaneously as when soup, stew or gravy is ladled over noodles or bread is dunked in. Eating in this way facilitates good digestion and assimilation. After the soup is gone, the grain may be eaten with other side-dishes, which, when properly chewed, will produce liquid in the mouth. (Thorough chewing, until food is totally liquified, should provide ample liquid in a meal. Good quality sea salt, miso, or tamari also stimulate the flow of saliva, producing additional moisture.)

Drinking liquids other than seasoned soup, stew, broth, or gravy with meals dilutes the digestive juices, smothers (puts out) the digestive fire, and usually discourages proper chewing of food. If we chew our food until it is liquefied, (and make grains and vegetables our staple foods), then we do not need a drink to wash down our meals. As Ghandi once said, "Drink your food and chew your soup." We should chew our food until it is liquid, like soup thoroughly, before swallowing. We should also chew our soup— as if it were food, mixing it with our saliva before swallowing. Eating this way, food will be more easily digested, and tastier too. You may be amazed to discover that chewing your food until it becomes a "soup" reduces the desire for liquids with meals or after meals.

The best time to drink water, tea, or grain coffee, is about 60 minutes before a meal, at least 30 minutes after a meal, between meals, or upon arising in the morning. If you are very thirsty before a meal, you can sip a small volume of warm or hot water without risk of harming digestion. But remember, beverages should not be so hot that they burn your lips or so cold that they chill your teeth, nor should they be gulped.

How much liquid is enough?

As for the amount of fluid one should drink, it is important to follow your thirst, rather than someone else's notion of the appropriate number of cups of water or liquid per day. Forcing yourself to drink fluids is not only unnecessary but may, in fact, be harmful. Most people find that once they begin to eat a grain-based and vegetable-rich diet, with only small amounts of sweets and less animal products, two or three cups of water, tea, or grain coffee per day is sufficient to quench thirst. (Carbohydrates are broken down into carbon dioxide and water in the body, so a carbohydrate rich diet actually creates water in the body). Of course, you may want or need slightly more, especially if you are pregnant, lactating, or extremely active. But don't force it. You may be amazed at how little you really need or desire.

Causes of excessive thirst

If you find yourself drinking large mugs of water, tea, or grain coffee, you might be eating more sweets and/or fruit than you realize, or eating a lot of hard and dry foods such as baked bread, chips, crackers, rice cakes, toast, or popcorn. (Salty popcorn can make you thirsty but the dryness, rather than the saltiness, may be the real culprit as even unsalted or lightly salted dry foods can stimulate thirst.) However poor quality, overly refined, kiln dried salt or salt added to food at the table may cause excessive thirst. Try eating fewer sweets and more moist and soft grains and vegetables. Skip the crackers or toast; or dunk them into a moist cup of soup, stew, or gravy when you do eat them. And use sea salt, tamari and shoyu in cooking, not at the table.

The way to quench excessive thirst before it happens is to base your diet on cooked whole grains, soft porridge, and vegetables and soups, and to limit your intake of hard and/or dry or overly sweet foods. For the moderate thirst that arises in such a context, your vital life force will benefit from lukewarm pure water and mild herb or grain teas or grain "coffees," such as follow.

Healthy beverages

Grain coffees and herb teas do not have the undesirable side effects that come with coffee, decaf, soda pop, or sugared or artificially sweetened or flavored beverages. In fact, grain coffee and many herb teas actually confer benefits. Most stimulate proper digestion, and some stimulate peristalsis and proper elimination. Some teas and most grain beverages help cool you off if you are too hot, others can warm you if you are too cold. In general, bitter, sour, or cool flavored beverages have a cooling effect while roasted beverages have a more warming effect. Examples of some cooling beverages include rosehip, camomile, and peppermint. Japanese style kukicha twig tea is neutral. Roasted chicory, dandelion, and barley coffee are slightly warming. Examples of some very warming or hot beverages include those with cinnamon, cardamom, and black pepper. Yogi tea (a popular commercial tea), is a example.

In this book we have provided mild, everyday and seasonal beverages. For more specific medicinal teas for fever, chills, flu, bronchitis, allergies, or other aggravating conditions, it is best to go to an herbalist or practitioner of acupuncture or Oriental medicine rather than to self-medicate or take health food store herb preparations. This is because no two people are alike. Colds, flu, allergies and other illnesses can have very different signs, symptoms, and causes and two people with the "same" illness may need two very different herb preparations to balance and ameliorate their pathogenic condition.

Kicking the Coffee Habit

If you find that you just can't function in the morning without your cup of coffee, you're not alone. Many Americans suffer from this problem. Unfortunately, this unhealthy addiction depletes the body and can lead to innumerable physical, mental, and emotional disorders. The problem can only be overcome if you understand and get at the root cause and find a more nourishing solution. If you try to kick the habit with sheer will, you may quickly find that you have taken up another habit to replace it or that you soon return to the coffee.

A coffee "habit" or addiction is functional. That is, it is a response to something that is present or lacking in your current diet and lifestyle. It makes up for some deficiency, but in a dysfunctional way. Both coffee and sugar are qi tonics (that means that they produce a feeling of energy or "qi"). However, they are empty, devoid of substance. Both create many more problems than they solve. For example, both deplete body stores of iron, calcium, vitamin C and other vitamins and minerals. They are also major contributors to iron deficiency anemia, osteoporosis, and kidney and adrenal exhaustion (called qi-deficiency in Oriental medicine). Please refer to the "Causes of Sweets Cravings" in the dessert chapter for more on this topic; many of the roots of coffee cravings parallel those of sugar and sweets cravings.

Coffee cravings often result from late night eating and food stagnation. Eating a large meal late in the evening—after 6:00 or 7:00 p.m., or close to bedtime—is at the root of numerous diseases and health complaints. The metabolism slows down as darkness and night fall. Further, we are usually inactive in the evening. Thus, food eaten late at night is rarely used and is never used as efficiently as food taken earlier in the day when the digestive system is strongest and most able to transform food into qi (energy) and blood. If you go to bed on a full stomach your food is left to sit, undigested or only partially digested. This leads to poor digestion, stagnation and low energy, poor blood and energy flow, and the accumulation of toxic by-products in the body. This in turn creates fatigue, sluggishness and pathological physical, mental, and emotional conditions.

The common practice of eating late in the evening and close to bed also interferes with a good night's sleep. Since your energy is split between trying to digest your food and trying to sleep, neither job is done to its fullest. When food stagnates in the stomach or intestines, the flow of qi (energy) and blood is impaired. This can make your sleep poor and lead you to awaken tired and feeling groggy. Sleeping on and waking up with a belly full of undigested food will probably also leave you without a strong morning appetite, without the energy to pop out of bed without an alarm, and without the mental clarity to take on physical activity or intellectual challenges first thing in the morning.

It is not unusual to feel a strong need for drugs such as coffee and/or sugar to jump-start your engine in the morning, or to keep it running throughout the day, after eating late at night for a period of time. Though coffee and sugar may provide you with a burst of energy and a shot of "get up and go," their effects are depleting in the long run, and often in the short run as well. The need or desire for a second cup of coffee and/or a pastry, danish, candy bar, or cigarette mid-morning or later on shows this short term depleting effect. These stimulants create a vicious cycle of needing even more stimulants to release your pent up energy or to make up for a lack of it. These stimulants also aggravate existing health problems, putting excessive stress on the body as a whole.

Eating rich and fatty foods or excessively sweet, damp, or highly processed foods will have the same stagnating effect as eating late at night. If these two practices are combined, as they often are, the problems of morning sluggishness and coffee dependency will only be compounded.

Other causes of coffee dependency may include:

(a) overwork

(b) erratic eating

(c) working and sleeping schedules

(d) a lack of sufficient exercise, rest, or fresh air

(e) Being out of sync with your environment, such as working night shifts and odd hours.
(f) A chemically toxic home or work environment can also contribute to morning sluggishness, fatigue, depression, and low energy by bombarding the body with pollutants that it must then labor to process and eliminate.

To kick the coffee habit, it is crucial to eat a light and early dinner. If this is not possible, it would be better to have an afternoon snack and to skip dinner altogether or have a cup of light vegetable soup, broth, or a kuzu drink in lieu of dinner. (A hot bath can be a good follow-up.) It is far better to go to bed on an empty stomach; that way you will sleep more soundly and awaken more alert in the morning. You will also be hungrier in the morning and able to eat a more substantial breakfast and a larger lunch, thereby creating the energy required to jump off the stimulant-dependent merry-go-round. You will be amazed at the difference once you readjust your eating schedule and your body clock.

Chlorinated Water and Cancer

A recent review of 10 studies of the relationship between the consumption of chlorinated water and incidence of cancer has revealed that individuals who drink chlorinated water have a significantly increased risk of cancer at all sites. The correlation is especially strong between bladder and rectal cancers.

It is not necessary to use chlorine for public water purification. Ozone can be used, with even better results; however, it is more expensive.

You can protect yourself from the risks associated with chlorine by purchasing a home water filtration system. A solid carbon block filter, such as the Multi-Pure water filter, removes chlorine and organic pollutants at a cost of pennies per gallon.
Source:American Journal Public Health 82 (7):955-

Cultivate healthy habits

It is important to cultivate habits that will help you to eliminate the need for coffee or other addictive drugs and stimulants. These include:

1. Nourishing, grain-based regularly scheduled meals every day (3 meals, 2 meals, or 2 meals and 1 snack)

2. *At least* thirty to sixty minutes of daily exercise—walking, jogging, yoga, martial arts, bicycling, etc. Vigorous walking is perhaps one of the easiest exercises to perform and least stressful on your joints.

3. A brief period of daily meditation, breathing exercises, stretching, or relaxation.

4. Ample time for sleep each evening, at a reasonable and predictable time.

5. Healthy beverages that you can drink at times when you are accustomed to drinking coffee.

If you have difficulty putting these tips into practice, shiatsu and/or herbs can provide further support when used in conjunction with dietary and lifestyle changes. However, herbs are not a panacea. You may also have to re-evaluate the amount of time you work, your work load, or the kind of work that you do in order to steer clear of the stress and fatigue that have "driven you to drink." If your life-style and work-style do not allow you ample time to take care of yourself with proper food, exercise, fresh air, and relaxation, then no amount of herbs or "willing" yourself to give up coffee will work. In the end, an energy-depleting diet and life-style will only drain you dry and shorten the quality and quantity of life that you do have.

Basic Procedure, Brewed Grain Coffee/Beverage (Any Season)***

Prep: 5 minutes
Cooking: 20 minutes
Yield: 5-6 cups
Serving size: 1/2-1 cup per person

Grain coffees have a taste and aroma similar to coffee yet have none of the harmful side effects of coffee and decaf. But you don't have to be a coffee lover to enjoy grain coffee. We were never "into" coffee but always enjoyed grain coffee. (It tonifies the digestive system, stimulating peristalsis and elimination.)

Unlike coffee, you don't have to make it fresh every day. We make a pot to last for several days at a time. Brew it in a stainless steel stove-top percolator, glass pot, Chinese clay tea pot, coffee maker, or a stainless steel pot with a tight lid.

The roasted grains and roots called for in the following recipe can be purchased in the bulk herb and spice or macrobiotic section of health food stores, in Oriental markets, or by mail. Roasted barley (a.k.a. mugi cha), roasted whole corn and other roasted grains are different from those varieties that are commonly eaten. The brewing varieties are unhulled and dry roasted until almost black, a process which gives them a coffee-like flavor. Health food stores also stock instant and non-instant grain coffee.

5-6 cups pure water

4-5 Tbsp. roasted grains, roots, or grinds—see favorite combinations below *(roasted dandelion or chicory root, roasted barley or corn or a combination of 2-3 of these)*

1. **To cook directly in a pot:** Combine ingredients in a glass, ceramic or stainless steel pot. Cover, bring to boil, reduce heat to low and simmer 10-15 minutes, or until dark. If too dark, add a bit more water. For ease of serving and cleanup, put the grain, roots, and/or grinds in an oversized tea ball or tea infuser before boiling.

   To percolate: Place grains, roots, and/or grinds in the metal basket of a stainless steel percolator. Cook on top of the stove if using a stove top percolator; if it is an electric percolator, just plug it in and let it brew.

   To brew in a coffee maker: Use dioxin-free coffee filters and follow manufacturer's instructions for your unit, using roasted grains, roots, or grinds in place of coffee. (We have no experience with these.)

2. If grains and grinds are brewed loose, pour through a small tea strainer into serving cups, otherwise pour the beverage right into cups.

Serving suggestions: It is best to take grain coffee "straight," without any sweetener, cream, milk, or soy milk. On occasion, you may add some soy or almond milk, rice milk beverage, or amasake nectar; however, we do not recommend these for everyday use. You will get used to drinking your brew straight (without "milks" or sweeteners) if you take the "cold turkey" approach. Serve your "coffee" warm or at room temperature.

Storage: Store the pot on the counter or stove. Heat as needed. When the pot runs low, add more water and a small amount of grains or grinds. Simmer as above. After three or four days, toss the old brew and make a new batch.

Favorite combinations:

- **Roasted Barley Coffee:** 100% whole roasted barley or roasted barley grinds.

- **Roasted Barley & Chicory Coffee:** 50:50 toasted barley with roasted chicory root.

- **Roasted Barley & Dandelion Coffee:** Use a half roasted barley and half roasted dandelion root, or 3 parts barley to 1 part dandelion root.

- **Roasted Barley & Corn Tea:** Use half of each, or slightly more barley than corn.

- **Roasted Chicory & Dandelion Coffee:** 3/4 roasted chicory root and 1/4 dandelion root.

- **Roasted Chicory & Corn Coffee:** 50:50 or 3 parts chicory to 1 part roasted corn. Roasted corn is mild so you may need to use slightly more than is called for in the basic recipe.

- **Roasted Corn Tea:** Use 100% roasted corn.

- Cafe Du Grain, Bambu, Barley Brew, Ohsawa Coffee, mugi cha, and other natural grain coffees. Follow package instructions for brewing or use the portions suggested above. ❑

Basic Procedure, Instant Grain Coffee (Any Season)***

Prep: 3-4 minutes
Cooking: 3 minutes (to boil water)
Serving size: 6-8 oz.
Serves: 1

Instant grain coffee is incredibly convenient. You might want to keep some at the office and some at home for the times when it is inconvenient to brew a pot from scratch. Instant grain coffee will cost more than home-brewed, but it's often worth it. The brands available aretoo numerous to mention. Try several varieties until you find a favorite. There is quite a difference in taste and ingredients from one brand to the next.

6-8 oz. boiling water

2-3 tsp. instant grain coffee

(Kafree Roma, Cafe Du Grain, Inca, Postum, Pero, Bambu, etc.)

Note: Most manufacturers suggest one teaspoon per cup; however, we like grain coffee best when made dark, so we always use more grain coffee powder. We find this makes for a more flavorful cup, though you may prefer it lighter.)

1. Add instant grain coffee to your tea cup. Add boiling water. Stir and serve.

Serving suggestion: It is best to avoid adding soy, dairy, rice, nut or seed milk to your daily brew. If you make a strong and flavorful cup, it won't take long for you to get accustomed to taking it straight.

Variation

Soy Mocha or Almond Mocha: For an occasional treat, use lite, vanilla, original or plain Rice Milk Beverage, Almond Milk Beverage, soy milk, or amasake nectar. Stir the grain coffee powder into the liquid as you heat it in a saucepan over medium heat. Stir to dissolve and thicken. Do not boil or the "milk" will curdle.

Note: This is not recommended for frequent or daily use. These milks can be hard to digest, particularly when made from soy beans or nuts and/or when sweetened. ❏

Basic Procedure, Herb Tea (Year Round)

Prep: under 5 minutes
Steeping: 10-15 minutes

Serves: 4-8
Serving size: 1/2-1 cup per person

A wide assortment of herb teas can be found but be careful that they do not contain caffeine, sweeteners, or artificial flavors. Although herb teas seem fairly innocuous, some can have very strong effects if taken in excessive amounts or by someone with strong imbalances. Thus, mild varieties of herb tea are most suited for regular use.

Blends which contain fruits are best kept to occasional use while spicy teas are suited for those with a "cold" condition (poor digestion, easily chilled, frequently cold, weak, fatigued, pale tongue, or generally deficient). In contrast, spicy teas or "hot" herbs can aggravate the condition of someone with "heat" symptoms (marked by a dark red tongue, red face, feelings of excess heat, dryness, restlessness, or sweating). Peppermint tea, which is very cooling, should be avoided by those who tend to be cold and deficient.

Generally, cooling teas are best in hot weather and warming teas are best in cold weather, although there are exceptions. If you wish to use herb teas medicinally, it is best to study their effects and/or seek the advice of a qualified herbalist.

5-6 cups pure water

2 Tbsp. loose herbs
(camomile, rosehips, alfalfa, red clover, peppermint, spearmint, or others)

1. Bring water to boil in a tea pot or a stainless steel, glass, porcelain or clay pot.

2. Put loose herbs in a tea ball or tea infuser and add to pot or place herbs loose in a pot. Turn off heat. Allow tea to steep in a covered pot for 10-15 minutes or until it reaches the desired strength. Or, fill a tea ball with 1-2

tsp. of loose, dried and ground herbs. Place the tea ball in a cup of boiling water and allow it to steep until it reaches the desired strength.

Serving suggestions: Serve warm or close to room temperature. Remove tea ball. Do not boil the leftover tea as this may destroy the volatile oils in the herbs. If you must reheat the tea, just simmer it briefly.

Storage: Store leftover tea at room temperature.

Variations:

- **If using tea bags:** Boil water as above then add 1 tea bag per 1 1/2-2 cups of water. Turn off the heat and brew as above.

- **For a sweet tea:** Combine the above volume of water with 2 tsp. of licorice root.

1. Cover, bring to boil, then reduce heat to low and simmer for 15-20 minutes.

2. Add loose peppermint, camomile, spearmint, or other herb tea (in a tea ball), turn off heat and steep for 10 minutes. Or, simmer up a pot of licorice tea, then pour the warm liquid over a tea ball or tea bag placed in a single cup. Reheat the licorice portion each time you want a cup of tea.

- **Green Tea:** Often served in Japanese restaurants, this tea contains some caffeine, but far less than coffee or black tea and confers benefits that these others do not. Medicinally this cooling tea dissolves fats and mucous, acts as a diuretic and is said to aid in weight loss. It is best used moderately and cautiously by anyone with a cold or deficient condition. Some authorities have reported the effectiveness of green tea in helping to lower cholesterol (an extreme accumulation of fat and mucous in the blood vessels) and relieve hypertension.

Brew as for herb tea or purchase it in tea bag form and follow the above instructions. ❏

Bancha Twig Tea (a.k.a. Kukicha) (Year Round)

Prep: under 5 minutes
Cooking: 15 minutes
Serves: 6-8
Serving size: 1/2 cup per person

This Japanese tea is made from the twigs of the kukicha plant. The taste is quite mild. Some people take to it immediately while others find it too bland. It can be served warm or room temperature in any season. Many find this mild tea to benefit digestion when taken after a meal.

6 cups water
2 Tbsp. kukicha twigs

1. Combine in a pot. Cover and bring to boil over medium heat. Reduce heat to low and simmer 10-15 minutes.

Serving suggestions: To serve, place a small bamboo or metal tea strainer in each cup then ladle or pour tea in. Return the twigs to the tea pot to be used again. The twigs may be used several times.

Storage: Store at room temperature. Reheat as desired or serve at room temperature.

Variations:

- **Kukicha & Camomile Tea:** Add 1-1 1/2 Tbsp. loose camomile in step #1 above. Or, add 2 chamomile tea bags after simmering and allow the pot to steep, covered, with the heat off, for 10 minutes before serving.

- **Tamari & Kukicha Tea:** This is a good strengthening tea which can relieve food poisoning, gastric pains, headache, according to Japanese folk medicine. To 1/2-1 cup of warm tea, add 1/2-1 tsp. tamari or shoyu. Drink on an empty stomach. (Use infrequently.)

- **Ume-kukicha Tea:** This is another good tea for heartburn, acid indigestion, stomach ache, headache, or food poisoning. Chop 1/2 umeboshi plum or apriboshi or place 1/2 tsp. of ume or apriboshi paste in a tea cup. Top with 1/2-1 cup of kukicha tea. Stir well and drink. ❏

Ume-Sho Kuzu Drink (Any Season)***

Prep: 5 minutes or less
Cooking: 5-10 minutes
Serves: 1
Serving size: 1 cup per person

This soothing drink can relieve an upset stomach, painful gas, heartburn, indigestion, fatigue, colds, and even headaches or food poisoning. It can also be used to ward off hunger pangs if you get hungry in the evening but want to avoid eating close to bed time.

Kuzu is a hearty plant with incredible medicinal properties. Kuzu leaves and roots are rich in minerals such as iron, calcium, and phosphorus. The starch from the root strengthens the digestive system and alkalinizes the blood, particularly when combined with umeboshi, apriboshi, and/or tamari soy sauce. Kuzu root has been shown to help in the treatment of alcoholism.

Note: Most of the kuzu root found in stores and macrobiotic catalogs comes from Japan. Hopefully that will change soon. Kuzu root grows wild in the Southern part of the United States where it known as a pesky weed.

1 cup water or vegetable soup stock
   (if stock is too strong or dark, dilute with water)
1-3 tsp. kuzu root powder (see step #2 below), depending upon desired thickness
1/4-1 tsp. tamari *or* shoyu
1 umeboshi plum or apriboshi, chopped, mashed or puréed *or* 1 tsp. paste
1/4-1/2 tsp. fresh ginger juice *or*~1/8 tsp. dried ginger powder

Note: Ginger juice is extracted from fresh ginger root which has been grated very finely (with a special grater), then squeezed in one's fist (use only the juice).

1. Grate ginger root with a porcelain or stainless steel ginger grater or the smallest hole on your all-purpose grater. Squeeze the juice into a cup, then wet the wad of ginger and squeeze again. Discard pulp.

2. In a cup, mash kuzu lumps into powder and dissolve into cool or cold water or soup stock.

Add umeboshi or apriboshi and tamari. (If using dried ginger, add it now.) Bring to boil over medium heat and stir until thick and transparent, several minutes. Add ginger juice (if dried ginger powder was not used) and turn off heat.

Serving suggestions: Serve warm, with a spoon, savoring every drop.

Variations:

• Use arrowroot to replace kuzu (if kuzu is unavailable or the cost is prohibitive).

• **Garlic-Kuzu Drink** (Any Season): Omit ginger; instead, add 1 clove of garlic to the water or stock. Simmer over low heat for 10 minutes before adding umeboshi or apriboshi, tamari, and kuzu. ❏

Licorice & Ginger Tea

Prep: under 5 minutes
Cooking: 15 minutes
Serves: 6-12
Serving size: 1/2 cup per person

This tea is sweet and particularly good for colds, flus, and upper respiratory infections marked by cold symptoms (aversion to cold temperatures, desire for more clothing or covers, chills, clear or watery mucous, a pale tongue, pale urination or related cold symptoms). Licorice soothes the throat and stomach (too much can cause burping, though). Ginger root help stimulate digestion and circulation and revs up the metabolism. Ginger can also stimulate sweating, to expel cold-type pathogens.

If symptoms such as fever, sweating, aversion to bed covers, a desire to wear less clothing, dark yellow or thick mucous, a dark red tongue and/or a flushed face, or other heat symptoms appear then this is not a suitable tea for you. For hot and dry symptoms, peppermint and licorice tea would be appropriate because they clear heat rather than generate more of it. For hot and damp symptoms, peppermint and honey tea would be a better bet.

1 1/2-2 tsp. dried licorice root (comes ground or in bits)
2-3 penny-sized slices of fresh ginger root
4-6 cups water

1. Bring to boil in a glass, clay or ceramic pot. (If possible, avoid using a metal or stainless steel pots for this tea; it can chemically interact with the herbs and make them less effective.) Reduce heat to low and simmer for about 15 minutes.

2. Pour servings through a bamboo or mesh tea strainer if the licorice and ginger are not contained in a tea ball. Serve warm.

Storage: Store leftovers at room temperature and reheat briefly as needed. You can often make a second batch with the same licorice and ginger if you add a lesser amount of water than was called for in the original recipe. ❑

Cinnamon Spice Tea (Mainly Fall & Winter)

Prep: under 5 minutes
Cooking: 15 minutes
Serves: 6-12
Serving size: 1/2-1 cup per person

This warming tea is just the thing to stoke your digestive fires and metabolism in the cold months, or any time when you're feeling cold. It has a spicy, sweet taste that is sure to please. Licorice root soothes and tonifies the digestive organs and can help to regulate blood sugar levels.

1-1 1/2 heaping tsp. dried licorice root
2-3 cinnamon sticks (bark)
2 penny-sized slices of fresh ginger root
Optional, 3-4 cardamom pods
Optional, 1/8 tsp. black pepper
5-6 cups of water

1. Combine all ingredients in a Chinese clay pot (a special pot found in most Asian markets which is used for making medicinal herb teas so that they do not interact with the metals in most tea pots) or in a glass tea pot or saucepan.

2. Cover and bring to boil, reduce heat to low and simmer for 10-15 minutes.

Serving suggestions: Serve warm and reheat as needed. Reheat before serving. Add 4 cups of water for a second pot. After two pots have been made, discard the remains and start over.

Note: It is not a good idea to use more licorice than the recipe above states because too much licorice root can cause acid heartburn and burping. If this occurs, you drank too much of the tea or made it too strong (with too much licorice).

Storage: Store at room temperature or refrigerate for up to three days. ❑

Rose Hip Tea (Spring, Summer)

Prep: 5 minutes
Cooking: 15 minutes
Serves: 6-10
Serving size: 1/2-1 cup per person

For a tangy, tart tasting tea try this recipe. Dried, whole or seeded, rosehips can be found in most health food stores and herb shops. This tea has a cooling and astringent effect. It can help to moderate heat symptoms such as painful fibrocystic breasts, PMS, and irritability. Rosehips contain bioflavinoids, substances which help to regulate the Blood, clear pathogenic Heat, stop bleeding, relieve stagnation of Qi or Blood. For a lighter tea use a lesser amount of rose hips. Leftover tea can be used to replace lemon juice in soups, sauces, salad dressing, or desserts, or used as the base for light and cooling soups in spring and summer. (In other seasons, rosehips can be used by those with heat conditions or if moderated with a bit of cinnamon or other warming spices.)

6 cups water
3 Tbsp. dried, whole or seeded rose hips

1. Put rosehips in an over-sized tea ball or tea infuser or directly in a tea pot or glass, ceramic or stainless steel pot.

2. Cover and bring to boil over medium heat, then reduce heat to low and simmer, covered, 12-15 minutes. If too dark or thick, add more water.

3. Ladle through a tea strainer (if the tea is loose) or remove the tea ball and pour tea into cups.

Storage: Store at room temperature. Reheat as desired or serve at room temperature. If it is too strong, add a bit of water. You can reuse rosehips to make a second pot of tea.

Variations:

- **Rosehip & Licorice Tea:** For a sweeter tea, add 1-2 tsp. dried licorice root to the tea pot before brewing. Prepare as above.

- **Rosehip & Honey Tea:** Good for a sore throat with hot sensations and symptoms. Stir half a teaspoon of honey into your cup of warm rosehip tea. ❏

Cornsilk or Corn Cob Tea or Stock (Summer and Fall)

Prep: under 5 minutes
Cooking: about 15 minutes
Serves: 3-8 (or several times for 2)
Serving size: 1/2-1 cup per person

Although most people discard the silk lining tucked inside the husks of fresh corn, this silk makes the most marvelous warm weather tea. It's great for after summer meals or heavy exercise, and also makes a soothing stock for instant or simmered vegetable soups or for cooking hot cereal. Corn silk tea is light and easy to digest. It lubricates dryness and clears heat, relieves summer heat or fever, and drains dampness. Since it has a diuretic action it is good for relieving edema and promoting urination. Although fresh corn silks are a must, dried ones can be used in a pinch. Corn cobs also make great tea. For this you will want to use the cobs soon after cutting the corn off. You can use them alone or combined with the corn silk. Either way you will have a sweet and nourishing tea.

silk removed from 2-4 fresh ears of corn (roughly 1-1 3/4 cups)
Optional, 2-4 bare corn cobs (these must be fresh)
4-6 cups water (or as needed for desired strength)

1. Combine corn silk and water. If desired, add fresh, bare corn cobs (after the corn has been removed for use in other dishes). Cover the pot, bring to boil over medium heat, reduce heat to low and simmer for 15 minutes or until pale yellow.

2. Remove corn cobs if used. Strain off corn silk.

Serving suggestions: Serve warm or close to room temperature.

Storage: Store leftovers at room temperature. Use within 4 days. Leftover tea can be used as soup stock or breakfast cereal stock (really good with millet, rolled oats, or leftover rice with either of these).

Variation:

- For sweet cravings—particularly good for people who are weaning themselves from juices and other sweets—you may wish to cook corn cobs with the corn still on. For this you can experiment with the proportion of water to corn. We suggest 1 ear of corn per 3-4 cups water. Make only enough to last for one to three days at a time. Drink it warm or at room temperature, never ice cold.

- Use corn cobs alone, without the silks. ❏

Warm Soy Milk (Any Season)

Prep: 5 minutes
Cooking: 4-6
Serves: 1
Serving size: 3/4-1 cup per person

Soy milk is fairly rich, so it's not recommended for regular use by those who have a hard time losing weight, tend to be phlegmy, have poor digestion, allergies, or cold symptoms. But, for those who are very active, pregnant, lactating, or just have a hard time keeping weight on, it can be good medicine. (In some cases it can also help with insomnia in the same way that the old "milk & honey" remedy worked, except that in most cases the honey wouldn't be necessary.)

Soy milk is best and most digestible when lightly seasoned with sea salt or miso, then warmed. Adding a bit of spice is also advisable because soy milk is very cooling and can put out the digestive fire and/or create copious amounts of intestinal gas if taken cold. Further, many brands of soy milk are made from soy beans that have undergone only partial cooking. This poses serious health problems because raw or under-cooked soy beans contain a thyroid inhibiting substance. (The addition of sea salt or miso makes it more alkalinizing and helps with digestion. The spice sparks digestion and counters the soy milk's damp, mucousy qualities. And heating cooks the milk brings it closer to body temperature, and also counters the cooling effects.)

3/4-1 cup plain, unsweetened, oil-free soy milk
1/8 tsp. sea salt *or* 1 tsp. light or dark miso
1/8 tsp. dried ginger powder, ground black pepper or nutmeg or cinnamon

Note: You may use azuki, brown rice, black soy-bean, chickpea, barley or other varieties of miso. Any will do and all will be very tasty when combined with soy milk. Just pick one.

1. Combine ingredients and heat in a saucepan over medium heat, stirring often to keep the milk from boiling and curdling. (If using miso, dissolve it just before serving or keep mixture under a boil to preserve miso's beneficial enzymes.)

Note: If your soy milk tastes "beany" and raw, heat it for 20 minutes using the covered-bowl-within-a-pot method.

Serving suggestions: Serve as a light snack or with a meal, in place of soup. This is delicious served with Squash-Wiches or Yam-Wiches and a pressed, marinated, tossed, or boiled salad, It is also good with Huminta Tamales and sautéed or stir fried greens.

Variation:

- Add 1-2 tsp. raw honey, barley malt, or rice syrup to 3/4-1 cup of warm soy (or goat or cow's) milk. (This is good for insomnia with hunger or as an occasional snack or dessert.) Sprinkle with cinnamon, nutmeg, or dried ginger.

- Use goat milk for soy milk but be careful not to boil it. This variation can be made without the miso or sea salt, if you like.

- Use unpasteurized goat or cow's milk in the above recipe. Omit miso. Add the spice for best digestion. Serve warm or at room temperature. ❏

Cooling Carrot Cocktail (Infrequent Use, Spring, Summer or Fall)

Prep: 5 minutes
Cooking: zero
Serves: 2
Serving size: 3/4-1 cup per person

Juice is not a regular part of the Nourishment For Life diet. If is far too concentrated and wasteful for frequent, daily, or even weekly use. Who would eat five or six apples or oranges at one time, let alone eight carrots. (It really does take 6-8 carrots, apples, or oranges to make a single cup of juice!) Besides that, juice is raw and very cooling and can weaken the body by putting out the digestive fires and draining body heat. Drink juices only occasionally and in warm weather or when you're running hot or feverish. Avoid drinking this or other juices if you tend to be cold or easily chilled, are plagued by weak digestion, falling hair, allergies, diarrhea, or frequent cold.

1 1/2-2 cups fresh carrot juice

2-3 tsp. spirulina **or** Green Magma powder

1. Mix ingredients with a whisk or in a blender. Pour into two cups. If juice has been refrigerated, allow it or the mixed cocktail to come to room temperature for 1/2-1 hour before serving to avoid chilling the stomach and lowering the body temperature.

Serving suggestions: Serve with a meal, in place of soup. Try it for lunch or supper with whole grain, pizza, pasta, or bread, and greens. Or serve it as a snack. ❏

Holiday Spiced Cider (Infrequent use, Fall & Winter)

Prep: 5 minutes
Cooking: about 15 minutes or 2-8 hours in a crock pot
Serving size: 3/4-1 cup per person
Serves: 5-8

Warm up to the holidays with this sweet and spicy drink. For best results use fresh, locally made apple juice or apple cider. Because the juice is so sweet, we prefer to dilute it with water. You can vary the juice to water ratio if you like. Bear in mind, however, that drinking too much of this sweet brew can stimulate an almost unquenchable thirst; both fruit juice and especially hot spices like cinnamon and ginger can be very drying if taken to excess or taken by certain people who tend to have a drier condition.

3-4 cups apple juice or apple cider

2-3 cups water

2 cinnamon sticks

2 penny sized slices of fresh ginger root

Optional, 3 cloves

1. Combine ingredients in a pot, preferably glass, ceramic, clay or enamel lined, or stainless steel if that is all you have. Cover and bring to boil over medium heat. Immediately, reduce heat to low and simmer, covered, for 15-20 minutes or until dark and aromatic. Or cook, covered, for 2-8 hours on low in a crock pot.

Serving suggestions: Serve warm. (At holiday parties, for convenience and to avoid boiling the cider pot dry, you may wish to heat and serve from a crock pot/slow cooker.)

Storage: Refrigerate and reheat before serving.

Sweet-n-Spicy Mu & Apple Cider (Fall & Winter, Festive Use)

Prep: 5 minutes
Cooking: about 15 minutes *or* 2-8 hours in a crock pot
Serves: 8-12 people
Serving size: 3/4-1 cup per person

Mu tea is a exotic blend of herbs that are typically used in Oriental medicinal as a kidney and lung tonic, for wheezing coughs and respiratory troubles accompanied by difficult breathing or for qi deficiency, prolonged feelings of coldness, weakness, or fatigue.When taken as medicine-mu tea should be cooked without juice.However, in this recipe, the mu tea is brewed with apple juice for a spicy winter party beverage.

Mu tea comes in two varieties, one which contains 9 herbs, and another which contains 16 herbs. It can be purchased in macrobiotic supply stores, the macrobiotic section of some health food stores, or through the mail.Mu 9 contains herbaceous peony root, cinnamon, Japanese parsley root, hoelen, licorice root, peach kernels, ginger root, Japanese ginseng, and rehmannia. Mu 16 contains these herbs plus seven others.

Note: Although this tea has a wonderful spicy flavor, it is neither recommended for everyday use nor for all people. It best avoided by those with heat conditions. If you like the taste of the herbs and they are suited to your condition, you can make this tea without the juice for more frequent consumption.

6 cups juice and 2 cups water, or half water and half juice

or 2 quarts (8 cups) apple juice/apple cider (fresh, local if possible)

4-5 Tbsp. mu tea

1. Place the tea in a tea ball or directly in a glass, ceramic, clay, enamel lined, or stainless steel pot. Add juice or juice and water. Cover and bring to boil over medium heat. Reduce heat to low and simmer for 15-20 minutes or until the drink reaches the desired strength. Or, cook 2-8 hours on low in a crock pot.

2. If the tea has been placed loosely in the pot, strain the entire batch or place a small strainer over a tea cup and ladle the tea in. Repeat for additional cups. Serve warm.

Storage: Refrigerate leftovers and reheat to serve, or store at room temperature if the drink will be used within 36 hours.

Variation:

- **Mu Tea**: Replace juice with water in the above recipe. Cook for 30 minutes, on low.Serve 1/2-1 cupful between meals, as desired.

Fluoridated Water & Osteoporosis

Several recent studies reported in the *Journal of American Medicine*, the *New England Journal of Medicine*, and the *Journal of Epidemiology*, have shown that both men and women have up to a 100% greater risk of hip fractures if they drink fluoridated city water. Researchers at the University of Utah and University of Michigan have found that fluoride from water can accumulate to toxic levels and cause bone degeneration.

A Multi-pure water purifier can be fitted with a filter to remove fluoride (these can be ordered from the company; see our resource section). This may be part of your best insurance against osteoporosis—pure food and drink and plenty of vigorous exercise.

Source: JAMA, Aug. 12, 1992. NEJM, Mar. 22, 1990. Science News, May 25, 1991.

Chapter 12
Reading List & Resources:

Recommended Reading List for a Nourishing Life:

The health benefits of various diets have been debated for years, and conflicting information is rampant. We think that it is important to conduct one's own research, and not to rely on only one source to establish a method and philosophy of eating or living.

We have provided a list of books which we think may be helpful in your study, understanding, and practice of a more sustainable and nourishing diet and lifestyle. The books in each section are listed in the order of our preference. No one book captures the essence of what we believe and practice. In the books on diet and nutrition, for example, we have found each book offers some valuable information and insights into our cultural heritage; however, some outline dietary practices which do not accord with the principles of Nourishment For Life, though they all contain some valuable information.

Used bookstores are excellent places to shop for inexpensive books for education and inspirational reading. Many cities also boast half-price bookstores where slightly damaged or overstocked books are sold at a fraction of their suggested retail price. Many popular books can be found at either of these places, often within a short time of publication. It pays to look there first.

You needn't throw out all your old cookbooks upon venturing into the world of ecological-wholefoods cookery. Some of your most treasured books may still offer new ideas and inspiration. Many of the ethnic meals and dishes we have created were adapted from or inspired by various ethnic cookbooks (even classics like the Joy of Cooking). We especially enjoy ethnic cookbooks with pictures and thorough descriptions of how people have traditionally prepared foods in different countries and regions.

Below you will find some of our favorite books on cooking, nutrition, natural living, and gardening. We sometimes cook directly from a book without changing ingredients, though in most cases—even with vegetarian or natural foods books—we find it necessary to modify the recipes. Other books can give us a basic idea, then we use our standard proportions and procedures to create suitable dishes for health, harmony and pleasure.

If you can afford it, buy an extra copy or copies of your favorite cookbooks and health books, then donate them to your local library. If they like them, they may be encouraged to buy additional copies for other branch libraries. You'll help spread the good word and share valuable information with others at the same time.

If possible, set aside thirty minutes each day for reading about natural health, cookery, and healing. Reading and studying will expand your knowledge and help you to become a more informed cook, consumer, and healthy eater. Your new-found knowledge and cooking techniques will be reinforced through repeated exposure and you will then be able to deal with friends and family members who express concern or fear about your un-orthodox dietary and lifestyle practices. If you know why you are doing what you are doing, you are more likely to continue. Take it upon yourself to re-educate yourself and your family. You will be rewarded with good health and delicious meals.

Cooking:

1. *Basic Macrobiotic Cooking* by Julia Ferre. Oroville, CA: GOMF Press, 1987.

The recipes and techniques are excellent. This is the perfect gift for the novice natural foods cook who doesn't have a lot of time to cook. It is not a glamorous book but it is one of the best we have found to introduce people to macrobiotic/wholefoods cookery. We have studied and cooked from this book extensively and have adapted many of Julia's recipes. Simple illustrations and instructions take you through the basics of using the proper equipment and techniques necessary for delicious and nutritious wholefoods.

2. *American Macrobiotic Cooking* by Meredith McCarty. Eureka, CA: Turning Point Publications, 1987

This book contains a variety of ethnic and American regional meals built around whole grains, vegetables, and beans. Recipes are easy to follow and always delicious. This book contains valuable information (much like our formulas) to help you figure out how much of each food to prepare per person.

3. *FRESH: From A Vegetarian Kitchen* by Meredith McCarty. Eureka, CA: Turning Point Publications, 1989.

This book provides a fresh and innovative approach to gourmet vegan/macrobiotic cooking. Meredith's friendly tone and unpretentious attitude will welcome you into the world of whole foods cookery. Included are countless recipes for non-dairy sauces, spreads, salad dressings, casseroles, natural barbeque sauce, and much more. With this book will woo your family and wow your friends. It would make an excellent gift too!) Natural leavened bread making recipes and procedures are also provided.

4. *Cooking with Rachel: Creative Vegetarian & Macrobiotic Cuisine* by Rachel Albert. Oroville, CA: G.O.M. F. Press, 1989.

This was one of my earlier books and does not reflect my current knowledge, practice, or style of cooking. It offers many delicious recipes but watch out for the yields (there are no guidelines). Some recipes serve twelve to fifteen; thus, you may need to reduce some of the bean, amasake, pudding, and gravy recipes by one-half *or more*. I do not recommend the cake and cookie recipes on a regular basis (if used, the fats and oils should be reduced or replaced with apple sauce), nor do I recommend the use of tofu in any desserts. Otherwise, it is a great book and full of many tasty recipes for soups, stews, grains, beans, dairy-free casseroles, dips, and fruit desserts.

5. *Cooking with Japanese Foods: A Guide to the Traditional Natural Foods of Japan* by Jan and John Belleme. Garden City, New York: Avery Publishing,1986.

If you're looking for great recipes using tofu, miso, tamari, shoyu, umeboshi, Japanese mushrooms, daikon radish, noodles, rice, rice syrup, and the like, this is the book for you. The easy-to-follow recipes are delightful and sure to please even the most finicky family members and guests. The marinades, sauces, stir frys, cooked vegetables, and tofu dishes are especially good.

6. *Culinary Treasures of Japan* by John and Jan Belleme. Garden City, New York: Avery Publishing Group, 1992.

This delightful book details the history, production, and medicinal uses for traditional Japanese foods such as miso, tamari, shoyu, umeboshi, brown rice vinegar, kuzu, toasted sesame oil, and Japanese noodles. Cooking methods and short, easy-to-follow recipes are offered for each food. This book will provide the novice and seasoned whole foods cook with much needed information and new ideas. However, you needn't rely on Japanese foods to use the book; for the health of our fragile planet, it is a good idea to substitute American miso, tamari, umeboshi, shiitake, sea vegetables and mochi for Japanese imports as much as possible.

7. *Natural Healing From Head to Toe* by Cornellia and Herman Aihara. Garden City, N Y: Avery Publishing, 1994.

This book offers an array of tasty macrobiotic recipes using fresh, wholesome grains, beans, land and sea vegetables, and some fish and eggs.

8. *The Thousand Recipe Chinese Cookbook* by Gloria Bley Miller. New York: Grosset & Dunlap, 1977, with reprints up to the present.

This is one of the most simple and comprehensive books on Chinese cooking. Recipes are clearly explained; the ingredients are in intelligible English; and the basic cooking techniques are lucidly described. (You can to replace the meats with vegetarian products like tempeh or wheat meat/seitan, though) The text is so enticing and full of enthusiasm that one can read this classic book for pleasure, like a good novel; you will no doubt learn a lot this way. It's enough to make a good cook out of anyone!

Oriental Nutrition, Home Remedies & Herbology:

1. *Arisal of The Clear: A Simple Guide to Healthy Eating According To Traditional Chinese Medicine* by Bob Flaws. Boulder, CO: Blue Poppy Press, 1991.

This is a straightforward, clear and easy to understand book for the layperson who wishes to apply the wisdom of Oriental dietetics to his/her daily life. It can also benefit health practitioners and health care providers. It explains the theory behind traditional Chinese diet and tells you how to apply the two thousand plus years of Eastern dietary wisdom in modern times. This is a must for anyone who wants to understand more about the effects of diet and lifestyle on the human organism. It's quick reading too.

2. *Natural Healing From Head to Toe* by Cornellia and Herman Aihara. Garden City, N, Y: Avery Publishing, 1994.

This encyclopedia of common ailments offers offers the traditional Japanese folk medicine perspective on the causes and remedies available.

3. *The Way of Herbs* by Michael Tierra, C.A., N.D. New York: Washington Square Press, WSP, Simon & Shuster, 1983.

A good introduction into the theory behind herbal medicine and the appropriate use of culinary herbs and herbal remedies, this book makes an excellent reference for laypeople and health practitioners alike.

4. *Planetary Herbology* by Michael Tierra, C.A., N.D. Twin Lakes, WI: Lotus Press, 1988.

5. *The Breast Connection: A Laywoman's Guide to the treatment of Breast Disease* by Honora Lee Wolfe. Boulder, Colorado: Blue Poppy Press, 1989.

A must for every American woman. It gives Oriental medicine view of the progression of breast disease from PMS breast tenderness to breast cancer, noting that PMS is a prelude to more serious problems. Ms. Wolfe may underestimate the role of dietary factors in female disorders in America but she definitely offers sensible lifestyle and dietary guidance for the prevention of breast disease.

6. *A Second Spring* by Honora Lee Wolf. Boulder, CO: Blue Poppy Press, 1991.

Another must for American women. This gives the Oriental medicine view of menopause and ways to help yourself to a "second spring" through diet, exercise, and relaxation. It also discusses estrogen replacement therapy as well as holistic options. Gives good advise on the prevention and treatment of osteoporosis.

Diet & Nutrition:

1. *Fats That Heal, Fats That kill* by Udo Erasmus, Ph.D., Vancouver, British Columbia: Alive Publications, 1986, 1993.

This groundbreaking, eye-opening book uncovers the truth about fats and oils. They're not all created equal. Find out about the good, the bad, and the ugly. Deficiency of essential fatty acids is linked a wide variety of illnesses, including cancer, MS, lupus, PMS, AIDS, depression, acne, eczema, anxiety, and other modern diseases. This book can help set you on the right course. Must reading!

2. *Transition To Vegetarianism* by Rudolph Ballantine, M.D., Honesdale, PA: Himalayan International Institute,

This is a good reader for those embarking on a vegetarian or semi-vegetarian diet and for the avid student of nutrition.

3. *Native Nutrition* by Ronald Schmid, N.D. Rochester, Vermont: Healing Arts Press, 1994.

Regardless of whether you choose to eat a vegetarian, vegan, or omnivorous diet, it is well worth reading this book. The author details the dietary practices of some of the healthiest people around the world and makes a case for the inclusion of at least some animal products in the diet. Various diets, diseases and foods are discussed in detail. Included is extensive information on the benefits of essential fatty acids, raw dairy foods from pastured animals, sea vegetables, deep sea fatty fish, and other traditional foods.

4. *Nutrition & Physical Degeneration* by Weston Price, DDS. (Price Pottenger Foundation, 1945, 1970, 1982, TypeCraft Inc. Pasadena, CA P.O. Box 2614, La Mesa, CA 91943-2614. Tel # (619) 582-4168.

This is a collectors item, one you will want to have on your shelf for years to come. (You could also donate one to your local library.) This is perhaps one of the most comprehensive books on the effects of refined foods on the human organism and its physical and psychological development and functioning. Price also discusses the problems of soil depletion and food quality and its resultant effect on human health.

5. *McDougall's Medicine, A Challenging Second Opinion* by John McDougall, M.D. Piscataway, NJ: New Century Publishers.

This book will inspire you to take your health into your own hands. It challenges the currently accepted treatments for the most commonly diagnosed diseases such as cancer, osteoporosis, arthritis, heart disease, atherosclerosis, hypertension, urinary problems, and diabetes. Filled with information on the causes, prevention and treatment of these ailments with thorough documentation with both scientific clinical and experimental data. Read this before you consider western drugs or surgery.

6. *RX: Charcoal* by Agatha Thrash, M.D., & Calvin Thrash, M.D., Sunfield, Michigan: Family Health Publications, 1988. (8777 E. Musgrove Hwy, Sunfield, MI 48890).

7. *Diet & Nutrition: A Wholistic Approach* by Rudolph Ballantine. Honesdale, PA: Himalayan International Institute, 1978.

8. *Sea Salts Hidden Powders* by Jacques De Langre, Phd. Magalia, CA: Happiness Press, 1990.

This book details the benefits of true sea salt and its effects on the human organism. It also explains about the drawbacks of highly refined salt.

9. *An Introduction to Macrobiotics: The Natural Way to Health & Happiness* by Oliver Cowmeadow. Northamptonshire, Wellingborough, England: Thorsons Publishing, 1987.

10. *Let Food Be Thy Medicine* by Alex Jack. Beckett, Mass: One Peaceful World Press, 1991. (Box 10, Becket, Mass 01223. Tel.# (413) 623-2322)

Alex Jack cites 185 independent scientific, medical and other studies that have linked a wide variety of illnesses, including cancer, MS, lupus, PMS, AIDS, depression, anxiety, delinquency, crime, schizophrenia, agricultural decline, world hunger, and war-making behavior with impoverished and unbalanced diets rich in processed foods, sugars, and/or saturated animal fats.

Lifestyle:

1. *The Catalog of Healthy Foods on Farms, in Stores & Restaurants* by John Tepper Marlin, Ph.D., and Daniel Bertelli. New York: Bantam Books, 1990.

Find out how to mail order health foods from stores and small family-owned farms. Find out where some of the most healthy restaurants are around the country. This book is meant to be a supplement to the more current information in our resource/mail order section.

2. *Beyond Beef: The Rise and Fall of the Cattle Culture* by Jeremy Rifkin. New York: Penguin Books, 1993.

Rifkin's well documented book shows that the beef industry—including ranching, feed farming, feedlots, and processing—is responsible for turning rangelands into dry deserts, poisoning and eroding topsoil of fertile agricultural lands, extermination of millions of range wildlife (including endangered species), destruction of native cultures and farming lands, razing of the rainforests, draining of rivers and aquifers, pollution of groundwater, abuse of migrant and immigrant labor, diversion of cropland from efficient production of grains for people to inefficient production of cattle feed and consumption of oil in an amount equal to our total oil imports.

Books on the effects of sugar:

1. *Lick the Sugar Habit* by Nancy Appleton, Ph.D. New York: Warner Books, 1985.

   Highly readable; a must for those addicted to and unaware of the dangers inherent in soda, artificial sweeteners, candy, and sugars of all sorts, including fruit sugars. Sugar may be a major contributor to your de-generation..

2. *Sweetness and Power: The Place of Sugar in Modern History* by Sidney Mintz. New York: Elizabeth Sifton Books/Viking Penguin, Inc., 1985.

   This book presents a thorough discussion of the history of the sugar industry and its corrosive effect on traditional "third world" cultures, Euro-American politics and economics, and the freedom of the common person everywhere. This book is an absolute must!

3. *Sweet and Dangerous: The New Facts About the Sugar You Eat As A Cause of Heart Disease, Diabetes and Other Killers* by John Yudkin, M.D. New York: Peter H. Wyden, Inc., 1972.

   Though the author perpetuates several myths about whole grain bread and naturally farmed animal products, this book is worth reading. Full of information on the effects of sugar.

4. *Pure, White & Deadly,* by John Yudkin, M.D. New York: Penguin Books, 1983.

   Here's another great book on the deleterious effects of sugar. Must reading.

Other:

1. *International Macrobiotic Directory.* Compiled, edited & published by Bob Mattson. 1050 40th St., Oakland, CA 94608. Tel. # 510-601-1763.

   This valuable resource lists macrobiotic contacts and information, natural food stores, supplies, restaurants, educational organizations, teachers, cooks, counselors, natural practitioners, etc. Updated four times a year.

2. *Voluntary Simplicity* by Duane Elgin. New York: William Morrow & Company, 1981.

3. *How Much is Enough : The Consumer Society & The Future of The Earth* by Alan Durning. New York: Norton Books, 1992.

4. *Eating Oil: Energy use in food production* by Maurice Green. Boulder, CO: Westview Press, 1978.

   Reveals the energy intensive nature of our food processing system. The commercial meat and sugar industries are the most energy intensive of all.

• Books by Wendell Berry, a farmer and poet, with practical suggestions on reinhabiting the Earth through a return to local agriculture.

Magazines:

1. *Vegetarian Times*, P.O. Box 570, Oak Park, IL 60303

2. *Vegetarian Voice*, P.O. Box 72, Dolgeville, NY 13329

3. *Veggie Life*, EGW Publications, 1041 Shary Circle, Concord, CA 94518

4. *Macrobiotics Today*, 1511 Robinson St., Oroville, CA 95965

5. *MacroChef*, 243 Dickinson St, Phila, PA 19147

6. *Vegetarian Journal*, Vegetarian Resource Group, P.O. Box 1463, Baltimore, MD 21203

7. *Qi: The Journal of Eastern Health & Fitness 14014-D Sullyfiled Circle, Chantilly, VA 22021.*

Mail Order Resources:

Before ordering supplies by mail, it is helpful to first inquire into the availability of organic and natural foods products in your area. If you cannot find what you are looking for in your city or town, select from quality mail order suppliers. Choose products made in your own country over those that are imported from other countries and continents and, whenever possible, select companies that are closest to home (in a neighboring state for example). That way, you' will save money on shipping; you'll help save energy and precious resources; and you'll be supporting the local and regional economies. Shipping prices will be outrageous if you order from companies across the country or half-way around the world so it just makes sense to shop close to home. It makes little sense for Americans to subsist New Zealand apples or Japanese miso, sea vegetables, pickles, or umeboshi when quality American varieties exist. Admittedly, there are some quality natural foods products that you may enjoy using but which are not yet grown or produced in America. In such cases, it may be best to limit your consumption of some of these products and to avoid using others. You will have to weigh the costs and benefits here.

When ordering foods that you are unfamiliar with, inquire about the availability of recipes; many companies offer them free of charge or at a minimal cost. Some catalogs also offer extensive nutritional information about their products. This literature can give you new ideas, even if you end up adapting the recipes to make them healthier and more nourishing.

Send for a catalog. If you do not have a business license (which will make it possible to secure wholesale prices for bulk orders), you may be able to form a buying club with a handful of friends so that you can purchase goods at a reduced price. When you start eating a grain based diet, you will undoubtedly go through grains, sea vegetables, dried foods, and seasonings at a rapid rate. Buying in bulk will save you money in the short run and time in the long run, so don't be afraid to buy large bags of staple foods. (See the section on stocking your pantry for more on this.)

General Supplies
from Kitchen to Pantry

Note an asterisk (*) after companies whose catalogs offers helpful hints, recipes, and general information about wholefoods cooking and healthy living.

- **Gold Mine Natural Food Co.***
  1947 30th St. San Diego, CA 92102. Tel. #
  619-234-9711; Order line: 1-800-475-FOOD

Non-food items: Stainless steel and enamel-lined pressure cookers, pots, pans, bamboo mats, rice paddles, Ohsawa pots, pressure cooker inserts, grain mills, vegetable knives, suribachis, salad presses, water purifiers, non-toxic household cleaning and personal care products, books, and much much more.

Food items: One of the best selections of macrobiotic and natural foods, many of which are organic. They sell whole grains, flour, noodles, masa harina, dried chestnuts chestnut flour, beans, sea vegetables, miso, tamari, shoyu, umeboshi, natural vinegars and pickles, sea salt, sweeteners, dried fruits, oils, nuts, seeds, herb teas, grain coffee, etc. They offer a wide selection of American made products and Japanese-macrobiotic imports.

- **Smokey Mountain Natural Foods***
  15 Aspen Court, Ashville, North Carolina
  28806. Tel. # 1-800-926-0974

Non-foods items: See above listing for Gold Mine Natural Foods.

Food items: See above listing for Gold Mine Natural Foods.

- **Mountain Ark Trading Company***
  P.O. Box 3170, Fayetteville, AR 72702.
  Tel. # 1-800-643-8909

Non-foods items: See above listing for Gold Mine Natural Foods.

Food items: See above listing for Gold Mine Natural Foods.

- **Natural Lifestyle Supplies***
  16 Mt. Lookout Drive, Ashville, North
  Carolina 28804-3330. Tel. # 1-800-752-2775

Non-foods items: See above listing for Gold Mine Natural Foods.

Food items: See above listing for Gold Mine Natural Foods.

- **Granum Company**
  2901 N.E. Blakely St., Seattle, WA 98105. Tel. # (206) 525-0051

Non-foods items: Slightly limited selection; mostly wholesale; sells some of the items sold by Gold Mine Natural Foods and other natural foods companies listed above.

Food items: Limited selection; mostly wholesale; sells some of the items listing for Gold Mine Natural Foods and other natural foods companies listed above.

- **Walnut Acres Natural Foods**
  Organic Farming Since 1946, Penns Creek, PA 17862. Tel. # 1-717-0601.

Non food items: Stainless steel cookware; some other kitchen gadgetry.

Food items: Organically raised, home grown meats and poultry, dry beans, whole grain, flour, pasta, hot cereals, herbs, spices, oils, cheeses, dried fruits, nuts, seeds, and more.

Specialty Items

SUN DRIED SEA SALT & SEA MINERALS
(wholesale or retail)

- See listings for **Great Life Products; Gold Mine Natural Foods; Smokey Mountain Natural Foods; Ozark Co-op; Granum Company; and Natural Lifestyle Supplies.**

- **Grain & Salt Society,** P.O. Drawer S-DD, Magalia, CA 95954. Tel. # (916) 873-0294.

American Sea Vegetables
(bulk, direct, retail or wholesale):

Great selection, reasonably priced, many varieties, ask for recipes with your order! Stock up, seaweeds last indefinitely in airtight bags or canisters.

- **Maine Seaweed Company**
  Larch Hansen, P.O. Box 57, Steuben, Maine 04680. Tel. # (207) 546-2875.

Food items: Kelp, alaria, dulse, digitata kelp, and wild nori. Very high quality and very delicious.A family of 2 can easily go through a $40 family pack from Larch in 4 months).

- **Mendocino Sea Vegetable Co**.
  255 Wedling St. , or P.O. Box 372, Navarro, CA 95463. Tel. # (707) 895-3741.

- **Rising Tide Sea Vegetables**
  P.O Box 1914, Mendocino, CA 95460. Tel. # 707-964-5663

- **Ocean Harvest Sea Vegetables**
  P.O. Box 1719, Mendocino, CA 95460. Tel. # 707-937-1923

Food items: Wild nori, sea lettuce, wakame, sea whip, fucus tips, ocean ribbons, sea palm, sea palm fronds, and grapestone. Inquire about their recipe booklet and price list.

- See also **Gold Mine Natural Foods; Smokey Mountain Natural Foods; Ozark Co-Op.; Granum Company; Natural Lifestyle Supplies.** Buying directly from the harvesters is often most economical and ecological

BEANS

- **Beans & Beyond, Inc.**
  818 Jefferson Street, Oakland, CA 94607. Tel. # 1-800-845-BEAN(2326)

Incredibly selection of beans, bean mixes, true sun dried tomatoes, spices, herbs, crocks, bean cook books, and more. They offer the largest and most diverse selection of dried beans, peas, and lentils in the U.S.—over 75 varieties! Many are organic, most come from the U.S., some from around the world. Everything from the common chickpea, green pea and black eyed pea to anasazi, aduki/adzuki, appaloosa, cranberry, lupini, marrow, and rattlesnake beans.

- See also **Gold Mine Natural foods, Smokey Mountain Natural Foods, Ozark Co-Op., Granum Company, Natural Lifestyle Supplies.** They sell many other brands of grain coffee too.

ORGANIC AMERICAN MISO (direct)

One of the best quality hand made, unpasteurized miso comes from small miso makers like this. Available in numerous varieties: sweet rice, brown rice, millet, 3-year barley, black soybean, buckwheat, aduki bean, dandelion, and leek. Buy in 1, 3, 7, or 9 lb. tubs. Great prices! Ask for recipes and storage tips.

- **South River Miso Co.**
  South River Farm, Conway, MA 01341
  (413)369-4057

Food items: 3-year Barley, Black Soy Bean, Aduki, Dandelion-Leek, Golden Millet, Sweet Brown Rice, Buckwheat, and Chickpea Miso. Available in 1, 4, 9, 18, or 45 pound containers. Send a business size S.A.S.E with your request for a miso recipe booklet. This is absolutely the best miso made in America.

- **Junsei Yamazaki**
  Route 1, Box 1333, Orland, CA 95965

KOJI (for making amasake rice nectar, pudding, or sweetener, and miso):

- **South River Farms,** see listing above

- **Miyako Oriental Foods, Inc.**
  4287 Puente Ave., Baldwin Park, CA 91706.
  Tel.# (818) 962-9633

NATURAL, HANDMADE SOY SAUCE

- **Great Life Products**
  581-F North Twin Oaks Valley Road, San Marcos, California, 92069. Tel. # (619) 471-2637

Food items: Handmade soy sauce, and sun dried sea salt, made in America.

- See also **Gold Mine Natural foods; Smokey Mountain Natural Foods; Ozark Co-Op.; and Natural Lifestyle Supplies.**

AMERICAN MADE UMEBOSHI & APRIBOSHI
(pickled plums, apricots, and vinegar)

Note: These are tasty, preservative-free and far more ecological for Americans than imported macrobiotic products! Try Muramoto's apriboshi, pickled apricots and apriboshi vinegar or Yamazaki's ume plums and ume vinegar. (Avoid the cheap imitations found in Asian markets; they usually contain sugar, MSG, and/or preservatives or poor quality salt.)

- **Junsei Yamazaki**
  Route 1, Box 1333, Orland, CA 95965

- See **Great Life Products; Gold Mine Natural foods; Smokey Mountain Natural Foods; Ozark Co-Op.; and Natural Lifestyle Supplies.**

SPELT PRODUCTS

- **Purity Foods**
  2871 W. Jolly Road, Okemos, MI 48864-3547. Tel. # (517 351-9231

Food products: Whole grain spelt, spelt flour (ask for whole spelt flour or the slightly refined, unbleached variety), also spelt flakes, pasta, baking mixes, recipe booklets, dried fruits, and more.

WHEAT MEAT & SEITAN
(If you can't find it locally, mail order .)

- **Ivy Foods**
  7613 Prospector Drive, Salt Lake City, UT 84121. Tel. # 1-800-943-7311.

Food products: Wheat of Meat in sausage-style, chicken-style, and hearty-style; Grilled Burgers; Sun Burgers; and more. A 5-Pack Sampler is available.

- See also **Gold Mine Natural Foods; Mountain**

Ark Trading Company; Granum Co., Smokey Mountain Natural Foods; and Natural Lifestyle Supplies for Meat of Wheat brand. Sante Fe Naturals Seitan (original, curry, herb, garlic, ginger, and smoked flavors) are available from the general food suppliers listed above.

- **Knox Mountain Farms** products Franklin, NH 03235.

CHESTNUT PRODUCTS

- **Chestnut Hill Orchards**
  3300 Bee Cave Road, Austin, Texas 78746-6663. Tel.# (512) 477-3020

Foods items: Chestnut flour, dried chestnuts, and fresh-frozen steam peeled chestnuts This are the best quality and best tasting products. (Once you try them you'll want to keep a healthy supply on hand.)

- See also **GoldMine Natural Foods.**

GRAIN COFFEE

- **Sundance Roasting Company**
  (Home of Barley Brew)
  P.O. 1886 (or 855 Baldy Mtn. Road).
  Sandpoint, Idaho 83864. (208) 265-2445

- See also **Gold Mine Natural foods; Smokey Mountain Natural Foods; Ozark Co-Op.; Granum Company; or Natural Lifestyle Supplies.** These companies also sell numerous other brands of grain coffee, both instant and brewable varieties.

BREAD BAKER'S EQUIPMENT

- The King Arthur Flour Break Baker's Catalogue
  P.O. Box 876, Norwich, Vermont 05055-0876. Tel. #1-800-827-6836.

Products: Incredible selection of bread baking pots, pans, and paraphernalia. Pizza stones, two-tier cooling racks, stainless steel measuring cups and spoons, thermometers, La Cloche "brick-oven within an oven," whole grain flour (including hard white wheat flour), flour grinders, books and more.

MASA HARINA & TORTILLA & TAMALE MAKING KITS

- **Col. Sanchez**
  P.O. Box 5848, Santa Monica, CA 90409.
  Tel. # (310) 313-6772.

Products: You'll find organic yellow and blue masa harina (instant corn mix) for making tamales, arepas, corn tortillas, and dumplings; an inexpensive tortilla and tamale making kit, wooden tortilla press, chili and spices, corn husks, an electric tortilla, press, and frozen tamales.

- See also **GoldMine Natural Foods.**

NON-ELECTRIC & ENERGY EFFICIENT APPLIANCES

- **Lehman's Hardware & Appliances**
  One Lehman Circle, P.O. Box 41, Kidron, Ohio, 44636. Tel. # (216) 857-5757

Non-food products: Cast iron pots and pans; propane, gas, and kerosene stove; stove top pop corn poppers; cabbage shredders; the most efficient refrigerators on the market, etc.

- **Real Goods**

  966 Mazzoni St., Ukiah, CA 95482-3471.
  Tel. # 1-800-762-7325

Non-food products: Books on gardening; world's most energy efficient refrigerators and freezers; non-toxic cleaning products; cloth produce storage bags; and more.

Food products: Shiitake mushroom growing kits (incredible!)

Getting started:

Step #1: Read the Preface; chapters 1-3; and the introductions to chapters 4-11
Do this at whatever pace seems manageable. However, the more you read, the more you will learn about the way of cooking for personal and planetary health. Proper food preparation is as important as proper food selection.

Step #2: Glance over the first 1-2 weeks of menus, noticing
—the dishes that are made to last several meals or days and which for the entire week.
—how leftovers are mixed and matched for new meals each day or transformed into new dishes.
—that dishes in each meal are created from basic recipe procedures and can be varied with whatever vegetables, whole or cracked grains, breads, noodles, beans, soy foods, seeds, nuts, herbs, spices, fruits, are in season, on hand, or most appealing.

Step #3: Practice. Use the basic recipe procedures over and over so that you learn them by heart.
Doing this will eventually save you time and make cooking go more smoothly. For example,

1. Make week # 1 menus for two, three, or even four weeks in a row, but vary the dishes by trying
—different kinds of breads or different flour combinations in the same breads
—different whole or rolled grain combinations for breakfast, lunch, and/or dinner
—different vegetables in the same soup, stew, or side dish recipes
—different types of sea vegetables as condiments, garnishes, in soups, stews, etc.
—different beans or bean products in the same soup, stew, or side-dish recipes
—different herbs, spices, garnishes, or seasonings in the basic recipes

2. Make week #2 menus for several weeks repeating as above or rotate them with week #1 menus.

3. You may need to modify the menus slightly. Depending upon how much you make or eat of a given dish— such as rice or sea vegetable—you may go through something more rapidly or slowly than is depicted in the charts that follow. Be creative with leftovers, waste nothing, and make fill in items wherever and whenever needed.

4. Make week #3 menus repeating as for week #1. Repeat as desired or rotate with week #1 and/or #2 menus, then add week #4 menus. Repeat and rotate as desired.

5. Repeat the cycle again, including some of the occasional or seasonal use recipes as desired.

Notes:

• Whole grains may stand in for noodles, or noodles for whole grain, in almost any meal.

• Bread may be replaced with whole grain, or whole grain may be replaced with bread.

• Noodles may stand in for bread. They are quick and easy; good for any meal.

• Dinner grain may be replaced with porridge or porridge with dinner grain.

• Mochi can stand in for whole grain in a pinch, or vice-versa.

• Just be sure to serve grain at every meal, and in a substantial quantity.

• It is important to emphasize whole grains over flour products (pasta, bread, etc.). All of these grain products have their place in a healthy diet, but whole (unprocessed) grains are most ecological and nutritious and should form the bulk of our diet. If possible, serve some whole grains each day.

Week #1
(2-MEAL-A-DAY-PLAN +/- SNACK)

	SUNDAY	MONDAY	TUESDAY	WEDNESDAY
Breakfast	Puréed Squash Soup Parsley or chives Rice with 2nd grain Seed Condiment Quick-Boiled Greens Sea Flakes	Puréed Squash Soup Parsley or chives Rice with 2nd grain Seed condiment Quick-Boiled Greens Sea flakes	Millet & Oatmeal Roasted dulse or nori Scallions or chives Seed condiment Winter Squash Sautéed Greens	Rolled Grain Cereal Rroasted dulse or nori Scallions or chives Seed condiment Quick-Boiled Vegetables with 1-2-3 Dressing
Lunch	Pea Soup Parsley or chives Rice with 2nd grain Seed condiment Quick-Boiled Greens Radish Pickles Yogurt	Pea soup Parsley or chives Rice with 2nd grain Seed condiment or Bread +/- spread Quick-Boiled Greens Pickles	Cream of Veg. Soup Scallions or chives Millet with 2nd Grain Seed condiment Sea Vegetable Sautéed greens Steamed Egg *or* Yogurt Amasake Pudding	Cream of Veg. Soup Scallions or chives Millet with 2nd grain Seed condiment Sea vegetable Quick-Boiled Vegetables Amasake Pudding
Snack	Yogurt or soy milk Fruit Compote *or* Salad Tea	Bread, Yogurt *and/or S*alad Tea	Yogurt *with* Salad *or* Amasake	Yogurt Amasake Pudding *or* Fruit

	THURSDAY	FRIDAY	SATURDAY	SUNDAY
				Notes:
Breakfast	Millet Porridge Scallions or chives Roasted dulse or nori seed condiment Steamed Vegetables Pickles Yogurt or milk	Kasha & Oatmeal Scallions or chives Roasted dulse or nori Seed or Nut Condiment Quick-Boiled Greens Squash *or* Sweet Corn Yogurt	Squash or Yam-Wiches: Chapatis or other bread Squash or Sweet Potato Miso Nut Butter Spread Quick-Boiled Greens *or* Pressed Salad Yogurt *or* Soy Milk	Use up any leftovers from the previous day, as is or in new dishes. Leftover squash or yam may be cooked into or served atop morning porridge; made into a Soup for use at breakfast
Lunch	Any Bean Soup Rice Seed condiment Sea vegetable Steamed vegetables Pickles	Anybean soup Rice Seed condiment Sea flakes Quick-Boiled Greens Pickles Scallions or parsley Yogurt	Quick Miso Broth *or* Soup from leftovers Rice *or* Noodles Seed condiment PanFried Wheat Meat *or* Tempeh Cutlets Scallions or Parsley Boiled Salad Oil-Free Dressing	or lunch; or used as a spread for bread or waffles. Cooked pasta may be cooked into morning porridge or used at lunch with leftover cutlets. Make new condiments and side dishes as needed.
Snack	Yogurt *or* Quark Bread Pickles *or* Salad	Yogurt *or* Quark Rice ball or Bread *and/or* Salad	Yogurt *or* Grain Coffee *and* Nutty Fruit Mousse *or* Salad	Proceed with Week #2 Menus or Repeat Week #1 Menus.

Week #2
(2-MEAL-A-DAY-PLAN +/- SNACK)

	SUNDAY	MONDAY	TUESDAY	WEDNESDAY
Breakfast	Overnight Rice Porridge *or* Counter Top Oats Seed or Nut Condiment Scallions or chives Steamed Vegetables with 1-2-3 Dressing Onion Pickles Yogurt	Overnight Rice Porridge Scallions or chives Seed or nut condiment Roasted dulse or flakes Quick-Boiled Greens Squash or corn Yogurt	Barley & Oatmeal Roasted dulse or nori Seed or nut condiment Scallions or chives Quick-Boiled Greens +/- Bread +/- Squash or Corn Yogurt	Overnight Rice Porridge with kelp or kombu Scallions or chives Seed or nut condiment Seamed Greens Squash *or* corn Steamed Egg
Lunch	Millet "Mash Potatoes" Mock Poultry Gravy Scallions or chives Baked, Nishime cooked *or* Steamed Yam, Sweet Potato, or Corn Seamed Vegetables with 1-2-3 dressing Wheat Meat or Tempeh	Gravy (in soup cups) Scallions or chives Bread *and/or* Mllet Wheat Meat Cutlets Quick-BoiledGreens *or* PressedSalad	Cream of Veg. Soup Scallions or chives Steamed Buns *or* Loaf Bread Tofu or Tempeh Spread Quick-Boiled Greens Pickles	Cream of Vegetable Soup Scallions or chives Bread Tofu or Tempeh Spread Salad *and/or* Steamed veggies Scrambled Egg *or* Yogurt
Snack	Yogurt *or* Quark Bread *or* Rice Cakes	Millet Slices *or* Fruit Compote *with* Yogurt or Quark	Yogurt *or* Quark Fruit Dessert	Bread with Spread *or* Popcorn and Tea

	THURSDAY	FRIDAY	SATURDAY	SUNDAY
Breakfast	Sweet Vegetable Soup Scallions or parsley Rice with 2nd Grain Nut or seed condiment Sea Flakes Stir Fried Greens Pickles +/- Yogurt	Sesame Buttered- Noodles Nori or dulse flakes Scallions or chives Quick-Boiled Veggies Miso Soup +/- Bread Pickles	Rice Porridge Roasted dulse or flakes Seed or nut condiment Scallions or chives Steamed Vegetables with 1-2-3 Dressing +/- Bread +/- Pickles	**Notes:** Leftover noodles could be cooked into morning cereal, serveS with leftover vegetables and condiments. Leftover squash, yam, or corn can be cooked into cereal; served on the side; or used in soup.
Lunch	Land & Sea Veg. Soup Rice with 2nd Grain Seed or nut condiment Stir Fried Greens *and/or* Pressed Salad Parsley garnish Yogurt	Yogurt Rice with 2nd grain Seed or nut condiment Sea flakes Pressed Salad with oil *or* Quick-Boiled Veggies	Seitan Stroganoff Noodles or rice *and/or* Steamed Buns *or* Baked Bread Pressed *or* Boiled Salad with oil Sweet Potato *or* Corn	Leftover stroganoff could be served over fresh cooked rice or millet, with side dishes. Soup could be served alongside it if desired.
Snack	Yogurt, Fruit *or* Amasake Pudding Grain Coffee	Quark, Yogurt, *or* Tea Bread *or* Amasake Tea	Yogurt *or* Tea Rice Ball or Bread *and/or* Greens	Proceed with Week #3 Menus or repeat Week #2 Menus.

Week #3
(2-MEAL-A-DAY-PLAN +/- SNACK)

	SUNDAY	MONDAY	TUESDAY	WEDNESDAY
Breakfast	Cream of Veg. Soup Parsley or chives Rice with Millet Seed condiment Boiled Greens + 1-2-3 Dressing	Cream of veg. soup Parsley or chives Rice or Millet Nut or Seed Condiment Pickles Parsley or chive garnish Quick-Boiled Greens Yogurt	Mochi Waffles Parsley or chives Squash *or* Sweet Potato *or* Onion Butter Miso Seed Butter Spread Quick-Boiled Greens Nori or dulse Yogurt or milk	Mochi waffles or Bread Pparsley or chives Squash *or* Sweet Potato *or* Onion Butter Miso Seed Butter Spread Pressed Salad *or* Greens Nori or Dulse Yogurt or milk
Lunch	Hungarian Goulash Parsley or scallions Rice with 2nd grain +/- Bread Boiled greens Sea Vegetable Flakes	Hungarian Goulash Parsley or scallions Rice **or** Millet Slices +/- Bread Quick-boiled greens	Simmered Veg. Soup Parsley or scallions Beans-in-Rice Seed condiment Quick-boiled greens *or* Salad Steamed Egg	Simmered Veg. Soup Parsley or scallions Beans-in-rice Seed condiment Pressed Salad + oil *or* Sautéed Greens Sea vegetable
Snack	Yogurt *or* Quark Rice Ball or Bread	Millet Slices *or* Bread Salad with Grain Coffee	Yogurt or Quark Bread **and/or** Salad	Yogurt *or* Quark Amasake pudding *or* Bread

	THURSDAY	FRIDAY	SATURDAY	SUNDAY
Breakfast	Porridge from old grain Roasted nori or dulse Seed condiment Stir Fried Vegetables Steamed Squash Parsley or scallions Yogurt *or* Steamed Egg	Squash Soup Nutty or Seeded Rice Ume Paste with Nori *or* Dulse lakes Parsley or scallions Stir Fried Vegetables +/- Yogurt	Oat Porridge (any kind) Roasted dulse or nori Seed condiment Scallions or chives Boiled Greens Root Vegetable Yogurt *or* Egg	**Notes:** Use up any leftovers at breakfast, lunch, or both, incorporating them into new dishes or supplementing them with other dishes. Make new condiments and other dishes as needed.
Lunch	Any Bean Soup Steamed or Baked Buns *or* nutty or seeded rice Sea vegetahble Stir fried vegetables *or* Ssalad +/- Yogurt	Anybean Soup Nutty or Seeded Rice **and/or** bread Quick-boiled greens *or* Salad + oil Sea Vegetable Flakes +/- Yogurt	Cream of Veg. Soup Mochi Pizza Pie *or* Pizza Bianca Light Miso Broth Quick-Boiled Greens Pickles	Repeat Week #3 Menus or Proceed with Week #4 Menus.
Snack	Yogurt *or* Grain Coffee Chestnut Dessert *or* Salad	Rice Ball, Bread *or* Chestnut Dessert **with** Tea or Yogurt	Yogurt *or* Tea Popcorn *or* Bread **and/or** Greens	

Week #4
(2-MEAL-A-DAY-PLAN)

	SUNDAY	MONDAY	TUESDAY	WEDNESDAY
Breakfast	Nutty Rice Porridge Kelp **or** roasted dulse Ume/Apriboshi Paste **or** Onion Pickles Quick Boiled Greens Chives **or** scallions Root Vegetable Dish	Sweet Rice & Millet **or**Noodles Sea flakes or nori Seed condiment Quick-Boiled Greens Root Vegetable Soup Parsley or chives	Rice Porridge (with squash or corn) Roasted dulse Seed or nut condiment Stir Fried Vegetables Parsley or dill Quick Pickles	Countertop Oats **or** Noodles Sea Flakes Seed or nut condiment Stir Fried Vegetables Parsley or scallions Yogurt **or** Egg
Lunch	Cream of Veg. Soup Chives or scallions Sweet Rice & Millet **or** Millet & Chestnuts Quick Boiled Greens **or** pressed salad Sea Vegetable Yogurt **or** Steamed Egg	Cream of Veg.Soup Chives or scallions Leftover Rice **or** Millet Seed/nut condiment Sea Vegetable Quick-Boiled Veggies Quick Pickles Grated Cheese **or** Yogurt	Wheat Meat Stew Corn Bread, Arepas **or** Plain Steamed Buns Seed or nut condiment **or**Spread Salad or Stir Fry Pickles Scallions or Parsley Yogurt **or** Grated Cheese	Wheat Meat Stew Bread **or** Areaps Miso-Tahini or Oil Pressed or Raw Salad Seed/nut condiment Pickles Parsley or Scallions +/- Yogurt **or** Cheese
Supper	Yogurt **or** Quark Amasake **or** Fruit Dessert	Yogurt **or** Quark Bread, Rice Ball, **or** Fruit Dessert	Yogurt **or** Tea Popcorn **or** Rice Ball	Popcorn, Bread **or** Rice Ball, Yogurt, Milk, **or** Tea

	THURSDAY	FRIDAY	SATURDAY	SUNDAY
Breakfast	Rice **or** Rice Combo Kinpira or Nishime Sea Sprinkles Nut or seed condiment Boiled Whole Greens Parsley or Dill +/- Pickles Yogurt	Rice Soup from sweet roots Sea sprinkles or dulse Seed or nut condiment Steamed Veggies + 1-2-3 Dressing Parsley or dill Yogurt	Mochi Waffles Onion Butter **or** Mashed Squash + Miso Nut Butter Boiled Whole Greens **or** Ppressed salad Scallions or Parsley Yogurt	**Notes:** Incorporate leftovers into new meals. Make leftover millet/polenta into porridge with rolled oats or millet. Any sweet vegetables can be cooked into cereal or served on the side.
Lunch	Anybean Soup Parsley or dill Rice **or** rice combo Nut or seed condiment Salad **or** Boiled Greens Oil topping +/- Yogurt	Anybean soup Parsley or dill Rice, bread **or** Polenta Seed condiment Steamed veggies **or** Pressed Salad Oil **or** seeds	Simmered Veg. Soup Millet or polenta +/- Tortillas Refried Beans Tofu Sour Cream **or** Quark/Yogurt Scallions or Chives Boiled or Pressed Salad +/- Pickles	Leftover refried beans can be served on mochi waffles for lunch or turned into soup. Salad can be served with both meals. Be creative; also refer to leftover tips. Proceed with week #1 Menus or repeat any other week's menus.
Snack	Yogurt **or** Quark Fruiit Dessert **or** Bread	Bread **or** Dessert Milk **or** Yogurt	Yogurt **or** Soy Milk Salad **or** Cooked Greens **and/or** Bread **or** Rice Ball	

Week #1
(3-MEAL-A-DAY-PLAN)

	SUNDAY	MONDAY	TUESDAY	WEDNESDAY
Breakfast	Millet & Oatmeal Roasted dulse Seed Condiment Scallions or Parsley Quick-Boiled Greens +/- Pickles	Kasha & Oatmeal Roasted Kelp Seed condiment Chives or parsley Quick-Boiled Veggies Yogurt	Millet-Rice Porridge Roasted Dulse Seeds **or** Steamed Egg Scallions or parsley Stir fried vegetables Pickles	Cornmeal & Oatmeal Roasted dulse Seeds **or** Steamed Egg Scallions or chives Parboiled Greens Pickles
Lunch	Pea Soup + garnish Rice with Millet Seed condiment Quick-Boiled Greens Fruit Compote	Pea soup + garnish Corn bread **or** Rice Quick Boiled Greens Pickles, +/- Yogurt Yogurt **or** Cheese	Cream of Veg. Soup Rice with Second Grain Seeds Condiment Pressed or Raw Salad Sea Vegetable, Yogurt	Cream of Veg. Soup Tortillas **or** Buns Scrambled Tofu Parboiled Greens Sauerkraut or dill pickle
Dinner	Puréed Squash Soup Corn Bread **or** rice +/- goat or soy yogurt Pressed Salad Cheese **or** Yogurt Pickles Parsley garnish	Puréed Squash Soup Millet-Rice Seed condiment Stir Fried Vegetables Sea Vegetable Parsley garnish Quick Pickles	Sesame Buttered Noodles **or** Noodles Seed condiment Scrambled Tofu Nishime Vegetables Parboiled greens Sauerkraut	Rice with Second Grain Seed or nut condiment Nishime vegetables **or** Corn on the cob Boiled or Tossed Salad Pickles, +/- Yogurt Sea Vegetable Flakes

	THURSDAY	FRIDAY	SATURDAY	SUNDAY
Breakfast	Rice Porridge Roasted dulse Seed condiment Sautéed greens **or** Pressed Salad Scallions or chives +/- Pickles Milk **or** Yogurt	Mochi Waffles **or** Bread Squash **or** Sweet Potato Nut Condiment **or** Miso-Nut Butter Pressed or Boiled Salad Scallions or chives Sushi Nori or dulse Milk **or** Yogurt	Rolled Grain Cereal Roasted dulse Seed or nut condiment (or ume or apriboshi) Greens + oil & tamari Scallions or chives Pickles Milk **or** Yogurt	**Notes:** Incorporate leftovers from the previous day. Leftover millet could be made into porridge or just reheated and topped with seed condiment or a sauce or gravy. Pasta could be steam warmed
Lunch	Anybean Soup Rice +/- Second Grain Sea Vegetable Seed or nut condiment Boiled or Pressed Salad (+ oil) Yogurt	Anybean Soup Rice **or** bread Seed condiment **or** Quark or Cheese Stir Fried Veggies Sea Vegetable	Quick Soup Broth Millet Seed condiment Sea Flakes Pressed Salad +/- No-Baked Cookies +/- Yogurt	or made into porridge with oats. Ladle beet sauce over millet or polenta or serve it as a soup with cutlets and grain on the side plus salad or greens.
Dinner	Simmered Veg. Soup Rice Seed condiment Stir Fried Veggies Vegetable Pickles +/- Fruit Sauce	Simmered Veggie Soup Rice Seed condiment Panfried Tempeh **or** Wheat Meat Cutlets Boiled Greens Dill Pickles or Kraut	Pasta Beet Sauce Italiano Garlic Bread or Buns **or** French/Italian Bread Vegetarian "Sausage" **or** Tempeh "Bacon" Boiled Salad + Dressing	Make new condiments, whole grain and/or bread, pressed salad, and other dishes for the start of the week.

Week #2 (3-MEAL-A-DAY-PLAN)

	SUNDAY	MONDAY	TUESDAY	WEDNESDAY
Breakfast	Noodle & Oatmeal Roasted dulse Nut or seed condiment Scallions or chives Quick-Boiled Greens Yogurt	Noodles Sea Flakes seed or nut condiment Scallions or chives Steamed Veggies with 1-2-3 Dressing	Rolled Grain Cereal Roasted dulse Seed condiment Scallions or chives Sautéed Greens Pickles, +/- Egg	Overnight Rice Cereal with kelp/kombu seed condiment Scallions or parsley Sautéed Greens +/- Yogurt
Lunch	Hungarian Goulash Baked Bread **or** Steamed Buns Quark **or** Millet Butter Pressed Salad	Hungarian Goulash Buns **or** Loaf Bread Grated Cheese **or** Millet Butter Pressed salad Parsley garnish	Squash-Wiches **or** Yam-Wiches Pressed Salad **or** Steamed Greens +/- Onion Pickles Yogurt	Squash-Wiches **or** yam-wiches PressedSalad **or** Boiled Greens +/- Milk or Yogurt Parsley
Dinner	Cream of Veg. Soup Beans in Rice seed Condiment quick-boiled greens Sea Vegetable Nutty Apple Mousse	cream of veg. soup beans in rice sea vegetable steamed vegetables (1-2-3 Dressing) nutty apple mousse	Quick Soup Broth beans-in-rice seed condiment sea vegetable sautéed greens +/- Pickles	Simmered Veg. Soup Millet + Second Grain nut or seed condiment sea veg. condiment Stir Fried Vegetables +/- Pickles

	THURSDAY	FRIDAY	SATURDAY	SUNDAY
Breakfast	Buckwheat & Teff **or** Rice Porridge) Roasted dulse Nut or seed condiment Scallions or chives Quick-Boiled Greens Steamed Egg	Past-Rice Porridge Sea flakes seed or nut condiment Scallions or chives steamed vegetables +/- Onion Pickles Egg **or** Yogurt	millet-Oat Porridge Roasted dulse Seed or nut condiment Scallions or chives Steamed Vegetables (+ 1-2-3 Dressing) Yogurt **or** Egg	**Notes:** Incorporate leftovers into today's meals. Leftover kinpira or nishime can be served with morning cereal; on top of mochi waffles; or made into soup for breakfast, lunch, or dinner.
Lunch	Simmered Veg. Soup Millet + Second Grain Seed or nut condiment Sea Vegetable Pressed Salad + oil **or** Quic-Boiled Greens +/- Yogurt	Soup of pasta sauce Millet or millet slices Seed condiment Pressed Salad + oil **or** Steamed Vegetables Sea Vegetable Cheese **or** yogurt	Chili Bean Stew Corn Bread **or** Millet Bread **or** Arepas Steamed Vegetables (+ nut or seed butter in 1-2-3 Dressing) +/- Yogurt **or** Cheese	Serve rice as is or make some into breakfast porridge. Serve chili with rice today for a change. Serve any leftover green vegetables with any or all meals.
Dinner	Pasta with Creamy Green Garlic Sauce Cooked Beets or Carrots **with** Dressing	Mochi Pizza Pie **or** Pizza Bianca Quick-Boiled Veggies Pickles +/- Fruit Compote **or** Chestnut Dessert	Yogurt **or** Soup Kinpira or Nishime of root vegetables Rice **or** Rice Combo Seed or Nut Condiment Glazed Broccoli or Greens Amasake Pudding	Repeat Week #2 Menus or Proceed on to Week #3 Menus.

Week #3 (3-MEAL-A-DAY-PLAN)

	SUNDAY	MONDAY	TUESDAY	WEDNESDAY
Breakfast	Countertop Oats Roasted dulse Seed condiment Quick-Boiled Vegetables Parsley or chives +/-Yogurt	millet porridge Roasted dulse Nut or seed condiment yams, squash, or corn Parley or chive garnish +/-Yogurt	Vegetable Muesli Yogurt or Soy Milk Roasted dulse or flakes Veggies +/- fruit Parsley or chives Seeds or nuts	Rice & Millet Porridge Roasted kelp Scallions or chives Seed or nut condiment Salad **or** Stir Fried Vegetables
Lunch	Millet-Vegetable Slices **or** Millet Mash-Potatoes Squash, Yams, or Corn Mock Chicken Gravy Oven Fried Wheat Meat or Tofu Cutlets Pickles, +/- Cheese	gravy (in a soup cup) Buns or Loaf Bread Oven Fried Wheat Meat BoiledSsalad (+ Oil) Pickles Fruit Compote	Loaf Bread, Bagels **or** Steamed Buns Tempeh Tuna **or** Tofu Cream Cheese Steamed Mixed Veggies +/- Pickles Parsley or Scallions	Cream of Veg. Soup Buns or Loaf Bread Tempeh or Tofu Spread **or** Yogurt Cheese PressedSsalad +/- Fruit Gel, Compote **or** Amasake
Dinner	Anybean Soup Millet Slices Seed condiment BoiledSalad Dressing Fruit Sauce or Compote	AnybeanSoup Rice with Second Grain Seed or nut condiment Stir Fried Vegetables Sea Vegetable Flakes +/- Yogurt **or** Cheese	Cream of Veg. Soup Rice with Second Grain Seed or nut condiment Sa vegetable Steamed Mixed Veggies Yogurt **or** Egg	Rice Seed Condiment Baked Sweet Vegetables **or** Nishime dish Stir fried vegetables Sea Vegetable

	THURSDAY	FRIDAY	SATURDAY	SUNDAY
Breakfast	Nutty Congee Roasted dulse Ume or apriboshi paste Sweet vegetables **or** Quick-Boiled Greens Parsley or Scallions Pickles	Noodle & Oatmeal Sea flakes Seed or nut condiment BoiledSalad Parsley or Scallions +/- Steamed, Baked or Nishime Squash	Rice Porridge Kelp or Sea Flakes Seed Condiment Scallions Stir Fried Vegetables Pickles	**Notes:** Incorporate leftovers. into today's menus. Seeded rice could be made into morning cereal or served with lunch.
Lunch	Soup of sweet veggies Steamed or Baked Buns Seed condiment Pressed Salad + oil +/- Yogurt	Stroganoff Rice **and/or** Bread Tossed or Boiled Salad (Dressing or oil)	Nishime or Kinpira Root/Round Vegetables Seeded rice Sea Vegetable Pressed Salad Yogurt **or** Cheese	Serve kinpira or nishime over mochi waffles or tortillas. Quick miso broth can simplify the preparations today.
Dinner	Stroganoff Noodles +/-Bread, French, Peasant, or other Boiled Salad (+/- dressing) Pickles	Any Bean Soup Rice **or** Seeded Rice Sea Vegetable Stir Fried Vegetables +/- Quick Pickles Cheese **or** Yogurt	Veggie Burgers: (Basic Bean or Tempeh) Steamed or Baked Buns Mustard & Grain Mayo Quick-Boiled Vegetables +/- Pickles +/- Cheese +/- Amasake Pudding	Make new condiments, whole grain, greens etc. as needed for the start of the week. Proceed with week #4 or repeat Week #3 or #2.

Week #4 (3-MEAL-A-DAY-PLAN)

	SUNDAY	MONDAY	TUESDAY	WEDNESDAY
Breakfast	Nutty Rice Porridge Ume or Apriboshi (or Onion Pickles) Boiled Salad Chives or scallions	Sweet Rice Porridge (+/- Chestnuts) Nut vondiment Squash or yam Parsley, +/- Yogurt	Millet porridge Roasted dulse Seed or nut condiment Steamed vegetables Parsley or dill	Simmered Cereal Sea Flakes Seed Condiment Sautéed Greens Parsley or dill
Lunch	Millet Loaf Sauce or Gravy Boiled Salad with 1-2-3 Dressing Squash, Yam, or Corn	Cream of Veg. Soup Filled Steamed Buns *or* calzones Chestnut dessert *or* Amasake gel or pudding	Filled Steamed Buns or Calzones +/- Yogurt steamed vegetables + 1-2-3 Dressing	Stew with tempeh *or* Stew with wheat meat Bbread *or* rice Sautéed Greens *or* Salad Seed or nut condiment
Dinner	Cream of Veg. Soup Steamed Buns + filling (or Calzones) Boiled Salad Amasake Dessert +/- Yogurt	Millet Loaf Sauce or gravy Steamed Vegetables +/- Pickles Sea Flakes +/- Yogurt *or* Cheese	Meaty Stew with Tempeh or wheat meat Rice + seed condiment Pressed salad *or* Boiled Greens Sea Flakes	Simmered Veg. Soup Rice *or* rice balls Seed or nut condiment Sautéed Vegetables *or* Pressed Salad Yogurt, Sea Flakes

	THURSDAY	FRIDAY	SATURDAY	SUNDAY
Breakfast	rice & oatmeal Roasted Dulse Nut Condiment Quick-Boiled Greens Parsley or Dill	Millet-Chestnut Cereal *or* Rice-Chestnut Cereal Seed or nut condiment Onion or Squash Butter +/- Parsley	Porridge Under Pressure *or* cereal from leftovers Roasted dulse Steamed Vegetables Scallions or dill Yogurt *or* Steamed Egg	**Notes:** Incorporate leftovers into today's meals. Try polenta porridge or millet porridge.
Lunch	Simmered Soup Rice *or* Bread Nut condiment *or* Miso-Seed Butter Quick-boiled greens *or* Pressed Salad Yogurt	Cream of Veg. Soup Millet *or* Polenta Seed condiment Quick-Boiled Greens *or* Pressed Salad Sea Vegetable Egg *or* Yogurt	cream of veg. soup Millet *or* Polenta Seed condiment Steamed Vegetables Dressing or Oil +/- Sea Vegetable +/- Egg *or* Yogurt +/- Fruit Compote	Leftover rice can be made into rice balls for lunch or served as is with seed condiments and/or refried beans. Or, refried beans could be made into soup. Tofu sour cream could be used as is or as dressing for steamed mixed vegetables or beets.
Dinner	Mochi Waffles *or* Pancakes with Onion Butter *or* Mashed Squash + Nut Condiment *or* Miso-Tahini Quick-Boiled Greens Pickles, dulse or nori +/- Yogurt	Millet/Polenta Slices *or* Pancakes Refried Beans Steamed Mixed Veggies (+/- Dressing) *or* Seed condiment Squash (mashed or soup) Scallions or chives +/-Fruit Compote	Rice Refried Beans Flat Breads *or* Tortillas +/- Tofu Sour Cream Seed condiment Seasonal Raw Salad *or*Steamed Mixed Veg. Yogurt *or* Quark	Make new dishes as needed. Repeat the menus you like or come up with your own menu plans as desired.

Down Home "American Meals"

For Weekend Suppers or Entertaining

Note: *All of these meals can be made in 1 1/2-2 hours with some advance prep and very little hands-on. Dessert is optional and may be excluded if you are short on time. Also, you may replace wheat meat, tofu, or tempeh with poached, steamed, or broiled fish any menu, or serve grated cheese, yogurt, or milk with beans, tofu, tempeh, or wheat meat in any of these menus..*

Fall and Winter Menu #1

Soup: Puréed Squash Soup; Puréed Squash & Rutabaga Soup; *or* Parsnip & Carrot Soup
Vegetarian Protein: Oven "Fried" or Pan Fried Wheat Meat *or* Tempeh Sausage
Grain: Chestnut Rice: Posole Rice: Black Bean Rice; *or* Corn Batter Bread
Condiment for grain: Sunflower-Salt *or* Smokey Pumpkin Seed Condiment
Vegetables: Quick-Boiled Greens, Parboiled or Steamed Greens *or* Pressed Salad
Optional, Dessert: Rosehip-Apple Compote, Cranberry Apple Sauce, or Amasake Pudding
Beverage: Peppermint Tea, Cinnamon & Licorice Tea *or* Barley Brew

Fall and Winter Menu #2

Vegetarian Protein: Oven "Fried" or Pan Fried Wheat Meat Cutlets
Grain: Millet & Squash Slices (polenta style) *or* Millet & Black Bean Slices
Condiment for grain: Mock Poultry Gravy or Seed Condiment
Other vegetable dish: Baked or Steamed Sweet Corn (w/diluted white miso as a table spread)
Greens: Sautéed or Stir Fried Collards with onions and sweet red bell pepper or hot red pepper
Pickles: Dill Pickles (home made or store bought) *or* Onion Pickles
Optional, Dessert: Apple Crisp; Apple Compote; Chestnut Custard; *or* Amasake Pudding
Beverage: Roasted Chicory & Dandelion (or Barley) Coffee

Fall and Winter Menu #3

Vegetarian Protein: Oven "Fried" Wheat Meat (Chicken-style or Hearty/Original)
Grain: Steamed Corn, Barley, or Millet Buns, Dinner Rolls *or* Corn Batter Bread
Condiment (for bread): Millet Butter, Garbanzo Butter *or* Raw Butter
Orange Vegetable: Baked, Baked & Mashed, or Steamed Winter Squash *or* Sweet Potato
Greens: Pressed or Marinated Salad *or* Steamed Vegetables with Mustard Vinaigrette
Optional, Dessert: Stewed Pears with Anise, Apple Sauce *or* Amasake Pudding
Beverage: Chicory & Licorice Tea *or* Dandelion, Barley & Chicory "Coffee"

Fall and Winter Menu #4

Soup: Cream of Zucchini, Brussel Sprout, or Celery Soup *or* Light Miso Broth
Vegetarian Protein: Oven "Fried" Wheat Meat or Firm Tofu *or* Nutty Wheat Meat Cutlets
Grain: Millet & Turnip (or Cauliflower) "Mashed Potatoes" with Basic Lean Gravy
Vegetables: Pressed or Marinated Salad, Steamed Green, *or* Boiled Salad
Optional Side dish: Baked, Steamed or Grilled Corn on the cob, in the fall
Optional, Dessert: Pumpkin or Sweet Potato Pie or Custard *or* No-Bake Cookies
Beverage: Dandelion & Chicory "Coffee," Instant Grain Coffee, or herb tea

Summer or Early Fall Menu #1

Soup: Tomato-Cuke Soup; Tomato Zucchini Soup; or Cream of Corn or Zucchini Soup
Vegetarian Protein: Oven "Fried" Wheat Meat *or* Tempeh "Sausage" or "Bacon"
Grain: Rice with Sweet Corn, Rice with Green Peas, *or* Millet "Polenta"
Condiment for grain: Flax Seed Condiment *or* Pumpkin Seed Condiment
Greens: Marinated Salad with cabbage, lettuce, carrots, sweet bell pepper and onion *or* Boiled Salad with Oil-Free Mustard Vinaigrette
Optional, Dessert: Sunflower-Apple Mousse *or* Nutty Fresh Fruit Salad
Beverage: Corn Silk Tea, Peppermint Tea or other tea

Summer or Early Fall Menu #2

Soup: Raw Corn Soup, Cream of Corn Soup, *or* Corn, Squash & Tomato Soup
Vegetarian Protein: Sticky Black Bean Sauce (to serve over millet or polenta)
Grain: Polenta *or* Millet "Polenta"
Second grain: Flat Breads or Corn or Wheat Tortillas with Tofu Sour Cream or Yogurt
Greens: Marinated or Boiled Salad
Optional, Dessert: Peach & Blueberry Crisp *or* Nutty Fresh Fruit Salad
Beverage: Corn Silk Tea, Roasted Corn Tea, Or Grain Coffee

Festive Spring Menu #1

Soup: Raw Corn Soup, Cream of Corn Soup, *or* Corn, Squash & Tomato Soup

Vegetarian Protein: Sticky Black Bean Sauce (to serve over millet or polenta)
Grain: Polenta *or* Millet "Polenta"
Second grain: Flat Breads or Corn or Wheat Tortillas with Tofu Sour Cream or Yogurt
Greens: Marinated or Boiled Salad
Optional, Dessert: Peach & Blueberry Crisp *or* Nutty Fresh Fruit Salad
Beverage: Corn Silk Tea, Roasted Corn Tea, Or Grain Coffee

Festive Spring Menu #2

- **Soup:** Daikon-Onion Wakame Soup or Miso-Kelp & Shiitake Broth
- **Grain:** "Nutty" Roasted Brown Rice
- **Condiment:** Sesame Salt Condiment
- **Side Dish:** Spiced Black Bean or Tofu or Tempeh Filled Won Tons
- **Vegetable Dish #1:** Steamed Winter Squash Crescents or cubes
- **Vegetable Dish #2:** Stir Fried Chinese Style Vegetables s
- **Optional, Dessert:** Buckwheat-Chestnut Gems *or* Raisin Glazed Chestnuts
- **Beverage:** Kukicha Tea *or* Barley "Coffee"

Festive Spring Menu #3

- **Soup:** Red Bean & Burdog Soup
- **Grain:** Huminta Tamales *or* Rice with Smokey Sunflower Seed Condiment
- **Vegetable Dish:** Dulse with Sunchokes
- **Second Vegetable Dish:** Parboiled Collards & Carrots with Easy As 1-2-3 Dressing
- **Dessert:** Rosehip & Apple Compote *or* Steamed Corn Pudding

Summer Menu

- **Soup:** Cream of Carrot Soup
- **Grain:** Millet with Amaranth & Kelp
- **Condiment:** Smokey Sunflower or Pumpkin Seed Condiment + Nori or Alaria Condiment
- **Side Dish:** Steamed cauliflower & Green Beans with "Tofu Sour Cream" or "Ricotta"
- **Condiment #2:** Black Soy Bean Natto with tamari, mustard and scallions
- **Vegetable Dish #2:** Stir Fried Chinese Style Vegetables s
- **Optional, Dessert:** Peach & Apricot Gel *or* Peaches with Amasake
- **Beverage:** Kukicha Tea *or* Barley "Coffee"

Festive Fall or Winter Menu

- **Soup:** Creamy Winter Squash, Tomato-Squash, or Parsnip & Carrot Soup w/parsley
- **Beans:** Refried Beans, Herbed Tofu Dip, Garbanzo Butter, or Baked Beans
- **Grain:** Steamed Buns, Corn or Millet Batter Bread *or* Freeform Chestnut Bread
- **Greens:** Pressed Salad, Boiled Salad *or* Steamed Greens tossed with Onion Pickles
- **Optional, Dessert:** Apple Sauce or Compote, Anise-Pears *or* Rosehip & Apple Compote
- **Beverage:** Roasted Chickory & Dandelion "Coffee" *or* Spice Tea

Thanksgiving Feast (Fall)

- **Soup:** Puréed Beet-Squash Bisque, Rutabaga-Squash Soup, *or* Cream of Parsnip Soup
- **Vegetarian Protein:** Pan Fried Tempeh or Wheat Meat Cutlets *or* Wheatloaf
- **Grain:** Millet & Turnip "Mashed Potatoes" *or* Millet & Cauliflower "Mash"
- **Other grain:** Chick-n-Peas Sourdough Dressing *or* Easiest Ever Bread Cube Dressing
- **Gravy:** Mock Poultry Gravy
- **Greens:** Pressed Salad, Steamed Greens, Boiled Salad *or* Kale-Carrots-Caraway & Kraut
- **Optional, Dessert:** Squash Custard, Apple-Pie, Stuffed Apples *or* Cranberry Apple Sauce
- **Beverage:** Roasted Barley & Dandelion Coffee, Grain Coffee *or* Spice Tea

Native American Thanksgiving Feast (Fall)

- **Soup:** Three Sisters Soup *or* Corn-Squash & Tomato Soup*
- **Grain:** Chestnut Rice, Wild Brown Rice *or* Posole Rice
- **Second grain:** Arepas, Corn Batter Bread, *or* Flat Breads
- **Vegetarian Protein:** Wheat Meat Cutlets (* If soup is bean-free, also serve Baked Beans)
- **Condiment (for grain):** Sunflower or Pumpkin Seed condiment *and/or* Millet Butter
- **Sweet vegetable:** Baked, Mashed Winter Squash *or* Sweet Potatoes (with light miso)
- **Greens:** Pressed or Marinated Salad *or* Boiled Greens with Radish Pickles or Sauerkraut
- **Optional, Dessert:** Rosehip & Apple Compote, Chestnut Pudding, *or* Glazed Chestnuts
- **Beverage:** Roasted Corn Tea *or* Chicory Coffee

Festive Chinese Meal, Any Season

- **Soup:** Cream of Celery, Asparagus, Leek *or* Corn Soup
- **Grain:** Brown Rice *or* Roasted Brown Rice
- **Condiment (for grain):** Sesame-Salt *or* Flax Seed Condiment
- **Second Grain:** Chinaman's Purse *or* Steamed Buns with tempeh, tofu, or wheat meat filling
- **Mixed Vegetables:** Stir Fried Vegetables *or* Chow-Mein Style Vegetables
- **Pickles:** Daikon, Red Radish or Onion pickled in tamari or umeboshi
- **Dessert:** Amasake Pudding, Chestnut Custard or Pudding, *or* Raisin Glazed Chestnuts

Equivalents,
liquid and dry measure

Abbreviations

tsp. = teaspoon
Tbsp. = tablespoon
oz. = ounces

Liquid Measure Volume Equivalents

A few grains = less than 1/8 tsp.
1 small pinch (two fingers) = 1/8 tsp.
1 big pinch (three fingers) = 1/4 tsp.
1 tsp. = 1/3 Tbsp.
1 Tbsp.= 3 tsp.
4 Tbsp. = 1/4 cup
5 1/3 Tbsp. = 1/3 cup
8 Tbsp. = 1/2 cup or 4 oz. (volume)
16 Tbsp. = 1 cup or 8 oz. (volume)
1/4 cup = 4 Tbsp.
1/3 cup = 5 1/3 Tbsp.
3/8 cup = 1/4 cup + 2 Tbsp.
5/8 cup = 1/2 cup + 2 Tbsp.
7/8 cup = 3/4 cup + 2 Tbsp.
1 cup = 1/2 pint or 8 fluid oz.
2 cups = 1 pint or 16 fluid oz.
2 pints = 1 quart (liquid)
4 quarts = 1 gallon
1 gallon (liquid) = 16 cups

Dry Measurements

Used for raw, fruits and vegetables when
dealing with large volumes.

1 quart = 2 pints
8 quarts = 1 peck
4 pecks = 1 bushel

Equivalents, cups and pounds

Whole grain (brown rice, etc.) uncooked	2-2 1/2 cups	=	1 pound
Brown rice, uncooked	1 cup dry	=	6 oz.. by weight
Rolled grain (rolled oats, oatmeal, etc.)	4 3/4 cups	=	1 pound
Flour (whole wheat)	4 cups	=	1 pound
Chestnut flour	3 cups	=	1 pound
Dried chestnuts	2+ cups	=	1 pound
Cornmeal	3 cups	=	1 pound
Bread crumbs or cubes	1/3 cup hard	=	1 slice
Bread crumbs or cubes	3/4 cup soft	=	1 slice
Macaroni, dry	4 cups	=	1 pound
Dried beans (lentils, split peas, etc.)	2 cups	=	1 pound
Pecans, in shell	2 1/4-2 1/2 lbs	=	1 pound shelled
Pecans, shelled	2 1/2 cups	=	1 pound
Almonds, whole, shelled	1 cup	=	5-6 ounces by weight
Walnuts, pecans, almonds, shelled	3 1/2-4 cups	=	1 pound
Peanuts, shelled	2 1/4 cups	=	1 pound (16 oz.)
Seeds, raw (sesame, sunflower, etc.)	4 cups	=	1 pound
Seeds, raw	1 cup	=	4 ounces (1/4 lb.)
Seeds, raw	1/4 cup	=	1 ounce
Oil	2 cups	=	1 pound fat
Wheat meat/seitan, drained	3 cups	=	12 oz. (3/4 lb)
Wheat meat/seitan, drained	4 cups	=	16 oz. (1 lb.)
Tempeh	1/2 lb.	=	1 1/2-2 cups chopped
Tofu, soft, drained	1 pound	=	2 1/2 cups
Tofu, extra firm, drained	1 pound	=	1 1/2-1 3/4 cups
Kale	1 pound, raw	=	12-16 cups raw
Collard greens	1 pound, raw	=	12 cups raw
Hard cabbage	1 pound, raw	=	6-7 cups packed, chopped
Broccoli	1 pound, raw	=	4-6 cups, raw, chopped
Bok choy/Chinese greens	1 pound, raw	=	6-9 cups, chopped
Onions, white/yellow	1 pound, raw	=	2 medium or 1 extra large
Onion, 1 medium to large size, chopped	1/2 pound	=	1 1/2-2 cups
Carrots	1 pound, raw	=	6 medium sized carrots
Red radishes, 1 average bunch	8 oz.	=	1-1/2 cups raw
Cauliflower, 1 average head	1 lb. 8 oz.	=	5 cups raw
Broccoli, 4 stalks	1 lb.	=	5 1/2 cups raw, usable portion
Apples	1 cup sliced	=	4-5 ounces.
Apples	3 cups sliced	=	1 pound
Apples, 1 small	1 cup sliced	=	4-5 ounces
Apples, 1 large	6-10 oz.	=	1 1/2-2 cups sliced
Raisins, seeded	2 3/4 cup	=	1 pound
Ginger root	2 tsp. grated	=	1/2 tsp. ginger juice

Substitutions

Lemon juice	1 tsp. = 1/2 tsp. cider vinegar or brown rice vinegar
Yeast, active dry or rapid-rise	1 packet = 2 1/4 tsp.
Garlic	1/8 tsp. powder = 1 small clove
Herbs	1/2-1 tsp. dry = 1 Tbsp. fresh, minced
Sea salt	1/4 tsp. sea salt = 1-1 1/2 tsp. tamari, shoyu, or miso
Sea salt	1/4 tsp. sea salt = 1 umeboshi plum or 3/4-1 apriboshi
Miso	1 Tbsp. miso = 1/2 tsp. sea salt = 1 Tbsp. tamari
Miso	1 Tbsp. dark miso = 1 Tbsp. tamari = 4 tsp. shoyu
Miso	1 1/2-2 tsp. miso or tamari = 1/4 tsp. sea salt
Umeboshi plum	1 plum = 1 1/2 tsp. umeboshi paste = 1/4 tsp. sea salt
Umeboshi vinegar	1 1/3 tsp. ume vinegar = 1 ume plum = 1 1/2 tsp. paste
Umeboshi vinegar	1 tsp. ume vinegar = 2/3 umeboshi plum or 3/4 apriboshi
Syrups	1 Tbsp. maple syrup = 2 1/4 tsp. rice or barley malt syrup
Thickeners	1 Tbsp. kuzu root starch = 2-3 tsp. arrowroot powder

When the recipe calls for milk, buttermilk, cream, yogurt, or eggs, how to leave them out

Cooking dairy products such as milk, yogurt or cheese, particularly at temperatures above a simmer, denatures their proteins and renders them less healthful and less digestible. Therefore, we suggest that you use these products as table condiments or as a side dish, in an uncooked or only lightly heated form. It also bears mentioning that these foods are very concentrated and needed in only small amounts. When used in cooking they are often "wasted. It is really unnecessary to use dairy products or eggs in soups or in breads, pancakes, casseroles or other cooked or baked dishes. Doing so leads to general overconsumption of animal foods. Ghee, due to its heat stable nature, can be used in cooking, as a replacement for vegetable oil or as a table condiment to replace seed sprinkles. Soy milk is far better, easier to digest, more ecological and more suited for use in cooking and baking than are dairy products. Oatmeal, rice, parsnips, or soy flour can be used to create rich and dairy-like textures in a dishes, without the drawbacks of dairy foods. Creamy soups can even more simply be made by purée-ing cooked vegetables or vegetables with oatmeal. Other items—tofu, soy milk, grated mochi, light miso, or nutritional yeast can give you a cheesy, milky, or creamy taste used alone or in combination. It is not difficult to eliminate the milk, cream, yogurt, and eggs from desserts. Amasake pudding, commercial amazake nectar, almond milk, rolled oats, sweet rice, puréed chestnuts or chestnut flour, millet, other whole grain flours, arrowroot, or a flax seed binder can add texture, volume, creaminess, or binding power in puddings, cookies, cakes, and mousses. Small amounts of nut or seed butter or soy milk can also do the same. (Please refer to the dessert chapter and the condiment chapter for more specifics.)

Eggciting Substitutes!

Eggs add lightness and binding power to breads, cakes, and muffins, but most folks use far more eggs than they need to and in places where they're not really necessary. You don't really need any eggs in most dishes. Sure, you can use egg-whites, but way waste a precious egg by using only half of it? Try an egg substitute in baking and save your eggs for dishes where they're flavor is called for—like omelettes, frittata's, scrambles, stir frys, or egg salads (stretched with tofu). Alternately, eggs can be steamed or poached and used as a topping for hot cereal, rice, bread, or pasta, with various vegetable dishes if you choose to use them. While the following egg replacer won't produce the rise that eggs do in some dishes, it will provide the binding effect that eggs or egg whites provide in baking or cooking popular dishes like loaves, burgers, croquettes, cookies, cakes, bars, muffins, and the like.

Quick Binder & Egg-Replacer (replaces 2 eggs)

2 Tbsp. flax seeds

6 Tbsp. boiling water

Grind flax seeds in a blender or coffee-spice mill. Place in a small sauce pan and pour boiling water over. Whisk with a fork. Cover and let sit 15 minutes. Whisk again or whip in a blender until fluffy. Add to cookie, muffin, cake batter, meat loaf, rissoles, burgers, nut or bean loaves, or casseroles to replace eggs. Bake as per recipe.

Smooth Egg-Replacer (mock egg-white mixture, replaces 2 eggs)

3 Tbsp. whole flax seeds

1/2 cup + 2 Tbsp. water

Bring ingredients to boil. Simmer 15-20 minutes in a covered pot. Cook down to a little over 1/2 cup then pour through a strainer. Mixture should be egg white consistency. Whisk with a fork. Add to pie fillings, custards, puddings, cakes, cookies, brownies, quiches, or other dishes in place of eggs. Bake or cook as per the standard recipes. For savory main dishes it is unnecessary to strain the flax seed mixture.

Other Good Egg Replacers
Replace one egg with one of the following:

- 1/4 cup mashed soft tofu, blended with the liquids in a recipe

- 2 Tbsp. arrowroot added to dry mixture and 4 Tbsp. water or soy milk added to liquids

- 1 Tbsp. sesame tahini, sesame butter, or peanut butter in 3 Tbsp. water, soy milk, or juice

- 1 Tbsp. arrowroot + 1 Tbsp. soy flour + 2 Tbsp. water, soy milk, or juice

- 1/3 cup soft mashed potatoes or sweet potatoes (for cookies, burgers, or loaves)

Replace 1 cup milk with an equal volume of one of the following:

- water

- almond, sunflower, or sesame milk

- pasta cooking water

- potato cooking water

- rice milk or oat milk

- amasake nectar or beverage

- plain, unflavored, unsweetened soy milk

- soup stock

- water blended with 1 Tbsp. nut or seed butter

- **Note:** To replace 1 cup of buttermilk place 1 Tbsp. apple cider vinegar in a measuring cup or brown rice vinegar then add soy milk, rice milk or nut/seed milk to equal 1 cup.

If and when you do use dairy foods it is best to use them as condiments, added judiciously to foods at the table rather than in cooking. A little bit of grated cheese or a dollup of yogurt will go much farther when sprinkled over rice, beans, warm bread, or other dishes than when cooked in. Yogurt or buttermilk can be eaten or drank with a meal or as a snack, used to soak oats for vegetable muesli, or made into a salad dressing, for example (though soy, nut or grain based substitutes work just as well if not better). These practices make you more conscious of your use of these rich foods.

Note: If you do serve yogurt or milk, be sure to serve them at room temperature or briefly warmed rather than ice cold from the refrigerator. This makes them more digestible as does the addition of a pinch or two of ground black pepper, ginger, cinnamon, or fresh or dried chives It is also important to use unpasteurized, un-homogenized, non-fortified milk products, free of hormones or antibiotics, and preferably goat rather than cow origin. The milk or yogurt should also be full fat or low fat (only lightly skimmed) rather than skim or non-fat. The latter two milks are much more difficult to digest and assimilate. (The fat aids mineral absorption, particularly that of calcium.)

Nourishment from Restaurants

Can restaurants really nourish us?

Though occasional meals out may be a treat, eating out frequently, more than once a week, can send your food bills skyrocketing and your health plummeting. A typical meal out generally costs two to four times more than an entire day's worth of home cooked meals. This means that you will end up having to work more in order to afford the luxury of paying someone else to cook for you. Furthermore, few restaurant have the quality and freshness of home-cooked meals.

Most restaurants rely on canned, frozen, and packaged foods and refined grains. They also seem to sneak sugar, preservatives, additives, large amounts of fat, and overly processed foodstuffs into just about everything. Very few use fresh, seasonal, local or organic produce or naturally raised animal products. An added disadvantage to eating out is that many restaurants prepare foods in quantity, then let them sit in warmer trays for hours on end. The result: whatever Qi (life-giving force) these foods had is completely lost and much of the flavor is also sacrificed. Suffice it to say that eating most of one's meals out is leaving your health to chance. This is not to discourage you from ever eating out. Eating out can be fun and inspiring every now and then. Our intention is merely to make you aware of some of the drawbacks of relying on commercially prepared foods and to provide you with a road map to help you chart a more sound and healthful course if and when you do choose to venture into restaurants.

Making wise choices

It is entirely possible to eat a grain-based and vegetable-rich meal in almost any restaurant if you know what you want and how to ask for it. Armed with the right information, and a strategy, you can make wiser choices when you dine out. Indeed, in most cases, you have far more ordering options than you might imagine.

Patterning your meal

It is helpful to keep the basic meal format in mind when eating out, just as when eating in. This can assist you in creating more balanced and healthful meals. The basic lunch and dinner format is: soup or stew + grain + vegetable side dish(es) + condiments. While the soup is desirable, it is not always available and can be omitted and replaced with another side dish if you like. The basic breakfast pattern is: grain + vegetable side dish or dishes + condiments. Countless combinations of dishes are possible using this basic pattern for nourishment.

Drinking up

Avoid drinking ice water or any other iced, chilled or frozen beverages before, during, or after a meal. These chill the Stomach and interfere with proper digestion and assimilation of food. Drinking beverages with meals also dilutes digestive juices and discourages proper chewing. A cup of warm soup is a much better choice and can actually help improve your digestion and overall health. If you order soup, stew, chowder, or a light broth, ask that it be served with the rest of your meal so that you can slowly eat/drink it throughout your meal. If you are particularly thirsty, you might try a small cup of hot water before the meal, or a cup of hot water, tea, or grain "coffee" afterwards.

Though most restaurants serve herb teas, it never hurts to keep a few of your favorite herb tea bags tucked in your purse, brief case, back pack or fanny pack. This way, if the restaurant you are dining in doesn't have any suitable beverages, you can order a cup of hot water and have your tea. You can also request that your favorite restaurant carry a variety of non-caffeinated herbal teas and roasted grain "coffee" beverages.

Examining your options

Scan the menu before you order, and don't be afraid to ask for a special dish made from any of several ingredients found on the menu. Ask how particular grain, bean and vegetable dishes are prepared. Avoid anything fried (unless it is stir-fried). Bear in mind that even if the menu says "breaded and deep fried," you can ask for your dish to be prepared in a low fat or fat-free manner. Avoid items described as "smothered in cream sauce," "covered with a mountain of cheese," or "rich and buttery." Speak up. Request that your dish be steamed, poached, broiled, baked, sautéed, or grilled with herbs, spices and/or seasonings, minus the rich sauces and gravies. Ask for butter, yogurt, or grated cheese on the side if you want these.

Going with the grain

When dining out, just as when eating at home, try to build your meals around grains and have vegetables and/or beans as side dishes. Though you can do this anywhere, ethnic restaurants are often your best bet since so many of the world's great culinary traditions are based on grains. You might try a Chinese, Japanese, Korean, Thai, Mexican, Italian, Greek, Middle Eastern, Ethiopian, Indian, or Moroccan restaurant. But even good old American seafood and steak houses, pizza parlors, or greasy spoon diners can accommodate your need for grain-based and vegetable-rich vegetarian meals.

First, look over the menu carefully, in search of grains. These might include brown rice, basmati rice, wild rice, or white rice, millet, oatmeal, barley, bulghur, injera, pita bread, pizza, pancakes, pasta, couscous, kasha, chapatis, calzones, tortillas, tacos, tamales, steamed or baked buns, bagels, bread sticks, loaf bread, or dinner rolls.

Getting what you want

If you don't like or can't tolerate certain spices or foods, don't be afraid to let the wait person know this. Most restaurants are becoming familiar with special requests and will often go to great lengths to make your dish or meal meet your specifications. In fact, most chefs are more than happy to use their creativity to make something a bit out of the ordinary. This can make their work more interesting, and your dining experience more pleasant and health promoting.

Getting it all, at once

Ask that your meal be served all at once, rather than in courses. This way, you will have your soup and/or salad to eat with your other side dishes and your bread, pasta or whole grain.

This will help you balance your meal and reduce the amount of fat you take in since every dish in the meal won't need butter, dressing, sauce, or oil. Rich dishes like sautées, stir fries, and salad dressing be eaten with more bland or plain foods like rice or bread. It is also best to avoid starting any meal with raw salads which chill the Stomach and hamper digestion.

Souping it up

If you order soup, and it's a good idea to do this, choose clear soups over cream soups and skip any that are described as "creamy," or "rich" (unless you are in a vegan or macrobiotic restaurant). Ask for low-fat, dairy-free vegetarian options. And remember to ask for your soup to be served *with* the rest of your meal, rather than as a first course.

Avoiding the oil slicks

Don't assume that vegetarian or vegan (dairy-free vegetarian) dishes are automatically low in fat. Many are prepared with mountains of cheese, buckets of oil (usually poor quality oil too), heaps of nuts and seeds, or large servings avocado. Some vegetarian dishes are as high or higher in fat than the meat-based dishes they may seek to imitate. Further, some meals are served with french fries or fried corn chips—which aren't health promoting in the least. Ask for several extra slices of bread, more rice, or extra vegetables instead. It is best order with awareness in any restaurant, vegetarian or otherwise.)

Getting enough

Since many restaurants serve small portions of grain, you will probably want (and need) to order a double or triple portion of whole grain, pasta, or bread. (Ask about portion size first, just to be on the safe side.) Some ethnic restaurants already serve large portions of grain. For example, Mexican, Moroccan, and some French, American, and European, restaurants serve complimentary baskets of bread or tortillas. Ask about these and about brown rice or whole grain bread or pasta. Though whole grain products are ideal, if they are unavailable, refined or semi-refined grain products such as white bread, white pasta, and white rice will do. Grain is still the best staple food, even if it is refined.

Going plain

It is always helpful to ask to have your bread, pasta, or whole grains, prepared with little or no added oil or butter. Ask to have butter and any other sauces or spreads served on the side, that way you can use these sparingly and consciously. Also, don't overlook the possibility of using your side dishes as toppings for your grain. Use stir fried or sautéed vegetables or refried or baked beans as a topping for unbuttered bread or plain noodles, or rice. You can also dunk your bread into a hearty soup or stew, eat dressing topped vegetables with plain bread or noodles. Or, ask to have a rich soup served over a hot bowl of plain noodles.In most cases, it is best to pick one or two dishes in a meal which contain oil and just one dish which with nuts, seeds, or nut butters. It is unnecessary to have these concentrated foods in every dish in the meal.

Going green

Once you are set with grain, go for vegetables. Look and ask for dishes prepared with just a little oil, ghee, or butter. (You can even order steamed or stir fried vegetables for breakfast in many restaurants.) If you are still unsure how a dish will be prepared after reading the menu, ask. Be clear about what you want and don't want. Many restaurants automatically douse everything with butter or cream sauce, though they will happily leave these off at your request. Skip deep fried vegetables (or limit them to special occasions). Skip dishes served in sauces that described as "thick, rich, creamy, buttery, or cheesy." Try steamed, stir fried, lightly sautéed, or grilled vegetables instead.

If you don't see any vegetable dishes that sound appealing on the menu, ask that a special dish prepared. Special orders are usually accepted and often result in exceptionally artful and delicious dishes. Again, ask for dressings and sauces on the side, that way you can add as much or as little fat as you like. If a dish usually comes with cheese, you can order it without or grated and served on the side so you can use it sparingly. You can even do this in a pizza parlor. Or, order a cheese-less pizza; they are tasty and generally pose no problem for the kitchen. (Instead of cheese on pizza, or try pesto or a small amount of nuts or seeds with roasted, grilled, sautéed and/or fresh vegetables, plus herbs or spices.)

Scaling things down to size

If you do choose to order eggs, yogurt, cheese, fish or dishes which contain them, we suggest asking about the portion size before ordering. Find out how many eggs or ounces of cheese or yogurt a particular dish contains.

Many restaurants consider a portion to be very large! Fish and fowl are served in 6-12 ounce portions and many dishes contain eggs, cheese, cream, milk,butter or all of these. Many egg dishes contain three eggs, plus milk, cream and/or cheese. Often times a single serving of a dish may contain upwards of a quarter pound of cheese, per person! This is far more than anyone needs. Also ask how a dish will be prepared. To keep the fat low, you might opt for a poached egg rather than a fried egg; grated cheese, served on the side; a cup of yogurt; or some butter, ghee, or yogurt dressing on the side. In this way you can use these rich items as condiments for plain grain or vegetables, so they enrich rather than smother your food. If you choose to use animal foods, we suggest eating them in very small condiment sized portions (an ounce or two of cheese, one egg, or six to eight ounces of yogurt; or just 3-4 ounces of fish, if you eat fish. If you do order fish, cheese, milk, or yogurt or dishes which contain them, it is also a good idea to limit their use to just one dish in a meal. They are very concentrated.

Sane solutions:

(a) When ordering a vegetarian entrée, you can ask for a totally dairy-free dish or meal. (You may have to explain exactly what this constitutes.) If you want a bit of butter or grated cheese, ask for it "on the side," that way you can regulate the amount you use.

(b) If you order an item which comes with cheese, ask for a reduced portion (i.e., just 1-1 1/2 ounces rather than the usual 2-4 ounce mountain) on the side then order a double or triple portion of whole grain, bread, or pasta and/or extra veggies.

(c) If you want eggs, split an egg containing dish with several dining companions, then order grain, bean and vegetable side dishes from the a-la-carte or appetizer menu to round out the meal.

(d) Or, skip the eggs altogether then order tofu, tempeh, or beans to enrich and enhance the flavors of your grains and vegetables.

(e) When ordering eggs, order a single egg, or two at the most. Also ask that they be steam or poach it, or stir fry it with your vegetables rather than fried or scrambled.

(f) If you eat fish, ask for a half portion or less, (3-4 ounces) or share your order with a friend then order extra grains and veggies.

(g) Take home leftovers in a doggy bag—you can turn them into interesting soups, stews, stir frys, casseroles or sandwich fillers.

Desserting

As for desserts, most restaurants serve sticky, sweet, rich and fat-filled desserts. These won't help you maintain or regain your health and should be avoided. Ask yourself whether you really need dessert; maybe some extra bread or pasta in the meal will satisfy your need for a little something extra.

Some restaurants do offer low-fat, fat-free, sugar-free, dairy-free, or whole grain desserts on a regular basis. Look over the menu (before you order dinner), noticing what sorts of ingredients are listed that could constitute dessert— apples, pears, berries, fresh melon, fruit salad, etc. Many a chef will gladly poach a pear in wine sauce or cider. Some will even bake or steam an apple for you, sweetened only with dried fruit or juice. Others will gladly simmer or stew a sugar-free apple and raisin compote. (Ask for a sprinkling of chopped nuts if you like.) If you want a fat-free or special dessert, don't be bashful in making your request—just do so before you get your meal so that the kitchen staff will have time to prepare for your special request.

If you do decide to order a dessert that you wouldn't normally eat at home, it pays to get the highest quality that you can. You may even want to share a rich-treat with a friend so you are less likely to come away from the meal with a bad taste in your mouth and a belly-ache to boot!

A Case For
Using Animal Products

Veganism (the total abstinence from all animal products, including eggs and dairy products) is becoming increasingly popular. We ourselves have practiced such a diet; however, we no longer advocate this approach. There are many reasons for this.

Naturally raised animals are sources of many nutrients that are either absent from or less available from plant foods. From our reading and research it is clear that the healthiest and longest lived peoples in the world (the Soviet Georgians, the Hunzas, the Vilcabambans, etc.) were not and are not pure vegetarians (vegans); they all use cultured dairy foods daily, eggs frequently, and fish or fowl now and then.

A pure vegetarian diet can be marginal or deficient in sufficient calcium, vitamin A, D-complex vitamins, and vitamin B-12. Most experts agree that a B-12 supplement is essential if one does not eat animal products on a daily or frequent basis. However, taking a supplement does not assure that one will not come up deficient; in fact, these supplements can contain B-12 analogs and/or breakdown products of B-12 which can interfere with normal B-12 metabolism. Although certain vegetable foods are reputed to contain this vitamin, there is not conclusive evidence to this effect. Some foods that were thought to contain B-12 were, under further testing, found to be lacking in biologically active B-12.

As for calcium, increasingly research shows that people who eat calcium rich animal products--particularly milk products--have stronger bones later into life than those who abstain from them. Also, more and more studies are showing that calcium is better absorbed from animal products than from plant foods. Among Soviet Georgians, who use a fair amount of fermented goat milk products daily, and who live to a ripe old age of 100 years or more, osteoporosis, tooth decay, and loss of teeth is uncommon.

Because fiber in plant foods can hinder the absorption of certain key nutrients, it is prudent to have a diet which amply covers ours needs and is comprised of the most nutritious foods. Serious, even irreparable damage may result from a chronic lack of Vitamins A, D, B-12, calcium, and essential fatty acids nutrients. Since we believe that it is better to be safe than sorry, we recommend the inclusion of some high quality animal products in one's daily diet. Some may choose yogurt and other fermented dairy products; others may choose dairy products and eggs; others may choose fish or fish and poultry; still others may opt for a different combination according to preference, availability, and economical or health considerations.

Most of us have come from traditions where animal products--dairy, eggs, fish, fowl, or meat--played important roles. Although it is not necessary for us to eat all of these foods, it is important to adapt our dietary practice to our ancestry. It is possible to do this both ecologically and economically. If you have further questions about selection and use of high quality animal products and their role in a health supportive and/or therapeutic diet, we urge you to read *Native Nutrition* by Ronald Schmid, N.D., and *Nutrition & Physical Degeneration* by Weston Price, DDS. (See Resources section, ch. 12.)

What About Dairy Allergies?

While many people say that they are allergic to dairy foods, it is often the case that people do not have negative reactions, and actually thrive, when the products are:
(a) from naturally raised, pasture-fed animals
(b) unhomogenized and unpasteurized
(c) served raw and uncooked, or just briefly boiled (if desired, to sterilize or to counteract the effects of pasteurization)
(d) fermented to break down the lactose
(e) used in the context of a highly nutritious, grain-based, vegetable-rich, junk food-free diet
(f) used in small amounts.

A similar situation exists with eggs. Properly prepared (lightly cooked, whole eggs), from fertile, free-ranging birds eating a natural diet are far more nutritious and readily accepted by the body than eggs from diseased, underexercised, confined, drugged, factory farmed animals.

With all foods, and particularly with animal foods, the quality, quantity, and context are important considerations and change their effects on the human organism.

Special Foods

Basic Procedure, Ghee (Clarified Butter, Year Round)

Prep: 30-45 minutes
Cooking: same
Yield: from 1 pound of butter, 1 1/2-2 cups ghee + 1/2-2/3 cup ghee leavings
Serving size: 1/2-2 tsp. per person at a meal, in cooking or at the table

Unlike butter, ghee lasts for months when stored at room temperature. It is more heat stable than both butter and vegetable oils, making it the perfect cooking medium for sweet or savory dishes. Through simmering, the moisture, air and carbohydrate and protein portions (the solids or leavings) separate and float to the top of the pan, to be skimmed off. The remaining liquid fat solidifies as it cools to make "ghee,"

Ghee can be used in sautéing, baking, or cooking, or as a table condiment to replace seed or nut condiments or other oils. The solids can also be used as a table condiment, though they are not suitable for cooking (most of the fat has been removed and what is left contains carbohydrate and protein). Since ghee is more concentrated than butter—it is pure butterfat—only a small amount of this nourishing substance is needed at a time.

Some people who are allergic to milk can digest ghee because the proteins—the part they react to—have been removed. Also, butter from naturally raised, grass fed animals will be far more nutritious, digestible, and healthful than butter from penned up animals that are denied sunlight and fed hormones, antibiotics, grains, soy beans, and other inappropriate food.

Medicinally, ghee, and high quality butter, enhance immune function, promote the growth of beneficial digestive flora, and boost mineral absorption and mineral metabolism. In Chinese medicine we say that it assists the Yang, tonifies the Qi and Blood, removes Stagnant Blood, expels Cold, and sedates Yin. Over use, however, congests the Middle Burner organs and contributes to the formation of Phlegm.

Notes: Butter and ghee made from the butter of grass fed, free ranging animals will be bright yellow or orange in color (from the carotenes in the animal milk). Ghee from inferior butter will be dingy beige or grey. If the only quality butter you have available is pasteurized, turning it into ghee, whether you plan to cook with it or use it at the table, will make it more healthful and digestible by antidoting the pasteurization process.

1 lb. raw butter *or* pasteurized organic butter

1. In a 1 or 2-quart saucepan, melt butter over a low heat. (Do not use a high flame.) When completely melted, it will sizzle as the moisture and air are driven off. As the solids separate and float to the topp, stick a small spoon into the foam and remove the solids a little at a time, without taking the "oil."

2. Transfer solids to a small custard cup or a small wide mouth jar. Continue to skim until the oil is clear. This usually takes about 20 - 30 minutes, depending upon the volume.

3. It is done when the oil stops bubbling and sounds like frying oil. Turn off heat. Allow ghee to cool for 10-15 minutes before pouring it into a wide 8-16 ounce jar. Cover when completely cooled. It will solidify as it cools.

4. Scrape remaining solids from the bottom of the pot and transfer the bowl or jar with the rest of the solids. Instead of washing the pot right away, set it aside, for up to 24 hours, then cook hot cereal or soup in this pot.

Storage suggestions: Cover and refrigerate the solids (leavings) and use within one month. Store ghee at room temperature in a cool, dry place, away from direct sunlight. When traveling or in very hot weather, refrigerate ghee if desired. Use ghee within 6-12 months. Always use a clean knife or spoon to dip into the ghee jar to avoid contaminating it.

Serving suggestions: Use ghee solids to top a serving of rice, millet, hot cereal, or baked potato. (Add a sprinkle of sea flakes and/or black pepper, dill, chives, scallions, or parsley for best digestion). Melt the solids and pour over popcorn (about 2 tsp. solids per 6-8 cups popped corn.) Or, use solids to season an oil-free soup. Use ghee to replace oil when you sauté or stir fry. (You can usually reduce the amount of fat or oil by one half in your recipe.). You don't need much!)

Basic Procedure, Yogurt (Year Round)***

Prep: 10-15 minutes
Incubation: 8-12 hours if heated briefly; 12-24 hours if milk is unheated
Yield: 8 cups yogurt from 4 cups milk
Serving size: 1/2-1 cup per person

Homemade raw milk yogurt is far superior to commercial varieties which are made from pasteurized and often homogenized milk. Further, commercial milk and yogurt is often tainted with hormones, antibiotics, preservatives, and additives and taken from anemic cows on drugs that get little if any sunlight or exercise. Thus, most supermarket dairy products are of inferior nutritional value. In contrast, grass fed cows and goats are happier and produce far tastier and more nutritious milk and yogurt. (Look in your healthfood store for the most healthful milk.)

Certified raw milk, whole or with just the cream skimmed off the top, is ideal. Avoid pasteurized milk and milk which has been fortified. Locally raised milk is your best bet, organic, pasteurized milk is a good second choice. The culture or starter that you use may come from commercial, plain yogurt from the health food store (preferably raw, though for this purpose pasteurized yogurt will still work). After you make your first batch, save some to use as a culture for the next batch then keep doing this each time.

You don't need a fancy yogurt making machine. All you need is a large glass bowl with a plate to cover it or a few quart mason jars with lids. Another option is a glass lined thermos.

Goat milk—being rather astringent—tonifies the Yang. Cow's milk, which is richer, tonifies the Yin. Both tonify Qi and Blood and nourish the Essence Serving them warm or at room temperature and with a hint of spice or herbs helps counter their Damp and Mucousy qualities.

Note: We do not advocate using non-fat milk as these are virtually indigestible and stripped of the essential fats necessary for proper calcium and vitamin D metabolism. Use only full fat or part skim milk. Many of the so-called "allergies" that some people have to dairy foods are reactions to pasteurized, homogenized dairy foods from factory farm animals. Other reactions come from cooked or overcooked dairy products. We advise that you get your milk from animals that are allowed to eat pasturage and roam the range.

We also advise against cooking with milk or yogurt. They are best taken raw at room or body temperature or just briefly warmed. For many people, it is possible to eat real yogurt without a "reaction." Also, goat milk tends to be easier to digest and far cleaner than cows milk. Goats are almost always allowed to run around outside and eat a wide variety of wild vegetation. Their milk is also closer to human mother's milk in composition than is cow's milk.

Note: Make only as much yogurt as you will use within 1-1 1/2 weeks.

2 quarts (4 cups) raw milk (goat is best)
 or pasteurized organic milk, full fat or with only cream removed

1/2 cup plain goat or cow's milk yogurt
 (raw or pasteurized) *or* yogurt starter

2 wide-mouth quart jars with lids *or* 1 10-cup pyrex bowl with a plate to cover

1. **If the milk has been pasteurized:** Bring to a full boil then turn off heat Allow to cool to 110-120°F before proceeding with next step.

   If the milk is raw: Heat to 110 ° F if desired. (Use a thermometer.) This renders the milk more sterile and nutritious than pasteurization and preserves certain nutrients. You can also make yogurt without heating the milk.

2. Stir yogurt into cooked milk. Pour into sterilized jars and seal, or pour into a pyrex bowl and top with a dinner plate. Or, pour into one or more thermos bottles that have been pre-heated with boiling water then emptied.

3. Put in a warm place (90-120° F) and allow to incubate for 8-9 hours if heated, or up to 24-30 hours if the milk was not heated.

Good places to ferment yogurt:

(a) a gas oven with just the pilot light on;
(b) or, on top of an electric heating pad turned to medium then wrap containers with a blanket to insulate.
(c) a thermos that has first been pre-heated.

4. When done, it should be fairly thick, almost solid on top. (**Note:** It may be thinner than what you are accustomed to finding in the store, particularly if the milk was unheated.)

Storage tips: Refrigerate. Use within 1-1 1/2 weeks. Remove meal-size portions from the refrigerator 1/2-4 hours before serving to take the chill off and avoid creating mucous.

Serving suggestions: Serve as a beverage after a meal; alight snack with grain, vegetables, or fruit; a side dish in a meal; or use to make a dressing or sauce. Before serving, add a pinch of black pepper, cinnamon, ginger or ginger juice or chives to spark digestion.

Basic Procedure, Quark or Yogurt Cheese (Year Round)***

Prep: 10 minutes
Straining: 1/2-2 hours or longer
Yield: variable,~ 4-5 cups depending on thickness
Serving size: 1/3-1/2 cup per person

This cheese is a snap to make and very versatile. It can replace cream cheese, sour cream, whip cream, cottage cheese, farmers cheese.

2 quarts (8 cups) raw milk yogurt, goat is best

1. Line a fine mesh strainer or colander with several layers of cheesecloth. Put the colander or strainer over a bowl; slowly pour the yogurt into the cloth and allow whey (liquid) to drain into the bowl. The cloth will catch the "cheese."

   Soft farmer's-style, quark, or ricotta cheese: Drain for 15-30 minutes.

   Firmer cheese: Allow to drain for 2-6 hours in the refrigerator. (You may cover the top of the strainer with a dinner plate.)

3. Two quarts (8 cups) of yogurt yields about 3 cups of soft quark cheese or 2 cups of firmer yet still spreadable quark cheese.

Storage suggestions: Refrigerate the "cheese." and use within 1-2 weeks. Refrigerate the liquid, whey in a jar. Do not cook with this cheese (or any cheese). Cooking renders it less digestible and less nutritious by denaturing the proteins.

Serving suggestions: Figure about 1/4-1/2 cup soft curd yogurt cheese or 4 Tbsp. of firm cream-cheese cheese per person. Use as a spread for bread or a topping for beans, cooked vegetables, tempeh, wheat meat, tacos or enchiladas, raw fruit or a fruit gel, salad, or compote (It's also good spread on tortillas with mustard and pressed salad or cooked greens.) For a fancier dip, add a small amount of sea salt, light miso or ume vinegar and dried herbs or spices. Add back a bit of the whey if needed to make a smooth texture.

About the whey: Use this to thin puréed vegetable soups (squash, carrot, zucchini, etc.) or warm briefly (about 1/2 cup per person) and stir into hot cereal that was made too thick.

Basic Procedure, Steamed Eggs***

Prep: less than 5 minutes
Cooking: 6-10 minutes
Serves: 1
Serving size: 1 egg per person

Eggs are very nutritious if you get them from real barnyard chickens. They are also very concentrated, so you don't need much. One egg per person is plenty. (It is meant to be a condiment, not the main dish!) You can use chicken or duck eggs. They make a delightful topping for a heaping helping of hot cereal, brown rice, noodles, or for a burrito.

This cooking method beats poaching: it's less messy, less involved, and allows you to cook and serve the eggs from the same dish. You can cook several at once, with ease too. **Note:** Be careful not to overcook your eggs; they are less digestible and less nutritious when hard cooked.

1 whole fertile, free-range chicken or duck egg
Sesame oil or ghee to coat the custard cups

1. Liberally oil one 6-ounce heat-proof custard cup or ramekin dish for each person.

2. Crack one egg into each dish. (Don't discard the yolk; it is very nutritious!)

3. Put egg cups on a metal or bamboo steamer tray above rapidly boiling water. Cover lid or tray. Steam for 5-7 minutes or until the whites are firm and yolks are just barely set. (They will set more as they cool.) They can sit at room temperature for 10-30 minutes before serving.

4. Remove custard cups from steamers immediately to avoid overcooking the eggs.

Serving suggestions: Serve with whole grain, pasta, porridge, or bread and greens or pressed, marinated, or boiled salad, and condiments. Also serve a sweet root vegetable or soup for lunch or supper.

Steamed Omelet (Any Season)***

Prep: less than 5 minutes
Cooking: 20 minutes
Serves: 2

2-3 whole eggs
1/2-1 tsp. tamari or shoyu
1/4 tsp. dried spices *or* 1 tsp. dried herbs
1-2 Tbsp. soy milk
1/2-2/3 cup tofu, cooked beans or vegetarian sausage, chopped

1. Whisk first four ingredients. Add bean product (or blenderize tofu with eggs).

2. Pour into a well greased 12 to 16 -ounce, heat-proof custard cup. If desired, stir in 1/4 cup minced raw or leftover cooked vegetables. Don't add too much!

3. Cook as per Steamed Eggs, on a rack, over boiling water, for 15-20 minutes or until fluffy and light like a soufflé.

Serving suggestions:. Serve with whole grain, pasta, or bread; cooked greens or mixed vegetables or pressed or marinated, or raw salad. Serve with soup, stew, or a root or round vegetable dish and/or condiments.

Book Ordering Information

☐   Yes, send me a copy of *The Nourishment For Life Cookbook* $_____

     by Rachel Albert-Matesz & Don Matesz ($24.00 retail)

☐   Yes, I'd like to order in quantity (minimum of 4 books) $_____

     ($19.20 per book)

                 8.2% TAX (Washington Residents Only) $_____

                        SHIPPING (See below) $_____

Name_____

Address_____

City, State, Zip_____

Phone #_____

PLEASE PRINT LEGIBLY.

SHIPPING: Choose either U.S. Mail Bookrate or UPS.

Quantity	U.S. Mail Book rate to all states	WA	UPS RATES ID, MT, Ut NV, CA, OR	CO, AZ NM, WY	All other
1 book	$ 3.00	$ 3.25	$ 3.50	$ 4.50	$ 4.75
2 books	$ 3.75	$ 3.75	$ 4.50	$ 4.75	$ 5.00
3 books	$ 5.00	$ 4.00	$ 4.75	$ 5.50	$ 6.00
5 books	$ 6.75	$ 4.75	$ 5.25	$ 6.50	$ 8.00
10 books	$ 9.75	$ 7.00	$ 8.50	$ 11.50	$ 14.50
12 books	$11.25	$ 8.00	$ 10.00	$ 12.00	$ 15.00

Notes:

*   AK & HI UPS rates are for air mail only.

*   Other UPS rates: Call for rates for Overnight, 2-Day, or 3-Day Select.

*   Please allow 2-4 weeks for delivery.

*   Call for wholesale rates if you have a business and business license.

Make checks payable to:

Rachel Albert-Matesz or Don Matesz.

Send to Nourishment For Life Press, 2210 N. 42nd, Suite A, Seattle, WA 98103.

Call (206) 545-4325